Architecture
residential drawing and design

by
Clois E. Kicklighter
Dean, School of Technology
and Professor of Construction Technology
Indiana State University
Terre Haute, Indiana

Ronald J. Baird
Professor, Industrial Technology
Eastern Michigan University
Ypsilanti, Michigan

Joan C. Kicklighter, C.H.E.
Co-author of *Residential Housing*
Terre Haute, Indiana

South Holland, Illinois
THE GOODHEART-WILLCOX COMPANY, INC.
Publishers

Library of Congress Cataloging in Publication Data

Kicklighter, Clois E.
    Architecture: residential drawing and design/Clois
E. Kicklighter, Ronald J. Baird, Joan C. Kicklighter

    p.   cm.
Bibliography: p.
Includes index.
ISBN 0-87006-757-5
    1. Architecture, Domestic—Designs and plans.
I. Baird, Ronald J.   II. Title.
NA7115.K45   1990
728'.028--dc20   89-33743
                                               CIP

Introduction

ARCHITECTURE, Residential Drawing and Design provides basic information necessary for planning various types of dwellings. It presents basic instruction in preparing architectural working drawings using traditional as well as computer-based methods. Further, the text is designed to serve as a reference for design and construction principles and methods. It is intended to help develop the necessary technical skills to communicate architectural ideas in an understandable, efficient, and accurate manner.

ARCHITECTURE, Residential Drawing and Design is organized so that the content is presented in the logical order of use. The functional organization and layout of the text, the step-by-step procedures, and the easy-to-understand language in which it is written makes it easier for learners to learn and for teachers to teach.

ARCHITECTURE, Residential Drawing and Design is profusely illustrated. The text is printed in full color throughout to increase communication and add interest. In addition to providing information on architectural drawing, design, and construction, the text includes excellent coverage of computer applications, industrialized housing, tradework specifications, career opportunities, and an extensive reference section.

This edition adds four new chapters covering CADD hardware, CADD software, common CADD commands and functions, and architectural CADD applications. No other residential architectural text exceeds this edition in coverage of state-of-the-art technology. In addition, a new workbook designed specifically for use with this text is available. Together, they form a complete learning package for diverse classes in architectural design.

This text is intended for architectural drawing and design classes in high schools, vocational and technical schools, community colleges, universities, adult classes, and apprenticeship training. It will also serve as a valuable reference for builders, carpentry classes, skilled tradeworkers, and interior designers.

Clois E. Kicklighter

Contents

The sensitive skills of the architect are represented in this contemporary residence. Distinctive features blended with unique materials make this structure outstanding. (California Redwood Association)

The World of Architecture

After studying this chapter, you will be able to:
- Identify the historical influences that helped shape today's home designs.
- Recognize and describe the elements of contemporary dwellings.
- Discuss current trends in architecture.

The fascinating study of architecture encompasses a sensitivity to design, skill in drawing techniques, and a knowledge of the latest construction materials. It is the combination of these abilities that yields the outstanding architects of today's world. These architects design massive high-rise buildings, quaint lakeshore cottages, modern churches, and family homes as required to meet the needs of our society.

The world of architecture is all around us. It has been one of the major conquests of humanity to design structures to bring the thrill of lasting beauty to the eye of the beholder. Whether it is a symbolic monument, or a long awaited residence, Fig. 1-1, a rewarding experience belongs to the architect and years of pleasure to those who view the structure. Some structures are designed for commercial and industrial use, Fig. 1-2, while others are planned for organizations

Fig. 1-1. This stately stone home shows good design in its clean lines. (Pella/Rolscreen Company)

Fig. 1-2. Many commercial structures, such as this office building, result from combined architectural design efforts. (Eldorado Stone Corporation)

and private living. The emphasis of this book is on the design and architectural study of residential structures; however, the relationships of line, form, and material of almost any structure has an impact on home construction.

PEOPLE AND THEIR STRUCTURES

Over the years a number of architectural styles for house construction have been developed. Many of these structures were designed to meet climatic conditions and needs of families

in various parts of the country. Others were planned especially for luxurious living, Fig. 1-3. All of these factors provide a historical background that influences the design of today's homes. Some house styles became so popular that they took on names related to their shape, period of time, or area of the country in which they were built. The emphasis here is given to the design qualities that people have used over many years and now imitates or incorporates in modern homes.

THE CAPE COLONIAL

Two very popular home styles developed over 200 years ago are the Cape Cod and Cape Ann. These traditional homes have influenced structural design since they were first conceived. People have enjoyed them for their aesthetic appeal. They provide a comfortable and livable atmosphere, and the rooms are large and functional.

The Cape Cod, Fig. 1-4, is one of the earliest and best known of the traditional Colonial styles. It originated as a fairly small house with a steep roof and little overhang. A central chimney accommodated the necessary room fireplaces. These homes were normally built as one- or one-and-one-half-story buildings, however, the same features have been incorporated in two-story styles. The eaves line is always near the top of

Fig. 1-3. This large expensive home was designed for luxurious living. (Weather Shield Mfg., Inc.)

Fig. 1-4. Refined version of the traditional Cape Cod. Later Cape Cod houses have dormers on the second floor. Many also have shutters.

the windows, ending with a gable roof. Narrow trim lines of the siding, which appealed to New Englanders many years ago, are still used on these homes. Shutters are generally used on all windows, giving emphasis to the white or yellow painted siding which was preferred in earlier times. Many variations of the Cape Cod are used in today's structures.

Another example of the Colonial style used in modern construction is the Cape Ann, Fig. 1-5.

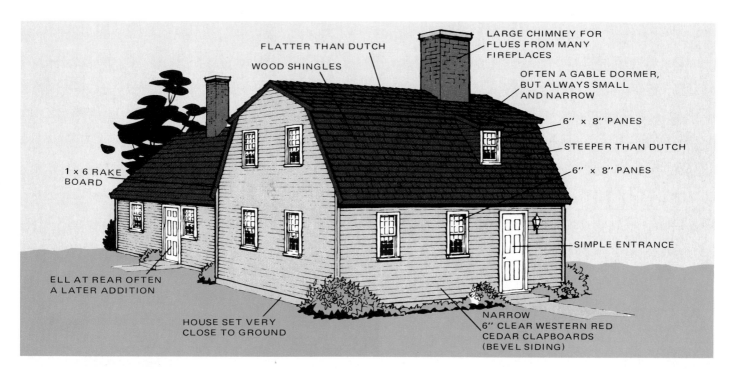

Fig. 1-5. Rendering of the traditional Cape Ann. Many modern homes are distinguished by features taken from this early structure. (Western Wood Products Assoc.)

This differs from the Cape Cod in many respects. The chimney is centrally located and is usually larger. The tapering gambrel roof encloses an attic that is often converted into extra rooms. A growing family may take this into consideration when planning their first home. Modern use of the Cape Ann characteristics provides a house with simple lines, sound construction, and a feel of colonial atmosphere. It makes a particularly attractive house along a tree shaded avenue or in a wooded development.

The New England Gambrel, as shown in Fig. 1-6, is a variation of other colonial styles. It features the gambrel roof where the pitch is abruptly changed between the ridge and eaves. Inherently American, the style is now used in most every section of the country. An advantage of the gambrel roof is the extra headroom and usable space available. The shorter rafter lengths required is an economic measure. Many adaptations of this architectural style provide pleasing and enduring homes for modern families.

THE GARRISON

An attractive house that includes a number of special features is a modern presentation of the traditional Garrison, Fig. 1-7. A distinguishing feature is the overhanging second story. This construction technique includes a number of advantages. (1) The separate corner posts on each floor make it possible to use shorter, stronger posts. (2) The short straight lines provide economy in framing materials. (3) Extra space is added at the second level by the overhang at very little extra cost. The steep pitch roof adds attic space. Narrow siding maintains the traditional styling. Fig. 1-8 shows the traditional Garrison from which modern design features have been developed.

THE SALT BOX

An interesting and easily recognizable Colonial is the Salt Box, Fig. 1-9. It is a direct offshoot of the basic colonial half house, resulting in a long

Fig. 1-6. Contemporary styling of the typical New England Gambrel house.

Fig. 1-7. The Garrison home in a contemporary setting retains the original straight line features and overhanging second story.

roofline sloping gently from ridge to eaves. Many of today's beautiful homes have borrowed from this distinctive style, developed by master builders of early American times. The Salt Box house gets its name from the shape of coffee, tea, cracker, and salt boxes found in Colonial stores. The side elevations of these containers had the same general shape as this fascinating architectural style. Variations of this style are used to enhance many new homes.

The long low roofline at the rear of the house came about by the addition of "lean-to" struc-

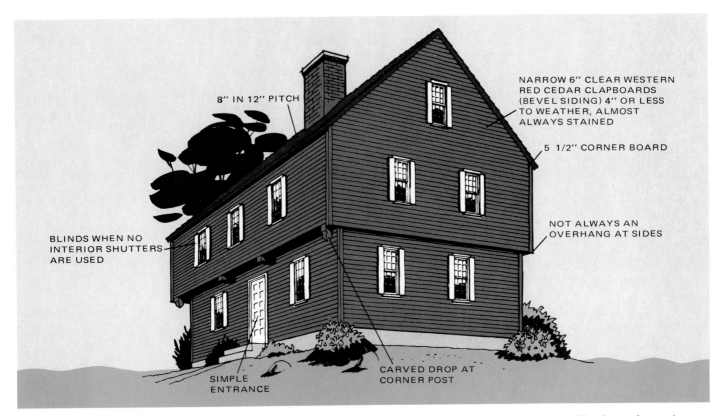

Fig. 1-8. The distinguishing characteristics of the traditional Garrison home. (Western Wood Products Assoc.)

Fig. 1-9. Beautiful reproduction of the early New England Salt Box home.

tures being attached to add more living space. As further developments evolved, the low slanting roof was helpful in combating the bitter winds common to New England winters. The basic style of the original Salt Box house is shown in Fig. 1-10.

THE SOUTHERN COLONIAL

One of the most gracious of all the Colonials is the traditional Southern Colonial. The style, which reflects the warmth, quaintness, and hospitality of the old south, is shown in Fig. 1-11.

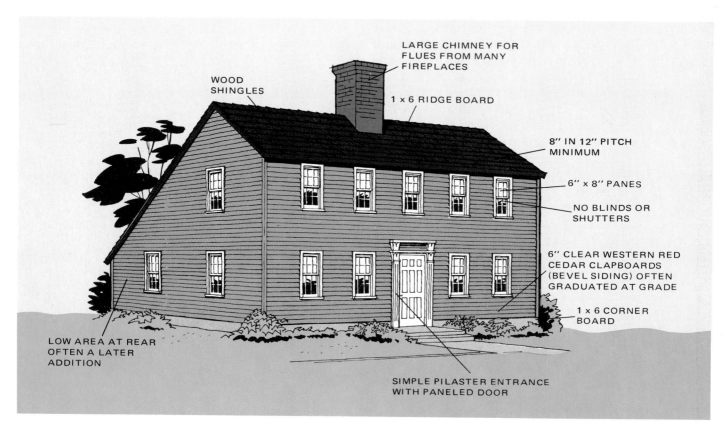

WOOD SHINGLES

LARGE CHIMNEY FOR FLUES FROM MANY FIREPLACES

1 x 6 RIDGE BOARD

8" IN 12" PITCH MINIMUM

6" x 8" PANES

NO BLINDS OR SHUTTERS

6" CLEAR WESTERN RED CEDAR CLAPBOARDS (BEVEL SIDING) OFTEN GRADUATED AT GRADE

1 x 6 CORNER BOARD

LOW AREA AT REAR OFTEN A LATER ADDITION

SIMPLE PILASTER ENTRANCE WITH PANELED DOOR

Fig. 1-10. Styling of the original Salt Box home with wood roof shingles, narrow wood siding, and no shutters. (Western Wood Products Assoc.)

Fig. 1-11. The most gracious of all the Colonial homes is this version of the Southern Colonial.

This modern example borrows many of the fine details of the Southern Colonial to express a mood of elegance and traditional charm. The outstanding architectural features are the front colonnade and the giant portico. The extended portico sheltered the front entrance from the weather and kept direct sunlight from glaring into the first and second story rooms. These homes were usually massive, with upper and lower balconies, three-story chimneys for bedroom fireplaces, ornate woodwork and iron trim, and a roof over the driveway to protect persons using the side entrance. Many of these features of the Southern Colonial may be adapted to the esthetic qualities of modern homes.

It is evident that the influences of the past, both in beauty and function, have had a profound effect on modern home designs. On the other hand, many new materials, appliances, and modes of living have caused the architect to "think out" ways to plan homes for all styles of modern living. The modern American home is a combination of many of these factors.

CONTEMPORARY STRUCTURES

The style of homes that is generally called contemporary, is the result of years of architectural planning, design, and evolution. Many are well planned while others lack imagination or design balance. Some inexpensive homes are functionally satisfactory for a family, yet for economical reasons, the exterior styling may have

to be quite conservative in the use of a variety of materials. See Fig. 1-12. The ability of the architect and the needs or finances of the family are two factors that generally dictate the type of construction being planned. Fig. 1-13 shows the

Fig. 1-12. An economical contemporary home, using standard materials. (Pella/Rolscreen Company)

Fig. 1-13. Multimaterials and coordinated lines give an architectural flair to this contemporary style home. (Carl Grooms)

use of various materials and expensive detailing in a modern home.

The term contemporary (modern) does not denote any one particular architectural style. Most modern homes borrow some distinctive features from more traditional structures, while others appear almost independent of past designs, Fig. 1-14. It makes little difference in our society just what constitutes contemporary styling. The most important job for the architect is to design homes that satisfy the customers—homes they may live in with pride and joy. In today's society, individual tastes vary to the extent that many people desire a house that is distinctly different from other houses. The owner may feel that the house represents a particular style of living and individuality, Fig. 1-15. One owner may enjoy the warmth of natural wood, Fig 1-16, another may like the solid structural design of a brick home, Fig. 1-17.

The rapid development of new construction materials and methods of fabrication has made it possible to design homes that require a minimum of maintenance, Fig: 1-18, make extensive use

Fig. 1-14. Unique styling is featured in this redwood residence. Note the strong vertical and horizontal lines. (California Redwood Association)

Fig. 1-15. Individuality is emphasized in this home through the unique treatment of space. (American Plywood Association)

Fig. 1-16. This attractive home makes use of wood siding combined with large areas of glass. (California Redwood Association)

Fig. 1-17. A traditional brick home communicates the feeling of permanence. (Pella/Rolscreen Company)

Fig. 1-18. This home requires a minimum of maintenance through the use of solid aluminum siding, gutters, downspouts, ornamental shutters, fascia, and soffits. (Alside)

*Fig. 1-19. Large exposed areas of glass are being used extensively in contemporary homes.
(California Redwood Association)*

of glass, Fig. 1-19, or place the emphasis on exposed structural members, Fig. 1-20.

THE RANCH DESIGN

One prominent modern architectural home style is the ranch home. This is basically a long, low, one-story house that grew out of the ''rancher's'' homes of the southwestern part of the country, Fig. 1-21. The plain ranch design generally has a low pitched roof with gables and overhanging eaves. It is normally built on a concrete slab with no basement. However, over the years ranch homes have taken on many newer features, Fig. 1-22. They usually have a one or two car attached garage. Basements are often

*Fig. 1-20. Visible roof support is a dominant design element in this home.
(Cultured Stone by Stucco Products, Inc.)*

Fig. 1-21. A Spanish ranch design with traditional materials and styling.

Fig. 1-22. Unusual and attractive architectural design for a ranch home. Note the variety of materials used.
(Western Wood Products Assoc.)

added, and many have gone to an L shape to add interest and break up the straight line effect. Skylights and cathedral ceilings provide variations.

New design concepts and additions to the basic ranch style have probably added more to the development of contemporary or futuristic homes than any other major factors, Fig. 1-23. The ranch has taken new twists, turns, angles, and curves to the enchantment of the architect of today and tomorrow.

TRENDS IN ARCHITECTURE

It is interesting to note that home styles for the near and distant future give the architect a freedom of design seldom known in the past. As indicated earlier, the multitude of individual preferences, materials, and structural techniques predicts a variety of unique expressions for architectural designing. Many of these homes are being designed for dramatic effects, as in Figs. 1-24 and 1-25, while others are styled for particular settings, Figs. 1-26 and 1-27, such as hillsides, seashores, and even cliffs.

Fig. 1-24. The stately appearance of this two-story home is achieved with use of various building materials and interesting design. (Pella/Rolscreen Company)

Fig. 1-23. Angular lines and a sharp, slanting roof give this ranch home a contemporary as well as attractive appearance. (Western Wood Products Association)

Fig. 1-25. This dramatic wood structure uses large areas of glass to add design and brighten the interior. (Vermont Castings Inc.)

The trends in architecture appear to be leaning toward the dramatic yet comfortable living styles. Homes designed to complement the site provide a feeling of openness and still retain the required privacy are always being developed. Fig. 1-28 gives an indication of spaciousness and is designed to take advantage of the site. Fig. 1-29 provides texture and curvature to exterior styling.

A current trend in architectural design that is receiving strong support is called post-modern architecture. This ''style'' combines traditional and contemporary influences, Figs. 1-30 and 1-31, into truly modern structures which are strongly reminiscent of popular styles of the past. However, modern materials and building

Fɪg. 1-26. Adaptation of an ultra-modern structure to a seashore setting. (American Plywood Assoc.)

Fig. 1-27. The roof design, use of glass, and structural materials are particularly suited for this arid climate. (Cultured Stone by Stucco Stone Products, Inc.)

Fig. 1-28. Flat and curved surfaces are blended together in this custom home to provide a sense of unity. (Pella/Rolscreen Company)

The World of Architecture 19

Fig. 1-29. The curved concrete arches and roof beam extensions provide a classic expression to this contemporary home. (Ideal Cement Co.)

Fig. 1-30. An example of post-modern architecture which combines traditional and contemporary influences. (Armstrong World Industries, Inc.)

Fig. 1-31. A post-modern structure strongly reminiscent of the Victorian era. (Marvin Windows)

techniques are used to produce energy efficient and weather resistant homes.

Another trend in residential architecture is the renovation of older homes. Many older homes are structurally solid and may be restored to their original beauty with some care and attention. Fig. 1-32 shows a historic Italianate home that was saved from demolition. Fig. 1-33 shows a California Victorian home which was authentically restored as a law office. The photos included in Figs. 1-34 through 1-37 illustrate the dramatic impact that thoughtful restoration can have even on a less dramatic, traditional home.

Experimentation with new materials and design concepts continues to produce radically new structures. The Xanadome (pronounced Zanadome) structure shown in Fig. 1-38 is an example. It is made from fiberglass-skin wedges

Fig. 1-32. A restored Italianate home showing one strong design influence of the past. (Marvin Windows)

Fig. 1-34. Traditional home before restoration. (Georgia-Pacific Corporation)

Fig. 1-33. Elements of Victorian architecture as shown in this authentic structure still appear today. (Marvin Windows)

Fig. 1-35. Unfinished attic before restoration. (Georgia-Pacific Corporation)

The World of Architecture 21

Fig. 1-36. Attic after restoration.
(Georgia-Pacific Corporation)

Fig. 1-38. The ''Xanadome'' is made from fiberglass-skin wedges which are filled with polyurethane foam. (Xanadome Structures, Ltd.)

which are filled with polyurethane foam and finished inside with a polyester material. The wedges are connected together to form a rigid structure which produces a high insulation R-value of 25. This modular concept provides flexibility in design and rapid construction.

Fig. 1-37. Exterior view of the restored home. (Georgia-Pacific Corporation)

Write your answers on a separate sheet of paper. Do not write in this book.

1. The needs of families and _____ _____ have contributed to the structural styles of homes.
2. List the three major factors that the study of architecture includes.
3. Which of the following factors led to the name Salt Box for a particular style home?
   a. Implement sheds.
   b. Containers in village stores.
   c. Early churches.
   d. The shape of barn roofs.
4. What are the three main advantages of the architectural design of the Garrison style house?
5. What are the outstanding architectural features of the Southern Colonial home?
6. What is unique about the shape of the roof on a Gambrel style home?
7. Why do the terms contemporary and modern not describe a particular architectural style?
8. The basic ranch home is a low, long one-story house with a _____ _____ roof and overhanging eaves.
9. Name two factors that have probably contributed most to the development of modern or futuristic homes.
10. List four factors that appear to be influencing new trends in architectural design.
11. A style that combines traditional and contemporary influences is called _____ _____.
12. A Xanadome structure is made from _____ skin wedges.

1. Call on an architect and ask the following questions: (a) What particular style home is most in demand today? (b) How does one become an architect and why? (c) In what way does one communicate with one's customers to provide the style home they desire? (d) How does one derive from a customer just what design features will be most appealing to a family? Write a brief report on the responses the architect has given you.
2. By using clippings from magazines and newspapers, make an architectural design folder indicating as many home styles as you can find. Indicate on each home any design feature that has been borrowed from the past or gives an indication of a futuristic trend.
3. Visit a local contractor and ask him to specify a few materials he is using for exterior structural features. Make a list of these materials and explain their use to your class.
4. Select a particular traditional style home and, using cardboard and glue, cut out and make a model of that design. Sketch in doors, windows, siding, etc. and put it on display in your classroom.
5. Make a collection of catalogs from lumber dealers and suppliers. From this material, prepare a list of new materials that are available to replace older exterior structural devices. An example might be the use of aluminum or plastic gutters that replace galvanized iron gutters. Present this as a discussion with your class.

The architect planned this space to take advantage of the natural beauty of the site. Using the most modern materials and components, the architect can use solar energy to heat many residences. (Janco Greenhouses)

2
CHAPTER

Basic House Design

After studying this chapter, you will be able to:
- Recognize the four basic house designs.
- List the chief advantages of each design.
- Map the traffic circulation for maximum efficiency.
- Compare the relative cost of heating and cooling for each design.

A residential home designer has four basic designs to choose from: the one-story or ranch, the one-and-one-half-story, the two-story, and the split-level. Each of these individual styles has strengths and weaknesses which should be considered before making a choice. Such factors as space available for the house, site contour, climate, convenience, cost, surroundings, and personal preference should all play a role in the final decision.

ONE-STORY RANCH DESIGNS

The one-story house has all the regular living space on one level, Fig. 2-1. It may have a basement, depending on the section of the country in which it is built and preference of the prospective owner.

One of the chief advantages of the ranch is that it lends itself beautifully to indoor-outdoor living. Patios, porches, and terraces may be added to virtually any room. With lots of glass, it is possible to bring the outdoor surroundings inside to make the house appear even larger than it is, Fig. 2-2. Another advantage of this design is

Fig. 2-1. One of the many style variations for a typical one-story ranch house.

Fig. 2-2. A sunroom extends the living space of this ranch-style house. (Pella/Rolscreen Company)

Fig. 2-3. This ranch house minimizes the height problem in construction. (Elk Corporation)

Fig. 2-4. This large ranch house combines simplified construction and minimal maintenance. (The Garlinghouse Company)

Fig. 2-5. This Florida ranch home is attractive, yet inexpensive to build.

the absence of stairs . . . unless it has a basement. The ranch without a basement is popular with many older and handicapped people.

The ranch usually has a low-pitched roof with wide overhangs since no headroom is necessary above the ceiling. The low-pitched roof and short walls make outside maintenance easy. Cleaning the gutters, removing the screens, and painting do not require long ladders or other special equipment. Low height also simplifies construction. See Figs. 2-3 and 2-4.

The low and long appearance of the ranch is pleasing to most people, Fig. 2-5. The ranch may be built with a full basement, Fig. 2-6; crawl space, Fig. 2-7; or on a slab, Fig. 2-8. Great variation is possible. The ranch easily lends itself to expansion and modification.

One disadvantage is that the one-story is usually more costly to build than other designs of the same square footage. This stems from the fact that the one-story requires more roof area and more foundation length, Fig. 2-9.

Another negative aspect of the ranch is that it requires a larger lot since it is spread out, rather than up. Furthermore, this increased area sometimes causes heating problems for certain areas of the house because of the distance from the furnace. There is generally no problem with electric heat.

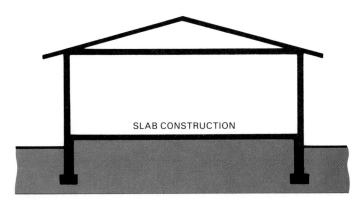

Fig. 2-8. The ranch on a concrete slab reduces cost and simplifies construction.

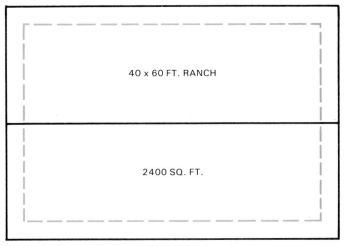

FOUNDATION LENGTH = 200 FT.
ROOF AREA = 2500 SQ. FT.

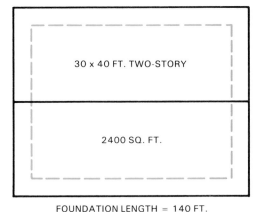

FOUNDATION LENGTH = 140 FT.
ROOF AREA = 1300 SQ. FT.

Fig. 2-9. A comparison of the foundation length and roof area of a ranch and a two-story house having the same square footage of living area reveals the reason a ranch is usually more expensive to build.

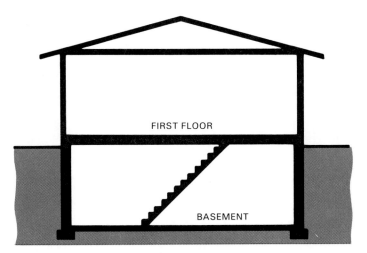

Fig. 2-6. Addition of a full basement provides valuable extra usable space to a ranch house.

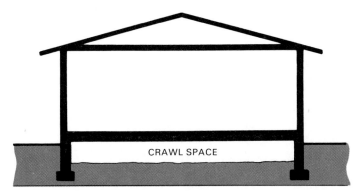

Fig. 2-7. A crawl space under the ranch house adds accessibility for service and maintenance.

Maintenance costs may be more on a ranch because of the larger roof and exterior wall surfaces, Fig. 2-10. Considerable hall space may be required in a large ranch style house to provide access to all rooms, Fig. 2-11. Careful planning should be done to keep hall space to a minimum.

ONE-AND-ONE-HALF-STORY DESIGNS

The one-and-one-half-story house (sometimes called a "Cape Cod") is essentially one-story with a steeper roof which allows for expansion of the attic, Fig. 2-12. Dormers are usually added to provide additional light and ventilation, Fig. 2-13. This has two distinct advantages; economy in cost per unit of habitable living space, and built-in expansibility.

Generally, bedrooms and a bath are provided in the attic space. Since any space with less than five feet of headroom is considered unusable, the total square feet of space in the attic is about one-half that of the first floor. See Fig. 2-12.

Fig. 2-10. This spacious ranch house has extensive roof and wall areas that may produce maintenance problems.

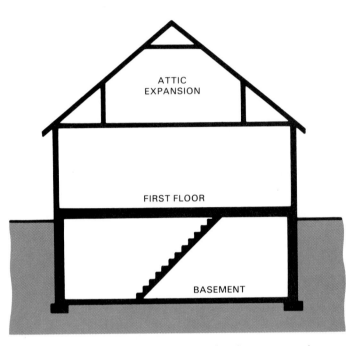

Fig. 2-12. Typical design section for a one-and-one-half-story house.

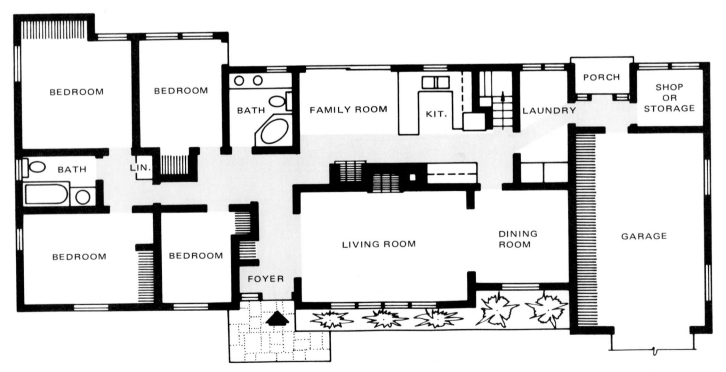

Fig. 2-11. Extreme hall space is required to make this ranch design serviceable. Better planning is desirable.

Fig. 2-13. One large dormer on this attractive one-and-one-half-story house provides natural light and ventilation to the upper living areas. (American Plywood Association)

Dormers, stairs, and a slightly steeper roof are the principal additional costs required to build a one-and-one-half-story house.

The one-and-one-half-story is quite versatile. It can begin as a two-bedroom, one-bath house with the upper area left unfinished. This minimum house will meet the needs of a newly married couple or a retired couple. As the family of the younger people expands, the ''expansion attic'' can be finished to provide more livable room.

Heating costs are minimized due to the small outside wall area compared to the amount of interior space. Cooling may be accomplished through the use of louvered ventilators at each end of the structure and the generous use of insulation. Adequate ventilation and insulation is necessary since about one-third of the ceiling area is directly under the roof. This area tends to be quite warm in the summer.

Care must be taken in designing the one-and-one-half-story structure to best accommodate the number of persons it can ultimately house. The electrical and plumbing systems should be planned with expansion in mind. Failure to consider expansion at the outset will greatly reduce the efficiency of these vital systems. Other areas of the house, such as kitchen, dining, and living rooms should also be planned for the ultimate number of occupants.

TWO-STORY DESIGNS

Compared to ranch and one-and-one-half-story houses, the two-story house is more economical to build, Fig. 2-14. It may be built with

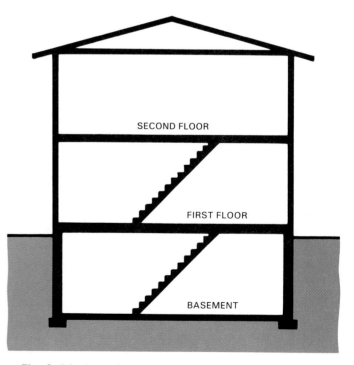

Fig. 2-14. A section of a ''standard'' two-story house.

Fig. 2-15. An attractively styled two-story house with attached garage. (Alside)

or without a basement. A two-story house requires a smaller lot and has a smaller roof and foundation area compared to interior space of most other designs. Fig. 2-15 shows a typical example.

Heating and cooling a two-story house is simple and comparatively economical. Heat from the first floor naturally rises to the second floor level. Even though the second floor is usually far from the furnace it is usually easy to heat. Cooling is facilitated due to the fact that the ceiling is not directly under the roof. Ventilation is easy and effective when ample windows are included in the design.

The two-story, however, in many localities is not as popular today as in former years. This is probably a result of the turn to more contemporary styles, Fig. 2-16. The two-story home is usually traditional in style, Fig. 2-17. The two-story home, unless located among other similar styles, may appear to be out of place.

General exterior maintenance is usually more difficult and costly because of the height. For some people the necessity of climbing stairs from level to level is considered a disadvantage. The two-story does not lend itself to variations in style as well as some other designs. However, architects have added a contemporary flair, and

as a result, have improved their overall appearance and salability, Fig. 2-18.

As the cost increases and availability of land becomes more of a problem, the two-story house may gain in popularity.

Fig. 2-16. A contemporary adaptation of the two-story house. Roof design and windows tend to disguise the resemblance to older styles.

SPLIT-LEVEL DESIGNS

The split-level was conceived for the sloping or hilly lot. It takes advantage of what might otherwise prove to be a troublesome difference in elevation and uses it to advantage, Fig. 2-19. As a general rule, a split-level should not be built on a flat lot. Mounding up soil in front of the high section to give the appearance of a hill usually yields poor results.

The split-level makes efficient use of space. The general arrangement of the split-level separates sleeping, living, and recreation on different levels, Fig. 2-20. Little or no hall space is required in a split-level house due to its basic design, a positive factor for consideration.

Fig. 2-17. Typical example of the more traditional two-story house. (Pella/Rolscreen Company)

Fig. 2-19. Contemporary split-level house well integrated with site atop a steep hill. (Cultured Stone by Stucco Stone Products, Inc.)

Fig. 2-18. The basic two-story house takes on a contemporary appearance with extended wings, overhanging porch roof, and post supports. (The Atrium Door & Window Corporation)

Fig. 2-20. This split-level house illustrates a standard arrangement of living quarters.

At the lowest level, there is a normal basement which houses the heating and cooling equipment, storage, and perhaps a shop or washroom, Fig. 2-21. This area is the usual depth of a basement. In some instances a basement may not be desired and a crawl space is provided for maintenance and ventilation. The basement ordinarily equals about 40 to 60 percent of the space occupied by the house. This is usually enough for efficient use without wasted space.

The next level up from the basement, the intermediate level, generally houses the garage and recreation area, Fig. 2-21. This area is ground level and thus lends itself to these functions. Patios and terraces may be attached to the

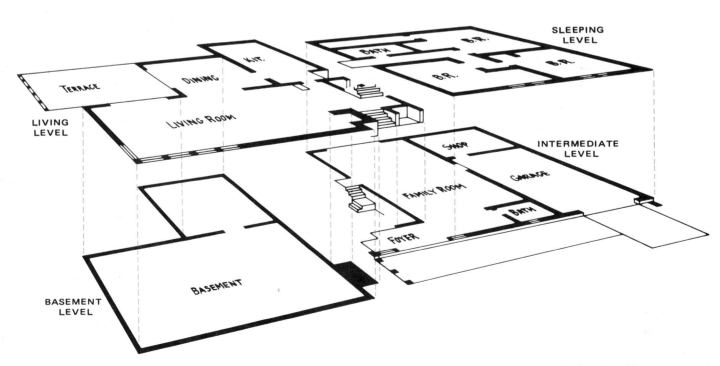

Fig. 2-21. This three-dimensional drawing provides good insight into the arrangement of a four-level house.

recreation area which further enhances its use. The intermediate level may also have a large foyer, mud room, or family room.

Slightly higher than the intermediate level is the living level, Fig. 2-21. Generally this area is located at grade also; the sloping grade makes this arrangement possible. The kitchen, dining room, living room, and full or half bath normally are located on the living level. The foyer, mud room, and washroom may also be located at this level depending on the layout or preference. Again the use of patios and terraces adds to the usefulness and amplifies the attractiveness of the split-level.

At the highest elevation in the house is the sleeping area and bath, Fig. 2-21. The half-level difference between the living and sleeping levels affords greater privacy and quietness.

Split-level houses do have some negative aspects. They are generally more expensive to build than the two-story. In most cases, however, they are cheaper than a ranch. Heating may be a problem if not handled properly. The use of zoned heating (separate thermostats for the various areas of the house) will usually solve the heating problem.

VARIATIONS OF SPLIT-LEVEL DESIGNS

There are basically three variations of the split-level design: the side-by-side, the front-to-back, and the back-to-front. Lots sloping from the left to right (viewed from the street) are suited for the side-by-side design. This design places the living area opposite the sleeping and intermediate areas, Fig. 2-22.

Variation number two, the front-to-back split-level, is suited for lots which are high in front and low in the back, Fig. 2-23. This house looks like a ranch from the front and a two-story from the back. The living area faces the street and the bedrooms are on the second level to the rear.

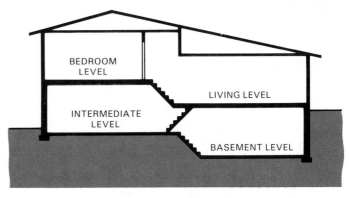

Fig. 2-23. Longitudinal section of a front-to-back split-level house. (side view)

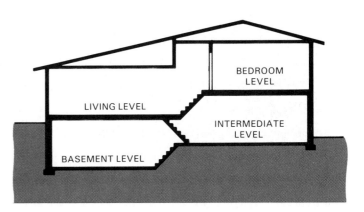

Fig. 2-24. The back-to-front split-level is adapted to a lot which slopes to the front. (side view)

The third variation, the back-to-front split-level, requires a lot that is low in front and high in back, Fig. 2-24. The intermediate level faces the street at grade. The bedrooms are above, also facing the street. The living level is at the rear. This model looks like a two-story in front and ranch in the rear.

Fig. 2-25 shows another style which some people call a traditional split-level. This is nothing more than a ranch with a raised basement which causes it to be taller than a ranch, yet not as high as a two-story. It also has a split entry (the foyer is half-way between levels) which is probably the reason for it being identified as a split-level.

TRAFFIC CIRCULATION

A primary consideration in designing a functional plan is traffic circulation. Traffic circulation involves those areas of the house that provide a means of moving from one area or room to another. Circulation must be planned for maximum efficiency. The pattern shown in Fig. 2-26 is an example of a well-planned arrangement. The distance from the garage to the

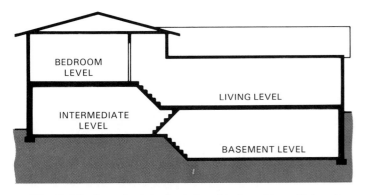

Fig. 2-22. A typical design of a side-by-side split-level house. (front view)

Fig. 2-25. A simple split-level (split entry) design which takes advantage of a raised basement to add height and better lighting. (Alside)

kitchen is short and direct. The foyer is centrally located and convenient to all parts of the house. All bedrooms are close to a bath. Few rooms have traffic planned through them. The family room and eating nook are exceptions. An analysis should be made of traffic circulation to determine if the plan is as functional as it could be. Frequently, a slight change in the floor plan can increase smooth flow of traffic to desired locations.

REVIEW QUESTIONS—CHAPTER 2

Write your answers on a separate sheet of paper. Do not write in this book.

1. List the four basic residential home designs.
2. Identify five advantages of the ranch-style house.
3. List five disadvantages of the ranch-style house.
4. A one-and-one-half-story house may be recognized by its _____ _____ and _____.
5. The one-and-one-half-story has two distinct advantages—_____ and _____.
6. One of the most economical houses to build is a _____ design.
7. List four negative aspects of the two-story house.
8. The _____ design was conceived for the sloping or hilly lot.
9. Name the four levels of the split-level design.
10. List three variations of the split-level.
11. What is one of the main advantages of the ranch-type home?
12. Why are dormers usually added to the one-and-one-half-story house?
13. In a split-level house, the basement usually equals what percentage of space occupied by the house?
    a. 10 to 20 percent.
    b. 20 to 40 percent.
    c. 40 to 60 percent.
    d. 60 to 80 percent.
14. What house design looks like a two-story from the front and a ranch from the rear?

SUGGESTED ACTIVITIES

1. Look through magazines and find an example (photo) of each of the basic house designs (one-story, one-and-one-half-story, two-story, and split-level). Mount the pictures on illustration board for display.

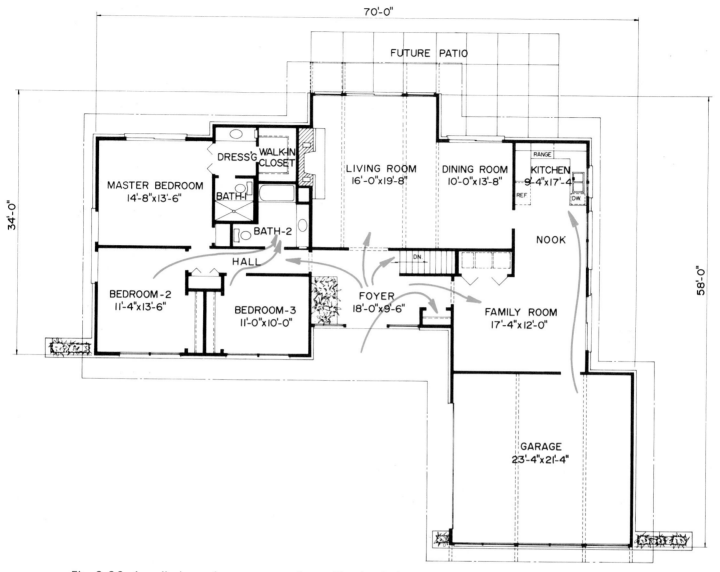

Fig. 2-26. A well-planned arrangement for traffic circulation through the major living areas of a home.

2. Identify houses in or near your community which are examples of the basic house designs. Describe materials used, colors, and location of each house.

3. Obtain a floor plan of a house from a magazine, newspaper, or other source. Determine the basic design and compile the following information about the house:
   a. How many square feet of living space is in the house?
   b. List the rooms identified in the house.
   c. How many sets of stairs are there in the house?
   d. Does the house have a basement?

4. Visit a contractor or architectural firm and ask for prints of basic house designs. Bring these to class and discuss the advantages and disadvantages of each in respect to the families of different members of the class.

5. Invite an architect to your class to discuss how basic house designs are chosen for various areas of your community.

6. Prepare a simple sketch of your own home showing the various levels for living and the contour of the property. Indicate what basic design your house resembles. If you live in an apartment, sketch the home of one of your friends.

7. Using your local newspaper for reference, read through the "houses for sale" section and make a list of the styles advertised. See if there seems to be a trend toward a particular basic design.

IV. Proposed Development Plan (scheme A)

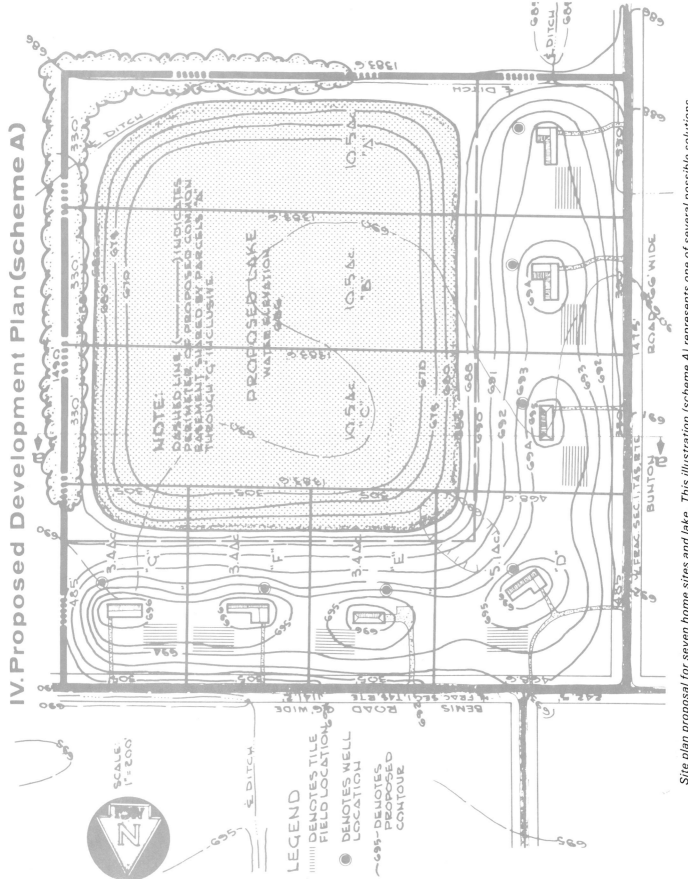

Site plan proposal for seven home sites and lake. This illustration (scheme A) represents one of several possible solutions presented by the designer. (Midwestern Consulting, Inc.)

Primary Considerations

After studying this chapter, you will be able to:
* Evaluate a given site with respect to important considerations.
* Discuss key site consideration, restrictions, zoning, and codes.
* Record topographical features of a site.
* List family needs that should be considered when planning a dwelling.
* Describe the basic construction drawings used to build a structure.

Most people have a "dream home" in the back of their mind which they hope to build some day. However, few people think beyond the house itself to the site location and characteristics, community attributes, zoning restrictions, family lifestyle, and quality of living. These considerations, in many instances, are just as important as the size and room arrangement of the house.

SITE CONSIDERATIONS

The site is more than just a plot of land—it is part of a larger community, Fig. 3-1. It is located in a certain school district and is either near or far from shopping areas. An airport or major traffic artery may be nearby. The site is in a growing community or a stagnant one. The topography is rolling or flat, high and dry or low and wet, big or small, wooded or treeless. It is located in a warm or cold climate. The site, next to the house itself, is probably the most expensive item of investment. It must be evaluated carefully to realize its potential as a vital part of the home and its setting.

The characteristics of a site frequently indicate the basic type of house that would be best suited for that site. For example, flat topography lends itself to a ranch or two-story house. A hilly

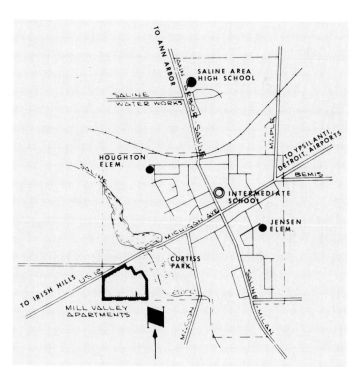

Fig. 3-1. A homesite is always a part of a larger community—subdivision, city, or state. (Midwestern Consulting, Inc.)

A hilly or sloping site is ideal for a split-level home. A site which has many trees may require a house with large windows and generous use of natural materials. Every effort should be made to take full advantage of site characteristics in planning the home. The structure should appear to be part of the site. It should blend in with the surroundings rather than stand apart from them.

THE COMMUNITY

The neighborhood should be evaluated on the following points: (1) Is the community a "planned" community, Fig. 3-2, or one that has sprung up with no central theme or forethought, Fig. 3-3? (2) Are the homes in this community in the price range of the proposed house? (3) Are the neighbors in about the same socioeconomic category as the prospective owner? (4) Is the community alive and growing or is it rundown and dying? (5) Does the community have room for growth or is it restricted? (6) Are the residents of the community people who take pride in their homes or seem indifferent toward them? (7) Does the community have modern churches, quality schools, and shopping areas? (8) Are such facilities as fire protection, water, sewer, natural gas, and garbage collection available in this community? (9) Is the site near the prospective owner's workplace? (10) Is public transportation available in the community? (11) Does the community have a high rate of turnover due to the resale of homes? These, and many other factors relate to the site selection and eventually to the happiness of the owner. These factors should be considered before selecting a site.

COST AND RESTRICTIONS

It is not possible to state exactly what percentage of the total cost of a home should be allowed for the site. This depends on many considerations. The price, however, should be examined carefully to determine if it takes into consideration needed improvements such as grading, fill, tree removal, and drainage. The cost of the lot should also take into account the amount of frontage it has and whether or not it is a corner lot. Assessments are usually proportional to length of frontage, therefore, corner lots are more expensive.

A title search should be instituted before purchasing the lot to determine if there are any legal claims against the property. The deed, Fig. 3-4, will show any restrictions or easements attached to the property. Restrictions may specify the style of house that may be built on the lot, size of the house, type of landscaping, or even the overall cost of the house. Easements may allow utilities to cross the property or may prevent the filling of a low area which must remain for drainage purposes. The title and deed are very important documents and should be examined carefully by a competent attorney before the lot is purchased.

ZONING AND CODES

Investigate the zoning ordinances in the area where the site is located. It may be zoned commercial or for multiple-family dwellings. This could prohibit building a single-family residential structure. Even if the selected site were zoned for single-family structures, you might find the large open area nearby which plays a large part in the selection of the site, is zoned for apartment buildings. Check the zoning!

Another area for consideration which many prospective buyers fail to explore is local building codes. It is possible that the codes (plumbing, electrical, and building codes) are so restrictive that the type of house that is being

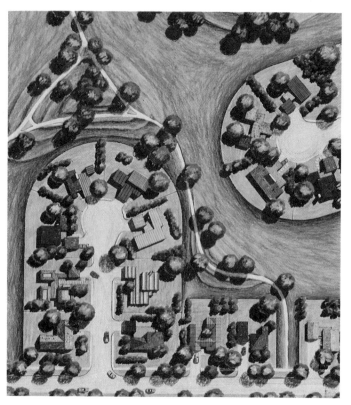

Fig. 3-2. A planned community neighborhood takes advantage of the natural site characteristics.
(Midwestern Consulting, Inc.)

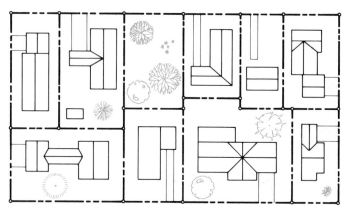

Fig. 3-3. This block of homes represents an example of little planning with no central theme.

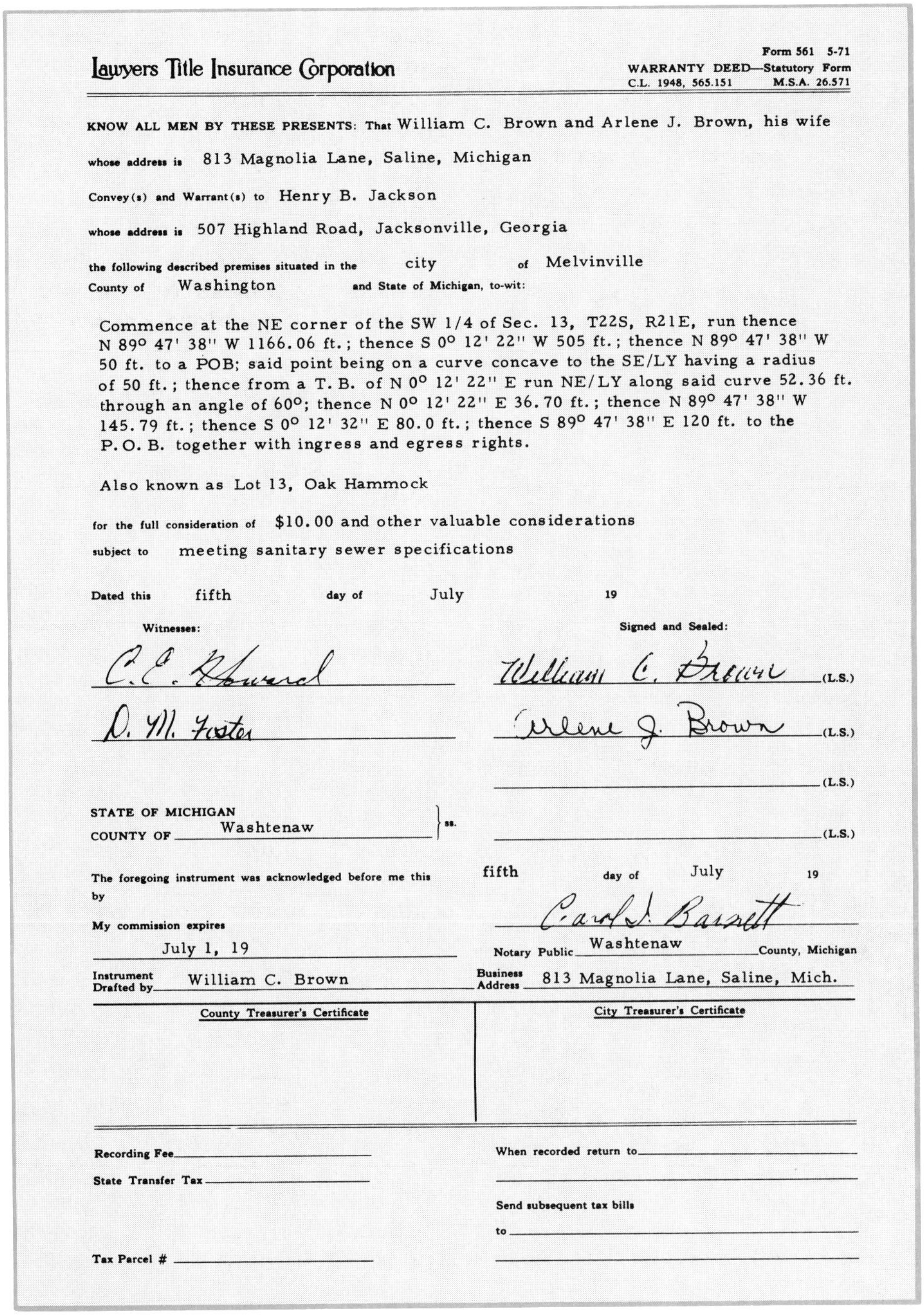

Lawyers Title Insurance Corporation

Form 561 5-71
WARRANTY DEED—Statutory Form
C.L. 1948, 565.151 M.S.A. 26.571

KNOW ALL MEN BY THESE PRESENTS: That William C. Brown and Arlene J. Brown, his wife

whose address is 813 Magnolia Lane, Saline, Michigan

Convey(s) and Warrant(s) to Henry B. Jackson

whose address is 507 Highland Road, Jacksonville, Georgia

the following described premises situated in the city of Melvinville
County of Washington and State of Michigan, to-wit:

Commence at the NE corner of the SW 1/4 of Sec. 13, T22S, R21E, run thence N 89° 47' 38" W 1166.06 ft.; thence S 0° 12' 22" W 505 ft.; thence N 89° 47' 38" W 50 ft. to a POB; said point being on a curve concave to the SE/LY having a radius of 50 ft.; thence from a T. B. of N 0° 12' 22" E run NE/LY along said curve 52.36 ft. through an angle of 60°; thence N 0° 12' 22" E 36.70 ft.; thence N 89° 47' 38" W 145.79 ft.; thence S 0° 12' 32" E 80.0 ft.; thence S 89° 47' 38" E 120 ft. to the P. O. B. together with ingress and egress rights.

Also known as Lot 13, Oak Hammock

for the full consideration of $10.00 and other valuable considerations
subject to meeting sanitary sewer specifications

Dated this fifth day of July 19

Witnesses: Signed and Sealed:

C. E. Howard — William C. Brown (L.S.)
D. M. Foster — Arlene J. Brown (L.S.)
(L.S.)

STATE OF MICHIGAN
COUNTY OF Washtenaw } ss. (L.S.)

The foregoing instrument was acknowledged before me this fifth day of July 19
by

My commission expires July 1, 19

Carol J. Barrett
Notary Public Washtenaw County, Michigan

Instrument Drafted by William C. Brown
Business Address 813 Magnolia Lane, Saline, Mich.

County Treasurer's Certificate | City Treasurer's Certificate

Recording Fee
State Transfer Tax
Tax Parcel #

When recorded return to
Send subsequent tax bills to

Fig. 3-4. A typical property deed containing a legal description of the site.

planned for the site cannot be built. The cost could also be much greater because of code requirements. On the other hand, the codes may be so lax that the quality of homes in the area is poor. Talk with the local building inspector to determine such things as cost of permits, inspections, and regulations. Fig. 3-5 illustrates a typical building permit form.

TOPOGRAPHICAL FEATURES

The topography of the site is a primary concern. Study the topographical drawings of the site to determine its slope, contour, size, shape, and elevation. Trees, rocks, and soil conditions may also be indicated on the drawings, Fig. 3-6. These factors may limit the type of structure that may be built on the site.

If the site is out of town and you must provide water and sewer, extra care must be taken in the selection of the proper site. Very hard water, iron water, or the lack of water are problems to be aware of before the house is built. Equipment to handle these problems is expensive and requires constant maintenance. A site smaller than one acre may not meet the code requirements.

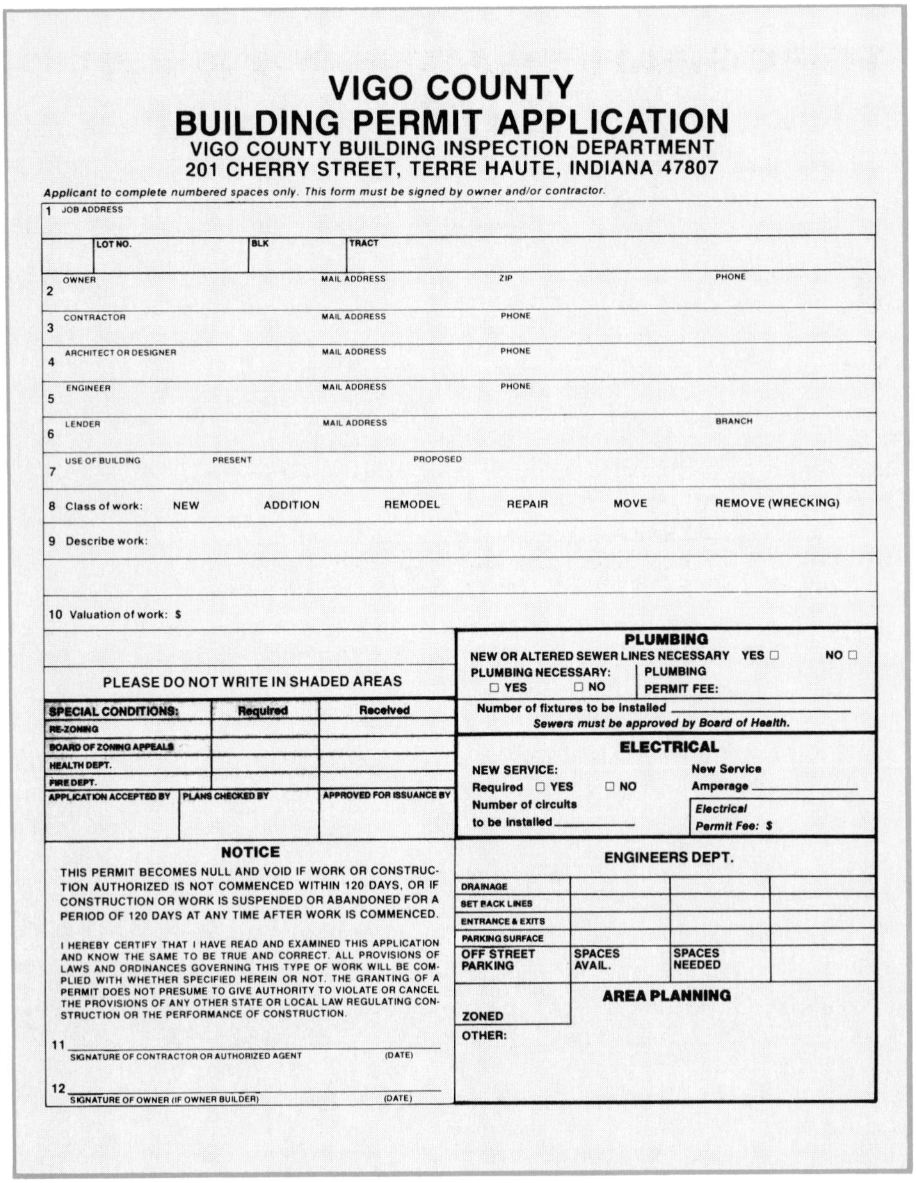

VIGO COUNTY
BUILDING PERMIT APPLICATION
VIGO COUNTY BUILDING INSPECTION DEPARTMENT
201 CHERRY STREET, TERRE HAUTE, INDIANA 47807

Applicant to complete numbered spaces only. This form must be signed by owner and/or contractor.

1 JOB ADDRESS			
LOT NO.	BLK	TRACT	

2	OWNER	MAIL ADDRESS	ZIP	PHONE

3	CONTRACTOR	MAIL ADDRESS	PHONE

4	ARCHITECT OR DESIGNER	MAIL ADDRESS	PHONE

5	ENGINEER	MAIL ADDRESS	PHONE

6	LENDER	MAIL ADDRESS	BRANCH

7	USE OF BUILDING	PRESENT	PROPOSED

8 Class of work: NEW   ADDITION   REMODEL   REPAIR   MOVE   REMOVE (WRECKING)

9 Describe work:

10 Valuation of work: $

PLEASE DO NOT WRITE IN SHADED AREAS

SPECIAL CONDITIONS:	Required	Received
RE-ZONING		
BOARD OF ZONING APPEALS		
HEALTH DEPT.		
FIRE DEPT.		
APPLICATION ACCEPTED BY	PLANS CHECKED BY	APPROVED FOR ISSUANCE BY

PLUMBING
NEW OR ALTERED SEWER LINES NECESSARY   YES ☐   NO ☐

PLUMBING NECESSARY: ☐ YES   ☐ NO   PLUMBING PERMIT FEE:

Number of fixtures to be installed _____

Sewers must be approved by Board of Health.

ELECTRICAL
NEW SERVICE: Required ☐ YES   ☐ NO

Number of circuits to be installed _____

New Service Amperage _____

Electrical Permit Fee: $

NOTICE
THIS PERMIT BECOMES NULL AND VOID IF WORK OR CONSTRUCTION AUTHORIZED IS NOT COMMENCED WITHIN 120 DAYS, OR IF CONSTRUCTION OR WORK IS SUSPENDED OR ABANDONED FOR A PERIOD OF 120 DAYS AT ANY TIME AFTER WORK IS COMMENCED.

I HEREBY CERTIFY THAT I HAVE READ AND EXAMINED THIS APPLICATION AND KNOW THE SAME TO BE TRUE AND CORRECT. ALL PROVISIONS OF LAWS AND ORDINANCES GOVERNING THIS TYPE OF WORK WILL BE COMPLIED WITH WHETHER SPECIFIED HEREIN OR NOT. THE GRANTING OF A PERMIT DOES NOT PRESUME TO GIVE AUTHORITY TO VIOLATE OR CANCEL THE PROVISIONS OF ANY OTHER STATE OR LOCAL LAW REGULATING CONSTRUCTION OR THE PERFORMANCE OF CONSTRUCTION.

11 _____   (DATE)
SIGNATURE OF CONTRACTOR OR AUTHORIZED AGENT

12 _____   (DATE)
SIGNATURE OF OWNER (IF OWNER BUILDER)

ENGINEERS DEPT.

DRAINAGE			
SET BACK LINES			
ENTRANCE & EXITS			
PARKING SURFACE			
OFF STREET PARKING	SPACES AVAIL.	SPACES NEEDED	

AREA PLANNING
ZONED

OTHER:

Fig. 3-5. A building permit must be obtained before construction may begin.

The shape of the site is important. Even though the site is large, it may be long and narrow or some odd shape that will limit construction possibilities, Fig. 3-7. Measure the site and have the measurements and lot lines checked by a surveyor to be sure the boundaries are located where you believe them to be.

FAMILY NEEDS

A truly functional house will represent the lifestyle of those who occupy it. Rather than try to change a lifestyle to fit the house, the structure should evolve from those who will use it.

Family size will be a major consideration in a house design. Ample space should be provided for each member of the family to perform their chosen activities. Consideration should be given to providing space for these individual and family activities:

Preparing Food	Sleeping
Dining	Relaxing
Entertaining	Working
Family Recreation	Storage
Hobbies	Bathing
Laundering	Housekeeping
Studying	Accommodating Guests
Dressing	Planning

These activities should not be thought of necessarily in relation to specific rooms. Some activities are performed throughout the house while others are restricted to certain areas. The important point is to provide for activities in which the family will be engaged. Let the structure take the shape and arrangement that best serves these needs.

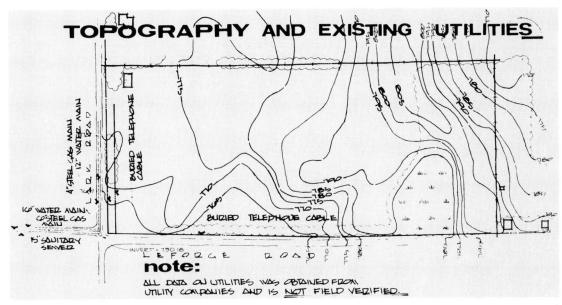

Fig. 3-6. A site plan which shows topographical features such as contour, elevations, trees, and property lines. (Midwestern Consulting, Inc.)

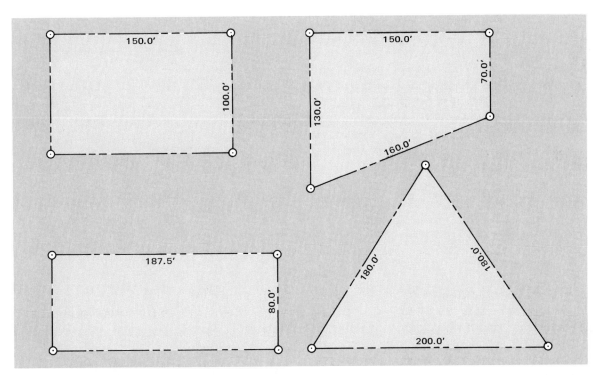

Fig. 3-7. Property shape is important in determining the size and style of the house to be designed. Note that each of these sites has 15,000 sq. ft. of area, yet the triangular plot appears the largest.

OTHER CONSIDERATIONS

A residential structure should not be planned entirely from an "inside-out" approach. Consideration should be given to the exterior design, size, and materials, Fig. 3-8. These additional factors add a unity to the structure and enhance its overall appearance. Consideration should also be given to the salability of the home.

MODULAR ASPECTS

Much is heard today about the advantages and disadvantages of *modular construction* (use of building materials based on 4 inch units of measurement, or modules). The fact remains that a house is a combination of many parts and these must fit together to form the whole. These parts are basic construction materials which are

Fig. 3-8. Design is important. Note how the lines and use of materials complement each other in this unique ranch structure. (The Atrium Door and Window Corporation)

available across the country and are produced in standard sizes. If home designers know what these standard sizes are and actively plan their structure around them, a more economical building with less wasted material will result. For example, it would probably cost no more to build a house with overall dimensions of 40' x 60' than a house of 39' x 59'. The 40' x 60' house will provide considerable extra floor space for the same cost.

A quick survey of representative construction material sizes as shown below will provide some guidelines for the designer:

Plywood — 4' x 8'

Paneling — 4' x 8'

Construction Lumber—lengths of 8', 10', 12', 14', 16'

Concrete Blocks—modules of 4'

Typical guidelines:

1. Exterior walls should be modular lengths (multiples of 4' or at least multiples of 2').
2. Plan for the use of materials with as little waste as possible.
3. Plan exterior rooms with an eye on standard sizes. (Example: carpet is produced in 12' and 15' widths.)
4. Walls should be modular heights (multiples of 4').

QUALITY OF LIVING

The location of the site, the characteristics of the site itself, Fig. 3-9, the size and layout of the house, and many other factors all add up to a certain quality of living. It is the designer's job to

Fig. 3-9. Imagine the site and design considerations necessary to construct this Frank Lloyd Wright home. (Western Pennsylvania Conservancy)

take advantage of as many aspects as possible to increase the quality of living in the structures being designed. The quality of living provided by the structure is a measure of the success of the designer in solving a problem.

DRAWINGS INCLUDED IN A SET OF PLANS

Most sets of plans for residential construction include these drawings:

Plot Plan
Foundation Plan
Floor Plan
Elevations
Electrical Plan
Construction Details
Pictorial Presentations

A set of construction drawings is not complete without specification sheets. Specifications describe the quality of work and materials. They provide additional details that are not shown on the prints. The drawings and the specifications form the basis of a legal contract between the owner and the builder.

BRIEF DESCRIPTION OF PLANS

The **plot plan** shows the location of the house on the site, Fig. 3-10. It usually also shows utilities, topographical features, site dimensions, and any other buildings on the property.

A **foundation plan** illustrates the foundation size and material, Fig. 3-11. It may also include the basement plan if the house has a basement. The foundation plan gives information pertaining to excavation, waterproofing, and supporting structures.

The **floor plan** shows all exterior and interior walls, doors, windows, patios, walks, decks, fireplaces, mechanical equipment, built-in cabinets, and appliances, Fig. 3-12. A separate plan view is drawn for each floor of the house.

Elevations are drawn for each side of the structure, Figs. 3-13 and 3-14. These plans are typical orthographic projections showing the exterior features of the building. They show placement of windows and doors, type of exterior materials used, steps, chimney, rooflines, and other exterior details.

The **electrical plan** is drawn from the floor plan, Fig. 3-15. It locates switches, convenience outlets, ceiling outlet fixtures, television jacks, service entrance location, panel box, and general information concerning circuits and special installations.

Construction details are usually drawn where more information is needed to fully describe how the construction is to be done. Typical drawings include details of kitchens, stairs, chimneys, fireplaces, windows and doors, foundation walls, and items of special construction, Figs. 3-16 and 3-17.

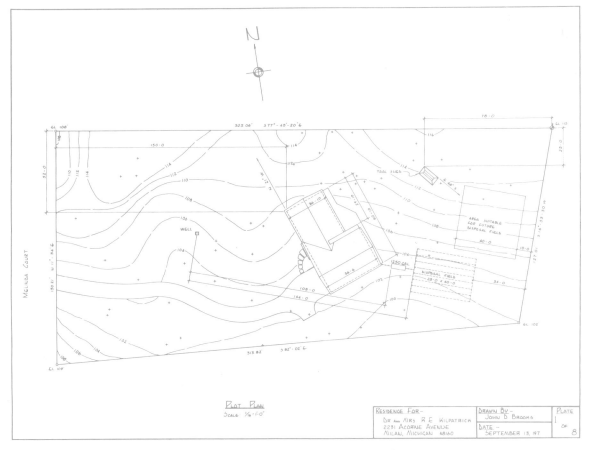

Fig. 3-10. A typical residential plot plan.

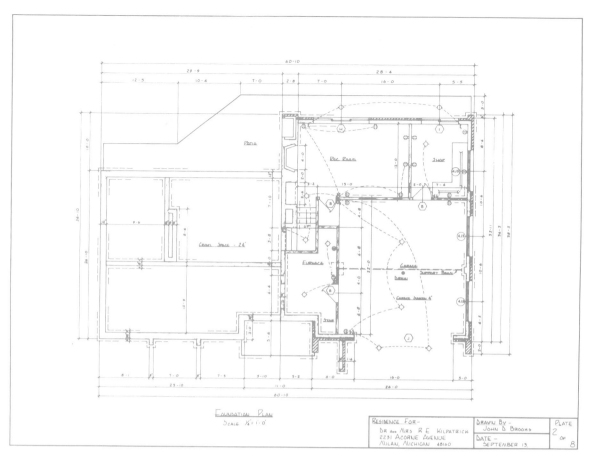

Fig. 3-11. A basement/foundation plan for a residence.

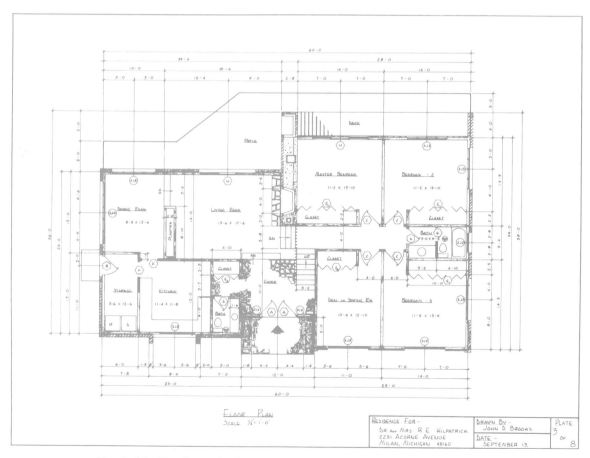

Fig. 3-12. The floor plan is the heart of a set of construction drawings.

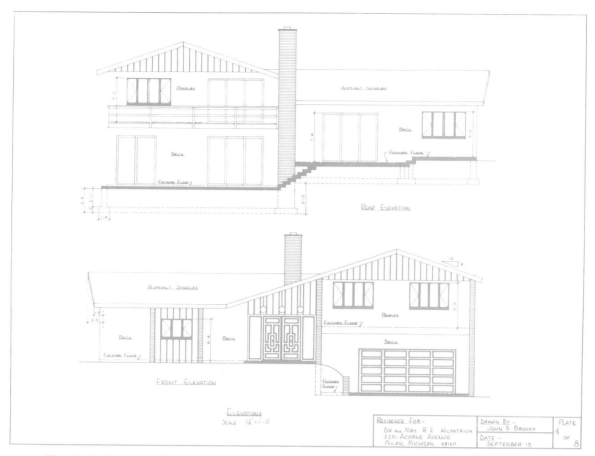

Fig. 3-13. Back and front elevations. A front elevation shows the most impressive side of the structure.

Fig. 3-14. Elevations are also drawn of the other sides of the house.

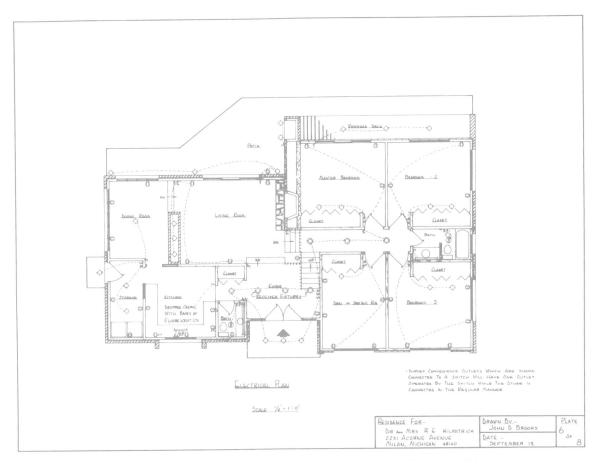

Fig. 3-15. An electrical plan is a necessary part of a well-designed home.

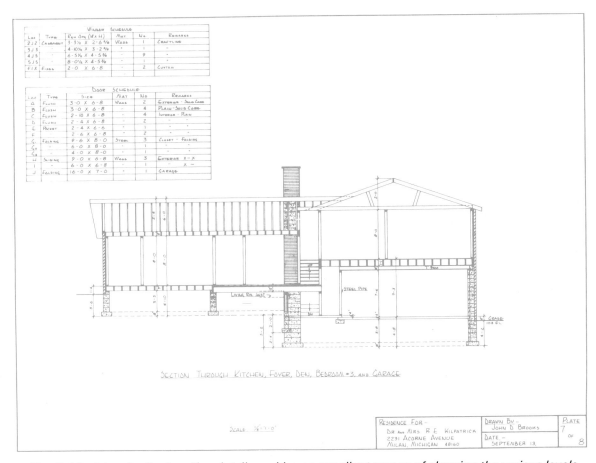

Fig. 3-16. A longitudinal section detail provides an excellent means of showing the various levels

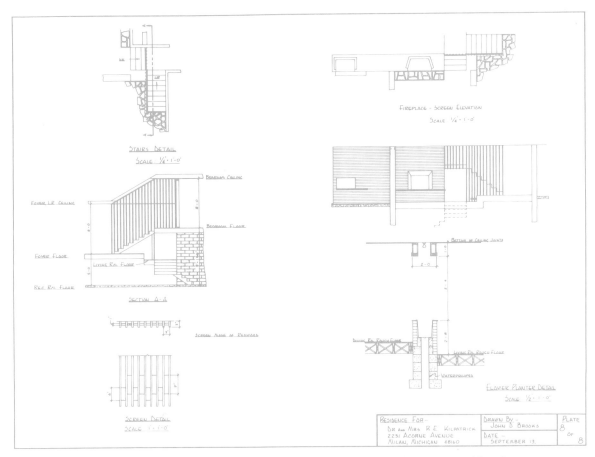

Fig. 3-17. Construction details provide the contractor with exact specifications.

A *pictorial presentation* is often included to show how the finished structure will appear. The pictorial method commonly used is the two-point perspective. Sometimes a model is used instead, or in addition to the perspective, to show the total structure.

Other drawings which may be included in a set of residential construction drawings are:

Roof Plan
Roof Framing Plan
Floor Framing Plan
Heating and Cooling Plan

Plumbing Plan
Landscaping Plan
Furniture Plan
Expansion Plan

A *roof plan* should be included if the roof is complicated and not clearly shown by the other standard drawings. The roof plan may be incorporated into the plot plan.

A *roof framing plan* should be included in a set of residential plans when the roof is complex and requires unique construction. A roof framing plan may be drawn to clarify construction aspects associated with the roof. The roof framing plan, normally shows the rafters, ceiling joists, and supporting members.

A *floor framing plan* shows direction of joists and major supporting members.

The *heating and cooling plan* illustrates components (furnace, air conditioner, heating and cooling ducts, or hot water pipes of the climate control system of the house). The design of this system is usually performed by the contractor who installs the system.

A *plumbing plan* shows such features as the hot and cold water system, waste lines, vents, storage tank if needed, placement of plumbing fixtures and cleanouts.

The *landscaping plan* is sometimes combined with the plot plan. Its purpose is to locate and identify plants and other elements included in landscaping the site.

A *furniture plan* identifies the furniture to be used and its placement in each area of the house. Even if no furniture plan is to be a part of the construction drawings, care should be taken in the design process to allow ample room for standard size furniture.

An *expansion plan* shows how the structure has been designed to accommodate future expansion. Information on the expansion plan could be presented as part of the regular construction drawings.

REVIEW QUESTIONS—CHAPTER 3

Write your answers on a separate sheet of paper. Do not write in this book.

1. List 12 factors, with respect to the house size and arrangement of rooms, that should

be considered when planning a residential structure.

2. The document that lists any legal claims against the property is called a _____.

3. The document that shows any restrictions or easements attached to the property is the _____.

4. List eight site features that are found on a topographical drawing of the site.

5. If a home is to have its own septic system and water supply, the lot should be at least _____ _____ in size. (The local code may require a larger site.)

6. What determines whether or not a house is functional?

7. List ten individual and family activities which should be provided for in a house.

8. Why should one plan a house using modular sizes?

9. Exterior walls should be lengths divisible by _____ feet.

10. List the drawings which are ordinarily included in a set of residential house plans.

11. Why should a title search be made before purchasing a lot?

12. The measure of success of the architect in designing a house is _____.

13. The cost of a site as a percentage of the total cost of a house will depend on _____ _____.

SUGGESTED ACTIVITIES

1. Obtain a map of your city or community and identify the approximate location of your house on the map.

2. Using your house as an example, determine the following characteristics:

a. How many square feet of living area does it have? (Do not include garage.)

b. What are the dimensions of the lot on which your house sits?

c. How far is it from your house to the closest grocery store?

d. How far is it from your house to the school that you attend?

e. Does your house have its own well and septic system?

f. How many homes are under construction and for sale within a 1/2 mile radius of your home?

3. Visit your local building inspector and ask to be shown copies of the codes which are used in your community. Ask how the cost of permits is calculated and what is required by the building department before a permit may be obtained.

4. Look around your neighborhood for a vacant lot or piece of property. Make a list of the ''site considerations'' that should be made if a house were to be constructed on this property. Include as many factors as necessary from this chapter that would apply to the property.

5. From your family needs, make a listing of the activity areas (space) that should be provided if you were planning a new home. Be sure to include all the needs of each member of your family and special group activity areas.

6. Prepare a display for the bulletin board that illustrates the advantages of proper site consideration when planning a house. Use clippings from magazines and other publications to show how the architect made good use of all aspects of the property to enhance the beauty of the house.

Drawing Instruments and Techniques

After studying this chapter, you will be able to:
* Define the three principal views in orthographic projection.
* List and explain the use of architectural drafting equipment.
* Discern the difference between size and scale.
* Reproduce the standard alphabet of lines.
* Demonstrate an acceptable architectural lettering style.
* Explain the use of several architectural drawing time-savers.

An understanding of basic drafting practices and the use of equipment is a necessary introduction to architectural drawing and style. Most of the equipment and many of the principles are similar to those used in a course in mechanical or technical drawing. A review of the basic drawing concepts will establish a foundation on which the techniques for architectural drawing may be developed.

ORTHOGRAPHIC PROJECTION

The use of orthographic projection is a means of representing an object from a point at infinity. For this reason, the projection lines are parallel to each other and no depth is represented in any of the primary views.

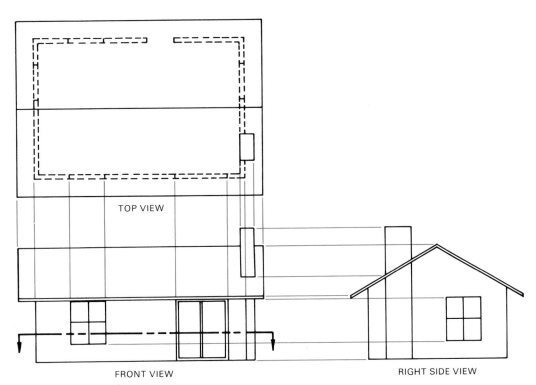

TOP VIEW

FRONT VIEW

RIGHT SIDE VIEW

Fig. 4-1. This camp cottage shows the arrangement of a regular orthographic projection.

Orthographic projection is basic to any type of drawing. It makes little difference whether you are drawing metal fasteners, electric motors, or residences, the principles remain the same. Architectural drawing applies these principles with the primary difference being the objects drawn and symbols used to represent the various parts.

THREE PRINCIPAL VIEWS

The three principal views in orthographic projection are the top, front, and right side views. In architectural drawing the names are changed slightly, but the views remain basically the same with minor exceptions.

The top view of an object in mechanical drawing is comparable to the roof plan of a house. The ''plan view'' or floor plan is the most important view and is actually a section view taken about halfway up the wall. The plan view is used as the basis for most of the other views in a house plan and for most purposes will take the place of the top view. Fig. 4-1 shows a small cottage drawn in orthographic projection using the normal arrangement. A cutting plane line is shown in the front view to illustrate how the plan view is derived for use in architectural drawings.

The front view of an object in mechanical drawing is the same as the front elevation in architectural drawing. Note that the word ''view'' is changed to ''elevation.'' Architectural drafters ordinarily drawn an elevation of all sides of the structure rather than just the front and right side as is the practice in mechanical drawing. These elevations are called the front elevation, the right side elevation, the left side elevation, and the rear elevation. Some complex structures require more than four elevations to provide a complete description. Fig. 4-2 illustrates how the plan view is used to project the elevations. It should be noted that the elevations are NOT presented upside-down and on their side as shown in this illustration. In actual drawing, the plan view is revolved so that each elevation will be drawn in its natural position.

ARCHITECTURAL DRAFTING EQUIPMENT

An architectural drafter uses equipment that is designed for specific purposes. Using this spe-

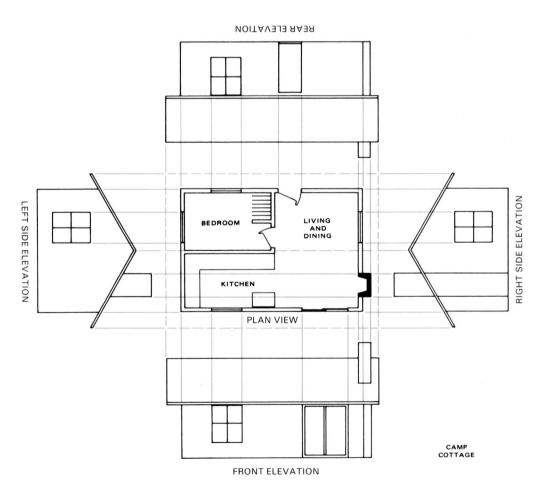

Fig. 4-2. How the four elevations of the camp cottage are projected from the plan view.

cialized equipment requires skill and understanding. Traditional drafting equipment such as triangles, scales, compass, etc. can be used to produce architectural drawings, Fig. 4-3. A computer-aided design and drafting (CADD) system can also be used, Fig. 4-4. A brief description of the major items used in each of these approaches follows.

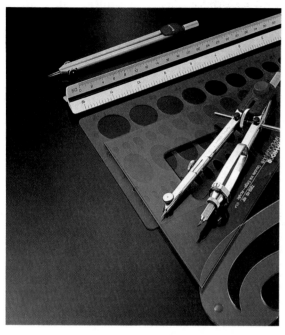

Fig. 4-3. Typical drafting equipment used for traditional architectural drawing. (Koh-I-Noor Rapidograph, Inc.)

PENCILS

Pencils used in drafting are of two principal types—the common wood pencil and the mechanical pencil. Wood pencils are still used by some drafters, but most are using the mechanical types. The mechanical pencil allows the drafter to change the hardness of lead at will, but more important, the lead is easier to sharpen and may be used close to the end. Either type of pencil will give the desired results if kept sharp and used properly. (Be sure to sharpen the proper end of a wooden pencil so as not to remove the hardness identification.) The hardness number is printed on the side of the wooden pencil and along the lead used in mechanical pencils. Fig. 4-5 illustrates the two types of pencils commonly used, lead for mechanical pencils, and a variety of pencil sharpening devices which may be used to obtain a fine conical point.

ERASERS

Most drafters prefer to use an eraser not attached to the pencil. Several common drafting erasers are shown in Fig. 4-6. Select an eraser that will remove all traces of lead without destroying the surface of the paper or leaving colored marks. Some pink erasers will leave a pinkish color which detracts from the appearance of the finished drawing. Many of the newer

Fig. 4-4. Modern CADD system used to produce drawings. (Hewlett-Packard)

Fig. 4-5. Pencils and pencil pointing devices used by an architectural drafter. (Berol USA)

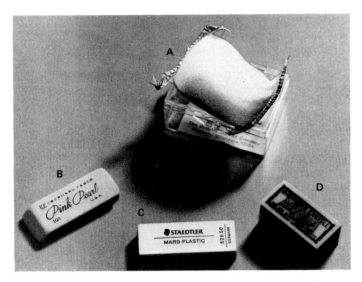

Fig. 4-6. An assortment of drawing erasers used by architects.

plastic erasers are suitable for this type of work. Electric erasers are preferred by some drafters because they quickly erase large areas, Fig. 4-7.

ERASING SHIELDS

Erasing shields, Fig. 4-8, are made of metal or plastic and are usually thin to provide for accurate erasing. The shield will allow lines to be removed without disturbing surrounding lines. Always use the erasing shield when there is a possibility of touching another line that you wish to save.

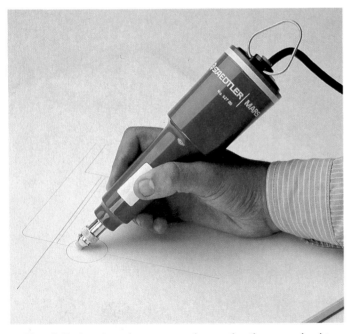

Fig. 4-7. An electric eraser reduces the time required to erase large areas. (J.S. Staedtler, Inc.)

PAPER

Drafting paper may be purchased in standard size sheets or rolls. The sheets are easier to use but are usually more costly, Fig. 4-9. The chart shows two systems of standard drawing sheet sizes.

Standard Drawing Sheet Sizes

Multiples of 8 1/2 x 11 Size	Letter Designation	Multiples of 9 x 12 Size
8 1/2 x 11	A	9 x 12
11 x 17	B	12 x 18
17 x 22	C	18 x 24
22 x 34	D	24 x 36
34 x 44	E	36 x 48

Both systems are approved by the American Standards Association and are commonly used. Most architectural drawings are executed on some type of tracing paper, vellum, or drafting film which provides for ease of reproduction.

Fig. 4-8. The use of an erasing shield will improve the quality of a drawing. (J.S. Staedtler, Inc.)

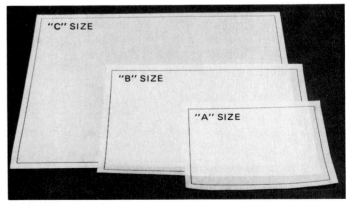

Fig. 4-9. Three standard sizes of tracing paper commonly used in architectural drawing are: ''A'' size (9 x 12), ''B'' size (12 x 18''), and ''C'' size (18 x 24'').

Preliminary drawings are sometimes made on opaque drawing paper and then later traced for reproduction. Presentation plans are often executed on illustration board or some other special type medium designed for the particular artistic technique used in the presentation. As a general rule, the type of paper selected will depend on the intended use for which the drawing is being prepared and presentation technique used.

DRAWING BOARDS

Drawing boards are made in standard sizes of 12 x 18, 18 x 24, 24 x 36, and 30 x 42''. Most boards have traditionally been white pine or basswood, but with the advent of vinyl covers, plywood, and other species are now acceptable. The use of drawing boards seems to be giving way to drawing tables with tops which serve as boards. These tables are usually larger and have a drafting machine, Fig. 4-10, or straightedge permanently attached. Such an arrangement provides adequate working area and does away with the need for a T-square.

THE T-SQUARE

T-squares are manufactured from wood, metal, plastics, and combinations of these materials. Fig. 4-11 shows one of the traditional mod-

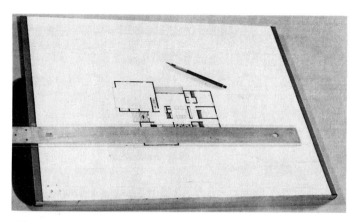

Fig. 4-11. The traditional T-square and drawing board are adequate for the beginning drafter.

els. The T-square is used to draw horizontal lines and provide an edge for guiding the triangles. The blade is held with the left hand and lines are drawn from left to right. (This is for a right-handed person. The process is reversed for a left-handed person.) The T-square should be used on only one side of the drawing board while making a drawing since the opposite edge may not be exactly parallel. Straightedges are used in much the same way as T-squares. Fig. 4-12 illustrates the use of a straightedge to draw a horizontal line.

Fig. 4-12. One procedure for drawing a horizontal line using a straightedge. (J.S. Staedtler, Inc.)

TRIANGLES

The 45 and 30-60 triangles are the common triangles used in drafting work. They may be purchased in metal or plastic. Plastic is preferred because of its transparency. Fig. 4-13 shows the adjustable triangle. Triangles are used for drawing lines that are not horizontal. Drawing

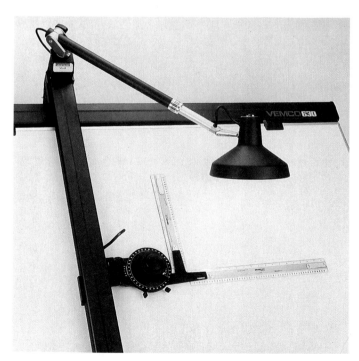

Fig. 4-10. A drafting machine allows the drafter to draw lines and measure angles conveniently. (Vemco Corporation)

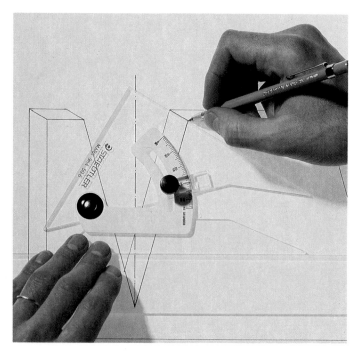

Fig. 4-13. The adjustable triangle allows the drafter to draw lines at any angle. (J.S. Staedtler, Inc.)

vertical lines in an upward direction with the hand sliding along the triangle is shown in Fig. 4-14. Adjustable triangles are also available which take the place of the 30-60 and 45 triangles. When using the adjustable type, care should be taken to adjust it accurately.

PROTRACTORS

Protractors are used for measuring angles. They are produced in semicircular and circular styles. The semicircular type is extensively used by most architectural drafters. Measurement finer than half a degree is not possible with most common protractors. However, metal protractors with a vernier scale may be purchased which will measure accurately to one minute. Fig. 4-15 illustrates the type of protractors commonly used by architectural drafters.

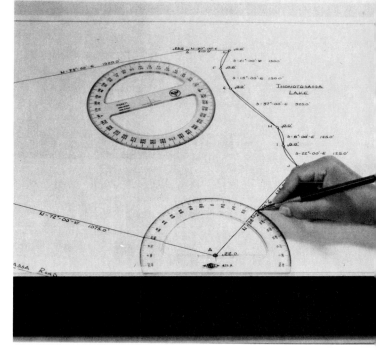

Fig. 4-15. Protractors are available in semicircular and full circle styles.

SCALES

Scales used in drawing are primarily of three types: the architect's scale, the engineer's scale, and the combination scale. Fig. 4-16 shows a typical architect's and engineer's scale. These are made of wood, plastics, metal, or a combination of materials. The architect's scale is usually divided into 3/32, 3/16, 1/8, 1/4, 1/2, 1, 3/8, 3/4, 1 1/2, and 3'' to the foot and one edge divided into 16 parts to the inch. The engineer's scale is divided into 10, 20, 30, 40,

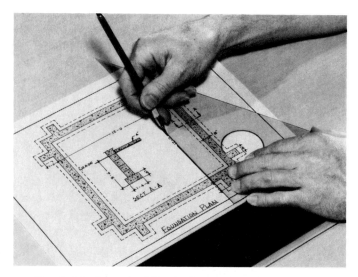

Fig. 4-14. A vertical line is drawn along the edge of a triangle from the bottom toward the top.

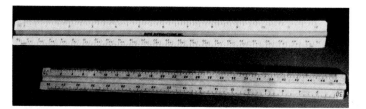

Fig. 4-16. An architectural drafter uses both an engineer's and architect's scale.

50, and 60 parts to the inch. The engineer's scale is divided into 10, 20, 30, 40, 50, and 60 parts to the inch. The combination scale is just what the name implies—a combination of the architect's and engineer's scales. It is divided into 1/8, 1/4, 1/2, 1, 3/8, and 3/4'' to the foot and 50 and 16 parts to the inch. Decimal measurements may be made using the 50th scale.

The most significant difference in these scales is that the divisions of the architect's scale is based on twelve units to the foot while the engineer's scale is based on ten units to the inch. The combination scale is designed to bridge the gap and provide both features. An architectural drafter usually needs both an architect's scale and an engineer's scale since certain drawings (topographical drawings and plot plans) require measurements in 10ths.

Scales are designed in various configurations which include two-bevel, four-bevel, opposite bevel, and triangular shapes.

How to Use the Scale

The use of words SIZE and SCALE should be clarified. In drafting terminology, one may say the drawing is ''half size.'' This means exactly what it says. The drawing is one half as large as the object in real life. When the notation at the bottom of the drawing indicates, Scale: 1/2'' = 1'-0'', then the drawing is 1/2 scale. One half scale means that 1/2'' on the drawing is equal to 1'-0'' on the object. If you were to draw a 40' x 60' house at a scale of 1/2'' = 1'' you would need a piece of paper a little over 20' x 30'. Most residential floor plans are drawn at 1/4

scale. (1/4'' on the drawing equals 1'-0'' on the house.)

Study the 1/4 scale shown in Fig. 4-17 and notice that the end 1/4'' is divided into twelve parts which represent the 12 inches of one foot. Be careful not to confuse the 1/4 scale with the 1/8 scale which appear together on the same face. The 1/4 scale has longer lines denoting each foot.

The scale shown in Fig. 4-18 indicates a measurement of 16'-4'' on the 1/4 scale. Always begin a zero on the scale and lay off the number of feet and then measure back from zero the number of inches. Use a sharp pencil and be very careful in pinpointing the exact length you wish to measure. ***Always draw as accurately as possible.*** This is a good habit to form.

DIVIDERS

Architectural drafters use dividers in basically two sizes—large (about 6'') and small (about 4''). The small dividers usually have an adjustment wheel in the center or on the side. The larger dividers often have a friction device of some type instead of the wheel. Both types are useful and considered standard equipment, Fig. 4-19.

The dividers are used to divide a line into proportional parts, provide a quick method of measuring a length which must be used a number of times, and other related uses.

Divider points are shaped like needles. They must be kept sharp to be useful.

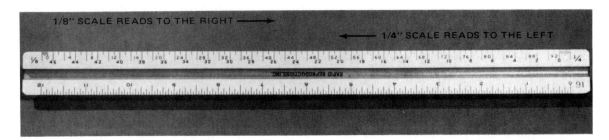

Fig. 4-17. The 1/8'' = 1'-0'' and 1/4'' = 1'-0'' scales are printed on the upper edge of this architect's scale. Note, however, that 1/4'' = 1'-0'' is standard in architectural work.

Fig. 4-18. The proper method of measuring 16'-4'' using the 1/4'' = 1'-0'' scale.

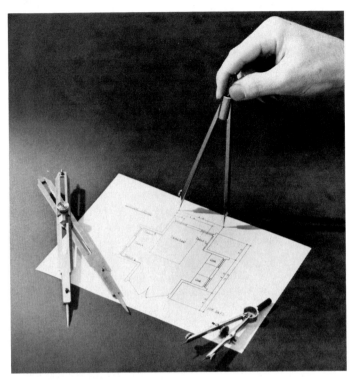

Fig. 4-19. Three types of dividers—a small center wheel divider, a large friction type divider, and a proportional divider.

THE COMPASS

The compass is produced in different styles and sizes to match the dividers. Some have center adjusting wheels and others have side adjusting wheels. The most common varieties used by architectural drafters are the giant bow (about 6'' in length), medium size friction compass and the smaller center wheel compass. Fig. 4-20 shows a large center adjusting wheel compass with three types of drawing points.

The compass is used to draw circles, arcs, or radii. Some practice is required to be able to draw sharp, smooth arcs. It is held between the thumb and forefinger and rotated in a clockwise manner while leaning it slightly forward. Large

arcs may be drawn using a beam compass as illustrated in Fig. 4-21.

Lead in the compass should be adjusted to the proper length (slightly shorter than the center point) and sharpened to a fine point. Use an F or H lead.

The center point of a compass is different from points on the divider. The compass center point may be cup shaped or have a point with a shoulder. The shoulder prevents the point from going too deep.

LETTERING GUIDES

Lettering guides are used to draw guide lines which assist in producing neat letters. The Braddock-Rowe Lettering Triangle and the Ames Lettering Guide are shown in Fig. 4-22.

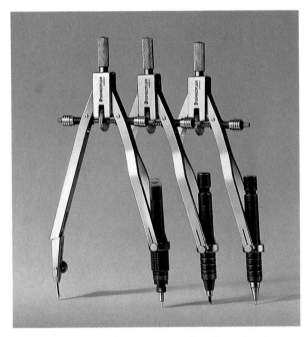

Fig. 4-20. A modern center adjusting wheel compass with three types of detachable points. (J.S. Staedtler, Inc.)

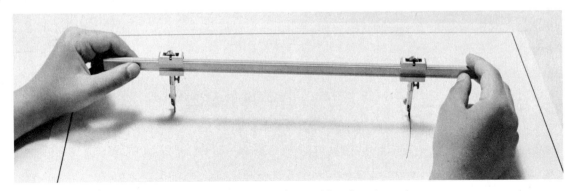

Fig. 4-21. A beam compass is used for drawing a large arc.

Fig. 4-22. Draw guidelines for lettering using either the Ames Lettering Guide or the Braddock-Rowe Lettering Triangle (above).

IRREGULAR CURVES

Irregular curves are used to draw lines which cannot be drawn with the compass. These lines usually have a series of centers and would be very difficult to construct with a compass. When using an irregular curve, line up at least four points and draw the line through three. Continue this process until the curve is completed. This procedure produces a smoother line. Fig. 4-23 shows how a flexible curve could be used to draw a long curved line.

Fig. 4-23. Flexible curves are used to draw curved lines which are not arcs of a circle.

CASE INSTRUMENTS

The case instruments may include dividers, compass, lining pens, pencil pointers, spare parts, small screwdriver, and various other instruments. Some students may wish to purchase a set of case instruments rather than individual parts. Fig. 4-24 shows a small set of case instruments.

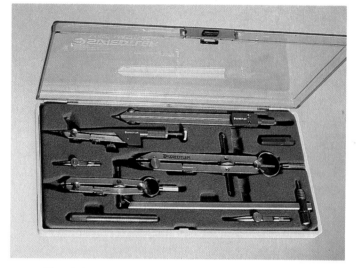

Fig. 4-24. A beginner's set of case instruments. (J.S. Staedtler, Inc.)

LETTERING DEVICES

Lettering devices are used when uniformity of letters is essential. Many styles and sizes of letters are available. Two popular types are shown in Figs. 4-25 and 4-26. Lettering in ink and pencil is possible with both types.

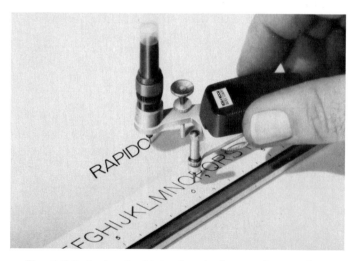

Fig. 4-25. A standard lettering device used to produce mechanical type letters. (Koh-I-Noor Rapidograph, Inc.)

Fig. 4-26. A stencil type lettering device used to form precise letters. (J.S. Staedtler, Inc.)

TECHNICAL PENS

Technical pens are used by the drafter to letter and draw straight and curved lines in ink, Fig. 4-27. They have about replaced the old lining pen of years past. Pen points are interchangeable and range in size from 000 (very fine) to 8 (about 1/16 in. wide), Fig. 4-28.

Fig. 4-28. A typical set of technical fountain pens. (J.S. Staedtler, Inc.)

COMPUTER-AIDED DESIGN AND DRAFTING

Architectural design and drafting as well as generating schedules and analyses can be done using a modern (CADD) computer-aided design and drafting system. The entire process—from conceptual design to the actual production of the construction drawings—can be completed on a computer system configured for CADD application, Fig. 4-29. New software designed specifically for architectural, engineering, and construction (AEC) applications makes the drafting process easy and efficient. These systems completely replace the equipment used by the traditional drafter.

Using a computer system to design structures and generate drawings still requires a knowledge

Fig. 4-27. Technical fountain pens used for inking lines and lettering. (J.S. Staedtler, Inc.)

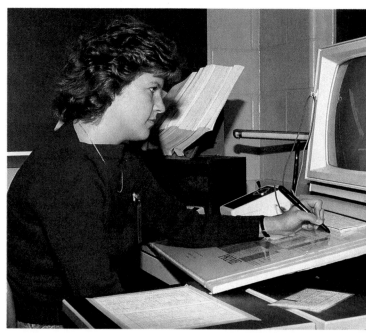

Fig. 4-29. A typical CADD workstation used to produce architectural drawings.

of the field. You must know orthographic projection, sections, auxiliary views, the use of standard architectural symbols and conventions, and dimensioning procedures. Knowledge of contemporary construction practices is essential. The drafter is still responsible for communicating his/her ideas in a manner that is recognized by practitioners in the field, Fig. 4-30. The computer system merely replaces traditional tools for recording, manipulating, and reproducing ideas.

COMPUTER

The computer or processor is probably the most critical component in a CADD system. The computer is composed of three components: a data processing or logic section, a memory or control section, and a data transfer mechanism or data bus. Each component serves a specific function.

The **data processing unit** executes the commands given the computer by the operator or software program. The type of operations performed in this section generally include:
Selecting memory locations for programs.
Transferring instructions and data to and from input and output devices such as disk drives, displays, plotters, digitizers, and printers.
Performing arithmetic and logic functions.

The **memory** or **control section** of the computer contains programs which are currently in use or on-line. Memory locations are assigned for data storage. The data in a memory location frequently changes, but the location itself remains constant.

The **transfer mechanism** or **data bus** is a bundle of circuits over which data travel. Data travel to and from the processor and peripherals and

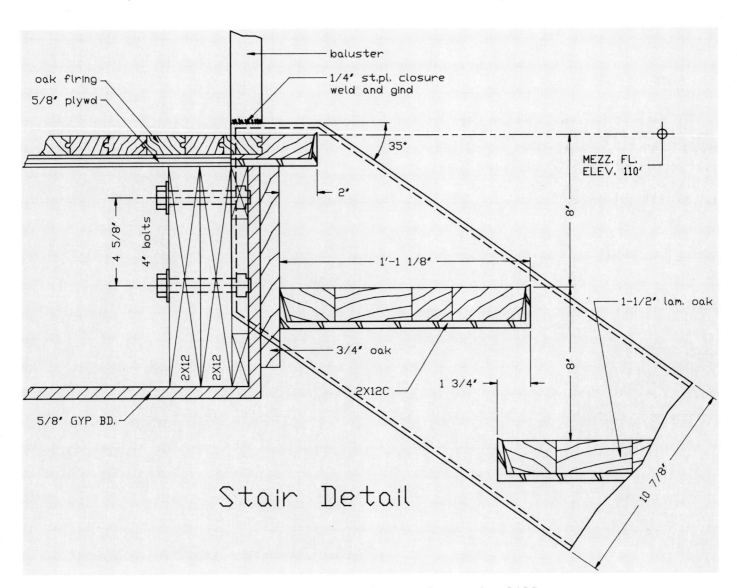

Fig. 4-30. A stair detail, designed and drawn using a modern CADD system.

the processing unit and memory section. The transfer mechanism is similar to a pipeline.

CADD SOFTWARE

The **CADD software** provides the operations to be performed on the data by the computer. In short, software is a computer program designed for a specific application. Each computer program is composed of a series of instructions which are to be executed in a specified sequence. These instructions are written in one of several computer languages.

Many CADD software packages are available for general and specific applications. General drafting packages are used for mechanical and technical drafting. Architectural, engineering, and construction (AEC) packages are specifically made for the design and illustration of structures—houses, commercial buildings, bridges, and roads, Fig. 4-31. Other software programs are even more specific and are used in conjunction with CADD AEC packages. An example is Andersen's window program which includes the dimensions and details of all their windows.

How user friendly any CADD system is largely depends on the design of the software program. In choosing a program, first decide what you want to accomplish. Then, select a program that was designed to perform that task.

OUTPUT DEVICES

Any CADD system must be able to output a paper hardcopy to be useful as a drafting machine. The most common used devices are pen plotters, electrostatic plotters, photoplotters, and printers.

The device which most experienced drafters choose is the **pen plotter,** Fig. 4-32. It draws in much the same way that a drafter does. It produces a very accurate drawing in ink on a variety of materials—paper, vellum, or polyester film. Pen plotters are classified as either drum or flatbed plotters. Either type will produce a quality drawing.

An **electrostatic plotter** is probably the most versatile type of plotter. It can function as a plotter or printer. This type of machine is much faster than a pen plotter, but does not produce as sharp a line. Electrostatic plotters do not draw one line at a time as the pen plotter does. Instead, it produces images in the form of small dots arranged in a matrix. Another consideration is the size of drawing that can be produced on the machine. Most electrostatic plotters are designed for ''A'' or ''B'' size paper, but some will handle ''C'' and ''D'' size. Architectural drawings generally require at least ''C'' size paper.

Photoplotters are not commonly used for architectural drafting. They are very accurate and, therefore, used for applications such as plotting printed-circuit-board masters. These machines use a light beam and special photosensitive paper. They can achieve an accuracy of plus or

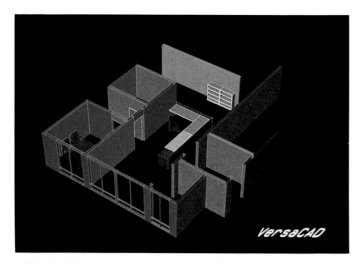

Fig. 4-31. A computer-generated pictorial of a structural drawing showing the basic space layout. (VersaCAD Corporation)

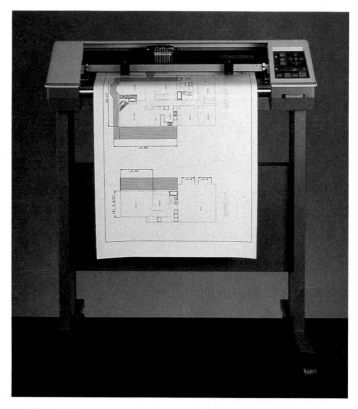

Fig. 4-32. A modern pen plotter used to produce very accurate CADD drawings. (Bruning)

minus .0005 inch. The main disadvantage is the high cost of the unit.

Printers are designed to produce a hardcopy for alphanumeric data—the typical computer printout. Two types of printers are commonly used for CADD drawings: impact printers and electrostatic printers. *Impact printers* produce images by striking character keys against an inked or carbon ribbon. *Electrostatic printers* form images by charging a special electrographic paper with an electron beam in the form of the desired character. A special ink spray is passed over the surface and is attracted to the electrostatically charged areas. This type of machine is faster than an impact printer.

LINES USED IN ARCHITECTURAL DRAWING

Architectural drafters use a number of different line symbols which assist in clarifying the drawing to the reader. Drawings are usually made for a customer or as a presentation. It is for the purpose of accurate communication that a specific line symbol is used in a given situation. Once the drafter learns these lines and uses them properly, he will begin to communicate with others in a more precise manner. *The purpose of a drawing is to communicate ideas accurately and clearly.*

Drafters refer to the line symbols used in drawing as the *alphabet of lines.* Many of the same symbols used in mechanical or technical drawing are also used in architectural drawing. However, one not familiar with architectural line symbols should study them carefully to be sure that their use is clearly understood. Some symbols may be slightly different in architectural work. Study Fig. 4-33 which illustrates the major lines used in architectural drawing.

BORDER LINES

Border lines are very heavy lines and are used to form a boundary for the drawing. They assure the reader that no part of the drawing has been removed and provide a ''finished'' appearance to the drawing. A #4 (.047'', 1.20mm) technical pen should be used for the border line.

OBJECT LINES

Object lines show the outline of the main features of the object. They are important lines and therefore should be easily seen. On an architec-

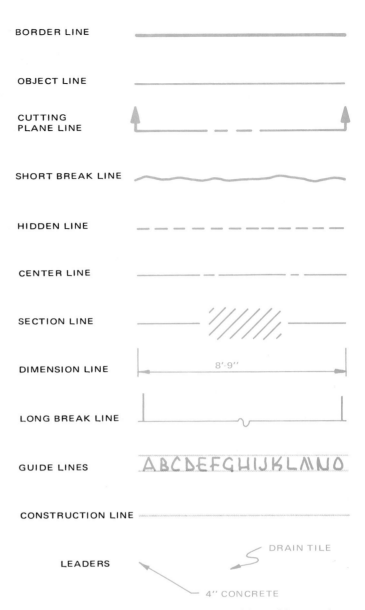

Fig. 4-33. General line symbols used in architectural drawing.

tural drawing, such things as interior and exterior walls, steps, driveways, patios, fireplaces, doors, and windows are represented by object lines. The width of an object line should be between .024'' (0.60 mm) and .028'' (0.70 mm) wide. A #2 or 2 1/2 pen point will produce these widths.

HIDDEN LINES

Hidden lines represent an edge that is not visible in a given view. Note that in a floor plan, hidden lines are also used to indicate features above the cutting plane, such as wall cabinets in a kitchen or an archway. Hidden lines are usually not as thick as object lines. A #1 pen (.020'', 0.50 mm) pen is recommended.

CENTER LINES

Center lines indicate the center of symmetrical objects such as windows and doors. Center lines simplify dimensioning, but should not be used as extension lines. Dimension to extension lines. Center lines may be drawn with a #0 pen (.014'' or 0.35 mm). A #00 (.012'' or 0.30 mm) may also be used for center lines and extension lines.

EXTENSION LINES

Extension lines are used to denote the termination point of a dimension line. They extend from a portion of the object to the dimension lines. Extension lines are thin lines, but are not construction lines, therefore, draw them sharp and clear to about 1/16'' past the dimension line. Use a #0 or #00 pen.

DIMENSION LINES

Dimension lines are used to show size and location. They are usually placed outside the object, but it is sometimes proper to place them within the object if the area is large and not too cluttered with other lines. All dimension lines have a dimension figure halfway between the ends with some form of symbol at the two terminal ends. Fig. 4-34 shows accepted methods of terminating dimension lines and placing the dimension figures. Dimension lines are drawn with a #0 or #00 pen.

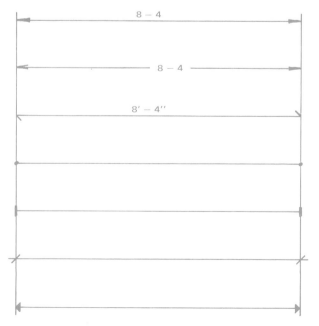

Fig. 4-34. Styles of dimension lines used in architecture.

LONG BREAK LINES

Long break lines are thin lines used to show that all of the part is not drawn. When the break is two or three inches in length, then a long break line is usually used. An example of a long break line might be found across a paved driveway indicating that the drive was longer than shown on the plan. Break lines may be drawn with a #0 or #00 pen.

SHORT BREAK LINES

Short break lines are used where part of the object is shown broken away to reveal an underlying feature or part of the object removed for some other reason. Short break lines are heavy lines drawn freehand. A #3 pen (.031'', 0.80 mm) is generally used for short break lines.

CUTTING PLANE LINES

Cutting plane lines are heavy lines used to show where the object is to be sectioned. Ordinarily, cutting plane lines are labeled with a letter at each end or a flag at one end and a direction arrow at the other so that the section detail will be easily identified. A #3 pen should be used.

SECTION LINES

Section lines or **crosshatch lines** are used to show that the feature has been sectioned. General section lines are usually drawn at a 45° angle, but specific symbols may represent various types of material. A #00 pen is generally used for section lines.

GUIDELINES

Guidelines are used in lettering. They are drawn very light and are for the drafter's use. Guidelines will help improve the quality of lettering and are, therefore, well worth the time and effort required to draw them. Guidelines are drawn in pencil only.

CONSTRUCTION LINES

Construction lines are very light lines used in the process of constructing a drawing. Again, they are for the drafter and should not reproduce when a print is made. Draw your construction lines sharp and light.

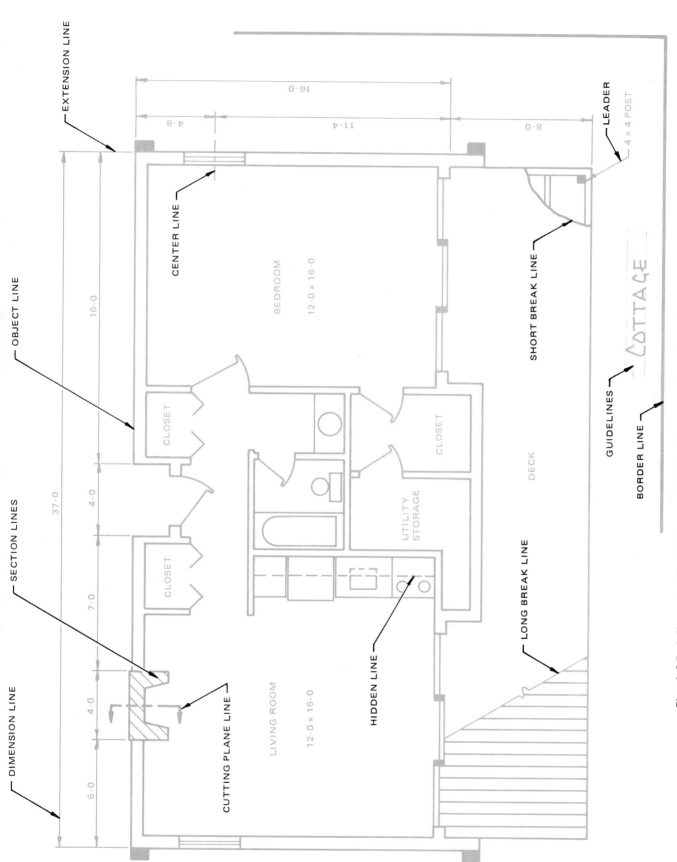

Fig. 4-35. A floor plan illustrating most of the line symbols used by the architectural drafter.

Fig. 4-35 shows most of the general line symbols applied in a floor plan. Other symbols will be found in areas pertaining to their specific use. A close examination of the lines shown in Fig. 4-35 shows that they vary in thickness (width) but not in shade. **All lines are black and vary only in width.** A thin line may look lighter than a thick line but in reality they are both black. Just remember that all lines (except construction lines and guidelines) must be dark so that reproduction of the drawing will be possible; light lines will not reproduce satisfactorily.

Certain types of lines lend themselves to hard or soft pencil leads. As a general rule, use 4H for dimension lines, extension lines, center lines, leader lines, long break lines, and section lines; 2H for object lines, hidden lines, cutting plane lines, short break lines and border lines; H for lettering; and 6H for construction and guidelines. These are not absolutes, but will vary with the type of paper being used and the pressure applied. The harder the lead, the more difficult it is to draw a dark line. The leads in the soft range (B-9B) are too soft to use in architectural drawing because they smear quite easily. Therefore, choose the lead which will allow you to draw a sharp dark line which will not smear. Note the following hardness range of pencil leads available to the drafter to meet the many needs in line weight.

9H 8H 7H 6H 5H 4H 3H 2H H F HB B 2B 3B 4B 5B 6B 7B 8B 9B
Very Hard   Medium   Very Soft

Always use the proper line symbol so that communication will be clear to the reader.

ARCHITECTURAL LETTERING

Architectural lettering is not the same as mechanical or technical lettering. The nature of an architectural drawing borders on art work and the "pure" letters used in mechanical drawing are not in keeping with architectural style.

There is no "one" correct architectural lettering style. Many acceptable styles present a certain artistic flair. Architects often like to develop their own personal style which is unique. Fig. 4-36 shows three individual styles developed by students of architecture. Each of the styles is different, but each is in keeping with the feeling of architecture.

SOME NOTES ON DEVELOPING A STYLE OF LETTERING

1. Draw guidelines and use them.
2. Experiment with variations of the capital letters of the alphabet to determine the ones you like best, Fig. 4-37. Lower case letters are seldom used in architectural lettering.
3. Select letter styles that are artistic but readily identifiable.
4. Apply a basic technique to all similar letters of the alphabet, Fig. 4-38.
5. Letter the entire alphabet large enough so that the proportion of the letters is distinct.
6. Make a mental picture of each letter so that you may reproduce it the same each time.
7. Practice "your" style until it becomes a part of you and flows easily.
8. Use your style.

Fig. 4-37. Variations of standard letters may add interest to your style.

Fig. 4-36. Architectural students should develop their own personal lettering style.

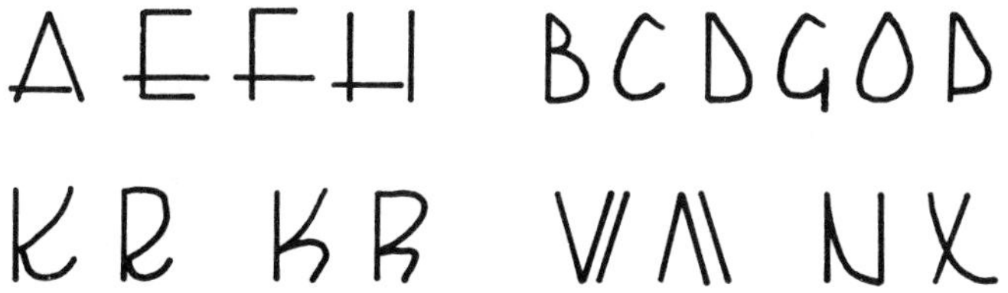

Fig. 4-38. Treat similar letters the same way to increase unity of style.

Architectural lettering should be vertical. If you learn to letter that way, you should never have to worry whether your method will be acceptable. Slanted letters usually indicate that the word is in italics. This is only used for emphasis applications.

LETTER SPACING

The space between letters in a word is not a constant. The ability to judge the space between letters must be carefully learned. Only practice will perfect this ability. Fig. 4-39 shows an example of spacing as a constant, and then in a more pleasing arrangement with variable spacing. Constant practice in lettering words helps develop the ability to space letters in a pleasing attractive manner.

LINE   LINE
POOR   GOOD

Fig. 4-39. Variable spacing of letters adds interest and is more pleasing to the eye.

WORD SPACING

The space between words is as important as the spacing between letters. Words must not appear to run together, nor should they be so far apart that valuable space is wasted. A good rule to follow in spacing words is to allow approximately the same distance between words as the letters are high.

LETTER SIZE

There are no absolute rules concerning lettering size. Generally, most information lettering on architectural drawing is 1/8'' or 3/32'' high. A technique that looks good and helps in the readability of lettering is to make the first letter of each word 1/8'' high and the remainder of the

Fig. 4-40. Draw the first letter of each word larger than the succeeding letters for emphasis.

word 3/32'' high. This emphasizes the beginning of each word and tends to separate them, Fig. 4-40.

Titles and important words are usually lettered larger, with bold lines being used to direct attention to their importance. Underlining also helps to call attention to important information.

ARCHITECTURAL DRAWING TIME-SAVERS

In years past, architectural drafters drew all details with standard instruments. This was time-consuming and hindered standardization of many common elements found on architectural drawings. Today we are fortunate in having at our fingertips many devices which speed up our work and add to the readability of our drawings. These devices are architectural time-savers.

TEMPLATES

Templates serve as a guide in drawing special lines or symbols. Most templates used in drawing are made of plastic. Fig. 4-41 shows a

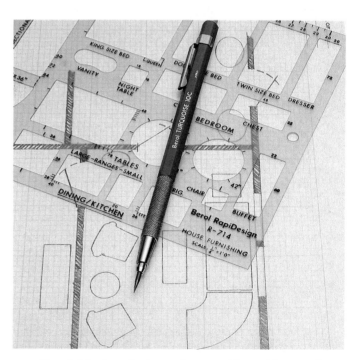

Fig. 4-41. A typical template used in architectural drawing. (Berol USA)

typical plastic template used in architectural drawing. The cutouts represent standard symbols and may be traced to form the symbol on the drawing. Some of the features on the templates are general in nature and may be used to form symbols not represented on the template. A wide variety of templates may be purchased in various scales to suit the requirements of most any drawing.

UNDERLAYS

Underlays are similar to templates. Symbols are printed or drawn on a sheet which is placed under the drawing and traced. Underlays are usually made for symbols that are used repeatedly. Symbols such as trees, bricks, stone, siding, and even doors and windows may be traced from underlays. Fig. 4-42 shows several underlays which are used by architectural drafters.

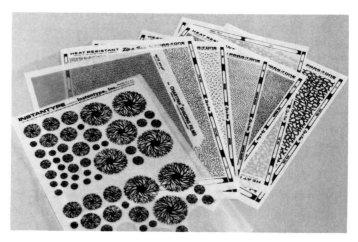

Fig. 4-43. A variety of permanent type overlays available to the drafter.

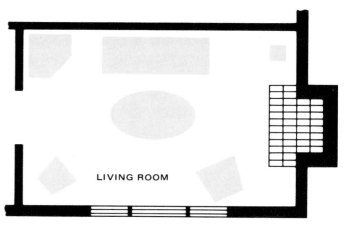

Fig. 4-44. Acetate overlays provide a technique for adding information to a drawing. Areas in color are on plastic overlay.

Fig. 4-42. Underlays are a useful aid to the drafter drawing difficult symbols.

OVERLAYS

Two types of overlays are commonly used in architectural drawing. The first type is printed on a transparent film and is attached directly to the original drawing by the use of an adhesive backing, Fig. 4-43. This overlay becomes a permanent part of the drawing and cannot be readily removed.

The second type of overlay is not permanently attached to the original drawing. The same materials may be used, but are attached to a transparent acetate sheet which is placed over the

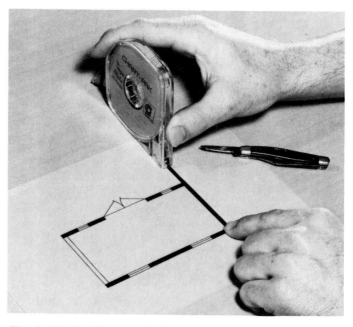

Fig. 4-45. Drafting tape being used to shade the wall thickness on a drawing of a storage house.

drawing, Fig. 4-44. This overlay may be used to emphasize specific features or provide alternate solutions. These overlays may be removed or used with a variety of other overlays.

DRAFTING TAPES

Drafting tapes are manufactured in opaque and transparent color from 1/64'' to 2'' wide. They may be used on vellum, plastic overlays, or illustration board, Fig. 4-45. The transparent tapes are especially effective on overlays to represent areas of interest or to emphasize certain elements.

Pattern tapes are available that represent such standard symbols as hidden lines, arrowheads, north symbols, section lines, dot patterns, and many others, Fig. 4-46.

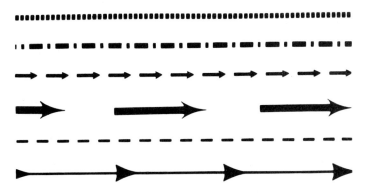

Fig. 4-46. Pattern tapes are available which represent many standard line symbols.

TRANSFER LETTERS AND SYMBOLS

Letters and symbols are easily applied to drawings using **transfer type.** Large title letters and difficult symbols are available for use by architectural drafters. A smooth rounded object is used to burnish them on. These reproduce well. In some cases they may be removed if desired. Fig. 4-47 shows a sample of the transfer materials available to architectural drafting students.

STENCIL LETTERING GUIDES

Stencil lettering guides are available in plastic, metal, and cardboard. Stencils are actually templates and are used in the same way. There are a variety of styles on the market. Lettering guides probably should not be listed as time-savers. A drafter who has developed a lettering style and practices it, will be able to letter faster freehand than when using a lettering stencil. A stencil also prevents the development of an individual style. In architectural drawing, the stencil should be reserved for special situations.

LETTERING MACHINES

Quality lettering is possible using a lettering machine similar to the one shown in Fig. 4-48. These devices combine "type-on-tape" lettering with the latest microelectronic technology. Several fonts are available and various styles of tape are possible: all purpose, diazo, photo, and labeling. The more sophisticated machines have an editor display screen that allows corrections to be made before printing.

PHOTO OR SCISSORS DRAFTING

Photo or scissors drafting is a technique that can be a time-saver in a variety of situations. It combines drafting, paste-ups, and photography or other copying. Rather than redraw an entire plate when revisions are needed, you produce a paste-up, make a photograph or copy, and in this way obtain a final drawing quicker. Old, dirty drawings can often be copied to obtain improved quality using photography. This technique can often be combined with other time-savers, Fig. 4-49.

GRIDS

Grids are available in a wide variety of sizes and forms and have many uses in architectural

Fig. 4-47. Transfer letters and symbols save time and add a professional touch to a drawing.

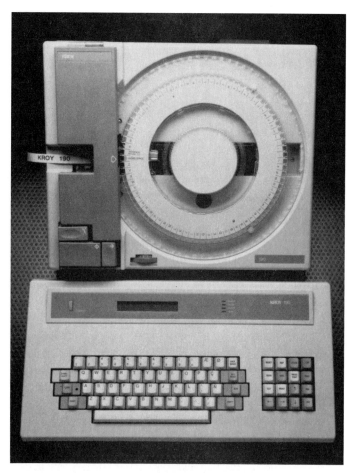

Fig. 4-48. A lettering stencil may be used for titles and for special effects as well as regular lettering. This is a type-on-tape lettering machine which produces press-ons for precise lettering jobs. (Kroy, Inc.)

drawing, Fig. 4-50. Some grids are designed to be used under a sheet of tracing paper as an underlay, while others are designed to be drawn on directly. Square grids are useful in sketching idea plans and in modular construction drawings. These grids are produced in standard size sheets with 2, 4, 8, 16, and 32 squares per inch including reproducible and nonreproducible grid lines.

Another type of grid used in architectural drawing is the perspective grid. These grids are quite useful and usually serve an underlays. Vanishing points are preselected on perspective grids. Numerous variations are available.

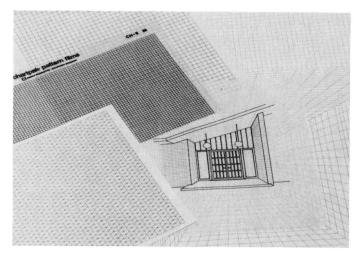

Fig. 4-50. A variety of useful grids.

A

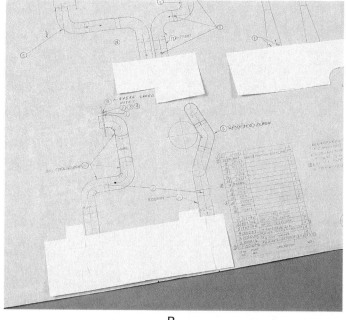

B

Fig. 4-49. A—Composites made from paste-ups make clear, sharp copies in a fraction of the time required to draw the component parts. B—Blocking, or masking, is another technique that provides a copy with cleared areas for revisions. (Bruning)

RUBBER STAMPS

A relatively new time-saving technique in architectural drawing is the use of rubber stamps. Stamps are available of many standard architectural symbols. They are especially useful on plot plans and presentation plans. Fig. 4-51 shows a sample of tree stamps which range in size from less than one inch to over four inches. Trees require a certain amount of artistic ability to draw attractively. The tree stamp helps to solve the problem in a minimum of time.

BURNISH PLATES

Burnish plates are a special type underlay device. The plates, Fig. 4-52, are raised in the

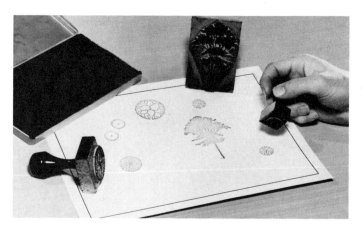

Fig. 4-51. Tree stamps are a popular new addition to the architectural drafter's equipment.

Fig. 4-52. Burnishing plates enable the drafter to add minute detail in a minimum of time.

sections where lines are desired and recessed in all other areas. A pencil is used as a burnishing tool which results in a transfer of the symbol onto the surface of the tracing. The method is easy to use and accurate. It also reduces the time required to draw siding, bricks, trees, roofing, and many other symbols to a fraction of the time required by conventional methods.

COMPUTER SYMBOL LIBRARY

A significant architectural drafting time-savers, and chief reason for using CADD, is a symbol library. Most CADD AEC software packages include a series of standard symbols designed for use in architectural, engineering, and construction drawings. These symbols, and those designed by the user, can be stored on disk in a library and called up when needed. This saves time since each symbol needs to be created only once. Furthermore, a user can have several symbol libraries for various applications—material sections, plan views of standard architectural symbols, or elevation views of structural elements. Symbol libraries are available for most CADD programs.

Each symbol stored in the symbol library has a corresponding menu position, Fig. 4-53, or identification number that is used to call it up. Once the symbol appears on the screen, it may be changed to the desired size, position, and angle.

REVIEW QUESTIONS—CHAPTER 4

Write your answers on a separate sheet of paper. Do not write in this book.
1. The three principal views in orthographic projection are _____, _____, and _____ _____ views.
2. The most important view or plan in a set of architectural drawings is the _____ _____.
3. To erase accurately, use a(n) _____ _____.
4. Drafting paper is produced in standard sizes. The dimensions of ''B'' size paper are _____ or _____.
5. A newer piece of drafting equipment which replaces the T-square, but not triangles, is the _____.
6. The two triangles most commonly used in architectural drawing are the _____ and the _____ triangles.
7. The most accurate measurement possible with a common drafting protractor is _____.

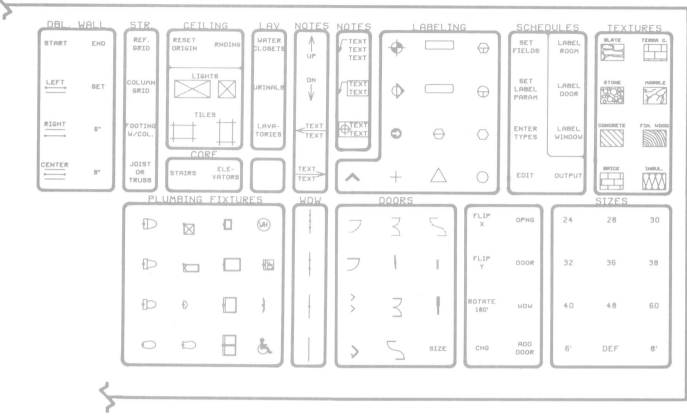

Fig. 4-53. Typical architectural symbols may be called up from the symbol library using an overlay on the digitizing tablet. (Sigma Design, Inc.)

8. A scale that is only divided into 10, 20, 30, 40, 50, and 60 parts to the inch is an _____ scale.
9. If a drawing is half as large as the object, then the scale is _____.
10. If 1/4 in. on the drawing equals 1 ft. on the object, then the scale is _____.
11. Other than the scale, the instrument that is used to divide a length into proportional parts is the _____.
12. The instrument used to draw circles and arcs is the _____.
13. Guidelines may be drawn with a pencil using a _____ _____.
14. The purpose of a drawing is to _____.
15. The _____ line is the widest line on a drawing and provides a ''finished'' look.
16. Visible lines are also called _____ lines.
17. Lines that are not visible are _____ lines.
18. Lines that are used to indicate the length of a line or edge are called _____ lines.
19. A number H pencil is usually used for _____ on an architectural drawing.
20. Architectural lettering is different from mechanical lettering. It is more _____.
21. Space between letters in a word is _____.
22. Letters on an architectural drawing are generally _____ or _____ high.
23. Symbols on an architectural drawing may be traced using what four devices?
24. Symbols may be attached to the surface of a drawing using what five devices?
25. What is the purpose of a CADD system?
26. List the three components of a computer (processor).
27. What is the purpose of CADD software?
28. What type of CADD package would be best for the design of a residential structure?
29. What type of hardcopy output device is most popular for architectural applications?

SUGGESTED ACTIVITIES

1. Letter the alphabet using architectural style letters on a sheet of grid paper. Make the letters at least 1/4'' high so the proportions will be distinct. Also letter the numbers using an architectural style.
2. Draw the ''alphabet of lines'' using proper line weights. Identify each line with its correct name. Design a title block which identifies the drawing. The following information should appear in this title block: your name,

title of the drawing, the date, the class name, and the plate number.

3. Visit a drafting supply store and make a list with prices of the types of time-savers they carry in stock that are used in architectural drawing.

4. Obtain a sketch pad with square grid lines. Measure your drafting lab and sketch a plan view showing the walls, doors, and windows. Dimension the plan as illustrated in this chapter. Use proper line symbols and line weights. Make the drawing at 1/4 scale.

5. Write letters to some of the major drafting equipment supply companies and ask for their specification literature. Prepare a bulletin board display by clipping and mounting illustrations of pieces of equipment and time-savers most used by the architectural drafter.

6. Visit a local computer store and ask for a demonstration of one of the popular CADD AEC software programs that they sell. Collect literature about the software program and the type of equipment required to run it. Make a report to your class on the program and equipment and share the literature.

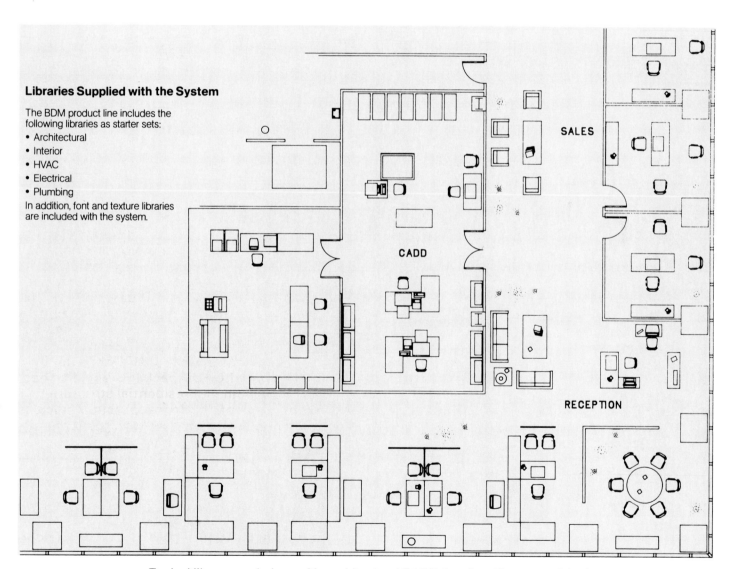

Typical library symbols used in architectural CADD drawing. (Computervision)

Fig. 5-1. A residence may be divided into three basic areas: the Sleeping Area, the Living Area, and the Service Area.

Room Planning, Sleeping Area

After studying this chapter, you will be able to:
- Discuss factors that are important in the design of bedrooms.
- Plan the size and location of closets for a typical residence.
- Apply the furniture cut-out method in planning a room arrangement.
- Implement important design considerations for bathrooms.
- Plan a bathroom that follows solid design principles.

A residential structure may be divided into three basic areas, the Sleeping Area, the Living Area, and the Service Area, Fig. 5-1. The Sleeping Area is where the family sleeps and rests. The Living Area is where the family relaxes, entertains guests, dines, and meets together. The Service Area is the part of the house where food is prepared, clothes are laundered, goods are stored, the car is parked, and equipment for upkeep of the house is maintained.

These three basic areas are generally divided into rooms. Rooms provide privacy and help to separate and contain various activities. A house designer must understand the purpose for each room if a functional plan is to be developed.

SLEEPING AREA

Usually about one-third of the house is dedicated to the sleeping area which includes bedrooms, bath, dressing rooms, and nurseries.

Normally the sleeping area is in a quiet part of the house away from traffic and other noise. If possible, the sleeping area should have a south or southwest orientation so that it may take advantage of cool summer breezes which usually prevail from this direction.

BEDROOMS

Bedrooms are so important that houses are frequently categorized as "two-bedroom," "three-bedroom," or "four-bedroom." The size of the family usually determines the number of bedrooms needed. Ideally, each person would have his or her own bedroom, Fig. 5-2. In the case of a couple with no children, at least two bedrooms are desirable. The second bedroom could be used as a guest room and for other activities when there are no guests. A home with only one bedroom may be difficult to sell. In most localities three-bedroom homes have the greatest sales potential. A three-bedroom home usually provides enough space for a family of four. It may be wise to include an extra bedroom in the plan which can be used for other purposes

Fig. 5-2. A bedroom designed for typical activities and interests. (Wilsonart)

Fig. 5-3. An extra bedroom may be used as a den or for guests. (Georgia-Pacific Corporation)

room plan, separates the master bedroom from the remaining bedrooms to provide even greater privacy. Another plan might utilize a bedroom in another area of the home for an employee, live-in relative, or overnight guests. Each bedroom should have its own access to the hall. An attempt should be made to place each bedroom close to a bathroom. Some bedrooms may have their own private baths.

One of the first problems in designing a bedroom is determining its size. How large is a "big" bedroom, Fig. 5-5? How little is a "small bedroom"? The FHA (Federal Housing Administration) recommends 100 square feet as the minimum size. A small bedroom is shown in Fig. 5-6. It has 99 square feet and the bare essentials in furniture. An average size bedroom, Fig. 5-7, contains between 125 and 175 square feet. Such a room provides ample space for a double or twin beds, chest of drawers, dresser, and other small pieces of furniture. A large bedroom has over 175 square feet of floor space, Fig. 5-8. A room of this size provides space for additional furniture. A desk, chair, or television set may be included as bedroom furniture. The largest bedroom is usually considered to be the

until needed, Fig. 5-3. It is usually more economical to add an extra room at the outset than to expand later.

Grouping bedrooms together in a separate wing or level of the house, Fig. 5-4, affords solitude and privacy. Another plan, the split bed-

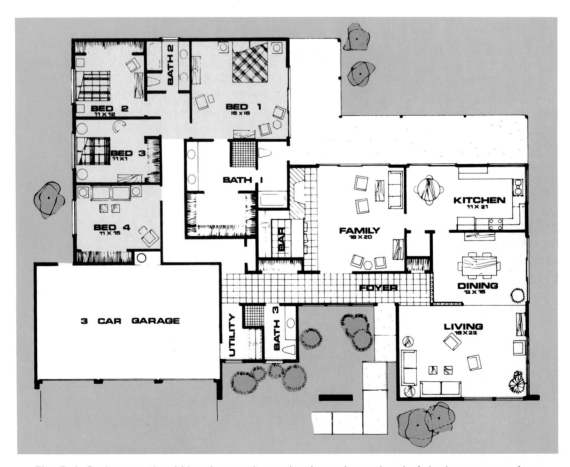

Fig. 5-4. Bedrooms should be clustered together in a wing or level of the house away from noise and other activities.

Fig. 5-5. A large bedroom allows for a variety of furniture and space for relaxation. (The Lane Company)

master bedroom. It may have its own private bath.

It is necessary for each bedroom to have a closet, Fig. 5-9. The FHA recommends a minimum of four linear feet of closet rod space for a man and six feet for a woman. The minimum depth of a clothes closet is two feet. If space is available, a 30'' depth is desirable. When possible, closets should be located along interior walls rather than exterior walls. This provides noise insulation between rooms and does not reduce exterior wall space. In addition, closets should be located near the entrance of the room for easy access. A bedroom will normally have no more than two exterior walls, and the use of one for closets will reduce the chance of cross ventilation through windows.

Access to the closet should receive serious consideration. A variety of doors may be selected: sliding, bi-fold, accordion or flush. The usual height of a door is 6'-8'', but bi-fold and accordion doors are also available in 8'-0'' heights. Using doors that provide easy accessibility, but require little space, is desirable.

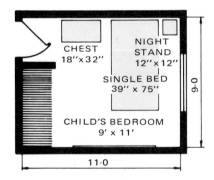

Fig. 5-6. A small bedroom with the minimum: single bed, night stand, and chest of drawers.

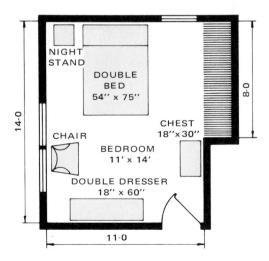

Fig. 5-7. The medium-size bedroom contains room for a double bed, chest, chair, double dresser, and night stand.

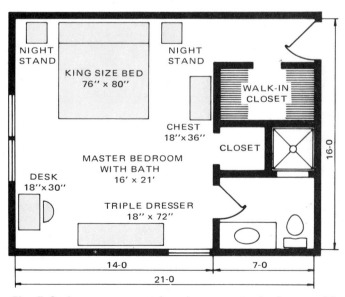

Fig. 5-8. An arrangement for a large master bedroom with private bath included. Note the area of floor space.

Fig. 5-9. A neat closet arrangement provides a place for each item as well as easy access.
(Schulte Corporation)

Good closet lighting is a necessity. Fixtures may be placed inside the closet.

Bedroom design is directly related to furniture size and arrangement. Determine common furniture sizes, Fig. 5-10, and design the bedroom with a specific arrangement in mind. Fig. 5-11 shows the furniture cutout method of planning a definite arrangement. The steps are simple: (1) Determine the size of furniture to be used. (2) Draw the plan view of each item to the same scale as the floor plan. (3) Cut out each furniture representation. (4) Place the cutouts on the floor plan in the desired arrangement. (5) Trace around each one to "fix" the location. (6) Remove the cutouts and darken the lines. Be sure

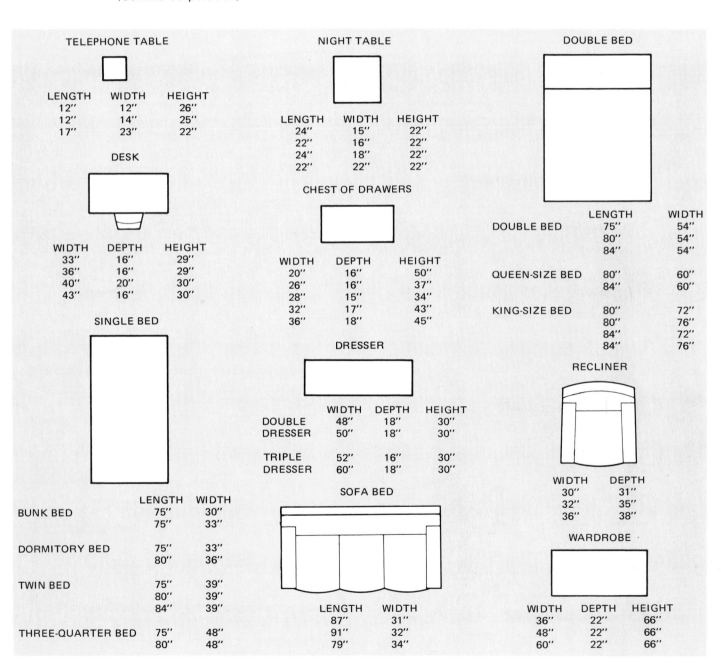

TELEPHONE TABLE

LENGTH	WIDTH	HEIGHT
12"	12"	26"
12"	14"	25"
17"	23"	22"

DESK

WIDTH	DEPTH	HEIGHT
33"	16"	29"
36"	16"	29"
40"	20"	30"
43"	16"	30"

SINGLE BED

	LENGTH	WIDTH
BUNK BED	75"	30"
	75"	33"
DORMITORY BED	75"	33"
	80"	36"
TWIN BED	75"	39"
	80"	39"
	84"	39"
THREE-QUARTER BED	75"	48"
	80"	48"

NIGHT TABLE

LENGTH	WIDTH	HEIGHT
24"	15"	22"
22"	16"	22"
24"	18"	22"
22"	22"	22"

CHEST OF DRAWERS

WIDTH	DEPTH	HEIGHT
20"	16"	50"
26"	16"	37"
28"	15"	34"
32"	17"	43"
36"	18"	45"

DRESSER

	WIDTH	DEPTH	HEIGHT
DOUBLE DRESSER	48"	18"	30"
	50"	18"	30"
TRIPLE DRESSER	52"	16"	30"
	60"	18"	30"

SOFA BED

LENGTH	WIDTH
87"	31"
91"	32"
79"	34"

DOUBLE BED

	LENGTH	WIDTH
DOUBLE BED	75"	54"
	80"	54"
	84"	54"
QUEEN-SIZE BED	80"	60"
	84"	60"
KING-SIZE BED	80"	72"
	80"	76"
	84"	72"
	84"	76"

RECLINER

WIDTH	DEPTH
30"	31"
32"	35"
36"	38"

WARDROBE

WIDTH	DEPTH	HEIGHT
36"	22"	66"
48"	22"	66"
60"	22"	66"

Fig. 5-10. Common sizes of standard bedroom furniture.

```
DOUBLE BED . . . . . . .54" x 75"
TRIPLE DRESSER . . . . .18" x 60"
NIGHT STAND . . . . . . .18" x 24"
CHEST OF DRAWERS . . .18" x 35"
```

STEP 1. DETERMINING FURNITURE SIZE

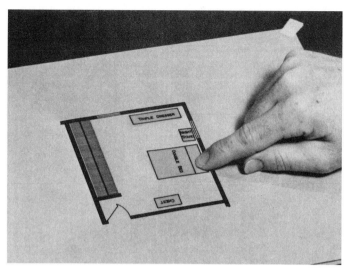

STEP 4. PLACE THE FURNITURE CUTOUTS
ON THE FLOOR PLAN

STEP 2. DRAW THE PLAN VIEW OF EACH
PIECE OF FURNITURE

STEP 5. TRACE AROUND EACH PIECE OF FURNITURE
TO LOCATE ITS POSITION

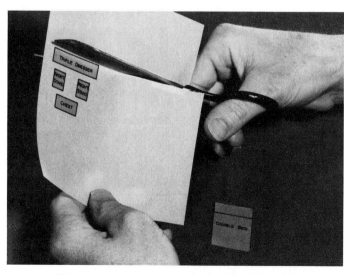

STEP 3. CUT OUT EACH PIECE OF FURNITURE

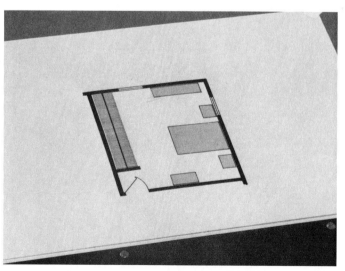

STEP 6. REMOVE THE CUTOUTS AND
DARKEN IN THE LINES

Fig. 5-11. Using the furniture cutout method for planning a room arrangement.

to allow adequate clearance between the various room elements, as in Fig. 5-12.

Windows and doors are important bedroom features. An ideal bedroom will have windows on two walls. These should be located so that a draft will not blow across the bed. If the bedroom is on the first-floor level, ribbon windows (wide, short windows) may be desired to provide added privacy. Window location and spacing is a definite consideration in all well-designed bedrooms.

Each bedroom will have at least one entry door. Interior doors are usually 1 3/8'' thick and 6'-8'' high. Standard widths range from 2'-0'' to 3'-0'' in increments of 2''. The minimum recommended bedroom door width is 2'-6''. A wider door, 2'-8'' or 2'-10'', provides for easier movement of furniture especially adjacent to a hall. To accommodate a wheelchair and space to turn, doorways should be at least 3'-0''. The door should swing into the bedroom. Allow space along the wall for the door when it is open. Locating a door near a corner of the room usually results in less wasted space. To further conserve space, pocket or sliding doors may be used.

A well-planned bedroom is a cheerful but restful place, Fig. 5-13. Carefully select colors which help to create a quiet and peaceful atmosphere.

Fig. 5-14 shows an average size bedroom. It could function as a master bedroom, guest room, or regular bedroom. It provides adequate ventilation with large sliding windows. A private bath and large closet are assets. The lounge chair and small table provide a comfortable place to read or relax. Furniture is arranged in such a way that all pieces are easily accessible.

Fig. 5-15 shows a bedroom with 156 sq. ft. plus closet and bath. It is a functional arrangement. Adequate space is provided for traffic by the furniture arrangement. Ventilation is sufficient, but could be improved if this were a corner room. The private bath is positioned in such a way that it could be shared with other rooms if desired.

BATHROOMS

The small, drab bathroom of a few years ago is almost a thing of the past. Modern homes today have larger, more pleasant, and functional

Fig. 5-13. A well-designed and decorated bedroom is an area of lasting beauty and charm. (Weather Shield Mfg., Inc.)

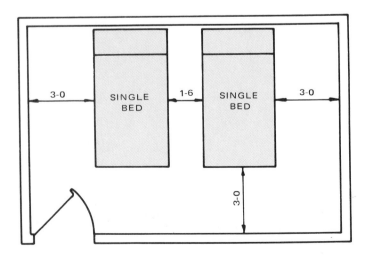

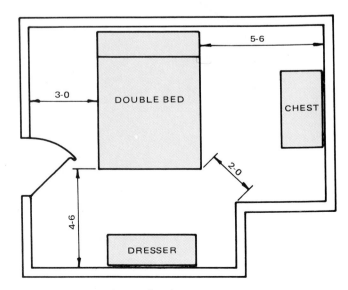

Fig. 5-12. Examples of minimum space clearances for bedroom furniture.

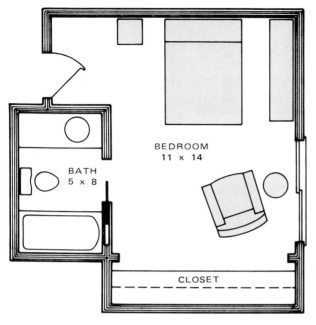

Fig. 5-14. An average size bedroom which is quite versatile.

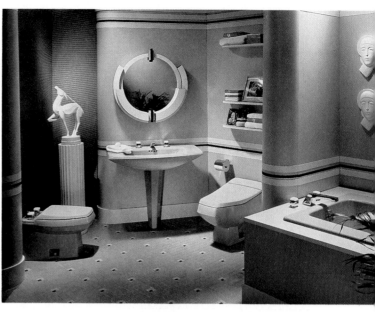

Fig. 5-16. This large, attractively decorated bathroom illustrates the use of functional planning for convenience. (Kohler Co.)

baths, Fig. 5-16. They also have more bathrooms than were used in the past. All homes require at least one bathroom; most modern homes have 1 1/2 or more. Ideally, every bedroom should have its own bath, however this is seldom possible.

Bathrooms should be located near the bedroom and living areas of the house. If the house is small, one bath may be sufficient. In this case, locate the bathroom in a place where it will be most convenient. See Fig. 5-17. Often the de-

sign of the house will indicate the minimum number of baths needed. A two-story design requires at least 1 1/2 baths—a full bath on the second level near the bedrooms, and a half bath on the first floor near the living area. A half bath is one that does not have all three major fixtures. It usually has only a water closet and lavatory. A split-level house will also require at least 1 1/2 baths. Since the bedrooms are located on the upper level away from the living area, the need for another bath on a lower level becomes evi-

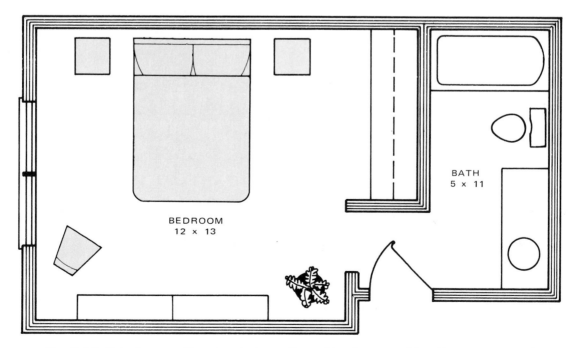

Fig. 5-15. A bedroom with one exterior wall provides for ease of furniture arrangement.

Fig. 5-17. A well-planned centrally located bath in a small house.

dent. A large ranch house will require a minimum of 1 1/2 baths. The bedrooms are usually located in a wing of the house away from the living area and convenience dictates a second bath. A three-quarters bath is functional for basement or attic conversions. A lavatory, water closet, and shower comprise a three-quarters bath.

For years designers have emphasized the importance of locating baths close together and near the kitchen to reduce cost. Granted, the cost will be less if baths share a common wall or are placed above or below one another. However, this is a rather minor consideration compared to convenience and function. It is desirable to design a functional bath, and to place the bath in the most convenient location.

A minimum size bath is 5' x 8', Fig. 5-18. A large bath may be 10' x 10', 10' x 12', or larger. A family bathroom will require more countertop and storage space than a guest bath. Most people prefer ample space for dressing, linen storage, and personal items, Fig. 5-19.

The three primary fixtures found in most bathrooms are the lavatory, water closet, and tub or shower. A fourth fixture, the bidet, is also included in some bathrooms. See Fig. 5-16. The arrangement of the fixtures determines whether or not the bath is truly functional. Locating the lavatory or water closet under a window should be avoided. A mirror should be placed above the sink, Fig. 5-20. Arrange the mirror so it will be well lighted and away from the tub to prevent fogging.

Fig. 5-19. A large functional bath provides room for dressing, bathing, and grooming. Note the pleasing use of coordinated colors. (American Olean Tile Company)

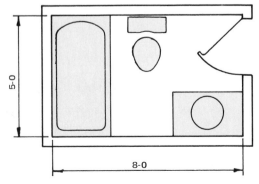

Fig. 5-18. Planned layout for a small size bathroom.

Fig. 5-20. The combination of the mirror and the smooth surfaces of the vanity unit provide an excellent grooming area. (Formica Corporation)

Provide ample space for each fixture in the room. Check the manufacturer's specifications and code requirements for placement of each of the fixtures. Most water closets require a space at least 30'' wide for installation, Fig. 5-21. Allow 36'' for a handicapped person.

Water closets should be placed so that they are not visible from another room when the bathroom door is open.

Water closets are produced in a number of styles. The older style had a separate tank and stool. Most newer models are one-piece units, either floor- or wall-mounted, Fig. 5-22. Wall-mounted water closets make cleaning easier and are more accessible for persons in wheelchairs.

Bathroom fixtures vary in size as shown in Fig. 5-23. For example, regular bathtubs range in

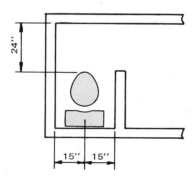

Fig. 5-21. Minimum clearance for water closet installation.

Fig. 5-22. Contemporary styling of a one-piece water closet and bidet. (Kohler Company).

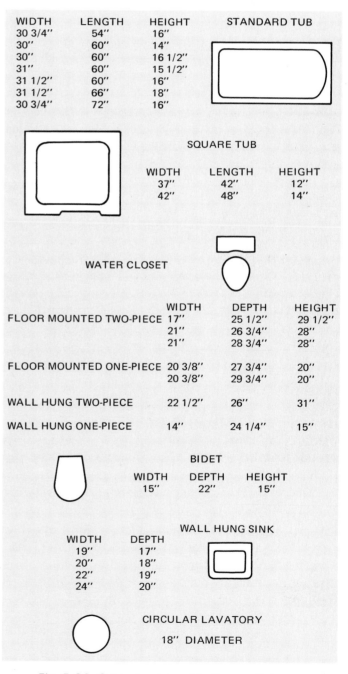

WIDTH	LENGTH	HEIGHT	STANDARD TUB
30 3/4''	54''	16''	
30''	60''	14''	
30''	60''	16 1/2''	
31''	60''	15 1/2''	
31 1/2''	60''	16''	
31 1/2''	66''	18''	
30 3/4''	72''	16''	

SQUARE TUB

WIDTH	LENGTH	HEIGHT
37''	42''	12''
42''	48''	14''

WATER CLOSET

	WIDTH	DEPTH	HEIGHT
FLOOR MOUNTED TWO-PIECE	17''	25 1/2''	29 1/2''
	21''	26 3/4''	28''
	21''	28 3/4''	28''
FLOOR MOUNTED ONE-PIECE	20 3/8''	27 3/4''	20''
	20 3/8''	29 3/4''	20''
WALL HUNG TWO-PIECE	22 1/2''	26''	31''
WALL HUNG ONE-PIECE	14''	24 1/4''	15''

BIDET

WIDTH	DEPTH	HEIGHT
15''	22''	15''

WALL HUNG SINK

WIDTH	DEPTH
19''	17''
20''	18''
22''	19''
24''	20''

CIRCULAR LAVATORY

18'' DIAMETER

Fig. 5-23. Common sizes of bathroom fixtures.

size from 54 to 72 inches long and 28 to 32 inches wide. The most common size is 30'' x 60''. It is accepted practice to install a shower above the tub. This provides the convenience of both and does not require two separate facilities. Tubs may also have such safety features as non-skid bottoms and grab rails.

Shower stalls are popular. Many homes have a tub and separate shower stall. Prefabricated showers are available in metal, fiberglass, and plastics. Fig. 5-24 shows a prefabricated shower unit. More luxurious showers are usually made of ceramic tile, terrazzo, marble, or similar materials, Fig. 5-25. Common shower sizes range from 30'' x 30'' to 36'' x 48''.

Fig. 5-25. The beautifully designed sunken shower makes use of durable ceramic tile. (Summitville Tile)

Fig. 5-24. This one-piece, prefabricated shower is installed as a complete unit during construction. (Kohler Co.)

Sink cabinets or vanities are popular and provide much-needed countertop and storage space. Twin lavatories are functional when more than one person must share the bathroom. A typical base unit is shown in Fig. 5-26. Lavatories can be circular or rectangular shape as well as other shapes. The wall-mounted and pedestal models, Fig. 5-27, are once again becoming popular. A variety of vanity base units is shown in Fig. 5-28.

Fig. 5-26. This lavatory-vanity combination illustrates how beauty and function enhance a bathroom. (H.J. Scheirich Company)

Fig. 5-27. This attractively designed bath is functional and easy to clean. (American Olean Tile Company)

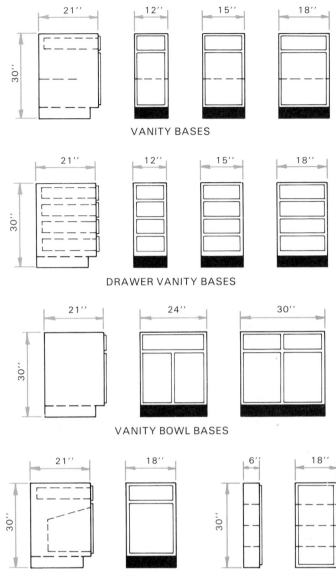

VANITY BASES

DRAWER VANITY BASES

VANITY BOWL BASES

VANITY HAMPER BASE   VANITY WALL CABINET

Fig. 5-28. Standard vanity sizes and designs.

Jacuzzis™ and saunas can be installed in or near the bathroom. They are available in precast units or wood kits ready for assembly. Some Jacuzzis™ may be used as a whirlpool or a bathtub. Saunas can be built in as part of the bath or purchased in kits. More luxurious designs include a combination of a sauna, whirlpool, and steam bath, Fig. 5-29.

A bathroom must have ventilation. This may be provided by windows or an exhaust fan. If windows are used, care must be taken to locate them properly. Window placement should be such that a draft is not produced over the tub and maximum privacy is secured. If an exhaust fan is used, it should be located near the tub and water closet area. ***Electrical switches should be placed so that they cannot be reached from the tub!*** Plus, ground fault circuit interrupter (GFCI) receptacles should be used in the bathroom.

Accessibility to the bathroom is important, Fig. 5-30. If there is only one bath for all the bedrooms, locate the door in a hall common to all the bedrooms. One should not be required to go through another room to reach the bath. Bathroom doors are ordinarily not as wide as bedroom doors. A door that is 2'-6'' or even 2'-4'' is usually sufficient. In some instances pocket

Fig. 5-29. The touch control panel in this ''Environment Masterbath'' simulates the elements of nature–rain, steam, and sun. Luxurious units also include a whirlpool bath. (Kohler Company)

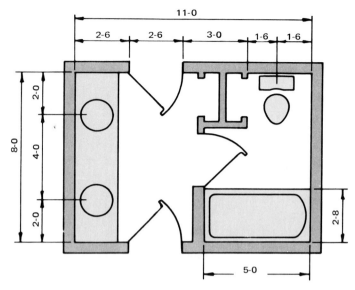

Fig. 5-30. A double-entry bath which provides maximum accessibility.

doors are used to subdivide the bath into two or more areas, Fig. 5-31, as in a two-compartment bath. Doors should swing into the bathroom and be designed so as not to interfere with the use of any fixture.

Bathrooms may be simple with only the necessary fixtures, Figs. 5-32 and 5-33, or elaborate in design and function, Fig. 5-34. A dressing or exercise area may be incorporated in the bath, Fig. 5-35. These activities require more space and added facilities. Plan the bath around the functions to be provided.

Safety should be a prime consideration when planning the bath. Flooring materials that become slick when wet should not be used. Grab bars should be installed around shower stalls, Fig. 5-36, and bathtubs. Generally, horizontal bars are more preferable than vertical bars. Devices should be installed in tub and shower

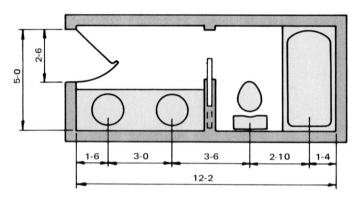

Fig. 5-31. Two-compartment bath using a pocket door as a divider.

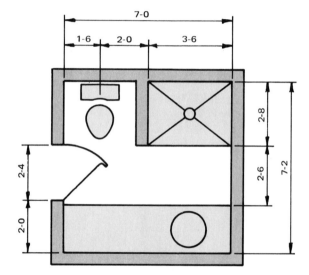

Fig. 5-33. A minimum size bath with shower.

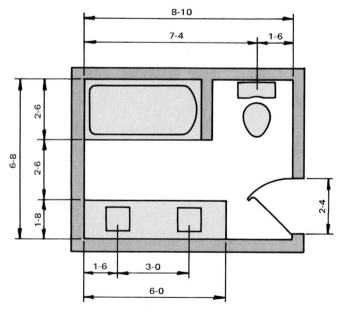

Fig. 5-32. A small bathroom containing only the necessary fixtures.

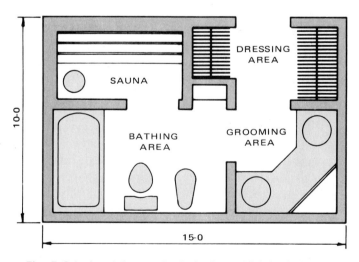

Fig. 5-34. An elaborate bath design which includes the bathing area, dressing area, grooming area, and sauna.

Fig. 5-35. A beautifully decorated bath provides ample space for bathing, dressing, grooming, and exercising. Plenty of natural and artificial lighting is available. (Armstrong World Industries, Inc.)

faucets to control water temperature thermostatically to eliminate burns from scalding water. Also, devices can be installed to control the water pressure so that when the cold water pressure is reduced, the hot water flow is automatically reduced. Nonshatter glass should be used in shower and tub enclosures. Special provisions should be made for any handicapped persons who might use the bathroom, Fig. 5-37.

The decor of a well-planned bath will provide for easy cleaning, resistance to moisture, and a pleasing atmosphere. Select fixtures of a color appropriate for the desired color scheme of the room. Plants and art pieces may be added to

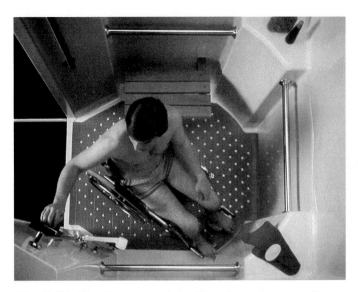

Fig. 5-36. The three examples of shower stalls accessible for the physically handicapped. Notice that the arrangement of each unit provides for safe, convenient use. All have slip-resistant floors. (Universal-Rundle Corporation)

Fig. 5-37. The floor area of the fiberglass shower unit permits a 5' turning radius for wheelchairs. Several grab bars are within easy reach and the fold-down seat is convenient for bathing. (Universal-Rundle Corporation)

enhance the beauty of the room, Fig. 5-38. The bathroom need not be a dull room which is void of design and beauty.

Fig. 5-39 shows a small bath which provides maximum convenience and practicality at a nominal cost. Economy is partially obtained by the supply and drains being placed on a single wall. Also, there is no wasted space in this functional bath. Zones may be created through the use of open-shelf cabinetry.

A large bath is shown in Fig. 5-40. This 12' x 15' bath groups all the plumbing fixtures into an island unit at the center of the room. The square tub and twin vanities create a unique design. The entrance and closets may be rearranged to suit the particular needs of a given plan. A vent fan,

heater, lighting, and shower curtain track are mounted in a cabinetized ceiling unit.

Fig. 5-41 represents a luxury bath. The 240 sq. ft. area provides separate, private dressing and grooming areas for the husband and wife. "Her area" may be decorated in a completely feminine decor while "his area" may be dis-

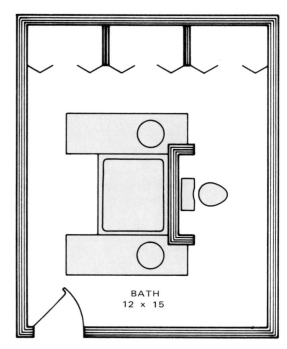

Fig. 5-40. A large island bath with plumbing fixtures in a center cluster.

Fig. 5-38. Live plants and the use of redwood provide a background of beauty for this bath. (California Redwood Association)

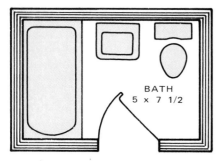

Fig. 5-39. An economical bath with the supply and drains on a single wall.

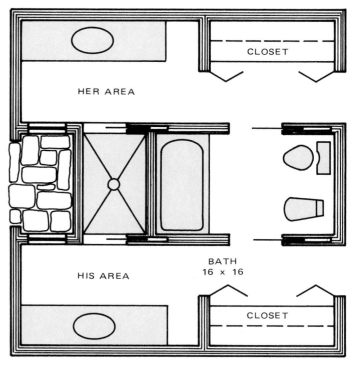

Fig. 5-41. This "his" and "her" bath represents a luxury dressing and grooming area.

tinctly masculine. The sanitary area, tub, and shower may be completely closed when desired. The shower and tub area are tiled and slightly sunken.

REVIEW QUESTIONS — CHAPTER 5

Write your answers on a separate sheet of paper. Do not write in this book.

1. In bathroom design, what two electrical safety features must always be followed?
2. List the three basic areas into which a residential structure may be divided.
3. In some design situations, _____ _____ are used to subdivide the bath into two compartments.
4. The most expensive bathroom showers are usually made of what three materials?
5. Less space is wasted when the bedroom door is located near a _____ of the room.
6. FHA specifications recommend a minimum of _____ linear feet of closet rod space for a woman and _____ for a man.
7. FHA recommends that the minimum bedroom size be no smaller than:
   a. 100 square feet
   b. 150 square feet.
   c. 200 square feet.
   d. 250 square feet.
8. A minimum size bathroom is about _____.
9. Bathtubs range in size from 28'' x 54'' to 32'' x 72''. The most common size is _____.
10. List four types of doors generally selected for closets.
11. The arrangement of fixtures will determine whether or not a bathroom is truly _____.
12. The standard height of a bathroom vanity is _____.
13. Name two advantages of a wall-mounted water closet.

SUGGESTED ACTIVITIES

1. Select a floor plan of a house from a newspaper, magazine, or other literature. Plan furniture arrangements for each of the bedrooms. Prepare a short writeup of each room describing the furniture and arrangement. Include sizes of all pieces of furniture.
2. Design a small bathroom (5' x 10'). Show the location and size of each fixture in a plan view.
3. Prepare a plan view for a clothes closet that is 3 feet deep and 8 feet in length. Show maximum door access, clothes rod, and shelf storage area.
4. Design an average size bedroom according to FHA specifications. Make a plan view drawing of the room including bed, dresser, chest of drawers, and other furniture to meet the needs of your own activities. You may want to include a study or reading area.
5. Look through a number of home design and planning magazines for closet arrangements. Prepare a display of clippings that illustrates maximum use of closet space for clothes, shoes, and other wearing apparel.
6. Enlist the help of your local librarian in finding addresses of one or more agencies that specify unique requirements for the handicapped relative to both facilities.

A formal dining room provides a feeling of warmth. (Thomasville)

6
CHAPTER

Room Planning, Living Area

After studying this chapter, you will be able to:
- Identify the rooms and areas that comprise the living area.
- Apply design principles to planning a living room.
- Integrate the furniture in a living room plan.
- Analyze a dining room using good design principles.
- Design a functional entryway and foyer.
- Communicate the primary design considerations for a family recreation room.
- Synthesize patios, porches, and courts into the total floor plan of a dwelling.

The living area is the part of the house that most friends and guests see. This is the area that usually becomes the showplace. Comprising roughly one-third of the house, this area serves a variety of functions. It is the location for family get-togethers and dining. It is the area for recreation, entertaining, and just relaxing. The living area is not restricted to the interior of the structure. It includes patios, decks, and terraces. This area is designed for all activities not encompassed in the sleeping and service areas.

The living area is composed of a number of rooms. They include the living room, dining room, foyer, recreation or family room, and special–purpose rooms such as a sunroom or home office. Some of the ''rooms'' may not be rooms in the true sense; however they serve the same purpose. Modern trends are moving away from many rooms toward a more open plan with fewer walls and doors. See Fig. 6-1.

Fig. 6-1. Note the ''openness'' of this bright dining and living area. (American Olean Tile Company)

LIVING ROOMS

The living room, for many families, is the center of activity. Depending on the specific occasion, it may be a play room for the children, a TV room, or a conversation place. Its size and arrangement will depend on the lifestyle of the members of the family who will ultimately use it. Figs. 6-2, 6-3, and 6-4 illustrate this point.

Fig. 6-2. The feeling of warmth is expressed in the styling of this pleasant conversation area.
(Georgia-Pacific Corporation)

Living rooms are of all sizes and shapes. A small living room may have as few as 150 square feet; an average size, Fig. 6-5, around 250 square feet; while a large one may exceed 400, Fig. 6-6. The most important questions to ask regarding size and design of a living room are: (1) What furniture is planned for this particular room? See Fig. 6-7. (2) How often will the room be used? (3) How many people are expected to use the room at any one time? (4) How many functions are combined in this one room? (Is it a multipurpose room?) (5) Is the living room size in proportion to the remainder of the house? Answers to these questions should help establish the broad specifications of the room.

Specific furniture will reflect the use to which the room will be subjected, Fig. 6-8. For instance, if it is to be used primarily for viewing television, the arrangement should indicate that use. Conversely, if a separate room is provided for TV then this activity will probably not be a consideration. It's important to analyze the functions to be performed and provide for them.

The location of the living room should not be such that a natural traffic pattern will be established through it to other parts of the house, Fig. 6-9. Instead, try to locate the living room where members of the family will not feel the need to use it as a hall. Slightly raising or lowering the living room level helps to set it apart and discourage ''thru traffic,'' Fig. 6-10. If possible, the living room should be positioned at grade level. This allows for expanding activities to a patio or terrace. Such an arrangement enhances the use

Fig. 6-3. Formality is emphasized in the design of this large living area. (Thomasville Furniture Industries, Inc.)

Fig. 6-4. The lifestyle of the owners is expressed in the color and design of the living area. (Preway, Inc.)

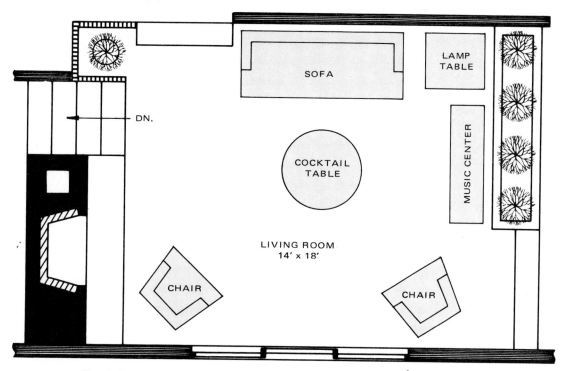

Fig. 6-5. A modern sunken living room with flower planter and fireplace.

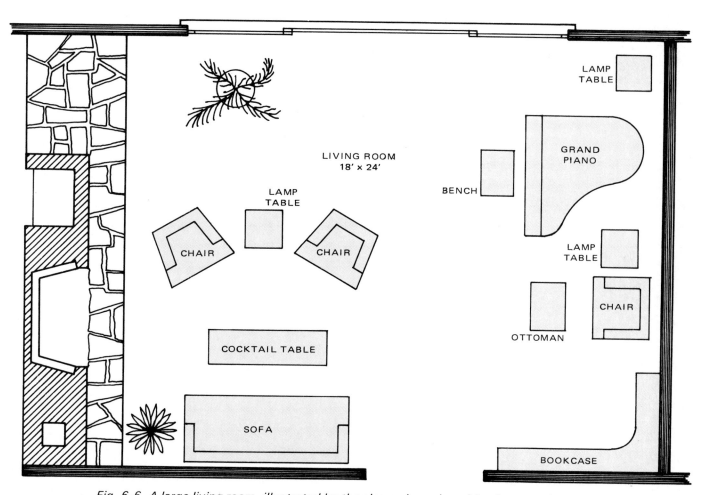

Fig. 6-6. A large living room, illustrated by the size and spacing of furniture requirements.

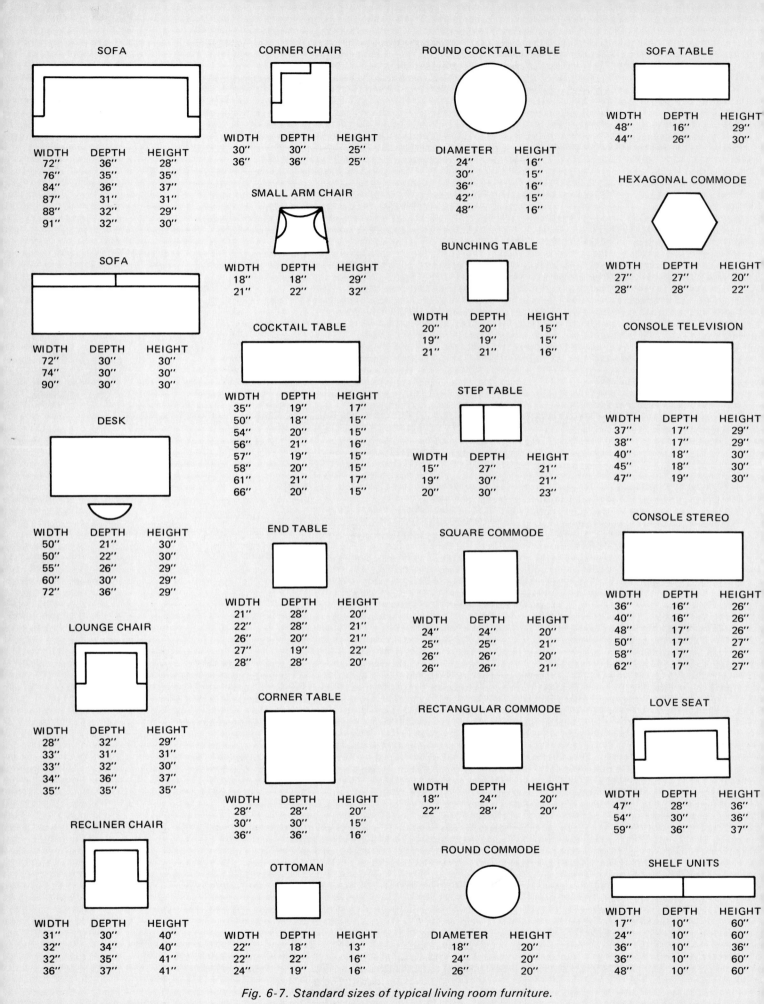

SOFA

WIDTH	DEPTH	HEIGHT
72″	36″	28″
76″	35″	35″
84″	36″	37″
87″	31″	31″
88″	32″	29″
91″	32″	30″

SOFA

WIDTH	DEPTH	HEIGHT
72″	30″	30″
74″	30″	30″
90″	30″	30″

DESK

WIDTH	DEPTH	HEIGHT
50″	21″	30″
50″	22″	30″
55″	26″	29″
60″	30″	29″
72″	36″	29″

LOUNGE CHAIR

WIDTH	DEPTH	HEIGHT
28″	32″	29″
33″	31″	31″
33″	32″	30″
34″	36″	37″
35″	35″	35″

RECLINER CHAIR

WIDTH	DEPTH	HEIGHT
31″	30″	40″
32″	34″	40″
32″	35″	41″
36″	37″	41″

CORNER CHAIR

WIDTH	DEPTH	HEIGHT
30″	30″	25″
36″	36″	25″

SMALL ARM CHAIR

WIDTH	DEPTH	HEIGHT
18″	18″	29″
21″	22″	32″

COCKTAIL TABLE

WIDTH	DEPTH	HEIGHT
35″	19″	17″
50″	18″	15″
54″	20″	15″
56″	21″	16″
57″	19″	15″
58″	20″	15″
61″	21″	17″
66″	20″	15″

END TABLE

WIDTH	DEPTH	HEIGHT
21″	28″	20″
22″	28″	21″
26″	20″	21″
27″	19″	22″
28″	28″	20″

CORNER TABLE

WIDTH	DEPTH	HEIGHT
28″	28″	20″
30″	30″	15″
36″	36″	16″

OTTOMAN

WIDTH	DEPTH	HEIGHT
22″	18″	13″
22″	22″	16″
24″	19″	16″

ROUND COCKTAIL TABLE

DIAMETER	HEIGHT
24″	16″
30″	15″
36″	16″
42″	15″
48″	16″

BUNCHING TABLE

WIDTH	DEPTH	HEIGHT
20″	20″	15″
19″	19″	15″
21″	21″	16″

STEP TABLE

WIDTH	DEPTH	HEIGHT
15″	27″	21″
19″	30″	21″
20″	30″	23″

SQUARE COMMODE

WIDTH	DEPTH	HEIGHT
24″	24″	20″
25″	25″	21″
26″	26″	20″
26″	26″	21″

RECTANGULAR COMMODE

WIDTH	DEPTH	HEIGHT
18″	24″	20″
22″	28″	20″

ROUND COMMODE

DIAMETER	HEIGHT
18″	20″
24″	20″
26″	20″

SOFA TABLE

WIDTH	DEPTH	HEIGHT
48″	16″	29″
44″	26″	30″

HEXAGONAL COMMODE

WIDTH	DEPTH	HEIGHT
27″	27″	20″
28″	28″	22″

CONSOLE TELEVISION

WIDTH	DEPTH	HEIGHT
37″	17″	29″
38″	17″	29″
40″	18″	30″
45″	18″	30″
47″	19″	30″

CONSOLE STEREO

WIDTH	DEPTH	HEIGHT
36″	16″	26″
40″	16″	26″
48″	17″	26″
50″	17″	27″
58″	17″	26″
62″	17″	27″

LOVE SEAT

WIDTH	DEPTH	HEIGHT
47″	28″	36″
54″	30″	36″
59″	36″	37″

SHELF UNITS

WIDTH	DEPTH	HEIGHT
17″	10″	60″
24″	10″	60″
36″	10″	36″
36″	10″	60″
48″	10″	60″

Fig. 6-7. Standard sizes of typical living room furniture.

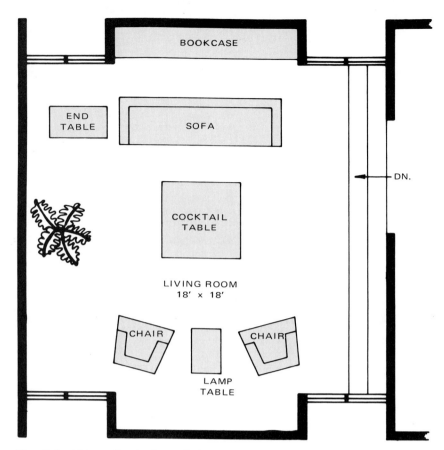

Fig. 6-8. Above. Designing a living room around ''conversation'' concept.

Fig. 6-9. Below. Notice how this ''poorly located'' living room is in the traffic pattern from all of the surrounding rooms.

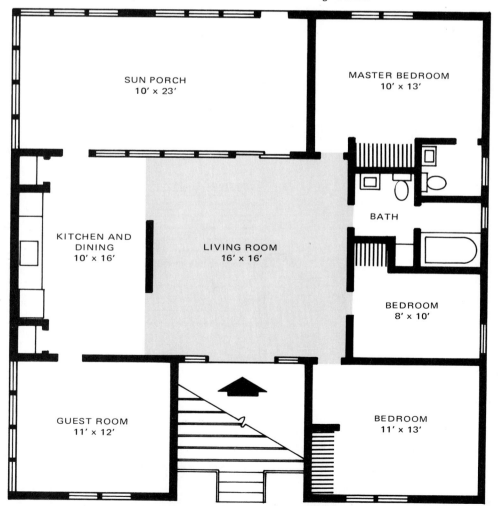

BEDROOM
11' x 14'

BEDROOM
9' x 11'

MASTER BEDROOM
11' x 15'

DINING
12' x 20'

KITCHEN
9' x 12'

GARAGE
26' x 27'

FOYER

LIVING ROOM
19' x 24'

Fig. 6-10. This living room, located near the kitchen and dining areas, is properly located to minimize through traffic.

and often the beauty of the living room. If the building site contains an area that has a pleasing view, then plan the location of the living room to take advantage of the view. The main outside entrance should not open directly into the living room, but through a hallway or foyer.

Consider the orientation of the living room for maximum comfort and energy conservation. In warm climates, use a northern orientation to keep the living areas cool. The north side is usually shaded and cool, while the south side receives sun almost constantly.

The use of large windows or sliding doors further encourages the feeling of ''spaciousness'' and increases the enjoyment of the living room, Fig. 6-11. Exterior wall areas should not be broken with too many small windows and doors and care should be taken to provide adequate wall space for required furniture.

The living room, like all other rooms in the house, should be used. It should not be planned just as a showplace. A properly designed living room can be a functional part of the house and at the same time a beautiful and charming area, Fig. 6-12.

Dining and entertaining are closely related; therefore, the living room should be located near the dining room. In some instances these areas may be combined to serve a dual purpose, as in Fig. 6-13. Usually some informal divider, short of a wall, is used to separate the two areas. A flower planter, furniture arrangement, screen, or variation in level will effectively serve this purpose. An open plan makes the house appear to

Fig. 6-12. An attractive living room designed for entertaining and relaxing. (California Redwood Association)

Fig. 6-11. Beauty and spaciousness are obtained in this living room by the use of large areas of glass.

Fig. 6-13. A well-designed living room/dining combination. (American Olean Tile Company)

be larger inside, while the closed plan tends to make the rooms look small.

Modern living rooms should be exciting, colorful, and inviting. See Fig. 6-14. The selection of bright, vivid colors will complement existing natural materials, Figs. 6-15 and 6-16. Color, texture, and design may be used to emphasize the good points and minimize weak aspects of the room, Fig. 6-17.

Fig. 6-16. Warm and cool colors form a pleasing contrast in this living room setting. (Georgia-Pacific Corporation)

Fig. 6-14. An inviting living room obtained by combining a variety of vivid colors with natural and artificial lighting. (Vermont Castings)

Fig. 6-15. Several colors that nature has provided in this charming view are repeated in the conversation area furnishings. (Pella/Rolscreen Company)

Fig. 6-17. The use of natural light and soft colors complement the beautiful stone wall in this pleasant setting. (The Atrium Door and Window Corporation)

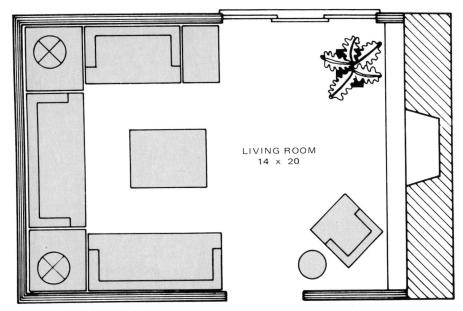

Fig. 6-18. An average-size living room designed for conversation.

The design of the living room should follow the exterior design. For example, the furnishings, wall and floor coverings, and window treatments of a Southern Colonial home would be traditional in design while contemporary design would be appropriate for a contemporary structure.

An average size living room designed for conversation is shown in Fig. 6-18. This layout lends itself to a corner location and restricts through traffic. Grade level placement permits access to a patio or porch. The fireplace is in an ideal spot for viewing from the conversation area.

Fig. 6-19 shows a well-planned living room adjacent to the dining area. An area rug unifies the furniture arrangement and adds interest. The screen defines the living room boundary and at the same time makes it appear larger. Large windows provide an excellent viewing area.

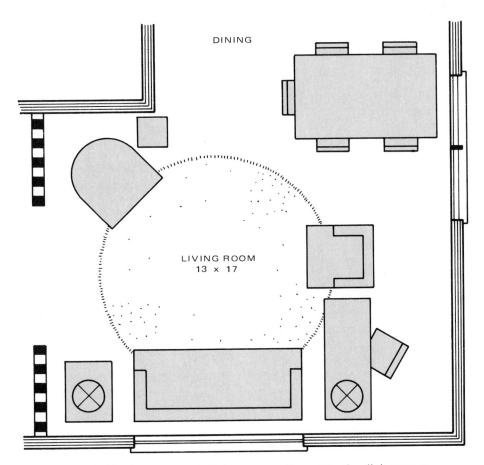

Fig. 6-19. An open-style living room adjacent to the dining room.

DINING ROOMS

Most modern homes today have a dining room. Shortly after World War II fewer houses were being built with dining rooms. In most localities that trend has been reversed and dining rooms have become popular again. However, in each individual case, the determining factor should be the lifestyle of those who will live in the house rather than fad or fancy.

The main function of a dining room is to provide a special place for eating. In some instances this activity is performed in the kitchen rather than in a separate room or area. At other times, eating is done in the kitchen as well as in some other location. Many modern homes provide eating facilities in the kitchen for informal meals and separate dining room for more formal gatherings, Fig. 6-20.

Dining rooms vary greatly in size. A small room, capable of seating four people around a table and providing space for a buffet would require an area of approximately 120 square feet, Fig. 6-21. A medium size room, 12' x 15', would provide space for six to eight people with buffet and china closet, as shown in Fig. 6-22. Large dining rooms range in size from 14' x 18' or larger, Fig. 6-23. In most cases, the dining room size would depend on the number of people who will use the facility at a given time, the furniture to be included in the room, and clearance allowed for traffic through the room.

Typical dining room furniture includes the table, chairs, buffet, china closet, and server or cart, Fig. 6-24. Arrangement and spacing will depend on the layout of the room, a pleasant outdoor vantage point, or orientation to other rooms, Fig. 6-25. At least 2'-3'' should be allowed from center line to center line of chairs around the table. Also, be sure to provide ample space for serving. Usually 2'-0'' is sufficient space between the back of the chairs and the wall.

Location of the dining room is important. For efficient use it should be adjacent to the kitchen and living room, as in Fig. 6-26. In some instances it may be desirable to locate it near the family room as well. An ideal arrangement is one that places the dining room between the living room and kitchen. This provides for natural movement of guests from living room to dining with minimum confusion. Furthermore, added space is available in the living room if needed.

Fig. 6-20. The large dining room pictured above is designed for formal gatherings. (Focal Point, Inc.)

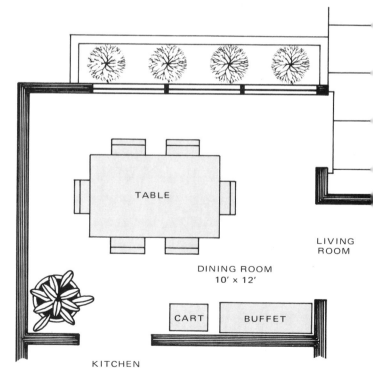

Fig. 6-21. Floor plan of a small dining room which seats four to six people.

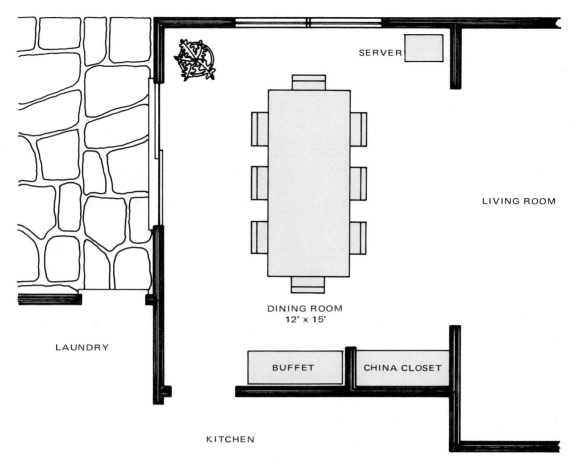

Fig. 6-22. Note planning for a medium-size dining room arranged in respect to other living areas.

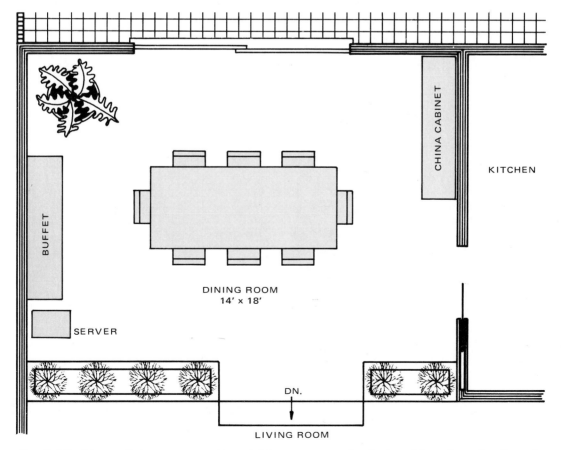

Fig. 6-23. A large dining room, seating eight or more people, designed for a large family or for those who entertain frequently.

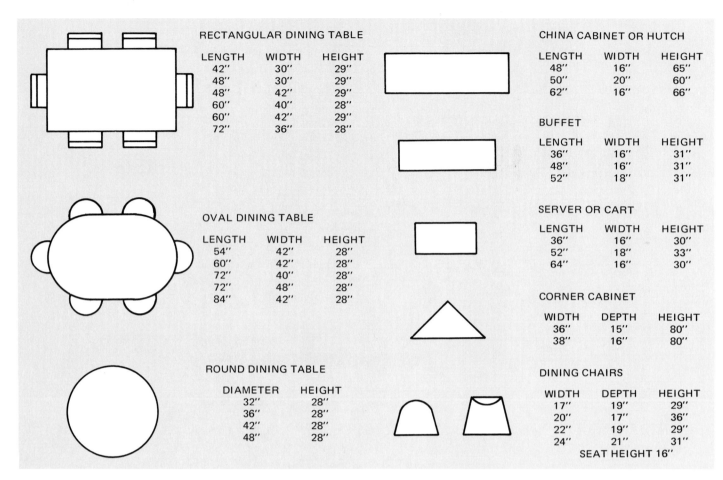

RECTANGULAR DINING TABLE

LENGTH	WIDTH	HEIGHT
42″	30″	29″
48″	30″	29″
48″	42″	29″
60″	40″	28″
60″	42″	29″
72″	36″	28″

OVAL DINING TABLE

LENGTH	WIDTH	HEIGHT
54″	42″	28″
60″	42″	28″
72″	40″	28″
72″	48″	28″
84″	42″	28″

ROUND DINING TABLE

DIAMETER	HEIGHT
32″	28″
36″	28″
42″	28″
48″	28″

CHINA CABINET OR HUTCH

LENGTH	WIDTH	HEIGHT
48″	16″	65″
50″	20″	60″
62″	16″	66″

BUFFET

LENGTH	WIDTH	HEIGHT
36″	16″	31″
48″	16″	31″
52″	18″	31″

SERVER OR CART

LENGTH	WIDTH	HEIGHT
36″	16″	30″
52″	18″	33″
64″	16″	30″

CORNER CABINET

WIDTH	DEPTH	HEIGHT
36″	15″	80″
38″	16″	80″

DINING CHAIRS

WIDTH	DEPTH	HEIGHT
17″	19″	29″
20″	17″	36″
22″	19″	29″
24″	21″	31″

SEAT HEIGHT 16″

Fig. 6-24. Typical dining room symbols and dimensions.

Fig. 6-25. This dining room is styled to reflect the decoration of an adjacent room. (The Lane Company, Inc.)

Fig. 6-26. The kitchen and living room surround two sides of this dining room. Note the planning for an outdoor view. (Armstrong World Industries, Inc.)

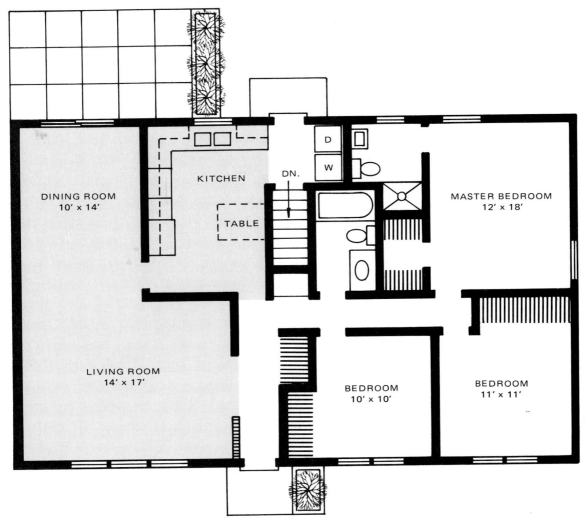

Fig. 6-27. An "open plan" layout showing the relationship between the dining room, kitchen, and living room.

This is especially true in an "open plan" layout as in Fig. 6-27.

When planning the dining room a decision should be made early as to whether an open or closed plan will be the most desirable. A closed plan places the dining room in a cubicle with little chance for overflow into other rooms, Fig. 6-28. The house appears smaller and less dramatic than in an open plan. Flower planters, screens, dividers, and partial walls may be used effectively to divide the dining area from the living room or kitchen and at the same time make the rooms appear larger, Fig. 6-29. The function and efficiency of the rooms will be enhanced by using the open plan, Fig. 6-30. However, it is best if the dining room is separated from the kitchen in order to reduce the sight and smell of food preparation.

Dining is generally a happy conversation time, hence the decor and lighting are important factors, Fig. 6-31. Controlled lighting is desirable and makes possible a variety of moods. The color scheme used in the dining room is often the same as the living room since it will most likely

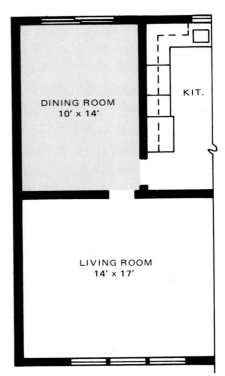

Fig. 6-28. Same basic plan as shown in Fig. 6-27 with a wall added to accomplish a "closed plan" dining room.

Fig. 6-29. A railing adds spaciousness to both the dining room and living area. (Morgan Products, Ltd.)

Fig. 6-31. Graciousness is the theme of this dining room as evident in the lighting and decor. (Focal Point, Inc.)

Fig. 6-30. A delightfully planned dining area with cheerful colors and extensive lighting.
(Armstrong World Industries, Inc.)

be an extension of that area. A bright, warm, and cheerful atmosphere is the desired result, Fig. 6-32. In frequently used dining areas, flooring should be durable to withstand daily wear.

Fig. 6-33 shows a medium-size dining room. The relationship to the kitchen is ideal, but cannot function as an overflow area for the living room. Boundaries of the dining room are defined by the area rug and is a good example of an open plan. Traffic is confined to the space along the

Fig. 6-32. A bright, cheery atmosphere is reflected in the open plan of this home. (Armstrong World Industries, Inc.)

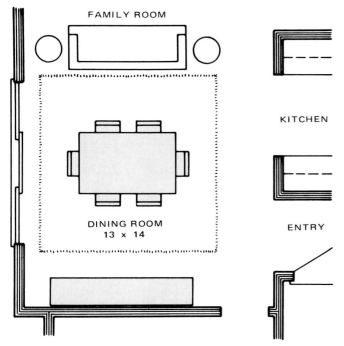

Fig. 6-33. An open plan dining room.

edge of the room and does not interfere with activities in the kitchen or dining room. The large sliding doors provide for a nice view of the patio or side yard.

The dining room in Fig. 6-34 is ideally located between the kitchen and living room. This semi-open plan is functional and creates a desirable atmosphere for dining. This arrangement is well suited for a site with a nice view to the rear. The room is large enough to allow for required traffic and to seat eight people.

ENTRYWAY AND FOYER

Every house has at least one entryway, but not all have a foyer. A well-planned house will have both.

There are three basic types of entryways: main entry, service entry, and special-purpose entry, Fig. 6-35. The main entry should be designed to be impressive because it is the first part of the house that guests see when they arrive. An entry need not be large to be attractive. Creative use of materials and a functional arrangement will enhance beauty and design.

The main entry should be centrally located to provide easy access to various parts of the house, Fig. 6-36. A main entry opening into a

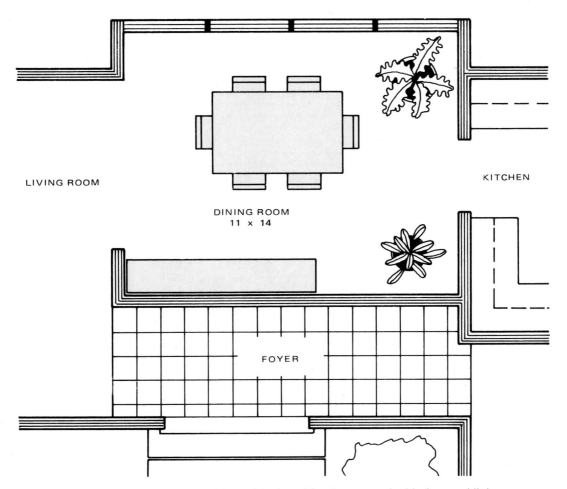

Fig. 6-34. A dining room located in an ideal position between the kitchen and living room.

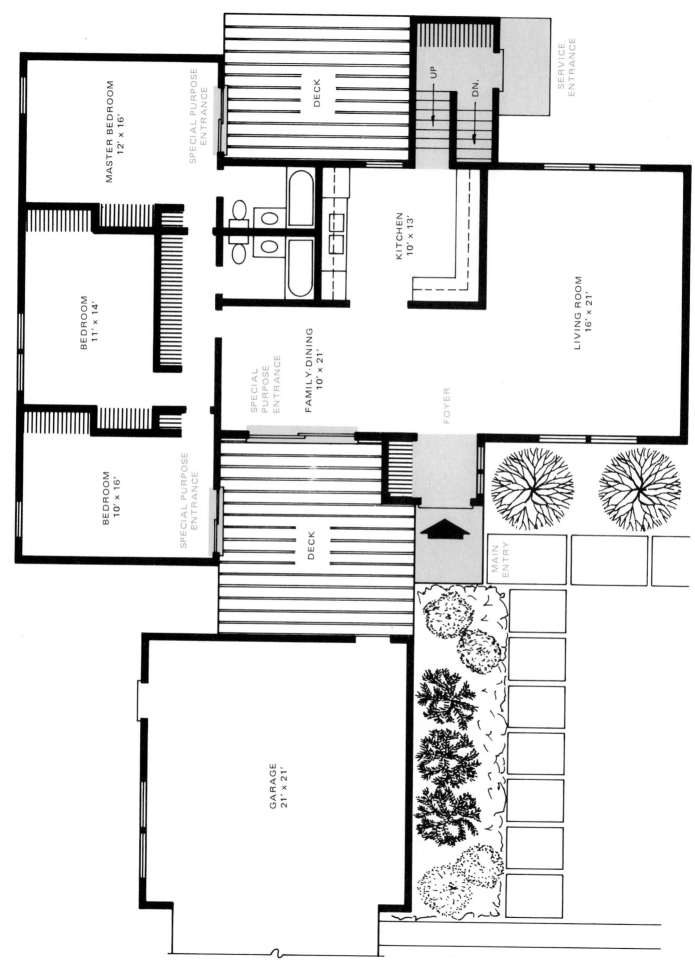

MASTER BEDROOM
12' x 16'

SPECIAL PURPOSE ENTRANCE

DECK

UP

DN.

SERVICE ENTRANCE

BEDROOM
11' x 14'

KITCHEN
10' x 13'

SPECIAL PURPOSE ENTRANCE

FAMILY-DINING
10' x 21'

LIVING ROOM
16' x 21'

BEDROOM
10' x 16'

SPECIAL PURPOSE ENTRANCE

DECK

FOYER

MAIN ENTRY

GARAGE
21' x 21'

Fig. 6-35. This floor plan illustrates a variety of entryways used in a modern home. Note the main entry and foyer.

Fig. 6-36. The main entry is clearly defined in the traditional style home above. It is centrally located to insure easy access to the different areas of the house. (Alside)

foyer is usually preferable to an entry leading directly into the living room. The entry should be designed in such a way that callers may be viewed without opening the door. Glass side panels provide visibility, natural light, and add to the design, Fig. 6-37.

Protection from the weather is a major consideration in the design of an entryway. Either a large overhang may be provided or the entry may be recessed, Fig. 6-38. A recessed entry is impressive and helps to break up a long plain front which might otherwise be uninteresting. An extended overhang may also add design and interest to a plain roof. Regardless of the technique used, the lines of the entry should be compatible

Fig. 6-37. Stained glass in the door and side panels of the foyer door provides visibility, natural light, and is decorative. (Stanley Door Systems)

Fig. 6-38. Functionally designed, this entryway provides protection from the weather, electric and natural light to the foyer, and visibility of callers.

with the remainder of the house, Fig. 6-39. The use of totally different materials or a drastic change in proportion usually will not produce the desired results.

The size of the entry will depend somewhat on the size and design of the house. However, sufficient space should be provided to accommodate several people at any given time.

Fig. 6-40. These double doors add a spacious appearance to the entryway and increase the function. (Weather Shield Mfg. Inc.)

Fig. 6-39. Note how the entryway carries through the same theme of styling as the rest of the house. (Elk Corporation)

Well-styled doors are a key element in any entry. Doors should be carefully selected to conform to the overall design of the house and add that special touch of creative design. Entry doors are normally 3'-0'' wide and 1 3/4 in. thick. Standard door height is 6'-8''. Added emphasis may be obtained by using two doors instead of one. This technique places more emphasis on the entry and also increases its function, Fig. 6-40.

The service entrance is usually connected to the kitchen. The overall design may be improved by placing a mudroom or utility room between the kitchen and service entrance.

Special-purpose entries are those providing access to patios, decks, and terraces. Sliding doors are often used for this type of entry. Service and special-purpose entrances are not intended to be as striking as the main entry, Fig. 6-41.

As stated earlier, a well-designed house should have a foyer. The foyer functions as a place to greet guests and (in colder climates) remove overcoats and overshoes. Conse-

Fig. 6-41. The service door to the rear of the house is designed to match the house style. (Therma-Tru, Division of LST Corporation.)

Fig. 6-42. Resilient flooring is a popular choice for flooring in the foyer. It is not affected by water and can be easily cleaned. (Pella/Rolscreen Company)

quently, the floor must be of a material that is not affected by water or dirt. Materials such as slate, terrazzo, ceramic or asphalt tile, or linoleum are generally used for foyer floors, Fig. 6-42. The foyer must have a coat closet. Minimum size required by FHA is 2' x 3' inside dimensions. A more desirable size would be 30 in. deep by 4'-0'' wide. The closet floor covering material should also withstand mud and water.

The foyer is an extension of the entry and, if possible, should capitalize on the design aspects of the entry, Fig. 6-43. For example, a two-story entryway may be extended to include the foyer as well, Fig. 6-44. This technique creates a unity between the inside and outside and increases a pleasing effect. Planters or potted plants may be used in the same way. They may also serve as informal dividers between the foyer and other rooms. Foyers with an open feeling are more

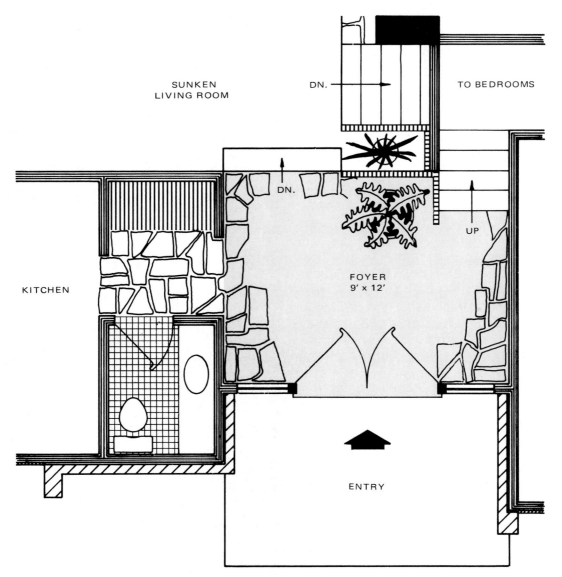

Fig. 6-43. Layout of a foyer designed as an extension of the entryway.

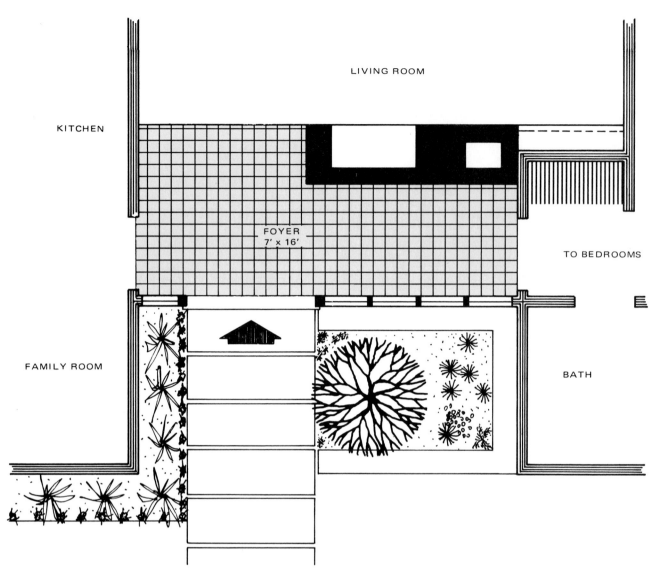

LIVING ROOM

KITCHEN

FOYER
7' x 16'

TO BEDROOMS

FAMILY ROOM

BATH

Fig. 6-44. Design of a large foyer leading to three living areas.

desirable than those that are small and closed. Using mirrors and windows helps create an open feeling. Lighting is an effective design tool which should not be overlooked. Plan the lighting for maximum effect both inside and outside the entry. Lighting outside walks and entries should be carefully considered.

The size of the foyer will depend on several factors: (1) The size of the house. (2) Cost of the house. (3) Location. (4) Personal preference. A minimum foyer is about 6' x 6'. An average size is 8' x 10'. Anything larger is considered a large foyer, Figs. 6-44 and 6-45.

Frequently the foyer provides access to other rooms of the house through halls. Hall space should be kept to a minimum, since any wasted area in halls reduces the space available for other rooms of the house. The FHA recommends a minimum hall width of 3'-0''. A width of 3'-6'' or 4'-0'' is more desirable.

Decor of the foyer will most likely reflect the color scheme and materials used in the living room or other adjacent rooms.

The foyer shown in Fig. 6-46 is well designed and functional. It is small to average in size, but well proportioned. The coat closet is easily accessible and the floor covering is durable. This is a functional design.

Fig. 6-47 shows a split-entry main and lower foyer. The main foyer is small, but adequate. The closet is convenient and the floor of both foyers is water and soil resistant. Even though the plan is complex with many walls and corners, this is a functional arrangement.

FAMILY RECREATION ROOM

In modern homes there is a trend toward providing a specially designed room called a recre-

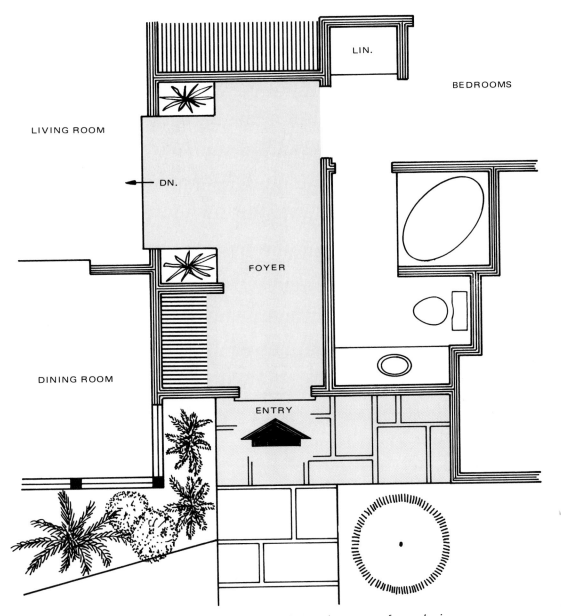

Fig. 6-45. An attractive entry and complementary foyer design.

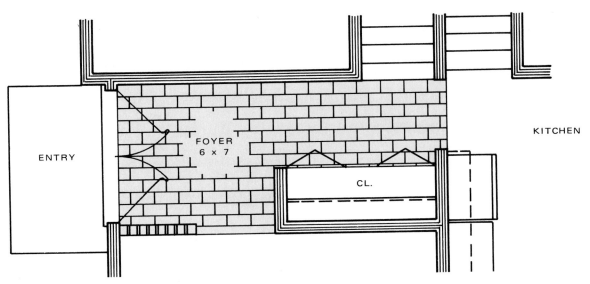

Fig. 6-46. A small well-designed foyer.

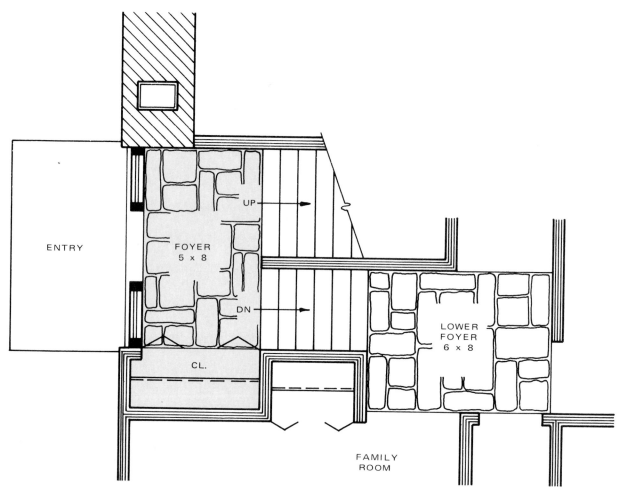

Fig. 6-47. This split-entry is functional and convenient.

ation room, family room, music room, hobby room, or rumpus room. In some instances a large house may have a number of these rooms each planned for specific activities, Figs. 6-48 and 6-49.

Fig. 6-48. A family room such as this appears warm and inviting for relaxing activities. (Pella/Rolscreen Company)

Fig. 6-49. The "entertainment wall" concept incorporates video cassette recorder, receiver, cassette deck, and turntable. (H.J. Scheirich Company)

The basic purpose of a family recreation room is to provide a place where the family can play or pursue hobbies. Design this room so that it is functional and easily maintained.

The family recreation room, if located near the dining or living room, will provide overflow space when needed. It may also be placed between the kitchen and garage, since this provides an ideal location for pursuing hobbies, Fig. 6-50. In some cases, it may be wise to locate the family recreation room adjacent to a patio to take advantage of swimming pools, indoor-outdoor picnics or sunbathing.

Some designers favor placing the recreation room in the basement, Fig. 6-51. This location takes advantage of a large area which separates noise from other living areas, contains the necessary structural details, and is easy to decorate and keep clean. Wherever the room is located it should be convenient to those who use it.

Family recreation rooms range greatly in size. The number of people planning to use the room and the types of activities in which the family members are to be engaged are important

Fig. 6-51. Basement recreation room. Note the cabinets for storing recreational equipment. (Formica Corporation)

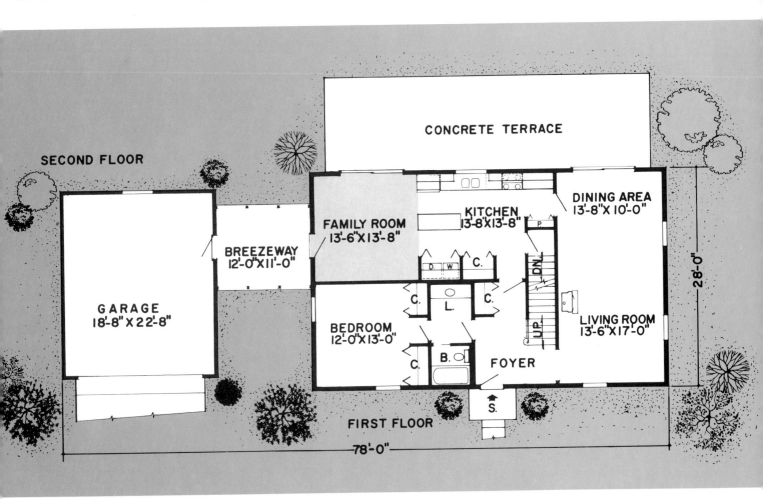

Fig. 6-50. The location of this family recreation room in the floor plan is ideal for games or family hobbies.
(The Garlinghouse Company)

considerations. A common size is 12' x 20', Figs. 6-52 , 6-53, and 6-54. Of major importance is the furniture. Again, furniture selection will depend upon the activities anticipated, Figs. 6-55 and 6-56. Choose furniture that is serviceable and resistant to wear. This room will probably receive a great deal of use.

Decor of the family recreation room should feature floors that are easy to clean, suitable for a variety of activities, resistant to wear, and not slippery. Linoleum and vinyl tile are commonly used for family recreation room floors. Deep pile carpeting should be avoided when persons in wheelchairs will be using the room. It is wise to select materials for the that are washable and mar resistant. Bright materials which are "alive with color" are desirable. Remember, this is a fun room!

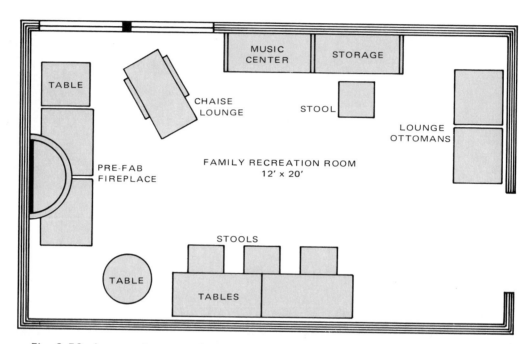

Fig. 6-52. A recreation room designed primarily for relaxation, writing, and reading. Note the furniture arrangement.

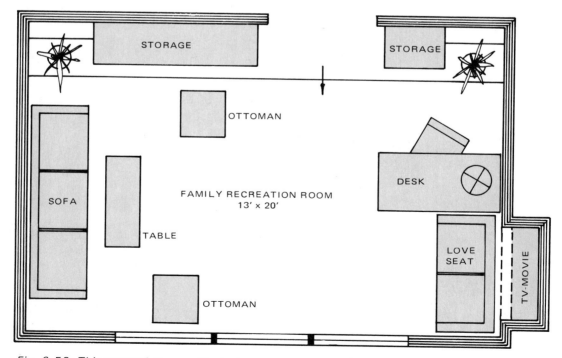

Fig. 6-53. This recreation room illustrates an arrangement for hobby work and a music center.

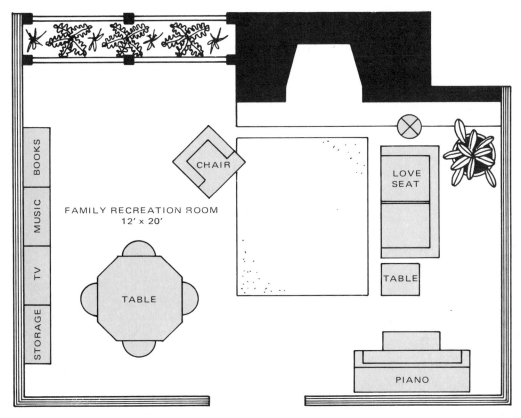

Fig. 6-54. Styled for board games, singing, or a fireside chat, this illustration suggests further design ideas.

Fig. 6-55. Note the furniture selection which offers a warm surrounding for the pocket billiards table in this game room. (Masonite Corp.)

Fig. 6-56. Functional furniture emphasizes the theme of this general-purpose recreation room. (California Redwood Association)

This room should include storage space for games and hobbies, Fig. 6-57. Lighting must be good for those activities that require sensitive viewing, such as table tennis or exacting hobby work.

The family recreation room is a good place to try out decorating ideas. Emphasize your creative talents to develop individual and personal designs, Fig. 6-58.

Fig. 6-58. Creative decorating gives the recreation room life and excitement. (Shakertown Corporation)

Fig. 6-57. Well-planned storage for recreational equipment keeps the room tidy and easy to clean. (Georgia-Pacific Corporation)

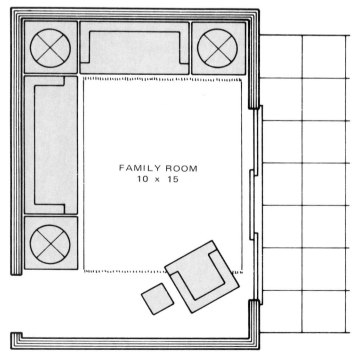

FAMILY ROOM
10 x 15

Fig. 6-59. A family room designed for reading, conversation, or relaxing.

Fig. 6-59 shows a compact family room designed for conversation, reading, and relaxing. Large glass sliding doors opening onto the patio are an added attraction. This arrangement is quite functional for a "quiet" type family room. More vigorous activities may be performed on the patio, weather permitting.

The recreation room shown in Fig. 6-60 is truly an action room. It is designed especially for young people. The built-in conversation area is the focus point, but the raised dance area is a close second. This room would be popular in most any home with teenagers.

SPECIAL-PURPOSE ROOMS

After the primary rooms of the living area have been planned, consider special purpose rooms. These rooms may include a home office, sunroom or atrium, greenhouse, ham radio room, etc. Some special-purpose areas may be placed in the corner of another room like the home offices shown in Figs. 6-61 and 6-62. Other special-purpose rooms such as a greenhouse, Fig. 6-63, or sunroom, Fig. 6-64, may be located to the side or rear of the house. Other rooms that require a great deal of privacy, such as a dark room or Jacuzzi™, should be placed in a remote area of the home, Fig. 6-65. Many special-purpose rooms have unique requirements—storage, lighting, ventilation, plumbing, and electrical facilities—and should receive attention in the design process.

Fig. 6-61. Little space was needed for the well-planned office area. The remainder of the room may be devoted to dining activities. (Cabinetry by St. Charles, Products of Whirlpool Kitchens, Inc.)

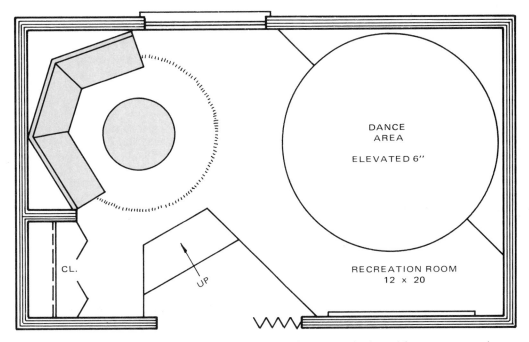

Fig. 6-60. This recreation room is truly an action room designed for young people.

Fig. 6-62. Storage for the computer, monitor, printer, telephone, and office supplies is necessary for the home office area. Space is also available for talking with clients or entertaining. (Georgia-Pacific Corporation)

Fig. 6-63. Special-purpose areas such as this greenhouse are often placed at the rear of the house. Entry is available from the interior and exterior of the home. (Janco Greenhouses)

Fig. 6-64. The light, cheery sunroom is ideal to display favorite plants and enjoy a quiet activity such as reading. (American Olean Tile Company)

Fig. 6-65. Privacy was a consideration when selecting the location of this Jacuzzi™. The use of large plants was a further effort to insure privacy. (American Olean Tile Company)

PATIOS, PORCHES, AND COURTS

A well-designed house will extend its living facilities beyond its walls as shown in Fig. 6-66. The use of patios, porches, and courts effectively enlarges the area and function of a house. In most localities, outdoor living is popular and should be planned for, Fig. 6-67.

Fig. 6-66. This enclosed court helps to provide the comfort of indoor-outdoor living.

Fig. 6-67. An attractive enclosed patio such as this complements the house and natural surroundings and provides extended outdoor living. (American Olean Tile Company)

Patios are usually near the house but not structurally connected. These are ordinarily located at ground level and are constructed for durability. Concrete, brick, stone, and redwood are commonly used materials.

Patios are used for relaxing, playing, entertaining, and living, Fig. 6-68. Each function requires special consideration as to location, size,

and design. Try to locate patios designed for relaxing, on a quiet side of the house near the bedrooms, where there is privacy, Fig. 6-69. Privacy may be achieved through the use of screens, walls, or plants.

A patio designed for living and entertaining will most likely be large and located off the living room, dining room, or family recreation room.

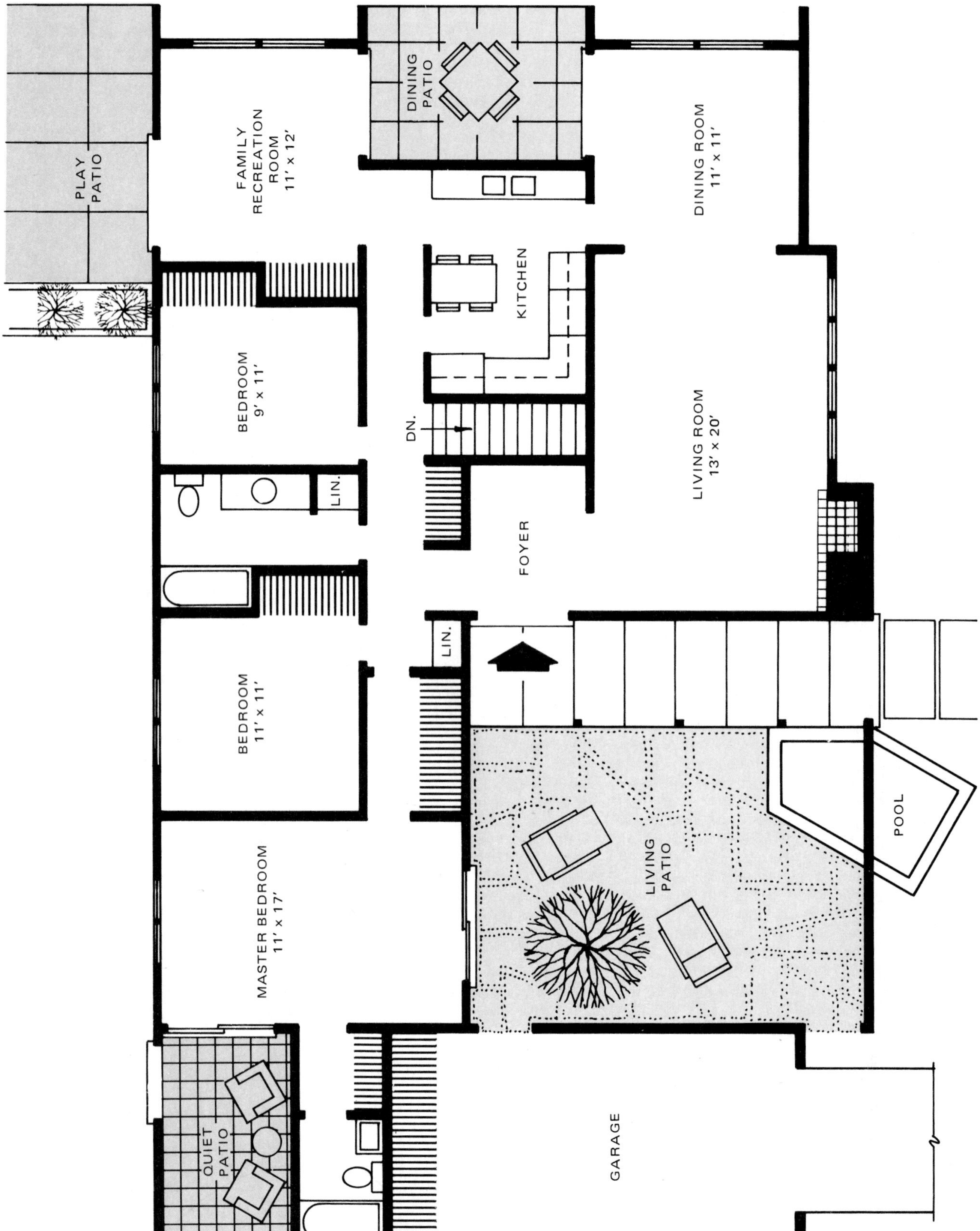

PLAY PATIO

FAMILY RECREATION ROOM
11' x 12'

DINING PATIO

BEDROOM
9' x 11'

LIN.

KITCHEN

DN.

DINING ROOM
11' x 11'

FOYER

LIVING ROOM
13' x 20'

BEDROOM
11' x 11'

LIN.

MASTER BEDROOM
11' x 17'

LIVING PATIO

POOL

QUIET PATIO

GARAGE

Fig. 6-68. This floor plan notes four different types of patios and their location to the house.

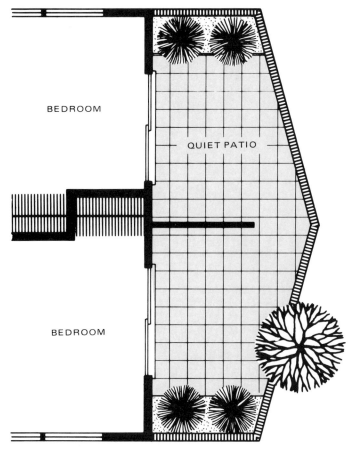

BEDROOM

QUIET PATIO

BEDROOM

Fig. 6-69. A quiet, secluded patio designed for privacy and comfort.

The wood plank patio, Fig. 6-70, is an example of the contribution that an architecturally designed patio can make to the overall function of a house.

A 10' x 14' patio is considered small, while a 20' x 30' is considered large. Design the size of the patio proportional to the size of the house. The living or entertaining patio most likely will be located on the back side of the house where more space is available, Fig. 6-71. Again, privacy is a consideration that must be actively pursued in the planning.

Consideration should be given to the orientation of sun, wind, and view. In warm climates, shade may be a major factor; while in the far north, ample sun may be a prime objective. A well-designed patio is a pleasant place, so if the surrounding area lacks natural beauty, more emphasis should be placed on design and styling. The use of flowers, pools, and screens helps to create a beautiful setting for dining, relaxing, or entertaining, Fig. 6-72.

If a swimming pool is planned, the encompassing area may be designed as a patio. Fig. 6-73 is an example of a patio with a swimming pool as the main feature. This type of patio may be a living-entertaining type patio or a play patio. Play patios are usually less encumbered with furniture, planters, and screens. The play patio is

Fig. 6-70. An extension of living off the dining room, this large patio adds beauty and function.

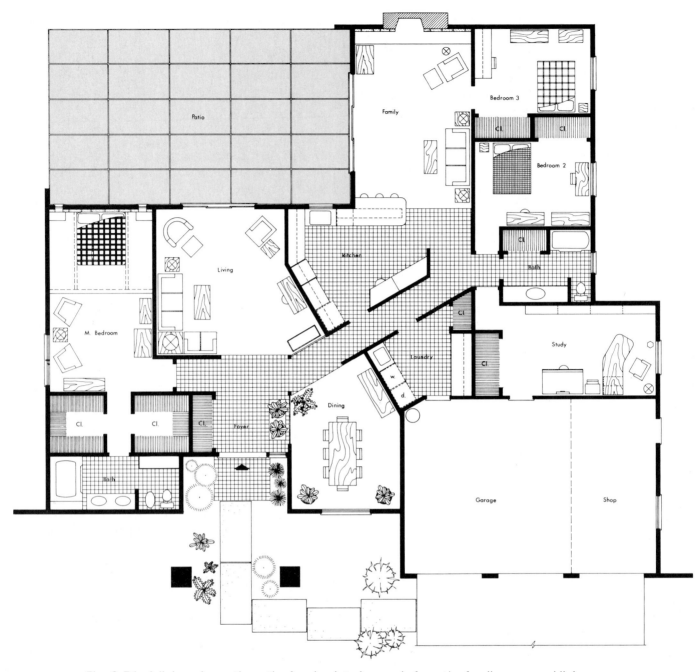

Fig. 6-71. A living-play patio as the focal point. Access is from the family room and living room.

usually designed for use by children and adults for physical activities which require more open space. A patio of this nature is ordinarily located near or adjacent to the family recreation room or the service entrance. It sometimes doubles as a service entrance terrace.

Porches differ from patios in at least two ways. First, they are generally structurally connected to the house and are raised above the grade level. Secondly, porches are usually covered. Fig. 6-74 shows a porch that is an integral part of a home which features a spectacular view. Porches that are not under roof are usually called **decks,** Fig. 6-75. Porches may function as outdoor dining areas, Fig. 6-76, and entryway extensions. Balconies and verandas

Fig. 6-73. Making use of the swimming pool surroundings to form a beautiful and useful patio. (Ideal Cement Co.)

Fig. 6-74. Covered porches are excellent places to relax and enjoy a beautiful view. (Marvin Windows)

Fig. 6-75. The deck with pool is an integral part of the landscape. Notice the several areas for seating. (Bill Whetstone, Greater Detroit Landscaping)

are types of porches that are generally higher than the standard porch.

Porches need not appear to be ''tacked-on.'' If the porch is planned as an integral part of the structure the result will be pleasing.

Usefulness of the porch (in northern states) may be increased by the addition of screens or glass, especially if the porch is to be used during the winter months.

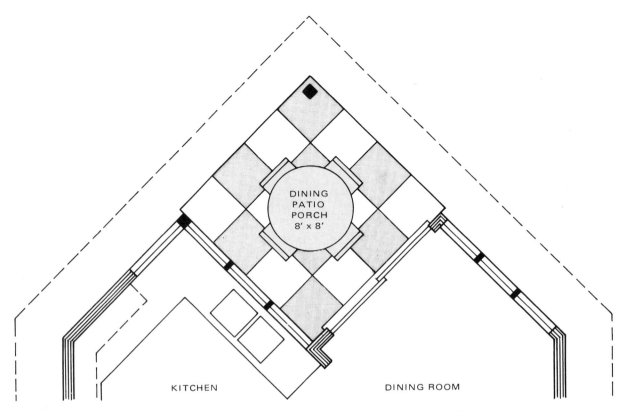

Fig. 6-76. A small roof-covered dining patio-porch located adjacent to the dining room and kitchen.

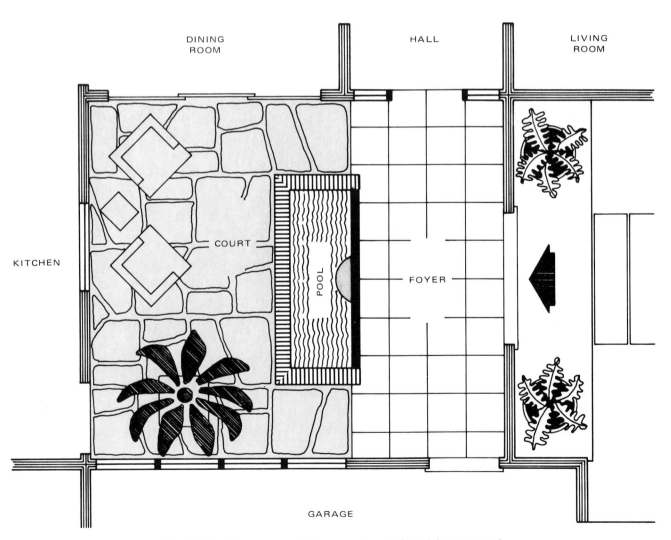

Fig. 6-77. New approach to romantic old Spanish courtyard.

If possible, the porch should be large enough to act as a patio when needed. Porches are worthy of consideration in all modern plans.

Courts are similar to porches and patios and may have characteristics of both. They are totally or at least partially enclosed by walls or roof. Fig. 6-77 is a good example of an interior court. Courts may be used for dining, relaxing, or entertaining, Fig. 6-78. They may also serve as interior gardens to add a touch of spring throughout the year. Courts are sometimes used to break up floor plans, add interest or serve the purpose of providing natural light to an interior part of the house which has no exterior wall space.

Lighting is an important feature of the patio, porch, and court. Without proper lighting, use after dark may be limited, and much of the dramatic effect will be lost. Lighting should be used as a design tool to assist in accomplishing an atmosphere and extend the usefulness of the structure.

A large porch is shown in Fig. 6-79. This porch would be a welcome addition to most any home located in a warm climate. It could also be enclosed. It is convenient to the living and dining rooms as well as the bedroom area.

Fig. 6-80 shows an extensive porch and patio. The patio is enclosed with a fence to increase privacy and define the boundaries. The porch and patio extends the living area of the house to the outside and encourages outdoor living. The patio also provides a nice view from the living room.

REVIEW QUESTIONS

Write your answers on a separate sheet of paper. Do not write in this book.

1. The normal width of an entry door is _____.

Fig. 6-78. View of a beautiful court from the front entryway. Plantings provide a feeling of indoor-outdoor living. (Portland Cement Association)

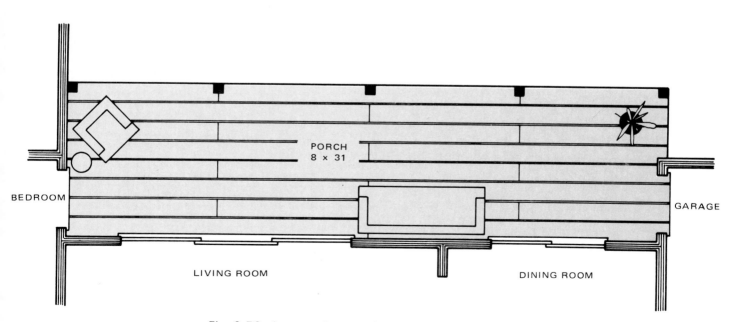

BEDROOM

PORCH 8 x 31

GARAGE

LIVING ROOM

DINING ROOM

Fig. 6-79. A convenient porch to increase outdoor living.

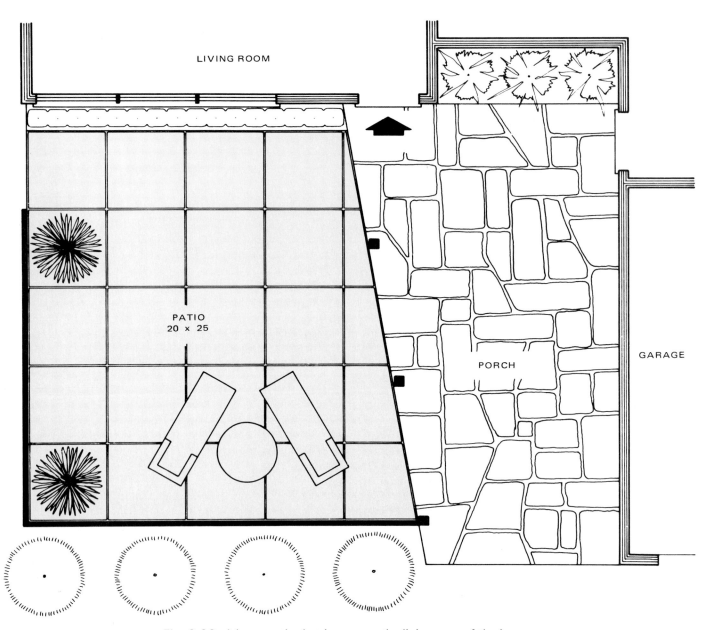

LIVING ROOM

PATIO
20 x 25

PORCH

GARAGE

Fig. 6-80. A large patio that increases the living area of the house.

2. What is the purpose of the foyer in a well-designed house?

3. A dining room measuring 16' x 20' would be considered a _____ room.

4. List four ways in which the dining area may be separated from the living room without using a full wall.

5. List four factors, other than the number of people expected to use the living room, to be considered for living room design.

6. The living area of a residential structure comprises about _____ of the total area of a house.

7. There are many modern trends in planning the living area of a house. List four.

8. List the three basic types of entryways.

9. Standard interior and exterior door height is _____.

10. Name the four parts of a typical house that most visitors or friends see.

11. Identify three special-purpose living area rooms.

SUGGESTED ACTIVITIES

1. Plan a medium-size living room with furniture. Present your plan in color for a bulletin board display. Prepare a short description of the intended use.

2. Draw the plans for a modern dining room which is designed to accommodate six people. Show the furniture.

3. Prepare a bulletin board display of entries from pictures cut out of magazines. Try to represent a broad range of designs.
4. Design a family recreation room for a specific hobby or activity. Describe the features of your design.
5. Select a house plan which has no patio and plan one. Draw the patio on tracing paper or film and present as an overlay on the house plan.
6. Plan a special-purpose room and specify the equipment and furniture required. Explain the special requirements which must be met in the room.

The natural light in this dining room makes a pleasant area for an early morning breakfast.
(Pella/Rolscreen Company)

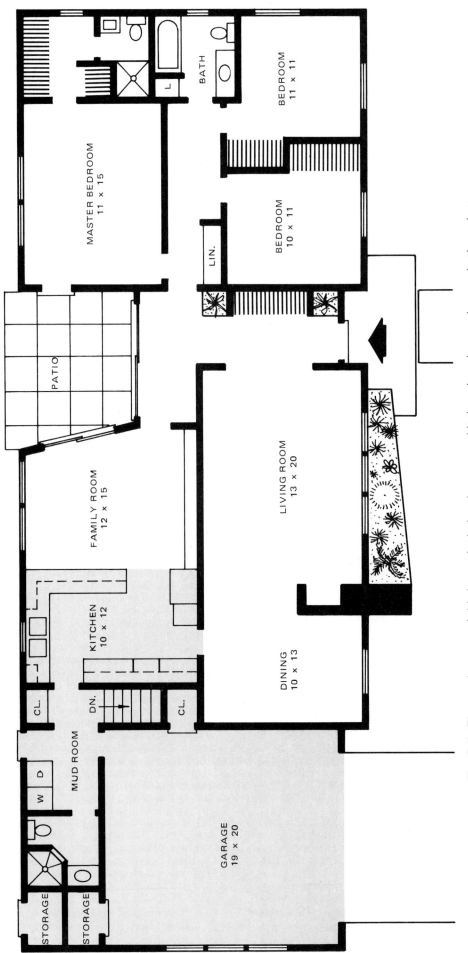

Fig. 7-1. The service area of this house includes the garage, kitchen, laundry, mud room, bath, and storage.

MASTER BEDROOM
11 x 15

BATH

BEDROOM
11 x 11

LIN.

BEDROOM
10 x 11

PATIO

FAMILY ROOM
12 x 15

KITCHEN
10 x 12

LIVING ROOM
13 x 20

CL.

DN.

CL.

DINING
10 x 13

MUD ROOM

W   D

GARAGE
19 x 20

STORAGE

STORAGE

Room Planning, Service Area

After studying this chapter, you will be able to:
* Apply good design principles to planning the service area of a home.
* Design a functional kitchen to meet a family's needs.
* Select appliances for a modern kitchen.
* Plan a modern, efficient clothes care center.
* Describe appropriate dimensions for garage space.

The Service Area supplements the Living and Sleeping Areas of the house. It supplies equipment and space for maintenance, storage, and service. This includes the kitchen, clothes care center, garage or carport, utility, and storage, Fig. 7-1. Due to its varied functions, the service area will require careful planning.

KITCHEN

A principal use for the kitchen is food preparation. It may, however, be extended to include dining, laundry, and storage, Fig. 7-2. Kitchen design presents problems that are unique. Inefficiency and added cost will result if the problems are not solved satisfactorily. From the standpoint of cost, the kitchen is usually the most expensive room in the house per square foot and receives the most active use of any room.

Efficient kitchen planning involves the placement of appliances, providing adequate storage cabinets, and food preparation facilities, Fig. 7-3. This placement creates the work centers— food preparation center, cleanup center, and cooking center. In designing kitchens, give considerable thought to the general location of each of the kitchen components. The arrangement should be logical and designed to minimize the

Fig. 7-2. A contemporary, functional kitchen designed for food preparation, dining, storage, and laundry.
(H.J. Scheirich Company)

amount of walking required by the homemaker, Fig. 7-4.

The work triangle is one measure of kitchen efficiency. It is determined by drawing a line from the front center of the range to the refrigerator to the sink and back to the range. The lengths of these three lines are added together to produce the length of the work triangle, Fig. 7-5. For practical kitchen design this distance should not exceed 22 feet.

Provision for food storage and cooking utensils should be located near the areas where they

Fig. 7-3. This contemporary kitchen has ample space for storage, food preparation facilities, and appliances. (Kitchenaid, Inc.)

Fig. 7-4. A compact kitchen which provides an exciting place to prepare food.

are to be used, Figs. 7-6 and 7-7. For example, the homemaker should not be required to walk across the kitchen to get pots and pans which are always used on the range. Store them near the cooking area.

The kitchen designer has six basic styles to choose from:

Straight Line U-Shaped
L-Shaped Peninsula
Corridor Island

THE STRAIGHT LINE KITCHEN

This design is frequently used in cottages and apartments. See Fig. 7-8. Little space is required and the design usually provides for an efficient arrangement of kitchen facilities. Two disadvantages are that it provides a limited amount of cabinet space and the result is usually not very interesting. The straight line kitchen is seldom chosen for modern residences.

Fig. 7-6. Any homemaker would love the convenience these storage units provide. (Whirlpool Corporation)

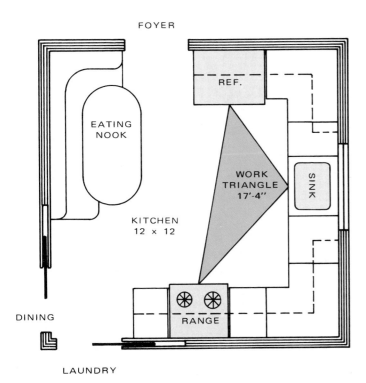

Fig. 7-5. The length of the work triangle is a good measure of the efficiency of a kitchen.

Fig. 7-7. The pull-out drawers provide storage which is convenient and organized. (Quaker Maid)

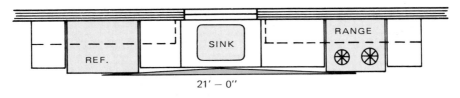

STRAIGHT LINE KITCHEN

Fig. 7-8. An example of a straight line or one-wall kitchen.

THE L-SHAPED KITCHEN

The L-shaped kitchen is located along two adjacent walls, Fig. 7-9. This design is efficient and an L-shaped kitchen is usually more attractive than a straight line kitchen. Two work centers are generally located along one wall and the third on the adjoining wall. The L-shaped design is not intended for large kitchens because of

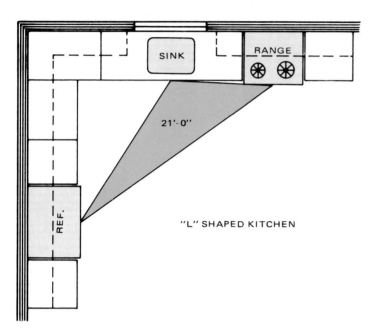

Fig. 7-9. The L-shaped kitchen provides a traffic-free work triangle.

Fig. 7-10. This L-shaped kitchen has sufficient light to decorate with plants. (H.J. Scheirich Company)

Fig. 7-11. An L-shaped kitchen which has a short work triangle to reduce steps. (Wood-Mode Cabinetry)

effectiveness of the plan is lost if the walls are too long. Figs. 7-10 and 7-11 show modern L-shaped kitchens.

THE CORRIDOR KITCHEN

As implied by the name, the corridor kitchen is located on two walls opposite each other, Fig. 7-12. Corridor kitchens are usually small to medium in size and are ideal for a long, narrow room, Fig. 7-13. This design lends itself to an efficient arrangement, but is not recommended if traffic is to be heavy through the kitchen. Open space between the cabinets should be at least four feet.

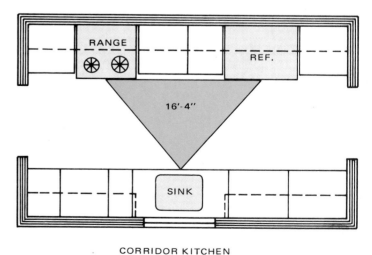

Fig. 7-12. Corridor kitchen design with plenty of cabinet space.

Fig. 7-13. A spectacular corridor with convenient storage and workspace. Notice the meal planning center. (Haas Cabinet Company)

THE U-SHAPED KITCHEN

Probably the most popular design, the U-shaped kitchen, retains a high level of efficiency and is one of the most attractive of the six designs, Fig. 7-14. There is no traffic through the kitchen to other areas of the house and the work

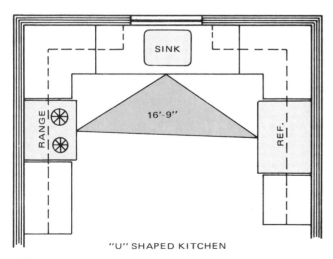

"U" SHAPED KITCHEN

Fig. 7-14. The U-shaped kitchen is a popular design.

triangle is compact and functional, Figs. 7-15 and 7-16. Most U-shaped kitchens are medium in size with the open space between the legs of the ''U'' being 5 or 6 feet.

THE PENINSULA KITCHEN

The peninsula kitchen is popular because it provides plenty of work space, is attractive, and is easily joined to the dining room using the

Fig. 7-15. Efficiency and beauty are the key elements of this unique U-shape design. (Whirlpool Corporation)

Fig. 7-16. This medium-size U-shape design is pleasant for preparing meals. The counter space on the left is useful for meal preparation or serving informal meals. (Quaker Maid)

peninsula as a divider, Fig. 7-17. The peninsula may be used as the cooking center, Fig. 7-18, eating area, Fig. 7-19; or as a food preparation center, Fig. 7-20. As in the U-shaped kitchen, the amount of traffic is reduced and the work triangle is compact.

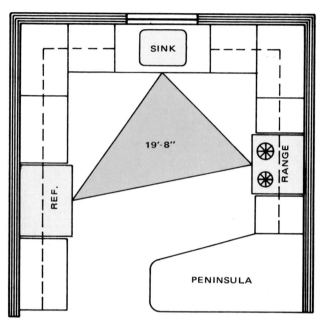

PENINSULA KITCHEN

Fig. 7-17. The peninsula kitchen is a popular style.

Fig. 7-19. Here the peninsula is utilized as a hobby area. (Quaker Maid)

Fig. 7-18. A peninsula kitchen using the peninsula for cooking and serving. A nice feature for this kitchen style is that it provides plenty of workspace. (Quaker Maid)

Fig. 7-20. The peninsula in this kitchen is used as a food preparation center. (Wood-Mode Cabinetry)

THE ISLAND KITCHEN

The island kitchen may be a modification of the straight line, the L-shaped or the U-shaped design, Fig. 7-21. The island may house the sink, cooking center or food preparation area, and in some instances it may serve as a countertop or snack bar, Figs. 7-22, 7-23, and 7-24. The island should be accessible from all sides. At least four feet clearance should be allowed on all sides of the island for easy access.

Nearly every one of the kitchen designs can easily be adapted for a handicapped person. Toe space of 6'' deep and 8'' to 11'' high is needed under the cabinets for wheelchair footrests. Knee space of 28'' to 30'' wide, 27'' to 30'' high, and 21'' to 24'' deep can be provided by an overhang or extended counterspace.

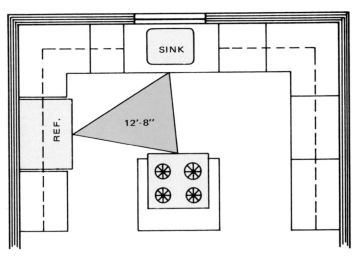

ISLAND KITCHEN

Fig. 7-21. An island kitchen design.

Fig. 7-23. An island kitchen tastefully decorated and designed to be functional. Note that the island serves as a cooking center. (H.J. Scheirich Company)

Fig. 7-22. Kitchen with contemporary styling and island with sink should excite most any homemaker. (Whirlpool Corporation)

Fig. 7-24. The beauty and functional arrangement of this modern island kitchen would be an asset to any home. (Cabinetry by St. Charles, Products of Whirlpool Kitchens, Inc.)

Room Planning, Service Area   133

CABINETS AND APPLIANCES

Kitchen appliances are available in a variety of styles, colors and sizes. Symbols and standard sizes of kitchen appliances and sinks are shown in Fig. 7-25.

Kitchen cabinets provide the majority of storage space in most modern kitchens. They are produced in standard sizes, but may be custom made in other than standard sizes if required. Most standard base cabinets are 34 1/2'' high,

24'' deep, and width increments in 3 inch multiples (15'', 18'' 21'', etc.). Wall cabinets are either 12 or 13 inches deep (both are standard). Cabinets 12 to 30 inches high in increments of 3 inches and 12 to 36 inches wide in increments of 3 inches are also available. A typical section through the base and wall cabinets is shown in Fig. 7-26. Fig. 7-27 illustrates the standard base and wall cabinets that most manufacturers

REFRIGERATOR

CU. FT.	WIDTH	HEIGHT	DEPTH
9	24''	56''	29''
12	30''	68''	30''
14	31''	63''	24''
19	34''	70''	29''
21	36''	66''	29''

STANDARD FREE-STANDING RANGE

WIDTH	HEIGHT	DEPTH
20''	30''	24''
21''	36''	25''
30''	36''	26''
40''	36''	27''

DOUBLE OVEN RANGE

WIDTH	HEIGHT	DEPTH
30''	61''	26''
30''	64''	26''
30''	67''	27''
30''	71''	27''

DROP IN RANGE

WIDTH	HEIGHT	DEPTH
23''	23''	22''
24''	23''	22''
30''	24''	25''

BUILT-IN COOK TOP

WIDTH	HEIGHT	DEPTH
12''	2''	18''
24''	3''	22''
48''	3''	22''

RANGE HOOD

WIDTH	HEIGHT	DEPTH
24''	5''	12''
30''	6''	17''
66''	7''	26''
72''	8''	28''

SINGLE COMPARTMENT SINK

WIDTH	DEPTH
24''	21''
30''	20''

DOUBLE COMPARTMENT SINK

WIDTH	DEPTH
32''	21''
36''	20''
42''	21''

Fig. 7-25. Appliance symbols and sizes.

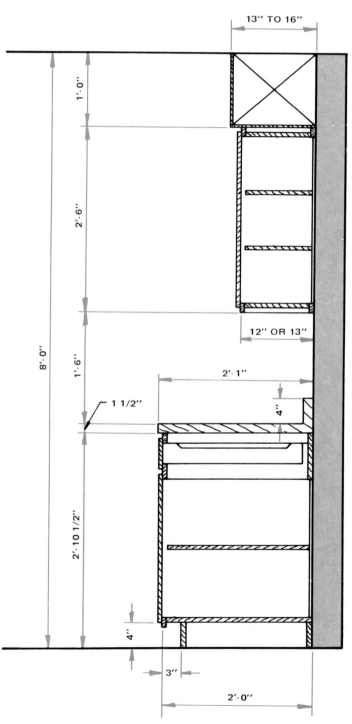

Fig. 7-26. A typical section through the base and wall cabinets.

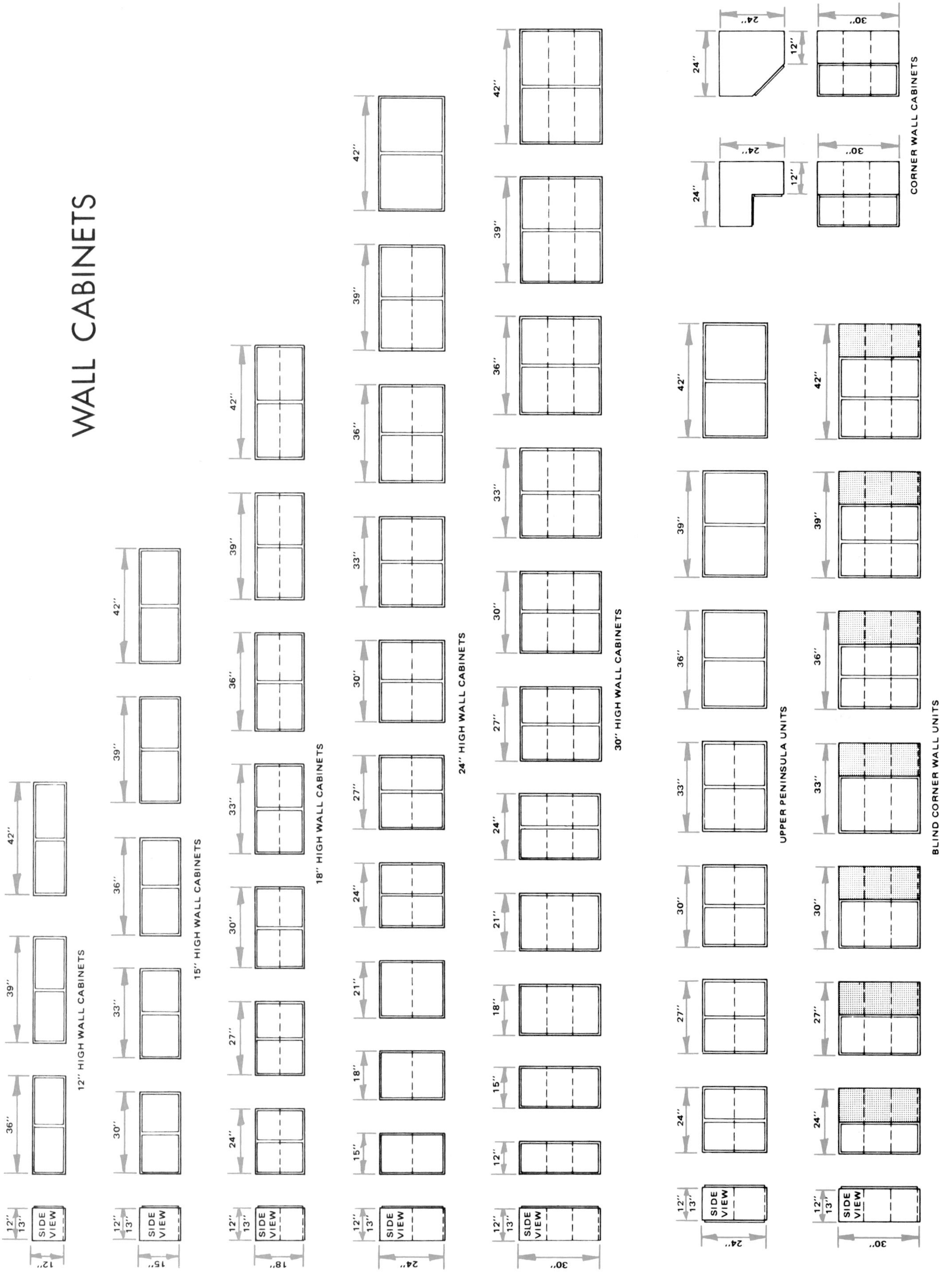
WALL CABINETS
12'' HIGH WALL CABINETS
15'' HIGH WALL CABINETS
18'' HIGH WALL CABINETS
24'' HIGH WALL CABINETS
30'' HIGH WALL CABINETS
UPPER PENINSULA UNITS
BLIND CORNER WALL UNITS
CORNER WALL CABINETS
SIDE VIEW

Fig. 7-27. Standard wall cabinet sizes and designs.

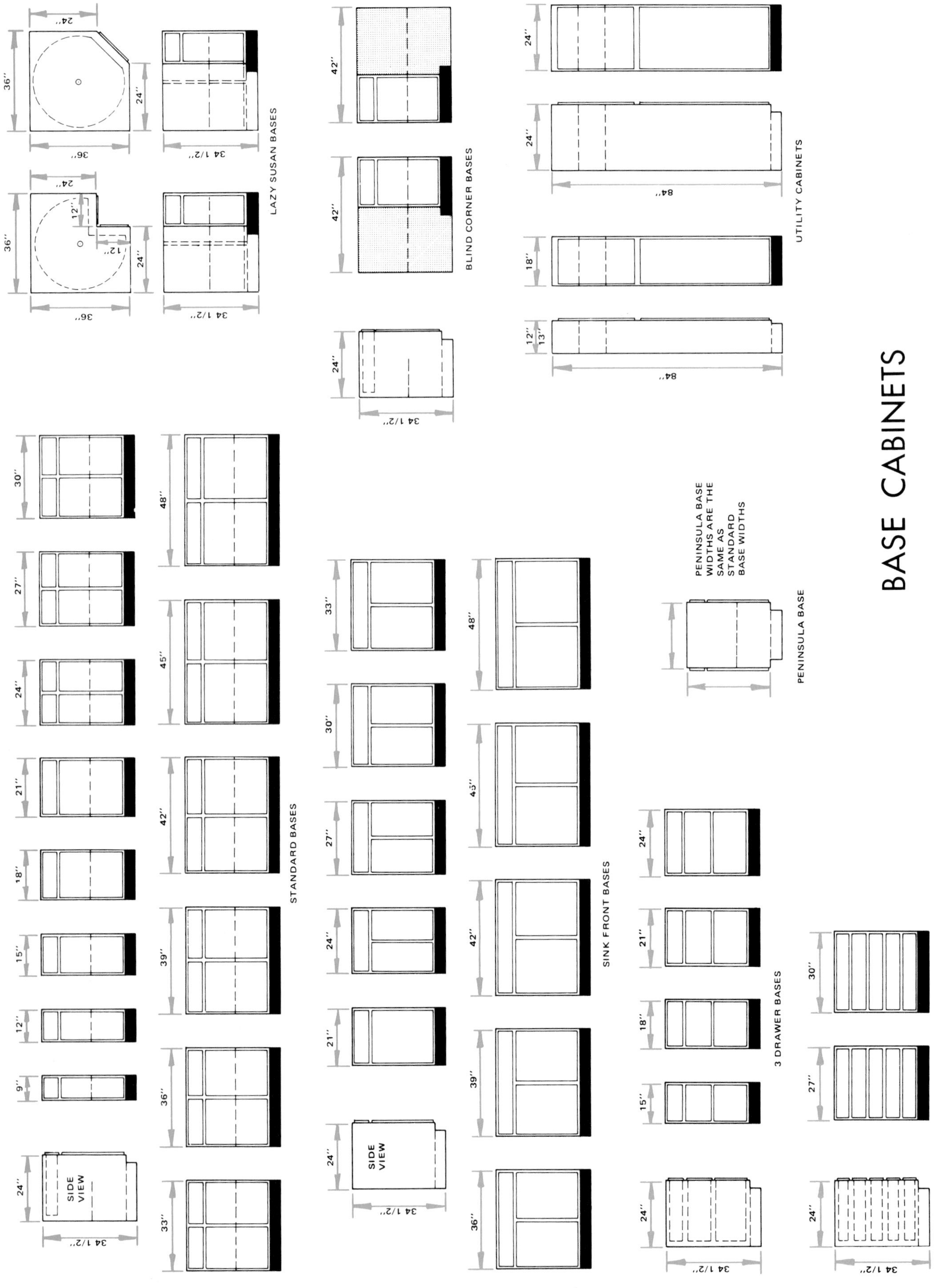
BASE CABINETS
LAZY SUSAN BASES
24"
36"
12"
34 1/2"
BLIND CORNER BASES
42"
24"
UTILITY CABINETS
84"
18"
13"
STANDARD BASES
9"
12"
15"
18"
21"
27"
30"
33"
39"
45"
48"
SIDE VIEW
SINK FRONT BASES
PENINSULA BASE
PENINSULA BASE WIDTHS ARE THE SAME AS STANDARD BASE WIDTHS
3 DRAWER BASES
5 DRAWER BASES

Fig. 7-27. (Continued) Standard base cabinet sizes and designs.

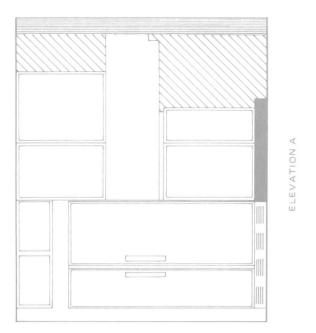

ELEVATION A

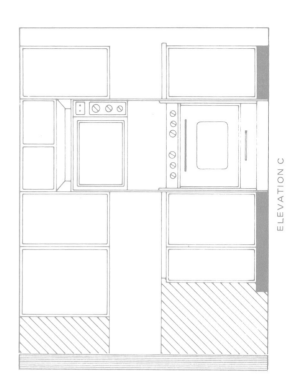

ELEVATION C

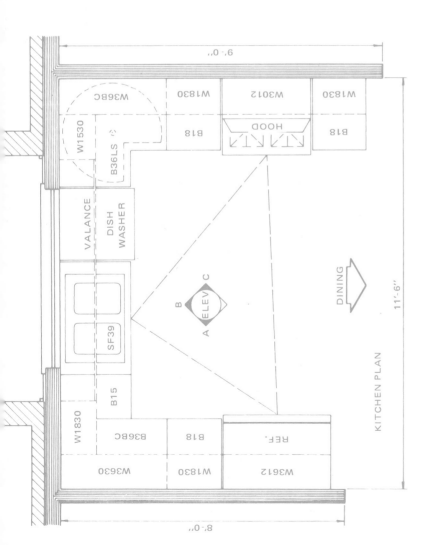

9'-0"

W3630 | W1830 | W3612

W1830 | B18 | REF.

B36BC

B15

SF39

W1830

VALANCE

DISH WASHER

W1530

B36LS

W36BC

B18 | W1830

HOOD | W3012

B18 | W1830

8'-0"

A ELEV C B

DINING

11'-6"

KITCHEN PLAN

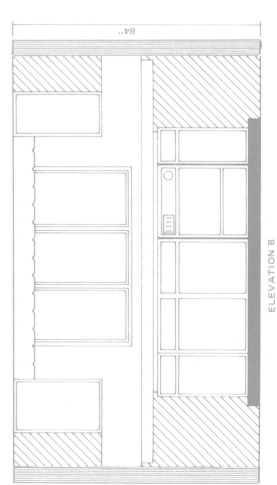

84"

ELEVATION B

Fig. 7-28. Construction drawings for a modern kitchen.

produce as standard units. Be sure to check the specifications of the cabinets selected before drawing the kitchen plan.

Fig. 7-28 shows the plan and elevation of a modern kitchen. Note how the wall and base cabinets are identified in the plan view. Numbers shown are manufacturer's stock numbers. The wall cabinets are illustrated with a hidden line symbol while the base units are shown as object lines. A kitchen plan should also show the work triangle and specify its length.

Proper location of the kitchen is important. It is the prime element of the service area and its relation to other areas of the house require careful evaluation. It is usually advisable to locate the kitchen near the service entrance and to provide easy access to outside trash containers. The kitchen should be located next to the dining room. Try to position windows in such a way that children in their play area may be observed from the kitchen. The laundry area and a bath should also be located in the general area of the kitchen.

Ventilation is a must in the modern kitchen. A wall fan is good, but a hood with a fan is better because it is more efficient in collecting fumes, Figs. 7-29 and 7-30. Provision for exhaust is necessary either through an outside wall or the roof. Exhaust from the kitchen fan should not be expelled into the attic.

Decor of the kitchen should be pleasant. The room should be well lighted. In addition to the main ceiling fixtures, lights over the sink, cooking center, and food preparation areas are needed. A dropped ceiling with banks of fluorescent lights is a popular way to supply an ample amount of light and at the same time add to the appearance of the kitchen. A lowered ceiling makes the room look larger.

Modern appliances are produced in many colors and styles. Select colors and styles that are consistent with the overall design of the kitchen. Choose materials which are easy to maintain and are durable, Fig. 7-31.

Fig. 7-30. A modern range hood which utilizes charcoal filters. The cooker hood has a transparent glass insert which allows you to see the cooking center. (Gaggeau USA)

Fig. 7-29. This kitchen will remain free of excessive cooking odors because it has a large efficient hood over the range. (Pella/Rolscreen Company)

Fig. 7-31. Modern kitchen refrigerators are designed to be functional. (Jenn-Air Company)

Fig. 7-32 shows a modified corridor kitchen. This efficient design provides a planning area, ample storage, and easy access to the work centers. The breakfast nook serves as a room divider and is convenient to the adjoining family room.

A U-shaped kitchen with extras is presented in Fig. 7-33. This plan is designed for the person who enjoys planning and preparing large meals. The design is efficient with lots of room provided for movement. The dining area is conveniently

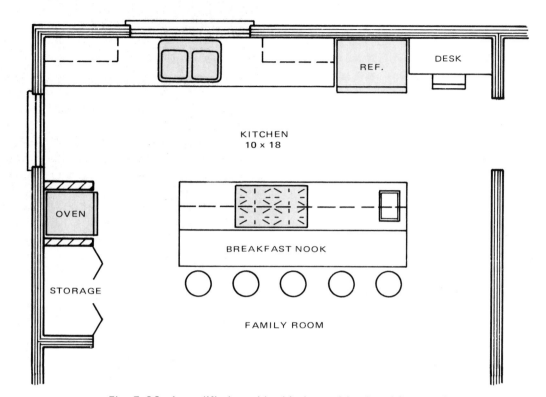

Fig. 7-32. A modified corridor kitchen with a breakfast nook.

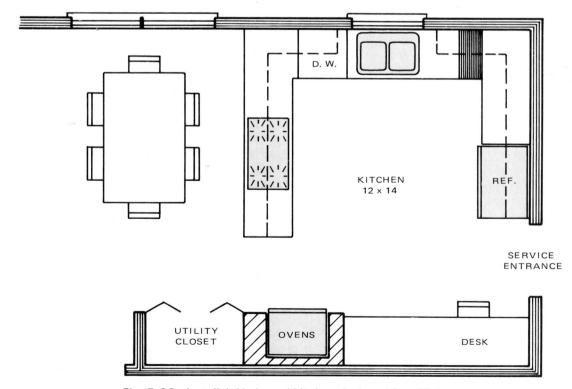

Fig. 7-33. A stylish U-shaped kitchen designed for efficiency.

located next to the food preparation center. Another advantage of this plan is the service entrance, which facilitates garbage removal and restocking supplies.

KITCHEN EATING AREAS

A kitchen eating area is convenient for serving informal meals and snacking. It should be located outside of the food preparation area, yet convenient to it. When planning an eating area in the kitchen, allow sufficient space. Thus, the overall size of the kitchen will be larger.

A kitchen eating area such as the one shown in Fig. 7-34 is popular with many families. The arrangement of table and chairs is flexible to accommodate the number of people.

Other households prefer an eating counter with chairs or stools, Fig. 7-35. The change in the height of countertop separates the cooking from the dining area in this cooking/dining island. Allow for knee space under the counter. If chairs are to be used at the eating counter, the counter height should be 26''. Lighting should be a consideration when planning either kitchen eating area arrangement.

CLOTHES CARE CENTER

A clothes care center provides the location and facilities for washing, drying, pressing, fold-

Fig. 7-35. Eating counters require less space than table and chairs, but may not serve as many people. (Whirlpool Corporation)

ing, storing, and mending clothes. It is intended to be more than a ''utility'' room. Many utility rooms are drab and are located away from other service areas of the house. The clothes care center is intended to be bright, cheerful, and convenient, Fig. 7-36. It should be large enough to provide adequately for the activities to be performed there, Figs. 7-37 and 7-38.

Fig. 7-34. An attractive kitchen eating area which allows for flexibility in serving people. Eating areas require lighting. (Whirlpool Corporation)

Fig. 7-36. This bright clothes care center provides ample workspace and convenient storage. (Wood-Mode Cabinetry)

Fig. 7-37. Natural light is available to help in the laundry process. (Wood-Mode Cabinetry)

It is desirable for the clothes care center to be ventilated and well lighted. The floor must be resistant to water and easily cleaned. Ceramic tile is preferred. Countertop space that is durable and soil resistant provides for a convenient work area, Fig. 7-39.

A well-designed clothes care center is illustrated in Fig. 7-40. Note that this room includes all the functions associated with clothes care. The built-in ironing board saves space and is functional. The laundry sink is near the washer for convenience. Cabinet storage space is provided above the washer and dryer.

Fig. 7-39. This clothes care center provides ample counter space and utilizes a durable floor covering. (Kitchenaid, Inc.)

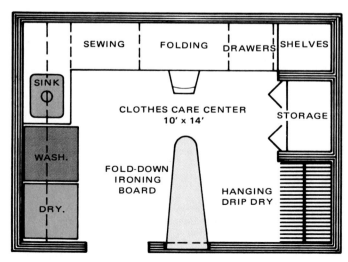

Fig. 7-40. A well-designed clothes care center with facilities for washing, drying, pressing, folding, storing, and mending.

Fig. 7-38. Storage space and convenience are the main features of this clothes care center. (Wood-Mode Cabinetry)

If possible, locate the clothes care center near the kitchen. A homemaker spends a large amount of time in the kitchen and this location may save many steps.

Fig. 7-41 shows the sizes and shapes of appliances and furnishings commonly used in a clothes care center. The clothes care center may be expanded into a full-fledged "homemakers center." Here is an all-purpose room where the homemaker can sew, arrange flowers, pursue hobbies, and do many other things in addition to washing and ironing clothes. Fig. 7-42 shows such a room.

A compact clothes care center is presented in Fig. 7-43. This room is organized for efficiency. The ironing board swings up into the wall out of the way. Soiled clothes are collected in the bin below the clothes chute which is convenient for

IRONING BOARD		
WIDTH	LENGTH	HEIGHT
15"	54"	23"- 37"

LAUNDRY TUB		
WIDTH	DEPTH	HEIGHT
24"	20"	34"
24"	23"	34"
28"	26"	34"

DRYER		
WIDTH	DEPTH	HEIGHT
29"	26"	43 1/2"

WASHER		
WIDTH	DEPTH	HEIGHT
29"	26"	43 1/2"

Fig. 7-41. Furniture and appliance symbols used in a clothes care center.

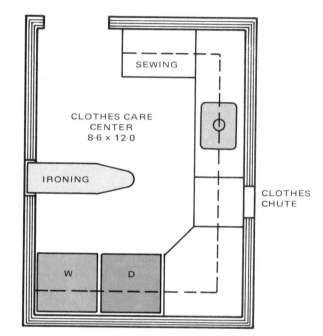

Fig. 7-43. A modern clothes care center which provides for washing, drying, sewing, storage, and ironing.

Fig. 7-42. This homemaker center is an all-purpose room. Here the homemaker can sew, and pursue creative activities. (Wood-Mode Cabinetry)

wash day. A sewing and mending area is flanked by generous counter space. Storage is more than average in this well-planned center.

The clothes care center shown in Fig. 7-44 is designed especially for a basement location next to the family or recreation room. A series of storage shelves screens the area and adds many

Fig. 7-45. A small garage with no storage facilities.

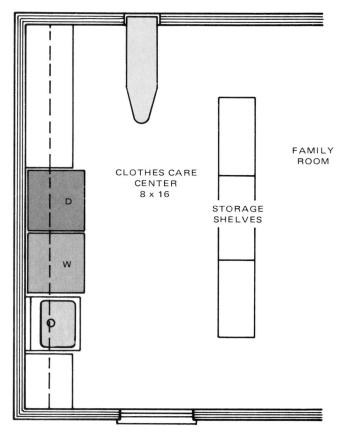

Fig. 7-44. A clothes care center designed for the basement.

cubic feet of storage space. Wall cabinets line one wall and create a trim appearance as well as adding storage space. Counter area is sufficient for folding clothes or mending. Organization is the key in this plan.

GARAGE OR CARPORT

The primary purpose of a garage or carport is to provide shelter for the family automobile(s). It may be small and simple, large and complex, attached to the house, or free standing.

The size and location of the garage or carport will depend on the number of cars to be housed, the size and layout of the house, and the space available. A single-car facility may range in size from 11' x 19' to 16' x 25', Figs. 7-45 and 7-46. A space designed for two cars may be as

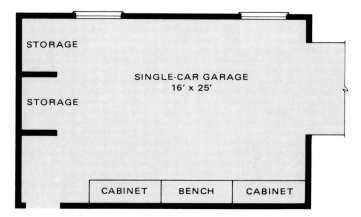

Fig. 7-46. Single-car garage with storage and workspace.

small as 20' x 20' or as large as 25' x 25', Figs. 7-47 and 7-48.

Several factors should be considered when deciding between a garage or a carport. A carport provides less protection for the car than a garage since it is open on one or more sides,

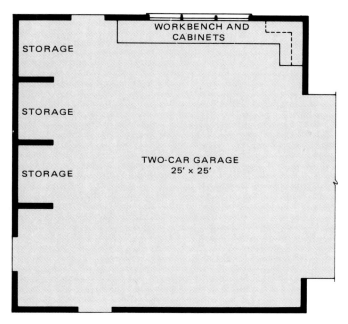

Fig. 7-47. Large two-car garage with workshop and storage.

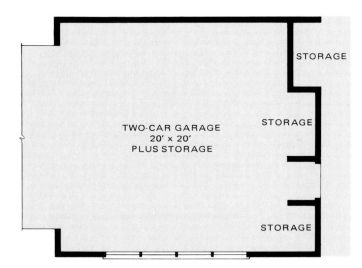

Fig. 7-48. A small two-car garage with a variety of storage space.

Figs. 7-49 and 7-50. A garage supplies more security than a carport. Certain house styles look better with one than the other. In cold climates, a garage may be more desirable. Carports are less expensive to build than garages and may be satisfactory for warm dry climates.

The overall space may be increased considerably if a work area or utility storage is planned into the facility. (See Fig. 7-47.)

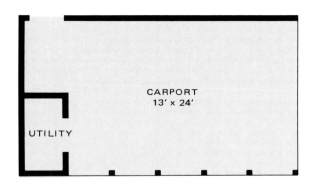

Fig. 7-49. Single stall carport open on two sides, with small utility area.

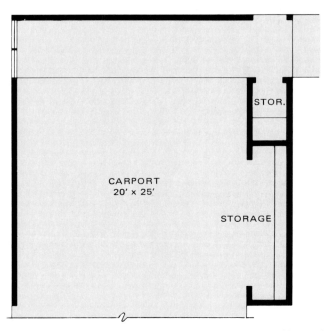

Fig. 7-50. A carport with space for two cars and lots of storage.

Fig. 7-51. Garage is an integral part of the house. (Weather Shield Mfg., Inc.)

A garage or carport should be designed in such a way that is an integral part of the total structure, Fig. 7-51. If care is not taken, a garage or carport could detract from the appearance of the house.

If the garage is a free-standing structure, providing a covered walkway to the house may be desirable, Fig. 7-52. The walkway should lead to the service entrance and provide easy access to the kitchen.

Plan the garage or carport with storage in mind, Fig. 7-53. Provide space for outdoor rec-reation equipment and gardening tools, if no other specific facility is provided for that purpose. Many homes have garages which are not used for storage of the automobile because they are full of tools and other equipment. This is often a result of poor planning.

A few design ideas may be worth mentioning. The floor of the garage or carport should be at least 4'' thick concrete reinforced with steel or wire mesh. Good floor drainage is important. Include ample windows and artificial lighting. If the garage is attached to the house, be sure to

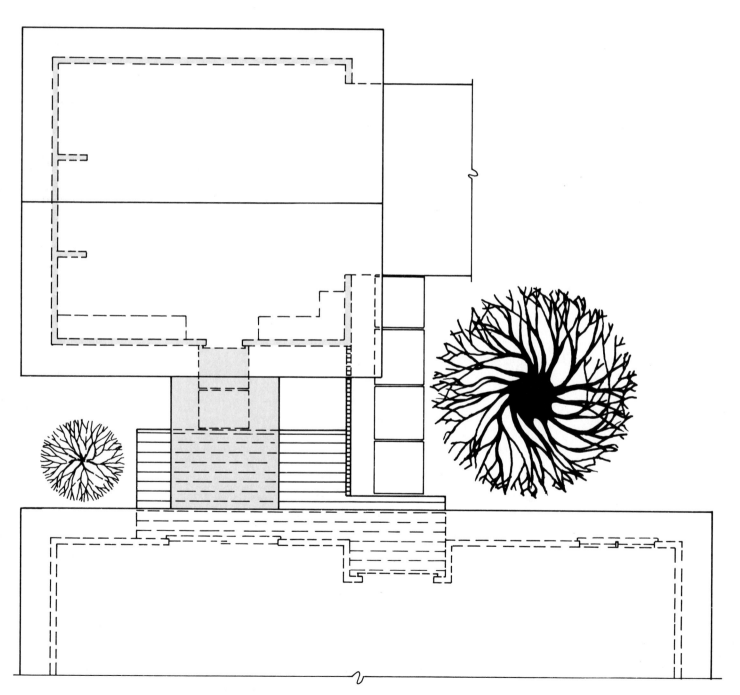

Fig. 7-52. This plan shows a free-standing garage that becomes an integral part of the house by adding a covered walkway between the two.

check the local building code for special requirements regarding fire protection. Garage doors should complement the design of the house.

Standard-size garage doors are available in wood, fiber glass, plastics, aluminum, and steel. Wood has been a traditional choice and is still preferred by many, but it requires frequent painting. Metal doors are popular and require little maintenance. Fiberglass is very durable and allows natural light to come through even with the door closed. A single-car garage door is usually 8 feet wide and 7 feet high. A two-car garage door is usually 16 feet wide and 7 feet high. Recreational vehicles may require garage doors higher than 7 feet. Garage doors are also produced in widths of 18 feet. Fig. 7-54 shows four modern double garage door styles.

The driveway and turnaround should be planned concurrently with the garage. If space is available, a turnaround is often recommended. Backing directly onto the street should be avoided when possible. Fig. 7-55 shows two

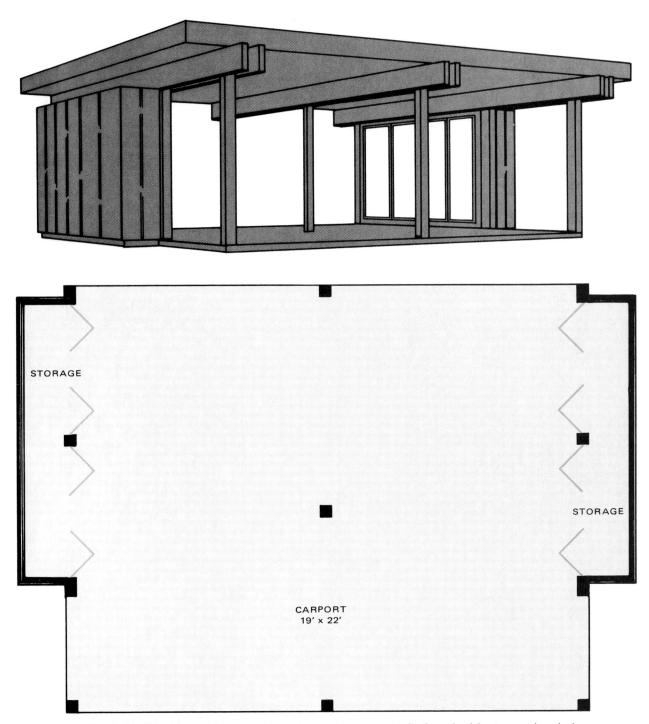

STORAGE

STORAGE

CARPORT
19' x 22'

Fig. 7-53. The plan and perspective of a modern carport designed with storage in mind.

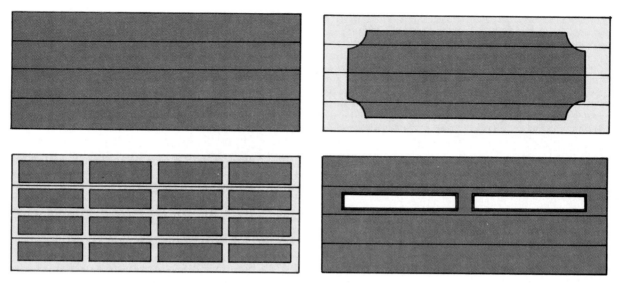

Fig. 7-54. Four modern double garage door designs.

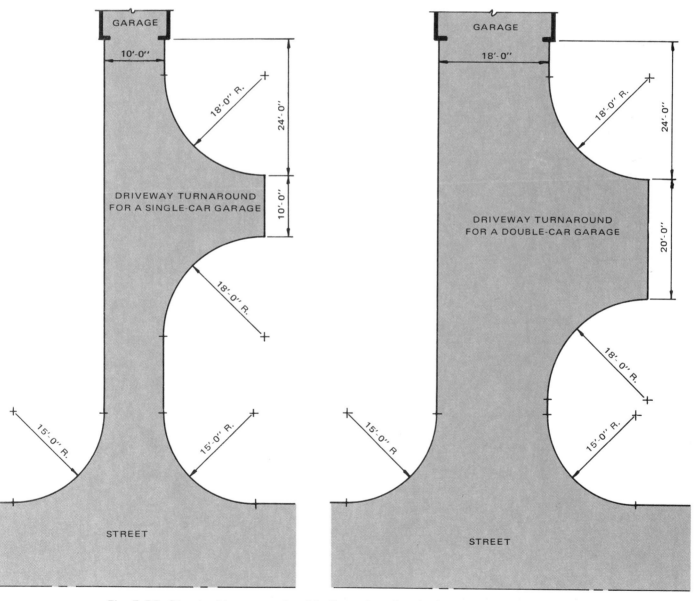

Fig. 7-55. Standard turnarounds with dimensions for single- and double-car garages.

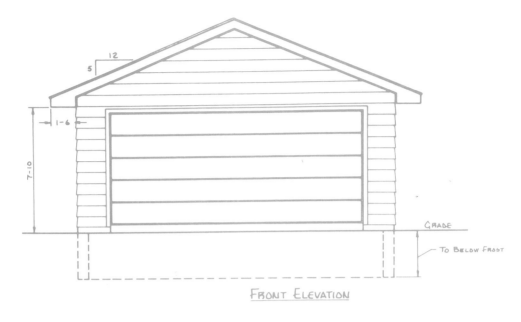

FRONT ELEVATION

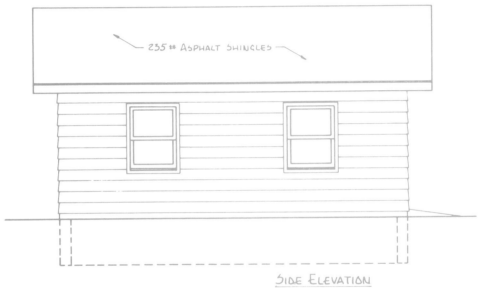

235# ASPHALT SHINGLES

SIDE ELEVATION

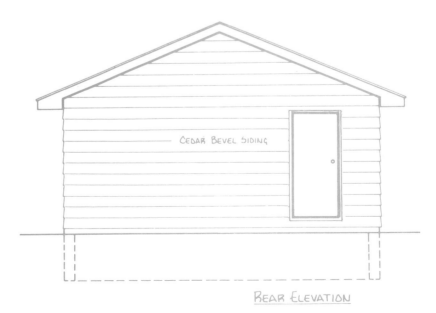

CEDAR BEVEL SIDING

REAR ELEVATION

Fig. 7-56. Plans for a conventional two-car garage.

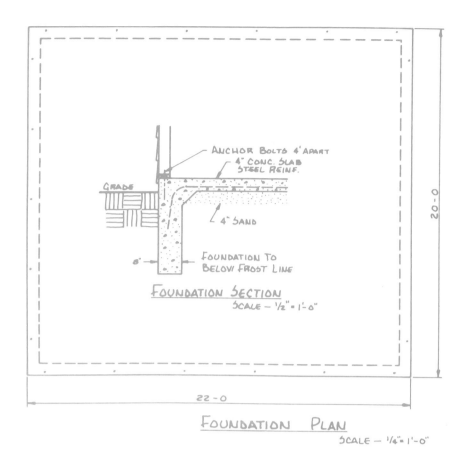

ANCHOR BOLTS 4' APART
4" CONC. SLAB
STEEL REINF.

GRADE

4" SAND

8"

FOUNDATION TO
BELOW FROST LINE

FOUNDATION SECTION
SCALE - 1/2" = 1'-0"

20-0

22-0

FOUNDATION PLAN
SCALE - 1/4" = 1'-0"

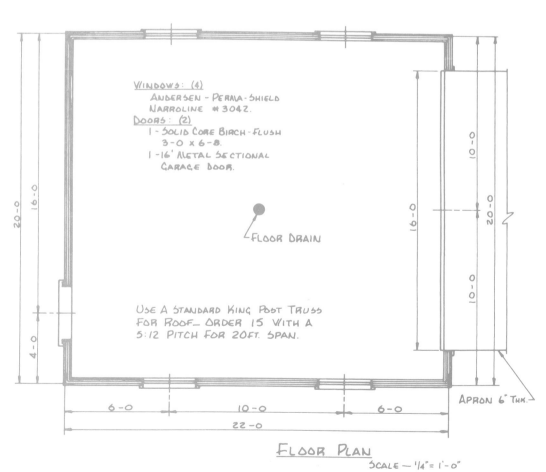

WINDOWS: (4)
ANDERSEN - PERMA-SHIELD
NARROLINE #3042.
DOORS: (2)
1 - SOLID CORE BIRCH - FLUSH
3-0 x 6-8.
1 - 16' METAL SECTIONAL
GARAGE DOOR.

FLOOR DRAIN

USE A STANDARD KING POST TRUSS
FOR ROOF. ORDER 15 WITH A
5:12 PITCH FOR 20 FT. SPAN.

20-0

16-0

4-0

16-0

20-0

APRON 6" THK.

6-0   10-0   6-0
22-0

FLOOR PLAN
SCALE - 1/4" = 1'-0"

Fig. 7-56. (Continued) Plans for a conventional two-car garage.

turnarounds with dimensions. Note that the minimum driveway width is 10 feet. Always plan garage facilities for a standard-size automobile even though the prospective owner may have a compact car.

The garage shown in Fig. 7-56 is designed to utilize common building materials and techniques. A slab foundation and stud walls with bevel siding constitute the basic structure. Standard trusses are used to form the gable roof. The design is both economical and attractive.

Basic proportions of a garage are relatively fixed, but several ideas may be applied to improve the appearance. For example, an innovative roof may be used such as the Dutch hip, butterfly, or mansard. The roof style will change the overall appearance considerably. The use of modern siding materials may also improve an otherwise drab structure. Textured siding with rustic stain or weathered redwood boards add character and charm. Windows may be conventional types or fixed panels of colored glass or plastics. It is possible, with the application of a few innovative ideas, to transform a garage into an attractive and functional structure adding much to the total home environment.

REVIEW QUESTIONS—CHAPTER 7

Write your answers on a separate sheet of paper. Do not write in this book.

1. Kitchen cabinets are produced in standard widths, heights, and depths. The standard modular width increment is _____ in.
2. The dimensions of a single-car garage are approximately _____.
3. The minimum width of a driveway is _____.
4. A clothes care center should provide for what activities?
5. Identify the six basic kitchen designs.
6. The maximum acceptable length of the work triangle in a kitchen is _____ feet.
7. The service area of a home generally includes what six individual areas?
8. Kitchen base cabinets are normally _____ in. high.
9. Exhaust fumes from a kitchen hood fan should not be expelled into the _____.
10. Standard size garage doors are available in what materials?
11. The standard width of a kitchen countertop is _____ in.
12. The counter height for an eating area in the kitchen should be _____ in.

SUGGESTED ACTIVITIES

1. Visit an appliance store and obtain literature on the latest kitchen appliances. Prepare a bulletin board display using pictures from the literature.
2. Secure specifications and price lists of kitchen cabinets from a manufacturer. Calculate the total cost for the cabinets shown in Fig. 7-28.
3. Plan a modern kitchen which includes the major elements of the work triangle. Draw the plan view and elevations. Identify the cabinets using the manufacturer's numbers and dimension the drawings.
4. Obtain three floor plans from magazines or other sources and analyze the provisions for clothes care in each plan. Explain the strengths and weaknesses of each. Propose improvements.
5. Measure the length and width of a standard size automobile and design a single-car garage which provides adequate space for the car and extra storage.

8
CHAPTER
Plot Plans

After studying this chapter, you will be able to:
- Identify the various features shown on a typical plot plan.
- Visualize land elevations from contour lines.
- Recognize typical topographical symbols and apply them to site considerations.
- Properly locate a building on a site.
- Draw a plot plan using correct symbols and conventions.

A plot plan is a plan view drawing which shows the site, location, and orientation of the buildings on the property. A plot plan shows several specific features, such as:

Length and bearing of each property line.
Location, outline, and size of buildings on the site.
Contour of the land.
Elevation of property corners and contour lines.
Meridian arrow (north symbol).
Trees, shrubs, streams, and gardens.
Streets, driveways, sidewalks, and patios.
Location of utilities.
Easements for utilities and drainage (if any).
Well, septic tank, and field.
Fences and retaining walls.
Lot number or address of the site.
Scale of the drawing.

The plot plan is drawn using information provided by a surveyor and recorded on a site plan, Fig. 8-1. Note that the site plan presents

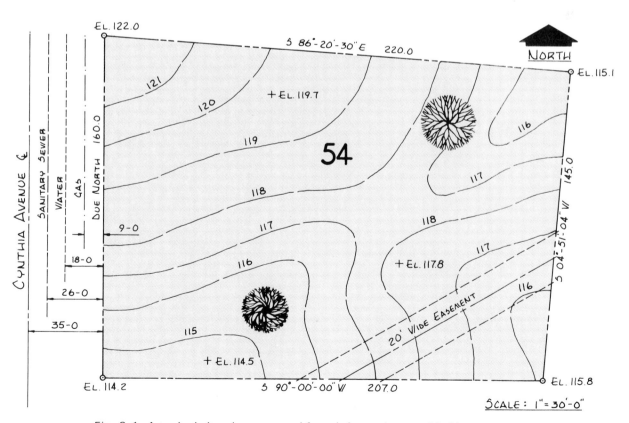

Fig. 8-1. A typical site plan prepared from information provided by a surveyor.

information only about the property and utilities. It does not show proposed construction. However, the plot plan shows both the property and proposed construction.

PROPERTY LINES

Property lines define the site boundaries. The length and bearing of each line must be identified on the plot plan. Property line lengths are measured with an engineer's scale to the nearest 1/100 foot. Fig. 8-2 shows a property line that is 175.25′ long and has a bearing of N 89° E.

Bearing angles are recorded in degrees and, if required, in minutes and seconds from north or south. An example of a typical bearing might be, (S 63° W), while a more specific bearing would read, (S 63° 13′ 05″ W). Fig. 8-3 shows a number of lines with bearings identified.

If the property corner begins or ends on a bench mark it is usually identified with a special symbol. All other corners may be represented by drawing a small circle, with the center of the circle being the property corner. See Fig. 8-4.

It is customary when drawing the property lines of a site to begin at a given corner and proceed in a clockwise manner until the begin-

ning point is reached. Fig. 8-5 shows the procedure for drawing the property lines of a site.

CONTOUR LINES

A *contour* is a line connecting points which have the same elevation. The shoreline of a lake is a good example of a contour. Contour lines help describe the topography of a site by depict-

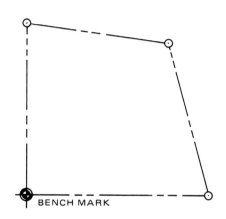

Fig. 8-4. Property corners which are located at a bench mark are identified with a bench mark symbol.

Fig. 8-2. This property line is 175.25′ long and has a bearing of N 89° E.

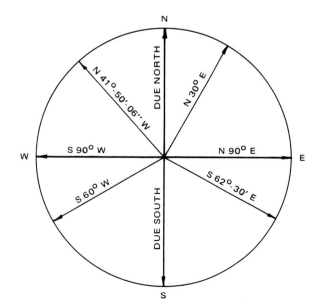

Fig. 8-3. Bearings are from North or South and may be as accurate as plus or minus one second.

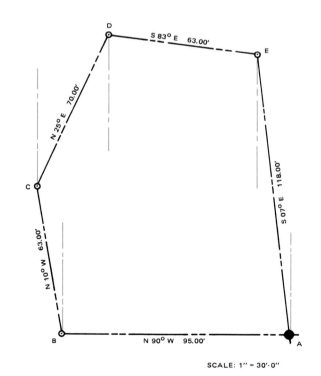

SCALE: 1″ = 30′-0″

PROPERTY LINE DESCRIPTION

FROM POINT A	A LINE BEARS N 90° W	95.00′	TO POINT B
FROM POINT B	A LINE BEARS N 10° W	63.00′	TO POINT C
FROM POINT C	A LINE BEARS N 25° E	70.00′	TO POINT D
FROM POINT D	A LINE BEARS S 83° E	63.00′	TO POINT E
FROM POINT E	A LINE BEARS S 07° E	118.00′	TO POINT A

Fig. 8-5. These property lines have been drawn to scale using the property line descriptions provided.

ing shape and elevation of the land. The accepted reference point for topographical surveys is mean sea level. Many times, however, it is not important to know how far a point is above or below sea level, but what the relative difference is between two or more points. In residential home construction, relative elevations are usually sufficient.

The examination of several characteristics of contour should help to clarify their use:

1. Contour interval is the vertical distance between two adjacent contours. This interval may be any distance which is functional for the specific drawing. Fig. 8-6 illustrates a contour interval of five feet. Be sure to identify the elevation of each contour line.

2. When contours are spaced closely together a steep slope is indicated, Fig. 8-7.

3. When contours are smooth and parallel, the ground surface is even. When contours are irregular, the ground surface is rough and uneven, Fig. 8-8.

4. Summits and depressions are represented by closed lines as shown in Fig. 8-9.

5. Contours of different elevations do not cross. Only in the instance of a vertical slope would the contours appear to touch.

6. Contours cross watersheds and ridge lines at right angles with the concave side of the curve facing toward the higher elevation, Fig. 8-10.

Contour lines that are the result of a survey are usually represented by a series of long (one

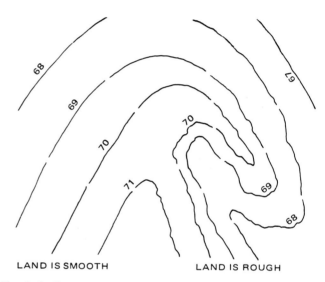

Fig. 8-8. Contour lines show relative roughness of the land as well as elevation.

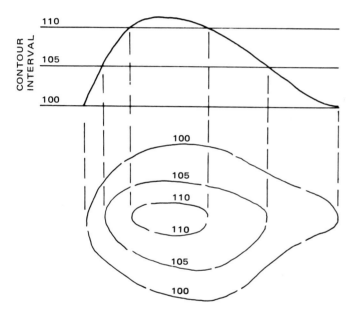

Fig. 8-6. The plan and elevation view of the contour using an interval of 5 feet.

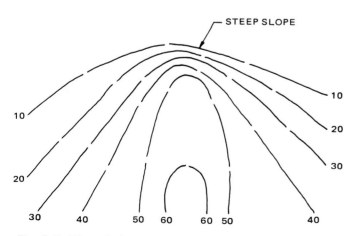

Fig. 8-7. The relative spacing of contour lines represents the slope angle.

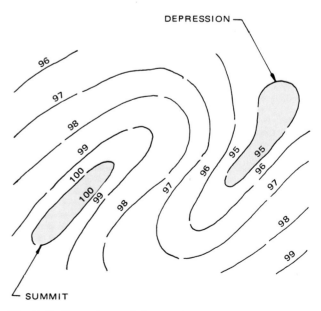

Fig. 8-9. Summits and depressions are represented by closed contour lines.

Plot Plans   153

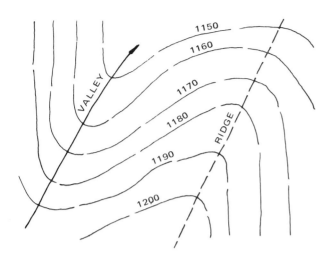

Fig. 8-10. Ridges and valleys should be identified using the proper symbols.

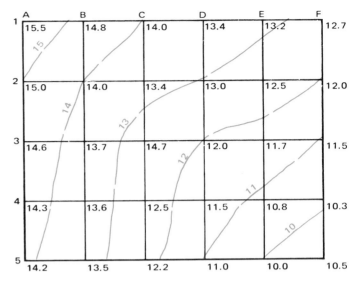

Fig. 8-12. Contour lines plotted from an elevation grid using data supplied by a surveyor.

to two inch), thin freehand lines. Estimated contours are represented by a short dashed line similar to a hidden line, Fig. 8-11.

Fig. 8-12 shows the plotting of contours from a grid of elevations developed by a surveyor. Too few measurements taken for a given area results in less accuracy of contour representations. When insufficient data is given, the resulting contour will be only moderately accurate.

TOPOGRAPHICAL FEATURES

Topographical features are represented by symbols. Many symbols are standardized and readily recognizable. A few are not. When a symbol is designed for a specific purpose and is not standard it should appear in a legend on the drawing.

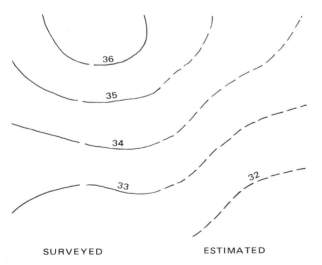

SURVEYED   ESTIMATED

Fig. 8-11. Estimated contours are shown with a dash line symbol. Surveyed contours are represented by solid or long dash lines.

In some topographical drawings color plays an important role. When color is used, the following guidelines should be applied: black is used for lettering and the works of man, such as roads, houses, and other structures; brown represents all land forms such as contour lines; blue is used for water features such as streams, lakes, marsh, and ponds; and green for vegetation.

Fig. 8-13 illustrates some of the more common topographical symbols which might be used on a plot plan.

LOCATION OF STRUCTURE ON SITE

A complete analysis should be made of the site to determine the ideal location and placement of the structure on the site. The analysis should include such things as natural contour, trees, view, surrounding houses, code restrictions, style of house to be built, solar orientation, winds, placement of well and septic system, if needed, and size and shape of the site. Not all of these factors will apply in every situation, but they should be examined to determine their importance.

Once a specific location is decided on, the structure may be drawn on the plot plan. There are three commonly accepted methods of representing the house on the drawing. The first method is to lay out the outside of the exterior walls omitting all interior walls and roof. Shade or crosshatch the space covered by the house, Fig. 8-14. The second method of representing the house on the site is to draw the exterior walls as hidden lines with the roof shown as solid lines (typical roof plan), Fig. 8-15. The third method

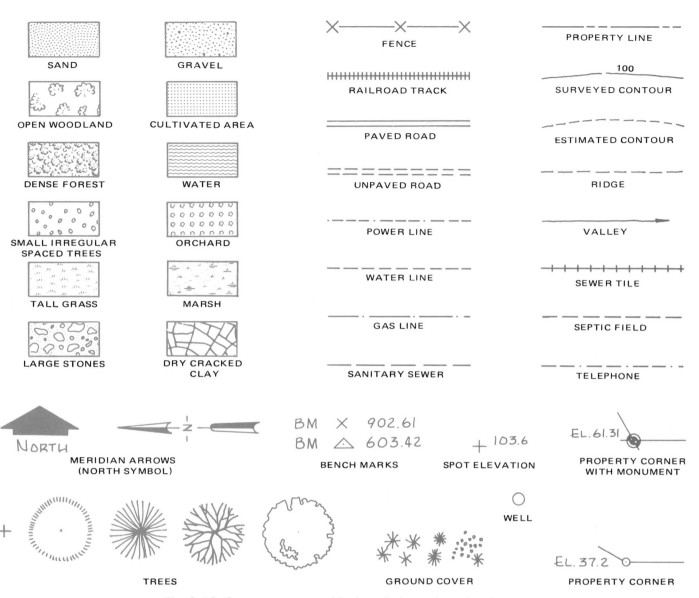

Fig. 8-13. Common topographical symbols used on plot plans.

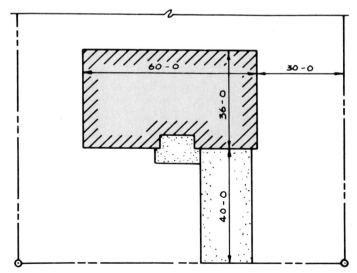

Fig. 8-14. A house may be represented on a plot plan by shading or crosshatching the area covered by the house. The roof is not included.

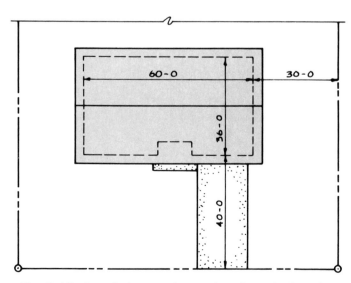

Fig. 8-15. A roof plan may be used to show the location and size of the house on a site. Exterior walls are represented as hidden lines.

shows exterior walls thickened with all interior walls, windows, and doors omitted, Fig. 8-16.

When the distance between house and property line is critical it may be advisable to use the second method or add the overhang line to either of the other two methods. The distance from the roof overhang to the property line may then be shown.

The location of the house on the site must be dimensioned. Standard procedure is to dimension the distance of one corner of the house from adjacent lot lines as shown in Figs. 8-14, 8-15, and 8-16. In some instances, this simple procedure will not be sufficient to clearly locate the structure. Fig. 8-17 shows a more complex situation and its solution. In each instance, dimension the distance from the outside of the exterior wall to the property line and, if required, show the overhang distance.

PROCEDURE FOR DRAWING A PLOT PLAN

These steps are recommended for drawing a plot plan; omit items which do not apply:

1. Select a scale which provides the largest drawing on the size paper that you have chosen. All of the sheets in set of drawings should be the same size for ease of handling. The property lines should be placed sufficiently inside the border to provide room for adding dimensions, notes, and a title block. Scales commonly used in drawing plot plans range from 1/8'' = 1'-0'' to 1'' = 30'-0'' and smaller.

2. Lay out the property lines using data supplied by the site plan or other source. Be extremely careful in this step to ensure an

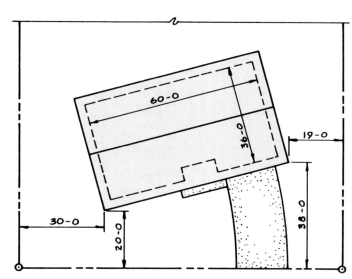

Fig. 8-17. A house which is not positioned parallel to the property lines may require more than two dimensions to properly locate it on the site. A bearing line could also be used to show the position of the house.

accurate drawing. Steps 2 through 4 are illustrated in Fig. 8-18.

3. Letter the bearing and length of each property line and affix the scale near the bottom of the drawing.

4. Locate the meridian arrow (north symbol) in a place on the drawing where it will be easy to find.

5. Select a contour interval which is appropriate for your specific situation and plot the contour lines. Draw the lines lightly at this point. These are to be darkened in later. Steps 5 and 6 are illustrated in Fig. 8-18.

6. Letter the elevation of each contour line and property corner.

7. Locate the house on the site using one of the methods discussed earlier. Steps 7 through 9 are shown in Fig. 8-19.

8. Dimension the overall length and width of the house and the distance from the house to the two adjacent property lines. The elevation of a reference corner of the house is sometimes given.

9. Draw surrounding features such as driveway, sidewalks, and patios. The size and elevation may be given for each if they are required.

10. Determine the center line of the street and location of utilities. Draw these features using proper symbols and dimension their location. If a well and septic system are required, draw them at this point. Steps 10 through 12 are illustrated in Fig. 8-20.

11. Draw other topographical features such as trees and shrubs. Now darken in all light contour lines.

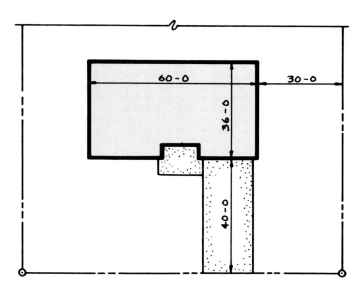

Fig. 8-16. Thickened exterior walls may show the location and size of a house on a site.

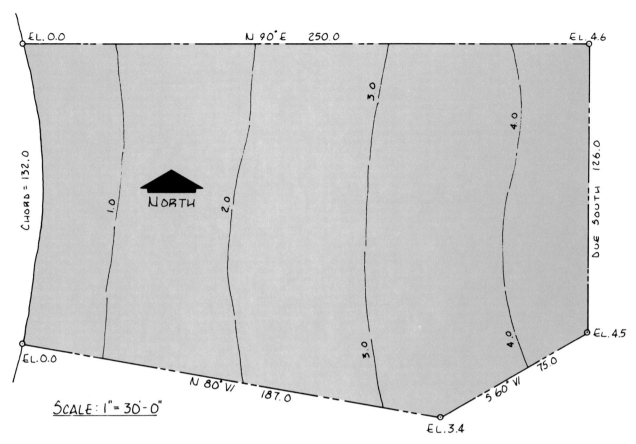

Fig. 8-18. A partially complete plot plan which has the property lines located and identified, meridian arrow positioned, the scale shown, and the contour lines and corner elevations added.

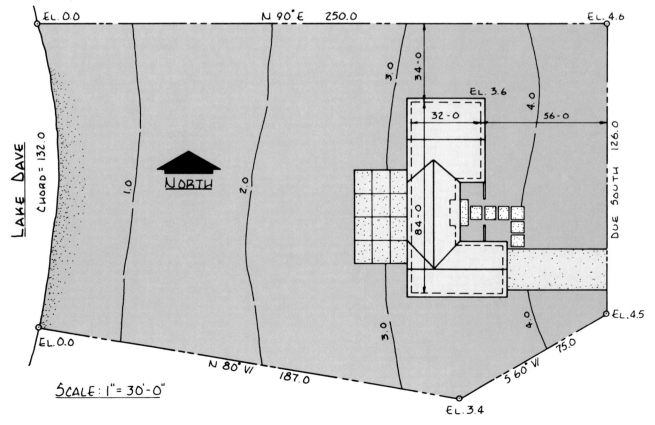

Fig. 8-19. The house, drive, and patio are positioned on the site and dimensioned.

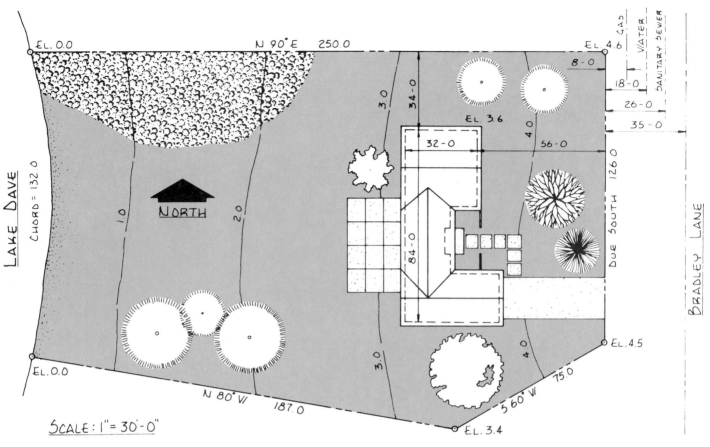

Fig. 8-20. The completed plot plan showing property lines, house location, north symbol, topographical features, center line of street, and utilities.

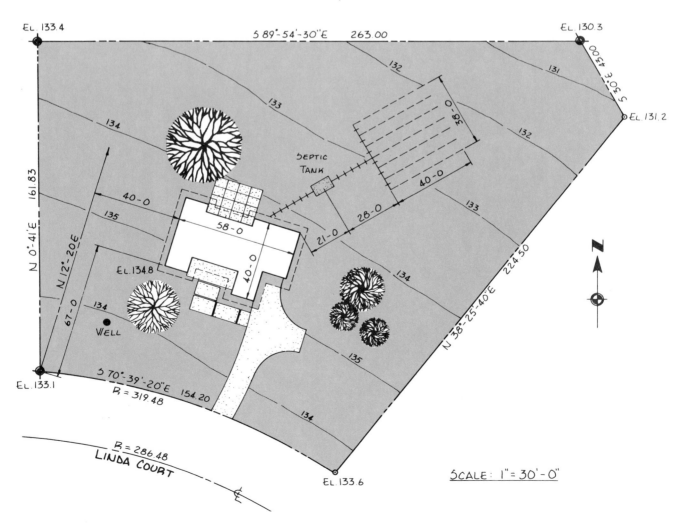

Fig. 8-21. A plot plan of a large site and house with its own septic system and well.

12. Check your drawing to be sure you have included all necessary elements.

Fig. 8-21 shows a plot plan of a large home site and house which has its own septic system and well. This drawing is a typical plot plan.

LANDSCAPE PLOT PLANS

The landscape plan is designed to show the type and placement of trees, shrubs, flowers, gardens, and pools on the site. A landscape plan (which is not always required) provides an excellent way to plan the total setting for the home.

Much of the information presented on the construction plot plan is required on the landscape plan. Boundary lines, meridian arrow, outline of the house, driveway, walks, patios, and contour lines are needed to place the landscape elements into their proper perspective.

Symbols are used to represent various types of plants. These symbols should be keyed to a chart to avoid confusion. There are not sufficient symbols to allow each ornamental plant to have its own symbol.

Fig. 8-22 shows a typical landscape plot plan. When practical the plant symbols should be drawn to proper scale. This produces a realistic idea of the components on the plan.

Fig. 8-23 shows the result of using a landscape plan to arrange the landscape elements to achieve a pleasing appearance.

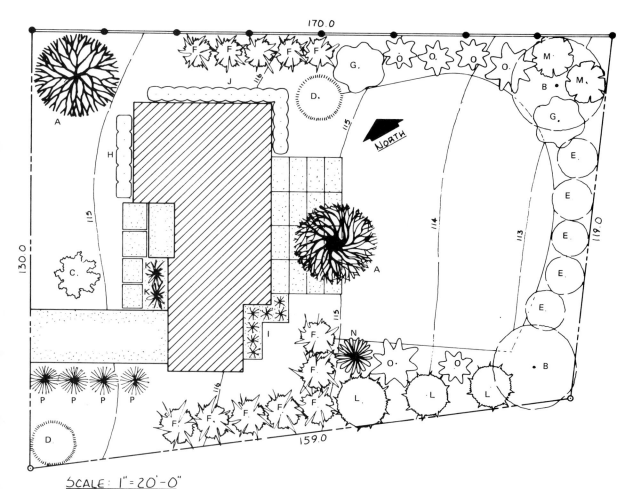

SCALE: 1" = 20'-0"

LANDSCAPING SCHEDULE

KEY	QUAN.	PLANT DESCRIPTION	KEY	QUAN.	PLANT DESCRIPTION
A	2	SHADE TREE	I	7	BUXUS
B	2	ORNAMENTAL TREE	J	15	PRIVET
C	1	FLOWERING CRAB	K	2	FLORIBUNDA ROSE
D	2	WILLOW TREE	L	3	PYRAMID YEW
E	5	RHODODENDRON	M	2	CAMELLIA
F	12	SPREADING JUNIPER	N	1	FRENCH HYBRID LILAC
G	2	FLOWERING SHRUB	O	6	VIBURNUM
H	5	TAXUS GLOBE	P	4	FORSYTHIA

Fig. 8-22. A typical landscape plot plan showing the type and location of trees and shrubs on the property.

Fig. 8-23. A landscape plan was used to achieve this striking layout. (Elk Corporation)

REVIEW QUESTIONS—CHAPTER 8

Write your answers on a separate sheet of paper. Do not write in this book.

1. A line connecting points that have the same elevation on a plot plan is:
   a. A bearing line.
   b. A property line.
   c. A contour line.
   d. None of the above.
2. The plot plan contains information collected by a _____ and recorded on a site plan.
3. What factors included in the analysis of a site help determine the ideal location and placement of a house?
4. Symbols for plants should be drawn to the proper _____ whenever possible.
5. What is the purpose of the meridian arrow?
6. Estimated contours are represented on the plot plan by using _____ _____ lines.
7. List four topographical features represented on plot plans. Indicate the color for the symbol if it were to be used.
8. The standard procedure for locating a house on a plot plan is to dimension the distance from one corner of the house to _____ lot lines.
9. The two types of information needed about property lines are the length and _____ of each line.

10. The plan that shows the type and placement of trees, shrubs, flowers, gardens, and pools is the _____ plan.

SUGGESTED ACTIVITIES

1. Select a vacant site in your community which is suitable for a home. Measure the site, determine north with a compass, and draw a site plan of the property to scale. Show any trees that may be on the site and indicate approximate contour lines.
2. Select a floor plan of a house from a newspaper, magazine, or other source which is appropriate for the site you drew in No. 1 above. Locate the house on the site. Draw a plot plan showing the house and property.
3. Define these terms: property lines, meridian arrow, contour, site plan, plot plan, landscape plan, utilities, bearing, bench mark, and depression.
4. Compile a list of fifteen ornamental trees and shrubs which grow in the area in which you live. Describe each one as to mature size and characteristics. Design a plan view symbol for each one.
5. Using the plot plan developed in No. 2 and the list of trees and shrubs hardy in your area, draw a landscape plan for the site.

Footings, Foundations, and Concrete

After studying this chapter, you will be able to:
- Describe the procedure for staking out a house location.
- List the major considerations when designing a footing for a residential foundation.
- Analyze a typical floor plan to determine the appropriate foundation.
- Discuss the design considerations for wood, concrete, and masonry foundation walls.
- Calculate the load to be supported by a beam.
- Explain the purpose of a lintel.

In residential construction, providing a good foundation is very important. This requires careful planning and design on the part of the architect, if the foundation is to support the structure as required. See Fig. 9-1.

STAKING OUT HOUSE LOCATION

The plot plan provides the necessary dimensions required for staking out the location of the house on the lot. The task is accomplished with a measuring tape, contractor's level, and transit (if required). When angles other than 90° must be measured, a surveyor's transit is used.

The first step in staking out the house is to locate each corner by laying off the distances indicated on the plot plan. A stake is driven into the ground at the location of each corner of the foundation to identify its position. Square corners may be laid out using the 9-12-15 unit method, Fig. 9-2. These proportions define a right triangle and establish a 90° angle corner. The position of all corners should be checked for accuracy by diagonal measurement, Fig. 9-3.

Batter boards are used to retain the location of the foundation during excavation and construction. These are constructed of 2 x 4 stakes sharpened on one end and driven into the ground about 4 feet outside the footing line. A 1 x 6 board is nailed horizontally to the stakes so all are level and in the same horizontal plane. (They will have the same elevation.) A strong cord or string is stretched across the boards at opposite

Fig. 9-1. Two different types of residential foundations. A—Typical masonry foundation. B—All weather wood foundation. (American Plywood Association)

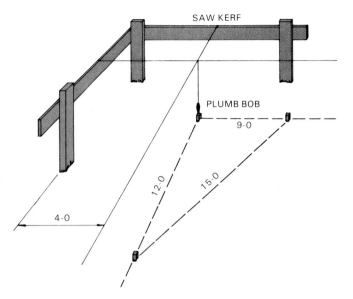

Fig. 9-2. Squaring a corner using the 9-12-15 unit method.

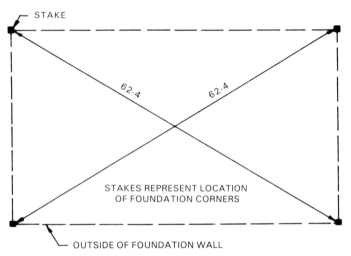

STAKE

62-4   62-4

STAKES REPRESENT LOCATION
OF FOUNDATION CORNERS

OUTSIDE OF FOUNDATION WALL

Fig. 9-3. The accuracy of layout may be checked by measuring the diagonals. They must be equal.

ends of the building and located directly above the corner stakes. A plumb bob is used for accurate placement of each stake. This is done for each side of the building. A saw kerf is usually made at the exact point on the horizontal batter board where the string is located. This prevents movement of the string along the board. After cuts are made in all eight batter boards, the lines of the house will be located, Fig. 9-4.

A control point is needed to determine the depth of excavation and foundation wall height. The corner with the highest elevation is usually selected for this purpose. The finished floor should be at least 8 inches above the grade.

EXCAVATION

In excavating for footings and foundation walls, the top soil is usually removed using a bulldozer or tractor with a blade. This soil is saved for final grading. A trencher or backhoe may be used to excavate for foundations when either slab construction or a crawl space is planned. In excavating for a basement, a backhoe or power shovel is generally used. Selection of excavating equipment is determined by the size of the excavation and type of soil.

Excavation for footings should extend down to a minimum of 6 in. into undisturbed earth. It must also be at least 6 in. below the average maximum frost penetration depth. See Fig. 9-5 for the approximate frost depth in your area. Local codes usually specify the minimum footing depth for a given area.

No backfilling should be permitted under the proposed footings, because uneven settling of

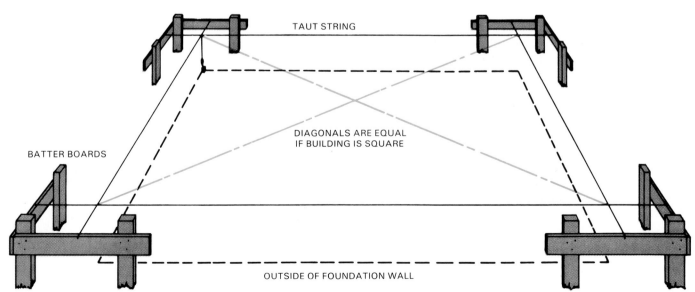

TAUT STRING

DIAGONALS ARE EQUAL
IF BUILDING IS SQUARE

BATTER BOARDS

OUTSIDE OF FOUNDATION WALL

Fig. 9-4. Batter boards in place around the location of the proposed foundation.

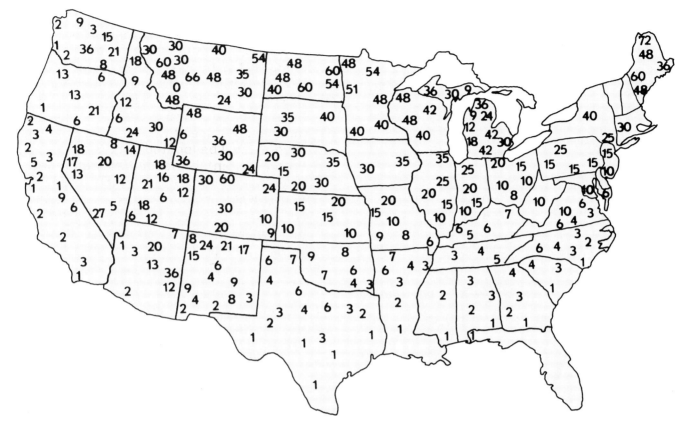

Fig. 9-5. Average depth of frost penetration in inches for locations throughout the United States. (U.S. Dept. of Commerce Weather Bureau)

the house may occur. In instances where part of the footings bear on rock, about 6 in. of the rock should be removed under the proposed footing and replaced with compacted sand to equalize settling.

On sites which have recently been filled and regraded, it is recommended that the footings extend down to the original undisturbed earth. The exception is when soil tests prove that the earth is sufficiently compacted to properly support the structure.

Excavation must be large enough to allow space to work when constructing the foundation wall and laying drain tile. The steepness of the back slope will depend on the type of soil encountered. Sandy soil is likely to cave-in and, therefore, requires a gentle back slope, while excavating in clay may be nearly vertical.

FOOTING SHAPES AND SPECIFICATIONS

Footings increase the supporting capacity of the foundation wall by spreading the load over a larger area, Fig. 9-6. If a foundation was built on rock, a footing would not be necessary. However, most houses are not built on such solid

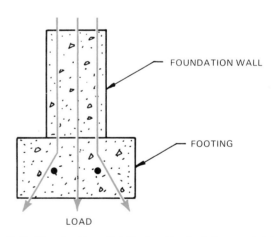

Fig. 9-6. The footing distributes the building weight over a broad area.

material and therefore need footings to support the heavy loads.

The size and type of footing should be suitable for the weight of the building and soil bearing capacity. Footings for most residential structures are made of poured concrete. The size of footing required is commonly determined by using the foundation wall thickness as a basis for its proportions. Fig. 9-7 illustrates the general proportions for a footing based on the foundation wall thickness. This size footing is

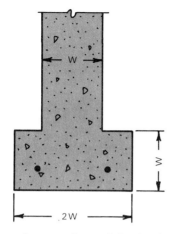

Fig. 9-7. General proportions of the footing as related to foundation wall thickness.

designed for most normal soil conditions ranging from sand to clay.

The footing thickness is equal to the foundation wall thickness and the footing width is twice the wall thickness. Foundation walls should be centered along the footing. Therefore, the footing will project beyond each side of the foundation wall a distance equal to one-half the thickness of the foundation wall. If the soil load bearing capacity is very poor, the size of footings should be increased and reinforced with steel.

During construction, the load increases on the footing and compresses the average subgrade soil. This compression causes a slight settlement of the structure. Whenever there are two or more different subsoils under various parts of the house, a variation in settlement may occur due to the unequal compressibility of the soil. Also, the weight of most homes is greater on two of the four walls which causes unequal loading. It is recommended that footings be large enough to minimize any of these differences in settlement to reduce cracking. Check your local code for recommended minimum footing size.

When footings must be located over soft or poorly drained soils, soils which are not uniform, or backfilled utility trenches, longitudinal reinforcement consisting of two No. 6 steel bars should be placed 2 in. from the bottom of the footing. The addition of continuous longitudinal reinforcing bars in the footings would be wise in most cases to provide further stability to the structure.

Footings for fireplaces and chimneys are more massive than regular house footings. They must support greater weight and are generally larger. A solid footing reinforced with steel is usually required. The footing should be 12 in. thick and extend 6 in. beyond the perimeter of the chim-

ney on all sides. The chimney footing should be cast integrally with the foundation wall footing if the chimney is located on an outside wall.

Stepped footings are frequently necessary when building on hilly terrain, Fig. 9-8. If stepped footings are required, the steps should be placed horizontally and the height of the vertical step should not be more than three-fourths of the distance between the steps. Step height and length should be multiples of 8 in. if the foundation is made of concrete block. Good building practice requires two 1/2 in. steel bars in the horizontal and vertical footing where steps are located. If steel bars are not used, the footing will very likely crack at these points.

FOUNDATION WALLS

Foundation walls are normally that part of the house which extends from the first floor to the footing. A foundation wall may also be a basement wall. Materials used to build foundation walls include cast (poured) concrete, concrete block, pressure-treated wood, and stone or brick in rare instances. Cast concrete and concrete block are widely used in residential structures. Pressure-treated wood foundations are gaining acceptance for residential structures. Brick is much more expensive than cast concrete, block, or wood, and is seldom used. Stone was once used extensively, but is no longer of significance as a foundation material. Fig. 9-9 illustrates these common foundation materials in section.

Foundation walls are of four basic types: the T-foundation, slab foundation, pier or post foun-

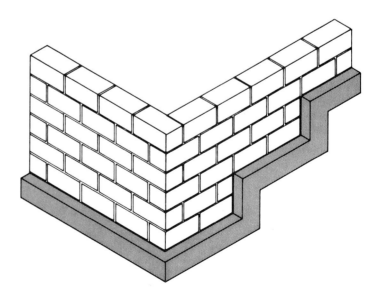

Fig. 9-8. A stepped footing and foundation wall for a sloping site.

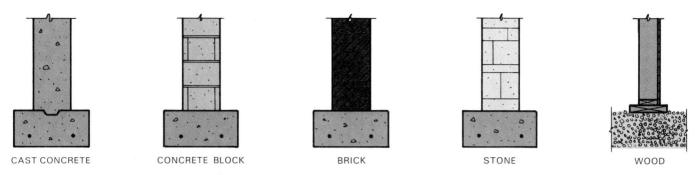

CAST CONCRETE   CONCRETE BLOCK   BRICK   STONE   WOOD

Fig. 9-9. Materials commonly used for foundation walls.

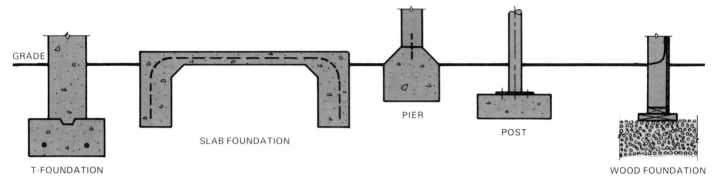

Fig. 9-10. Common foundation types used in residential construction.

dation, and permanent wood foundation, Fig. 9-10. The type chosen for a particular situation will depend upon the weight to be supported, load bearing capacity of the soil, location of the foundation in the building, climate, local codes, and preferred building practice. All should be considered when designing a foundation.

T-FOUNDATIONS

The most common foundation type is the T-foundation. The name is derived from the shape of the foundation and footing which looks like an inverted T. The foundation and footing are usually two separate parts but may be cast as a single unit.

Concrete for footings of a T-foundation is usually placed in forms made from construction lumber, Fig. 9-11. The form boards are nailed to stakes once they are level. Stakes prevent movement while the concrete is being cast.

Fig. 9-12 shows several applications of the T-foundation that are commonly found in residential construction.

SLAB FOUNDATIONS

A slab foundation is an extension of a slab floor. It is placed at the same time the floor is cast and is not a separate unit. It is sometimes called a thickened edge slab. The foundation wall should extend down below the frost line, as in the case of the T-foundation. Use of steel reinforcing bars or mesh is recommended for the slab foundation to prevent cracking due to settling.

Some of the primary advantages of the slab foundation are that it requires less time, expense, and labor to construct. Since no separate footing is required excavation is not as extensive as for the T-foundation. Less time is required since the entire foundation and floor is placed in one operation. Examples and dimension of typical slab foundations are illustrated in Fig. 9-13.

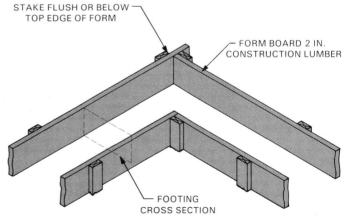

Fig. 9-11. Footings are usually placed using form boards made from construction lumber.

Footings, Foundations, and Concrete 165

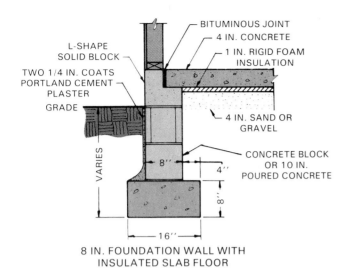

BITUMINOUS JOINT
4 IN. CONCRETE
1 IN. RIGID FOAM INSULATION

L-SHAPE SOLID BLOCK

TWO 1/4 IN. COATS PORTLAND CEMENT PLASTER
GRADE

VARIES

4 IN. SAND OR GRAVEL

8"   4"

CONCRETE BLOCK OR 10 IN. POURED CONCRETE

8"

16"

8 IN. FOUNDATION WALL WITH
INSULATED SLAB FLOOR

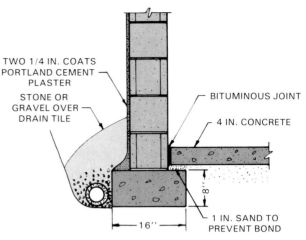

TWO 1/4 IN. COATS PORTLAND CEMENT PLASTER
STONE OR GRAVEL OVER DRAIN TILE

BITUMINOUS JOINT

4 IN. CONCRETE

8"

16"

1 IN. SAND TO PREVENT BOND

8 IN. BASEMENT WALL AND FOOTING

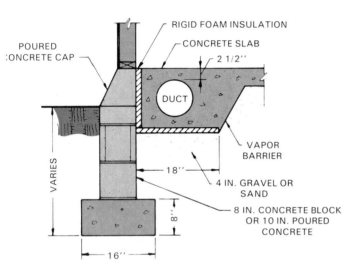

RIGID FOAM INSULATION
CONCRETE SLAB
2 1/2"

POURED CONCRETE CAP

DUCT

VARIES

VAPOR BARRIER

18"

4 IN. GRAVEL OR SAND

8 IN. CONCRETE BLOCK OR 10 IN. POURED CONCRETE

8"

16"

INSULATED SLAB FOR PERIMETER HEAT
WITH CONCRETE BLOCK FOUNDATION

POURED CONCRETE CAP
GRADE

VAPOR BARRIER

DUCT

VARIES

WASHED GRAVEL OR BASE
1 IN. RIGID FOAM INSULATION
8 IN. CONCRETE BLOCK OR 10 IN. POURED CONCRETE

8"

16"

INSULATED SLAB FOR PERIMETER HEAT
WITH CONCRETE BLOCK FOUNDATION

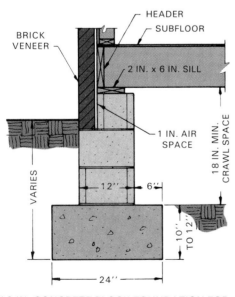

HEADER
SUBFLOOR

BRICK VENEER

2 IN. x 6 IN. SILL

1 IN. AIR SPACE

18 IN. MIN. CRAWL SPACE

VARIES

12"   6"

10" TO 12"

24"

12 IN. CONCRETE BLOCK FOUNDATION FOR
BRICK VENEER ON FRAME

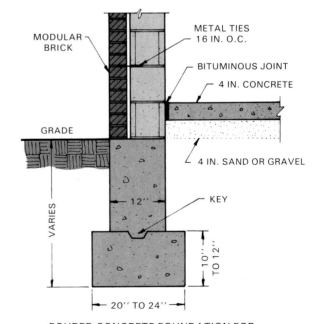

METAL TIES 16 IN. O.C.

MODULAR BRICK

BITUMINOUS JOINT

4 IN. CONCRETE

GRADE

4 IN. SAND OR GRAVEL

VARIES

12"

KEY

10" TO 12"

20" TO 24"

POURED CONCRETE FOUNDATION FOR
COMPOSITE BRICK AND BLOCK WALL

Fig. 9-12. Typical T-foundation details.

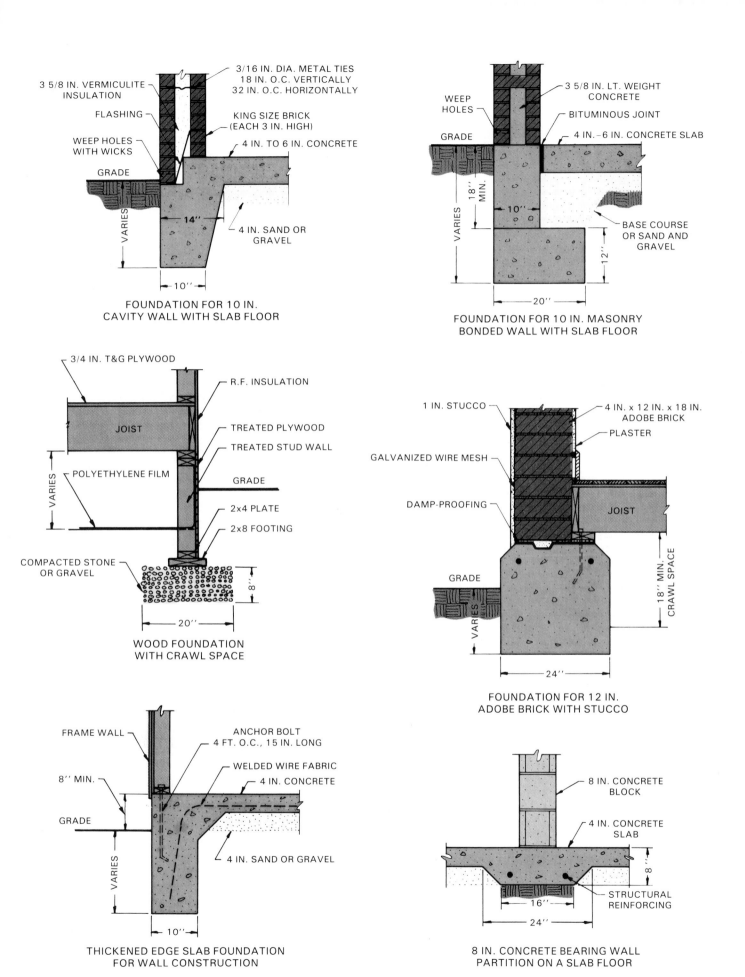

3/16 IN. DIA. METAL TIES
18 IN. O.C. VERTICALLY
32 IN. O.C. HORIZONTALLY

3 5/8 IN. VERMICULITE INSULATION

FLASHING

KING SIZE BRICK (EACH 3 IN. HIGH)

WEEP HOLES WITH WICKS

4 IN. TO 6 IN. CONCRETE

GRADE

VARIES

14''

4 IN. SAND OR GRAVEL

10''

FOUNDATION FOR 10 IN.
CAVITY WALL WITH SLAB FLOOR

WEEP HOLES

3 5/8 IN. LT. WEIGHT CONCRETE

BITUMINOUS JOINT

4 IN.–6 IN. CONCRETE SLAB

GRADE

18'' MIN.

VARIES

10''

BASE COURSE OR SAND AND GRAVEL

12''

20''

FOUNDATION FOR 10 IN. MASONRY
BONDED WALL WITH SLAB FLOOR

3/4 IN. T&G PLYWOOD

R.F. INSULATION

JOIST

TREATED PLYWOOD

TREATED STUD WALL

VARIES

POLYETHYLENE FILM

GRADE

2x4 PLATE

2x8 FOOTING

COMPACTED STONE OR GRAVEL

8''

20''

WOOD FOUNDATION
WITH CRAWL SPACE

1 IN. STUCCO

4 IN. x 12 IN. x 18 IN. ADOBE BRICK

PLASTER

GALVANIZED WIRE MESH

DAMP-PROOFING

JOIST

GRADE

VARIES

18'' MIN. CRAWL SPACE

24''

FOUNDATION FOR 12 IN.
ADOBE BRICK WITH STUCCO

FRAME WALL

ANCHOR BOLT
4 FT. O.C., 15 IN. LONG

WELDED WIRE FABRIC

4 IN. CONCRETE

8'' MIN.

GRADE

VARIES

4 IN. SAND OR GRAVEL

10''

THICKENED EDGE SLAB FOUNDATION
FOR WALL CONSTRUCTION

8 IN. CONCRETE BLOCK

4 IN. CONCRETE SLAB

8''

16''

STRUCTURAL REINFORCING

24''

8 IN. CONCRETE BEARING WALL
PARTITION ON A SLAB FLOOR

Fig. 9-13. Typical thickened edge slab, slab floor, and wood foundation details.

Footings, Foundations, and Concrete   167

Note that this type of foundation is also used for bearing wall partitions.

PIER AND POST FOUNDATIONS

Many situations in residential construction lend themselves to the use of piers, columns, and posts. Frequently it is cheaper and just as satisfactory to use piers rather than the T-foundation under parts of the building. For instance, when a crawl space is planned and the distance is too great for a single span, the pier foundation is a logical choice, Fig. 9-14. Another common application that involves columns is in a basement or garage where the distance is too great to span with floor joists. Lally columns are used to support a beam which in turn supports the joists, rather than construct a bearing wall partition, Fig. 9-15.

The basic difference between a pier and column is the length. Piers are usually much shorter and ordinarily located under the house. Fig. 9-16 illustrates a few of the common types of piers used in residential construction.

The column is composed of two pieces; a footing and post, Fig. 9-17. The footing is usually square or rectangular with a minimum thickness of 8 in. for one-story construction and a minimum projection of 5 in. beyond the face of

Fig. 9-14. Pier designed to support a heavy load.

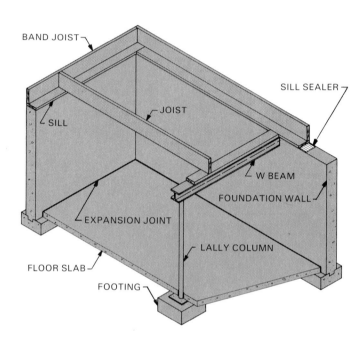

Fig. 9-15. Foundation cut-away showing a lally column used to support a beam.

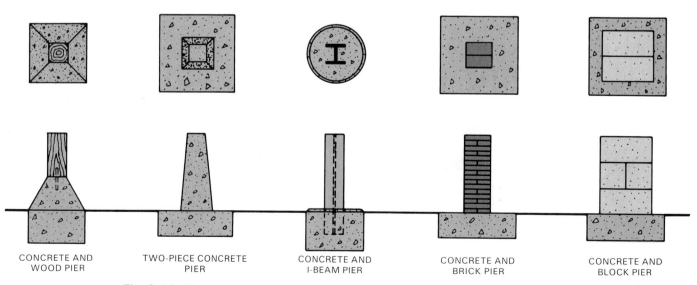

CONCRETE AND WOOD PIER

TWO-PIECE CONCRETE PIER

CONCRETE AND I-BEAM PIER

CONCRETE AND BRICK PIER

CONCRETE AND BLOCK PIER

Fig. 9-16. Piers may be constructed using a variety of techniques and materials.

the column. Two-story homes require a minimum thickness of 12 in. and a minimum projection of 7 in. beyond the face of the column. The post may be masonry, steel, or wood. If wood is used, it should be pressure-treated to resist decay.

WOOD FOUNDATIONS

Wood foundations are known by several names: the permanent wood foundation (PWF), the all-weather wood foundation (AWWF), and the treated wood foundation. Basically, a wood foundation is a below grade pressure-treated plywood-sheathed stud wall. The wood foundation is particularly attractive in climates where typical (concrete and masonry) foundation work stops in freezing or rainy weather. All wood parts are pressure-treated with chemical solutions that make the wood fibers useless as food for insects or fungus growth. The system is accepted by the Federal Housing Administration (FHA), the Department of Housing and Urban Development (HUD), Farmers Home Administration (FmHA), and by the major model building codes. It is rapidly gaining acceptance in state and local codes as well. The system may be used in full basement or crawl space construction and is adaptable to most any site and light-frame building design, Fig. 9-18.

Fig. 9-18. This modern home has an all-weather wood foundation. (Osmose Wood Products)

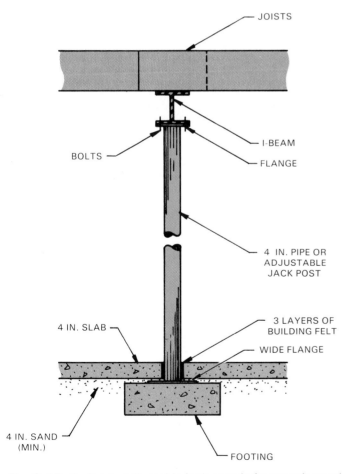

JOISTS

BOLTS

I-BEAM

FLANGE

4 IN. PIPE OR ADJUSTABLE JACK POST

4 IN. SLAB

3 LAYERS OF BUILDING FELT

WIDE FLANGE

4 IN. SAND (MIN.)

FOOTING

Fig. 9-17. A pipe or adjustable jack post is frequently used to support an ''I-beam.''

For a structure requiring a crawl space, a trench is excavated to receive the footing and foundation wall. The depth of the excavation should be below the average maximum frost penetration depth. The excavation should allow for 2 in. of sand or 6 in. of crushed stone or gravel raked smooth in the bottom of the trench. This provides a level base for the footing. The trench should be at least 12 in. deep regardless of the frost depth. See Fig. 9-19. It is essential that the sand base be perfectly level to insure that the top plate of the foundation unit is level and accurately located. The actual footing width (generally 10 or 12 in. wide) bearing on the ground must conform to the local code if the code requires a footing width greater than 12 in.

When a wood foundation is used for a basement, the site is excavated to the regular depth. Plumbing lines are installed and provisions are made for foundation drainage according to local requirements. A basement sump should be installed in poorly drained soils or where ground water is a problem. The bottom of the excavation is covered with 6 to 8 in. of porous gravel or crushed stone. This material is carefully leveled. Foundation footing plates made of 2 x 8, 2 x 10, or 2 x 12 pressure-treated material are placed

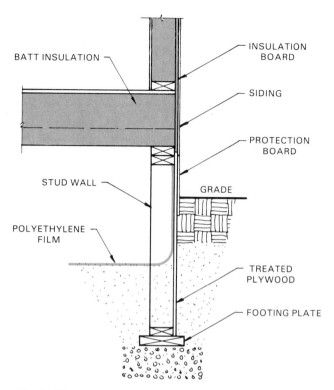

Fig. 9-19. Typical wood foundation for crawl space.

BATT INSULATION

INSULATION BOARD

SIDING

PROTECTION BOARD

STUD WALL

GRADE

POLYETHYLENE FILM

TREATED PLYWOOD

FOOTING PLATE

directly on the gravel, Fig. 9-20. The foundation walls (2 x 4 or 2 x 6 stud frame) are erected on these plates. Fig. 9-21 shows a typical wood foundation system for a basement.

Nails and other fasteners should be made of silicon bronze, copper, or hot-dipped zinc-coated steel. Special caulking compounds are used to seal all joints in the plywood sheathing. Lumber and plywood that comes in contact with the ground should be pressure-treated with water-borne preservative salts (ACA or CCA). All lumber and plywood in contact with the ground

Fig. 9-20. Placing the footing plate in the proper location for a wood foundation wall. (Osmose Wood Products)

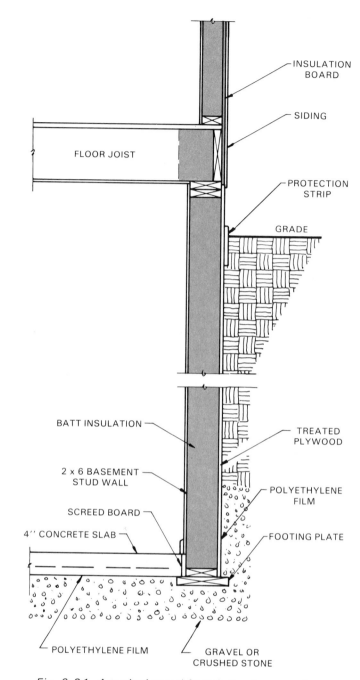

INSULATION BOARD

SIDING

FLOOR JOIST

PROTECTION STRIP

GRADE

BATT INSULATION

TREATED PLYWOOD

2 x 6 BASEMENT STUD WALL

POLYETHYLENE FILM

SCREED BOARD

4'' CONCRETE SLAB

FOOTING PLATE

POLYETHYLENE FILM

GRAVEL OR CRUSHED STONE

Fig. 9-21. A typical wood foundation basement.

should be pressure-treated in accordance with the American Wood Preservers Bureau (FDN Standard), Fig. 9-22.

After the basement wall is in place, the porous gravel or crushed stone base is covered with a polyethylene film (6 mil thick). A screed board is attached to the inside of the foundation wall to serve as an elevation guide for the basement floor slab. The floor joists or trusses are then installed on the double top plate of the foundation wall. Particular attention should be given to the attachment of the joists or trusses to insure that inward forces will be transferred to the floor structure. On the sides of the structure where

Fig. 9-22. All material in this basement wall has been pressure-treated to resist decay. (Osmose Wood Products)

MINIMUM THICKNESS OF BASEMENT WALLS*			
		Maximum Height of Unbalanced Fill, Ft.**	
Type of Unit	Minimum Wall Thickness, In. (Nominal)	Frame Super-structure	Masonry and Masonry Veneer Super-structure
Hollow load-bearing	8*** 10 12	5 6 7	5 7 7
Solid load-bearing	8*** 10 12	5 7 7	7 7 7

*Basement walls should be at least as thick as walls supported immediately above except as noted below.
**Heights shown may be increased to 7 ft. with approval of building official if justified by soil conditions and local experience.
***If the 8 in. basement wall supports an 8 in. wall, the combined height should not exceed 35 ft. If it supports brick veneer on wood frame or a 10 in. cavity wall, it may be corbeled out a maximum of 2 in. with solid units; but the total height of wall supported, including the gable, should not exceed 25 ft. Individual corbels should not project more than one-third the height of the unit. If a concrete first floor is used, it helps provide adequate bearing for these walls and corbeling can be omitted. (Portland Cement Association)

joists run parallel to the wall, blocking should be installed between the outside joists and first interior joists to resist lateral forces.

Before backfilling, a 6 mil polyethylene film should be applied to sections of the wall below grade to serve as a moisture barrier. All joints should be lapped at least 6 in. and sealed with adhesive. The top edge of the film should be bonded to the wall at grade level with adhesive. A treated wood strip is attached along this edge and caulked. This strip will later serve as a guide for backfilling.

CAUTION: Backfilling should not begin until the basement floor has cured and the first floor is installed. As with any foundation system, satisfactory performance requires full compliance with recommended standards covering design, fabrication, and installation. Standards for wood foundations are available from the National Forest Products Association and the American Plywood Association.

CONCRETE AND MASONRY BASEMENT WALLS

Concrete and masonry basement wall thickness depends on lateral earth pressure and vertical load to be supported. Recommended minimum thickness at various depths below grade are shown in the following chart.

These dimensions are based on conventional residential construction and average soils. The height of the unbalanced fill is measured from the finished grade (exterior) to the basement floor.

Several factors influence the strength and stability of a concrete or masonry basement wall to resist earth pressure. They include: height and thickness, the bond of the mortar, vertical loading, support from crosswalls, pilasters or wall stiffeners, and support provided by the first-floor framing. Lateral earth pressure may vary from almost zero to an amount equal to the hydrostatic pressure of a liquid with the density of mud.

When local conditions indicate strong earth pressures, pilasters, Fig. 9-23, can be used to strengthen the basement wall. Pilasters must be built at the same time the basement wall is laid. Pilaster block are frequently used for such construction. They should have a minimum width of 16 in. and project 8 in. inside an 8 in. thick basement wall. Ten-inch basement walls will have a 6 in. inside projection. With 12 in. concrete masonry basement walls, pilasters or other wall stiffeners are not usually required. In 8 in. thick walls over 30 ft. long, the distance between pilasters should not be greater than 15 ft. In 10 in. thick walls over 36 ft. long, this distance should not be greater than 18 ft. Pilasters are also used for additional support for girders or beams. Pilasters may also be required to stiffen concrete foundation walls. Since concrete walls

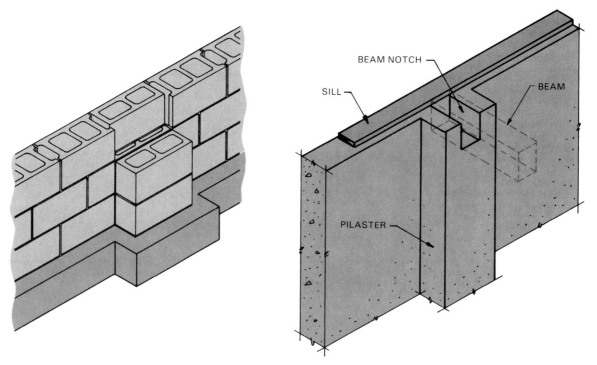

Fig. 9-23. Pilasters add strength to a basement wall and may be used to support a beam.

are generally 10 in. thick, cast-in-place pilasters are spaced every 18 ft. along the perimeter of the wall.

Wall stiffeners provide another method of strengthening the walls. This is accomplished by placing a No. 4 bar in one core of the block from the top of the wall to the footing and filling the core with concrete.

A third procedure is to use continuous horizontal steel joint reinforcement at 16 in. intervals vertically. This method will provide additional lateral support to the basement wall and help prevent cracking.

Basement walls should extend at least 8 in. above the finished grade when using wood frame construction. Wood sills should be anchored to the basement walls with bolts 1/2 in. by 15 in. long and spaced approximately 8 ft. apart. Each sill piece should have at least two bolts. Anchor bolts are placed in the cores of the top two courses of masonry and filled with mortar or concrete. Core filling may be supported by a piece of metal lath or similar material.

Basement walls may be slightly shorter than first and second floor walls. The distance from the top of the basement floor to the bottom of the floor joists above should be no less than 7 ft. A basement wall which is 11 courses above the footing with a 4 in. solid cap will provide a clear height of 7 ft. 5 in. from finished floor to the bottom of the floor joists, Fig. 9-24. This distance is more desirable since some space will

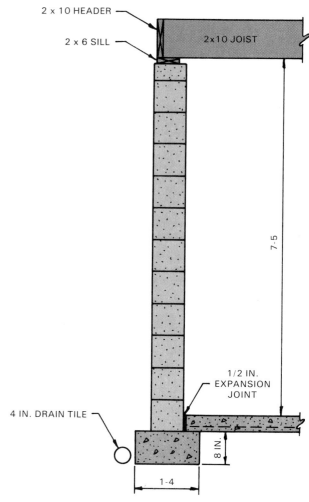

Fig. 9-24. A basement wall which provides a desirable floor to ceiling height.

generally be required for heating ducts, pipes, and beams.

Load-bearing crosswalls in the basement should not be tied to the exterior walls in a masonry bond. Instead, they should be anchored with metal tie bars. The tie bars are usually 1/4 in. thick, 1 1/4 in. wide, and 28 in. long. Each end has a 2 in. right-angle bend which is embedded in cores filled with mortar or concrete.

Floor loads are distributed more uniformly along the wall if the top course of block supporting the first floor is capped using: (1) 4 in. solid block, (2) solid top block, in which the hollow cores do not extend up into the top 4 in. of the block, (3) reinforced concrete masonry bond beam, or (4) cores in the top course filled with concrete or mortar. When the wood sill bears on both the inner and outer face shells of the block, capping may be omitted.

Basement walls require dampproofing on the outside to prevent ground water from seeping through the wall. Cast concrete walls may be dampproofed with a heavy coat of hot tar or two coats of cement-base paints, commercially prepared specifically for dampproofing basements. This is applied from the grade line to the footing. Concrete block walls are dampproofed by applying two 1/4 in. thick coats of cement-mortar or plaster to the wall and then covering it with hot tar, or a similar material when the cement is dry. This is called a **parge coat** (a thin coat of plaster over the foundation wall). In both instances, 4 in. perforated drain tile is used around the perimeter of the footing to remove excess ground water and reduce the chance of water problems, Fig. 9-25. The tile is covered with coarse stone or gravel to a depth of about 18 in. to allow water to seep into the tile. It is easier and faster to install and appears to function as well as cement tiles.

In poorly drained and wet soils, added precautions may be advisable to insure against water damage. A sump pump may be installed in the basement to remove any water which seeps in. The floor slab may be reinforced to resist uplift by ground water pressure. A check valve in the floor drain will prevent water from flowing in through the drain.

BEAMS AND GIRDERS

The size of most residences is such that the span is too great to use unsupported floor joists. Therefore, a beam or girder is required to support the joists and prevent excessive sagging. The beam is usually placed an equal distance from

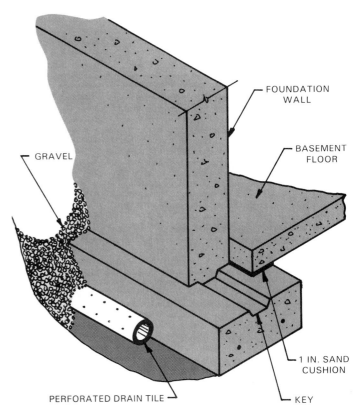

Fig. 9-25. A basement wall may be dampproofed by the application of a parge coat and drain tile placed along the footing.

each outside wall or under a bearing wall. A bearing wall is designed to support part of the load of the structure.

Beams may be either wood or metal. Wood beams are of two types; built-up and solid. Built-up beams are used more frequently than solid ones because they are easier to handle, more readily available, and do not check to the extent of solid beams. However, solid beams are generally stronger and more fire-resistant.

Two types of steel beams are commonly used. These are S-beams and wide-flange beams, Fig. 9-26. The wide-flange beam will support greater weight and is more stable than the standard S-beam. For these reasons it is more popular for residential construction.

Calculation of the size beam needed is based on the weight of the structure, Fig. 9-27.

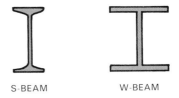

S-BEAM   W-BEAM

Fig. 9-26. Typical steel beams used in residential construction. An S-beam (formerly called an I-beam) is the standard shape. A W-beam is a wide flange shape.

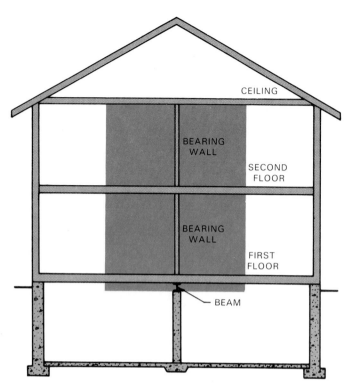

Fig. 9-27. Weight represented by the shaded area is supported by the S-beam.

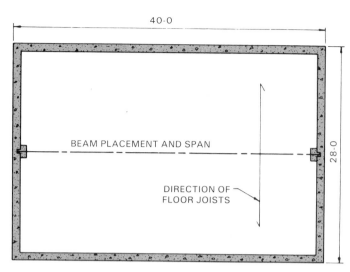

Fig. 9-28. A foundation wall with dimensions of 28'-0'' x 40'-0'' showing the direction of joists and placement of supporting beam.

Weights are designated either as live loads or dead loads. **Live loads** are those fixed or moving weights, which are not a structural part of the house. Examples include furniture, occupants, snow on the roof, wind, etc. **Dead loads** are those static or fixed weights of the structure itself. Examples of dead loads are the weights of roofing, foundation walls, siding, joists, etc. To simplify matters, it will be assumed that loads found in a typical residence are as follows.

FIRST FLOOR
    Live load plus dead load = 50 pounds per square foot.

SECOND FLOOR
    Live load plus dead load = 50 pounds per square foot.

CEILING
    Live load plus dead load = 30 pounds per square foot.

WALLS
    Dead load = 10 pounds per square foot.

ROOF
    No load on the beam. Exterior walls generally support the roof.

Use these figures for load calculations.

Weight Calculations

The example used is for a two-story frame structure which is 28'-0'' x 40'-0''. Fig. 9-28 shows the foundation walls and beam.
Width x length = Area of the house.
    28' x 40' = 1120 sq. ft. for each floor.
    8' x 40' = 320 sq. ft. of wall area for each wall.

(This calculation assumes a bearing wall running the length of the house on both floors.)

Weight per sq. ft. x number of sq. ft. = total wt.

Weight of first floor
    (1120 sq. ft. x 50 lbs./sq. ft.) =   56,000 lbs.
Weight of second floor
    (1120 sq. ft. x 50 lbs./sq. ft.) =   56,000 lbs.
Weight of ceiling
    (1120 sq. ft. x 30 lbs./sq. ft.) =   33,600 lbs.
Weight of roof on beam
    (none in this example)   =   0 lbs.
                         Total = 145,600 lbs.

One-half of the total weight bears on the center beam.
    (1/2 x 145,600 pounds)   = 72,800 lbs.
Weight of first floor wall
    (320 sq. ft. x 10 lbs./sq. ft.) =   3,200 lbs.
Weight of second floor wall
    (320 sq. ft. x 10 lbs./sq. ft.) =   3,200 lbs.
Weight bearing on beam   = 79,200 lbs.

Tables giving the greatest safe loads which beams will support usually record the weight in kips. One kip equals 1,000 pounds. Fig. 9-29 presents span data for American Standard S-

MAXIMUM ALLOWABLE UNIFORM LOADS FOR AMERICAN STANDARD I-BEAMS WITH LATERAL SUPPORT

SPAN IN FEET

SIZE OF BEAM	WEIGHT OF BEAM PER FT.	4	6	8	10	12	14	16	18	20	22	24	26	28	30	32	34	36	38	40
4 x 2 3/4	7.7	10	7	5																
	9.5	11	7	6																
5 x 3	10.0	16	11	8	6															
	11.3	20	13	10	8															
6 x 3 1/8	12.5	24	16	12	10	8														
	17.3	29	19	15	12	10														
7 x 3 3/4	15.3	35	23	17	14	12	10													
	20.0	40	27	20	16	15	13													
8 x 4	18.4	47	32	24	19	16	14	12												
	23.0	53	36	27	21	18	15	13												
10 x 4 3/4	25.4	80	54	41	33	27	23	20	18	16										
	35.0	97	65	49	39	32	28	24	22	20										
12 x 5	31.8	110	80	60	48	40	34	30	27	24	22	20								
	35.0	126	84	63	50	42	36	32	28	25	23	21								
12 x 5 1/4	40.8	144	100	75	60	50	43	37	33	30	27	25								
	50.0	168	112	84	67	56	48	42	37	34	31	28								
15 x 5 1/2	42.9	160	131	98	79	65	56	49	44	39	36	33	30	28	26	25				
	50.0	214	143	107	86	71	61	54	48	43	39	36	33	31	29	27				
18 x 6	54.7		196	147	118	98	84	74	66	59	54	49	45	42	39	37	35	33	31	
	70.0		226	170	136	113	97	85	76	68	62	57	52	49	45	43	40	38	36	
20 x 6 1/4	65.4		260	195	156	130	111	97	87	78	71	65	60	56	52	49	46	43	41	39
	75.0		281	211	169	140	120	105	94	84	77	70	65	60	56	53	50	47	44	42

LOADS ARE IN KIPS. 1 KIP = 1,000 POUNDS   (American Institute of Steel Construction)

Fig. 9-29. Span and load table for American Standard S-beams.

MAXIMUM ALLOWABLE UNIFORM LOADS FOR WIDE FLANGE I-BEAMS WITH LATERAL SUPPORT

SPAN IN FEET

SIZE OF BEAM	WEIGHT OF BEAM PER FT.	4	6	8	9	10	12	14	18	20	22	24	26	28	30	32	34	36	38	40
8 x 5 1/4	17	47	31	24	19	16	13	12												
8 x 6 1/2	24		46	35	28	23	20	17												
8 x 8	31		60	46	37	30	26	23	20	18	16									
10 x 5 1/4	21	62	48	36	29	24	21	18	16	14										
10 x 8	33		74	58	47	39	33	29	26	23										
10 x 10	49			88	73	61	52	46	40	36	33	30	28	26						
12 x 6 1/2	27		74	57	45	38	32	28	25	23	21	19								
12 x 8	40		87	69	58	49	43	38	35	32	29									
12 x 10	53			108	94	79	67	59	52	47	43	39								
12 x 12	65				117	98	84	73	65	59	53	49	45	42	39					
14 x 6 3/4	30		93	70	56	46	40	35	31	28	25	23	21	20	19					
14 x 8	43			105	84	70	60	52	46	42	38	35	32	30	28					
14 x 10	61				123	102	88	77	68	62	56	51	47	44	41					
14 x 12	78				156	135	115	101	90	81	73	67	62	58	54					
14 x 14 1/2	87					152	132	115	102	92	84	77	71	66	61	57	54	51		
16 x 7	36		124	94	75	63	54	47	42	38	34	31	29	27	25	24	22			
16 x 8 1/2	58			157	126	105	90	78	70	63	57	52	48	45	42	39	37			
16 x 11 1/2	88				202	168	144	126	112	101	92	84	78	72	67	63	59			
18 x 7 1/2	50			148	119	99	85	74	66	59	54	49	46	42	40	37	35	33	31	
18 x 8 3/4	64			188	156	130	111	98	87	78	71	65	60	56	52	49	46	43	41	
18 x 11 3/4	96				224	189	176	154	137	123	112	103	95	88	82	77	72	68	65	
21 x 8 1/4	62			211	169	141	120	105	94	84	77	70	65	60	56	53	50	47	44	42

LOADS ARE IN KIPS. 1 KIP = 1,000 POUNDS   (American Institute of Steel Construction)

Fig. 9-30. Span and load table for W-beams.

Beams. Fig. 9-30 presents span data for Wide Flange W-Beams. Loads shown are based on a fiber stress of 20,000 pounds, or the pressure they will withstand per square inch. This stress is usually sufficient for common residential construction situations.

The length of beam needed in the example is 40 feet. If no posts were used, the span would be 40 feet. From previous calculations, the weight bearing on the beam was found to be 79,200 pounds. This weight is represented by the shaded area in Fig. 9-27. Convert 79,200 pounds into kips by dividing the weight by 1000. The weight then is 79.2 kips. A beam large enough to support this weight over 40 feet is not practical. The logical course of action would be to shorten the span by adding one or more post supports. Study the chart below and Figs. 9-31, 9-32, and 9-33, and note how the beam size and weight on the beam decreases with the addition of post supports.

Any one of the beams above would support the load of the structure. However, steel is sold by the pound, so it is desirable to choose the

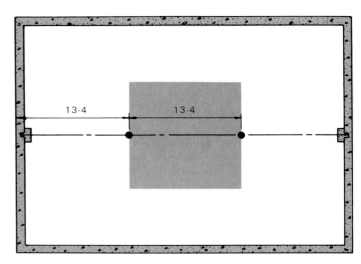

Fig. 9-32. The effective beam span with two posts. The span is 13'-4''.

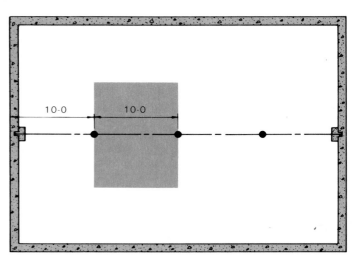

Fig. 9-33. Three supporting posts reduces the effective span to 10'-0''.

smallest beam which will adequately do the job with a reasonable span.

Once the size of beam and number of post supports have been determined, the size of each post must be calculated. This procedure is not as complex as the procedure for figuring beam sizes. In the previous calculations it was deter-

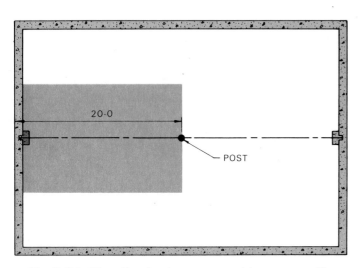

Fig. 9-31. The effective beam span with one post. The shaded area represents the weight supported by the 20'-0'' beam section.

COMPARISON DATA FOR EXAMPLE				
	Span	Weight on Beam	Size of Beam and Wieght	Kips Beam Will Support
One Post (Fig. 9-28) S-beam W-beam	20'-0'' 20'-0''	39.6 kips 39.6 kips	15'' x 5 1/2'' x 50.0 lbs./ft. 14'' x 8'' x 43.0 lbs./ft.	43 kips 42 kips
Two Posts (Fig. 9-29) S-beam W-beam	13'-4'' 13'-4''	26.5 kips 26.4 kips	10'' x 4 3/4'' x 35.0 lbs./ft. 8'' x 8'' x 31.0 lbs./ft.	28 kips 26 kips
Three Posts (Fig. 9-30) S-beam W-beam	10'-0'' 10'-0''	19.8 kips 19.8 kips	8'' x 4'' x 23.0 lbs./ft. 8'' x 6 1/2'' x 24.0 lbs./ft.	21 kips 23 kips

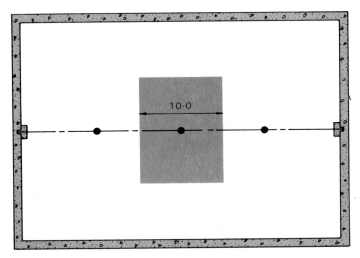

Fig. 9-34. Each post must support the weight represented by the shaded area.

mined that if three posts were used, each beam segment or 10'-0'' span would be required to support 19.8 kips or 19,800 pounds. This is the same weight that the center post must support since it must bear the weight on either side, half way to the next post. See Fig. 9-34 for a graphic representation of the load supported by the center post.

Steel post design information is presented in Fig. 9-35. The size post needed is determined by finding the weight to be supported and length of the post needed on the chart. (Loads are recorded in kips.) In the example, the weight is 19,800 pounds or 19.8 kips and the unbraced length is 8 feet. The smallest column shown on the chart (nominal size of 3 in.) is more than adequate since it will support 34,000 pounds. Therefore, the support posts should be 3 inches in diameter and weigh 7.58 pounds per foot.

Steel posts must have a flange welded on both ends and provision for attachment to the beam. It may be bolted or attached with clips. The bottom flange (8'' x 8'') should be larger than the

top flange to provide a larger bearing surface on the footing. Size of the top flange will be determined by the width of the beam to be supported.

Lintels

A *lintel* is a horizontal structural member that supports the load over an opening such as a door or window. Lintels may be constructed of precast concrete, poured concrete, lintel blocks, or angle steel, Fig. 9-36. When lintels are used in a masonry wall, the ends must extend at least 4 in. into the wall on either side of the opening.

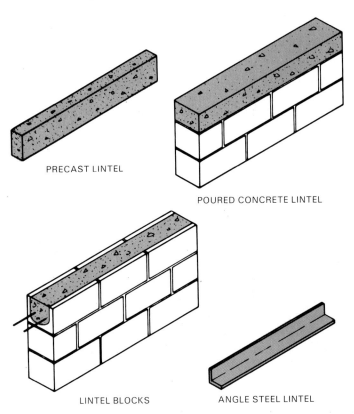

PRECAST LINTEL

POURED CONCRETE LINTEL

LINTEL BLOCKS

ANGLE STEEL LINTEL

Fig. 9-36. Four types of lintels frequently used in residential building construction.

		UNBRACED LENGTH IN FEET									
NOMINAL SIZE IN INCHES	WEIGHT PER FT. IN POUNDS	6	7	8	9	10	11	12	14	16	18
3	7.58	38	36	34	31	28	25	22	16	12	10
3 1/2	9.11	48	46	44	41	38	35	32	25	19	15
4	10.79	59	57	54	52	49	46	43	36	29	23
5	14.62	83	81	78	76	73	71	68	61	55	47
6	18.97	110	108	106	103	101	98	95	89	82	75

MAXIMUM ALLOWABLE CONCENTRIC LOADS FOR STANDARD STEEL PIPE COLUMNS

LOADS ARE IN KIPS. 1 KIP = 1,000 POUNDS
(American Institute of Steel Construction)

Fig. 9-35. Load table for standard steel pipe columns.

Footings, Foundations, and Concrete 177

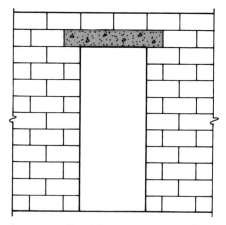

Fig. 9-37. A precast lintel in a masonry wall supporting the weight above a door opening.

Fig. 9-37 shows a precast lintel over a door in a concrete block wall. Common precast lintel sizes for residential construction are 4'' x 8'', 4'' x 6'', and 8'' x 8''. They are produced in a variety of lengths.

Lintels are also made of angle steel. They are available as equal angles (both legs the same size) or as unequal angles. The chart below identifies the size of angle required to support a 4 in. masonry wall above an opening.

STEEL ANGLES TO SUPPORT
4 IN. MASONRY WALLS

Span	Size of Angle
0'–5'	3'' x 3'' x 1/4''
5'–9'	3 1/2'' x 3 1/2'' x 5/16''
9'–10'	4'' x 4'' x 5/16''
10'–11'	4'' x 4'' x 3/8''
11'–15'	6'' x 4'' x 3/8''
15'–16'	6'' x 4'' x 1/2''

Fig. 9-38 shows a steel lintel supporting brick over a window opening. Openings in cast concrete walls do not require lintels.

CONCRETE AND MASONRY

The average modern home requires many yards of concrete. Fortunately, most contractors today are near a ready-mix plant. Concrete is ordered by the cubic yard and the consistency is generally specified by how many bags of cement are contained in each yard of mix. A ''five-bag mix'' is considered minimum for most jobs while a ''six-bag mix'' will produce a stronger product and should be used when high strength or reinforcing is required.

Concrete is the result of combining cement, sand, aggregate (usually stone or gravel), and water. Cement is composed of a mixture of lime, silica, alumina, iron components, and gypsum. The proportions of the ingredients will vary with the requirements. However; sidewalks, driveways, footings, and basement floors usually contain one part cement, three parts sand, and five parts aggregate. Footings as well as concrete floors must have both a minimum compressive strength of 3,000 psi and minimum cement content of 5 bags (470 lbs.) per cubic yard. The amount of water used will most likely be 6 or 7 gallons for each bag of cement (normally 94 pounds per bag).

Concrete cures over a long period of time and should be kept moist for several days after it is placed. Failure to do this reduces strength and may harm the exposed surface. Temperature also affects the setting time of concrete. Cold weather slows down the process and concrete should not be allowed to freeze before it has set.

When concrete is being placed, it commonly traps air pockets within the mixture. It is necessary to work these air pockets out by vibrating or tamping. This action helps to form a more dense material and removes weak spots due to air pockets.

After the concrete has been placed, a **screed** is used to smooth the surface. The screed is a long straightedge, usually a board, which is worked back and forth across the surface. This action brings excess water to the surface and settles the aggregate. Power screeds are also available for large jobs.

When screeding is finished, the surface is then worked over with a **float**. A float is a short board about a foot long with a handle attached to one of the flat sides. The purpose of floating is: (1) to embed the large aggregate just beneath the surface, (2) to remove any slight imperfections,

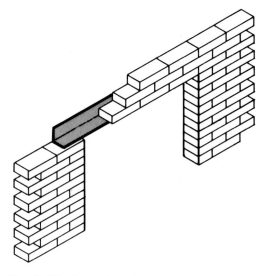

Fig. 9-38. A steel angle lintel in a brick wall.

lumps, and voids to produce a flat surface, and (3) to consolidate mortar at the surface in preparation for final steel-troweling. As the mixture reaches the proper consistency, the troweling process is started. The *trowel* is rectangular and is used in a circular motion. This troweling action further hardens the surface and develops a very smooth finish. If a slightly rough surface is desired, it may be swept with a broom to accomplish the desired texture.

As was indicated earlier, concrete is purchased by the cubic yard. A cubic yard is 27 cubic feet. When ordering concrete, one should figure only 25 cubic feet to the yard. Some of the material will remain in the mixer, some will be spilled, and forms may sag. Experience has shown that it is better to have a little more concrete than you need than to have too little.

Large areas of concrete are likely to crack from expansion and contraction due to changes in temperature and moisture content. This cracking may be minimized or controlled by introducing *contraction joints.* Contraction joints should be placed in line with interior columns, at changes in the width of the slab, or at maximum spacing of about 20 ft. These joints may be formed by cutting grooves in the freshly placed concrete with a jointing tool. They may also be cut into the slab with a power saw after the concrete has hardened. The depth of joints or grooves should be one-fourth the thickness of the slab.

A concrete slab is usually placed directly on firmly compacted sand 4 to 6 inches thick. Dry sand should be dampened to prevent absorption of too much mixing water from the fresh concrete. The slab base (sand) should be thoroughly compacted to prevent settlement of the slab. It should also be sloped toward the floor drains to ensure a uniform slab thickness. Floor slabs usually have a minimum thickness of 4 inches.

Floor slabs should not be bonded to footings or interior columns. A sand cushion 1 in. thick may be used to separate the slab from the footing, Fig. 9-39. A sleeve of three thicknesses of building felt may be wrapped around columns to break the bond.

CONCRETE BLOCKS

Concrete blocks are used extensively in residential buildings. They are used to form exterior, and in some instances, interior walls. They may

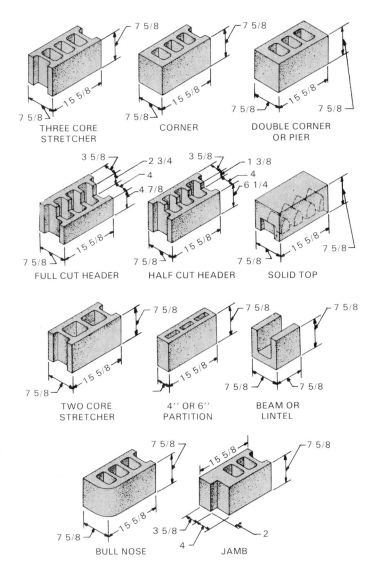

Fig. 9-40. Commonly used concrete blocks with actual sizes shown.

Fig. 9-39. Floor slabs should not be bonded to the footing or foundation wall.

be purchased in a variety of sizes and shapes. In general terms, concrete blocks refer to hollow concrete masonry units, usually 8'' x 8'' x 16'' in dimension. The actual size is 7 5/8'' x 7 5/8'' x 15 5/8''. These dimensions allow for a 3/8 in. mortar joint. Therefore, the distance from the center line of one mortar joint to the center line of the next will be 8 or 16 inches. Fig. 9-40 shows a variety of concrete blocks that are frequently used in a residential structure.

A wide variety of decorative concrete blocks are available. They may be used to form a screen, fence, or wall, Fig. 9-41. Use of decorative blocks should not be overlooked when searching for innovative materials. The application of concrete blocks is limited only to the designer's imagination.

REVIEW QUESTIONS — CHAPTER 9

Write your answers on a separate sheet of paper. Do not write in this book.
1. The necessary dimensions for staking out the house are found on the _____ plan.
2. What method may be used to check the accuracy of all corners of the house once it is staked out?
3. The purpose of batter boards is to _____.
4. The excavation must extend below the frost depth and down to _____.
5. The size and type of footing should be suitable for the weight of the building and _____.
6. The thickness of the footing is usually the same thickness as the _____.
7. Stepped footings are necessary when _____.
8. Concrete may be reinforced using _____ in. steel rod.
9. The most common foundation type is the _____ foundation.
10. List two advantages of the slab foundation.
11. The basic difference between a pier and column is the _____.
12. What type of foundation does the AWWF system represent?
13. What prevents the wood in a wood foundation from rotting?
14. Why does the sand or gravel under the footing for a wood foundation need to be perfectly level?
15. What three materials are used for nails and fasteners in a wood foundation?
16. The minimum clear height between a basement floor and bottom of the floor joists

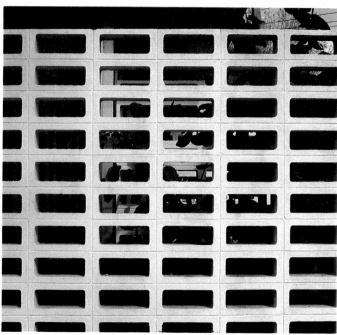

Fig. 9-41. Decorative concrete blocks may be used to add a new design dimension.

should be _____ ft. This height allows some space for heating ducts, pipes, and beams.
17. Long basement walls may need added lateral support. A _____ is used to provide this support.
18. The materials commonly used to dampproof basement walls are _____ and _____.
19. When the span is too far for unsupported floor joists, a _____ is used to provide support.

20. List two types of steel beams used in residential construction.
21. Weights are designated as live loads and dead loads. Snow on a roof is an example of a _____ load.
22. Safe loads that steel beams will support are usually given in _____.
23. A horizontal structural member that supports the load over an opening such as a door or window is known as a _____.
24. List the four ingredients in concrete.
25. Temperature affects the curing time of concrete. Cold weather _____ the process.
26. A _____ is a long straightedge (board) which is worked back and forth to smooth concrete.
27. Large areas of concrete are likely to crack from expansion and contraction due to temperature change. This cracking may be minimized or controlled through the use of _____.
28. The nominal size of a concrete block is 8'' x 8'' x 16''. The actual size of this block is _____.

SUGGESTED ACTIVITIES

1. Choose two or more friends and as a team stake out a one-car garage (12' x 20') using string, stakes, and a 50' measuring tape. (Use the 9-12-15 unit method of laying out a 90° corner. Refer to Fig. 9-2.) Check the accuracy by measuring the diagonals. Record the diagonal measurement.

2. Using a carpenter's level on a stool or other fixed surface, determine the difference in elevation at the four corners of the garage which you staked out in number 1 above. Procedure: Have one member of the team hold a pole or strip of wood vertically, with bottom end resting on the ground, over one of the corner stakes. Sight down the level and have your partner make a mark on the pole even with your line of sight. Be sure the level is not tilted. Duplicate this procedure for each corner. Using the tape, measure the difference between the marks on the rod. These distances represent the variation in elevation. The same procedure can be done much more accurately with a contractor's level. Record your results.

3. Visit an excavation site for a residence in your community. Measure the depth and size of excavation. Determine the size of footings and thickness of foundation walls. Prepare a sketch of the foundation layout with dimensions. Note the type of soil supporting the footings. (Secure permission before entering the site.)

4. Select a foundation plan of a small structure with a slab floor, such as a garage or storage building, and calculate the amount of concrete required for the footings, foundation wall, and floor. Show your calculation and the foundation plan.

5. Calculate the size of steel beam and columns required to support a frame house with foundation dimensions of 34'-0'' x 48'-0''. The spacing of your columns should not exceed 12'-0'' for this problem.

Spreading the gravel base for an all-weather wood foundation basement. (Osmose Wood Products)

The Foundation Plan

After studying this chapter, you will be able to:
* Identify the primary features included in a foundation plan.
* Discuss the difference between a foundation plan and a basement plan.
* Design and draw a foundation plan for a typical residential structure.

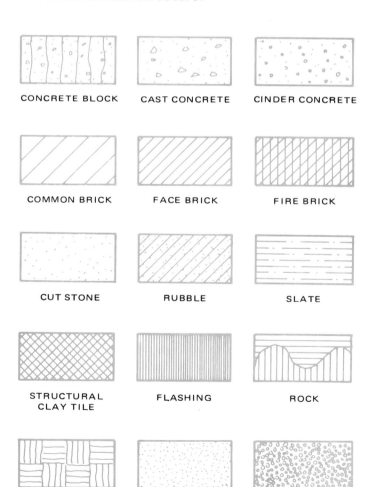

CONCRETE BLOCK	CAST CONCRETE	CINDER CONCRETE
COMMON BRICK	FACE BRICK	FIRE BRICK
CUT STONE	RUBBLE	SLATE
STRUCTURAL CLAY TILE	FLASHING	ROCK
EARTH	SAND	GRAVEL

Fig. 10-1. Material symbols commonly used on a foundation plan.

The foundation plan is a plan view drawing in section showing the location and size of footings, piers, columns, foundation walls, and supporting beams. It is usually drawn after the floor plan and elevations have been roughed out. A foundation plan ordinarily includes the following.

Footings for foundation walls, piers, and columns (hidden lines)
Foundation walls
Piers and columns
Dwarf walls (low walls built to retain an excavation or embankment)
Partial walls, doors, and bath fixtures if the house has a basement
Openings in foundation wall such as windows, doors, and vents
Beams and pilasters
Direction, size, and spacing of floor joists or trusses
Drains and sump (if required)
Details of foundation and footing construction
Complete dimensions and notes
Scale of the drawing

The foundation plan is prepared primarily for the excavator, masons, carpenters, and cement workers who build the foundation. Be sure to present the information they need to build the foundation. Symbols which are commonly used on a foundation plan are shown in Fig. 10-1.

PRELIMINARY STEPS TO DRAWING A FOUNDATION PLAN

The foundation plan is drawn from information presented on the floor plan, plot plan, and elevations. It is important that dimensions on the foundation plan and floor plan are accurate and consistent. The preliminary floor plan may be used as an underlay for drawing the foundation plan. This procedure is common and usually reduces the time required to make the drawing. It also helps to keep errors to a minimum.

Before drawing the foundation plan, examine the floor plan to determine the type of exterior walls specified. This step is important because the dimensions of the foundation may not be the same for different types of exterior walls. For example, the foundation size will be larger for a brick veneer house than a house with stud wall structure. The reason for the difference is that the basic house size is measured to the outside of the stud wall for both types of construction. A 4 in. brick ledge is required for the brick veneer house. This adds 8 in. to the length and width of the foundation. See Fig. 10-2.

The plot plan and elevation should also be examined to anticipate the need for stepped footings, retaining walls, and problems related to the grade, Fig. 10-3.

Determine the size of footings and foundation walls required from information available. Check the frost penetration depth for the area where the house is to be built. Refer to the building code to be sure that all requirements are met

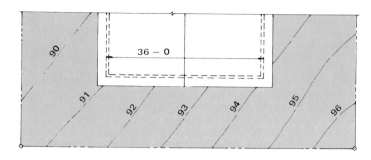

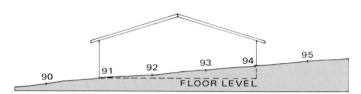

Fig. 10-3. No consideration for the existing grade has been made in this example. The finished floor level is below grade and most likely is in conflict with the building code.

before proceeding. If the soil bearing capacity is questionable, have a soil bearing test made. See Fig. 10-4.

DRAWING A FOUNDATION PLAN

Drawing a foundation plan includes the following steps. Not all items will apply to every situation:

1. Select the scale. Residential structures are usually drawn to 1/4'' = 1'-0'' scale. Be

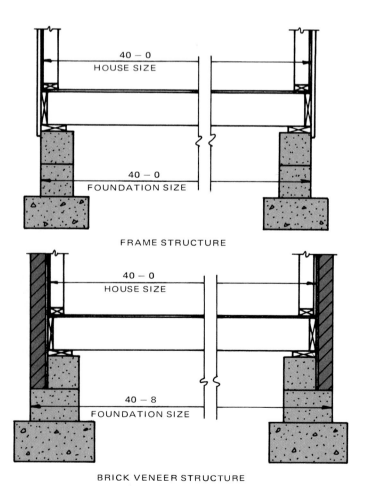

FRAME STRUCTURE

BRICK VENEER STRUCTURE

Fig. 10-2. A brick veneer house requires a foundation wall eight inches longer and wider than a frame wall structure.

Fig. 10-4. A soil test is being made to determine load-bearing capacity.

sure to use the same size tracing sheets for all drawings in the set.

2. Locate the outline of the foundation walls on the paper allowing ample space for dimensions, notes, and title block. Use the floor plan as an underlay or draw the foundation plan from dimensions obtained from the floor plan.

3. Draw the foundation walls, piers and columns, and the foundation for a chimney (fireplace).

4. Indicate breaks in the foundation wall for windows, doors, access holes, and vents. Steps 1 through 4 are shown in Fig. 10-5.

5. Lay out and draw the footings for the foundation walls. Use a hidden line symbol.

6. Draw the footings to be used for the piers and columns.

7. Draw the footings for the fireplace and chimney.

8. Locate the supporting beam if one is required. Draw the beam using a thick center line symbol.

9. Show the size, spacing, and direction of floor joists or trusses using the standard symbol.

10. Identify the location of sections needed to provide additional information. Steps 4 through 10 are shown in Fig. 10-6.

11. Draw the necessary sections and dimension them as shown in Fig. 10-7.

12. Determine the location of dimensions needed to show the size of all aspects of the foundation. The length and thickness of all foundation wall segments must be dimensioned. Piers are dimensioned to the center rather than to the edge.

13. Draw the dimension lines and add the required dimensions.

14. Letter any necessary notes.

15. Shade the foundation wall drawings with proper symbols.

16. Add the title block, scale, and name of drawing in the proper location.

17. Check drawing to be sure you have included all necessary information. Steps 12 through 17 are shown in Fig. 10-8.

THE BASEMENT/FOUNDATION PLAN

In cold climates where the frost penetration depth is several feet, basements are usually included in the plans. Since the footings must be below the frost depth, it is comparatively inexpensive to excavate the soil under the house and extend the foundation down a few more feet. This additional excavation provides additional usable space at much less cost per square foot than the first floor level. Basements are also popular in areas where space is crowded and building sites are small.

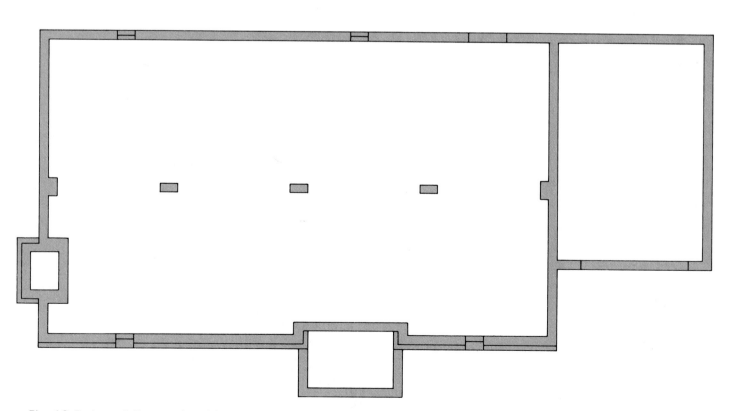

Fig. 10-5. A partially completed foundation plan which shows the foundation walls, piers, pilasters, and vent openings.

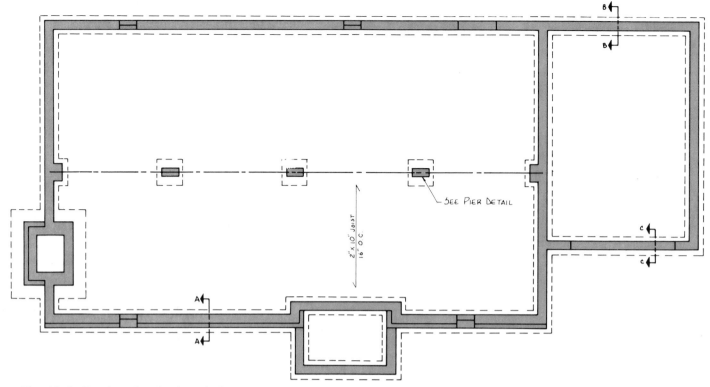

Fig. 10-6. Footings for the foundation walls and piers, supporting beam, section symbols, and floor joist data have been added to the foundation plan.

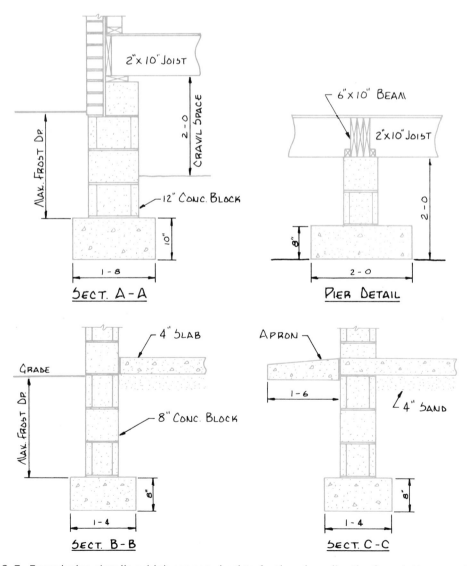

Fig. 10-7. Foundation details which are required to further describe the foundation construction.

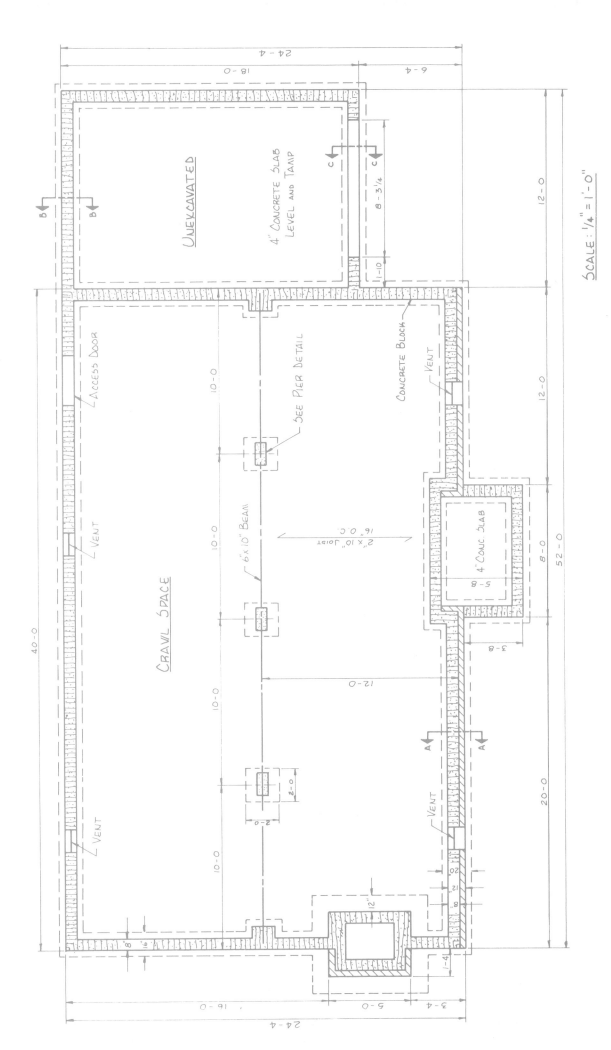

Fig. 10-8. The completed foundation plan showing dimensions, notes, foundation material symbol, and scale. The house is frame with brick veneer along the front.

The basement plan is a combination foundation and floor plan. It includes the information commonly shown on the foundation plan and at the same time shows interior walls, stairs, windows, and doors. The split-level house is a good example of a house that requires a foundation plan for one section of the house and a basement plan for the other. Fig. 10-9 illustrates the use of a basement and foundation plan to show construction for a split-level house foundation.

and insure the inclusion of all necessary information necessary for the drawing:

1. Select the proper scale to be used. Again, most residential plans are drawn at 1/4'' = 1'-0'' scale.
2. Draw the exterior foundation walls using the floor plan as an underlay or from information taken from the floor plan. Be sure the foundation walls are correctly positioned with respect to the first floor walls.

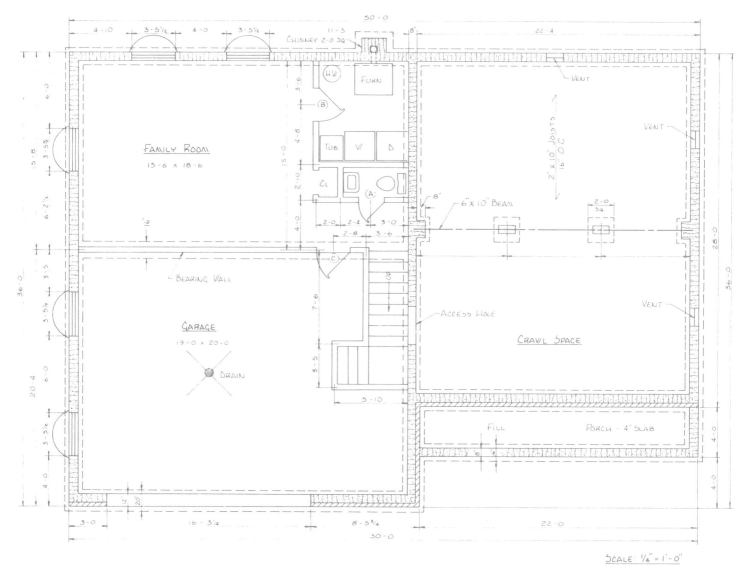

Fig. 10-9. A finished basement/foundation plan for a split-level house. The house is a frame structure with some brick veneer.

PROCEDURE FOR
DRAWING A BASEMENT PLAN

The procedure for drawing a basement plan is much the same as for a foundation plan except for the addition of several features. The following steps should help to clarify the procedure

3. Draw the footings for the foundation walls, chimney, and columns. Steps 1 through 4 are shown in Fig. 10-10.
4. Locate and draw the beam and supports or bearing wall partition(s).
5. Design the room layout in the basement area and darken in the lines.

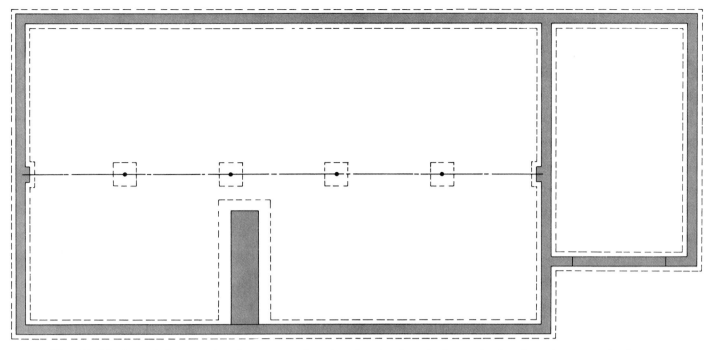

Fig. 10-10. A partially complete basement plan showing the foundation walls, footings, beam, and columns.

6. Indicate breaks in the basement walls where windows or doors are to be located.
7. Locate and draw the stairs leading to the basement.
8. Show size, spacing, and directions of floor joists or trusses using the standard symbol.
9. Identify the location of sections required to provide additional information about the

basement construction. Steps 5 through 9 are shown in Fig. 10-11.
10. Draw the necessary sections and insert dimensions, Fig. 10-12.
11. Locate and draw permanent bath fixtures such as water closet, tub, and lavatory. Also, locate the furnace, hot water heater, water storage tank, water softener, sump,

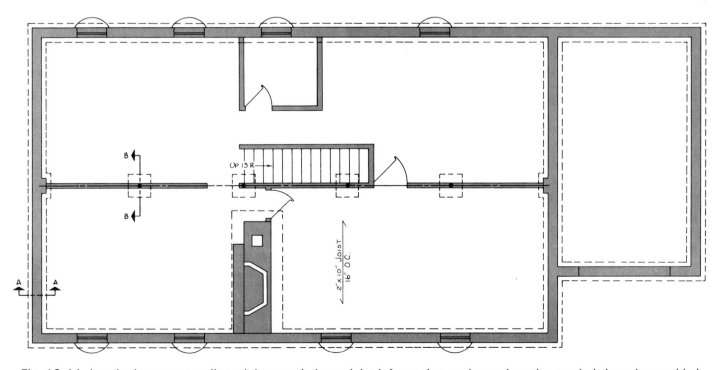

Fig. 10-11. Interior basement walls and doors, windows, joint information, stairs, and section symbols have been added to the partially completed plan.

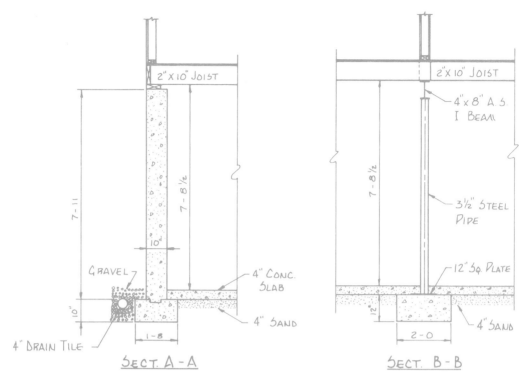

Fig. 10-12. Foundation details required for the basement plan shown in Figs. 10-11 and 10-13.

and floor drains. (All of these may not be necessary.)

12. Determine the location of dimensions needed to show all features. Dimension interior frame walls to the center of the walls. Do not dimension to the center of foundation walls.
13. Draw the dimension lines and add the required dimensions.
14. Letter any necessary notes.
15. Show electrical switches, outlets, and fixtures if no basement electrical plan is intended for the structure.
16. Shade the foundation walls with the proper symbol.
17. Add the title block, scale, and name of drawing in the proper location.
18. Check the drawing to be sure you have included all necessary information. Steps 11 through 18 are shown in Fig. 10-13.

REVIEW QUESTIONS — CHAPTER 10

Write your answers on a separate sheet of paper. Do not write in this book.
1. Define the foundation plan and explain its purpose.
2. Residential foundation plans are usually drawn at _____ scale.
3. List eight features which are usually shown on a foundation plan.
4. The foundation plan is prepared primarily for what persons?
5. The foundation plan is drawn from information presented on the _____ plan, _____ plan, and _____.
6. A brick ledge is at least _____ in. wide.
7. List three considerations that should be checked to help determine the height of foundation walls and size of footings.
8. The symbol for a supporting beam is _____.
9. The purpose of a section is _____.
10. The foundation wall should be shaded to _____.
11. How is a basement plan different from a foundation plan?
12. Why is a basement a logical choice for cold climates?

SUGGESTED ACTIVITIES

1. Select the floor plan for a garden or storage house and develop a foundation plan for the structure. Add necessary dimensions, symbols, and notes. Provide sufficient information so that the foundation could be constructed from your drawings without additional resources.
2. Using the floor plan for a cottage or vacation home, design and draw the foundation for this house. Completely dimension the

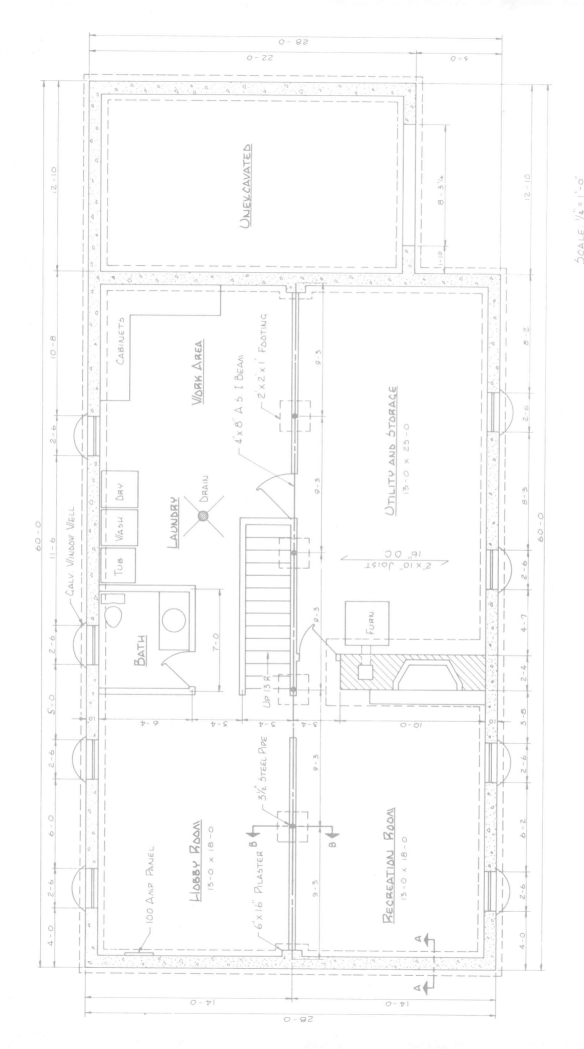

Fig. 10-13. A completed basement plan. The foundation walls are cast concrete and the structure is frame.

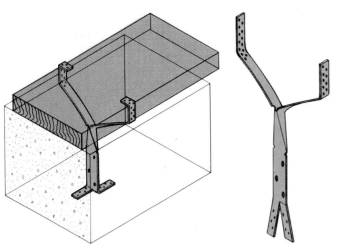

Fig. 10-14. Anchor clips are used along the perimeter of the foundation wall to secure the sill plate to the foundation. (The Panel Clip Company)

drawing and indicate details needed to explain the construction. Draw the details.

3. Draw the foundation plan for a double-car garage which has a slab foundation. Assume the garage is frame construction and is 20'-0'' x 20'-0''. Show anchor bolts or sill anchor clips, Fig. 10-14, every 4'-0'' along the perimeter. Check the required footing depth for your area.

4. Select a floor plan from a magazine or other source and draw the foundation plan for the house. Calculate the size of beam required, number, and size of piers or columns needed, and the size and spacing of floor joists or trusses. Include dimensions and notes.

This residence designed into a hill presented many unique opportunities to the architect. Note the cantilevered projections and the unusual roof on this distinctive dwelling. (California Redwood Association)

Sill and Floor Construction

After studying this chapter, you will be able to:
- Recognize platform and balloon framing.
- Plan the appropriate floor support using joists or trusses for a structure.
- Determine proper joist sizes using a typical span data chart.
- Describe the components of a floor system.
- Demonstrate an understanding of the principles involved in post and beam construction.

Methods of floor framing vary from one section of the country to another. Even builders in a given area may use different methods, based on personal preference and experience. The basic types of floor framing are *platform* and *balloon* framing. Of these two, platform framing is used more extensively. Plates, joists, and studs are the structural members used in both types of framing.

PLATFORM FRAMING

Platform framing is popular for several reasons. It is satisfactory for both one- and two-story structures and is easy and fast to construct. Shrinkage is uniform throughout the structure. A firestop is automatically provided. Construction is safe because the work is performed on solid surfaces.

In platform framing, the *sill* is the starting point in constructing a floor. A sill is the lowest member of the frame of a structure, resting on the foundation and supporting the floor joists or the uprights (studs) of the wall. The sill in most residential construction is a 2 x 6 (actual dimensions 1 1/2'' x 5 1/2''). Platform framing utilizes a method of sill construction known as *box sill* construction, Fig. 11-1. The box sill consists of a 2 x 6 plate (also called a sill or mudsill) and a

header which is the same size as the floor joists. Fig. 11-2 shows a detail of the first and second floor of a structure using platform framing and box sill construction. Fig. 11-3 shows one method of sealing the space between the foundation and sill plate.

BALLOON FRAMING

Balloon framing was once used extensively, but in recent years has diminished in importance. Its distinguishing feature is that the wall studs rest directly on the sill plate. In balloon framing, two types of sill construction are used, the solid or standard sill and the T-sill, Fig. 11-4.

The studs are nailed directly to the sill and joists in solid sill construction. No header is used. Joists are supported by a ribbon and nailed

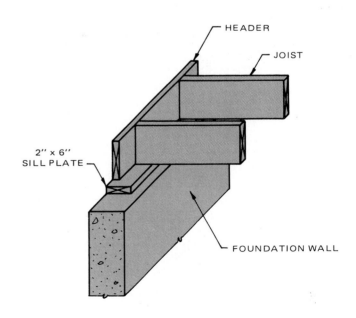

Fig. 11-1. Box sill construction.

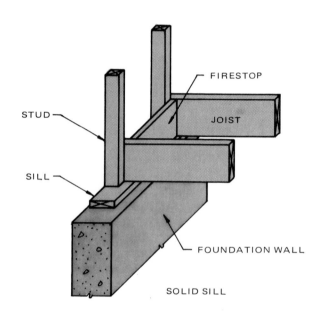

Fig. 11-2. Detail of first and second floors using platform framing and box sill construction.

Labels on figure:
- CEILING AND FLOOR JOISTS
- DOUBLE TOP PLATE
- SIDING
- STUDS
- WEATHER BOARD
- SOLE PLATE
- HEADER
- 2" x 6" SILL
- FLOOR JOIST 2" x 10" 16" O.C.
- ANCHOR BOLT 8-0 APART
- 9" FOUNDATION WALL

to the studs on the second floor level, Fig. 11-5. A firestop must be provided between the studs using pieces cut to the proper length.

In T-sill construction, a header is used which serves as a firestop. The studs rest on the sill plate and are nailed to the header as well as the sill plate. It should be noted that the sill in T-sill construction may be eight or ten inches wide to provide a broader supporting base upon which the joists may rest. Solid sill construction is used more extensively in two-story homes.

Two advantages of balloon framing are small potential shrinkage and vertical stability. Balloon framing is suitable for two-story structures with brick veneer or stucco exterior wall finishes. The vertical shrinkage in a two-story house using platform framing is sometimes great enough to

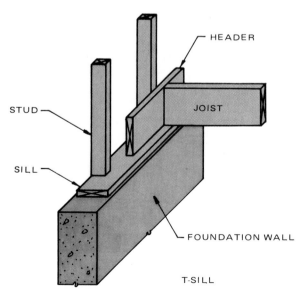

Labels: FIRESTOP, STUD, JOIST, SILL, FOUNDATION WALL, SOLID SILL

STUD, JOIST, HEADER, SILL, FOUNDATION WALL, T-SILL

Fig. 11-4. Two types of sill construction used in balloon framing.

Fig. 11-3. One-inch thick fiberglass insulation is frequently used as a sill sealer.

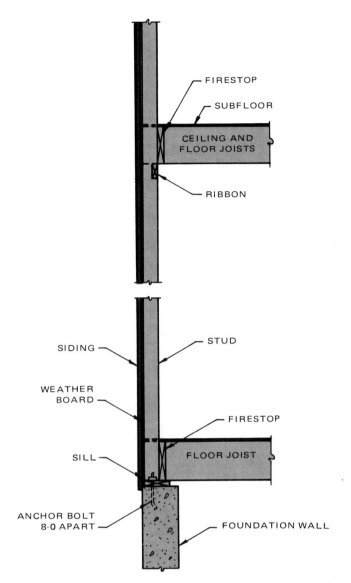

Fig. 11-5. A detail of the first and second floor using balloon framing and solid sill construction.

STANDARD LUMBER SIZES

DIMENSION LUMBER

PRODUCT CLASSIFICATION (NOMINAL SIZE)	ACTUAL SIZES	
	UNSEASONED*	DRY*
2 x 2	1 9/16 x 1 9/16	1 1/2 x 1 1/2
2 x 3	1 9/16 x 2 9/16	1 1/2 x 2 1/2
2 x 4	1 9/16 x 3 9/16	1 1/2 x 3 1/2
2 x 6	1 9/16 x 5 5/8	1 1/2 x 5 1/2
2 x 8	1 9/16 x 7 1/2	1 1/2 x 7 1/4
2 x 10	1 9/16 x 9 1/2	1 1/2 x 9 1/4
2 x 12	1 9/16 x 11 1/2	1 1/2 x 11 1/4

BOARD LUMBER

PRODUCT CLASSIFICATION (NOMINAL SIZE)	ACTUAL SIZES	
	UNSEASONED*	DRY*
1 x 2	25/32 x 1 9/16	3/4 x 1 1/2
1 x 3	25/32 x 2 9/16	3/4 x 2 1/2
1 x 4	25/32 x 3 9/16	3/4 x 3 1/2
1 x 6	25/32 x 5 5/8	3/4 x 5 1/2
1 x 8	25/32 x 7 1/2	3/4 x 7 1/4
1 x 10	25/32 x 9 1/2	3/4 x 9 1/4
1 x 12	25/32 x 11 1/2	3/4 x 11 1/4

*Dry lumber is defined as being 19% or less in moisture content. Unseasoned lumber is over 19% moisture content. The size of lumber changes approximately 1% for each 4% change in moisture content. Lumber stabilizes at approximately 15% moisture content under normal use conditions. (National Forest Products Assoc.)

Fig. 11-6. Actual size of common dimension and board lumber. (National Forest Products Association)

cause cracking. This is usually not the case with balloon framing.

Disadvantages of balloon framing include a less than desirable surface to work on during construction and the need for firestop blocks.

JOISTS AND BEAMS

Joists provide support for the floor. They are usually made from a common soft wood such as southern yellow pine, fir, larch, hemlock, or spruce.

The size of floor joists ranges from a nominal size of 2 x 6 to 2 x 12 for spacing from 12'' to 24''. See Fig. 11-6 for actual dimensions of construction lumber. The size joist required for a given situation will depend on the length of space, load to be supported, specie and grade of wood, and distance the joists are spaced apart. Spacing of floor joists may be 12, 16, or 24'' o.c. (on center). A spacing of 16'' o.c. is most common. Span data for floor joists is presented in Fig. 11-7. The span data presented assumes a maximum deflection of 1/360th of the span with a normal live load. This is the amount which most codes require. The normal live load is 40 pounds per square foot. The procedure for using the chart is as follows: (1) Determine the specie of wood to be used. The chart includes data for the three most common species. (2) Select the appropriate live load capacity required for the structure. (3) Determine the lumber grade to be used. Number 2 dense is the usual choice for fir, larch, and southern yellow pine. (4) Scan the row opposite the lumber grade and note the maximum allowable spans for various joist spacing. (5) Select the joist size and spacing, ordinarily 16'' o.c., which will adequately support the desired live load. Example: The span is 14'-0'' and No. 1 dense yellow pine is to be used for the joists. The live load is 30 pounds per square foot. The chart shows that the following choices would be within the limits chosen: 2 x 8 joists— 12'' o.c. and 16'' o.c.; 2 x 10 joists—12'' o.c., 16'' o.c. and 24'' o.c.; 2 x 12 joists—12'' o.c.,

FLOOR JOIST SPAN DATA

Douglas Fir — Larch — 30 lbs./Ft² — Live Load

	"Fb"	"E"*	2 x 6			2 x 8			2 x 10			2 x 12		
			12"	16"	24"	12"	16"	24"	12"	16"	24"	12"	16"	24"
Select Structural	2050	1.8	12-3	11-2	9-9	16-2	14-8	12-10	20-8	18-9	16-5	25-1	22-10	19-11
Dense #1	2050	1.9	12-6	11-4	9-11	16-6	15-0	13-1	21-0	19-1	16-8	25-7	23-3	20-3
Dense #2	1700	1.7	12-0	10-11	9-7	15-10	14-5	12-7	20-3	18-5	16-1	24-8	22-5	19-7
#2	1450	1.7	12-0	10-11	9-7	15-10	14-5	12-7	20-3	18-5	16-1	24-8	22-5	19-7
#3	850	1.5	10-4	9-0	7-2	13-8	11-10	9-8	17-5	15-1	12-3	21-3	18-3	15-0

Douglas Fir — Larch — 40 lbs./Ft² — Live Load

	"Fb"	"E"*	2 x 6			2 x 8			2 x 10			2 x 12		
			12"	16"	24"	12"	16"	24"	12"	16"	24"	12"	16"	24"
Select Structural	2050	1.8	11-2	10-2	8-10	14-8	13-4	11-8	18-9	17-0	14-11	22-10	20-9	18-1
Dense #1	2050	1.9	11-4	10-4	9-0	15-0	13-7	11-11	19-1	17-4	15-2	23-3	21-1	18-5
Dense #2	1700	1.7	10-11	9-11	8-8	14-5	13-1	11-5	18-5	16-9	14-7	22-5	20-4	17-9
#2	1450	1.7	10-11	9-11	8-6	14-5	13-1	11-4	18-5	16-9	14-5	22-5	20-4	17-6
#3	850	1.5	9-2	7-11	6-7	12-3	10-7	8-8	15-7	13-6	11-0	18-11	16-4	13-5

Southern Yellow Pine -- 30 lbs./Ft² — Live Load

	"Fb"	"E"*	2 x 6			2 x 8			2 x 10			2 x 12		
			12"	16"	24"	12"	16"	24"	12"	16"	24"	12"	16"	24"
Select Structural	2150	1.8	12-3	11-2	9-9	16-2	14-8	12-10	20-8	18-9	16-5	25-1	22-10	19-11
#1 Dense	2150	1.9	12-6	11-4	9-11	16-6	15-0	13-1	21-0	19-1	16-8	25-7	23-3	20-3
#2 Dense	1750	1.7	12-0	10-11	9-7	15-10	14-5	12-7	20-3	18-5	16-1	24-8	22-5	19-7
#2	1500	1.6	11-10	10-9	9-4	15-7	14-2	12-4	19-10	18-0	15-9	24-2	21-11	19-2
#3	875	1.5	10-6	9-0	7-4	14-0	11-11	9-9	17-7	15-3	12-5	21-9	18-7	15-1

Southern Yellow Pine — 40 lbs./Ft² — Live Load

	"Fb"	"E"*	2 x 6			2 x 8			2 x 10			2 x 12		
			12"	16"	24"	12"	16"	24"	12"	16"	24"	12"	16"	24"
Select Structural	2150	1.8	11-2	10-2	8-10	14-8	13-4	11-8	18-9	17-0	14-11	22-10	20-9	18-1
#1 Dense	2150	1.9	11-4	10-4	9-0	15-0	13-7	11-11	19-1	17-4	15-2	23-3	21-1	18-5
#2 Dense	1750	1.7	10-11	9-11	8-8	14-5	13-1	11-5	18-5	16-9	14-7	22-5	20-4	17-9
#2	1500	1.6	10-9	9-9	8-6	14-2	12-10	11-3	18-0	16-5	14-4	21-11	19-11	17-5
#3	875	1.5	9-4	7-11	6-8	12-4	10-10	8-9	15-9	13-9	11-0	19-3	16-7	13-8

California Redwood — 30 lbs./Ft² — Live Load

	"Fb"	"E"*	2 x 6			2 x 8			2 x 10			2 x 12		
			12"	16"	24"	12"	16"	24"	12"	16"	24"	12"	16"	24"
Cl. Heart Struct.	2650	1.4	11-3	10-3	8-11	14-11	13-6	11-10	19-0	17-3	15-1	23-1	21-0	18-4
Select Structural	2000	1.4	11-3	10-3	8-11	14-11	13-6	11-10	19-0	17-3	15-1	23-1	21-0	18-4
#1	1700	1.4	11-3	10-3	8-11	14-11	13-6	11-10	19-0	17-3	15-1	23-1	21-0	18-4
#2	1400	1.25	10-10	9-10	8-7	14-4	13-0	11-4	18-3	16-7	14-6	22-2	19-2	17-8
#3	800	1.1	10-0	8-8	7-1	13-3	11-6	9-4	16-11	14-9	11-11	20-7	17-8	14-7

California Redwood — 40 lbs./Ft² — Live Load

	"Fb"	"E"*	2 x 6			2 x 8			2 x 10			2 x 12		
			12"	16"	24"	12"	16"	24"	12"	16"	24"	12"	16"	24"
Cl. Heart Struct.	2650	1.4	10-3	9-4	8-2	13-6	12-3	10-9	17-3	15-8	13-8	21-0	19-1	16-8
Select Structural	2000	1.4	10-3	9-4	8-2	13-6	12-3	10-9	17-3	15-8	13-8	21-0	19-1	16-8
#1	1700	1.4	10-3	9-4	8-2	13-6	12-3	10-9	17-3	15-8	13-8	21-0	19-1	16-8
#2	1400	1.25	9-10	8-11	7-10	13-0	11-10	10-4	16-7	15-1	13-2	20-2	18-4	16-0
#3	800	1.1	9-0	7-10	6-5	11-9	10-3	8-5	15-0	13-1	10-8	18-2	15-10	13-2

*Modulus of Elasticity "E" in 1,000,000 psi. or 1.0 is equal to 1,000,000 psi.

Fig. 11-7. Span data in feet and inches for floor joists of Douglas Fir—Larch, Southern Yellow Pine, and California Redwood. Spans are calculated on the basis of dry sizes with a moisture content equal to or less than 19 percent. Floor joist spans are for a single span with calculations performed based on the modulus of elasticity (E) and maximum fiber bending stress F_b allowed. Deflection is limited to 1/360 of the span. Span data assumes a dead load of 10 lbs./Ft². For other species and applications see "Span Tables for Joists and Rafters, American Softwood Lumber Standard Sizes PS 20-70." (National Forest Products Association)

16'' o.c., and 24'' o.c. The most reasonable selection would be 2 x 8 joists placed 16'' o.c. Such a joist will span 15'-0'' which exceeds the span by 1 foot.

A floor system may also be constructed using girders or trusses (usually 4 x 6, 8, or 10 depending on the span) in the place of floor joists. The purpose of this approach is to use fewer support members (joists). The typical spacing of girders or trusses in this system is 48'' o.c. with 1 1/8'' thick tongue-and-groove plywood as the floor decking.

The distance which joists must span is usually so great that a beam or load bearing wall is needed to reduce the span. The beam may be a solid timber, a built-up beam from dimension lumber, or a metal S-beam. Load-bearing walls may be concrete block, cast concrete, or frame construction.

Several methods of supporting floor joists with a beam are commonly used. Fig. 11-8 shows some of these methods.

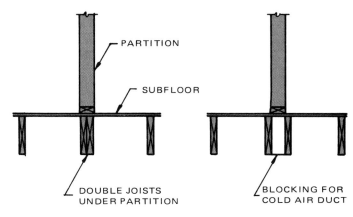

Fig. 11-9. Joists should be doubled under partition walls which run parallel to the joists.

Partition walls which are supported by the floor joists require added support. It is good practice to double the joists under parallel partition walls. If space between the joists is used as a cold air duct, solid blocking is used between the joists, Fig. 11-9.

Openings in the floor for stairs and chimneys require double joist framing. Fig. 11-10 shows how such an opening is framed and identifies the various parts.

Cross bridging is commonly used to stiffen the floor and spread the load over a broader area, Fig. 11-11. Bridging boards are ordinarily 1'' x 3'' in size with the ends cut at an angle so they fit snugly against the joist. They are nailed securely in place midway between the beam and wall. Metal bridging is also available, Fig. 11-12.

FLOOR TRUSSES

Engineered wood floor trusses for light-frame construction are widely used for residential

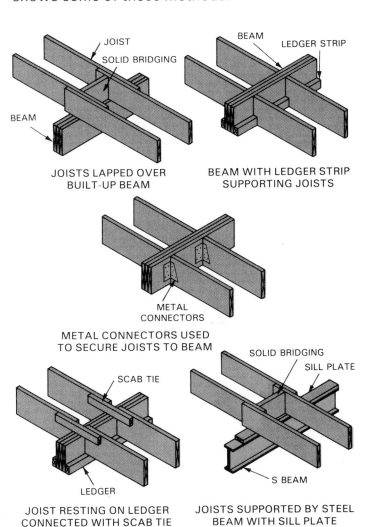

Fig. 11-8. Common methods of supporting floor joists with beams.

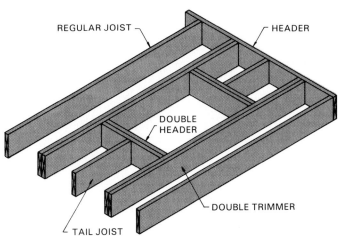

Fig. 11-10. Floor framing around openings such as fireplaces and stairs.

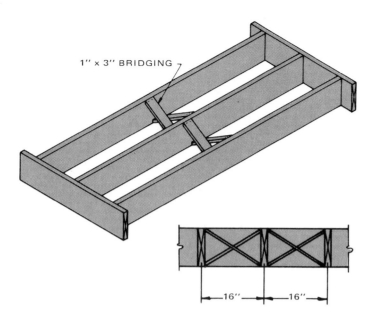

1" x 3" BRIDGING

|←—16"—→|←—16"—→|

Fig. 11-11. Bridging is required by many codes.

Fig. 11-13. Lightweight engineered wood floor trusses are easy to handle and install. (Osmose Wood Products)

structures. With a minimum of depth, in a lightweight assembly that is easy to handle, they provide clear spans, Fig. 11-13. The open web construction reduces transmission of sound through floor/ceiling assemblies. It also makes the installation of plumbing, heating, and electrical systems easy.

Computers are used to design modern engineered floor trusses to assure load capabilities for a given design. Fig. 11-14 shows typical specifications for engineered wood floor trusses. Each truss has a built-in camber so that the floor/ceiling will be level once a load is applied. Stress-graded lumber is used in their construction so that a minimum amount of material is required. Some trusses are fabricated with lumber chords and patented galvanized steel webs, Fig. 11-15, instead of the typical wood webs. The webs have metal teeth which are pressed into the sides of the chords. A reinforcing rib withstands both tension and compression forces. Engineered wood floor trusses are usually fabricated from 2 x 4 or 2 x 6 lumber and generally spaced 24" o.c.

Fig. 11-12. Metal bridging may be quickly installed.

MANUFACTURED 2'' x 4'' WOOD FLOOR TRUSSES

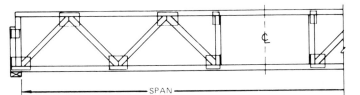
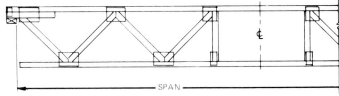

Bottom Chord Bearing Type			
DEPTH	CLEAR SPANS	# DIAGONAL WEBS	CAMBER
12''	7'-2''	4	0.063''
	9'-8''	6	0.063''
	12'-2''	8	0.063''
	14'-8''	10	0.134''
	17'-2''	12	0.237''
	19'-8''	14	0.365''
	21'-4''	16	0.507''
14''	9'-8''	6	0.063''
	12'-2''	8	0.063''
	14'-8''	10	0.095''
	17'-2''	12	0.178''
	19'-8''	14	0.288''
	22'-7''	16	0.449''
	24'-0''	18	0.569''
16''	12'-2''	8	0.065''
	14'-8''	10	0.070''
	17'-2''	12	0.132''
	19'-8''	14	0.228''
	22'-2''	16	0.346''
	25'-1''	18	0.505''
	26'-1''	20	0.596''
18''	14'-8''	10	0.065''
	17'-2''	12	0.120''
	19'-8''	14	0.176''
	22'-2''	16	0.268''
	24'-8''	18	0.367''
	27'-6''	20	0.600''
	27'-10''	22	0.630''
20''	14'-8''	10	0.063''
	17'-2''	12	0.081''
	19'-8''	14	0.140''
	22'-2''	16	0.226''
	24'-8''	18	0.327''
	27'-6''	20	0.451''
	29'-6''	22	0.630''
22''	17'-2''	10	0.066''
	19'-8''	12	0.114''
	22'-2''	14	0.184''
	24'-8''	16	0.266''
	27'-6''	18	0.367''
	30'-0''	20	0.520''
	31'-1''	22	0.630''
24''	17'-2''	12	0.063''
	19'-8''	14	0.095''
	22'-2''	16	0.153''
	24'-8''	18	0.235''
	27'-2''	20	0.325''
	30'-0''	22	0.431''
	32'-6''	24	0.630''

Top Chord Bearing Type			
DEPTH	CLEAR SPANS	# DIAGONAL WEBS	CAMBER
12''	6'-10''	4	0.063''
	9'-4''	6	0.063''
	11'-10''	8	0.063''
	14'-4''	10	0.122''
	16'-10''	12	0.233''
	19'-10''	14	0.376''
	21'-4''	16	0.507''
14''	9'-5''	6	0.063''
	11'-11''	8	0.063''
	14'-5''	10	0.088''
	16'-11''	12	0.167''
	19'-5''	14	0.273''
	21'-4''	16	0.429''
	24'-0''	18	0.569''
16''	12'-0''	8	0.063''
	14'-6''	10	0.067''
	17'-0''	12	0.126''
	19'-6''	14	0.219''
	22'-4''	16	0.337''
	24'-10''	18	0.489''
	26'-1''	20	0.596''
18''	14'-6''	10	0.063''
	17'-0''	12	0.098''
	19'-6''	14	0.170''
	22'-0''	16	0.260''
	24'-10''	18	0.378''
	27'-8''	20	0.617''
	27'-10''	22	0.630''
20''	14'-6''	10	0.063''
	17'-0''	12	0.079''
	19'-6''	14	0.136''
	22'-0''	16	0.221''
	24'-10''	18	0.337''
	27'-4''	20	0.442''
	29'-6''	22	0.630''
22''	17'-1''	12	0.065''
	19'-7''	14	0.112''
	22'-1''	16	0.181''
	24'-10''	18	0.275''
	27'-4''	20	0.381''
	30'-2''	22	0.534''
	31'-1''	24	0.630''
24''	17'-1''	12	0.063''
	19'-7''	14	0.093''
	22'-1''	16	0.150''
	24'-7''	18	0.231''
	27'-5''	20	0.335''
	30'-2''	22	0.443''
	32'-6''	24	0.630''

Wood floor trusses are typically manufactured from #3 Southern Yellow Pine. Pieces are joined together with 18 and 20 gauge galvanized steel plates applied to both faces of the truss at each joint. Where no sheathing is applied directly to top chords, they should be braced at intervals not to exceed 3'-0''. Where no rigid ceiling is applied directly to bottom chords, they should be braced at intervals not to exceed 10'-0''.

Manufactured wood floor trusses are generally spaced 24'' o.c. and are designed to support various loads. Typical trusses shown here were designed to support 55 psf (live load - 40 psf, dead load - 10 psf, ceiling dead load - 5 psf). A slight bow (camber) is built into each joist so that it will produce a level floor when loaded. Allowable deflection is 1/360 of the span.

Some of the longer trusses require one or more double diagonal webs at both ends. Wood floor trusses are a manufactured product which must be engineered and produced with a high degree of accuracy to attain the desired performance. See your local manufacturer or lumber company for trusses available in your area.

Fig. 11-14. Design specifications for typical engineered wood floor trusses for light-frame construction.

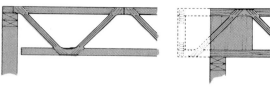

TOP CHORD

FIELD CUT TRUSS DETAIL

CENTER BEAM

BOTTOM CHORD WITH
CONTINUOUS BANDING

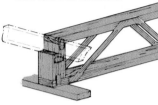

BOTTOM CHORD CANTILEVER
—ON PANEL

BOTTOM CHORD W/O
BANDING BLOCK

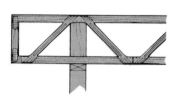

BALCONY JOIST DETAIL

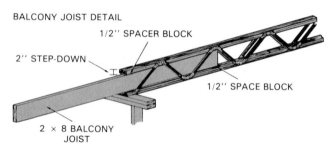

1/2'' SPACER BLOCK

2'' STEP-DOWN

1/2'' SPACE BLOCK

2 × 8 BALCONY
JOIST

*Fig. 11-15. Truss chords are made of lumber, but webbing
is a patented galvanized steel design.
(TrusWal Systems, Inc.)*

*Fig. 11-16. Many structural wood panels are manufac-
tured for construction uses. Products shown (top to
bottom) include: waferboard, structural particleboard,
composite plywood, oriented strand board, and plywood.
(Georgia-Pacific Corporation)*

SUBFLOOR

Plywood, tongue-and-groove boards, common boards, and other panel products are used
for subfloors. The large size of plywood and
other panel sheets (4' x 8'), and comparatively
short time required to nail the sheets in place has
drastically increased the use of these materials
for subfloors. One-half inch thick plywood, composite board, waferboard, oriented strand broad,
and structural particleboard, Fig. 11-16, may be
used when joists are spaced 16'' o.c. but some
builders prefer 5/8 in. stock. When these products are used, it is important that the joist spacing is very accurate. All edges of the panels must
be supported, Fig. 11-17.

In some localities there is a trend to combine
the subfloor and underlayment (usually 5/8''

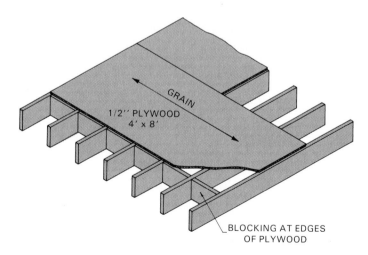

*Fig. 11-17. Blocking is used to support the edges of 1/2''
plywood used for subfloor.*

particleboard) into a single thickness which is
generally 1 1/8'' thick. The sheets have tongue-
and-groove edges and require no blocking between the joists. A single thickness sheet of
3/4'' tongue-and-groove plywood may also be
used for some applications.

Plywood should be installed so that the grain direction of the outer plies are at right angles to the joists. It is stronger when positioned in this manner. Panel products should also be staggered so that end joints in adjacent panels break at different joists. A slight space must be allowed between sheets for expansion.

Subfloor panels may also be glued and nailed to the joists. Structural tests have shown that stiffness is increased by 25 percent with 2 x 8 joists and 5/8'' plywood. Another advantage to gluing is that the system produces a squeak-free structure, eliminates nail-popping, and reduces labor costs.

CANTILEVERED JOISTS

Some home designs include a section of the floor that projects beyond a lower level. There is no particular problem when the floor joists run perpendicular to the cantilevered section, but when the joists are parallel to the overhanging area the situation requires cantilevered joists. Fig. 11-18 illustrates a typical framing technique for an overhanging section. A rule of

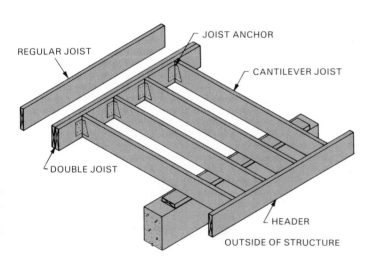

Fig. 11-18. Cantilevered joists should extend at least twice as far inside the house as they extend outside.

thumb to follow in determining the necessary length of the cantilevered joists is to extend the joists inside at least twice the distance they overhang outside. If the inside distance is too short the result may be a sagging floor along the outside wall. If a ledger strip is used, it should be located along the top of the inside double header joist since the force will be up rather than down as in a normal situation.

FRAMING UNDER SLATE OR TILE

Certain areas of the home frequently have ceramic tile, slate, or stone floors. These materials require a substantial base. If a concrete base is provided, the floor framing must be lowered to provide for the concrete. Several techniques are used to provide the needed support. A smaller size joist may be used and the space between joists reduced to provide adequate support, Fig. 11-19. This is a common solution to the problem. Another technique is to use one or more beams under the section to support the added weight. The dead weight may be as much as 40 or 50 pounds per square foot in a bathroom with a tile floor and heavy fixtures.

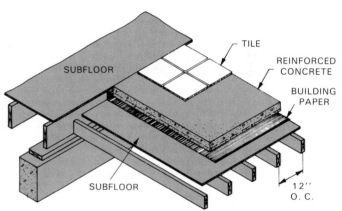

Fig. 11-19. A framing technique commonly used to support slate and ceramic tile areas. . . smaller size joists and placed closer together.

The concrete base for the tile or stone should be reinforced with wire mesh and cast on a plywood subfloor covered with building paper. A special type of concrete is generally used. It is a mixture of 1 part portland cement and 6 parts sand, known as a **cement mortar mix.**

POST AND BEAM CONSTRUCTION

In post and beam construction large framing members (posts, beams, planks) are spaced farther apart than conventional framing members, Figs. 11-20 and 11-21. Post and beam construction provides a greater freedom of design than conventional framing techniques. The system is basically simple, but presents problems related to larger structural sizes, framing connectors, and methods of joinery.

Most of the weight of a post and beam building is carried by the posts. The walls are called

Fig. 11-20. An example of post and beam construction. (American Plywood Association)

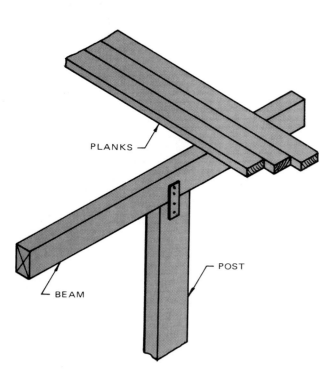

Fig. 11-21. The three components of post and beam construction.

PLANKS

BEAM

POST

curtain walls. Curtain walls provide for wide expanses of glass without the need for headers, Fig. 11-22. Wide overhangs are also possible by extending the large beams to the desired length. Spacing of the posts is determined by the design of the building and the load to be supported.

The foundation for a post and beam structure may be a continuous wall or a series of piers where each post is to be located. Size of footings will be determined by the weight to be supported, soil bearing capacity, and local building codes. Check local codes.

The size of posts required will be at least 4'' x 4''. If the floor is also to be supported by the posts, they should be at least 6'' x 6''. Vertical height of the posts will be a factor in determining the size. Again check local codes.

Beams may be solid, laminated, reinforced with steel, or plywood box beams. Fig. 11-23 shows a variety of beam types. Spacing and span of the beams will be determined by the size and kind of materials and load to be supported. In most normal situations, a span of 7'-0'' may be used when 2'' thick tongue-and-groove subfloor or roof decking is applied to the beams.

Fig. 11-22. Post and beam construction permits broad expanses of glass and provides the warm glow of natural wood. (Potlatch Forests, Inc.)

Thicker beams must be used if a span greater than 7'-0'' is required. See the span tables shown in Fig. 11-24.

Two systems of beam placement are possible with post and beam construction. The first system is the ***longitudinal method.*** Here the beams are placed at right angles to the roof slope. Roof decking is laid, therefore from the ridge pole to the eaves line. The second system is called the ***transverse method.*** The beams follow the roof

slope and decking runs parallel to the roof ridge. See Fig. 11-25.

A post and beam structure has a limited number of joints. The conventional method of fastening small members by nailing does not provide a satisfactory connection. Therefore, metal plates or connectors are used. These are fastened with lag screws or bolts. Fig. 11-26 shows a number of metal fasteners used to connect various beam segments.

SOLID BEAM

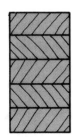
HORIZONTAL LAMINATED BEAM

VERTICAL LAMINATED BEAM

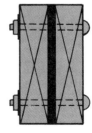
STEEL REINFORCED BEAM

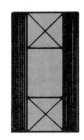
BOX BEAM

Fig. 11-23. A variety of beams used in post and beam construction.

SPAN DATA FOR GLUED LAMINATED ROOF BEAMS*
MAXIMUM DEFLECTION 1/240TH OF THE SPAN

BEAM SIZE (ACTUAL)	WGT. OF BEAM PER LIN. FT. IN POUNDS	SPAN IN FEET											
		10	12	14	16	18	20	22	24	26	28	30	32
		POUNDS PER LIN. FT. LOAD BEARING CAPACITY											
3 x 5 1/4	3.7	151	85										
3 x 7 1/4	4.9	362	206	128	84								
3 x 9 1/4	6.7	566	448	300	199	137	99						
3 x 11 1/4	8.0	680	566	483	363	252	182	135	102				
4 1/2 x 9 1/4	9.8	850	673	451	299	207	148	109					
4 1/2 x 11 1/4	12.0	1,036	860	731	544	378	273	202	153				
3 1/4 x 13 1/2	10.4	1,100	916	784	685	479	347	258	197	152	120		
3 1/4 x 15	11.5	1,145	1,015	870	759	650	473	352	267	206	163	128	104
5 1/4 x 13 1/2	16.7	1,778	1,478	1,266	1,105	773	559	415	316	245	193	154	124
5 1/4 x 15	18.6	1,976	1,647	1,406	1,229	1,064	771	574	438	342	269	215	174
5 1/4 x 16 1/2	20.5	2,180	1,810	1,550	1,352	1,155	933	768	586	457	362	290	236
5 1/4 x 18	22.3	2,378	1,978	1,688	1,478	1,308	1,113	918	766	598	478	382	311

EXAMPLE: CLEAR SPAN = 20'-0''
BEAM SPACING = 10'-0''
DEAD LOAD = 8 LBS./SQ. FT. (ROOFING AND DECKING)
LIVE LOAD = 20 LBS./SQ. FT. (SNOW)
TOTAL LOAD = LIVE LOAD + DEAD LOAD x BEAM SPACING
= (20 + 8) x 10 = 280 LBS./LIN. FT.
THE BEAM SIZE REQUIRED IS 3 1/4'' x 13 1/2'' WHICH SUPPORT 347 LBS./LIN. FT. OVER A SPAN OF 20'-0''

*BEAMS MAY BE DOUGLAS FIR, LARCH OR SOUTHERN YELLOW PINE.

SPAN DATA FOR GLUED LAMINATED FLOOR BEAMS*
MAXIMUM DEFLECTION 1/360TH OF THE SPAN

BEAM SIZE (ACTUAL)	WGT. OF BEAM PER LIN. FT. IN POUNDS	SPAN IN FEET											
		10	12	14	16	18	20	22	24	26	28	30	32
		POUNDS PER LIN. FT. LOAD BEARING CAPACITY											
3 x 5 1/4	3.7	114	64										
3 x 7 1/4	4.9	275	156	84	55								
3 x 9 1/4	6.7	492	319	198	130	89							
3 x 11 1/4	8.0	590	491	361	239	165	119						
4 1/2 x 9 1/4	9.8	738	479	298	196	134	96						
4 1/2 x 11 1/4	12.0	900	748	541	359	248	178	131	92				
3 1/4 x 13 1/2	10.4	956	795	683	454	316	228	169	128	98			
3 1/4 x 15	11.5	997	884	756	626	436	315	234	178	137	108		
5 1/4 x 13 1/2	16.7	1,541	1,283	1,095	732	509	367	271	205	158	123	96	
5 1/4 x 15	18.6	1,713	1,423	1,219	1,009	703	508	376	286	221	173	137	109
5 1/4 x 16 1/2	20.5	1,835	1,568	1,340	1,170	939	678	505	384	298	235	187	151
5 1/4 x 18	22.3	2,058	1,710	1,464	1,278	1,133	886	660	503	391	309	247	200

EXAMPLE: CLEAR SPAN = 20'-0''
BEAM SPACING = 10'-0''
DEAD LOAD = 7 LBS./SQ. FT. (DECKING AND CARPET)
LIVE LOAD = 40 LBS./SQ. FT. (FURNITURE AND OCCUPANTS)
TOTAL LOAD = LIVE LOAD + DEAD LOAD x BEAM SPACING
= (40 + 7) x 10 = 470 LBS./LIN. FT.
THE BEAM SIZE REQUIRED IS 5 1/4'' x 15'' WHICH WILL SUPPORT 508 LBS./LIN. FT. OVER A SPAN OF 20'-0''

*BEAMS MAY BE DOUGLAS FIR, LARCH OR SOUTHERN YELLOW PINE.

Fig. 11-24. Span data for glued laminated floor and roof beams. Local building codes should be checked for specific requirements. (Potlatch Forests, Inc.)

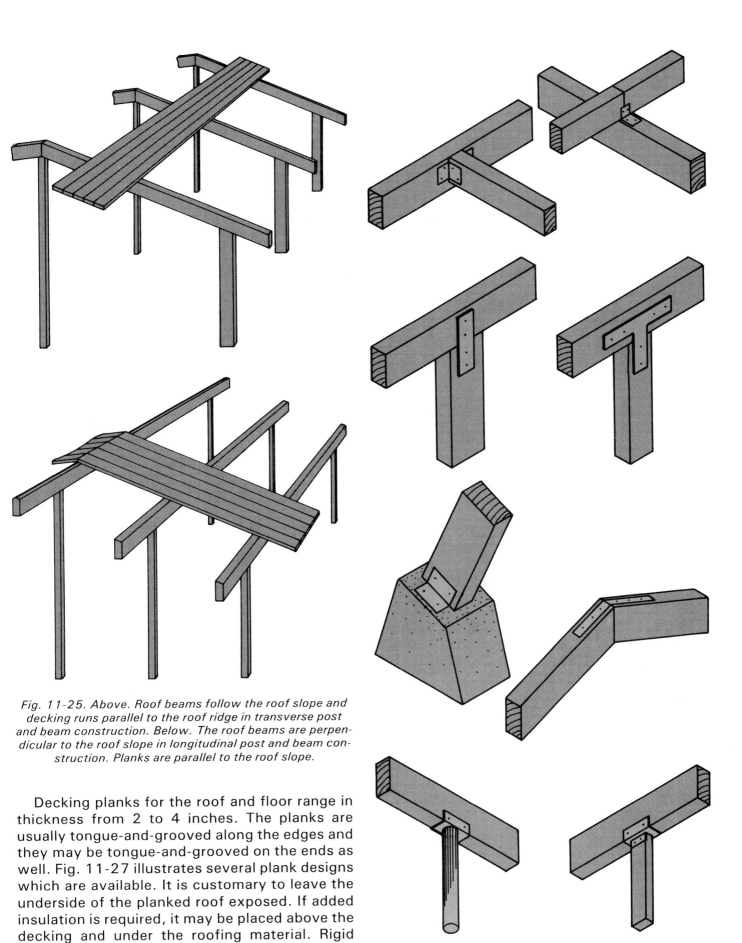

Fig. 11-25. Above. Roof beams follow the roof slope and decking runs parallel to the roof ridge in transverse post and beam construction. Below. The roof beams are perpendicular to the roof slope in longitudinal post and beam construction. Planks are parallel to the roof slope.

Decking planks for the roof and floor range in thickness from 2 to 4 inches. The planks are usually tongue-and-grooved along the edges and they may be tongue-and-grooved on the ends as well. Fig. 11-27 illustrates several plank designs which are available. It is customary to leave the underside of the planked roof exposed. If added insulation is required, it may be placed above the decking and under the roofing material. Rigid type insulation should be used. Roof decking span information is given in Fig. 11-28.

Fig. 11-26. Metal fasteners (typical) used to connect large beam segments.

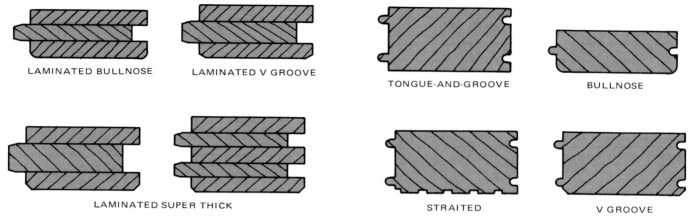

LAMINATED BULLNOSE   LAMINATED V GROOVE   TONGUE-AND-GROOVE   BULLNOSE

LAMINATED SUPER THICK   STRAITED   V GROOVE

Fig. 11-27. Several plank designs produced commercially for use in post and beam construction.

SPAN DATA FOR ROOF DECKING
WITH A MAXIMUM DEFLECTION OF 1/240TH OF THE SPAN
LIVE LOAD = 20 LBS./SQ. FT.

THICKNESS IN INCHES (NOMINAL)	LUMBER GRADE	SIMPLE SPANS	
		DOUGLAS FIR, LARCH, SOUTHERN YELLOW PINE	WESTERN RED CEDAR
		SPAN	SPAN
2	CONSTRUCTION	9'-5''	8'-1''
2	STANDARD	9'-5''	6'-9''
3	SELECT DEX.	15'-3''	13'-0''
3	COMPL. DEX.	15'-3''	13'-0''
4	SELECT DEX.	20'-3''	17'-3''
4	COMPL. DEX.	20'-3''	17'-3''

THICKNESS IN INCHES (NOMINAL)	LUMBER GRADE	RANDOM LENGTHS	
		DOUGLAS FIR, LARCH, SOUTHERN YELLOW PINE	WESTERN RED CEDAR
		SPAN	SPAN
2	CONSTRUCTION	10'-3''	8'-10''
2	STANDARD	10'-3''	6'-9''
3	SELECT DEX.	16'-9''	14'-3''
3	COMPL. DEX.	16'-9''	13'-6''
4	SELECT DEX.	22'-0''	19'-0''
4	COMPL. DEX.	22'-0''	18'-0''

THICKNESS IN INCHES (NOMINAL)	LUMBER GRADE	COMB. SIMPLE AND TWO-SPAN CONTINUOUS	
		DOUGLAS FIR, LARCH, SOUTHERN YELLOW PINE	WESTERN RED CEDAR
		SPAN	SPAN
2	CONSTRUCTION	10'-7''	8'-9''
2	STANDARD	10'-7''	6'-9''
3	SELECT DEX.	17'-3''	14'-9''
3	COMPL. DEX.	17'-3''	13'-6''
4	SELECT DEX.	22'-9''	19'-6''
4	COMPL. DEX.	22'-9''	18'-0''

Fig. 11-28. Span data for Douglas fir, larch, southern yellow pine, and western red cedar planking.

Write your answers on a separate sheet of paper. Do not write in this book.

1. The two basic types of floor framing being used today are _____ and _____ framing.
2. The lowest member of the frame of a structure, and which rests on the foundation and supports the floor joists and wall studs, is the _____.
3. The actual dimensions of a 2 x 6 framing member are _____.
4. Platform framing utilizes a method of sill construction known as _____ sill construction.
5. Two types of sill construction used with balloon framing are _____ and _____ sill construction.
6. List two advantages of balloon framing.
7. The floor of a house is supported by _____ or trusses.
8. Name three softwoods which are commonly used for joists.
9. Spacing of floor joists is usually _____ in. o.c.
10. Dry lumber is defined as wood which has no more than _____ percent moisture content.
11. What size floor joist should be used if the span is 14'-0'', No. 1 dense yellow pine is to be used, the live load is 30 pounds per square foot, and the joist spacing is 16'' o.c.? (Use the span data chart.)
12. The purpose of cross bridging is to stiffen the floor and _____.
13. The thickness of plywood commonly used for subfloors is _____.
14. Identify five types of panel products that may be used for subflooring.
15. Name four advantages of engineered wood floor trusses.
16. Why do floor trusses have a built-in camber?
17. When a part of the house extends out over a lower section, the term _____ is used to describe the structure.
18. List the three elements of post and beam construction.
19. Identify four types of beams used in post and beam construction.
20. Two systems of beam placement are used in post and beam construction. They are the _____ and the _____ method.
21. Roof decking is manufactured in various thicknesses and widths. The span chart for planking presents data for three thicknesses. List them.
22. What type of insulation is used with a planked roof?

SUGGESTED ACTIVITIES

1. Obtain a set of house plans and identify the following:
   a. Size of floor joists or trusses required.
   b. Spacing of floor joists or trusses.
   c. Type of sill construction specified.
   d. Thickness and type of subfloor material to be used.
   e. Size of sill plate.
   f. Type and size of bridging.
   g. Specie and grade of lumber specified for joists or trusses.
   h. Method of framing used (such as balloon or platform).
   i. Type of construction details shown relating to sill and floor.
2. Define the following terms:
   a. span
   b. live load
   c. dead load
   d. cantileverage
   e. beam
   f. partition
   g. post
   h. reinforced concrete
   i. construction grade
   j. nominal dimension
   k. firestop
   l. dimension lumber
   m. header
   n. sill
   o. laminated
   p. slope
   q. tongue-and-groove
   r. straited
3. Select a floor plan of a house and prepare a list of materials for the first floor. (Sill, header, joists, and subfloor.)
4. Design and draw the floor framing for a house of your design. Show the spacing, size, specie, and grade of joists used. Draw the necessary construction detail.

House wrap seals drafts through wall seams and openings, reduces air change rate, impedes air movement through insulation, and helps protect the R-value. (DuPont Company)

Wall and Ceiling Construction

After studying this chapter, you will be able to:
- Name the members of a typical frame wall.
- Explain methods of frame wall construction.
- Interpret information shown on a ceiling joist span data chart.
- Sketch the various types of exterior walls used in residential construction.

Residential wall construction is usually one of three types: frame, masonry, or combination frame and masonry. The wall panels may be constructed on site or prefabricated at another location and transported to the site for erection. The trend is toward more prefabrication and less on-site construction.

FRAME WALL CONSTRUCTION

Frame wall construction involves the proper arrangement of the wall framing members which are typically construction lumber, Fig. 12-1. Fig.

12-2 shows the various framing members used in conventional construction. This includes the sole plate, top plates, studs, headers, and bracing. Plates and studs are usually nominal 2 x 4 inch lumber. Headers or lintels are ordinarily

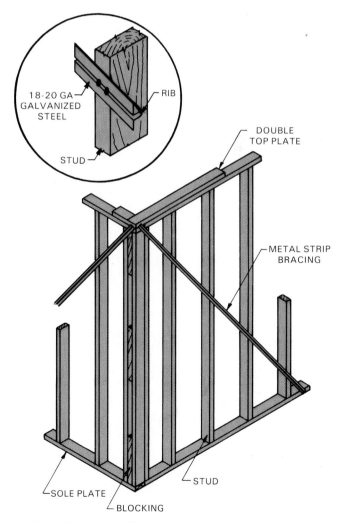
Fig. 12-2. A frame wall corner showing the various framing members and their relationship to each other.

Fig. 12-1. A typical light-frame wood structure which incorporates standard construction practices.

constructed from larger stock. Bracing may be 1 x 4 stock, metal strap, or plywood sheathing. Fig. 12-2 shows a frame wall with the framing members identified.

Wall framing lumber must have good stiffness and nail-holding properties, be free from warp, and easy to work. Species that meet these criteria include Douglas fir, southern yellow pine, hemlock, spruce, and larch. The most common lumber grade used is #2 grade or its equivalent. Moisture content should be between 15 and 19 percent.

Frame wall construction usually begins with the sole plate. The spacing of the studs is marked off on the sole plate, Fig. 12-3. Construction of the wall is ordinarily performed on

the subfloor since it provides a large, flat work surface. Exterior frame walls are flush with the outside of the foundation wall or moved 1/2'' to 3/4'' inside to allow for the thickness of sheathing, weatherboard, or rigid foam insulation, Fig. 12-4. The sole plate acts as an anchor for the wall panels and a nailer for interior and exterior wall sheathing. A wall panel may extend along an entire side of the building if sufficient help is available to raise the wall. Otherwise, the wall may be built in smaller sections.

Wall studs are cut to length (usually 7'-9'' when 1 1/2'' material is used) and are nailed to the sole and top plate. A second plate is added after the wall is in place. The distance from the top of the subfloor to the bottom of the ceiling joists is usually 8'-1 1/2''. This distance provides a finished wall height of 8'-0''.

Openings for doors and windows are framed before the wall is moved to the vertical position. Two basic approaches are used in constructing headers are **solid blocking** and **cripple construction.** In solid blocking, the header size is increased to completely fill the space from the top of the rough opening to the top plate. See Fig. 12-5. Two 2 x 12 pieces of dimension lumber are nailed together with a piece of 1/2'' plywood between them to form a 3 1/2'' thick header. This method reduces construction time, but increases shrinkage. Fig. 12-6 illustrates the older method of header construction which uses cripple studs and trimmers firmly nailed to the sole and top plates. **Cripples** are studs that are not full length due to a wall opening. **Trimmers** are studs that support the header over an opening in the wall.

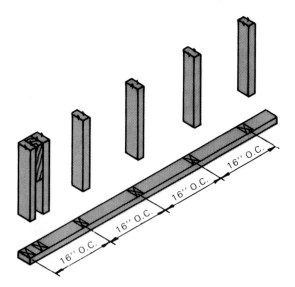

Fig. 12-3. A sole plate showing the location of studs.

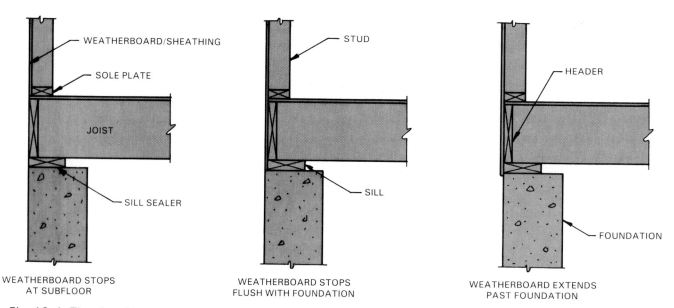

WEATHERBOARD STOPS AT SUBFLOOR

WEATHERBOARD STOPS FLUSH WITH FOUNDATION

WEATHERBOARD EXTENDS PAST FOUNDATION

Fig. 12-4. The sheathing, weatherboard, or rigid insulation may terminate at the subfloor, the top of the foundation, or extend below the top of the foundation. The treatment used will most likely depend on the construction procedure.

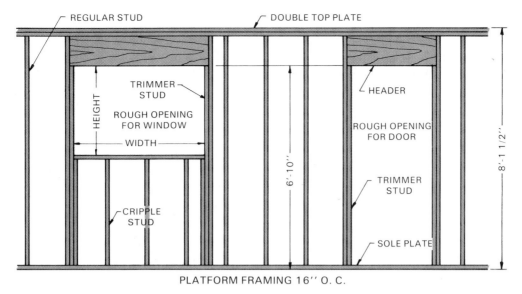

Fig. 12-5. Solid blocking is used to form the header over a window and door opening in this example.

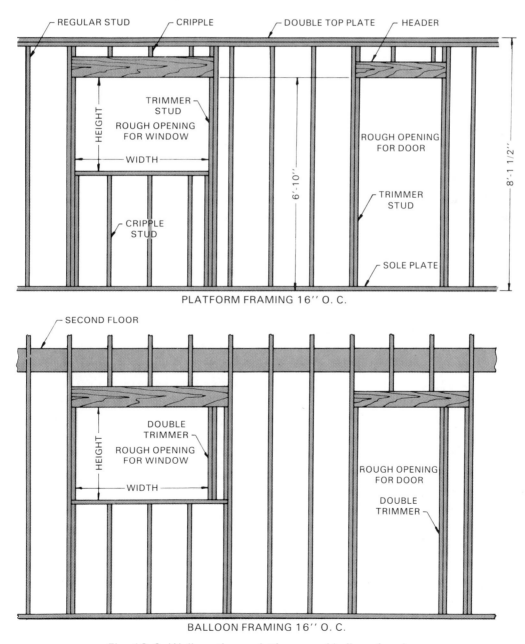

Fig. 12-6. Wall sections, platform, and balloon framing.

Corner bracing is required by most codes. Two methods of bracing are commonly used to provide added support. Diagonal corner braces of 1 x 4 inch material or metal straps are used from the top corner of the wall down to the sole plate. This method is shown in Fig. 12-2. The second method, which seems to be gaining in popularity, makes use of a sheet of 1/2'' plywood or other similar panel nailed to the studs at each corner, Fig. 12-7.

Typical methods of framing used to form exterior wall corners are shown in Fig. 12-8. The corner must provide a nailing edge for the interior wall material and adequate support for the structure.

Interior frame walls are constructed the same way as exterior walls. They also have sole plates, studs, and double top plates. Interior walls must be securely fastened to the exterior walls that they intersect. Again, a nailing edge must be provided for the plaster base, drywall, or paneling. This may be accomplished by using a 2 x 6 secured to cross blocking or by doubling the exterior wall studs at the intersection of the partition. Fig. 12-9 illustrates both methods. The same arrangement is used at the intersection of all interior walls.

Rough openings for windows and doors shown on the floor plan are dimensioned to the center of the opening when located in a frame wall. Specific dimensions are usually provided by the window and door schedule. The width is listed first and the height second. The rough opening height of most doors is 6'-10''. Tops of all windows will probably be the same distance above the floor. Each wall opening requires a header above the opening to support the weight above. The length of the header will be equal to the width of the rough opening plus the thickness of two trimmers, Fig. 12-10. Header sizes vary with the span and load requirements. The chart shown in Fig. 12-11 provides sizes for various situations. **Check the code to be sure**

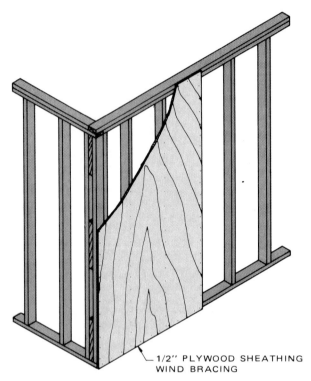

1/2'' PLYWOOD SHEATHING
WIND BRACING

Fig. 12-7. One-half inch plywood sheathing may be used as bracing for the exterior wall corners.

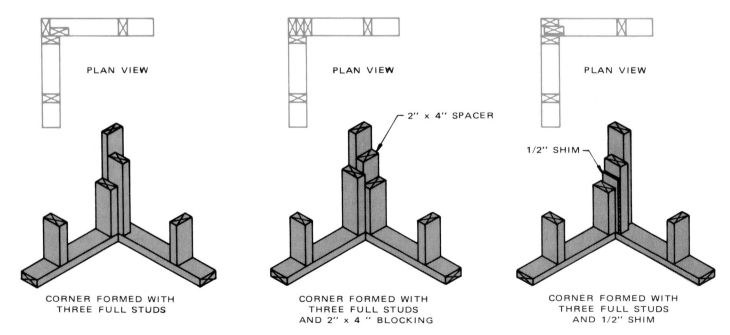

PLAN VIEW

PLAN VIEW

PLAN VIEW

2'' x 4'' SPACER

1/2'' SHIM

CORNER FORMED WITH
THREE FULL STUDS

CORNER FORMED WITH
THREE FULL STUDS
AND 2'' x 4'' BLOCKING

CORNER FORMED WITH
THREE FULL STUDS
AND 1/2'' SHIM

Fig. 12-8. Corner posts are framed in a variety of ways. This illustration shows three accepted methods.

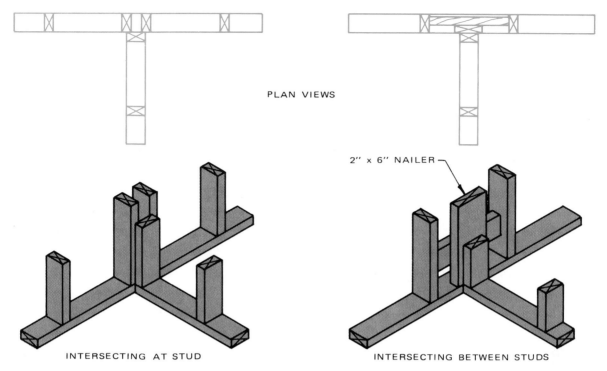

PLAN VIEWS

2" x 6" NAILER

INTERSECTING AT STUD

INTERSECTING BETWEEN STUDS

Fig. 12-9. The framing for the intersection of partitions and exterior walls is accomplished by using extra studs or blocking and a nailer.

these specifications are permitted in your area. Trussed headers are required for openings wider than 8'-0'' or in situations involving extremely heavy loads. Fig. 12-12 illustrates two types of trussed headers.

HEADER SIZES AND SPANS	
HEADER SIZES	MAXIMUM SPAN
2'' x 6''	3'-6''
2'' x 8''	5'-0''
2'' x 10''	6'-6''
2'' x 12''	8'-0''

NOTE: Header size refers to size of material used and not the overall size of the header. Each header is constructed of two pieces, on edge, with plywood spacer between.

Fig. 12-11. Typical header sizes for given spans.

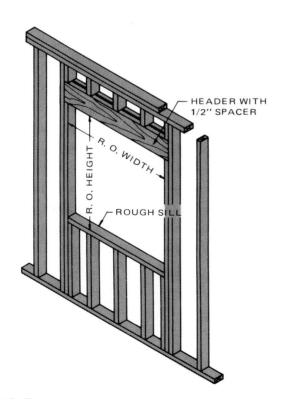

HEADER WITH 1/2'' SPACER

R. O. WIDTH

R. O. HEIGHT

ROUGH SILL

Fig. 12-10. The rough opening for a window is the area between the trimmers and the rough sill and header.

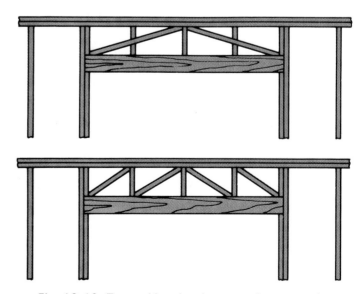

Fig. 12-12. Trussed headers increase the supporting strength and increase the span.

Limited Attic Storage Where Development of Future Rooms is Not Possible
Douglas Fir — Larch — 20 lbs./Ft² — Live Load

	"Fb"	"E"	2 x 4			2 x 6			2 x 8			2 x 10		
			12"	16"	24"	12"	16"	24"	12"	16"	24"	12"	16"	24"
Select Structural	2050	1.8	10-3	9-4	8-1	16-1	14-7	12-9	21-2	19-3	16-10	27-1	24-7	21-6
Dense #1	2050	1.9	10-5	9-6	8-3	16-4	14-11	13-0	21-7	19-7	17-2	27-6	25-0	21-10
Dense #2	1700	1.7	10-0	9-1	7-7	15-9	14-4	11-11	20-10	18-11	15-9	26-6	24-1	19-10
#2	1450	1.7	9-11	8-8	7-0	15-7	13-6	11-0	20-7	17-10	14-5	26-3	22-8	18-6
#3	850	1.5	7-8	6-7	5-5	11-11	10-7	8-5	15-8	13-8	11-4	20-2	17-5	14-2

Limited Attic Storage Where Development of Future Rooms is Not Possible
Southern Yellow Pine — 20 lbs./Ft² — Live Load

	"Fb"	"E"	2 x 4			2 x 6			2 x 8			2 x 10		
			12"	16"	24"	12"	16"	24"	12"	16"	24"	12"	16"	24"
Select Structural	2150	1.8	10-3	9-4	8-1	16-1	14-7	12-9	21-2	19-3	16-10	27-1	24-7	21-6
#1 Dense	2150	1.9	10-5	9-6	8-3	16-4	14-11	13-0	21-7	19-7	17-2	27-6	25-0	21-10
#2 Dense	1750	1.7	10-0	8-1	7-9	15-9	14-4	12-1	20-10	18-11	16-4	26-6	24-1	20-4
#2	1500	1.6	9-10	8-9	7-2	15-6	13-9	11-3	20-5	18-2	14-9	26-0	23-2	18-10
#3	875	1.5	7-9	6-8	5-6	12-0	10-8	8-6	15-9	13-9	11-5	20-3	17-6	14-3

Maximum Deflection is 1/240 of span.

Flat or Sloped Rafters (Flat Roof or Cathedral Ceiling with no Attic Space) Supporting Drywall Ceiling
Douglas Fir — Larch — Live Load = 20 lbs./Ft²

	"Fb"	"E"	2 x 6			2 x 8			2 x 10			2 x 12		
			12"	16"	24"	12"	16"	24"	12"	16"	24"	12"	16"	24"
Select Structural	2050	1.8	16-1	14-6	12-2	21-2	19-1	16-0	27-0	24-7	20-6	32-10	29-9	24-10
Dense #1	2050	1.9	16-5	14-10	12-2	21-7	19-7	16-0	27-6	25-0	20-6	33-4	30-5	24-10
Dense #2	1700	1.7	15-8	13-7	11-1	20-8	17-10	14-7	26-4	22-10	18-7	32-0	27-9	22-8
#2	1450	1.7	14-5	12-6	10-2	19-1	16-6	13-5	24-4	21-0	17-2	29-7	25-7	20-10
#3	850	1.5	11-1	9-7	7-10	14-7	12-7	10-3	18-7	16-2	13-1	22-6	19-7	16-0

Flat or Sloped Rafters (Flat Roof or Cathedral Ceiling with no Attic Space) Supporting Drywall Ceiling
Southern Yellow Pine — Live Load = 20 lbs./Ft²

	"Fb"*	"E"	2 x 6			2 x 8			2 x 10			2 x 12		
			12"	16"	24"	12"	16"	24"	12"	16"	24"	12"	16"	24"
Select Structural	2150	1.8	16-1	14-6	12-5	21-3	19-2	16-5	27-0	24-5	20-11	32-10	29-9	25-5
#1 Dense	2150	1.9	16-4	14-10	12-5	21-6	19-7	16-5	27-5	25-0	20-11	33-4	30-5	25-5
#2 Dense	1750	1.7	15-10	13-9	11-3	20-11	18-1	14-9	26-8	23-1	18-10	31-7	28-1	22-11
#2	1500	1.6	14-8	12-9	10-5	19-5	16-9	13-8	24-9	21-5	17-6	30-1	26-0	21-3
#3	875	1.5	11-3	9-8	7-11	14-9	12-10	10-5	18-10	16-4	13-3	23-0	19-11	16-3

Flat or Low Sloped Rafters (No Attic Storage) Slope 3 in 12 or less
Douglas Fir — Larch — Live Load = 20 lbs./Ft²

	"Fb"*	"E"	2 x 6			2 x 8			2 x 10			2 x 12		
			12"	16"	24"	12"	16"	24"	12"	16"	24"	12"	16"	24"
Select Structural	2050	1.8	16-2	14-7	12-10	21-3	19-3	16-10	27-1	24-7	21-6	33-0	29-11	26-1
Dense #1	2050	1.9	16-5	14-10	13-1	21-7	19-7	17-3	27-7	24-10	22-1	33-6	30-4	26-10
Dense #2	1700	1.7	15-10	14-6	11-11	20-10	19-0	15-9	26-7	24-2	20-1	32-5	29-6	24-5
#2	1450	1.7	15-7	13-6	11-0	20-7	17-10	14-7	26-3	22-9	18-7	31-11	27-8	22-7
#3	850	1.5	11-11	10-4	8-6	15-9	13-6	11-2	20-1	17-5	14-2	24-5	21-1	17-3

Flat or Low Sloped Rafters (No Attic Storage) Slope 3 in 12 or less
Southern Yellow Pine — Live Load = 20 lbs./Ft²

	"Fb"*	"E"	2 x 6			2 x 8			2 x 10			2 x 12		
			12"	16"	24"	12"	16"	24"	12"	16"	24"	12"	16"	24"
Select Structural	2150	1.8	16-2	14-7	12-10	21-3	19-3	16-10	27-1	24-7	21-6	33-0	29-11	26-1
#1 Dense	2150	1.9	16-5	14-10	13-1	21-7	19-7	17-3	27-7	24-10	22-1	33-6	30-4	26-10
#2 Dense	1750	1.7	15-10	14-6	12-1	20-10	19-0	16-0	26-7	24-2	20-4	32-5	29-6	24-9
#2	1500	1.6	15-7	13-9	11-3	20-9	18-2	14-10	26-6	23-2	18-11	31-5	28-2	23-0
#3	875	1.5	12-0	10-5	8-7	15-10	13-7	11-3	20-2	17-6	14-3	24-6	21-2	17-4

Medium or High Sloped Rafters (No Attic Storage) Slope over 3 in 12
Douglas Fir — Larch — Live Load = 20 lbs./Ft²

	"Fb"*	"E"	2 x 4			2 x 6			2 x 8			2 x 10		
			12"	16"	24"	12"	16"	24"	12"	16"	24"	12"	16"	24"
Select Structural	2050	1.8	11-2	10-3	8-10	17-9	16-0	13-10	23-5	21-2	18-2	29-11	27-0	23-4
Dense #1	2050	1.9	11-6	10-7	8-10	18-0	16-6	13-10	23-10	21-9	18-2	30-5	27-9	23-4
Dense #2	1700	1.7	11-2	9-10	8-0	17-4	15-5	12-7	22-10	20-4	16-7	29-2	25-3	21-2
#2	1450	1.7	10-5	9-1	7-4	16-5	14-3	11-7	21-8	18-9	15-4	27-8	24-0	19-7
#3	850	1.5	8-0	7-0	5-8	12-7	10-11	8-11	16-7	14-4	11-9	21-2	18-4	15-0

Medium or High Sloped Rafters (No Attic Storage) Slope over 3 in 12
Southern Yellow Pine — Live Load = 20 lbs./Ft²

	"Fb"*	"E"	2 x 4			2 x 6			2 x 8			2 x 10		
			12"	16"	24"	12"	16"	24"	12"	16"	24"	12"	16"	24"
Select Structural	2150	1.8	11-2	10-3	9-0	17-9	16-0	14-2	23-5	21-2	18-6	29-11	27-0	23-8
#1 Dense	2150	1.9	11-6	10-7	9-0	18-0	16-6	14-2	23-10	21-9	18-8	30-5	27-9	23-10
#2 Dense	1750	1.7	11-2	9-11	8-1	17-4	15-8	12-9	22-10	20-7	16-10	29-2	25-3	21-6
#2	1500	1.6	10-8	9-3	7-6	16-8	14-6	11-10	22-1	19-1	15-7	28-2	24-5	19-11
#3	875	1.5	8-1	7-1	5-9	12-8	11-0	9-0	16-8	14-5	11-10	21-3	18-5	15-1

*The required extreme fiber stress in bending, "Fb", in pounds/In². Modulus of elasticity is in 1,000,000 psi where 1.8 is equal to 1,800,000 psi.

Fig. 12-13. Ceiling joists and rafter span data in feet and inches for Douglas Fir — Larch and Southern Yellow Pine. Spans are based on dry lumber size with a moisture content equal to or less than 19 percent. Calculations were based on the modulus of elasticity (E) and maximum fiber bending stress (Fb) allowed for ceiling joists. Rafter spans were based on the fiber bending stress (Fb) and allowable modulus of elasticity (E). Rafter spans are horizontal distances. See the Reference Section for a rafter conversion table.

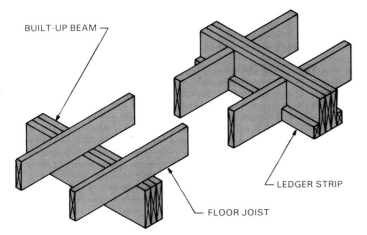

Fig. 12-14. Two methods of supporting ceilings joists with built-up beam.

CEILING CONSTRUCTION

After the exterior and interior walls are erected, plumbed, braced, and top plates added, ceiling joists may be put in place. These are usually positioned across the width of the house and in the same direction as the rafters. The size of ceiling joists required will depend on the load to be supported, span distance, wood specie, spacing of joists, and grade of lumber used. Span data for ceiling joists is presented for three common species of wood in Fig. 12-13. Examine the local code to be sure that your selection is acceptable.

Basic construction of the ceiling is similar to floor construction. The main differences are that a header is not required around the perimeter and smaller lumber is used. Long spans may require a bearing wall partition or beam. If a beam is used, it may be located below the joists or placed flush with them using ledger strips. Both methods are illustrated in Fig. 12-14.

The upper corner of the ceiling joists often interferes with the roof slope. To prevent this interference, the corner is usually cut to match the slope as shown in Fig. 12-15.

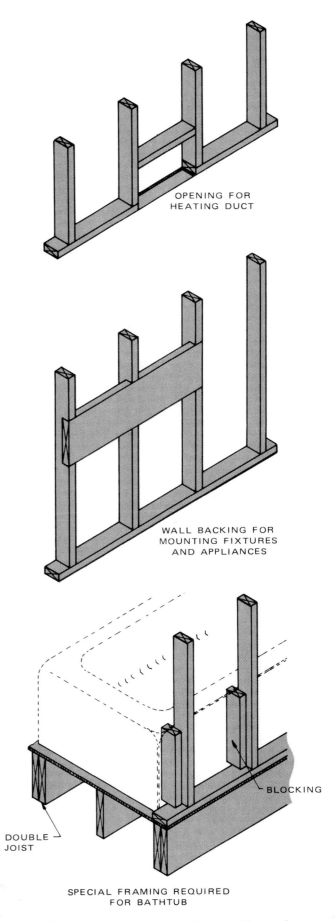

OPENING FOR HEATING DUCT

WALL BACKING FOR MOUNTING FIXTURES AND APPLIANCES

SPECIAL FRAMING REQUIRED FOR BATHTUB

Fig. 12-16. Areas in the house which usually require special framing consideration.

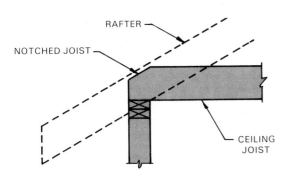

Fig. 12-15. Ceiling joists are usually notched to match the roof slope to prevent interference with the roof sheathing.

Roof trusses are being used in residential construction to a much greater extent. This approach eliminates the traditional ceiling joist and rafter. See the chapter on roof design for design and construction procedures.

FRAMING CONSIDERATIONS

An access hole must be provided in the ceiling (usually in closet) to afford entry to the attic. The size of this opening may be as small as 2 feet square. Framing around the opening is the same as for openings in the floor. Double headers are used for large holes (for example, when installing a disappearing stairway) but are usually not required for minimum size openings.

There are a number of areas in the house that require special framing. Openings for heating ducts, wall backing for various fixtures, and extra support for the bathtub are examples of situations which require attention. Fig. 12-16 illustrates some of these special framing details.

Framing for a bay window presents special problems. Fig. 12-17 shows one accepted method for this type of framing. Note that the floor joists extend beyond the wall to provide

support for the unit. If the unit is to be set at right angles to the joists, then cantilevered joists should be used, Fig. 12-17.

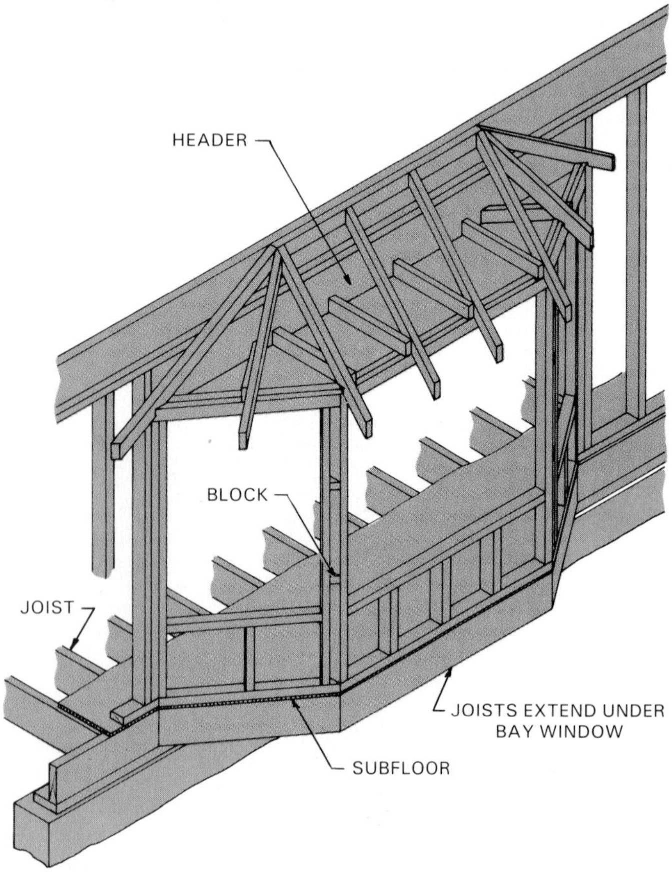

MASONRY WALL CONSTRUCTION

A masonry wall is constructed entirely of brick, concrete block, stone, clay tile, terra cotta, or a combination of these materials. Walls that require more than one thickness of masonry must be bonded together. They may be bonded by using a header course every 16'' vertically, Fig. 12-18, or corrugated metal wall ties may be placed in the mortar joints, Fig. 12-19. Metal wall ties should be placed no more than 16'' apart vertically and 32'' horizontally.

Solid masonry walls for residential construction are usually 8'' thick. Concrete block walls (cavity walls) are popular in many sections of the country. Block walls are relatively inexpensive to construct and a variety of textures and designs are possible. One disadvantage of a solid masonry wall is that furring strips (usually 2'' x 2'' or 1'' x 3'') are required on the inside of the wall if dry wall, plaster, or paneling is used. Insulation may be added as shown in Fig. 12-20.

Solid brick and stone walls have been used extensively in years past, but because of the cost of construction they are diminishing in im-

Fig. 12-17. Typical framing for a bay window.

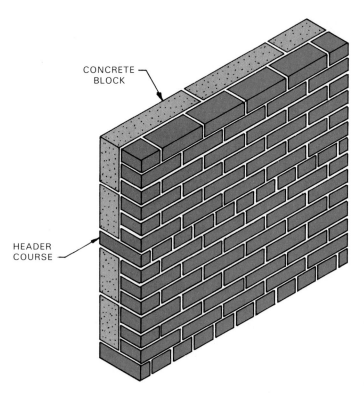

Fig. 12-18. A solid masonry wall using a header course to bond the two thicknesses together.

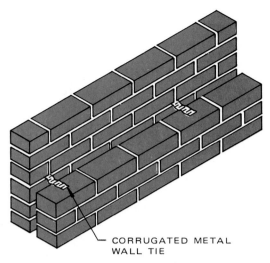

Fig. 12-19. Using corrugated metal wall ties.

Fig. 12-20. Insulation applied between furring strips on a masonry wall to reduce heat loss.
(CertainTeed Corporation)

Fig. 12-21. Insulation with a reflective-type vapor barrier being applied to the brick veneer on a frame structure. (CertainTeed Corporation)

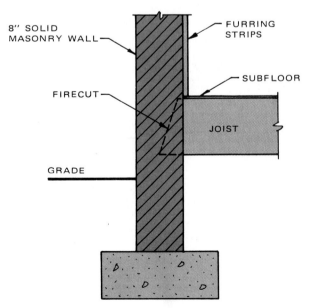

Fig. 12-22. Floor joists in a solid masonry wall require a firecut to prevent excessive wall damage in the event of a fire.

portance for residential purposes. The same exterior effect may be obtained with a brick or stone veneer on frame construction and the wall will be better insulated, less expensive to construct, and present fewer construction problems. Fig. 12-21 shows how a brick veneer wall is typically insulated on the frame wall side.

Floor joists are placed directly into openings in solid brick and stone walls. Each joist is cut at an angle on the end to prevent toppling the wall if the house should catch fire. The cut is known as a *firecut,* Fig. 12-22.

Stonework involves artistry on the part of the mason due to the various size and texture of the material ordinarily used.

Stonework is commonly referred to as *ashlar* or *rubble*. Ashlar stonework uses dressed, cut, or squared stones. Each stone is a specific size and fits in an exact place in the pattern, Fig. 12-23. Rubble stonework is made up of irregular shaped stones. If the stones are basically flat, the result may look like courses of stone, then the term *coursed rubble* is applied, Fig. 12-24. Fig. 12-25 shows random rubble stonework. Another type of rubble stonework is called *uncoursed cobweb* or *polygonal rubble.* These stones are dressed with relatively straight edges and are selected to fit a particular place, Fig. 12-26.

Masonry veneer is usually placed one inch away from the frame wall to provide a dead air space for insulation and a means of escape for moisture which condenses on the inside of the masonry. The term *veneer* is commonly used to indicate that a less expensive or desirable material has been covered up with some type of facing material. The facing is usually 4'' thick (but may range from approximately 1'' to 6''). The veneer does not help support the weight of the building. Fig. 12-27 shows a construction detail

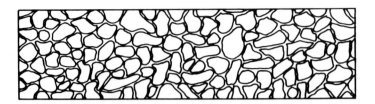

Fig. 12-25. Random rubble stonework.

Fig. 12-26. Cobweb or polygonal rubble.

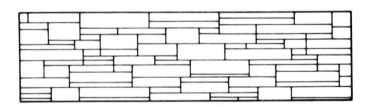

Fig. 12-23. Ashlar stonework.

Fig. 12-24. Coursed rubble stonework.

of brick veneer being used as a facing material over frame construction.

Flashing and termite shields should be used at the base of solid masonry or brick veneer walls. Flashing prevents moisture from entering the structure. Termites are a threat in a large part of the country and cause millions of dollars in damage to homes each year. Fig. 12-28 shows flashing and a termite shield in brick veneer and solid masonry walls.

If a solid masonry wall is used, the top plate must be anchored securely to the wall, Fig. 12-29. The usual procedure in a brick wall is to place anchor bolts between the bricks and bolt the plate in place. A lintel block is used in concrete block construction and anchor bolts are cast in place. The plate is then secured by the use of bolts.

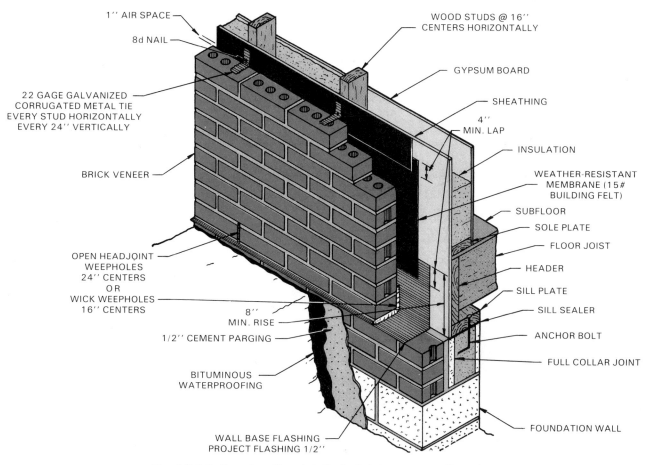

Fig. 12-27. Construction detail of a brick veneer wall section.

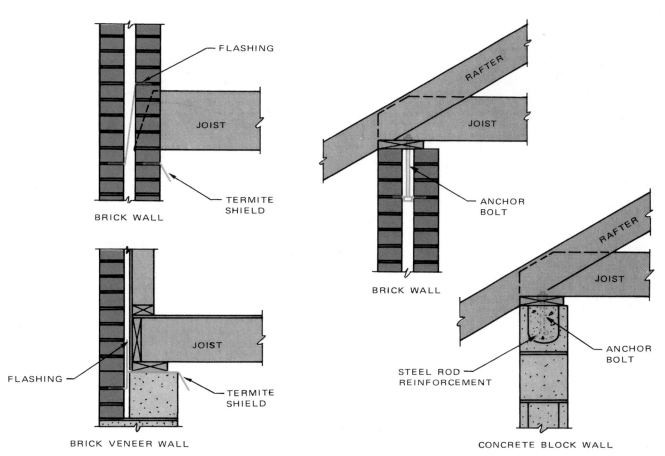

Fig. 12-28. Flashing is used to control moisture. Termite shields are required where termites are a threat.

Fig. 12-29. The top plate is attached to masonry walls with anchor bolts embedded in the wall.

Wall and Ceiling Construction **219**

BRICK NAMES AND SIZES

Brick is a fired clay product. The color is ordinarily determined by the natural color of the clay, but sometimes earth colors are added to produce a wider variety. Brick may be purchased in single colors or in a mixture to produce a blend.

There are two basic types of brick used for wall construction; *common brick* and *face brick.* Face brick is usually uniform in size and has sharp corners and lines. Common brick is not as uniform in size and color and may have a lip on one or more edges. In recent years, common brick has been used more widely as a facing material. They produce a character which is quite different from the face brick. They produce a rustic appearance and the texture is much more distinct. They look especially good with a deep rake joint which accents the individual character of each brick.

The names of brick shapes are well established, but sizes are not standardized. Sizes of brick frequently used in residential construction are shown in the following chart.

BRICK NAMES AND SIZES		
NAME	NOMINAL SIZE	ACTUAL SIZE
Roman	4 x 2 x 12''	1 5/8 x 3 5/8 x 11 5/8''
Modular	2 2/3 x 4 x 8''	2 1/4 x 3 5/8 x 7 5/8''
SCR Brick	2 2/3 x 6 x 12''	2 1/8 x 5 1/2 x 11 1/2''
Standard	2 2/3 x 4 x 8''	2 1/4 x 3 3/4 x 8''
Norman	2 2/3 x 4 x 12''	2 1/4 x 3 5/8 x 11 5/8''
Firebrick*	2 2/3 x 4 x 9''	2 1/2 x 3 5/8 x 9''

*Firebrick is not used for exterior wall construction but is included because it is used in fireplaces.

Specific terms apply to the position or way the brick is laid. Fig. 12-30 illustrates accepted terminology. Note that the term ''stretcher,'' ''header,'' etc. applies to the position of the

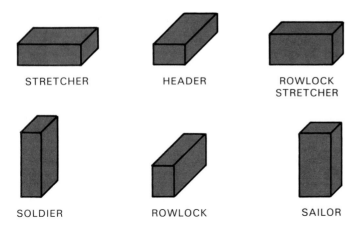

STRETCHER   HEADER   ROWLOCK STRETCHER

SOLDIER   ROWLOCK   SAILOR

Fig. 12-30. Bricks are laid in six basic positions. Each position has a specific name.

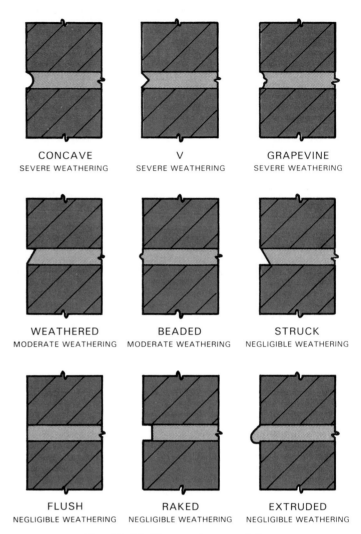

CONCAVE
SEVERE WEATHERING

V
SEVERE WEATHERING

GRAPEVINE
SEVERE WEATHERING

WEATHERED
MODERATE WEATHERING

BEADED
MODERATE WEATHERING

STRUCK
NEGLIGIBLE WEATHERING

FLUSH
NEGLIGIBLE WEATHERING

RAKED
NEGLIGIBLE WEATHERING

EXTRUDED
NEGLIGIBLE WEATHERING

Fig. 12-31. Types of mortar joints.

brick in the wall and not the type or size of the brick.

Numerous types of mortar joints are used in brickwork. Fig. 12-31 shows some joints used in residential construction. Masons have tools designed specifically for making the joints.

A discussion of brickwork would not be complete without mentioning some of the brick bonds which are recognized standards. Fig. 12-32 illustrates a few of the many bonds. The *running bond* is used extensively in brick veneer construction. The *common bond* is popular for solid masonry walls.

REVIEW QUESTIONS—CHAPTER 12

Write your answers on a separate sheet of paper. Do not write in this book.
1. List five factors that affect the size of ceiling joists.
2. Name the five standard parts of a frame wall.

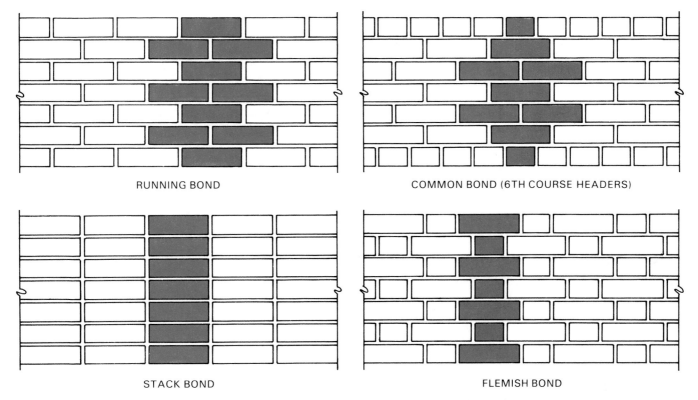

RUNNING BOND

COMMON BOND (6TH COURSE HEADERS)

STACK BOND

FLEMISH BOND

Fig. 12-32. Four of the most frequently used brick bonds.

3. Wood framing lumber must have what properties?

4. Name three softwoods commonly used as framing lumber.

5. The acceptable range of moisture content for framing lumber is _____ percent.

6. Finished wall height in most residential structures is _____.

7. The framing member used to span the distance over an opening in the wall, such as a door or window, is called a _____ or _____.

8. Identify an advantage of using a large solid header instead of a smaller header with cripples.

9. Studs that are not full length and are used above or below wall openings are called _____.

10. The rough opening height for most doors is _____.

11. If a window has a rough opening width of 5'-2", the Header Sizes and Spans Chart indicates that the header size should be _____.

12. Name three areas of the house that require special framing consideration.

13. The purpose of a header course of brick in a masonry wall is to _____.

14. The spacing of metal wall ties should be no greater than _____ apart vertically and _____ horizontally.

15. Solid masonry walls for residential construction are usually _____ in. thick.

16. Concrete block walls are sometimes called _____ walls.

17. An angle cut on the end of floor joists in a solid masonry wall is called a _____.

18. Two types of stonework are called _____ and _____.

19. In a brick veneer wall, the space between the brick veneer and stud wall is usually about _____ wide.

20. The top plate is secured to a solid masonry wall by the use of _____.

21. Brick is made primarily of _____.

22. There are basically two types of bricks. They are _____ and _____.

23. The most popular brick mortar bond is called the _____ bond.

SUGGESTED ACTIVITIES

1. Build a scale model, 1" = 1'-0", of a wall section which has at least one door, one window, and an intersecting partition. Identify the parts.

2. Select a simple floor plan for a frame house and lay out the wall framing indicating trimmers, cripples, spacing blocks, and full studs.

3. Collect samples of building materials to be displayed in class. Identify each of the materials and explain where each might be used in the construction of a house.

4. Build scale models, 1/4 size, of framing for corners, wall intersections, and openings for doors and windows. Prepare plan view drawings for display with the models.
5. Visit a building site where a house is being constructed using conventional methods and determine the specie and grade of the framing lumber and identify the type of framing used. (balloon or platform)
6. Photograph as many different brick bonds as you can find in the area surrounding your home. Identify the bonds and prepare them for display.

This terrace door with round top transom overlooks one of nature's beautiful views. (Marvin Windows)

Doors and Windows

After studying this chapter, you will be able to:
- Recognize the functions that doors and windows perform.
- Compare the types of doors used in a residential dwelling.
- Draw proper door and window symbols on a typical floor plan.
- Interpret the information shown in a window or door detail.

Doors and windows perform several functions in a residential structure. They shield an opening from the elements, add decoration, emphasize the overall design, provide light and ventilation, and expand visibility. Windows and doors are necessary features of all residential structures and should be planned carefully to insure maximum contribution to the overall design and function of the structure.

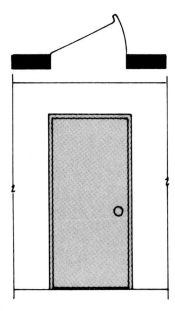

Fig. 13-1. Flush door with plan view symbol.

INTERIOR AND EXTERIOR DOORS

A number of classification systems may be used to identify the various styles and types of doors in residential construction. Two broad classes are interior and exterior doors. Doors may be grouped according to method of construction, uses, function, or location.

INTERIOR DOORS

Interior door types include flush, panel, bi-fold, sliding, pocket, double-action, accordion, Dutch, and French.

Flush doors

Flush doors are smooth on both sides and are usually made of wood, Fig. 13-1. Standard interior wood flush doors are 1 3/8'' thick and 6'-8'' high. They are hollow-core doors which have a wood frame around the perimeter and wood or composition material placed in the cavity to support the faces of the door. Interior flush doors are produced in a wide range of widths from 2'-0'' to 3'-0''. The standard increment width is 2''. Both surfaces of the door are usually covered with 1/8'' mahogany or birch plywood.

Panel doors

A panel door has a heavy frame around the outside and generally has cross members which form small panels, Fig. 13-2. The vertical members are called *stiles* and the horizontal pieces are *rails.* Panels which are thinner than the frame are placed in grooves on the inside edges of the stiles and rails to enclose the space. The panels may be wood, glass, metal, or other material. Panel doors are usually produced in white pine,

Fig. 13-2. A typical panel door used in residential construction. (Morgan Products, Ltd.)

but may be constructed of oak or other woods. Fig. 13-3 shows the plan view symbol and elevation view of a panel door.

Bi-fold doors

A bi-fold door is made of two parts which together form the door. They may be attached to the side jambs with conventional hinges or secured to the head jamb and floor using a pivot hinge. Bi-fold doors may be flush, paneled, Fig. 13-4, or louvered. They are popular as closet doors, and are seldom used for other applications. Bi-fold doors are installed in pairs with each door being the same width. Usual widths are 1'-0'' to 2'-0''.

Wood and metal bi-fold doors are produced in the standard 6'-8'' height as well as 8'-0''. The usual thickness is 1 1/8'' for wood and 1'' for metal. See Fig. 13-5 for the symbol and elevation view.

Sliding doors

Sliding or bi-pass doors are popular where there are large openings, Fig. 13-6. They are frequently used as closet doors. Any number of doors may be used. The width is not critical, because the doors are hung from a track mounted on the head jamb. Door pulls are recessed to allow the doors to pass without interference. Glides are installed on the floor to prevent swinging.

Fig. 13-4. These bi-fold doors have panels. (Morgan Products, Ltd.)

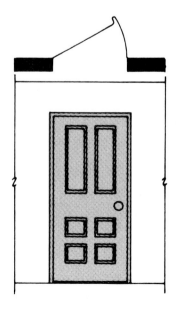

Fig. 13-3. Panel door with plan view symbol.

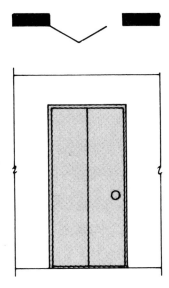

Fig. 13-5. Bi-fold doors with symbol.

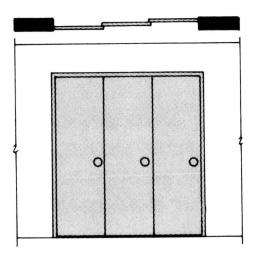

Fig. 13-6. Sliding doors and symbol.

Sliding doors may be flush, paneled, or louvered. They are usually constructed from wood, but other materials may be used. The major problem with wood sliding doors is warping since they are not restrained by hinges.

Pocket doors

The pocket door, usually a flush door, is a variation of the sliding door. Ordinarily, only one door is used to close an opening. It is hung from a track mounted on the head jamb and rests in a wall pocket when open, Fig. 13-7.

Pocket doors are frequently used between rooms such as the kitchen and dining room. The chief advantage is that they require no space along the wall when open. However, they are difficult to operate and present problems if outlets or cabinets are to be located on the wall

space outside the pocket cavity. Pocket door frames of metal and wood are usually purchased already assembled.

Double-action doors

Double-action doors are hinged in such a way that they may swing through an arc of 180°, Fig. 13-8. A special double-action, spring-loaded hinge is used and is mounted in the center of the side jamb. This door is generally used between rooms that experience a great deal of traffic and require the door to be closed most of the time. Double-action doors may be single or

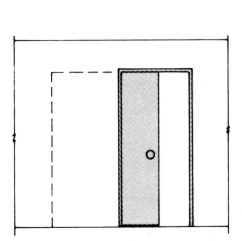

Fig. 13-7. Pocket door.

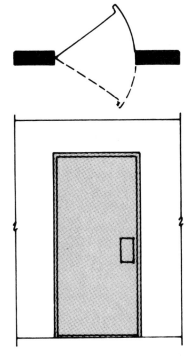

Fig. 13-8. Double-action door.

double doors. A flush, panel, or louvered door can be used.

Accordion doors

Accordion doors are frequently used to close large openings where bi-fold or sliding doors would not be acceptable, Fig. 13-9. They require little space and are produced in a large variety of materials and designs. They may be constructed from wood, plastics, or fabric. Individual hinged panels are sometimes used as well as a large folded piece of fabric or other material. The door is supported on a track mounted on the head jamb, Fig. 13-10.

Fig. 13-9. These beautiful paneled accordion doors are an effective way to close off a large opening. (Pella/Rolscreen Company)

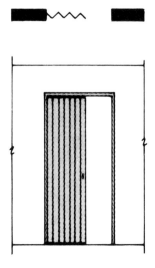

Fig. 13-10. Accordion door.

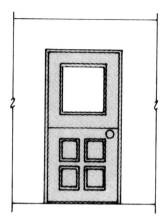

Fig. 13-11. Dutch door.

Dutch doors

A Dutch door is composed of two parts—an upper and lower half. The top section may be opened independently of the bottom to allow for light and ventilation, Fig. 13-11. This door may be used between the kitchen and dining room or as an exterior door.

French doors

French style doors are panel doors with the panels made from glass, Fig. 13-12. They are

Fig. 13-12. French doors are functional as well as decorative. When closed, they provide privacy for this sitting room. (Morgan Products, Ltd.)

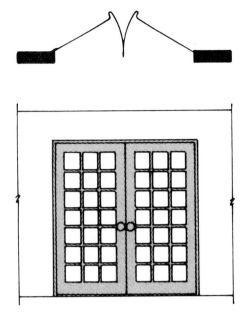

Fig. 13-13. French doors.

popular where the door leads to a patio or terrace. They may also be used between rooms. Fig. 13-13 shows the plan view symbol and elevation view of French doors.

EXTERIOR DOORS

Exterior residential doors are similar to some of the interior types, but have decided differences. Exterior wood doors are usually not hollow core as are many interior doors. They are also thicker than interior doors and may have one or more glass panels to provide visibility. Doors commonly used include: flush doors, panel doors, swinging and sliding glass doors,

and garage doors. Fig. 13-14 shows plan view symbols for various types of exterior doors.

Flush doors

Standard exterior flush wood doors are usually 1 3/4'' thick and 6'-8'' high. Ordinarily, they are 3'-0'' wide. The flush door is one of the most popular exterior doors. These are produced from birch, mahogany, oak, and several other woods as well as metal. Moldings or other decorative mill work may be added to the flush door to enhance its appearance, Fig. 13-15.

Fig. 13-15. This exterior flush door not only has decorative molding to enhance its appearance, but also includes an attractive leaded glass lite. (Weather Shield Mfg., Inc.)

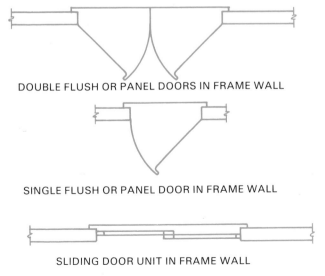

DOUBLE FLUSH OR PANEL DOORS IN FRAME WALL

SINGLE FLUSH OR PANEL DOOR IN FRAME WALL

SLIDING DOOR UNIT IN FRAME WALL

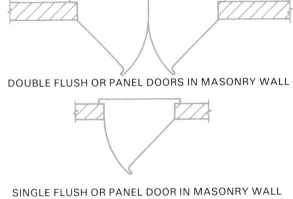

DOUBLE FLUSH OR PANEL DOORS IN MASONRY WALL

SINGLE FLUSH OR PANEL DOOR IN MASONRY WALL

SLIDING DOOR UNIT IN MASONRY WALL

Fig. 13-14. These are standard plan view symbols of common exterior doors.

Fig. 13-16. A traditional panel door made of wood and in use today. (Andersen Corporation)

Panel doors

Exterior panel doors are available in a great variety of styles. They are constructed from white pine, oak, fir, and various other woods. These doors are produced in the same sizes as flush doors. Fig. 13-16 shows a traditional panel door which is still popular today.

Sliding and swinging glass doors

In recent years, sliding and swinging glass doors have gained popularity, Figs. 13-17 and 13-18. Sliding doors are usually made of wood and follow typical sliding glass door sizes. Metal units are also available. Fig. 13-19 shows some of the standard sizes of exterior sliding glass doors which are available.

Garage Doors

Two types of garage doors which account for most of the doors used are the **overhead sectional** and the **one-piece overhead door,** Fig. 13-20. Garage doors are available in wood, metal, and plastics. Each material has its advantages and personal choice is usually the determining factor in selection. The following chart shows standard garage door sizes.

Fig. 13-17. These glass "sliding" doors provide a panoramic view and easy access to the deck. (Pella/Rolscreen Company)

GARAGE DOOR SIZES	
Single Doors	Double Doors
Height x Width	Height x Width
6'-6'' x 8'-0''	6'-6'' x 15'-0''
*7'-0'' x 8'-0''	7'-0'' x 15'-0''
8'-0'' x 8'-0''	
6'-6'' x 9'-0''	6'-6'' x 16'-0''
7'-0'' x 9'-0''	*7'-0'' x 16'-0''
6'-6'' x 10'-0''	6'-6'' x 18'-0''
7'-0'' x 10'-0''	7'-0'' x 18'-0''

*These sizes are the most frequently used.

Fig. 13-18. These swinging glass doors allow access to the deck and let in natural light for the dining room. (The Atrium Door and Window Corporation)

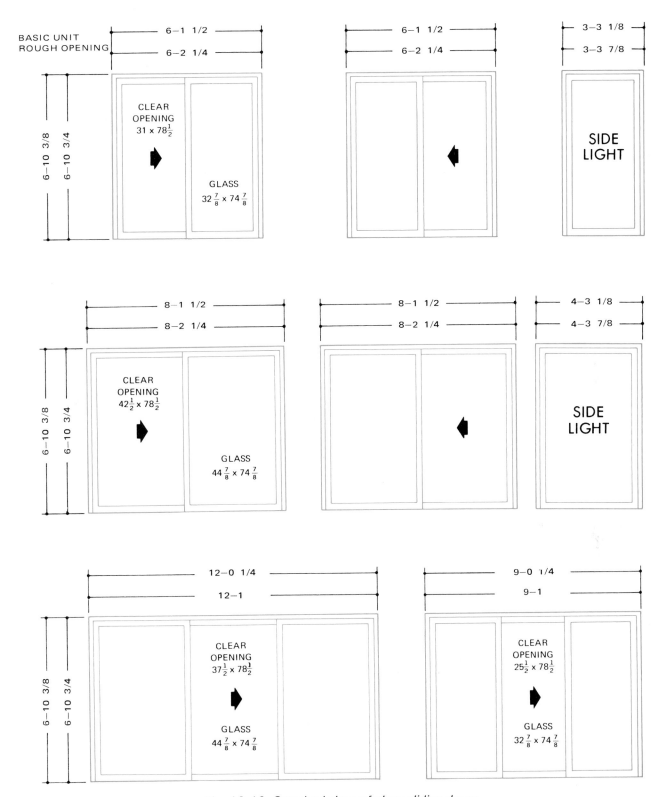

Fig. 13-19. Standard sizes of glass sliding doors.

If an automatic garage door opener is to be installed, proper space and wiring must be provided. Additional headroom is required to mount the motor drive on the ceiling above the open door. An electrical outlet is required to operate the opener. Check the manufacturer's installation requirements for the specific door.

SPECIFYING DOORS

Each door identified on the foundation plan and floor plan should appear on a *door schedule.* Information included on the door schedule should be obtained from manufacturers' literature. Specifications vary and it is important to

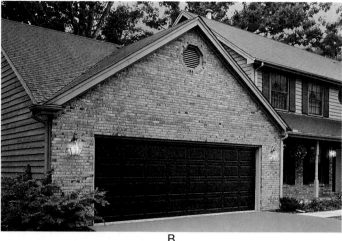

A B

Fig. 13-20. A—One-piece garage doors with decorative trim attached to complement the building style. (The Garling-house Company) B—This overhead sectional garage door is made of steel. It will provide years of maintenance-free beauty and complements the exterior trim. (Raynor Garage Doors)

DOOR SCHEDULE						
SYM.	QUAN.	TYPE	ROUGH OPENING	DOOR SIZE	MANUFACTURER'S NO.	REMARKS
A	2	FLUSH	3'-2 1/2'' x 6'-9 1/4''	3'-0'' x 6'-8''	EF 36 B	1 3/4'' SOLID CORE, BIRCH
B	6	FLUSH	2'-10 1/2'' x 6'-9 1/4''	2'-8'' x 6'-8''	IF 32 M	1 3/8'' HOLLOW CORE, MAHOGANY
C	2	FLUSH	2'-8 1/2'' x 6'-9 1/4''	2'-6'' x 6'-8''	IF 30 M	1 3/8'' HOLLOW CORE, MAHOGANY
D	8	BI-FOLD	SEE MANUFACTURER'S SPECS.	6'-0'' x 6'-8''	BF 36 AL	TWO UNITS EACH 36'' WIDE, ALUMINUM
E	2	SLIDING	4'-2 1/2'' x 6'-9 1/4''	4'-0'' x 6'-8''	IF 24 M	1 1/8'' HOLLOW CORE, MAHOGANY
F	1	GARAGE	SEE MANUFACTURER'S SPECS.	16'-0'' x 7'-0''	G 16 S	TWO-LITE OVERHEAD SECTIONAL, ALUM.

Fig. 13-21. A typical door schedule for a set of residential house plans.

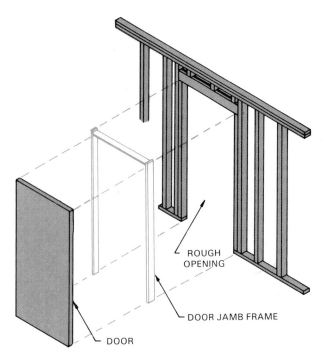

ROUGH OPENING

DOOR JAMB FRAME

DOOR

Fig. 13-22. The door jamb fits inside the rough opening and supports the door.

have exact information for the schedule. A typical door schedule is shown in Fig. 13-21. The door schedule should be placed on the sheet with the floor plan or elevations, if space permits. Otherwise, it should be located in the details section.

DOOR DETAILS

An interior or exterior door is placed inside a door jamb. A **door jamb** is the frame which fits inside the rough opening, Fig. 13-22. Jambs may be constructed from wood or metal. Wood jambs are more common in residential construction. A jamb consists of three parts—two side jambs and a head jamb across the top. Jambs for exterior doors are ordinarily 1 1/8'' thick while interior jambs are 3/4''. The door stop is rabbeted into the thicker exterior jambs, but is applied to the face of interior jambs, Fig. 13-23.

Jambs are available already assembled with the door hung and ready for installation. These are called **prehung units.** Pre-hung units are ad-

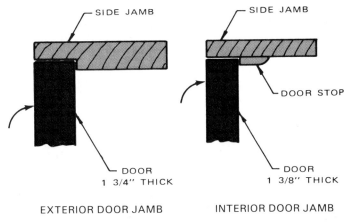

Fig. 13-23. Detail of interior and exterior wood door jambs.

justable for slight variations in wall thickness. Consult the manufacturer's literature to determine the preferred rough opening size.

Rough openings for interior doors are usually framed 3'' more than the door height and 2 1/2'' more than the door width. This provides ample space for the jambs and the necessary leveling and squaring. The space between the jamb and rough framing is covered with trim called **casing**. Exterior casing is usually thicker. When installed in a masonry wall it is called **brick mold**. A **drip cap** is used over the top piece of trim to shed water in frame construction. Such a strip is not necessary in masonry construction.

Exterior doors require a sill at the bottom of the door opening between the two side jambs. A sill is designed to drain water away from the door and provide support for the side jambs. Sills

are constructed from wood, metal, concrete, and stone. Fig. 13-24 shows a typical exterior flush door detail in frame and brick veneer construction. Door and window construction details are usually drawn in section through the head jamb (the jamb across the top of the opening), the side jamb, and the sill. The drawings show head, jamb, and sill details.

Construction details for exterior sliding door units are slightly more complicated than other doors, Fig. 13-25. Exterior sliding door jambs vary from one manufacturer to another. The number of door units may also affect the size and shape of the jambs. When specifying exterior sliding doors, it is advisable to secure specifications from manufacturers to assure accuracy.

Ordinarily it is not necessary to draw detailed window and door section drawings in conventional construction. However, if special framing or uncommon construction is involved, then these drawings are a necessary part of a set of construction drawings.

WINDOWS

When selecting windows for a dwelling it is important to remember the functions which windows perform. They admit light from the outside; provide fresh air and ventilation to the various rooms; help to create an atmosphere inside by framing an exterior view; and add detail, balance, and design to the exterior of the house.

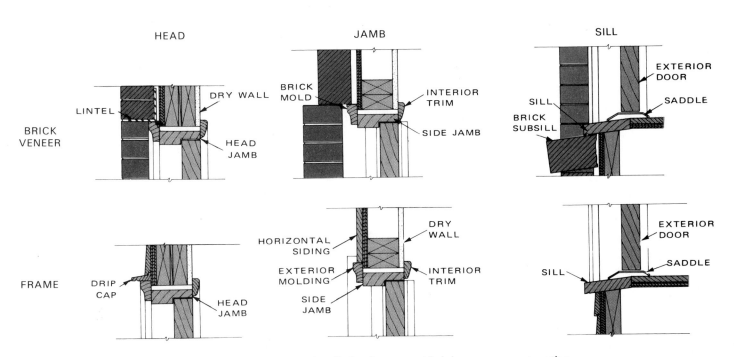

Fig. 13-24. Exterior door details for frame and brick veneer construction.

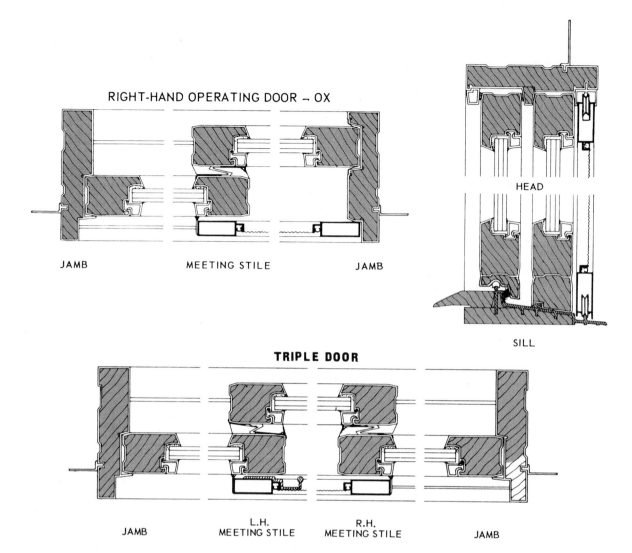

RIGHT-HAND OPERATING DOOR ~ OX

JAMB   MEETING STILE   JAMB

HEAD

SILL

TRIPLE DOOR

JAMB   L.H.   R.H.   JAMB
              MEETING STILE MEETING STILE

Fig. 13-25. Vinyl clad glass sliding door details.

Fig. 13-26. The windows of this attractive colonial complement the basic wall areas and add to the overall design balance. (The Garlinghouse Company)

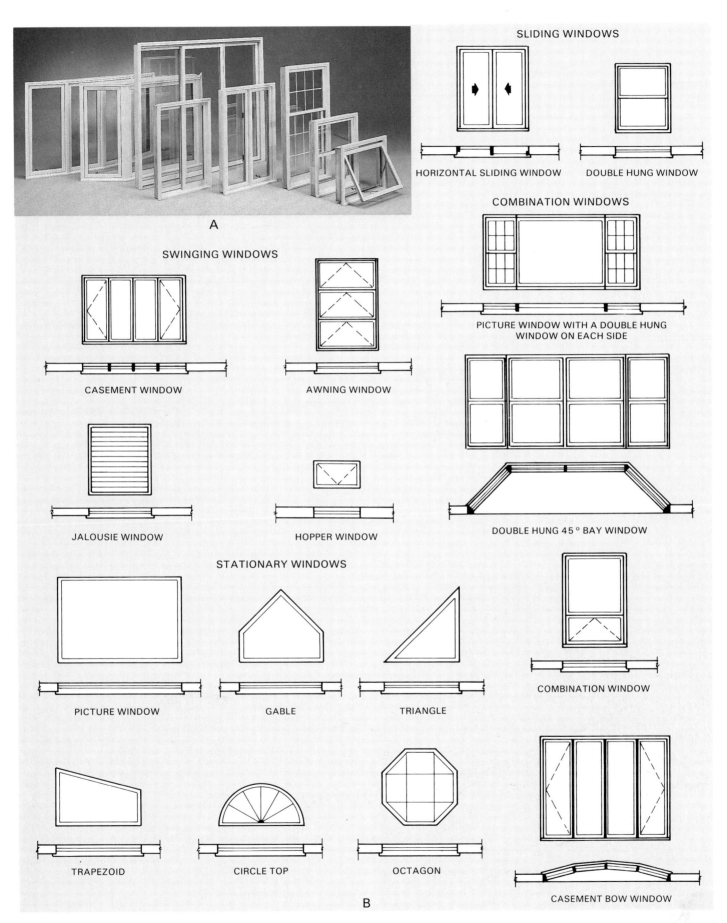

SLIDING WINDOWS

HORIZONTAL SLIDING WINDOW

DOUBLE HUNG WINDOW

COMBINATION WINDOWS

PICTURE WINDOW WITH A DOUBLE HUNG
WINDOW ON EACH SIDE

SWINGING WINDOWS

CASEMENT WINDOW

AWNING WINDOW

JALOUSIE WINDOW

HOPPER WINDOW

DOUBLE HUNG 45° BAY WINDOW

STATIONARY WINDOWS

PICTURE WINDOW

GABLE

TRIANGLE

COMBINATION WINDOW

TRAPEZOID

CIRCLE TOP

OCTAGON

CASEMENT BOW WINDOW

A

B

Fig. 13-27. A—Typical windows used in residential construction. Most are available primed ready to paint or as vinyl clad for maintenance-free beauty. (Caradco) B—Exterior and plan views of windows frequently used in residential construction.

Doors and Windows 233

A uniform amount of light across a room is desirable. Proper design and placement of windows will help to eliminate dark corners and extremely bright areas. The following guidelines will help achieve a more evenly lighted room:

1. Glass area should be at least 20 percent of the floor area of the room. This amount of glass will provide an adequate amount of natural light even on cloudy days. When the light outside is very bright, the intensity may be controlled with shades or draperies.

2. For increased light, face principle window areas toward the south. More light also means more heat, therefore, in warm climates a northerly orientation may be preferred.

3. One large window opening will produce less contrast in brightness than several smaller openings.

4. Better distribution of light will be accomplished if windows are placed on more than one wall.

5. Windows placed high on a wall will provide a greater degree of light penetration into the room than windows placed low.

6. Select the window shape which gives the type of light distribution desired in the room. Tall, narrow windows tend to give a thin and deep penetration while short, wide windows produce a shallow penetration over a broad area.

Natural ventilation in a home is necessary all year long, but is especially important during the summer months. If windows are located with adequate ventilation in mind, comfort will be increased considerably. Apply these guidelines for efficient ventilation:

1. Openings for ventilation should be at least 10 percent of the floor area.

2. Placement of openings for ventilation should take advantage of prevailing breezes.

3. Locate windows in such a way that the best movement of air across the room will be achieved. Furniture should be planned so it will not interfere with the flow of air through the room.

Windows may often be used to enhance an existing view or provide a selective one. Large glass areas tend to make a room look larger. The size and shape of the windows will frame the view so it is important to select a window of the proper proportions . . . one which does not have obstructions which interfere with the view.

The following points will aid the designer in specifying the proper window for a particular view:

1. A large area of fixed glass provides clear viewing without obstructions.

2. Horizontal and vertical divisions in the window or between windows should be thin to minimize obstruction.

3. Sill heights of windows should be determined on the basis of furniture, room arrangement, and view.

Designing a home to be functional, efficient, and pleasing to the eye on the exterior is no small task. Some of the guidelines provided may conflict. A home which has been designed for light, view, and ventilation may not have a pleasing exterior appearance. The challenge is to meet all the requirements of good design in a creative

The placement and number of windows affect the overall design appearance of the home. Even though windows should be selected to fulfill interior needs, the size, placement, and type may be varied slightly to improve the outside appearance of the home. Windows can add to the continuity of the design. They should relate to the solid wall areas rather than appear to be just a variety of openings in a wall, Fig. 13-26.

WINDOW TYPES

Many types of windows are available for residential construction, Fig. 13-27. Most types have unique proportions and may be constructed differently, depending on the material (wood, metal, or plastic). Windows of the same general type, purchased from different manufacturers, will seldom be exactly the same. For these rea-

Fig. 13-28. This style of double-hung window is reminiscent of the Victorian era. (Weather Shield Mfg., Inc.)

WINDOW UNIT SIZES

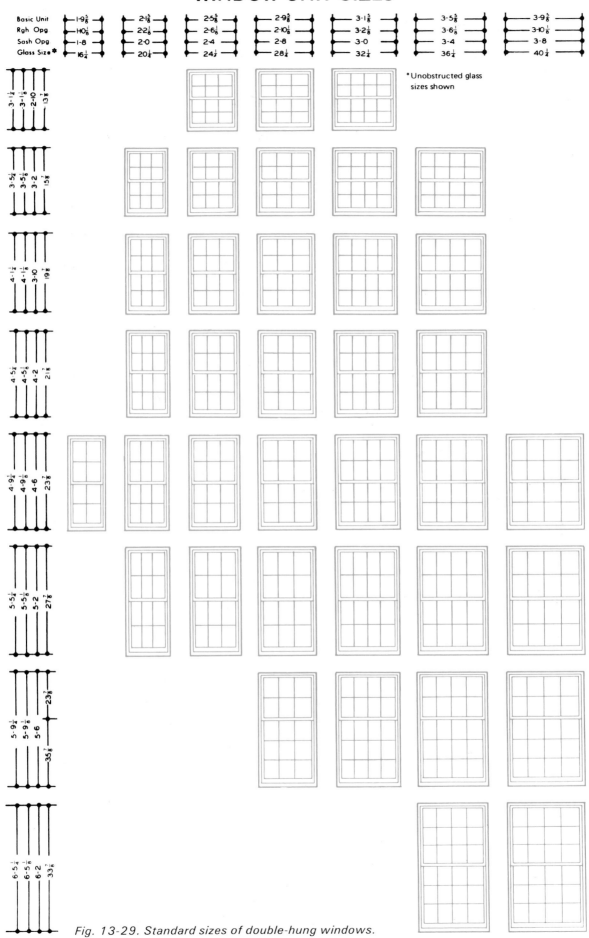

*Unobstructed glass sizes shown

Fig. 13-29. Standard sizes of double-hung windows.

sons, it is very important to obtain window specifications from the manufacturer.

Three basic types of windows are typically used in residential construction: *sliding windows, swinging windows,* and *fixed windows.* A fourth category — *combination windows* — is possible using two or more types of windows to form a unit. Windows placed in a location other than a typical wall account for a fifth category. These windows include *skylights, sky windows,* and *clerestory windows.* The specific window selected for a given application will depend on:

• The function(s) to be performed.
• Architectural style of the structure.
• Construction considerations.
• Building codes.
• Personal taste.

Sliding windows

The most common types of sliding windows include *double-hung* and *horizontal sliding windows.*

Double-hung windows. Double-hung windows have two sashes, Fig. 13-28. The sashes slide up and down in grooves formed in the window frames. The weight of the sashes are usually counterbalanced or have friction devices which hold them in the desired positions.

Muntins are small vertical and horizontal bars which separate the total glass area into smaller units. *Mullions,* not to be confused with muntins, are larger horizontal or vertical members which are placed between window units.

Fig. 13-29 gives the sizes of double-hung windows produced by one manufacturer. Note that four different sizes are given for each window. The *basic unit* size represents the overall dimen-

Fig. 13-31. Cut-away of vinyl clad sliding window with insulated glass. (Caradco)

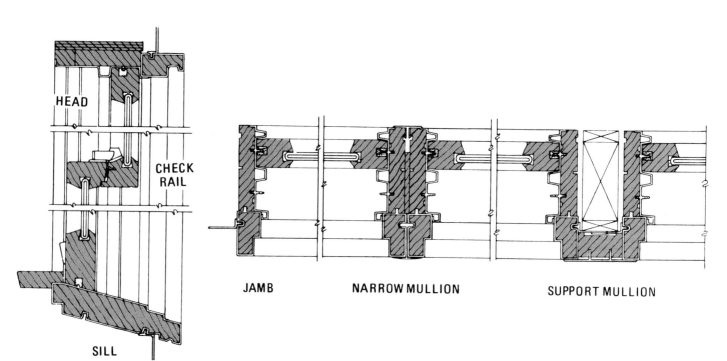

Fig. 13-30. Double-hung window details for a vinyl clad wood window.

SIZES AND LAYOUTS

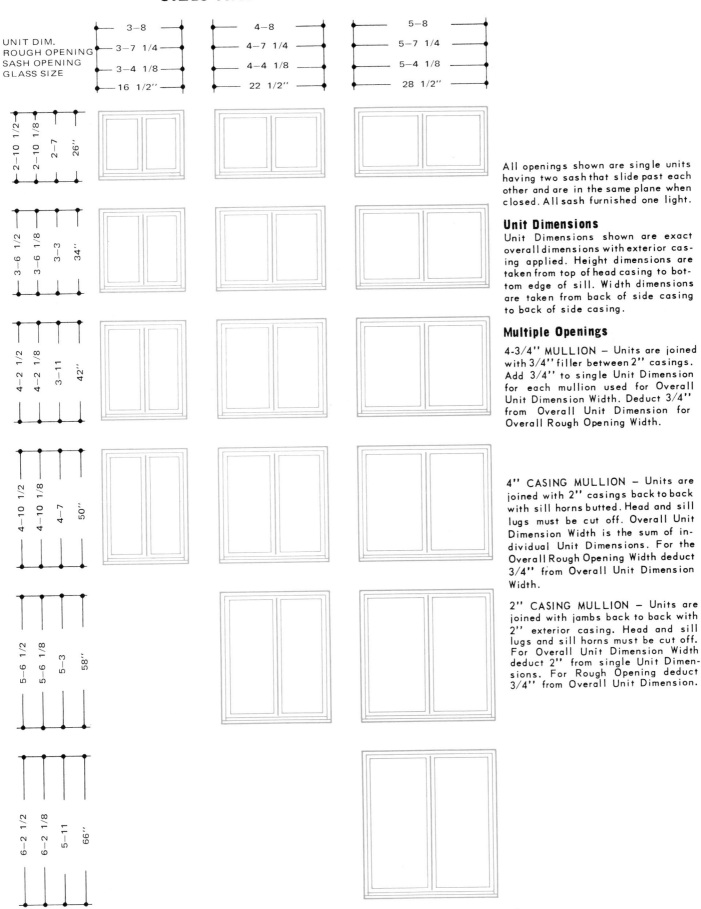

All openings shown are single units having two sash that slide past each other and are in the same plane when closed. All sash furnished one light.

Unit Dimensions

Unit Dimensions shown are exact overall dimensions with exterior casing applied. Height dimensions are taken from top of head casing to bottom edge of sill. Width dimensions are taken from back of side casing to back of side casing.

Multiple Openings

4-3/4" MULLION — Units are joined with 3/4" filler between 2" casings. Add 3/4" to single Unit Dimension for each mullion used for Overall Unit Dimension Width. Deduct 3/4" from Overall Unit Dimension for Overall Rough Opening Width.

4" CASING MULLION — Units are joined with 2" casings back to back with sill horns butted. Head and sill lugs must be cut off. Overall Unit Dimension Width is the sum of individual Unit Dimensions. For the Overall Rough Opening Width deduct 3/4" from Overall Unit Dimension Width.

2" CASING MULLION — Units are joined with jambs back to back with 2" exterior casing. Head and sill lugs and sill horns must be cut off. For Overall Unit Dimension Width deduct 2" from single Unit Dimensions. For Rough Opening deduct 3/4" from Overall Unit Dimension.

Fig. 13-32. Sizes of horizontal sliding windows.

sions of the window unit. The **_rough opening_** size is the rough framed space in a wall required to install the window. **_Sash opening_** refers to the size of the opening inside the frame or outside dimensions of the sash. **_Glass size_** is the unobstructed glass size. This would be the same as the inside dimensions of the sash.

Double-hung window details are presented in Fig. 13-30. Sections are traditionally drawn at the head jamb, side jamb, and sill, in a similar fashion as drawing doors. When a number of windows are placed together to form a unit it is often necessary to draw a section of the support mullion also.

Horizontal Sliding or Glider Windows. Horizontal sliding windows ordinarily have two sashes, Fig. 13-31. In some models both sashes are movable; in others, one sash is fixed. A track attached to the head jamb and sill provides for movement. Rollers are usually not required for windows unless they are quite large. Fig. 13-32 gives the standard sizes of one brand of horizontal sliding windows. Construction details are presented in Fig. 13-33.

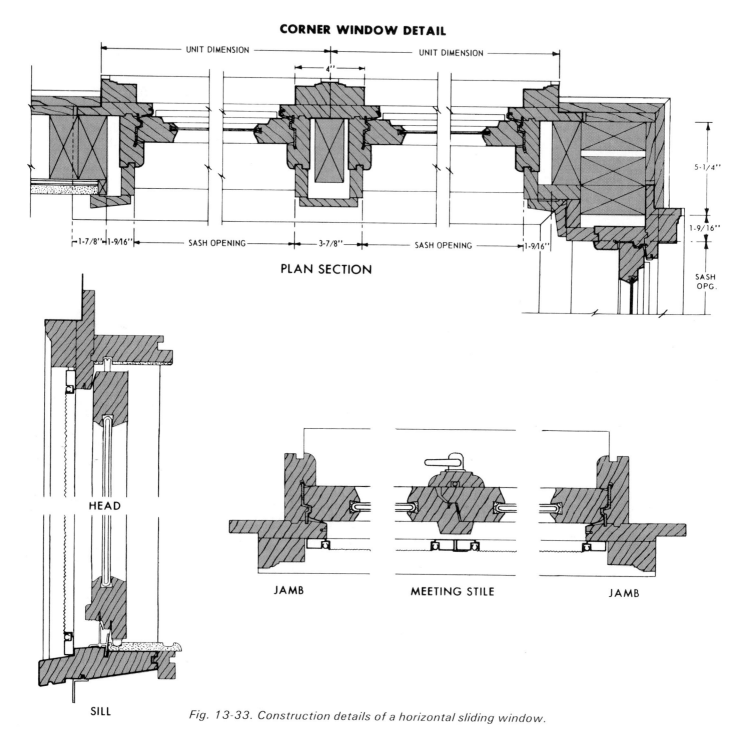

CORNER WINDOW DETAIL

PLAN SECTION

HEAD

SILL

JAMB   MEETING STILE   JAMB

Fig. 13-33. Construction details of a horizontal sliding window.

Fig. 13-34. Modern casement windows provide ample ventilation and natural light.
(Andersen Corporation)

Swinging windows

The most common types of swinging windows used in residential construction include: *casement, awning, hopper,* and *jalousie windows.*

Casement windows. A casement window has sashes hinged at the side which swing outward, Fig. 13-34. A single window unit may have several sashes separated by vertical mullions or a single sash.

A casement window may be opened or closed by using a crank, a push-bar on the frame, or a handle on the sash. See Fig. 13-35.

Casement windows are produced in a wide variety of sizes, Fig. 13-36. Single units may be placed together to form a larger section. Fig. 13-37 shows the construction details for one type of casement window.

Hinge position on a hinged window may be shown in the exterior elevation view by using a

Fig. 13-35. Casement windows operated with hand crank.
(Marvin Windows)

dashed line as shown in Fig. 13-38. It is usually advisable to indicate the direction of swing.

Awning windows. An awning window may have several sashes or only a single sash. Each sash is hinged at the top and swings out at an angle like an ''awning,'' Fig. 13-39.

Crank-operated awning windows are manufactured in a wide variety of sizes. The head, jamb, sill, and *transom bar* (horizontal divider) details are shown in Fig. 13-40 for the awning crank-type window. Fig. 13-41 shows some of the standard sizes offered by one company.

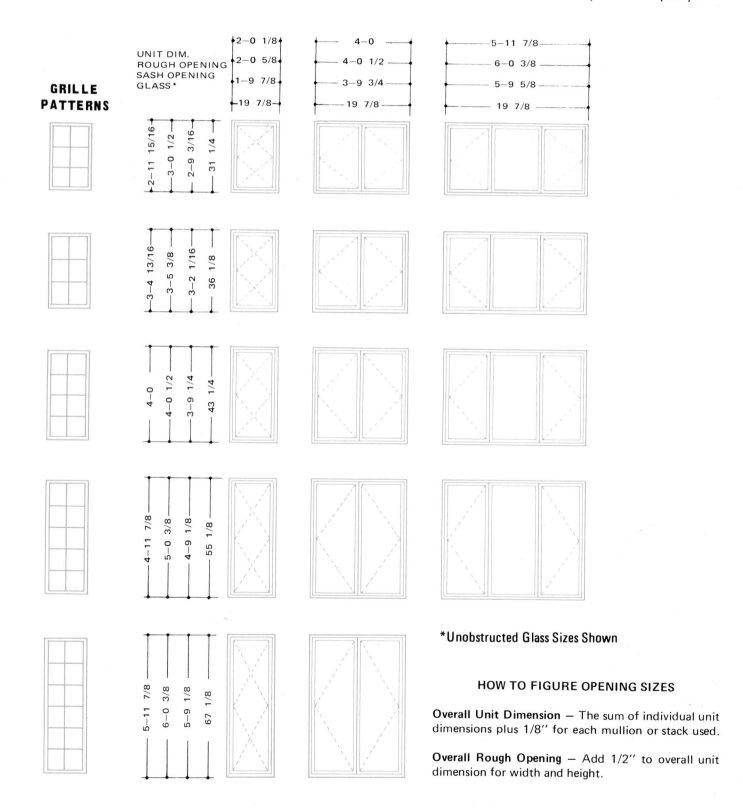

*Unobstructed Glass Sizes Shown

HOW TO FIGURE OPENING SIZES

Overall Unit Dimension — The sum of individual unit dimensions plus 1/8'' for each mullion or stack used.

Overall Rough Opening — Add 1/2'' to overall unit dimension for width and height.

Fig. 13-36. Standard casement window sizes.

Hopper windows. The hopper window is usually an in-swinging window. It is hinged at the bottom and is opened by a lock-handle at the top of the sash. It is usually manufactured only as a single unit, Fig. 13-42. Hopper windows are popular for basement use.

Fig. 13-39. This is an excellent location for an awning window. (Caradco)

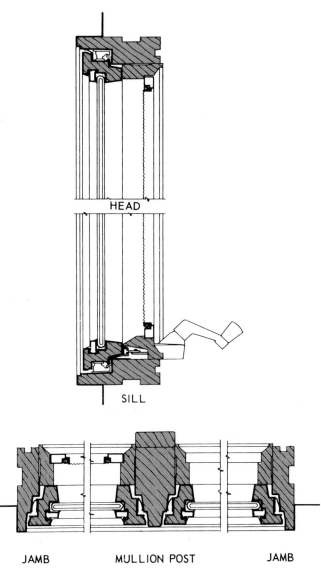

Fig. 13-37. Casement window details.

Fig. 13-38. A dashed line symbol may be used to indicate hinged side of windows as shown above.

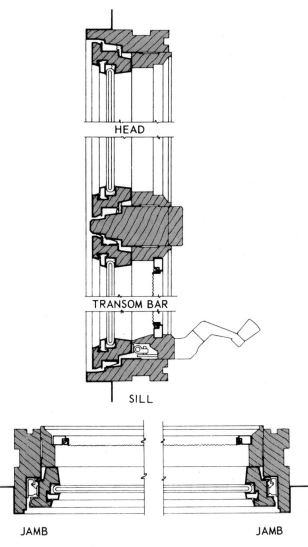

Fig. 13-40. Awning window details.

GRILLE PATTERNS

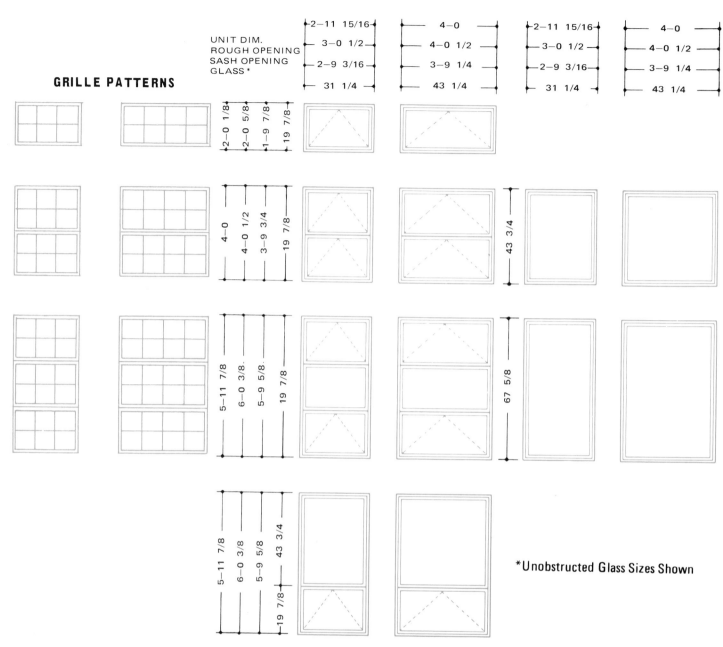

UNIT DIM.
ROUGH OPENING
SASH OPENING
GLASS *

Fig. 13-41. Standard awning window sizes.

*Unobstructed Glass Sizes Shown

Fig. 13-42. Wood hopper windows are popular for basement applications. (Andersen Corporation)

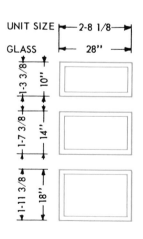

Fig. 13-43. Hopper window sizes.

Hopper windows direct air upward and should be placed low on the wall for best ventilation. They are easy to open and wash from the inside. The major disadvantage is that they swing inward. This interferes with the use of space in front of the window.

Hopper windows are produced in a relatively small number of sizes. Fig. 13-43 shows the sizes available from one company. Section details are shown in Fig. 13-44 for frame wall construction. Fig. 13-45 shows a section detail through a hopper window in a concrete block wall. This detail shows a typical basement installation.

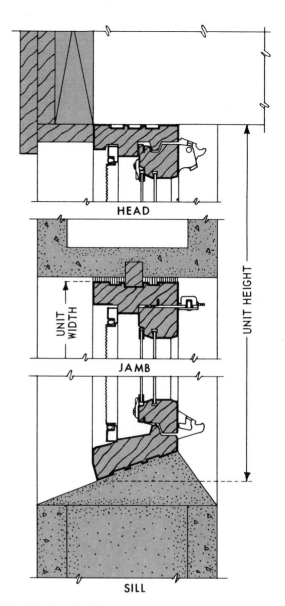

Fig. 13-45. A typical hopper window installation in a concrete block wall.

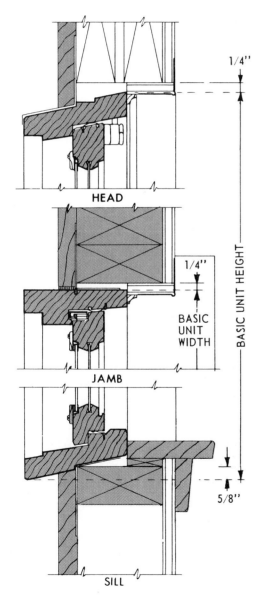

Single frame wall construction with dry wall interior returned into jambs. Note position of unit in wall.

Fig. 13-44. Details of hopper window used in frame wall construction.

Jalousie windows. A jalousie window has a series of narrow horizontal glass slats (usually 3'' wide in residential windows), which are held in metal clips and fastened to an aluminum frame. The slats operate in unison similar to Venetian blinds.

Jalousie windows are produced in a variety of sizes. Widths range from 18'' to 48'' in increments of 2 inches. Lengths are available from 17'' to 99 1/2'' in increments of 2 1/2 inches. Louver lengths are usually 2'' shorter than the window width (buck size). Head, jamb, sill, and mullion details for an aluminum jalousie window are shown in Fig. 13-46.

Fixed windows

The purpose of fixed windows is to provide a view and/or admit light. They do not permit

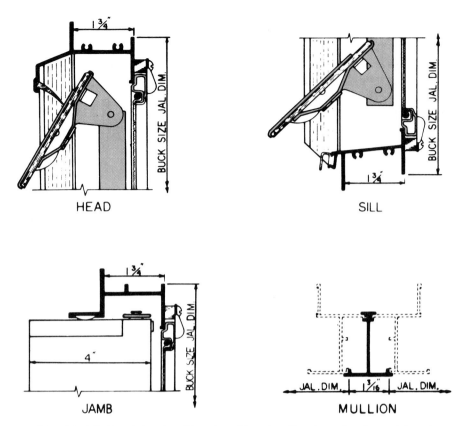

Fig. 13-46. Head, jamb, sill and mullion details of an aluminum jalousie window.

Fig. 13-47. This attractive picture window consists of a fixed glass section in the center and double-hung units on either side. They provide natural light to the dining room and a pleasant view of the outside. (Pella/Rolscreen Company)

ventilation. Fixed windows are more likely to be custom made and, therefore, may be sized for a specific application. Since they do not open, weather stripping, hardware, and screens are not required. Examples of fixed windows include *picture windows, circle top windows,* and *random shapes.*

Picture windows. The term ''picture window'' is used because the view is ''framed'' like a picture. Picture windows are fixed-glass units and are usually rather large. They are often the center unit of a group of regular windows. See Fig. 13-47.

Picture windows may be purchased in fixed sizes or custom-made on the job. Fig. 13-48 gives the standard sizes of picture window units produced by one manufacturer. Fig. 13-49 illustrates the construction details of a manufactured picture window.

Circle top windows. Circle top windows can be installed as single units, Fig. 13-50, or joined to other types of windows, Fig. 13-51. Circle

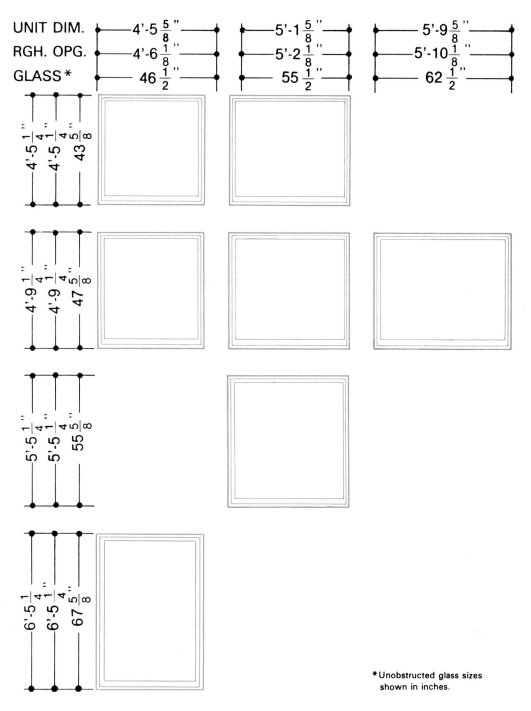

*Unobstructed glass sizes shown in inches.

Fig. 13-48. Standard picture window sizes in sash units.

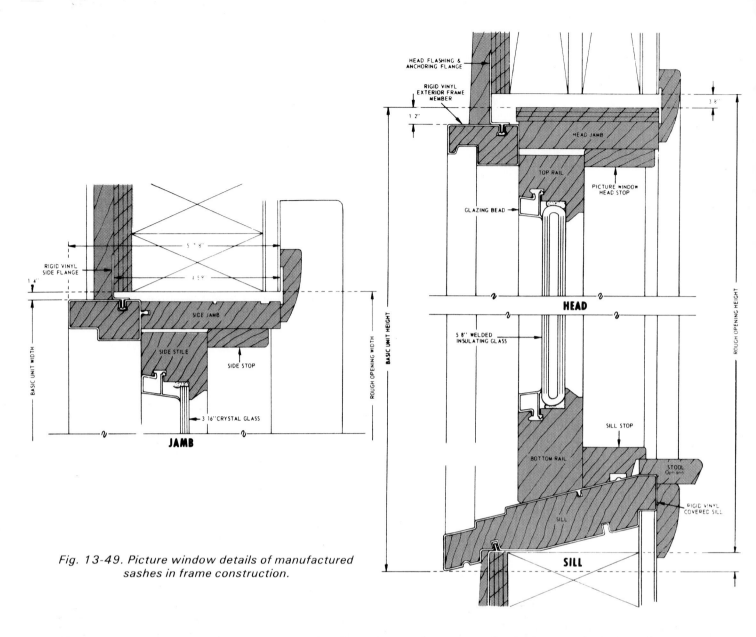

Fig. 13-49. Picture window details of manufactured sashes in frame construction.

Fig. 13-50. A circle top window and casement window in a single unit. (Andersen Window Corporation)

Fig. 13-51. Circle top windows used in combination with a door and double-hung windows. (Peachtree Doors, Inc.)

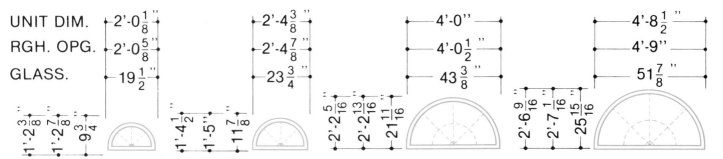

UNIT DIM.	2'-0$\frac{1}{8}$"	2'-4$\frac{3}{8}$"	4'-0"	4'-8$\frac{1}{2}$"
RGH. OPG.	2'-0$\frac{5}{8}$"	2'-4$\frac{7}{8}$"	4'-0$\frac{1}{2}$"	4'-9"
GLASS.	19$\frac{1}{2}$	23$\frac{3}{4}$	43$\frac{3}{8}$	51$\frac{7}{8}$

1'-2$\frac{3}{8}$" 1'-2$\frac{7}{8}$" 9$\frac{3}{4}$"

1'-4$\frac{1}{2}$" 1'-5$\frac{7}{8}$" 11$\frac{7}{8}$"

2'-2$\frac{5}{16}$" 2'-2$\frac{13}{16}$" 21$\frac{11}{16}$"

2'-6$\frac{9}{16}$" 2'-7$\frac{1}{16}$" 25$\frac{15}{16}$"

Fig. 13-52. Typical standard sizes of circle top windows.

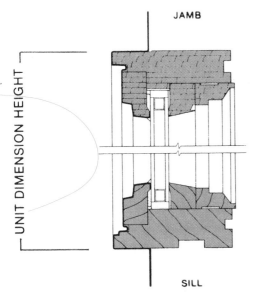

Fig. 13-53. Jamb and sill detail of a circle top window.

tops are available in quarter circles, half circles, ellipses, or full circles. Fig. 13-52 shows the standard sizes produced by one manufacturer. A typical construction detail of a manufactured circle top window is shown in Fig. 13-53.

Special-shape windows. Special-shape windows provide a wide range of interesting design options that can be used to individualize residential structures, Fig. 13-54. These units are fixed windows in made-to-order shapes and sizes, Fig. 13-55. If produced by the same manufacturer as other windows in the house, they may be combined with most any standard window to create a dramatic effect. Fig. 13-56 shows some of the most popular special-shape windows.

Combination windows

Combination windows are a mixture of two or more types of windows. The most popular types

A

B

Fig. 13-54. A—The unique shapes of these windows enhance the design of this modern structure. (California Redwood Association) B—The triangular windows in this gable add visual height to an airy room. (Georgia-Pacific Corporation)

include *bay windows, bow windows,* and picture windows combined with swinging or sliding windows.

Bay and bow windows. Bay and bow windows are combination windows that project out from the structure. They may be constructed using most any kind of windows including double-hung, casement, and fixed panels. Bay windows are frequently used in traditional-styled homes,

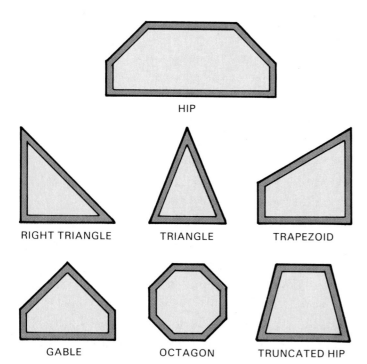

Fig. 13-55. This unique custom window adds an individual touch. (Weather Shield Mfg., Inc.)

HIP

RIGHT TRIANGLE   TRIANGLE   TRAPEZOID

GABLE   OCTAGON   TRUNCATED HIP

Fig. 13-56. Popular special shaped windows available from several manufacturers.

Fig. 13-57. Bay windows generally use two double-hung windows with a fixed window in the center. The side windows are normally placed at 45 degrees to the exterior wall. A typical 45 degree bay window detail is shown in Fig. 13-58. A newer design of the bay window called

A

B

Fig. 13-57. A—This bay window adds a touch of traditional styling. (Andersen Corporation) B—A unique bay window especially suited for this location. (Marvin Windows)

45° ANGLE BAY DETAILS

Metal or wood support brackets must be used below angle bay units.

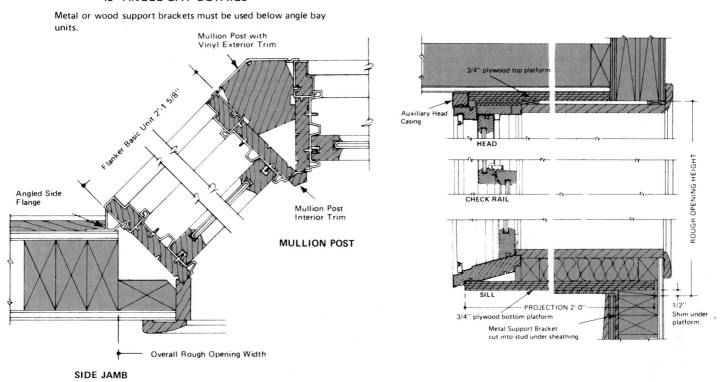

Fig. 13-58. Details of a typical 45 degree bay window.

the **box bay,** is shown in Fig. 13-59. It combines a picture window with two casement windows placed at 90 degrees to the wall.

Box windows are usually constructed with casement windows. Combinations of four to seven units are common, Fig. 13-60. Bow windows form an arc that extends beyond the out-

side wall. Fig. 13-61 shows a typical plan view for several bow windows using casements.

Skylights and clerestory windows

Skylights and clerestory windows are generally used to admit light into areas of the structure that receive little or no natural light. Skylights

Fig. 13-59. A typical "box bay" window provides an excellent location for plants. (Andersen Corporation)

Fig. 13-60. This large bow window provides a panoramic view. (Andersen Corporation)

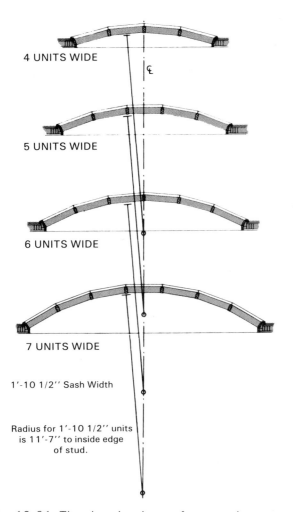

4 UNITS WIDE

5 UNITS WIDE

6 UNITS WIDE

7 UNITS WIDE

1'-10 1/2'' Sash Width

Radius for 1'-10 1/2'' units
is 11'-7'' to inside edge
of stud.

Fig. 13-61. The plan view layout for several casement
bow windows.

are located on the roof while clerestory windows are placed high on a wall, Fig. 13-62. The use of these windows, especially clerestory windows, can produce pleasing architectural effects. Some skylights and clerestory windows may open for ventilation.

Skylights are available in several basic sizes and shapes. The most common shape is rectangular and designed to fit between the roof trusses, Fig. 13-63. Custom-made skylights are possible to meet most any design situation, Fig. 13-64. Clerestory windows may be custom-made fixed windows or a series of standard windows, Fig. 13-65.

Fig. 13-63. This rectangular skylight is designed to fit between the roof trusses. (Pella/Rolscreen Company)

Fig. 13-62. A unique application of clerestory windows and skylights. (Pella/Rolscreen Company)

Fig. 13-64. This custom skylight provides an interesting accent to the ceiling. (California Redwood Association)

Fig. 13-65. Clerestory windows are placed as a series of standard windows.

Window Schedules

A *window schedule* provides pertinent information about the windows in a structure such as type of window, size, identifying symbol, manufacturer's number, and installation.

The window schedule may be placed on the same sheet as the floor plan or elevation if space permits. Otherwise, it may be located on one of the other drawings.

Care must be taken to ensure that all windows are listed on the schedule and are properly

WINDOW SCHEDULE						
SYM.	QUAN.	TYPE	ROUGH OPENING	SASH SIZE	MANUFACTURE NO.	REMARKS
A	6	CASEMENT	3'-6 1/8'' x 5'-1''	3'-2 1/4'' x 4'-9 1/4''	3N3	PRIMED, SCREENS, INSULATING GLASS
B	1	CASEMENT	3'-6 1/8'' x 3'-3 1/4''	3'-2 1/4'' x 3'-1 1/2''	2N3	PRIMED, SCREENS, INSULATING GLASS
C	1	CASEMENT	5'-6 1/2'' x 8'-4 1/2''	5'-2 5/8'' x 8'-1''	5N5	PRIMED, SCREENS, INSULATING GLASS
D	1	CASEMENT	2'-5 7/8'' x 3'-5 1/4''	2'-2'' x 3'-1 3/4''	2N2	PRIMED, SCREENS, INSULATING GLASS
E	5	HOPPER	1'-8'' x 5'-5''	1'-4'' x 5'-2''	314	EXTERIOR CASING OR SUBSILL NOT INCLUDED
F	2	FIXED	2'-4'' x 6'-9 1/4''	SEE REMARKS	CUSTOM	GLASS SIZE − 2'-0'' x 6'-8'', INSUL.

Fig. 13-66. A typical window schedule layout which includes spaces for information required.

identified. A sample window schedule is shown in Fig. 13-66.

REVIEW QUESTIONS—CHAPTER 13

Write your answers on a separate sheet of paper. Do not write in this book.
1. List five functions of doors and windows.
2. Name eight types of interior doors.
3. Interior flush doors are usually _____ in. thick.
4. The horizontal members in panel doors are called _____ and vertical members are called _____.
5. The main use of bi-fold doors in residential construction is _____.
6. Standard height for most interior and exterior doors is _____.
7. A door that hangs from a track mounted on the head jamb, and slides into the wall when open, is a _____ door.
8. A door that swings through a 180 degree arc is called a _____ door.
9. Name two ways in which exterior doors are different from interior doors.
10. Exterior doors are usually _____ wide.
11. What two types of garage doors are most common?
12. Door details are usually section drawings cut through the _____, _____, and _____.
13. What is the function of a drip cap?
14. Glass area should be at least _____ percent of the floor area of any room.
15. Name one type of window which does not provide ventilation.
16. Name eight different types of windows.
17. The small vertical and horizontal bars which separate the total glass area into smaller units are called _____.
18. What does the ''rough opening'' size of a window represent?
19. What type of window is hinged at the side and swings out?
20. A window that is commonly used in basements is the _____ window.
21. Information about windows shown in the architectural drawings is recorded on a _____ schedule.

SUGGESTED ACTIVITIES

1. Make a list of the types and sizes of doors and windows in your home.
2. Build a scale model of an exterior or interior door, jambs, and rough framing. Present the model with plan, elevation, and section drawings for display.
3. Select a floor plan for a small- to medium-size house and plan the windows following the guidelines presented for ventilation, light, and view. Record the information on a window schedule.
4. Visit a local lumber company and examine the cut-away models of the windows they handle. Measure the various parts of one model and prepare a sketch. Identify the type of window and the manufacturer. Collect any specification data about the windows that you can and bring it to class for reference purposes.

14
CHAPTER
Stairs

After studying this chapter, you will be able to:
- Define common stair terminology.
- Discuss the appropriate use of the various stair designs.
- Design a stairway for a residential structure.
- Draw structural details for a main stairs.
- Perform stair calculations for a residential stairway.

A **stairway** is a series of steps with or without landings or platforms which is installed between two or more floors of a building. Stairways provide easy access to various levels of the home. All styles of homes, except the ranch with no basement, have stairs. Prime considerations in stair design should be easy ascent or descent and safety.

A house may have a **main stairs** (from the first floor to the second floor or from a split foyer to the first floor) and/or a **service stairs.** The main stairs, Fig. 14-1, are usually assembled with prefabricated parts and are of a much better quality generally than are the service stairs. They are generally made of hardwoods such as oak, maple, or birch. Service stairs are frequently constructed on location and are ordinarily made of Douglas fir or pine (construction lumber).

TYPES OF STAIRS

Six general types of stairs are commonly used in residential construction. They are **straight run stairs, L stairs, double-L stairs, U stairs, winder**

Fig. 14-1. This beautiful main stairway is visible from the entrance and constructed with quality materials. (Arcways, Incorporated)

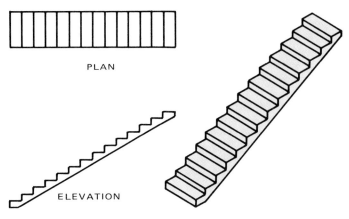

Fig. 14-2. Straight run stairs.

stairs, and *spiral stairs. Circular stairs* are also available for very large expensive homes.

Straight run stairs, Fig. 14-2, are the stairs used most in home construction. Straight stairs, as the name implies, have no turns. These stairs are not as expensive to construct as other types of stairs, but require a long open space which may be difficult to accommodate in the floor plan.

L stairs have one landing at some point along the flight of steps, Fig. 14-3. If the landing is near the top or bottom of the stairs, the term **long L** is used to describe the difference, Fig. 14-4. L stairs are used when the space required for a straight run stairs is not available.

Double-L stairs, Fig. 14-5, require two 90° turns along the flight. They may be used when space is not available for either the straight or L stairs. Double-L stairs are not frequently used in residential construction. They are expensive to build and break up the floor plan.

U stairs may be constructed either as **wide U** or **narrow U** stairs. Both have two flights of steps parallel to each other with a landing between, Fig. 14-6. The difference between wide and narrow U stairs is the space between the

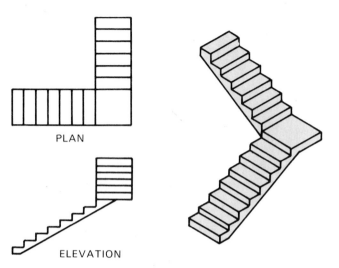

Fig. 14-3. L stairs.

Fig. 14-4. These long L stairs were designed specifically for this home. Notice that the stairs complement the design of adjacent areas. (Morgan Products, Ltd.)

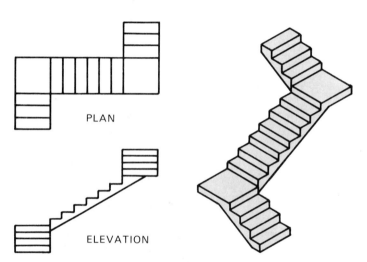

Fig 14-5. Double-L stairs.

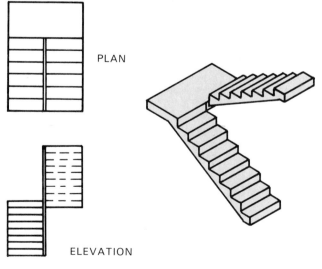

Fig. 14-6. U stairs.

two flights. Narrow U stairs have little or no space between the flights, Fig. 14-7, while wide U stairs have a well hole between.

Winder stairs have ''pie-shaped'' steps which are substituted for a landing, Fig. 14-8. This type of stairs is used when the space is not sufficient for the L stairs. If winder stairs are used, the width of the triangular steps should be sufficient at midpoint to provide a tread width equal to the regular steps. For instance, if the regular tread width is 10 in., then the winder step should also be 10 in. at its midpoint. Winder stairs are not as safe as other types and should be avoided whenever possible.

Spiral stairs are gaining in popularity and the components are now manufactured by several companies, Fig. 14-9. They may be used where little space is available, Fig. 14-10. Most spiral

Fig. 14-9. Spiral stairs are constructed where space is limited. They may be the focal point of an area. These spiral stairs are made from prefabricated parts. (Arcways, Incorporated)

Fig. 14-7. The U stairs with open risers are attractive and functional. They are sturdy and will last for many years. (Western Wood Products Association.)

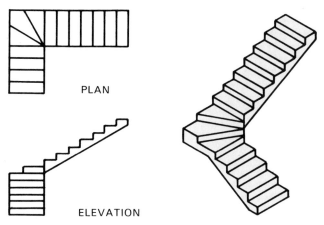

Fig. 14-8. Winder stairs.

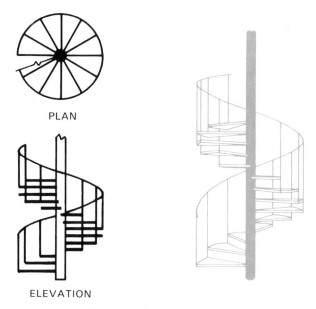

Fig. 14-10. Spiral stairs.

Fig. 14-11. Ample space is available for this circular stairway and a gracious home is the perfect setting. (Arcways, Incorporated)

stairs are made from steel and welded together, however, it is possible to construct them from modular wood components. Spiral stairs, as a rule, are not very safe since they generally have winder steps.

Circular stairs are custom-made, using trapezoid-shaped steps. An irregular curve or arc is the primary shape of the stairway. Many fine, large homes utilize these stairs, Fig. 14-11. Fig. 14-12 shows a plan view drawing of a typical circular stairs.

STAIR TERMINOLOGY

Several terms are associated with stairs which must be understood before considering design. The following list includes most of these terms:

- *Balusters:* vertical members that support the handrail on open stairs, Fig. 14-13.
- *Enclosed stairs:* stairs that have a wall on both sides (also known as *closed, housed,* or *box stairs*), Fig. 14-14.
- *Headroom:* the shortest clear vertical distance measured between the nosing of the treads and the ceiling, Fig. 14-15.
- *Housed stringer:* a stringer that has been routed or grooved to receive the treads and risers, Fig. 14-16.

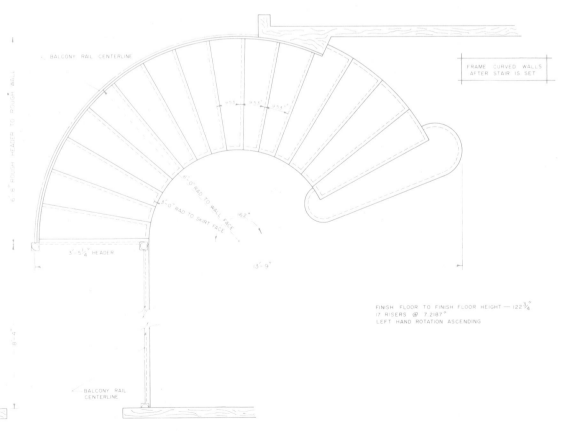

Fig. 14-12. Plan view drawing of typical circular stairs. (Arcways, Incorporated)

- **Landing:** the floor area at either end of the stairs and possibly at some point between, as in the case of an L stairs.
- **Newel:** the main posts of the handrail at the top, bottom, or at points where the stairs change direction. See Fig. 14-13.
- **Nosing:** the rounded projection of the tread which extends past the face of the riser, Fig. 14-17.

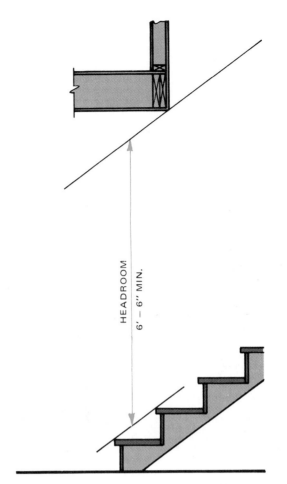

Fig. 14-15. Sufficient headroom is an important consideration in the design of stairs.

Fig. 14-13. A traditional-type open stairs with newel, handrail, and balusters identified. (Morgan Products, Ltd.)

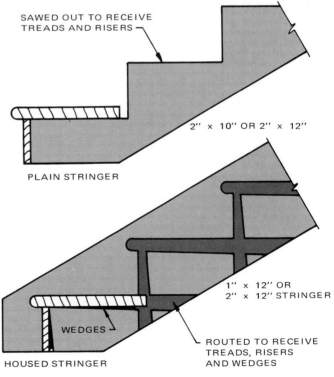

Fig. 14-16. The two most frequently used types of stringers are the plain and housed stringer.

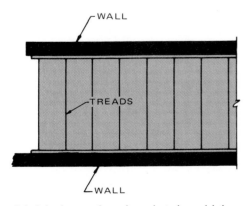

Fig. 14-14. A set of enclosed stairs which are built between two walls.

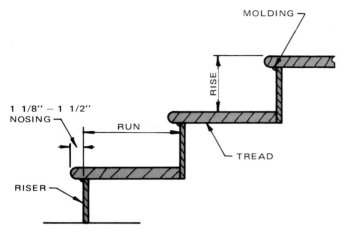

Fig. 14-17. Terms relating to treads and risers.

- **Open stairs:** stairs that have no wall on one or both sides. See Fig. 14-13.
- **Plain stringer:** a stringer that has been cut or notched to fit the profile of the stairs. See Fig. 14-16.
- **Rise:** the distance from the top surface of one tread to the same position on the next tread. See Fig. 14-17.
- **Riser:** the vertical face of a step, Fig. 14-17.
- **Run:** the distance from the face of one riser to the face of the next, Fig. 14-17.
- **Stringer:** a structural member, also called the **carriage,** which supports the treads and risers.
- **Total rise:** the total floor-to-floor vertical height of the stairs, Fig. 14-18.
- **Total run:** the total horizontal length of the stairs, Fig. 14-18.
- **Tread:** the horizontal member of each step. See Fig. 14-17.

STAIR DESIGN

A set of stairs which are properly designed and properly constructed will support the required weight, have width enough to provide ease of passage and movement of furniture, and slope between 30 and 35 degrees, Fig. 14-19.

Fig. 14-19. Beautiful traditional stairs which are properly designed and constructed. (Focal Point, Inc.)

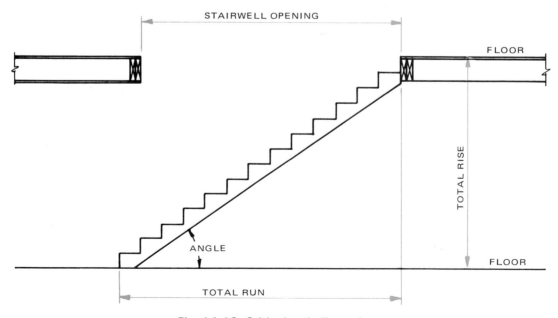

Fig. 14-18. Critical stair dimensions.

The main supporting members of the stairs are the *stringers.* Several types of stringers are used, but the *plain stringer* and *housed stringer* account for the majority. Fig. 14-16 shows these two types of stringers. Fig. 14-20 illustrates a type of stringer which is simple in design and appropriate for some types of construction. Usually two stringers are sufficient, however if the width of the stairs exceeds 3'-0'' a third stringer is required. (A main stairs should not be less than 3'-0''.) The extra stringer is placed midway between the outside stringers and under the treads and risers.

Fig. 14-20. The simple techniques used in this modern stairs complements the post and beam construction of the house. (Western Wood Products Association)

Plain stringers are generally cut from 2 x 12 straight-grain fir and the treads and risers are nailed directly to the stringers. This type of construction is used for service stairs and occasionally for main stairs if they are to be carpeted. Plain stringer stairs are sturdy, but they tend to squeak and do not have a finished appearance. The treads are usually 2 in. fir or other softwood and the risers 1 in. white pine.

Housed stringers are made from finished lumber and are generally purchased precut or preassembled. However, the stringers may be cut

from 1 x 12 or 2 x 12 lumber. One-half inch deep grooves are usually routed in the stringers to hold the treads and risers. The bottom and back sides of the grooves are wider than the thickness of the treads and risers so that wedges may be driven in to hold them in place. Fig. 14-21 illustrates how the wedges are inserted in the grooves. The treads, risers, and wedges are glued and nailed in place.

The two other primary parts of a set of stairs are the *treads* and *risers.* Standard treads are available in 1 1/4 in. oak in two widths — 10 1/2 in. and 11 1/2 in. Both widths are 1 1/16 in. thick (actual size). The nose which is rounded is not included in calculations. A tread width of 10 1/2 in. is the most popular choice. Risers are 3/4 in. thick actual size and vary in width depending on the slope of the stairs. The ideal riser height is between 7 and 7 5/8 in. Clear white pine is the customary riser material.

Several rules have been devised for calculating the rise-run (riser-tread) ratio. Four of these rules are:

Rule No. 1 The slope of the stairs (rise-run ratio) should be between 30 and 35 degrees.

Rule No. 2 The sum of two risers and one tread should equal 25 in.

Rule No. 3 The product of the riser height multiplied by the tread width should equal approximately 75 in.

Rule No. 4 The sum of one riser and one tread should equal 17 to 18 in.

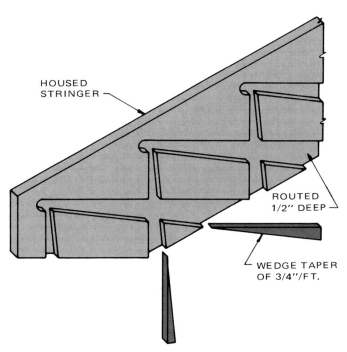

HOUSED STRINGER

ROUTED 1/2'' DEEP

WEDGE TAPER OF 3/4''/FT.

Fig. 14-21. A housed stringer showing how the wedges are positioned.

The first rule generally will not be applied for service stairs since they are ordinarily steeper than main stairs. However, if the treads are 10 in. wide, the riser should be between 5 3/4 in. and 7 in. to produce a 30-35 degree slope. A riser height of less than 7 in. is considered too short, therefore, a 7:10 ratio and 35° slope is acceptable.

If a 10 in. tread is used for each of the rules, these riser heights will be required:

	Tread Width	Riser Height	Approx. Angle
Rule No. 1	10 in.	7 in.	35 deg.
Rule No. 2	10 in.	7 1/2 in.	37 deg.
Rule No. 3	10 in.	7 1/2 in.	37 deg.
Rule No. 4	10 in.	7-8 in.	35-38 deg.

A riser height of 7 in. is the only example used which falls within the proper slope angle. The angle can be reduced by increasing the tread width. For example, if the tread width is 10 1/2 in. then the riser height would be 7 1/4 in using Rule No. 2. This combination would result in an angle slightly less than 35 degrees. A ratio of 7 1/4 in. to 10 1/2 in. is considered ideal.

A stairway must provide a handrail for support while ascending or descending the stairs. Unless the stairs are very wide, one rail is sufficient. Recommended height of the handrail is shown in Fig. 14-22. Note that the height is greater at a landing than along the incline.

STAIR CALCULATIONS AND DRAWING PROCEDURE

The following procedure may be used to determine the number and size of treads and risers for a set of stairs:

1. Determine the distance from finished floor to finished floor. This is the total rise of the stairs. The total rise is computed by adding the distance from finished lower floor to finished ceiling, plus the thickness of the ceiling material, plus the width of the floor joists, plus the thickness of the subfloor and finished floor. See the following examples:

Finished lower floor to finished ceiling	8' – 0 in.
Thickness of ceiling material (dry wall)	0 – 1/2 in.
Width of the floor joists	0 – 9 1/4 in.
Thickness of the subfloor (1/2" plywood)	0 – 1/2 in.
Thickness of the finished floor, subfloor, and underlayment	0 – 1 in.
Total rise =	8' – 11 1/4 in.

Since the size of each step is computed in inches, the total rise is converted to inches. Total rise = 107 1/4 in. Fig. 14-23 shows the first step in drawing stairs.

2. Determine how many risers will be required by first dividing the total rise by 7. The reason 7 is used is because 7 in. is an ideal riser height and it is therefore a logical place to start. When 107 1/4 in. is divided by 7 the result is 15.32 risers. The number of risers must be an exact number, so either 15 or 16 risers will be required. When 107 1/4 in. is divided by 15 a riser height of 7.15 in. is produced. This figure seems to be acceptable so further calculations will be based on it. Fig. 14-24 shows how the total rise is divided into 15 equal parts. *Each riser must be exactly the same height.*

3. Determine the tread size and total run which will yield a stair slope between 30 and 35

STEP 1

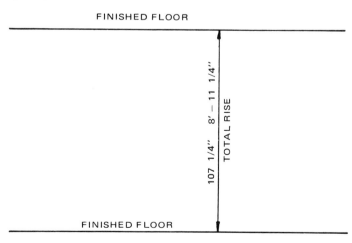

Fig. 14-23. Determine the total rise and lay out the finished floor lines.

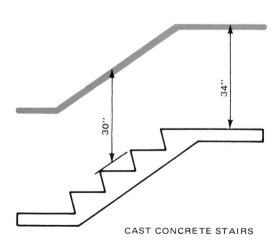

CAST CONCRETE STAIRS

Fig. 14-22. Recommended handrail heights for all stairs.

STEP 2

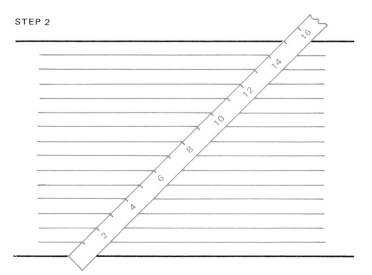

Fig. 14-24. Divide the total rise into the specified number of risers. The number of risers in this example is 15.

STEP 3

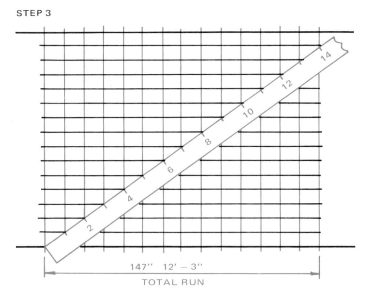

147" 12' — 3"

TOTAL RUN

Fig. 14-25. Lay out the total run and divide it into the number of tread widths required. In this case, 14.

degrees. It was determined earlier that a 10 1/2 in. tread was a commonly used width so it will be used for a trial calculation. *There is always one less tread than the number of risers.* This is because the floor serves as the top tread. Using Rule No. 2, the sum of two risers (7.15 in. + 7.15 in.) and one tread (10 1/2 in.) equals 24.80 in. This is very close to the required sum of 25 and indicates that this combination will be acceptable. For comparison Rules 3 and 4 will be applied. Rule No. 3 says that the product of the riser height and tread width should be approximately 75 in. Therefore if 7.15 is multiplied by 10.5 the produce is 75.1. This is acceptable. Rule No. 4 indicates that the sum of one riser and one tread should equal 17 to 18 in. If 7.15

is added to 10 1/2 the result is 17.65 in. This is within the required range. The tread width will be 10 1/2 in.

The total run is determined by multiplying the tread width (10 1/2 in.) by the number of treads (14). The product is 147 in. for the total run. Fig. 14-25 shows how the total run and tread widths are drawn.

4. Darken the tread and riser lines, draw the bottom edge of the stringer, and locate stairwell rough opening size. This dimension is a function of the headroom dimension. Minimum headroom is 6'-6''. Step 4 is shown in Fig. 14-26.

5. Remove all construction lines and add dimensions and notes, Fig. 14-27.

STEP 4

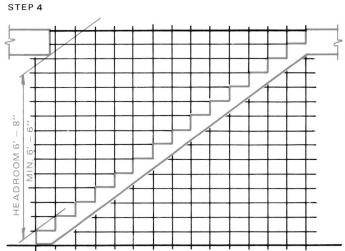

Fig. 14-26. Darken the treads and risers and indicate the stairwell rough opening.

STEP 5

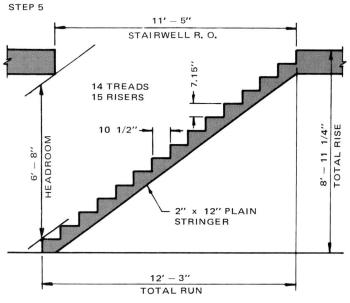

11' — 5"
STAIRWELL R. O.

14 TREADS
15 RISERS

7.15"

10 1/2"

6' — 8"
HEADROOM

2" x 12" PLAIN STRINGER

8' — 11 1/4"
TOTAL RISE

12' — 3"
TOTAL RUN

Fig. 14-27. Remove all construction lines and add dimensions and notes.

STRUCTURAL DETAILS

Procedures for building stairs vary widely from one part of the country to another. Local codes often specify restrictions. Carpenters have their own preferences which add to the variations. Regardless of the procedure followed, the construction techniques must be sound. Fig. 14-28 shows the rough framing for a plain stringer, open, straight run stairs. Ordinarily, this rough framing is not shown on a set of house plans, but a plan view and elevation with various section details are shown. Fig. 14-29 represents a typical stair detail drawing found in a set of residential plans.

REVIEW QUESTIONS—CHAPTER 14

Write your answers on a separate sheet of paper. Do not write in this book.
1. Stairs which connect the first and second floor are known as _____ stairs.
2. Identify the six general types of stairs.
3. Which type of stairs always has two landings along the flight of steps?
4. The type of stairs that has two parallel flights of steps is the _____ stairs.
5. ''Pie-shaped'' steps are generally associated with _____ stairs.
6. Vertical members which support the handrail on open stairs are known as _____.
7. Stairs which have a wall on both sides are known as _____ stairs.
8. Minimum headroom for stairs is _____.
9. The two main types of stringers used in home stair construction are _____ and _____ stringers.
10. The rounded projection of the tread which extends past the face of the riser is the _____.
11. A stair which has no wall on either side is a(n) _____ stair.
12. A stringer which has been cut or notched to match the profile of the stairs is a _____ stringer.
13. Define rise.
14. Define run.

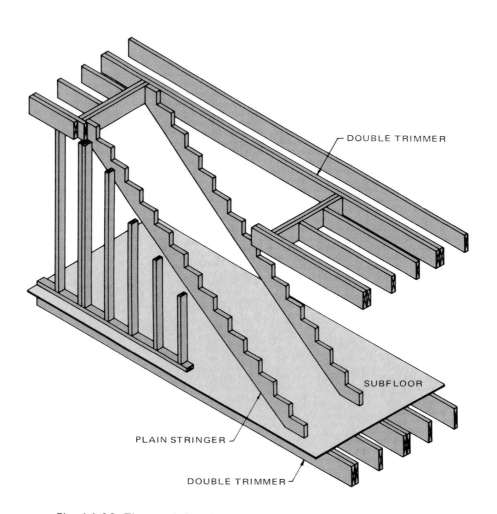

DOUBLE TRIMMER

SUBFLOOR

PLAIN STRINGER

DOUBLE TRIMMER

Fig. 14-28. The rough framing for a plain stringer straight run stairs.

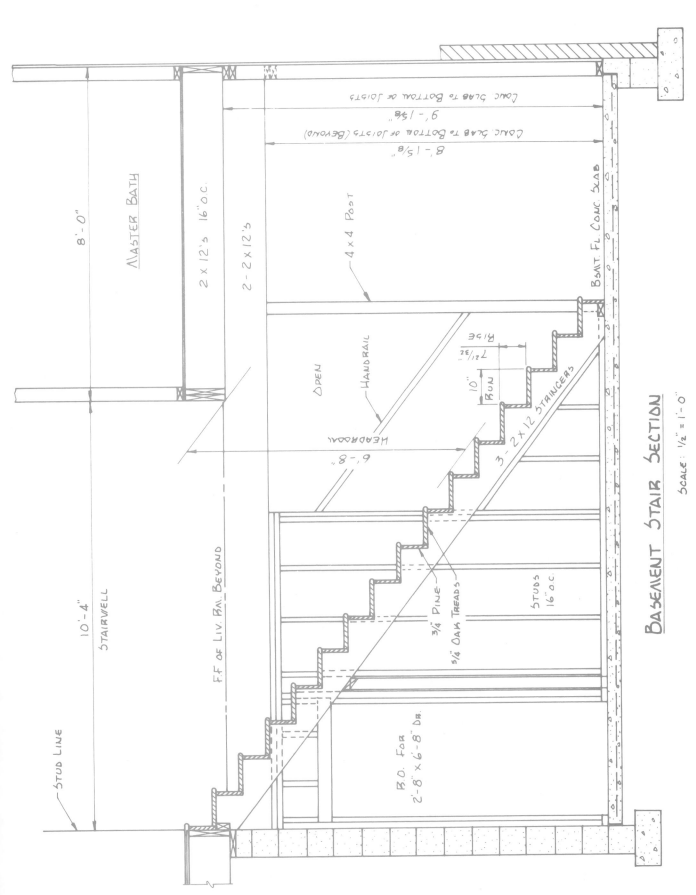

BASEMENT STAIR SECTION

SCALE: 1/2" = 1'-0"

Fig. 14-29. Typical stair detail which might be found on a set of residential drawings.

15. The total floor-to-floor vertical height of the stairs is known as the _____.
16. The total horizontal length of the stairs is the _____.
17. The proper slope angle for a set of main stairs should be between _____ and _____ degrees.
18. The minimum recommended width for main stairs is _____.
19. Treads on service stairs are frequently made from softwood, but main stair treads are usually _____.
20. The ideal tread-to-riser ratio is _____ to _____.

SUGGESTED ACTIVITIES

1. Locate as many different stair designs as you can. Measure the width of tread and riser height. Draw a profile of the tread and riser and measure the angle with a protractor. Identify the materials used and rate the stairs as to ease of travel and safety.

2. Locate a house in your community which is under construction and examine the stair framing. Measure the floor-to-floor distance and width of the stairs. If possible, interview the head carpenter and ask how a set of stairs is laid out. Report your findings to the class. Be sure to secure permission to enter the construction site.

3. Design a housed stringer, enclosed, straight run stairs for a house which has a finished floor-to-finished floor distance of 9'-1 1/4''. Distance between the finished walls is 3'-4''. Provide the necessary drawings, dimensions, and add notes.

4. Visit a local lumber company which sells precut stairs. Collect information and literature about these stairs. Bring this literature to class to help build a file on stairs.

5. Select a basic type of stairs and build a scale model as accurately as possible. Display this model along with drawing of the construction.

Fireplaces and Chimneys

After studying this chapter, you will be able to:
- Compare the various types of fireplaces appropriate for a modern residence.
- Identify the parts of a standard masonry fireplace and chimney.
- Apply the appropriate principles to design a typical fireplace.
- Use a fireplace design data chart.
- Recognize the difference between a radiant and circulating stove.

Most everyone enjoys the sound and warmth of a blazing fire. The fireplace is often a focal point in the living room or family room. In modern home planning it is an important design consideration, Fig. 15-1.

Many homes have fireplaces that are pleasing to the eye, but fail to operate properly. Care must be taken in the design and construction of a fireplace and chimney to make sure the fireplace will perform as desired.

FIREPLACE DESIGN CONSIDERATIONS

Several types of fireplaces are being constructed in modern residences. Some are traditional in design, Fig. 15-2, while others are

Fig. 15-2. This large, traditional fireplace is attractive and complements the decor of this living room.
(Portland Williamette Company)

Fig. 15-1. An attractive fireplace may be the focal point of a living room. (Heatilator, Inc.)

Fig. 15-3. The contemporary fireplace is appropriate for the setting. Note the brick hearth for fire protection and the log storage in the side wall. (Heatilator, Inc.)

contemporary, Fig. 15-3. Increasingly, metal fireplaces are finding their way into the home. Some of these are wood burning, but many are gas-fired, designed to look like a wood fire. Often fireplaces draw on the building materials for their charm, Fig. 15-4.

Generally, fireplaces may be identified as single face, two face opposite, two face adjacent, three face, or prefabricated metal fireplaces, Fig. 15-5. Each type has specific design requirements which must be met if the fireplace is to be safe and perform properly. (Design specifications are included later in this chapter.)

HEARTH AND FIRE CHAMBER

The function of the hearth is to protect the floor from sparks. It should extend at least 16 in. in front of the fireplace and be constructed from a noncombustible material. In conventional construction, the hearth extends beneath the fireplace to form an inner hearth, Fig. 15-6. It is usually covered with firebrick inside the fireplace, and stone, slate, or ceramic tile in front of

Fig. 15-4. This modern fireplace would be a welcome addition to most any room.
(Superior Fireplace Company)

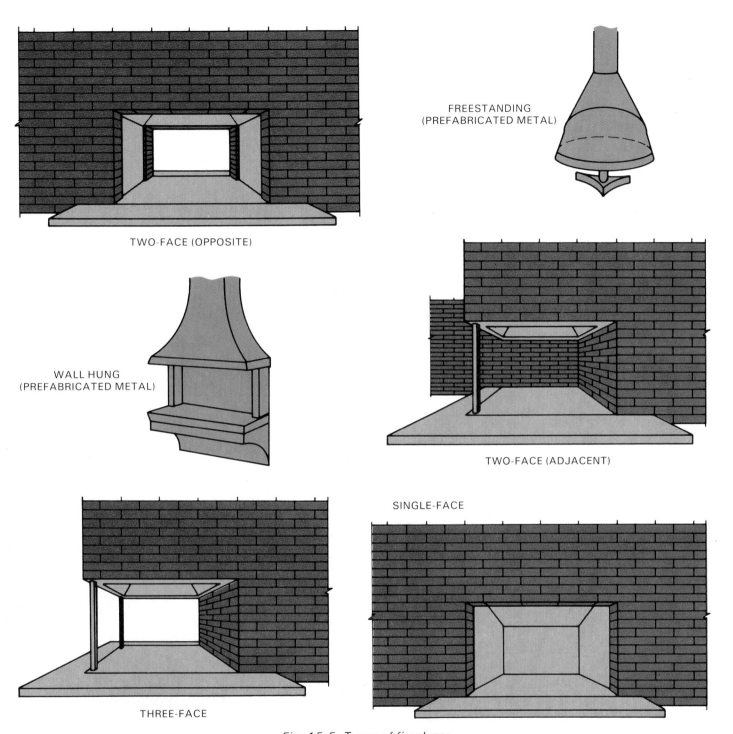

TWO-FACE (OPPOSITE)

FREESTANDING
(PREFABRICATED METAL)

WALL HUNG
(PREFABRICATED METAL)

TWO-FACE (ADJACENT)

SINGLE-FACE

THREE-FACE

Fig. 15-5. Types of fireplaces.

the fireplace. The hearth may be flush with the floor or raised to a desirable height.

The fire chamber is usually lined with firebrick set in fireclay, (fire-resistant mortar). *Fireclay* is a mortar-like refractory material used as a bonding agent between the firebrick. The shape of this area is critical and must be designed to lead hot gases and smoke into the throat for passage up the chimney. If the chamber is too deep, little heat will be reflected out into the room. If it is too shallow, the fireplace is likely to smoke. Wall

thickness should be a minimum of 8 in. on the back and sides of the fire chamber, Fig. 15-6.

When space is available below the fireplace and finished floor, an ash dump is desirable. A metal trap door is located in the middle of the fireplace floor and connected to the ash chamber below. A cleanout is provided in the ash chamber for the removal of ashes.

In modern residential construction extensive use is made of prefabricated steel heat-circulating fireplaces. The units include not only the

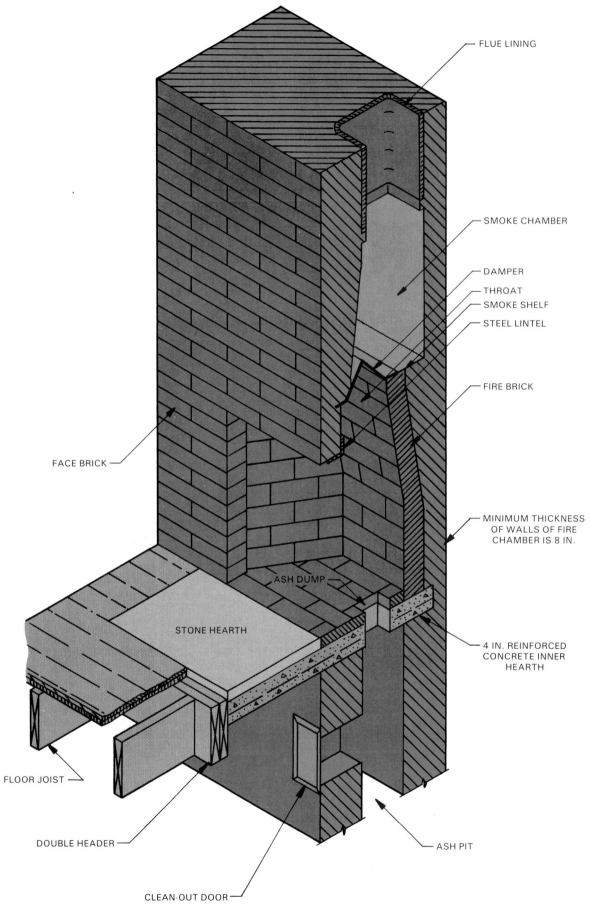

FLUE LINING

SMOKE CHAMBER

DAMPER
THROAT
SMOKE SHELF
STEEL LINTEL

FIRE BRICK

MINIMUM THICKNESS
OF WALLS OF FIRE
CHAMBER IS 8 IN.

FACE BRICK

ASH DUMP

STONE HEARTH

4 IN. REINFORCED
CONCRETE INNER
HEARTH

FLOOR JOIST

DOUBLE HEADER

ASH PIT

CLEAN-OUT DOOR

Fig. 15-6. Three-dimensional section drawing of fireplace details.

Fig. 15-7. A cut-away view showing the prefabricated steel heat-circulating fireplace. (Heatilator, Inc.)

firebox and heating chamber, but also the throat, damper, smoke shelf, and smoke chambers, Fig. 15-7. Installation is generally easy. Fig. 15-8 shows the step-by-step procedure for installing a prefabricated stack heat-circulating fireplace in frame construction. These units are very efficient because the sides and back consist of a double-wall passageway where the air is heated. Cool air is drawn into the chamber, heated and returned to the room through registers located at a higher level.

DAMPER AND SMOKE SHELF

Every modern fireplace should have a *damper* to regulate the flow of air and stop down drafts of cold air when the fireplace is not in operation. The damper is located in the throat of the fireplace and opens toward the back of the throat. The damper opening should be larger than the area of the flue lining and as long as the width of the fireplace. Standard damper sizes are shown

Fig. 15-8. Installation of a prefabricated steel heat circulating fireplace in frame construction. (Vega Industries, Inc.)

DAMPER SPECIFICATIONS

STEEL DAMPERS					
WIDTH OF FIREPLACE IN INCHES	DAMPER DIMENSIONS IN INCHES				
	A	B	C	D	E
24 TO 26	28 1/4	26 3/4	13	24	9 1/2
27 TO 30	32 1/4	30 3/4	13	28	9 1/2
31 TO 34	36 1/4	34 3/4	13	32	9 1/2
35 TO 38	40 1/4	38 3/4	13	36	9 1/2
39 TO 42	44 1/4	42 3/4	13	40	9 1/2
43 TO 46	48 1/4	46 3/4	13	44	9 1/2
47 TO 50	52 1/4	50 3/4	13	48	9 1/2
51 TO 54	56 1/4	54 3/4	13	52	9 1/2
57 TO 60	62 1/2	60 3/4	13	58	9 1/2
CAST IRON DAMPERS					
WIDTH OF FIREPLACE IN INCHES	DAMPER DIMENSIONS IN INCHES				
	A	B	C	D	E
24 TO 26	28	21	13 1/2	24	10
27 TO 31	34	26 3/4	13 1/2	30	10
31 TO 34	37	29 3/4	13 1/2	33	10
35 TO 38	40	32 3/4	13 1/2	36	10
39 TO 42	46	38 3/4	13 1/2	48	10
43 TO 46	52	44 3/4	13 1/2	48	10
47 TO 50	57 1/2	50 1/2	13 1/2	54	10
51 TO 54	64	56 1/2	14 1/2	60	11 1/2
57 TO 60	76	58	14 1/2	72	11 1/2

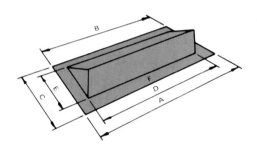

Fig. 15-9. Damper design specifications which are typical of products on the market. (Donley Brothers Co.)

in Fig. 15-9. It should be placed 6 or 8 in. above the top of the fireplace opening. Dampers are produced in both steel and cast iron.

The smoke shelf height is determined by the location of the damper, Fig. 15-6. The **smoke shelf** causes cold air flowing down the chimney to be deflected upward into the rising warm air.

CLAY FLUE LINER SIZES

NEW SIZES	ROUND (DIA.)	OLD SIZES
8 x 12	8	8 1/2 x 8 1/2
12 x 12	10	8 1/2 x 13
12 x 16	12	13 x 13
16 x 16	15	13 x 18
16 x 20	18	18 x 18
20 x 20	20	20 x 20
20 x 24	22	24 x 24

NEW FLUE SIZES CONFORM TO NEW MODULAR DIMENSIONAL SYSTEM. SIZES SHOWN ARE NOMINAL. ACTUAL SIZE 15 1/2'' LESS EACH DIMENSION. ALL FLUE LININGS LISTED ABOVE ARE 2' – 0'' LONG.

Fig. 15-10. Flue liners are available in round and rectangular shapes. Most are made of clay.

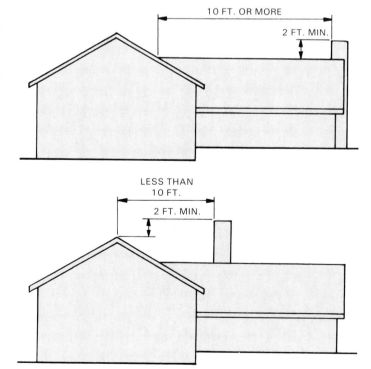

Fig. 15-11. Recommended chimney heights above the roof.

This action prevents down rushing cold air from forcing smoke into the room.

The smoke chamber is the area just above the smoke shelf and damper. This is basically pyramidal in shape with the back side usually being vertical. It is normally constructed from brick or other masonry.

FLUE

The flue usually has a clay lining which provides an avenue for smoke to pass up the chimney, Fig. 15-6. It begins at the top of the smoke chamber and extends to the top of the chimney. Each flue requires at least 4 in. of brick on all sides. If no liner is used the wall thickness must be a minimum of 8 in. *Each fireplace must have its own flue.* Ideally, the flue will be centered directly above the fireplace and proceed upward in a straight line. A small amount of offset is permissible; however, efficiency is reduced when the flue is not straight.

The size of flue is important since is must be large enough to provide the necessary draft. A rule of thumb to follow in selecting the proper flue size is to choose a flue that has at least 1/10th the sectional area of the fireplace opening. For example, if the fireplace opening is 32'' x 48'' the area is 1536 sq. in. One tenth of 1536 sq. in is 153.6 sq. in. A standard flue size

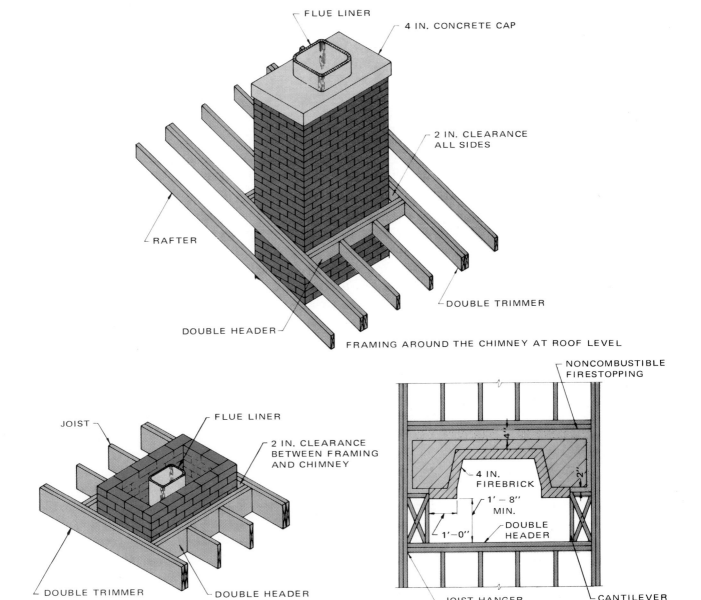

Fig. 15-12. Typical framing technique used at the floor, ceiling, and roof.

Fireplaces and Chimneys 271

that has at least this area is a 12'' x 16'' flue. It is better to have a flue that is too large than one that is too small. Standard flue sizes are shown in Fig. 15-10.

Flue size is also related to several other factors. If the height of the flue is less than 14 ft., the size should be increased to provide the necessary draft. The draft is increased by making the flue higher. Prevailing winds and surrounding trees and buildings also affect the draft. If the flue is sheltered, the size should be increased. Most codes require that the flue extend at least 2 ft. above the highest point of the roof, Fig. 15-11. This is a safety factor, since sparks fly out the top and may cause a roof fire.

A single chimney may have several flues. A flue is required for a gas furnace, a gas water heater, an incinerator, and each fireplace. Efficiency of a chimney may be increased if it is placed within the house rather than on an outside wall. The warmer the chimney, the better the performance.

FRAMING AROUND FIREPLACE AND CHIMNEY

The chimney is a free-standing structure. It does not support any part of the house. In fact, fire codes prohibit direct contact of framing with surfaces of the fireplace or chimney. A minimum of 2 in. of clearance is required between the chimney and framing. This space should be filled with a noncombustible material. The opening through which the chimney passes through the

Fig. 15-14. A single-face fireplace is decorated in Southwestern motif. Decorator glass doors provide visual enhancement and heating efficiency. (Superior Fireplace Company)

floor, ceiling, and roof requires double headers and trimmers to give the necessary support, Fig. 15-12.

If a chimney is located along the ridge line (the peak or highest point) of a roof, the chance of water problems is minimized. However, if the chimney must be located along a single slope of the roof, special precautions must be taken to prevent leaking. Water can back up along the chimney and roof intersections and seep under the shingles. To prevent this from happening, a *saddle* or *cricket* is built on the high side of the chimney to shed water. A saddle is especially necessary if the roof slope is low or the chimney is wide. Fig. 15-13 shows a saddle.

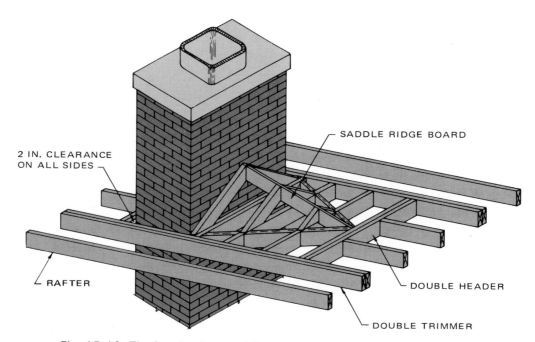

Fig. 15-13. The framing for a saddle to shed water away from the chimney.

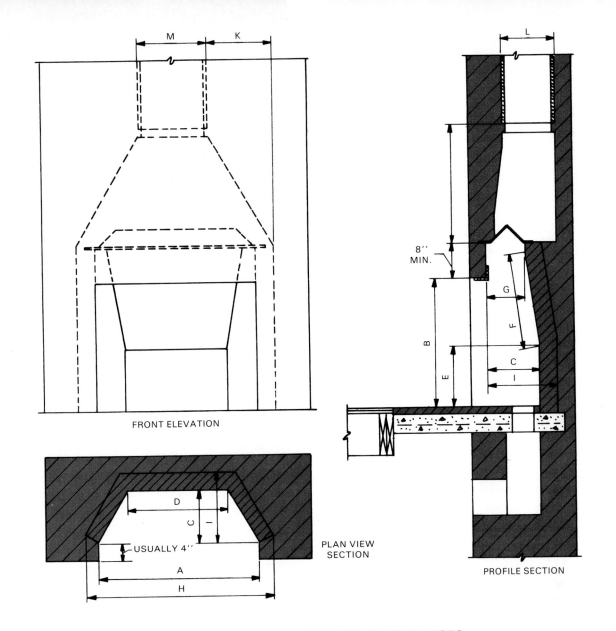

FRONT ELEVATION

PLAN VIEW
SECTION

PROFILE SECTION

8'' MIN.

USUALLY 4''

DESIGN DATA FOR SINGLE-FACE FIREPLACES

WIDTH	HGT.	DEPTH	BACK	VERT. BACK	SLOPE BACK	THROAT	WIDTH	DEPTH	SMOKE CHAMB.	FLUE LINING SIZES				
										RECT.		RND.	MODULAR	
A	B	C	D	E	F	G	H	I	J	K	L x M	K	L x M	
24	24	16	11	14	15	8 3/4	32	20	19	11 3/4	8 1/2 x 8 1/2	8	10	8 x 12
26	24	16	13	14	15	8 3/4	34	20	21	12 3/4	8 1/2 x 8 1/2	8	11	8 x 12
28	24	16	15	14	15	8 3/4	36	20	21	11 1/2	8 1/2 x 13	10	12	8 x 12
30	29	16	17	14	18	8 3/4	38	20	24	12 1/2	8 1/2 x 13	10	13	12 x 12
32	29	16	19	14	21	8 3/4	40	20	24	13 1/2	8 1/2 x 13	10	14	12 x 12
36	29	16	23	14	21	8 3/4	44	20	27	15 1/2	13 x 13	12	16	12 x 12
40	29	16	27	14	21	8 3/4	48	20	29	17 1/2	13 x 13	12	16	12 x 12
42	32	16	29	14	23	8 3/4	50	20	32	18 1/2	13 x 13	12	17	16 x 16
48	32	18	33	14	23	8 3/4	56	22	37	21 1/2	13 x 13	15	20	16 x 16
54	37	20	37	16	27	13	68	24	45	25	13 x 18	15	26	16 x 20
60	37	22	42	16	27	13	72	27	45	27	13 x 18	15	26	16 x 20
60	40	22	42	16	29	13	72	27	45	27	18 x 18	18	26	16 x 20
72	40	22	54	16	29	13	84	27	56	33	18 x 18	18	32	20 x 20
84	40	24	64	20	26	13	96	29	67	36	20 x 20	20	36	20 x 20
96	40	24	76	20	26	13	108	29	75	42	24 x 24	22	42	20 x 20

DIMENSIONS ARE IN INCHES.
FLUE SIZES FOR CHIMNEY HEIGHT OF AT LEAST 14' – 0''.

Fig. 15-15. Design specifications for single-face fireplace.

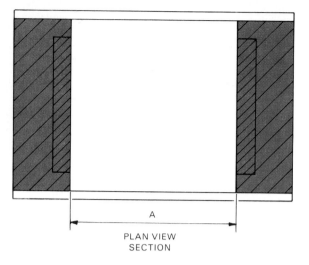

PLAN VIEW
SECTION

Fig. 15-16. Two rooms may benefit from a two-face (opposite) fireplace. The fireplace is both stylish and functional. (Superior Fireplace Company)

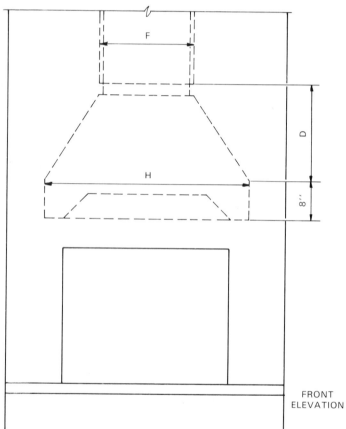

FRONT
ELEVATION

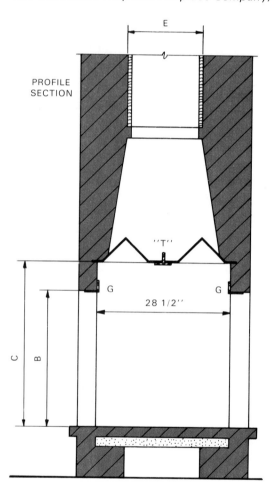

PROFILE
SECTION

DESIGN DATA FOR TWO-FACE OPPOSITE FIREPLACES

A	B	C	D	OLD FLUE SIZE		RND.	NEW MOD. SIZE		ANGLE G	H	TEE
				E	F		E	F	2 REQ'D.		LENGTH
28	24	35	19	13	13	12	12	16	36	36	35
32	29	35	21	13	18	15	16	16	40	40	39
36	29	35	21	13	18	15	16	20	42	44	43
40	29	35	27	18	18	18	16	20	48	48	47
48	32	37	32	18	18	18	20	20	54	56	55

DIMENSIONS ARE IN INCHES.
FLUE SIZES FOR CHIMNEY HEIGHT OF AT LEAST 14' – 0''.
ANGLE G IS 3'' x 3'' x 1/4''

Fig. 15-17. Design specifications for two-face opposite fireplaces.

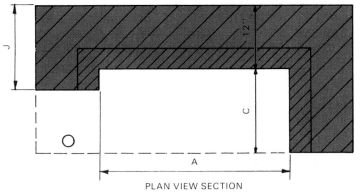

PLAN VIEW SECTION

Fig. 15-18. A two-face (adjacent) fireplace is suitable for this space. The fireplace materials are attractive and fire resistant. The screen is an additional safety feature. (Superior Fireplace Company)

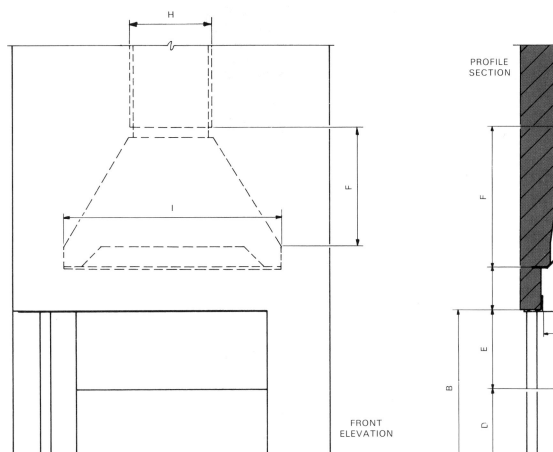

FRONT ELEVATION

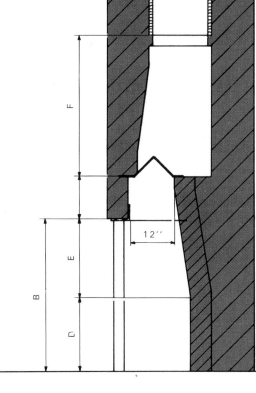

PROFILE SECTION

DESIGN DATA FOR TWO-FACE ADJACENT FIREPLACES

| A | B | C | D | E | F | OLD FLUE | | RND. | MOD. FLUE | | I | J | CORNER POST |
						G	H		G	H			HEIGHT
28	26 1/2	16	14	20	29 1/4	13	13	12	12	12	36	16	26 1/2
32	26 1/2	16	14	20	32	13	13	12	12	16	40	16	26 1/2
36	26 1/2	16	14	20	35	13	13	12	12	16	44	16	26 1/2
40	29	16	14	20	35	13	18	15	16	16	48	16	29
48	29	20	14	24	43	13	18	15	16	16	56	20	29
54	29	20	14	23	45	13	18	15	16	16	62	20	29
60	29	20	14	23	51	13	18	15	16	20	68	20	29

DIMENSIONS ARE IN INCHES.
FLUE SIZES FOR CHIMNEY HEIGHT OF AT LEAST 14' – 0''.

Fig. 15-19. Design specifications for two-face (adjacent) fireplaces.

Fireplaces and Chimneys   275

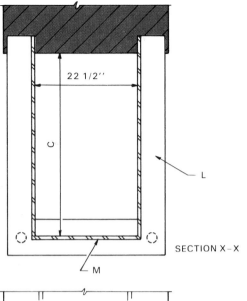

SECTION X–X

Fig. 15-20. A three-face fireplace is appropriate for this open plan. (Superior Fireplace Company)

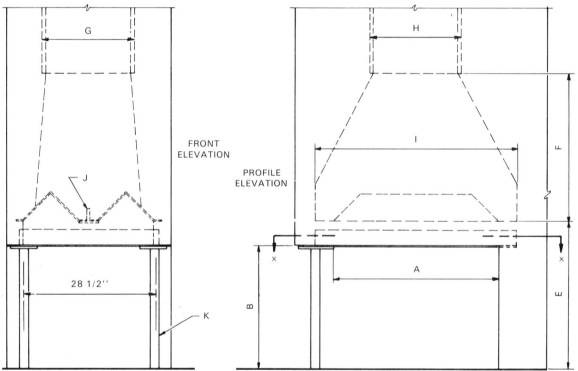

FRONT ELEVATION

PROFILE ELEVATION

DESIGN DATA FOR THREE-FACE FIREPLACES

A	B	C	E	F	OLD FLUE SIZE		RND.	NEW MODULAR FLUE SIZE		I	STEEL TEE	POST HEIGHT	ANGLE 2 REQ'D.	SPECIAL WELDED TEE
					G	H		G	H		J	K	L	M
28	26 1/2	32	32	24	18	18	18	16	20	36	35	26 1/2	36	34
32	26 1/2	36	32	27	18	18	18	20	20	40	39	26 1/2	40	34
36	26 1/2	40	32	32	18	18	18	20	20	44	43	26 1/2	44	34
40	26 1/2	44	32	35	18	18	18	20	20	48	47	26 1/2	48	34
48	26 1/2	52	32	35	20	20	20	20	24	56	55	26 1/2	56	34

DIMENSIONS ARE IN INCHES.
FLUE SIZES FOR CHIMNEY HEIGHT OF AT LEAST 14′ – 0″.

Fig. 15-21. Design specifications for three-face fireplaces.

Masonry above a fireplace opening must be supported by a lintel just the same as over a door or window. The common type of lintel used is angle steel. The size of angle required will vary with the length of opening. A 3'' x 3'' x 1/4'' angle will be sufficient for an opening of 60 in. wide. See Fig. 15-6.

FIREPLACE SPECIFICATIONS

The type of fireplace and size of opening is the beginning point in designing a fireplace. The following specifications are intended to facilitate the design process.

SINGLE-FACE FIREPLACE

The single-face fireplace is the most popular type, Fig. 15-14. It is the least complicated to construct and usually functions better than the other types. Fig. 15-15 gives the specifications for several single-face fireplaces. Damper size may be determined by studying the chart presented earlier.

TWO-FACE (OPPOSITE) FIREPLACE

A two-face (opposite) fireplace is open on both the front and back sides, Fig. 15-16. Its primary advantage is that it opens into two rooms. Care must be taken to prevent a draft from one side to the other which may result in smoke. Fig. 15-17 presents specifications pertaining to this type fireplace.

TWO-FACE (ADJACENT) FIREPLACE

A two-face (adjacent) fireplace is open on the front and one side, Fig. 15-18. It may be open on the right or left side. This type is also known as a *projecting corner fireplace.* Design specifications are shown in Fig. 15-19.

THREE-FACE FIREPLACE

A three-face fireplace is open on three sides, Fig. 15-20. Ordinarily, two long sides and one short side are open. This is also known as a *three-way fireplace.* This type is somewhat of a novelty, however, it can add interest and design if the interior room layout is properly arranged. Fig. 15-21 gives design specifications for the three-face type.

PREFABRICATED METAL FIREPLACES AND STOVES

Prefabricated metal fireplaces and stoves are becoming more popular as a greater number of styles are produced. Some metal fireplaces are

Fig. 15-22. A modern prefabricated steel heat-circulating fireplace with efficient design features. (Superior Fireplace Company)

Fig. 15-23. Free-standing metal fireplaces are popular for recreation rooms and cottages. (Preway)

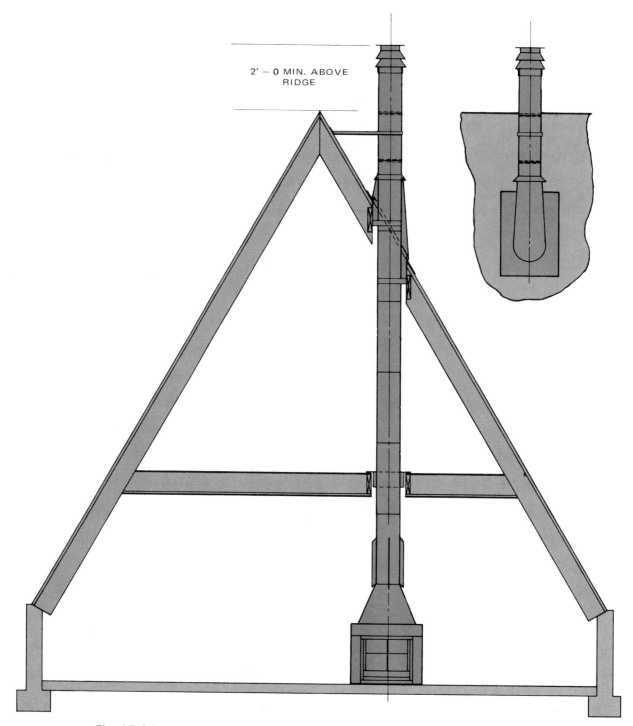

Fig. 15-24. A typical installation of a prefabricated metal fireplace in a cottage.

wall-mounted; some are enclosed in masonry, Fig. 15-22, and others are free-standing models, Fig. 15-23. These units may be purchased complete with all the necessary parts required to install them. No masonry work is needed for the wall-mounted types. The local code should be consulted prior to installation. Fig. 15-24 shows installation details of a typical prefabricated metal fireplace.

Prefabricated steel heat-circulating fireplaces are manufactured in several designs, Fig. 15-25. These units require framing or masonry enclosures. See Fig. 15-22. Vents are visible at the

top and bottom of the unit. Fireplace inserts are also efficient in circulating warmed air. These units are designed for existing masonry fireplaces. Fig. 15-26 shows a metal insert with glass doors and vents.

STOVES

Wood- or coal-burning stoves generally produce more usable heat than fireplaces. They are frequently located in such a manner that heat is radiated from all sides. They are ordinarily used

Fig. 15-25. Three common designs of prefabricated steel heat-circulating fireplaces; the single-face, two-face adjacent, and two-face opposite. (Superior Fireplace Co.)

Fig. 15-26. Fireplace inserts are popular for masonry fireplaces. This model provides efficiency and is visually appealing. (Superior Fireplace Company)

Fig. 15-27. A wood-burning stove suitable for heating this large family room. Heat radiates from all sides of the stove. (Vermont Castings)

as local sources of heat rather than total heating systems, Fig. 15-27. The efficiency among models varies greatly.

There are two main types of stoves: *radiant stoves* and *circulating stoves.* Both types of stoves produce radiant heat. (Radiant heat passes through the air with no assistance from air flow.) However, circulating stoves use air flow as well as radiation to distribute heat

Fig. 15-28. Circulating stoves tend to provide more heat than radiant stoves and may be placed closer to combustible materials. This wood-burning stove combines function with beauty. (Heatilator, Inc.)

throughout a room. A circulating stove has an outer jacket to facilitate air movement. This air flow provides more even heat than is possible with a radiant stove. Circulating stoves are safer and may be placed closer to combustible material than radiant stoves because of their lower surface temperature, Fig. 15-28.

Stoves are frequently classified according to their heating efficiency. Low-efficiency stoves range from 20 to 30 percent efficient. Examples include simple box stoves, Franklin stoves, pot belly stoves, and some parlor stoves. Medium-efficiency stoves range from 35 to 50 percent efficient. They provide better combustion and have less air leakage into the stove. Most include a device to insure a constant burning rate. High-efficiency stoves are over 50 percent efficient. They include all of the features of the medium-efficiency stoves, but also use baffles, long smoke paths, and heat exchange devices to increase heat output, Fig. 15-29.

A stove may be located inside, Fig. 15-30, or in front of an existing fireplace. When the stove is positioned in front of the fireplace, the opening should be covered with sheet metal to reflect the heat back into the room. It is very important

Fig. 15-29. A high efficiency stove made of cast iron with large glass doors to view the fire. Note the fire-resistant materials beneath and behind the stove. (Vermont Castings)

Fig. 15-30. Classical styling and graceful proportions of the antique green porcelain enamel stove blend nicely with the atmosphere and color scheme of this pleasant room. (Vermont Castings)

to follow the manufacturer's installation instructions as well as the local code requirements when installing a stove.

REVIEW QUESTIONS—CHAPTER 15

Write your answers on a separate sheet of paper. Do not write in this book.

1. Identify five types of fireplaces which can be installed in a home.
2. The part of the fireplace designed to protect the floor from sparks is the _____.
3. If the fire chamber is too shallow, a condition that may result is _____.
4. One major advantage of a prefabricated metal firebox is _____.
5. The _____ deflects cold air flowing down the chimney into the rising warm air.
6. The area in the fireplace above the smoke shelf and damper and below the flue is called the _____.
7. A rule of thumb to follow in selecting the proper flue size is to choose a flue which has at least _____ the sectional area of the fireplace opening.
8. Increasing the flue height will _____ the draft.
9. Most codes require that the flue extend at least _____ ft. above the highest point of the roof.
10. Why will a chimney placed within the house function better than one on an outside wall?
11. Allow a minimum clearance of _____ in. between the chimney and framing.
12. The purpose of a saddle or cricket is to _____.
13. The type of lintel used above the openings of most fireplaces is _____.
14. A fireplace which has only a single opening is known as a _____.
15. A fireplace which is open on the front and one side is a _____.

16. A type of fireplace that requires no masonry and is popular for cottages is _____.
17. Wood or coal burning stoves are ordinarily used as _____ sources of heat.
18. Name the two main types of stoves.
19. Name three features that are unique to a high efficiency stove.

SUGGESTED ACTIVITIES

1. Select a residential plan that has a fireplace. Draw the fireplace details and dimension the drawings.
2. Build a scale model of a fireplace and describe the materials to be used in the actual fireplace. Draw the plan view and front elevation of the fireplace.
3. Collect literature and materials commonly used in modern fireplaces and bring to class. Display the literature and materials and describe them in class.
4. Locate a residence under construction which has a fireplace. Measure the opening and depth. Sketch the fireplace and be prepared to discuss the construction techniques used.
5. Visit your local building department and secure local code restrictions about the installation of wood burning stoves. Summarize the main points in class.

A traditional home with more than one fireplace allows the architect to design creative floor plans for the occupants.

The Floor Plan

After studying this chapter, you will be able to:
- List the information required on a typical floor plan.
- Represent typical materials using standard architectural symbols.
- Design and draw a residential floor plan using accepted symbols and techniques.
- Dimension a floor plan in a clear and precise manner.
- Recognize the difference between a good and poor drawing of a floor plan.

The floor plan is the heart of a set of construction drawings. It is the one plan to which all tradeworkers refer. When designing a residence, the floor plan is usually started first. It may be completed near the end of the designing, since modifications are frequently required during the development of the other plans in the set.

The floor plan is actually a section drawing. An imaginary cutting plane is passed through the structure about four feet above the floor and parallel to it. The plane may be higher or lower as necessary to ''cut'' through the required details. In some instances, the plane is offset (changes levels) as in the case of a split-level house.

The purpose of the floor plan is to show the location and dimensions of exterior and interior walls, windows, doors, major appliances, cabinets, fireplace, and other fixed features of the house. See Figs. 16-1 and 16-2. Fig. 16-2 identifies many common features found on a floor plan. Sometimes when the structure is not complex, the floor plan may include information which would ordinarily be found on other drawings. For example, the electrical plan, heating/cooling plan, or plumbing plan might be combined with the floor plan. Be careful not to

Fig. 16-1. Study this photo, then examine the floor plan, Fig. 16-2.

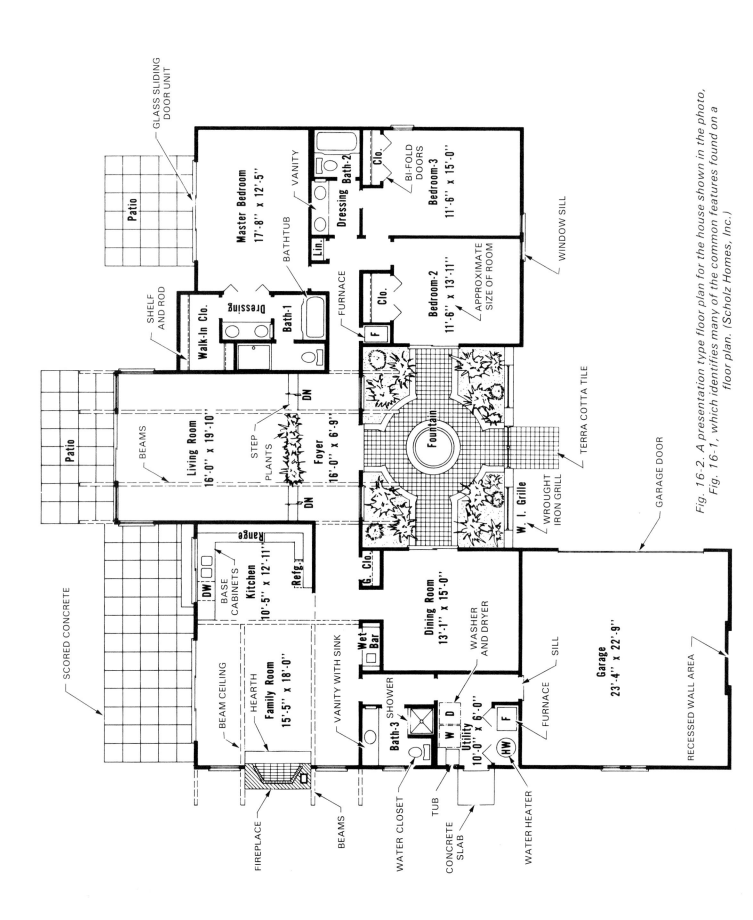

Fig. 16-2. A presentation type floor plan for the house shown in the photo, Fig. 16-1, which identifies many of the common features found on a floor plan. (Scholz Homes, Inc.)

include too much information on a single drawing or the drawing will become cluttered and confusing.

REQUIRED INFORMATION

Information about the following features should be included on the floor plan; exterior and interior walls; size and location of windows and doors; built-in cabinets and appliances; permanent fixtures; stairs and fireplaces; walks, patios, and decks; room names and material symbols; location and size dimensions; and scale. Frequently, related structures such as a free-standing garage or swimming pool are also shown on the floor plan.

LOCATION AND SIZE OF WALLS

Walls should be drawn accurately. You may use the following chart as a guide to wall thickness:

WALL THICKNESS CHART	
Wood Frame Walls	
Exterior walls (with sheathing and siding)	6 in.
Interior walls (with dry wall both sides)	5 in.
Concrete Block Walls	
Exterior walls	8, 10, or 12 in.
Interior walls	4 or 8 in.
Brick Veneer Exterior	
Veneer on frame	10 in.
Veneer on concrete block	12 in.
Brick Exterior Walls	
Two courses of brick	8 in.
Two courses with 2 in. air space	10 in.
Three courses of brick	12 in.

When drawing, a recommended technique for measuring wall thickness is to set your dividers to the proper dimension and use them rather than try to measure each time with your scale. Variations in wall thickness will be readily evident and will detract from the neatness of the drawing.

Since the floor plan is a section drawing, symbols should be used to indicate materials used. See Fig. 16-3.

LOCATION AND SIZE OF WINDOWS AND DOORS

When locating windows and doors on the drawing, use a center line through the middle of the opening. The sash opening is shown for windows and the actual door width is used for

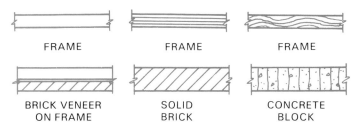

Fig. 16-3. Several methods of indicating interior and exterior walls on a floor plan.

doors. Sills are indicated for windows and exterior doors. Refer to Chapter 13 for appropriate window and door symbols. The door swing must be indicated on the floor plan. Fig. 16-4 shows how a window and door are represented on the floor plan.

Occasionally, a plain opening or archway may be desired rather than a door. In this case, hidden lines are used to show that the opening does not extend to the ceiling, Fig. 16-5. Hidden lines are used on the floor plan to indicate that a feature is above the cutting plane or hidden by some other detail.

CABINETS, APPLIANCES, AND PERMANENT FIXTURES

The location and size of kitchen cabinets, bathroom vanities, fixtures, and appliances must be indicated on the floor plan. These features are drawn using standard symbols which represent sizes. Never guess at the size of an appliance or fixture. Obtain information related to each item

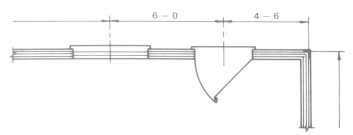

Fig. 16-4. Windows and doors should be located using a center line, type of window indicated, and door swing shown.

OPENING FROM FLOOR TO CEILING

ARCHWAY OR PLAIN OPENING

Fig. 16-5. Method of representing interior wall openings, other than windows and doors.

and record the necessary dimensions and specifications for inclusion in the plans.

Refer to symbols and location procedures presented in Chapters 5 and 7. Examine local codes relative to clearances and installation procedures acceptable in your area.

STAIRS AND FIREPLACES

If a stairway or fireplace is to be included, only basic size and location information needs to be recorded on the floor plan, because details will be included in the set of drawings for these two features.

Normally, the direction of flight, number of risers, and width of the stairs, is given on the floor plan. See Fig. 16-6. The basic width, length, location, and shape of opening of the fireplace is also shown on the floor plan. A simplified or more detailed symbol may be used to identify the fireplace, Fig. 16-7. Other flues that may be housed in the chimney are frequently added to the drawing.

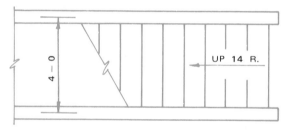

Fig. 16-6. Information about a set of stairs which is usually included on the floor plan.

WALKS, PATIOS, AND DECKS

Several features which are outside the house are commonly included on the floor plan. Walks, patios, and decks are examples. Sizes and materials to be used should be indicated on the plan. These features help to present the total plan and are important elements.

ROOM NAMES AND MATERIAL SYMBOLS

Room names add information which is important in communicating the plan to others. The room name should be lettered slightly larger (3/16 in.) than surrounding lettering. The ideal location for the room name is the center of the room. This may be shifted to one side or lowered if center space is unavailable. If desired, the approximate size of the room may be added immediately below the name. This is helpful to those not too familiar with construction drawings.

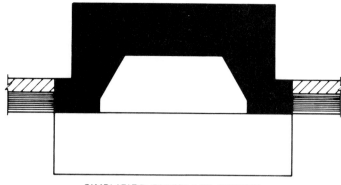

SIMPLIFIED FIREPLACE SYMBOL

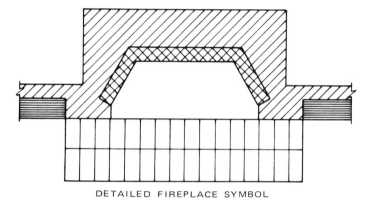

DETAILED FIREPLACE SYMBOL

Fig. 16-7. A fireplace may be represented using a simplified or detailed symbol. The detailed symbol is usually preferred.

Material symbols are a type of shorthand for the drafter. Symbols are used rather than try to describe each material with words. Use a material symbol whenever the material should be identified. If the symbol is not a standard one, identify it. Several common building material symbols are shown in Fig. 16-8.

DIMENSIONING

Dimensions on a floor plan may show the size of a feature or its location. *The importance of proper and careful dimensioning cannot be overemphasized.* Placement of dimensions requires good judgment. Locate dimensions where one would logically look for them. Dimension lines in architectural drawing are generally continuous lines with the dimension figure placed above the line. Dimensions are always parallel (never perpendicular) to the dimension line. Any of the termination symbols may be used as long as you are consistent. Review Chapter 4 for additional information.

When drawings are so crowded with dimensions it is difficult to see the objects, move

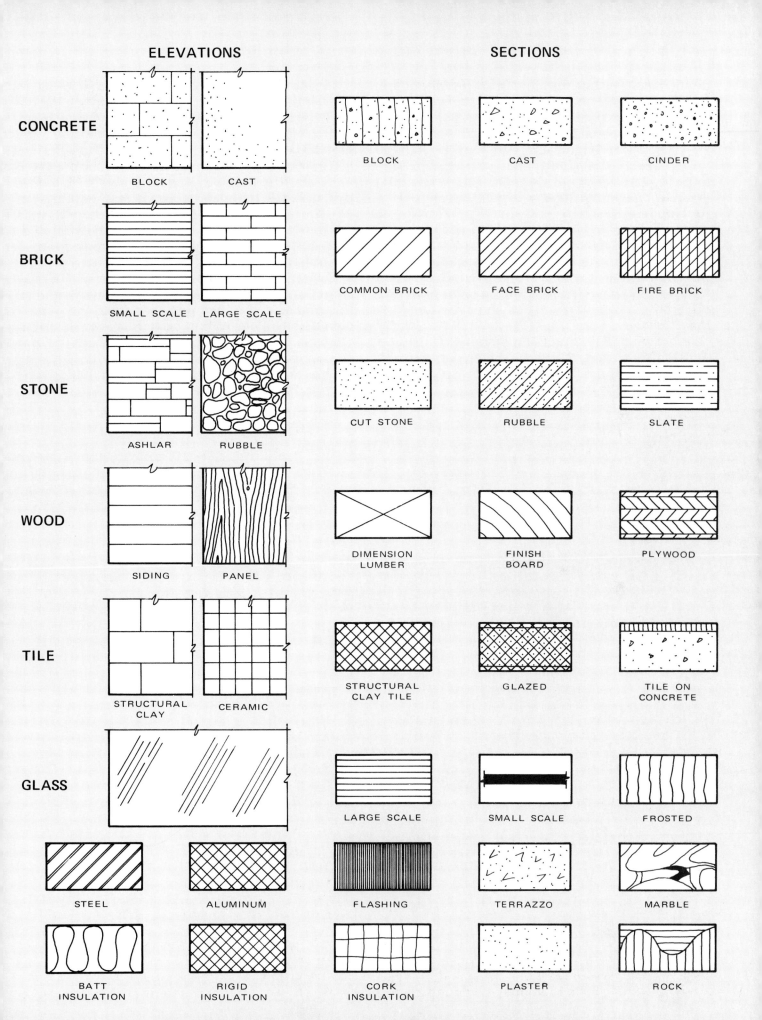

ELEVATIONS

SECTIONS

CONCRETE

BLOCK CAST

BLOCK CAST CINDER

BRICK

SMALL SCALE LARGE SCALE

COMMON BRICK FACE BRICK FIRE BRICK

STONE

ASHLAR RUBBLE

CUT STONE RUBBLE SLATE

WOOD

SIDING PANEL

DIMENSION LUMBER FINISH BOARD PLYWOOD

TILE

STRUCTURAL CLAY CERAMIC

STRUCTURAL CLAY TILE GLAZED TILE ON CONCRETE

GLASS

LARGE SCALE SMALL SCALE FROSTED

STEEL ALUMINUM FLASHING TERRAZZO MARBLE

BATT INSULATION RIGID INSULATION CORK INSULATION PLASTER ROCK

Fig. 16-8. Several common building material symbols used on residential plans.

dimension lines out from the drawing far enough (at least 3/4 in.) so the dimension, as well as the object lines, may be clearly seen. Spacing between the dimension lines may be 1/4 in. or 3/8 in. as desired. Dimension lines may be located within the house area if that seems to be the logical place for them. Refrain from using long leaders. Maximum length of leaders should be two inches.

Dimensions in architectural drawing are recorded in feet and inches. When the dimension is less than one foot, one of two procedures may be used. Either place a zero in the foot location followed by the number of inches (0-6) or record the length as so many inches and show the inch mark (6'').

In drawing plans, feet and inch marks may be omitted as a general rule. A dimension such as 12-6 could not mean anything other than the dimension 12 ft. 6 in.

Interior walls are commonly dimensioned to the center. A short line is drawn down the middle of the wall at the termination point of the dimension to show that the center is indicated. See Fig. 16-9.

Exterior walls, if they are frame, are dimensioned to the outside of the stud wall. This usually includes the weatherboard or sheathing but not the siding, Fig. 16-9. Solid masonry walls are dimensioned to the outside of the wall, Fig. 16-10. Brick veneer walls are dimensioned to the outside of the stud wall, Fig. 16-9.

Overall dimensions are necessary for the length and width of the structure. Always add all the dimensions which together equal the overall dimension. One of the most frequent errors in dimensioning is that partial dimensions do not add up to equal the total distance.

The overall length and width of major wall segments should be lengths that are multiples of

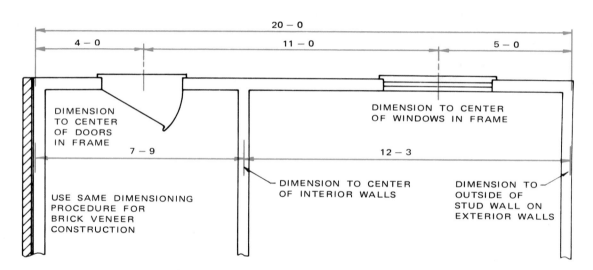

Fig. 16-9. Recommended method of dimensioning frame wall construction.

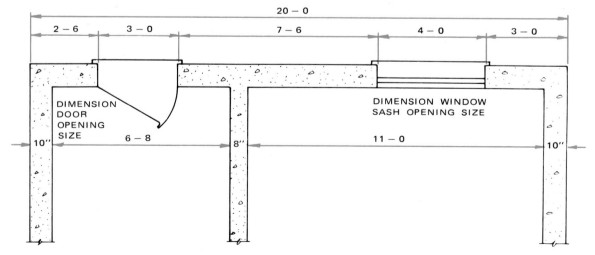

Fig. 16-10. Solid masonry walls (cast concrete, block, brick, or stone) are usually dimensioned as shown.

4 ft. Building material sizes are keyed to this dimension and much unnecessary waste will result if this rule is not applied.

Frequently, notes are required to present information that cannot be represented by a conventional dimension or symbol. These notes should be brief and located where they will be easy to see. Include only information that is required. Notes may be lettered 1/8 in. high or slightly smaller. They should be read from bottom of sheet—not from edge.

SCALE AND SHEET IDENTIFICATION

Residential floor plans are usually drawn to a scale of 1/4'' = 1'-0''. A detail may be a larger scale and the plot plan smaller, but the other drawings should be 1/4'' = 1'-0''. The size of paper selected for the plans will be determined by the size of the structure. A sheet of 18'' x 24'' paper is large enough for most plans. The scale must appear at the bottom of each drawing. An exception is the pictorial representation of the total house.

Numbering the sheets so the reader may determine if the set is complete is important. A method that works well is to number each sheet like this: Sheet 1 of 6, 2 of 6, etc. The sheet number should appear in the lower right hand corner of each sheet.

METRIC SYSTEM OF DIMENSIONING

Each year the metric system of measurement is used more world wide. It is anticipated that the United States will eventually convert to the metric system. Even though no standards have been agreed upon in the lumber and building industry, a simple floor plan has been presented, Fig. 16-11, to illustrate metric dimensioning. The basic unit of measure will most likely be the *meter*. However, before universal adoption of the system may be made by the building industry, new lumber sizes and standards must be decided upon and accepted.

PROCEDURE FOR DRAWING FLOOR PLAN

The first step in designing a house is to determine the requirements of the structure and record them as preliminary sketches. These rough sketches will provide direction for drawing the plan to scale. The following steps are presented as an aid to the student in drawing a floor plan once the basic requirements are determined and some preliminary sketches are developed.

1. *Lay out the exterior walls.* Draw the walls as light construction lines. Be sure that the overall length and width of the house is measured to the proper place on the walls and that walls are the correct thickness.

2. *Locate the interior walls.* Also draw these as light construction lines. Set your dividers to the desired wall thickness and use them to transfer the dimension. Use the center of the wall for locating its position. Steps 1 and 2 are shown in Fig. 16-12.

3. *Determine the location of the windows and doors.* Both of these features will be dimensioned to the center line of the opening (in frame wall construction), so locate it first. Indicate the swing of doors and type of window used. Darken in lines used for windows and doors.

4. *Draw the stairs.* Measure the width of the stairs and lay out the treads. The finished floor-to-finished floor height must be determined and the tread and riser height calculated before this step may be completed accurately. See Chapter 14 for an explanation of stair design and construction. Draw equally spaced lines to represent the stair treads. Show direction of travel and number of risers. If the house has no stairs, then go to the next step.

5. *Locate and draw the fireplace.* Review Chapter 15. If the house is to have a fireplace, draw the outline in lightly. Since the dimensions of a fireplace must be exact to ensure proper operation, some preliminary work must be done before it can be drawn on the floor plan. Identify the type and size of fireplace which is desired and record these dimensions for further use. Darken in the fireplace outline and fire chamber size. You may now darken in all exterior and interior walls. Steps 3, 4, and 5 are shown in Fig. 16-13.

6. *Locate and draw walks, patios, or decks.* These elements of the plan should be well thought out and materials and designs selected which will complement the total structure. Lay out and draw these parts.

7. *Draw the kitchen cabinets, appliances, and bathroom fixtures.* Kitchen base cabinets are usually 24 in. deep and wall cabinets 12 in. deep. The base units are shown as solid lines while the wall cabinets are indicated using a hidden line symbol. The refrigerator and range are usually deeper than 24 in. and should be represented as such. Bathroom vanities and fixtures should be located and drawn in the same way as kitchen cabinets and appliances. Be sure to check the code for clearances required for fixtures. Refer to Chapters 5 and 7 for information about bathrooms and kitchens.

Fig. 16-11. Units for linear measurement in the construction industry should be restricted to the meter (m) and the millimeter (mm). Thus on drawings, whole number dimensions will always indicate millimeters, and decimalized numbers (to 3 places of decimals) will always indicate meters.

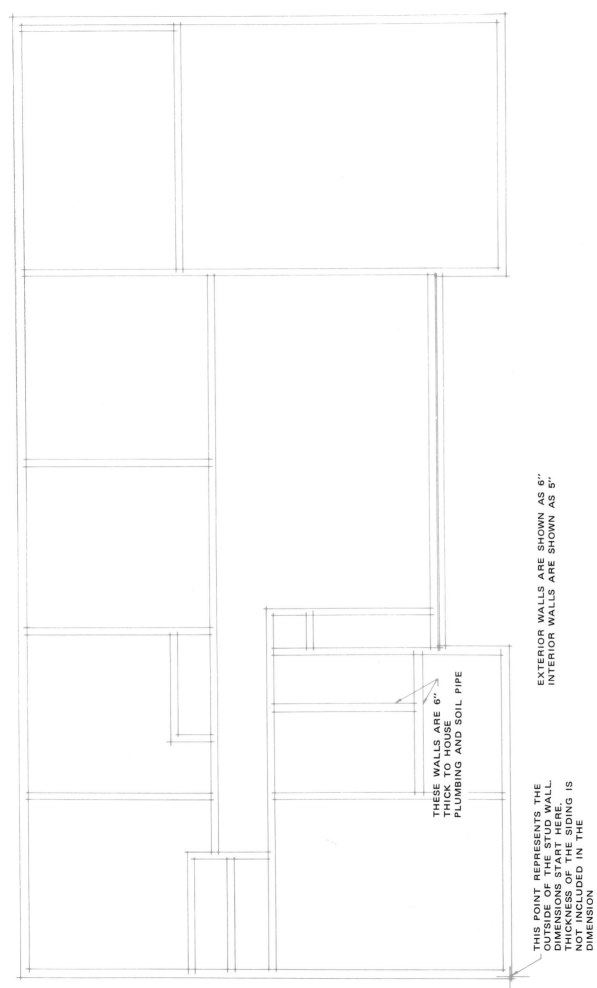

THIS POINT REPRESENTS THE
OUTSIDE OF THE STUD WALL.
DIMENSIONS START HERE.
THICKNESS OF THE SIDING IS
NOT INCLUDED IN THE
DIMENSION

THESE WALLS ARE 6"
THICK TO HOUSE
PLUMBING AND SOIL PIPE

EXTERIOR WALLS ARE SHOWN AS 6"
INTERIOR WALLS ARE SHOWN AS 5"

Fig. 16-12. A layout of the interior and exterior wall locations using light construction lines for a small ranch-type house with a basement.

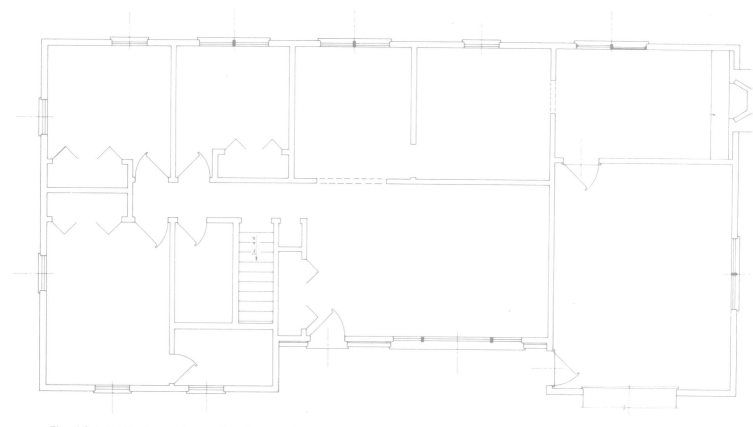

Fig. 16-13. Windows, doors, fireplace, and stairs have been added to the layout. Lines showing walls and symbols have been darkened.

8. **Add dimensions, notes, and room names.** Keep in mind the guidelines for dimensioning that were presented earlier in this chapter. Make sure the dimensions are accurate and complete. Letter the room name in the center of each room and show the approximate room size below the name if desired. Look over the drawing and add any general or specific notes that seem warranted. Steps 6, 7, and 8 are shown in Fig. 16-14. Note: It is important to show dimensions for all exterior wall features on the wall where they are located.

9. **Add material and identification symbols.** It is better to wait until the drawing is nearly finished to add material symbols so they do not interfere with dimensions or notes. Add the necessary symbols and darken in lines which are light. **All object lines, hidden lines, center lines, etc. on a drawing should be black and only vary in width.** Exceptions are guidelines and construction lines. You may wish to remove the construction lines, but do not remove the guidelines.

10. **Draw the title block and add the scale.** The scale is important and should be placed in a prominent location near the bottom of the drawing. It may be located in the title block if all drawings on the sheet are the same scale. The title block should include the following informa-

tion: sheet number, name of drawing, scale, date, who the drawing is for, who made the drawing, and any other information which is deemed necessary. Steps 9 and 10 are shown in Fig. 16-15.

11. **Check the entire drawing.** Examine all aspects of the drawing for accuracy and completeness.

The floor plan for a split-level house is presented in Fig. 16-16. This illustration shows the typical way of drawing a floor plan for a split-level house. First and second level floor plans of a common two-story house are shown in Figs. 16-17 and 16-18.

The plan shown in Fig. 16-19 is designed for expansion. The basic house, 28 x 52 ft. contains the necessary space for a small family. As the family grows, the house may be enlarged to meet the family's needs. A bedroom and bath could be added first and the breezeway, bath, and mudroom added later. Finally, the garage, storage, and porch may be built to complete the expanded plan which measures approximately 34 x 74 ft.

Expansion plans have much to offer. When additions are planned for in the initial design stage, the expanded house does not appear ''added on to.'' Also, fewer basic changes are required when additions are ultimately made.

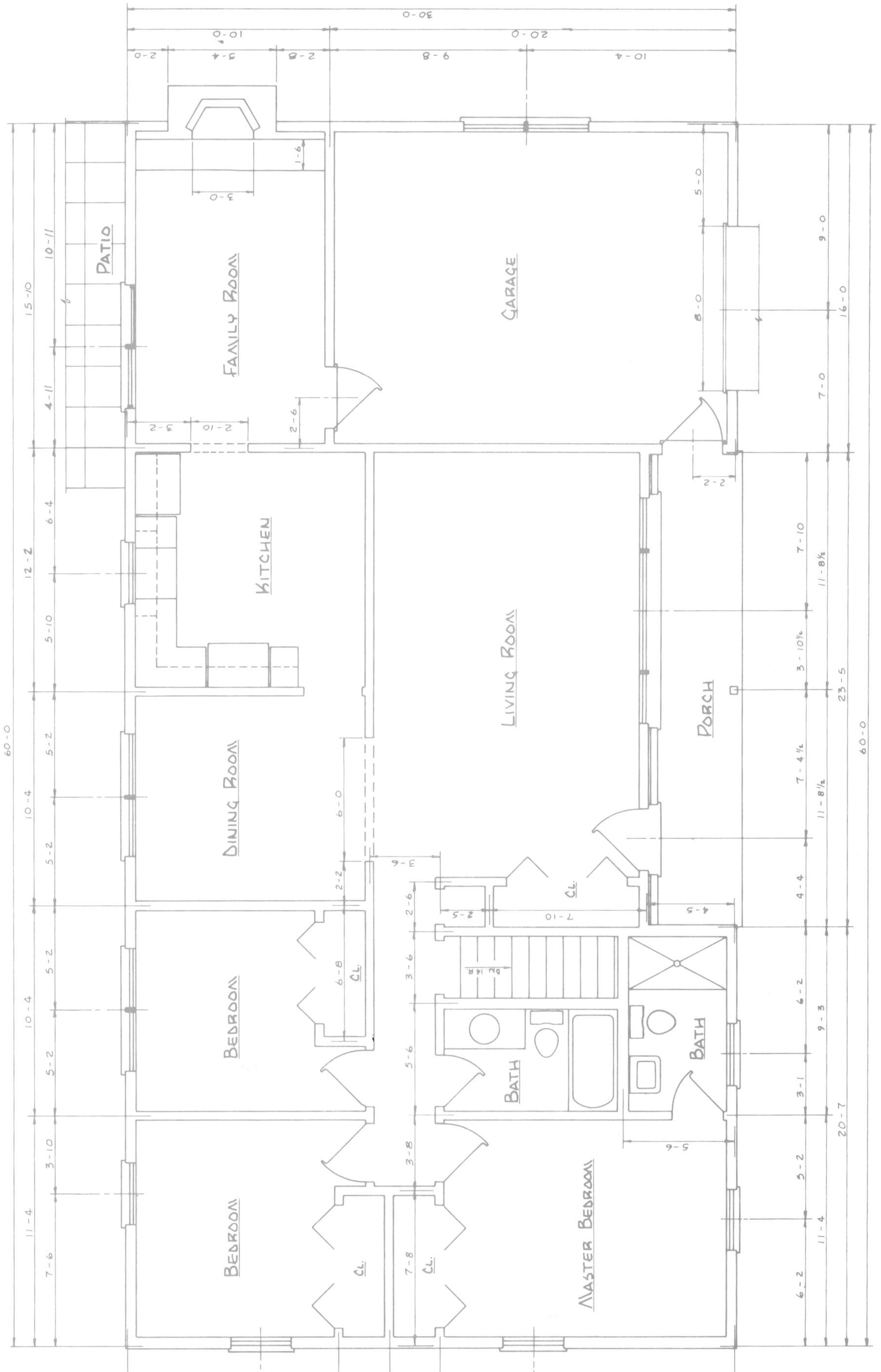

Fig. 16-14. A patio and porch, kitchen cabinets, bathroom fixtures, room names, and dimensions have been added to the plan.

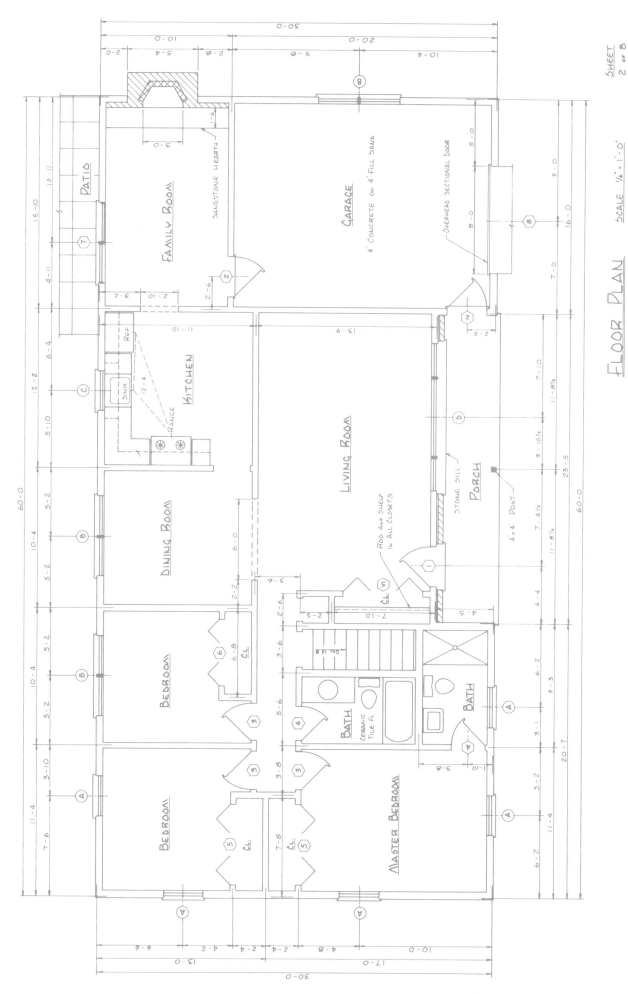

Fig. 16-15. The floor plan is completed by adding material and identification symbols, notes, scale, and name of the drawing.

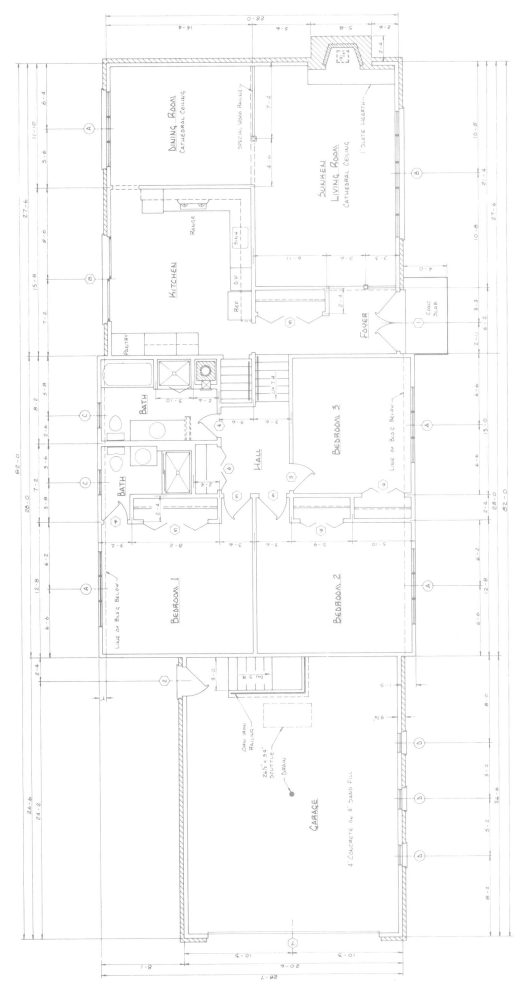

FLOOR PLAN
SCALE — ¼" = 1'-0"

Fig. 16-16. Upper level floor plan for a split-level house. The basement/foundation plan of this house would present the lower level layout. (Donald F. Sowa, A.R.A.)

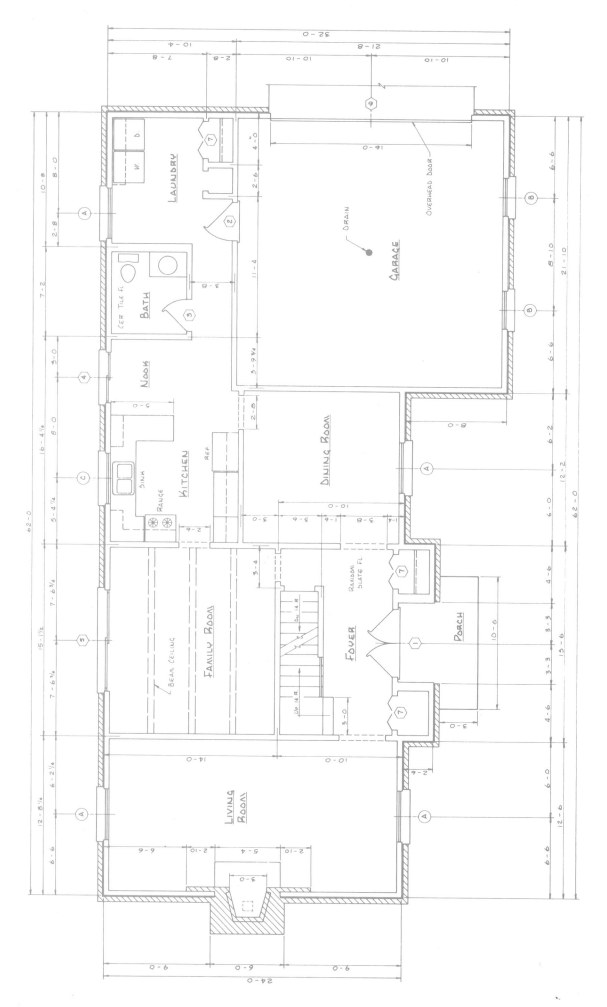

FIRST FLOOR PLAN
SCALE — ¼" = 1'-0"

Fig. 16-17. The first floor plan for a brick veneer, two-story house. Second floor plan is shown in Fig. 16-18.

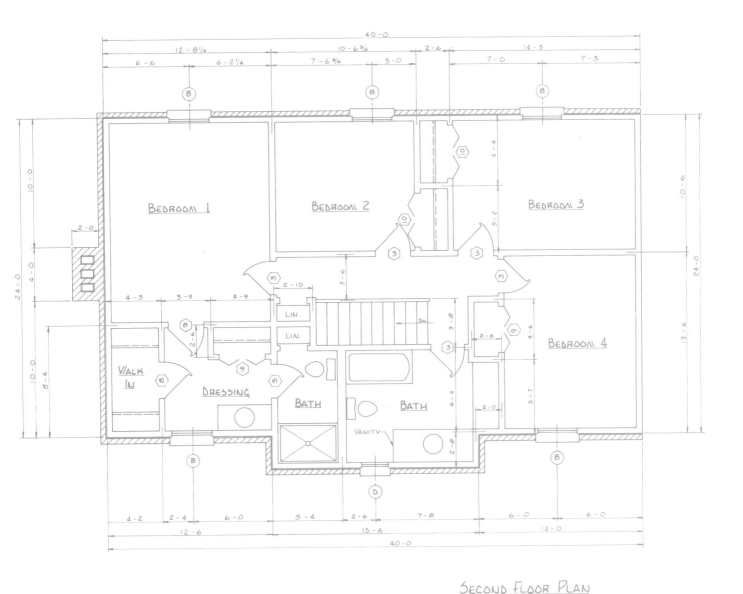

SECOND FLOOR PLAN
SCALE — 1/4" = 1'-0"

Fig. 16-18. The second floor plan for the two-story home shown in Fig. 16-17.

REVIEW QUESTIONS—CHAPTER 16

Write your answers on a separate sheet of paper. Do not write in this book.

1. A floor plan is not a typical top view, but a _____ drawing.
2. What is the purpose of a floor plan?
3. The scale of most residential floor plans is _____.
4. The actual thickness of an exterior frame wall with 1/2'' insulation board, 1/2'' dry wall, and 5/8'' siding on a 1 1/2'' x 3 1/2'' framing member (stud) is 5 1/8'', however an exterior frame wall may be represented as _____ on the floor plan.
5. Windows and doors are dimensioned to the _____ in frame construction.
6. Windows and doors are dimensioned to _____ in a solid masonry wall.
7. Indicate the symbol commonly used to show an archway.
8. List information generally given on the floor plan about a set of stairs.
9. Indicate the section symbol for the following materials:
   a. Plaster
   b. Aluminum
   c. Rigid Insulation
   d. Dimension Lumber
   e. Common Brick
   f. Cast Concrete
10. Show the two ways of representing a dimension of 4 in. on a floor plan.

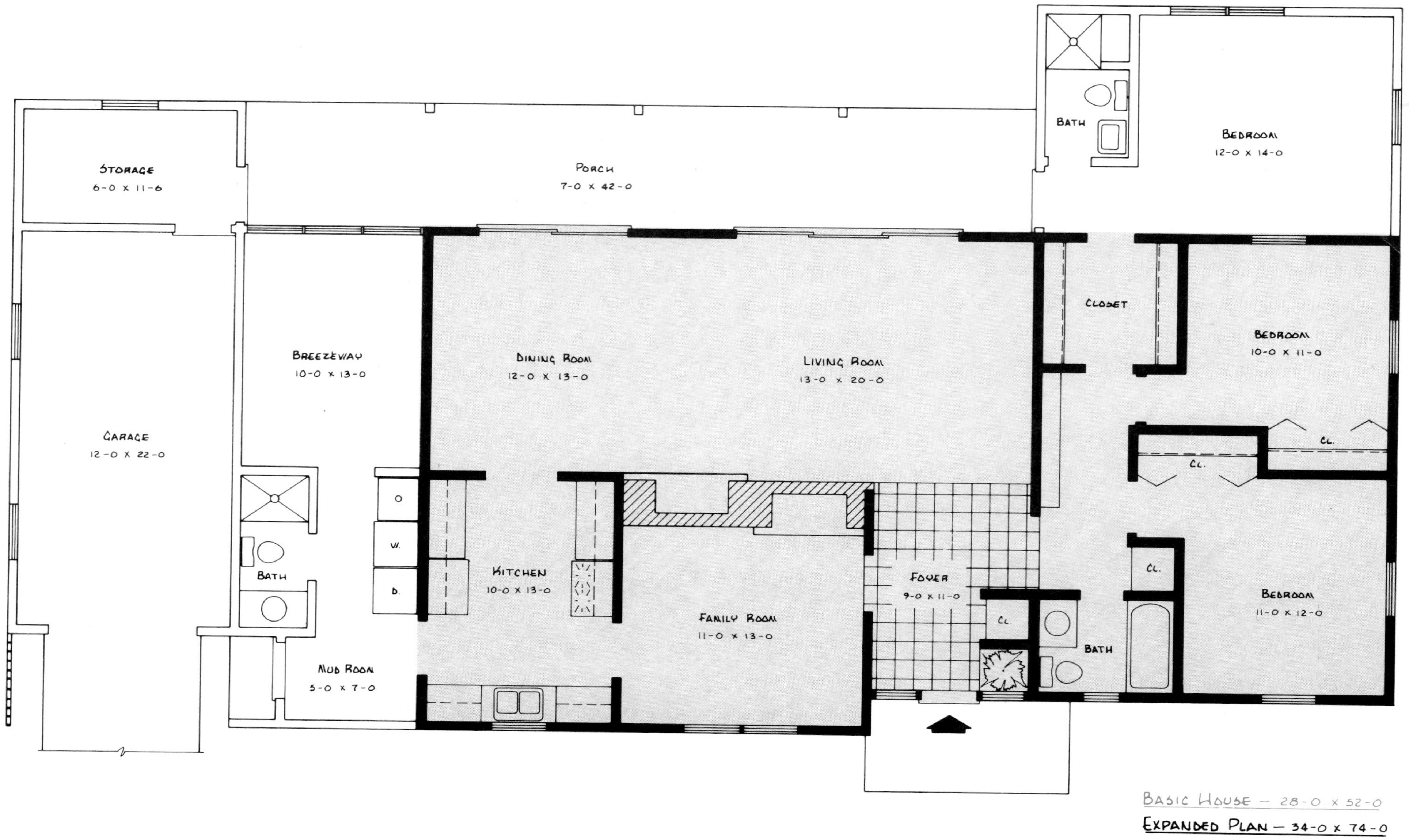

BASIC HOUSE — 28-0 × 52-0
EXPANDED PLAN — 34-0 × 74-0

BEDROOM
12-0 × 14-0

BEDROOM
10-0 × 11-0

BEDROOM
11-0 × 12-0

CL.

CL.

CL.

BATH

CLOSET

BATH

CL.

FOYER
9-0 × 11-0

LIVING ROOM
13-0 × 20-0

FAMILY ROOM
11-0 × 13-0

PORCH
7-0 × 42-0

DINING ROOM
12-0 × 13-0

KITCHEN
10-0 × 13-0

BREEZEWAY
10-0 × 13-0

BATH

MUD ROOM
5-0 × 7-0

STORAGE
6-0 × 11-6

GARAGE
12-0 × 22-0

Fig. 16-19. This basic house may be expanded from 1456 to 2516 sq. ft. The additions (which were preplanned) include a bedroom, two baths, a breezeway, mudroom, storage, garage, and porch.

1. Find a floor plan for a small house or cottage in a magazine, newspaper, or other source. Draw it to 1/4'' = 1'-0'' scale. Show all necessary dimensions, notes and symbols. Prepare a window and door schedule. Present your drawing along with the original.
2. Design a modern ranch style house for the following specifications:

Flat lot	Two-car garage
Three bedrooms	Slab floor construction
1 1/2 baths	No basement
Living room	Frame construction
Kitchen	Patio
Dining Room	Fireplace

3. Draw a floor plan for a one-bedroom apartment with a living room, kitchen and dining area, bath, and storage area. Interior walls are frame and exterior walls are brick veneer on 8 in. concrete block. Calculate the living space.
4. Secure the floor plan for a house or apartment which you feel has a poor arrangement and utilization of space. Redesign this plan and present both for comparison.

Examine the features of this contemporary split level and then compare to the construction drawings shown in Chapter 3.

Roof design is an important element in the overall architectural appearance of the structure. (Elk Corporation)

Roof Designs

After studying this chapter, you will be able to:
- Sketch ten different types of basic roof designs.
- Describe the construction of a typical frame roof.
- Draw a roof using a typical roof slope or pitch.
- Interpret information found on a rafter span chart.
- Explain the importance of proper ventilation and flashing.
- Compile the appropriate information to order roof trusses for a specific dwelling.

TYPES OF ROOFS

The overall appearance of a home is greatly affected by the roof lines and materials used for roof construction, Fig. 17-1. The designer has many standard designs to choose from. He/she should be able to find one which will complement the basic design of the home being constructed. Fig. 17-2 shows traditional and modern roof types commonly used in residential construction.

Fig. 17-1. An architect's design of the roof and selection of roofing materials has a significant impact on the finished appearance of the residence. (Red Cedar Shingle and Handsplit Shake Bureau)

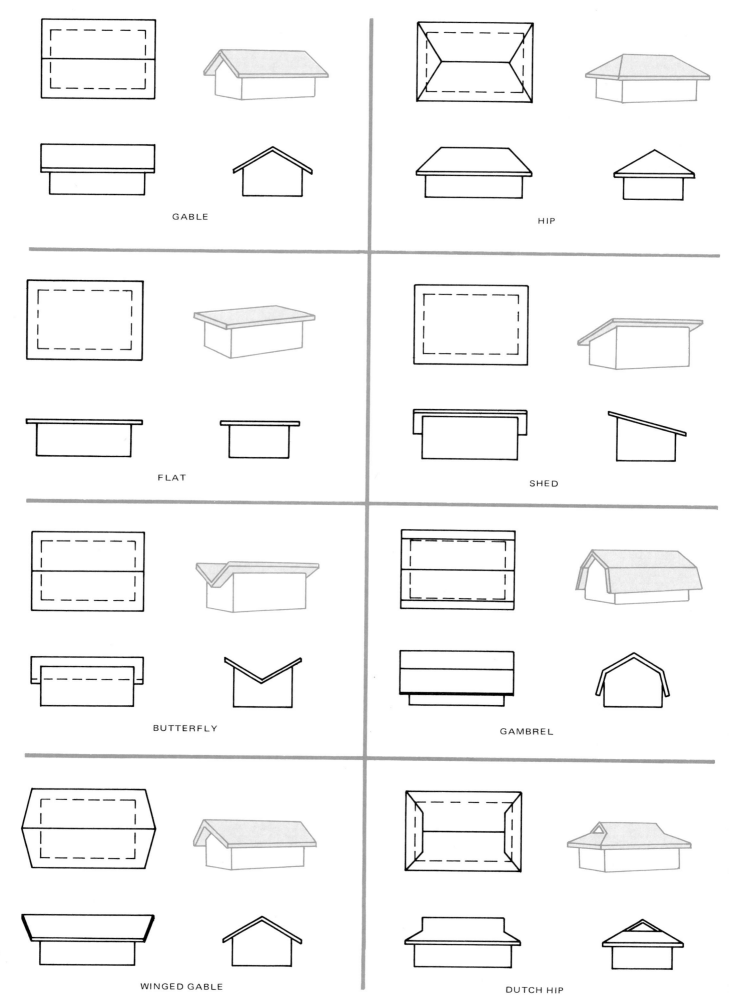

GABLE

HIP

FLAT

SHED

BUTTERFLY

GAMBREL

WINGED GABLE

DUTCH HIP

Fig. 17-2. Roof designs which may be used in residential construction. (Continued)

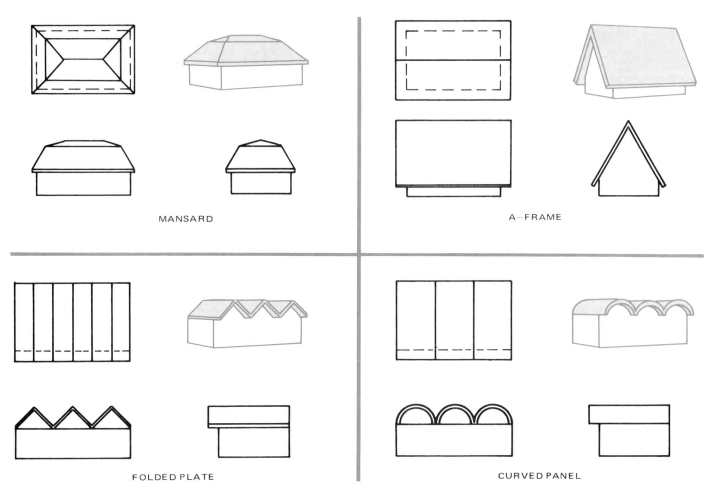

MANSARD

A—FRAME

FOLDED PLATE

CURVED PANEL

Fig. 17-2. Continued.

GABLE ROOF

The gable roof is a very popular type of roof. It is easy to build, sheds water well, provides for ventilation, and is applicable to a variety of house shapes and designs.

HIP ROOF

The hip roof is slightly more difficult to build than a gable roof, but is still a popular choice. It does not provide for ventilation as well as some other designs and increases the chance for leakage due to the hips and valleys.

FLAT ROOF

A flat roof is the most economical roof to construct, but does not add much to the design of most houses. It requires a "built-up" or membrane roof covering rather than conventional shingles. A built-up roof consists of layers of roofing felt and tar or some other material, such as rubber topped with gravel. Actually, most so-called flat roofs are pitched at about 1/8 to 1/2 in. per foot to aid in drainage. The flat roof is popular in warmer areas of the country where wide overhangs are desirable for shade and where little or no snow falls.

SHED ROOF

A shed roof is similar to a flat roof, but has more pitch. It is frequently used for additions to existing structures or in combination with other roof styles. A built-up roof is generally required unless the roof has a pitch of over 3:12. (Three feet rise for each 12 feet of run.)

MANSARD ROOF

The mansard roof is gaining in popularity after being used infrequently for several years. It is a French design and is more difficult to construct than the hip or gable, but does have interesting lines.

GAMBREL ROOF

The gambrel roof is sometimes called a barn roof because it has been used extensively on barns. It provides the additional headroom needed for the Dutch colonial.

BUTTERFLY ROOF

The butterfly roof has not been used widely in the past, but seems to be gaining in acceptance. It has the advantage of providing plenty of light and ventilation, but drainage is a problem. Flashing should extend far up each slope along the valley to prevent leaking.

A-FRAME ROOF

The A-frame provides not only a roof but the walls as well. Originally, it was used for cottages, but in recent years it has been applied to homes, churches, and other structures.

FOLDED PLATE ROOF

The folded plate roof is a contemporary design which is finding limited application in residential buildings. However, it is quite popular for motels and small commercial buildings. Modular, prefabricated roof units are being produced which will probably increase the popularity of this design.

CURVED PANEL ROOF

Curved panel roofs are similar to the folded plate in style and application. To this point in time they have had only limited use in home construction. They too are being produced in prefabricated modules.

OTHER CONTEMPORARY ROOF TYPES

Several other modern roof types are being experimented with and should be identified. The *parasol roof* looks like an upturned parasol. It is usually constructed from concrete. *Warped roofs* are limitless in design. They may be constructed from concrete, molded plywood, or plastics. Complete freedom is possible with the *free-form roof.* Urethane foam is a popular

Fig. 17-3. The importance of a well-designed roof is illustrated by each of these contemporary homes.
(Red Cedar Shingle and Handsplit Shake Bureau; The Celotex Corporation; California Redwood Association)

choice of material for this roof. It is sprayed over a network of pipes and net material. It is strong and weather resistant. Fig. 17-3 shows several modern residential structures with interesting roof styles.

TRADITIONAL
FRAME ROOF CONSTRUCTION

Rafters

Roof covering material is supported by roof framing. The framing must be strong and rigid. Roof framing consists of several distinct structural elements. The first and most basic of these elements is the *rafter.* Common rafters are perpendicular to the top wall plate. They extend from the plate or beyond to the ridge of the roof. Fig. 17-4 shows a plan view of the roof framing for a simple structure. Note that several types of rafters other than common rafters are identified.

Rafters are cut to the proper dimensions by locating the ridge cut, seat cut, plumb cuts, and tail cut, Fig. 17-5. The precise layout of these cuts is determined by the *slope* or *pitch* of the roof and the *inside width* or *clear span* of the building. Terms that must be understood before

calculating rafter dimensions and roof pitch are rise, run, and span. The *rise* of a roof is the vertical distance measured from the top of the wall plate to the underside of the rafters. The *run* of a roof is one-half the distance of the clear span. The *clear span* is the horizontal distance from the inside of one stud wall to the inside of the opposite stud wall. Fig. 17-6 graphically illustrates these terms.

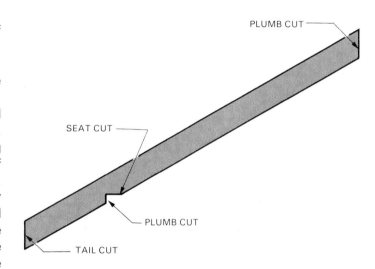

Fig. 17-5. A common rafter with the various cuts labeled.

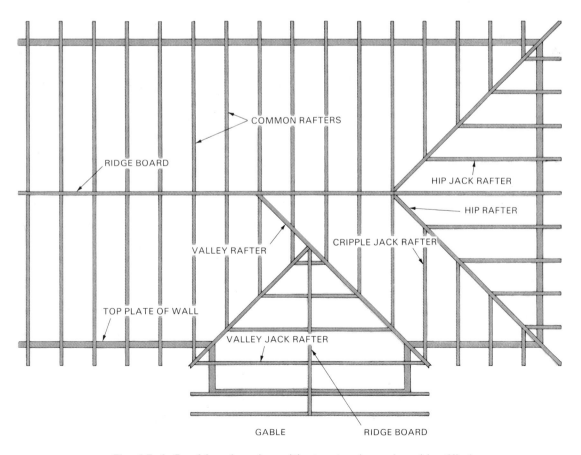

Fig. 17-4. Roof framing plan with structural members identified.

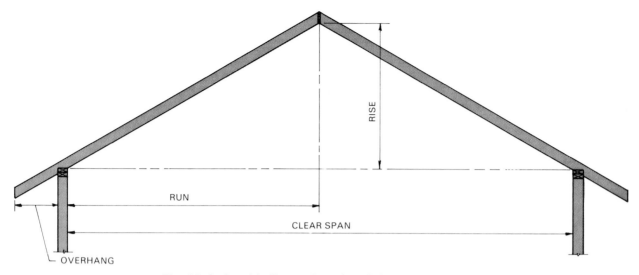

Fig. 17-6. Graphic illustration of roof rise, run, and span.

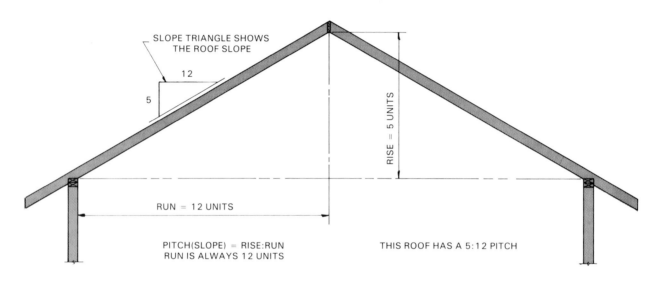

Fig. 17-7. The roof slope diagram represents the relationship of the rise to the run.

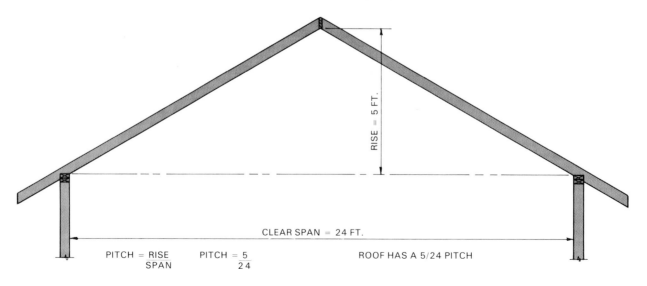

Fig. 17-8. The roof slope shown as a fractional pitch denotes the relationship between the rise and span.

Roof slope may be given on a drawing by showing a slope ratio diagram or a fractional pitch indication. The slope diagram, Fig. 17-7, represents the ratio between the rise and run of the roof. The fractional pitch is calculated using the following formula:

$$\text{Pitch} = \frac{\text{Rise}}{\text{Clear Span}}$$

Fig. 17-8 illustrates the fractional pitch for the same roof slope shown in Fig. 17-7.

Roof slope may also be shown using an angular dimension. However, this method is seldom used because it is difficult to measure as accurately as either of the other methods. A roof with a 45 degree slope has a 12:12 or 1/2 pitch. Fig. 17-9 shows several common roof pitches used in residential construction. When designing a

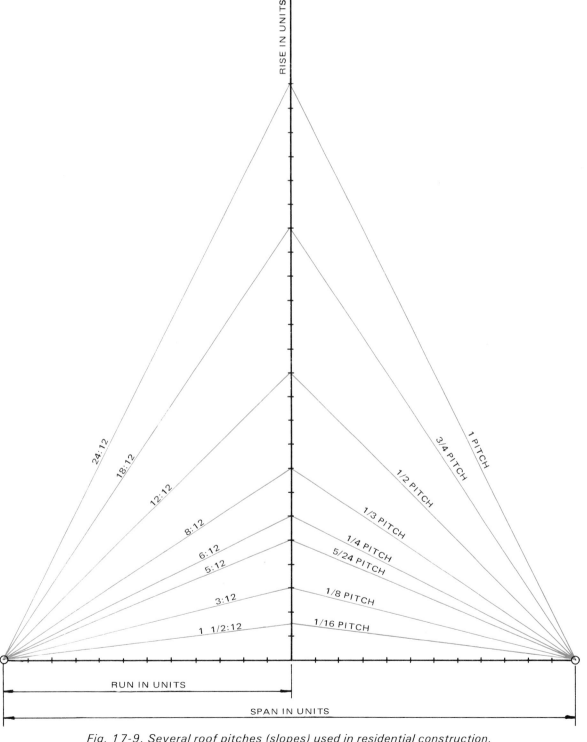

RISE IN UNITS

24:12
18:12
12:12
8:12
6:12
5:12
3:12
1 1/2:12

1 PITCH
3/4 PITCH
1/2 PITCH
1/3 PITCH
1/4 PITCH
5/24 PITCH
1/8 PITCH
1/16 PITCH

RUN IN UNITS

SPAN IN UNITS

Fig. 17-9. Several roof pitches (slopes) used in residential construction.

roof, try to use one of the standard roof pitches (slopes).

Rafter sizes will depend on the distance to be spanned, the spacing of the rafters, and the weight to be supported. Rafter span data is presented in Fig. 17-10. Rafters for low slope roofs may also serve as a base for the finished ceiling. In this instance, they are acting as rafters and ceiling joists, Fig. 17-11. Normal rafters are listed in the table under roof slope of over 3:12 pitch. A light roofing is one which weighs less than four pounds per square foot, Fig. 17-12.

RAFTER SPAN DATA

ROOF SLOPE OF 3:12 OR LESS*

NOMINAL SIZE IN INCHES	SPACING IN INCHES O.C.	NONSUPPORTING FINISHED CEILING					SUPPORTING FINISHED CEILING				
		DOUGLAS FIR AND LARCH									
		SELECT STRUCT.	DENSE CONSTR.	CONSTR.	STANDARD	UTILITY	SELECT STRUCT.	DENSE CONSTR.	CONSTR.	STANDARD	UTILITY
		SOUTHERN YELLOW PINE									
		NO. 1 K.D.	NO. 2 K.D.	NO. 1	NO. 2		NO. 1 K.D.	NO.2 K.D.	NO. 1	NO. 2	
2 x 6	12	14 4	14 4	14 4	14 4	9 6	13 8	13 8	13 8	13 8	8 10
	16	13 0	13 0	13 0	12 10	8 4	12 4	12 4	12 4	11 10	7 8
	24	11 4	11 4	11 4	10 6	6 8	10 10	10 10	10 8	9 8	6 2
2 x 8	12	18 4	18 4	18 4	18 4	14 4	17 8	17 8	17 8	17 8	13 2
	16	17 0	17 0	17 0	17 0	12 4	16 4	16 4	16 4	16 2	11 6
	24	15 4	15 4	15 4	15 4	10 0	14 8	14 8	14 6	13 2	9 4
2 x 10	12	21 10	21 10	21 10	21 0	19 6	21 0	21 0	21 0	21 0	18 0
	16	20 4	20 4	20 4	20 4	16 10	19 6	19 6	19 6	19 6	15 8
	24	18 4	18 4	18 4	18 4	13 10	17 8	17 8	17 8	16 8	12 10
2 x 12	12	24 0	24 0	24 0	24 0	22 8	24 0	24 0	24 0	24 0	21 0
	16	23 6	23 6	23 6	23 6	19 8	22 6	22 6	22 6	22 6	18 2
	24	21 2	21 2	21 2	21 2	16 2	20 4	20 4	20 4	20 2	14 10

SPANS ARE IN FT. AND INCHES.

(National Forest Products Assoc.)

*CALCULATIONS ARE BASED ON:

LIGHT ROOFING – LESS THAN 4 POUNDS PER SQ. FT.

A DEAD LOAD OF 15 POUNDS PER SQ. FT. AND A LIVE LOAD OF 20 POUNDS PER SQ. FT. FOR A FINISHED CEILING.

DEFLECTION NOT TO EXCEED 1/240TH OF THE CLEAR SPAN

ROOF SLOPE OVER 3:12*

NOMINAL SIZE IN INCHES	SPACING IN INCHES O.C.	LIGHT ROOFING					HEAVY ROOFING				
		DOUGLAS FIR AND LARCH									
		SELECT STRUCT.	DENSE CONSTR.	CONSTR.	STANDARD	UTILITY	SELECT STRUCT.	DENSE CONSTR.	CONSTR.	STANDARD	UTILITY
		SOUTHERN YELLOW PINE									
		NO. 1 K.D.	NO. 2 K.D.	NO. 1	NO. 2		NO. 1 K.D.	NO.2 K.D.	NO. 1	NO. 2	
2 x 6	12	16 10	16 10	16 10	16 10	11 2	15 6	15 6	15 6	14 10	9 6
	16	15 8	15 8	15 8	15 0	9 8	14 4	14 4	14 0	12 10	8 4
	24	13 10	13 10	13 6	12 2	7 10	12 6	12 6	11 6	10 6	6 8
2 x 8	12	21 2	21 2	21 2	21 2	16 8	19 8	19 8	19 8	19 8	14 4
	16	19 10	19 10	19 10	19 10	14 4	18 4	18 4	18 4	17 6	12 4
	24	17 10	17 10	17 10	16 8	11 0	16 6	16 6	15 8	14 4	10 0
2 x 10	12	24 0	24 0	24 0	24 0	22 10	23 6	23 6	23 6	23 6	19 6
	16	23 8	23 8	23 8	23 8	19 8	21 10	21 10	21 10	21 10	16 10
	24	21 4	21 4	21 4	21 0	16 2	19 8	19 8	19 8	18 8	13 10

SPANS ARE IN FEET AND INCHES

(National Forest Products Assoc.)

*CALCULATIONS ARE BASED ON:

LIGHT ROOFING WHICH IS LESS THAN 4 POUNDS PER SQ. FT. OR HEAVY ROOFING – OVER 4 POUNDS PER SQ. FT.

A DEAD LOAD OF 15 POUNDS PER SQ. FT. AND A LIVE LOAD OF 15 POUNDS PER SQ. FT. FOR HEAVY ROOFING

DEFLECTION NOT TO EXCEED 1/240TH OF THE CLEAR SPAN

Fig. 17-10. The maximum allowable rafter span may be determined by referring to these charts. Rafter span is the horizontal distance between supports. This is not to be confused with rafter length, which must be calculated using the rise and run of the roof.

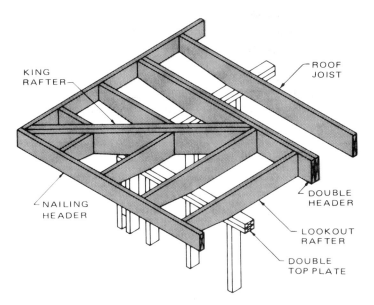

Fig. 17-11. Framing detail of the cornice for a flat or low pitched roof.

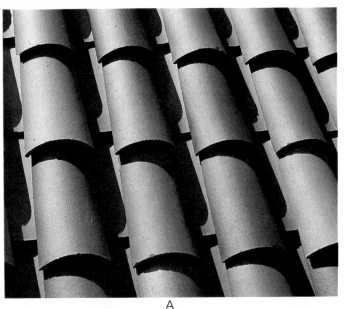

A

B

Fig. 17-13. Clay roofing tile. A–Two-piece taper mission tile. (Craycroft Brick Company) B–Flat clay shingle with equal widths. (Craycroft Brick Company)

Fig. 17-12. Common example of light roofing which weighs less than four pounds per square foot. (Marvin Windows)

Anything more is considered heavy roofing. A slate or clay tile roof is an example of a heavy roofing material, Fig. 17-13.

Cornice

The cornice is the overhang of the roof at the eaves line that forms a connection between the roof and side walls. In a gable roof it is formed on two sides of the building. The cornice continues around all four sides on a hip or flat roof.

The three types of cornices frequently used in residential buildings are the **open cornice, box cornice,** and **close cornice.** The open cornice, Fig. 17-14, may be used with exposed beam construction, contemporary, or rustic designs. Rafter ends are exposed and are usually tapered or curved to prevent a bulky appearance.

There are three basic types of box cornices: the **narrow box, wide box with lookouts,** and **wide box without lookouts.** A narrow box cornice is usually between 6 and 12 in. wide. The soffit board is nailed directly to the bottom side

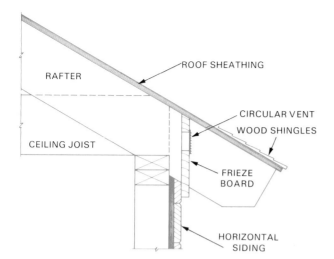

Fig. 17-14. Section through an open cornice.

of the rafters, Fig. 17-15. A wide box cornice with lookouts normally requires additional support members (lookouts) for fastening the soffit. Fig. 17-16 shows a wide box cornice with lookouts. A wide box cornice without lookouts has a sloped soffit. The soffit material is nailed to the underside of the rafters. This type of cornice is frequently used when the overhangs are very wide, Fig. 17-17.

A close cornice is one in which the rafter does not project beyond the wall. The roof is terminated by a frieze board and molding, Fig. 17-18.

RAKE OR GABLE END

The *rake* or gable end is the extension of a gable roof beyond the end wall of the house. The

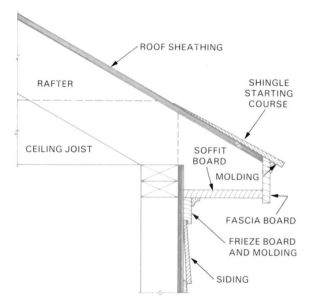

Fig. 17-15. Section through a narrow box cornice.

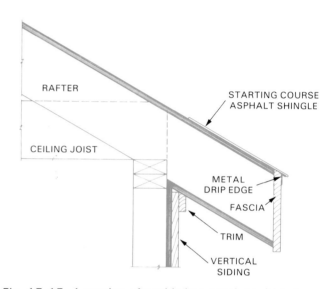

Fig. 17-17. A section of a wide box cornice without lookouts.

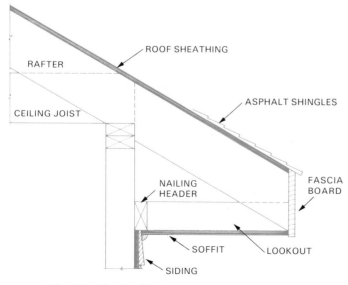

Fig. 17-16. A wide box cornice with lookouts.

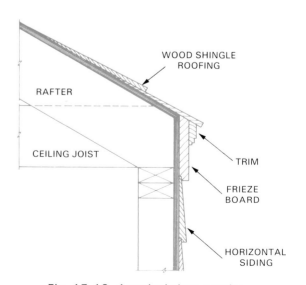

Fig. 17-18. A typical close cornice.

amount of overhang and treatment at the gable end should be about the same as the cornice. For example, if a close cornice is used, then a close rake should also be used. Fig. 17-19 shows the framing for a gable end with a wide overhang. A close rake is less expensive to build, but wide overhangs provide for side wall protection and less frequent painting.

The style of house must be considered when designing the gable end. A narrow box cornice is normally used for Cape Cod or colonial homes. The same proportions should be extended to the gable end.

ROOF TRUSSES

The roof truss is an assembly of members which forms a rigid framework of triangular shapes. This arrangement permits wide unsupported spans with a minimum amount of material. Fig. 17-20 shows several roof truss designs.

Lightweight wood roof trusses are designed to span distances of 20 to 32 ft. and in some instances even more. Many times they are less expensive than conventional framing. Time and expense is saved in the erection. Prefabricated trusses are readily available for standard widths and pitches. Trusses for nonstandard dimensions may be built on the site or factory produced. Most lightweight trusses are made from 2 x 4 in. lumber, however, 2 x 6 in. lumber may be used for wider spans and heavier loads.

Wood trusses which are commonly used in residential construction are the W-Type truss, Fig. 17-21; the King-post truss, Fig. 17-22; and the Scissors truss, Fig. 17-23. Most trusses are designed to be placed 24 in. o.c. Ceiling materials are nailed directly to the bottom of the trusses.

Information needed to purchase the proper truss for a house includes the span, roof pitch, spacing of the trusses, and the anticipated roof load. A roof load of 40 pounds per square foot is adequate for most applications.

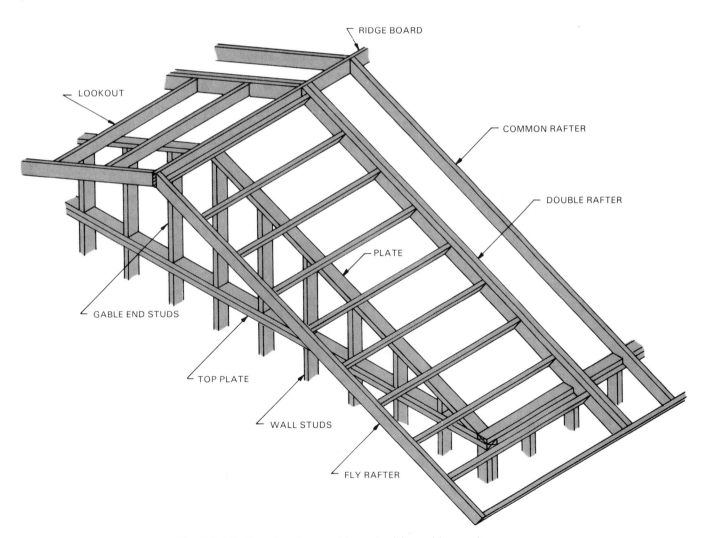

Fig. 17-19. Framing for a gable end with a wide overhang.

REPRESENTATIVE TRUSS CONFIGURATIONS

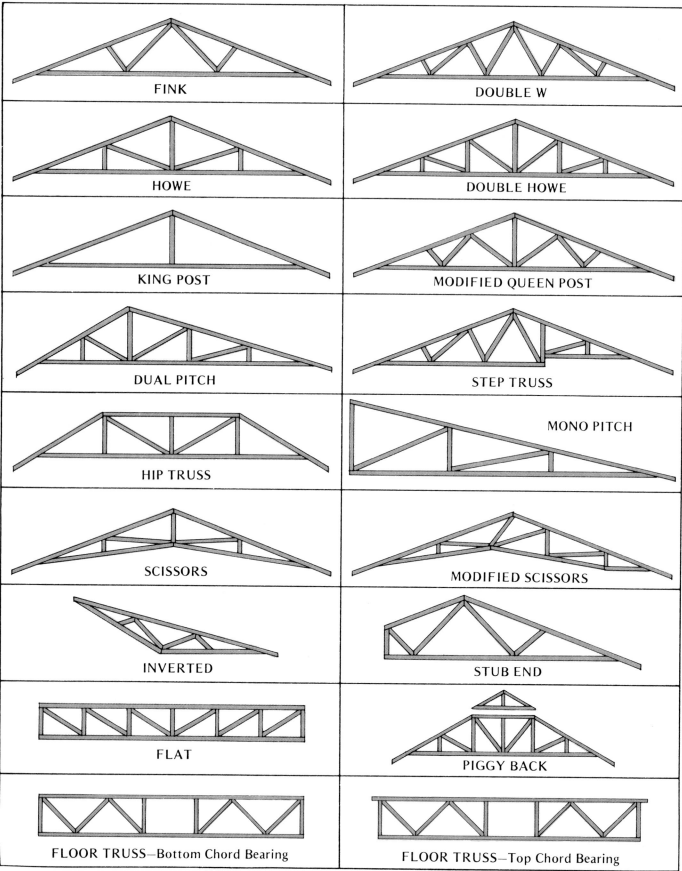

FINK

DOUBLE W

HOWE

DOUBLE HOWE

KING POST

MODIFIED QUEEN POST

DUAL PITCH

STEP TRUSS

HIP TRUSS

MONO PITCH

SCISSORS

MODIFIED SCISSORS

INVERTED

STUB END

FLAT

PIGGY BACK

FLOOR TRUSS—Bottom Chord Bearing

FLOOR TRUSS—Top Chord Bearing

NOTE: The number of webs and web configurations can vary from those shown.

Fig. 17-20. Common roof truss designs used in residential construction.

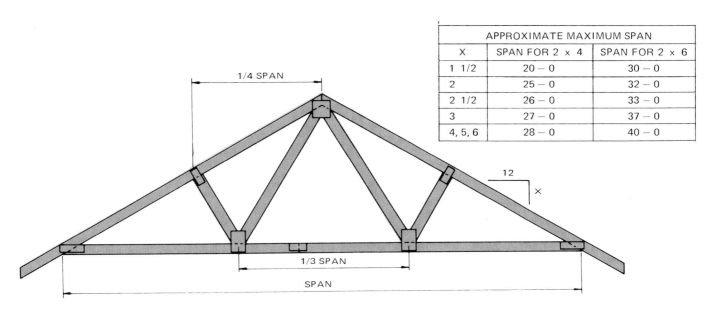

APPROXIMATE MAXIMUM SPAN		
X	SPAN FOR 2 x 4	SPAN FOR 2 x 6
1 1/2	20 — 0	30 — 0
2	25 — 0	32 — 0
2 1/2	26 — 0	33 — 0
3	27 — 0	37 — 0
4, 5, 6	28 — 0	40 — 0

Fig. 17-21. Design data for a W-type truss.

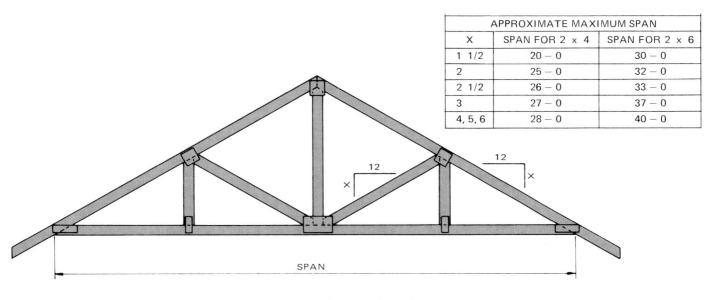

APPROXIMATE MAXIMUM SPAN		
X	SPAN FOR 2 x 4	SPAN FOR 2 x 6
1 1/2	20 — 0	30 — 0
2	25 — 0	32 — 0
2 1/2	26 — 0	33 — 0
3	27 — 0	37 — 0
4, 5, 6	28 — 0	40 — 0

Fig. 17-22. Design data for a K-post truss.

APPROXIMATE MAXIMUM SPAN		
X	SPAN FOR 2 x 4	SPAN FOR 2 x 6
4, 5, 6	28 — 0	40 — 0

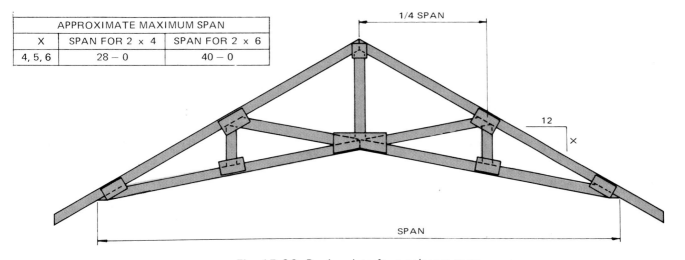

Fig. 17-23. Design data for a scissors truss.

Wood trusses are frequently fastened together with **gussets,** Fig. 17-24. These gussets are made from 3/8 or 1/2 in. plywood using exterior-type glue, or from metal, Fig. 17-25.

Roof trusses that extend the bottom chord beyond the exterior wall provide additional space for ceiling insulation. This construction, Fig. 17-26, allows 12 in. of batt insulation to be

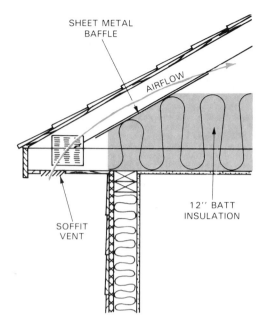

Fig. 17-26. By extending the bottom chord beyond the exterior of the structure with roof trusses, additional space is allowed for ceiling insulation. This method permits 12 in. of insulation and does not interfere with ventilation.

Fig. 17-24. Light wood trusses fastened together with plywood gussets form the roof framing for this house. (American Plywood Assoc.)

extended to the outside of the exterior wall without interfering with attic ventilation. This amount of insulation is generally not possible with traditional roof framing methods. The increased airflow reduces moisture condensation on the underside of the roof sheathing and prevents damage to the structure.

VENTILATION

Providing for adequate ventilation in the attic space is a necessity. If sufficient ventilation is not provided, moisture will probably form on the underside of the roof sheathing and in time damage will result. Also, a well-ventilated attic will help to cool the interior of the housing during the summer.

Ventilation in the attic space is usually accomplished through the use of louvered openings in the gable ends and along the underside of the overhang. Ridge ventilators are also available which provide an efficient means of expelling hot air when coupled with soffit openings. The difference between the temperature of air in the attic and the outside causes air movement and thus reduces the temperature inside.

Experience has shown that the total area of ventilator openings should be at least 1/300th of the ceiling area. For example, if the ceiling area is 1200 sq. ft., then the ventilator area should be a minimum of 4 sq. ft. Fig. 17-27 shows several louvered gable-type ventilator

Fig. 17-25. Metal gussets are also commonly used in residential construction to fasten together wood trusses.

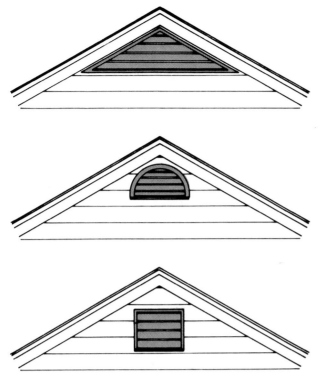

Fig. 17-27. Typical gable-type louvered ventilators.

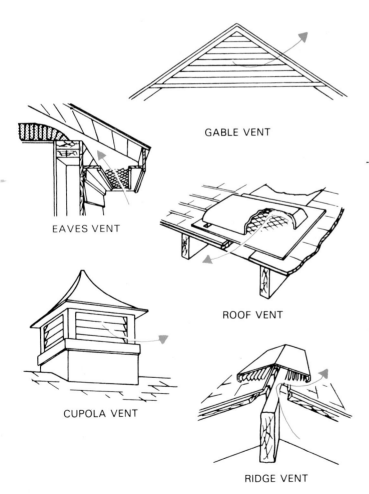

GABLE VENT

EAVES VENT

ROOF VENT

CUPOLA VENT

RIDGE VENT

Fig. 17-28. Several different methods of roof ventilation are possible.

openings. Fig. 17-28 shows a number of other types of ventilators that can be added to the roof to improve air flow.

FLASHING

Flashing should be used where the roof comes in contact with a wood or masonry wall, chimney, or roof valley—any element that penetrates the roof. Wide strips of weather-resistant metal such as aluminum, copper, and galvanized sheet steel are commonly used as flashing. This is worked beneath the surface material a distance sufficient to prevent the penetration of water. Fig. 17-29 shows flashing around a chimney.

Roof valleys may be flashed with metal or two thicknesses of roll type roofing. The width of valley flashing should be no less than specified below:

ROOF SLOPE		FLASHING WIDTH
Less than 4:12	–	24 inches wide
4:12 to 7:12	–	18 inches wide
Over 7:12	–	12 inches wide

Frequently a ribbon of asphalt-roofing mastic is used under the shingles adjacent to the valley

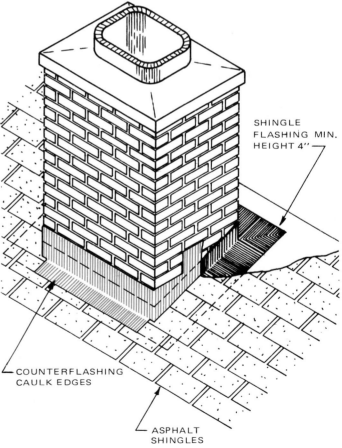

SHINGLE FLASHING MIN. HEIGHT 4"

COUNTERFLASHING CAULK EDGES

ASPHALT SHINGLES

Fig. 17-29. Flashing around a chimney is composed of shingle flashing and counterflashing.

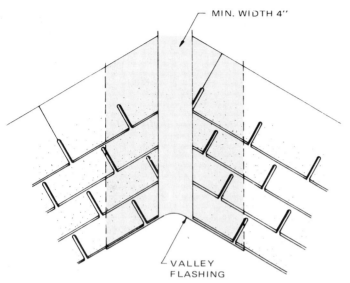

Fig. 17-30. The width of valley flashing is dependent upon the roof slope.

flashing, to aid in waterproofing the roof. Fig. 17-30 shows valley flashing under an asphalt shingle roof.

A small metal edging is normally used at the gable and eaves line to act as a drip edge. This flashing prevents water from entering behind the shingles and protects the fascia and rake boards, Fig. 17-31.

GUTTERS AND DOWNSPOUTS

Gutters collect the water from the roof and direct it to an outlet. This prevents water from running directly off the eaves and splattering the

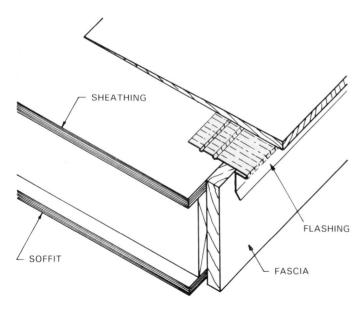

Fig. 17-31. Drip edge flashing prevents water from entering behind the shingles and protects the fascia.

house and running down the foundation wall. Gutters are usually pitched 1 to 1 1/2 in. in 20 ft. This slope permits even flow and prevents water from standing in the gutter.

Several styles of gutters and downspouts are available in copper, vinyl, aluminum, and galvanized sheet metal. The ogee style gutter is a popular type, Fig. 17-32. Several common shapes and sizes of gutters are shown in Fig. 17-33. Wood gutters are attractive on some home styles, but they are diminishing in importance due to high original and maintenance costs.

Fig. 17-32. Ogee style gutter made from aluminum. (Alside)

ROOF SHEATHING AND ROOFING

Roof sheathing is placed over the rafters to support the roofing material. Sheathing may be planks as in post and beam construction, individual boards, plywood, or other approved panel product. Except in the case where wood shingles are used as the roofing material, plywood is a popular choice. Usually 1 x 3 in. strips, spaced several inches apart, are used for wood shingle roofs, Fig. 17-34.

The thickness of sheathing will vary with the spacing of the rafters or supporting beams. However, in most situations (rafters spaced 16 or 24'' o.c.), 1/2 in. standard sheathing grade plywood is used. The plywood must be laid with the face grain perpendicular to the rafters as in

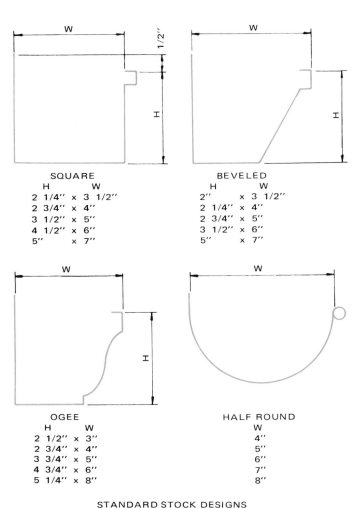

SQUARE
H	W
2 1/4''	x 3 1/2''
2 3/4''	x 4''
3 1/2''	x 5''
4 1/2''	x 6''
5''	x 7''

BEVELED
H	W
2''	x 3 1/2''
2 1/4''	x 4''
2 3/4''	x 5''
3 1/2''	x 6''
5''	x 7''

OGEE
H	W
2 1/2''	x 3''
2 3/4''	x 4''
3 3/4''	x 5''
4 3/4''	x 6''
5 1/4''	x 8''

HALF ROUND
W
4''
5''
6''
7''
8''

STANDARD STOCK DESIGNS

Fig. 17-33. Typical gutter designs and sizes. Lengths are usually 10 feet.

floor sheathing. The sheets should be staggered so that two sheets side-by-side do not end on the same rafter.

When individual boards are used as sheathing, they are usually no wider than 6 or 8 in. Minimum thickness is 3/4 in. for rafters 16 or 24'' o.c. Each board should be long enough to span a minimum of two rafters. Longer boards are desired for gable ends.

Roofing material used should be long-lived and provide a waterproof surface. Materials which have stood the test of time and have proven to be satisfactory include; asphalt shingles, wood shingles, Fig. 17-35, tile, slate, roll roofing, copper, aluminum, galvanized steel, layers of felt and tar, and rubber membrane roofing. Factors which influence the selection of the roofing material are cost, local codes, roof pitch, design, and individual preference.

More homes have asphalt shingle roofs than any other type. The usual recommended minimum weight of asphalt shingles is 235 pounds per square for square-butt strip shingles. A

Fig. 17-34. A shingled roof showing the exposed construction. (Southern Forest Products Assoc.)

square of shingles will cover 100 sq. ft. The square-butt strip shingle is 12'' x 36'' and is laid on 5'' intervals. A layer of building paper (15 pound saturated felt) is ordinarily placed on the sheathing before laying the shingles. This acts as a moisture barrier.

The other roofing materials are less frequently used and are usually applied in special situations. Instructions for installation may be obtained from manufacturers.

Fig. 17-35. Wood roof shingles are visually appealing and popular for residential construction. They blend nicely with the building materials in this dwelling. (Red Cedar Shingle and Handsplit Shake Bureau)

REVIEW QUESTIONS—CHAPTER 17

Write your answers on a separate sheet of paper. Do not write in this book.

1. Identify, by name, ten distinct roof types.
2. The purpose of roof framing is _____.
3. The roof framing member that extends from the top plate to the ridge is called a _____.
4. If a roof has a pitch of 3:12 and the rise is 6 ft., the span is _____ ft.
5. The roof span is measured from _____ to _____.
6. The _____ of a roof is one-half the span.
7. The formula for calculating the fractional pitch of a roof is _____.
8. The pitch of a roof which has a slope of 45 degrees is _____.
9. Rafter size depends on what three things?
10. A lightweight roofing material is one that weighs less than _____ pounds per square foot.
11. The _____ is the overhang of the roof at the eaves line that forms a connection between the roof and sidewalls.
12. List the three types of cornices that are frequently constructed on homes.
13. List the two purposes of attic ventilation.
14. The total area of ventilator openings should be a minimum of _____ of the ceiling area.
15. Name two materials commonly used for roof flashing.
16. Roof sheathing on most homes is _____ in. plywood.
17. Identify five roofing materials which are used on residential structures.
18. The recommended minimum weight of asphalt shingles is _____ pounds per square.
19. List two advantages of the roof truss over conventional framing techniques.
20. Identify three types of trusses which are commonly used in residential construction.
21. List information required to purchase roof trusses for a home.
22. What is a gusset?

SUGGESTED ACTIVITIES

1. Look through magazines to which you have access and cut out pictures of houses which represent various roof styles. Mount the pictures on illustration board for display.
2. Write to several manufacturers of roof covering materials and ask for specifications and descriptive literature about their products. Display the literature and then add it to the classroom collection.
3. Build a scale model of an open cornice, a box cornice, or close cornice. Use a scale of 1'' = 1'-0'' and label the various parts. Display your model along with a section drawing.
4. Design a contemporary roof for a 24' x 36' cottage or a small house of your choice. Try to be innovative in design. Draw a plan view, elevations, and a section of the roof. Dimension the drawings and describe the materials used.
5. Design three different types of trusses. Compare their strength by building a scale model of each and applying weight until each breaks. Write a description of your testing procedure and report your results. Show the drawings and models.

Elevations

After studying this chapter, you will be able to:
- List features that should be included on an exterior elevation.
- Identify the dimensions commonly shown on elevations.
- Illustrate symbols that are often found on elevations.
- Draw a typical exterior elevation which demonstrates proper techniques.

An elevation is an orthographic projection (drawing) which shows one side of the building. When the term ''elevation'' is used in connection with a set of construction drawings, it ordinarily refers to an exterior elevation. Various interior elevations may be drawn, but they are usually considered to be details.

The purpose of an elevation is to show the finished appearance of a given side of the building and furnish vertical height dimensions. Four elevations are customarily drawn—one for each side of the house. In some instances, however, more than four elevations may be required to describe the structure.

Elevation drawings provide height information about basic features of the house which cannot be shown very well on other drawings. They also indicate exterior materials such as siding and roof covering. Figs. 18-1 and 18-2 show the floor plan, front elevation, and photograph of a typical residence. Compare the features shown on each.

REQUIRED INFORMATION

Several features should be included on elevation drawings: identification of the specific side of the house that the elevation represents, grade lines, finished floor and ceiling levels, location of exterior wall corners, windows and doors, roof features, vertical dimensions of important features, porches, decks and patios, and material symbols.

ELEVATION IDENTIFICATION

Each elevation must be identified as to the particular wall it represents. The two methods commonly used are front, rear, right side, and left side or north, south, east, and west identification. The first method of designation is preferred by most designers as there is a possibility of confusion when specifying directions. The right and left side elevations are determined by facing the front of the building. The right side elevation is then on the right side. Identify each elevation immediately below the drawing to avoid confusion.

GRADE LINE, FLOORS, AND CEILINGS

The reference point for most elevations is the grade line. Study the plot or site plan to determine the existing grade along each exterior wall of the house. If the existing grade is not satisfactory, a final grade line should also be indicated on each elevation affected. It is frequently helpful to indicate the desired elevation height of the grade at each corner of the house. This information is recorded on the plot plan as well as the elevation drawing if the site is not relatively level.

All features which are below grade should be drawn in hidden lines. Examples are foundation walls, footings, and window wells (areaways).

Floor-to-ceiling height is an important feature of the elevation. Two methods of representing this height are commonly used. The first is to indicate the finished floor-to-finished ceiling

Fig. 18-1. Photo above and floor plans below for the front elevation in Fig. 18-2.

distance. (The floor and ceiling are represented using a center line symbol.) The usual distance from the finished floor to finished ceiling is 8'-0'' for the first floor and 7'-6'' or 8'-0'' for the second floor. The second method shows the construction dimension. This is measured from the top of the subfloor to the top of the wall plate. In this instance, the construction dimension for the first floor is 8'-1 1/2'' and 7'-7 1/2''

or 8'-1 1/2'' for the second floor. Carpenters usually prefer the later method because it does not require them to do any calculation.

Minimum recommended height for garage ceilings is 8'-0''. Basements must have a clear headroom space of at least 6'-2'' with all beams and heating ducts above this height. A full height ceiling is more desirable and should be specified where practical.

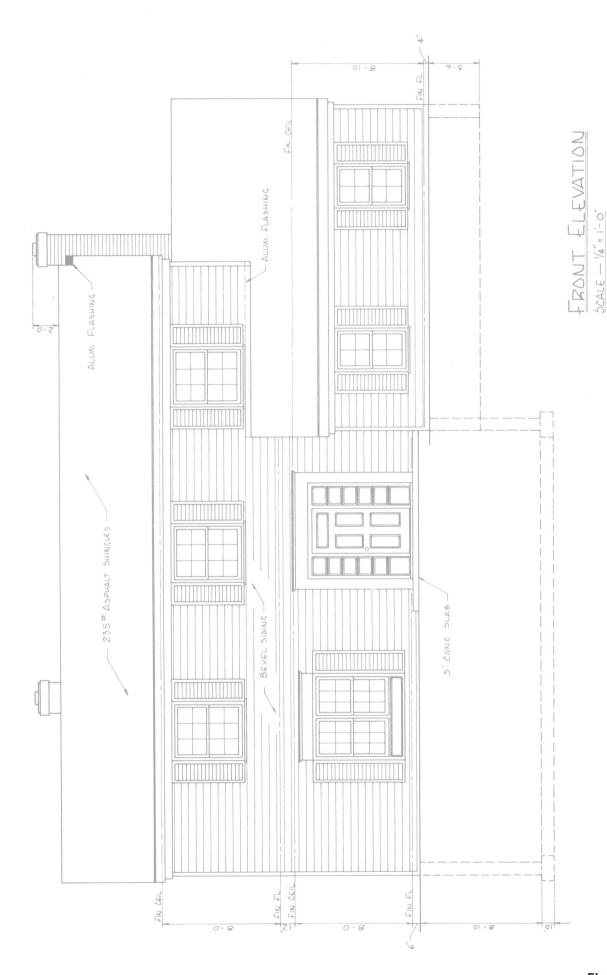

Fig. 18-2. The front elevation for the house shown in the photo and floor plans shown in Fig. 18-1.

Most codes require that the top of the foundation wall be at least 8'' above the grade. This is to protect the framing members from moisture. This requirement should be kept in mind when drawing elevations. The garage floor may be slightly higher than the grade, but should be at least 4'' lower than an interior floor when the garage is attached to the house.

WALLS, WINDOWS, AND DOORS

All visible wall corners are shown on the elevation using object lines. In rare instances it may be desirable to show hidden walls. Exact wall height should be determined by drawing a section through the wall and locating the grade, sill, floor joists, and top plate, Figs. 18-3 and 18-4. The section will be more helpful since the overhang will extend below the top of the wall in most instances. Determine the exact location.

Windows and doors that are located on an exterior wall must be included on the elevation. Placement along the wall may be projected from the floor plan, but the vertical height is shown only on the elevation drawing. It is customary to place tops of windows the same height as the tops of doors. The lower face of the head jamb is considered the height of the opening. This dimension is usually 6'-0'' from the top of the subfloor.

Show sufficient detail on windows and doors to accurately indicate details. If windows are hinged, show the swing using the proper symbol. See Chapter 13. If the windows or doors have brick mold or other trim then show this on the elevation. The glass elevation symbol may be used if desired. Sometimes it is desirable to show the window and door identification symbols on the elevation as well as the floor plan.

ROOF FEATURES

Showing roof features on an elevation drawing is important. It is here that the roof style and pitch are shown as well as chimney height and size. The roof pitch may be indicated using the fractional pitch or slope triangle. The slope triangle is usually preferred.

Gable ends must be drawn first to determine roof height. If more than one roof height is anticipated, the highest section should be drawn first. When a roof is complex, a single elevation may not be completed without constructing several details to determine various heights and termination points.

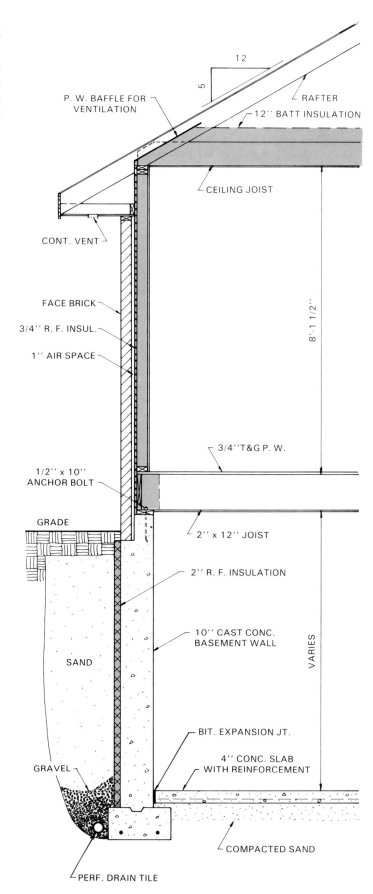

Fig. 18-3. Wall section for a typical brick veneer structure with a basement. This type of section would be included in a set of construction drawings.

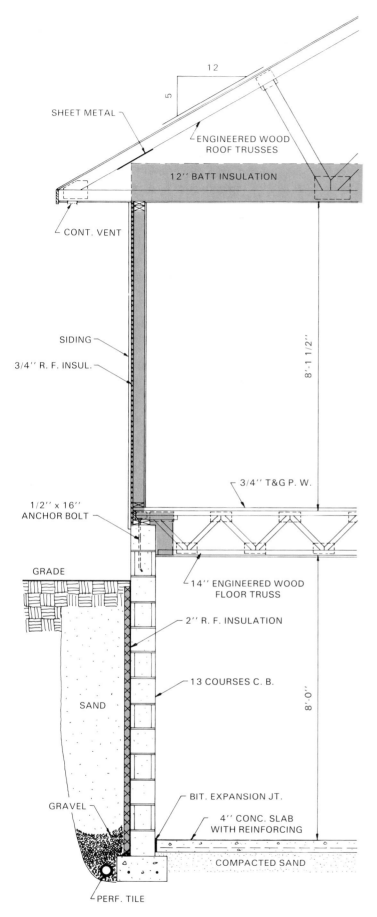

SHEET METAL

ENGINEERED WOOD
ROOF TRUSSES

12" BATT INSULATION

12
5

CONT. VENT

SIDING

3/4" R. F. INSUL.

8'-1 1/2"

3/4" T&G P. W.

1/2" × 16"
ANCHOR BOLT

14" ENGINEERED WOOD
FLOOR TRUSS

GRADE

2" R. F. INSULATION

13 COURSES C. B.

8'-0"

SAND

BIT. EXPANSION JT.

GRAVEL

4" CONC. SLAB
WITH REINFORCING

COMPACTED SAND

PERF. TILE

Fig. 18-4. Wall section for a typical frame structure with basement. This type of section is used to determine vertical height when drawing elevations.

The procedure for drawing a gable end is as follows:

1. Locate the top of the upper wall plate and center line of the proposed ridge location (usually in the center between the walls).

2. Lay out the desired slope starting from the top inside corner of the wall plate. A line from this point to the ridge will determine the underside. Note: A variation of this procedure will be necessary for certain roof trusses.

3. Measure the width of the rafter perpendicular to the bottom edge and draw the top edge parallel to the bottom edge of the rafter.

4. Measure the amount of desired overhang. Do not forget to add the thickness of roof sheathing.

5. Repeat the procedure for the other side of the roof.

Chimneys that intersect the roof usually require more than one view to determine the points where they pass through the roof. Draw the view where the roof slope is shown first. This view will indicate where the chimney passes through the roof. These points may then be projected to other views.

The chimney height above the highest roof point must be dimensioned. A minimum height above the ridge is usually 2'-0".

Chimney flashing, roof covering material, and gable ventilators are also shown on the elevation. Use proper symbols and adequate dimensions and notes on the drawings to describe these features. Other details such as roof ventilators, vent pipes, and gutters may be shown if desired.

DIMENSIONS, NOTES, AND SYMBOLS

Dimensions on the elevation drawing are mainly vertical height dimensions. Features that must be dimensioned include: thickness of the footing, distance from the footing to the grade, finished floor-to-finished ceiling distances, overhang width, height of the top of windows and doors, and height of chimney above the roof. Other dimensions may be required for details such as deck railing, retaining walls, and planters.

Notes should be included where additional information is needed or would be helpful to the builder. Some of the typical notes found on an elevation drawing are: grade information, exterior wall material notation, roof covering material identification, fascia material, and flashing material. Other notes may be required for specific situations.

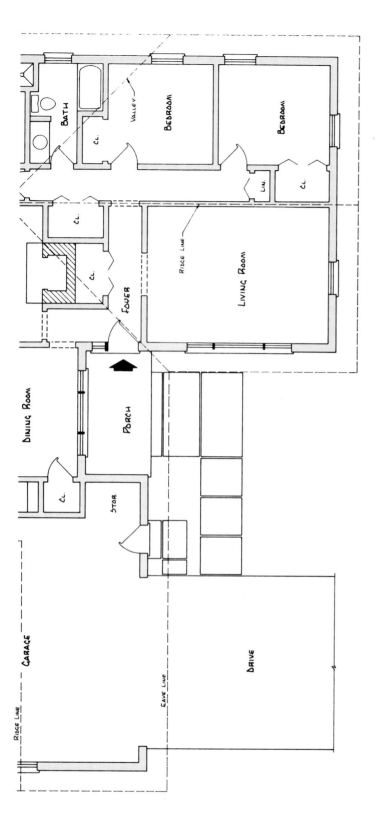

ELEVATION WILL BE DRAWN HERE

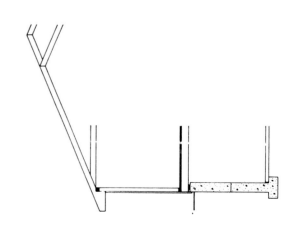

Fig. 18-5. The floor plan is placed above the space where the elevation is to be drawn and the section is to the left. This will provide a fast method of locating the various features on the elevation.

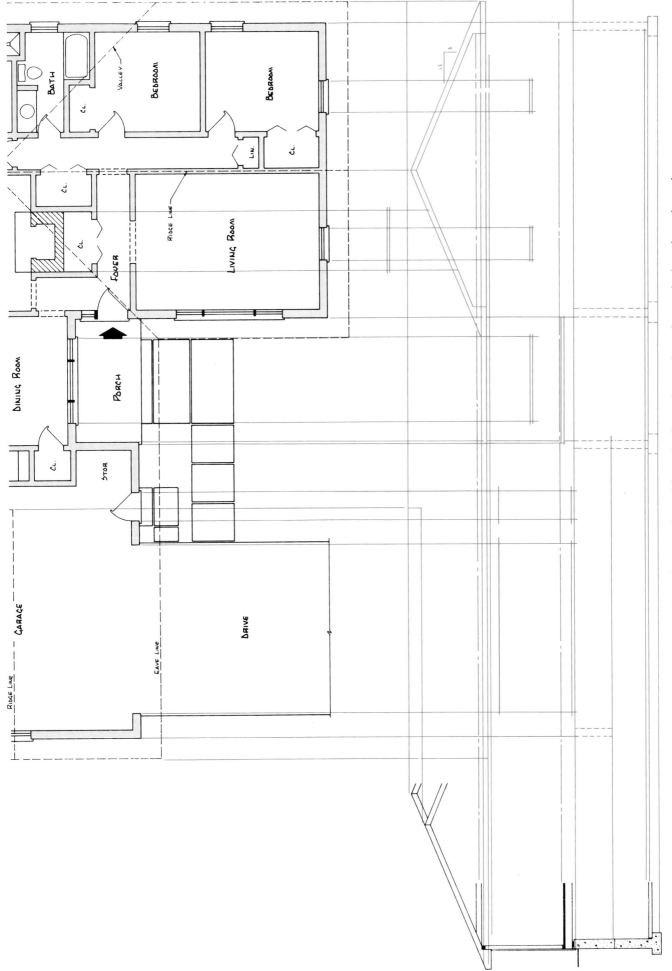

Fig. 18-6. Basic features of the house have been projected from the floor plan and section to the location where the elevation is to be drawn. Light construction lines are used.

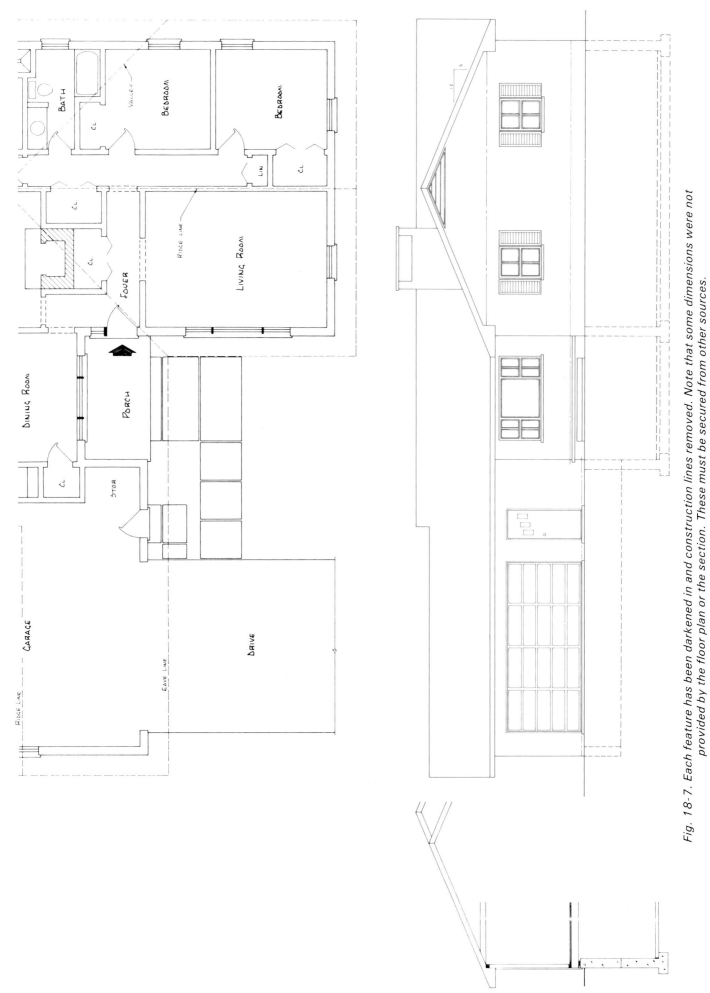

Fig. 18-7. Each feature has been darkened in and construction lines removed. Note that some dimensions were not provided by the floor plan or the section. These must be secured from other sources.

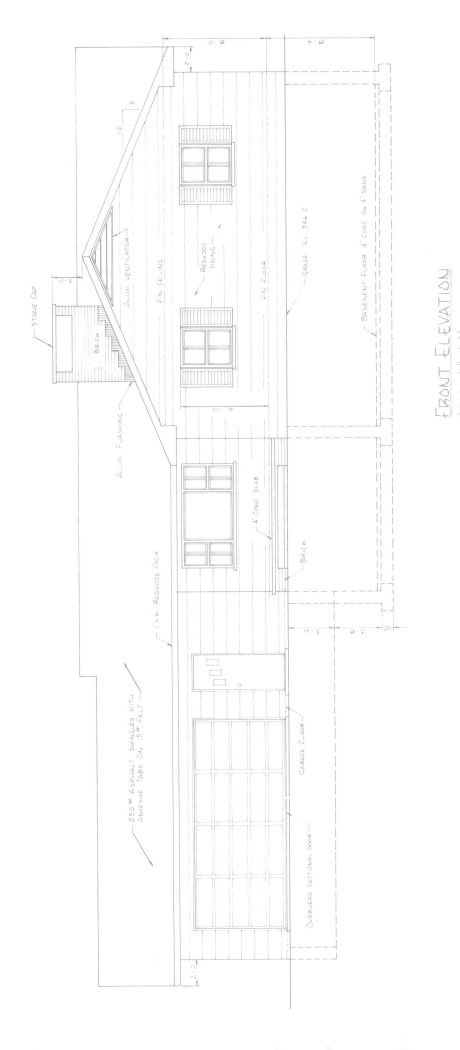

Fig. 18-8. Dimensions, notes, and symbols have been added to complete the elevation.

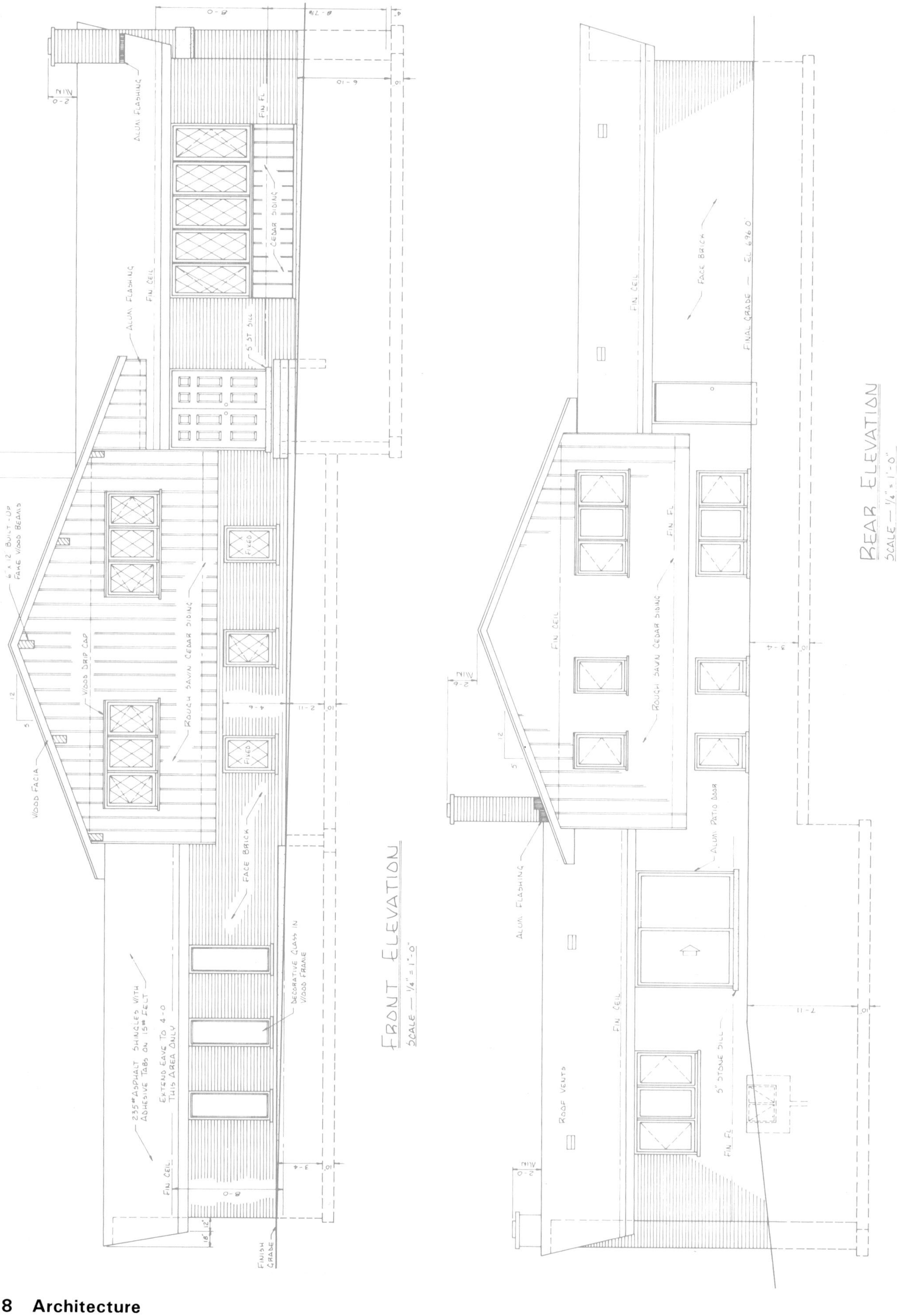

FRONT ELEVATION
SCALE — ¼" = 1'-0"

REAR ELEVATION
SCALE — ¼" = 1'-0"

Fig. 18-9. Front and rear elevation of a modern split-level house.

Several symbols are commonly used on elevations. The roof pitch symbol is always shown and the exterior wall covering is usually symbolized. Many designers show material symbols extensively on the front elevation but sparingly on the remaining views. Window swing symbols and cutting plane symbols are also drawn if needed.

PROCEDURE FOR DRAWING AN ELEVATION

There are numerous accepted procedures for drawing elevations. The procedure presented here is a logical approach which yields fast and accurate results if followed carefully. The steps include the following:

1. Draw a section through the wall to be represented by the elevation. This section should be the same scale (1/4'' = 1'-0'') as the floor plan and proposed elevation. The section drawing must be very accurate since it will be used to project the height of wall and roof elements to the elevation. If all the exterior walls of the house are the same type construction and height, then only one section will be required. However, if each wall is different, a section for each wall will be needed. These section drawings may be discarded after the elevations are complete. Similar drawings will be made at a larger scale later.

2. Place the floor plan directly above the space where the elevation is to be drawn. The exterior walls to be represented by the elevation should be facing down toward the elevation. Some drafters prefer to draw the elevation on top of the floor plan rather than below it. Either method is acceptable. Steps 1 and 2 are shown in Fig. 18-5.

3. Project the heights of the grade line, depth and thickness of footings, window and door heights, eaves line, and roof height across from the section drawing to the space reserved for the elevation. These should be very light construction lines.

4. Project the horizontal length of exterior walls, windows, doors, and other elements down from the floor plan. These may be drawn in dark since their proper length will already have been determined. Steps 3 and 4 are shown in Fig. 18-6.

5. Darken in each feature and remove the construction lines. At this point, the elevation is complete enough to determine if changes are desired in the overall design. Make any changes now before proceeding on.

6. Add details such as railings, window muntins, trim, window wells (areaways), and gable ventilators, Information on many of these features must be secured from reference sources such as Sweets Architectural File. Steps 5 and 6 are shown in Fig. 18-7.

7. Add dimensions, notes, and symbols. It is good practice to draw material symbols last since they may interfere with other information if drawn earlier.

8. Check the drawing to be sure that all features are shown as desired. Add the title block and scale. See Fig. 18-8 which shows the finished elevation.

Repeat the eight steps for each elevation. It is customary to draw two elevations on a single sheet if space permits.

The front and rear elevations of a typical, modern split-level home are presented in Fig. 18-9. Note that material symbols are more brief on the rear elevation than appear on the front.

REVIEW QUESTIONS–CHAPTER 18

Write your answers on a separate sheet of paper. Do not write in this book.

1. What is the primary purpose of an elevation drawing?
2. How many exterior elevations are usually required for a home? Name them.
3. The reference point for most elevations is the _____.
4. Features on the elevation drawing that are below grade are represented with a _____ line.
5. On most houses, the distance from the finished floor-to-finished ceiling is _____.
6. Sometimes, the second floor ceiling height is less than the first floor. The recommended minimum dimension is _____.
7. The minimum recommended clear ceiling height of a basement (after ductwork and beams are installed) is _____.
8. The foundation wall should be at least _____ in. above the grade.
9. A section through the wall is a helpful drawing for constructing the elevation because _____.
10. The lower face of the head jamb is considered to be the height of the opening for a window or door. The distance from the floor to this point is usually _____.
11. Where is the slope triangle located on an elevation drawing?
12. The minimum height that a chimney must extend above the highest point of the roof is _____.

SUGGESTED ACTIVITIES

1. Select a floor plan of a house and draw a section through the front wall. Draw the section at a scale of 1/2'' = 1'-0 . Add dimensions and notes. Present the floor plan with the section.
2. Draw the four elevations for one of the floor plans that you drew for the chapter on Floor Plans. Follow the procedure presented in this chapter. Add all dimensions, notes, and submit the elevations with the floor plan.
3. Select a home from the newspaper or a magazine (photo and floor plan) and draw a front elevation of the home using a different style roof and exterior materials. Do not change the floor plan. Present your revision along with the original.
4. Select an older home in your community and sketch an elevation as it now appears. Measure the house to determine the required dimensions. Redesign the front using good design and unique application of materials. Draw an elevation of your new design.
5. Draw a front elevation of the house shown in Fig. 18-10. Omit the garage. The width of the house is 32'-0''. The windows and door are 3'-0'' wide. Dimension the features identified in the section ''Procedure for Drawing an Elevation.''

Fig. 18-10. This modified colonial has aluminum shutters and siding to simulate original materials.
(Alside)

Residential Electrical

After studying this chapter, you will be able to:
• Define typical residential electrical terms.
• Plan for the electrical needs of a modern home.
• Identify and explain the three types of electrical circuits used in a residential structure.
• Calculate circuit requirements for a residence.

Planning for the electrical needs of a modern home requires a basic understanding of several factors. These factors include familiarization with related terms, electrical requirements for lighting and appliances, code restrictions, and safety considerations.

ELECTRICAL TERMS

The following terms are identified to assist in familiarization and understanding of electrical terminology.

Ampere: The unit of current used to measure the amount of electricity flowing through a conductor per unit of time.

Circuit: A path through which electricity flows from a source to one or more outlets and then returns to the source.

Circuit breaker: A device designed to open and close a circuit by nonautomatic means, and to open the circuit automatically on a predetermined overload of current.

Conductor: A material that permits the flow of electricity (usually refers to a wire).

Convenience outlet: A device attached to a circuit to allow electricity to be drawn off for appliances or lighting.

Fuse: A safety device that breaks the circuit when it is overloaded by melting a fusible link.

Lighting outlet: An outlet intended for the use of a lighting fixture.

Receptacle: A contact device installed at an outlet for the connection of an attachment plug and flexible cord (same as a convenience outlet).

Service drop: The overhead service conductors between the last pole and the first point of attachment to the house.

Service entrance: The fittings and conductors that bring electricity into the building.

Service panel: The main distribution box that receives the electricity and distributes it to various points in the house through branch circuits. The service panel contains the main disconnect switch fuse or breaker which supplies the total electrical system of the house.

Voltage: Pressure that forces current through a wire. One volt is the force that causes one ampere of current to flow through a wire with one ohm resistance. An ohm is the measure of electrical resistance in a circuit.

Watt: One ampere under one volt of pressure. Amperes times volts equal watts. Most appliances are rated in watts.

SERVICE ENTRANCE AND DISTRIBUTION PANEL

The foundation for a residential electrical system is the service entrance and distribution panel. Residential service entrance equipment may be of the circuit breaker, Fig. 19-1, or switch and fuse type. Either method provides overcurrent protection by opening the circuit if the current reaches too high a value.

A residence may have 120 or 240 volt service. Only two conductors are required for 120 volt service, but three are necessary for 240 volt service. Fig. 19-2 illustrates how 120 volts is derived from 240 volt service. Even if no 240 volt appliances are to be installed when the

Fig. 19-1. Residential service entrance equipment. Top– Distribution panel. Bottom–Circuit breaker. (Square D Co.)

home is built, 240 volt service entrance equipment is recommended. This is becoming standard procedure and it is less expensive to install initially than at a later date.

The most common arrangement of electrical service to a house is with the service conductors first terminating at the meter. The incoming service may be overhead or underground. Several

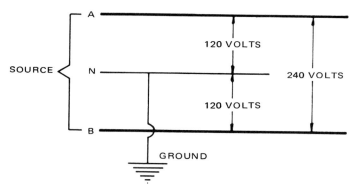

Fig. 19-2. Two voltages are available from this 240 volt, three-wire service drop. Half of the 120 volt circuits are connected to A and N and the other half to B and N. All 240 volt circuits are connected to A and B.

service entrance designs are possible. Fig. 19-3 shows a common method of anchoring the service drop to the house for overhead service. The use of a service head is a must if the service entrance is located along the eaves line of a single-story home. The service drop must be at least 10 feet above the ground at all points and 12 feet above driveways. No conductors may be closer than 3 feet to windows, doors, porches, or similar structures where they may be touched. Fig. 19-4 shows an underground service layout.

Electrical cable (copper or aluminum) is used to bring the current from the service head or

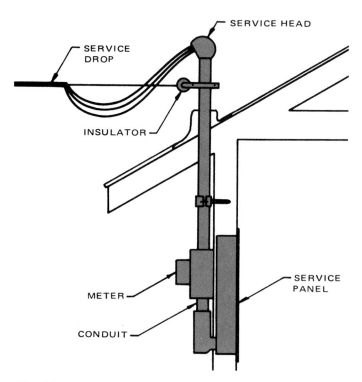

Fig. 19-3. The service head is commonly used for houses with low-pitched roofs or when the service entrance equipment is located along the eaves line.

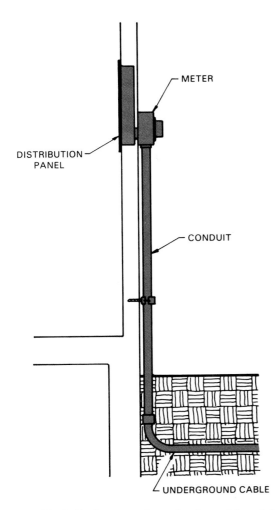

Fig. 19-4. Underground service layout is gaining popularity. It is safe and out of sight.

underground cable to the meter and on to the distribution panel. The size of this cable will depend on the size of service entrance equipment to be used in the home and the amount of amperage supplied by the electric company. The following table shows the size wire usually recommended for various amperage ratings.

SERVICE ENTRANCE CONDUCTOR SIZES				
(WHEN DEMAND FACTOR IS 80 PERCENT OR LESS)				
Number of Wires	Open Air Installation		Installed in Conduit	
	Size	Amperage	Size	Amperage
3	4	70	4	110
3	2	100	2	140
3	1/0	150	1/0	200
3	2/0	175	2/0	225
3	3/0	200	3/0	260

These sizes are for copper wire. If aluminum wire is used, at least two sizes larger will be required to handle the amperage indicated.

Fig. 19-5 shows how conductor size is indicated. Number 12 is generally recommended for branch lighting circuits of modern residential

Fig. 19-5. Relative wire sizes and designations.

installations. No. 14 is the smallest circuit conductor permitted by the National Electrical Code.

Conductor size is important in a residential electrical system because current flowing through the wires produces heat. If the wire is too small for the amount of current it may cause a fire. Even if a fire does not result, the heat increases resistance in the wire and electricity is wasted.

From the meter, the conductors are terminated at the distribution panel, Fig. 19-6. The main disconnect switch or breaker is usually located in the distribution panel. This switch disconnects all current to the house and should be

Fig. 19-6. A typical distribution panel box with the cover removed to show service entrance conductors, main disconnect switch, and wiring.

located as close to the incoming service as possible.

The capacity of the service entrance equipment should be sufficient to supply present and future demands. The National Electrical Code recommends that a minimum of 100 ampere service be provided for all residences. Many homes will require 150 or 200 ampere service.

The type of overcurrent protection devices most frequently used today is the circuit breaker. The heart of the system is the individual branch circuit breaker, Fig. 19-7. Breakers are safe, reliable, and easy to use which accounts for their popularity. Fig. 19-8 shows a modern panel box designed for circuit breakers.

BRANCH CIRCUITS

A modern residence has several branch circuits. Appliances and outlets are grouped together so that smaller breakers or fuses and smaller conductors may be used. If a house had only one giant circuit which could supply 100 amperes or current, the wire would be very costly and impossible to handle. Switches and outlets are not designed for such large wire.

Fig. 19-8. Circuit breaker panel box with cover. Shown are the main breaker, two 240 volt circuits, and eight 120 volt circuits. Four spaces remain for future use.

Fig. 19-7. A circuit breaker capable of providing overcurrent protection for two different branch circuits. (Square D Co.)

Also, if the fuse were to blow or breaker were to trip, the total structure would be without power. Just as important, it would not be possible to install the proper fuse protection for various appliances which require far smaller amounts of current. These reasons indicate the need for branch circuits.

The National Electrical Code specifies three types of branch circuits which should be used in a residential structure:

1. *Lighting circuits:* These are primarily for lighting and serve permanently installed lighting fixtures, as well as receptacle outlets into which you plug lamps, radios, television, clocks, and similar 120 volt devices (but not kitchen appliances).

2. *Special appliance circuits:* Special appliance circuits are located in the kitchen, usually above the countertop. These are designed for electric fry pans, mixers, blenders, toasters, and similar appliances which require large amounts of current. Special appliance circuits may also be used along a workbench in the home shop.

3. *Individual appliance circuits:* These are circuits which serve permanently installed appli-

ances such as a range, water heater, washer, dryer, or water pump.

LIGHTING CIRCUITS

In modern systems lighting circuits are frequently conductors with No. 12 copper wire with 20 amp. overcurrent protection. This combination will provide 2400 watts of lighting capacity (120 x 20 = 2400). The Code requires a minimum of 3 watts of lighting power for each square foot of floor space. One lighting circuit would be sufficient for 800 sq. ft. of floor space if this minimum were applied. Again, this is a minimum and probably not satisfactory of most homeowners. One lighting circuit for each 400 sq. ft. would be more advisable.

Calculation of the number of lighting circuits required for a typical 48' x 60' residence is performed as follow:
1. Figure the total area included in the house. (48' x 60' = 2880 sq. ft.)
2. Divide the total area in the house by 400. (2880 ÷ 400 = 7.2 lighting circuits.)

The number of lighting circuits required for a house with 2880 sq. ft. is seven. The following table shows the number of lighting circuits recommended for various size houses:

RESIDENTIAL LIGHTING CIRCUITS		
No. of Sq. Ft.	Number of Lighting Circuits	
	Code Minimum	Recommended
1000	2	3
1200	2	3
1600	3	4
2000	3	5
2400	4	6
2800	5	7

SPECIAL APPLIANCE CIRCUITS

Special appliance circuits require No. 12 copper conductors with a 20 amp. circuit breaker or fuse. The National Electrical Code specifies a minimum of two special appliance circuits in the kitchen or similar type room. No lighting outlets may be operated from these circuits. Each of these circuits is capable of supplying 2400 watts (20 x 120 = 2400). This number of special appliance circuits may not be sufficient for a large modern kitchen.

Special appliance circuits may be appropriate in other areas of the house such as sewing room, garage, and shop.

INDIVIDUAL APPLIANCE CIRCUITS

Some appliances require such a large amount of electricity that they must have their own circuit. Such circuits are called *individual appliance circuits.* The following appliances are usually operated on individual appliance circuits:

Range	Garbage Disposal
Countertop Oven	Air Conditioner
Water Heater	Furnace
Water Pump	Clothes Washer
Dishwasher	Attic Fan
Clothes Dryer	

In addition to these, any 120 volt permanently connected appliance that is rated at over 1,400 watts or has an automatically starting electric motor should have its own circuit.

Individual appliance circuits may be 120 or 240 volts depending on the requirements of the device it is to operate. Always check the rating of the appliance to determine these factors. The chart in Fig. 19-9 shows the approximate requirements of several appliances.

CIRCUIT REQUIREMENT CALCULATIONS

The size of service entrance equipment and number and type of branch circuits are dependent upon the size of the house, appliances, and lighting to be installed and planning for the future. In an effort to show how circuit requirement calculations are performed the following example is included:

Example of a Typical Residence – 1500 Sq. Ft.

Lighting Circuits:
1500 sq. ft. at 3 watts per sq. ft. = 4500 watts
Special Appliance Circuits:
2 circuits for kitchen – 4800 watts
(120 volts x 20 amp. x 2 = 4800 watts)

Individual Appliance Circuits:
1 circuit (240 volts) for
   self-contained range   = 12,000 watts
1 circuit (240 volts) for dryer = 5,000 watts
1 circuit for water heater   = 2,000 watts
1 circuit for clothes washer = 700 watts
1 circuit for garbage disposal = 300 watts
1 circuit for dishwasher   = 1,200 watts
1 circuit for furnace   = 800 watts
           Total = 31,300 watts

For 120/240-volt 3-wire system feeders, 31,300 watts ÷ 240 = 130.4 amps.

This house will require 150 amp. service. Service breakers are produced in ratings of 30, 40, 50, 60, 70, 100, 125, 150, 175, and 200 amp. Since 130.4 is between 125 and 150, the logical choice is 150 amp. service. This would also provide a spare circuit for future use.

OUTLETS AND SWITCHES

All convenience outlets, switches, and joints where conductors are spliced must be housed in an electrical box. Also, all lighting fixtures must be amounted on a box. There are several types of boxes for various uses. The three most common types of boxes are shown in Fig. 19-10. Most are made from metal with a galvanized coating, but some styles are made from Bakelite and other insulating materials, Fig. 19-11.

Placement of convenience outlets, switches, and lighting fixtures require some thought. Code requirements, furniture arrangements, and personal preference all play a role in the location. The Code states that in living areas no point along a wall should be more than 6 ft. from a convenience outlet and each room should have a minimum of three outlets. Fig. 19-12 shows various outlets, each having a distinct design or purpose. Placement of outlets about 8 ft. apart is more satisfactory and recommended. The height of most convenience outlets is 12 or 18 inches above the floor. The kitchen is an exception where the special appliance outlets are usually placed above the countertop. It is common practice to switch one or more outlets in each room where lamps are to be located. This saves wear on the lamp and is more convenient.

Frequently home designers forget to include weatherproof outlets and ample exterior lighting. These outlets provide a source of power for outside work or play. Placing at least one outlet on each side of the exterior is recommended.

TYPICAL APPLIANCE REQUIREMENTS				
Appliance or Equipment	Typical Watts	Usual Voltage	Wire Size	Recommended Fuse Size
Electric Range (with oven)	12,000	240	6	50-60 Amp.
Range Top (separate)	5,000	120/240	10	30 Amp.
Range Oven (separate)	5,000	120/240	10	30 Amp.
Refrigerator	300	120	12	20 Amp.
Home Freezer	350	120	12	20 Amp.
Automatic Washer	700	120	12	20 Amp.
Automatic Dryer (elec.)	5,000	120/240	10	30 Amp.
Dishwasher	1,200	120/240	12	20 Amp.
Garbage Disposal	300	120	12	20 Amp.
Roaster	1,400	120	12	20 Amp.
Rotisserie	1,400	120	12	20 Amp.
Furnace	800	120	12	20 Amp.
Dehumidifier	350	120	12	20 Amp.
Waffle Iron	1,000	120	12	20 Amp.
Band Saw	300	120	12	20 Amp.
Table Saw	1,000	120/240	12	20 Amp.
20,000 Btu Air Conditioner	1,200	120/240	12	20 Amp.
Bathroom Heater	2,000	120/240	12	20 Amp.
Ironer	1,500	120	12	20 Amp.
Water Heater	2,000-5,000	120	10	30 Amp.
Television	300	120	12	20 Amp.
Hand Iron	1,100	120	12	20 Amp.
Toaster	1,000	120	12	20 Amp.
Microwave Oven	1,450	120	12	20 Amp.
Trash Compactor	400	120	12	20 Amp.

Fig. 19-9. Chart showing the approximate requirements for several appliances.

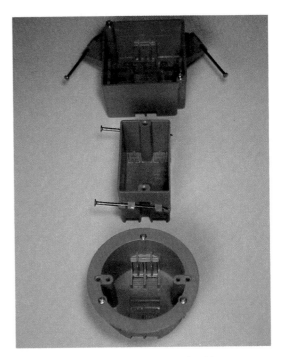

Fig. 19-10. Typical electrical boxes used in residential construction.

Fig. 19-11. Residential electrical boxes are also available in plastic.

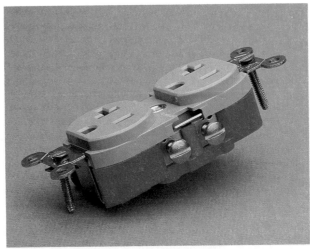

Fig. 19-12. Several types of outlets which are used in residential electrical systems. (Leviton Mfg. Co., Inc.)

Fig. 19-13. A duplex outlet protected by a ground-fault interrupter.

Exterior lighting enhances the appearance of the house and reduces the chances of vandalism. Lighting fixtures and convenience outlets should also be located in the attic and crawl spaces of the house.

Switches should be located in a logical place 48 in. above the floor. Care must be taken not to mount them behind doors or other hard-to-get-to places. Bathroom switches should not be located within reach of the bathtub or shower. This is an unsafe situation and must be avoided. A ground-fault interrupter should be installed on each circuit serving the bathroom or other areas that are likely to be wet--patio or swimming pool. These devices open the circuit when they detect a leakage of electrical current to the ground. Ordinarily the electrical fault will not be great enough to trip the circuit breaker, but could produce a severe electrical shock, Fig. 19-13.

Most switches in a house operate one fixture and are the *single-pole type.* Fig. 19-14 shows a variety of switch types. A single-pole switch simply opens and closes the circuit. In some

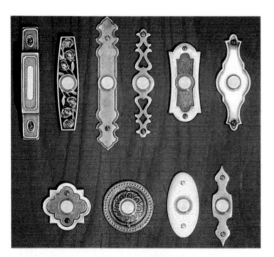

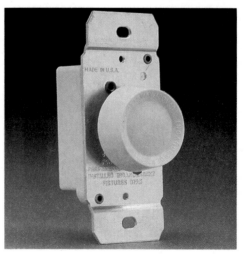

Fig. 19-14. Various styles of residential switches. (Leviton Mfg. Co., Inc., Nutone)

instances **three-way switches** may be used for extra convenience. By using three-way switches a fixture may be switched from two locations, Fig. 19-15. Common locations for three-way switches are entrances, garages, stairs, and rooms which have more than one entrance. Fixtures may also be switched from three locations using two three-way switches and one four-way switch, Fig. 19-16.

A special switch called a **dimmer switch** is commonly used for a main dining room ceiling fixture, Fig. 19-17. This allows the light to be adjusted to the desired brightness. The dimmer switch will fit into a regular electrical box.

There are several types of outlets which may be classified as "special outlets." These include telephone jacks, Fig. 19-18, television antenna outlets, built-in hi-fi or stereo outlets for speakers, entrance signals (bells or chimes), burglar alarm systems, and automatic fire-alarm systems. These are specialized installations. Information is usually supplied by the manufacturer or the systems are installed by them.

Fig. 19-17. A typical dimmer switch used to vary the intensity of an incandescent lighting fixture. (Leviton Mfg. Co., Inc.)

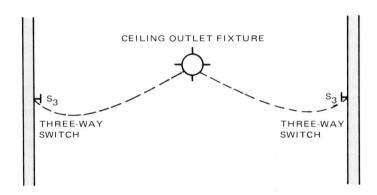

Fig. 19-15. A fixture or outlet may be switched from two locations using two three-way switches.

Fig. 19-18. An assortment of special residential outlets. (Leviton Mfg. Co., Inc.)

SIGNAL AND COMMUNICATION SYSTEMS

Signal and communication systems indicate that a visitor is present, allow persons to communicate within the home, or permit the owner to monitor the various systems within the dwelling and property. A popular signal and communication system is the doorbell or buzzer, or possibly sophisticated chimes. Doorbells, buzzers, chimes, and similar signal systems may require different tones for different entrances to the home.

An audio or visual system consists of a master station, Fig. 19-19, and numerous intercom

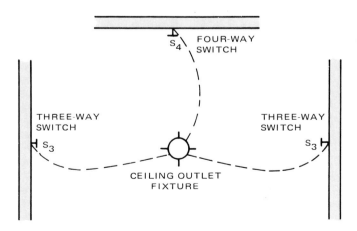

Fig. 19-16. One or more fixtures or outlets may be operated from three locations using two three-way switches and one four-way switch.

Fig. 19-19. Radio-intercom unit with built-in cassette recorder. This home communication system provides up to 20 stations plus door speakers, one-button intercom operation, and function display. (Nutone)

stations located throughout the house and at entrances. Some larger systems include a radio and cassette tape recorder.

Security systems are equipped to alert the resident of fires and unwanted intruders with detection devices and alarms, Fig. 19-20. Detection devices include heat sensors which can be set for normal temperatures in the sleeping, living, and service areas, and higher temperatures for attics and furnace rooms. The security system also includes intrusion detectors that signal when an intruder has entered the property or home. Security systems may be equipped with an automatic telephone dialing machine that repeats a taped emergency message to local authorities. Cables may be installed during construction or remodeling of the home to provide for the systems just discussed as well as a television antenna, cable, satellite dish, or telephone.

LOW VOLTAGE SWITCHING

In using low voltage switching, convenience outlets are wired in the conventional way with No. 12 or 14 conductors, and switches are wired to relays (electrically operated switches) using conductors similar to that used for wiring door bells and chimes. These conductors carry only 24 volts provided by a transformer which supplies current for the relays. The switches do not require boxes.

Low voltage switching, or remote control wiring as it is sometimes called, has possibilities for modern and unique installations. Remote control systems (low voltage switching) provide a simplified way of controlling lights in all parts of the home from one or more locations. For example,

Fig. 19-20. Basic home security system is composed of a control unit, detectors, and alarms. The circuit can be divided to guard the perimeter as well as the interior. (Nutone)

it is possible to operate fixtures located at various points in the house from the master bedroom. This is one of the advantages of the system. Fig. 19-21 shows a typical remote control wiring diagram.

REVIEW QUESTIONS—CHAPTER 19

Write your answers on a separate sheet of paper. Do not write in this book.

1. The term given to the pressure that forces current through a conductor is _____.
2. Two types of overcurrent protection devices are _____ and _____.
3. Material that carries the flow of electricity is called a _____. Copper wire is an example.
4. The result of multiplying amps by volts is _____.
5. How many service entrance conductors are required for 240 volt service?
6. The service drop must be at least _____ ft. above the ground at all points and _____ ft. above driveways.
7. Most wires used in residential wiring are made from what material?
8. Which conductor is larger in diameter: a No. 12 or No. 14 conductor?
9. If the wiring in a circuit is too small for the load, what is likely to happen?
10. The smallest conductor that may be used in a residential lighting circuit is No. _____ wire.
11. The purpose of the main disconnect switch is _____.
12. The National Electrical Code recommends a minimum of _____ amp. service for all residences.
13. The type of overcurrent protection used in most homes today is the _____.
14. List three types of circuits used in a home.
15. The minimum number of special appliance circuits required for a kitchen is _____.
16. A lighting circuit has _____ amp. overcurrent protection if No. 14 conductors are used.
17. The Code requires a minimum of _____ watts of lighting power for each square foot of floor space in the home.
18. One lighting circuit should provide lighting for _____ sq. ft. if the Code were followed.
19. A 1500 sq. ft. house would require _____ lighting circuits.
20. A special appliance circuit is usually wired with No. _____ copper conductors with a _____ amp. fuse.
21. How many watts can be supplied if the voltage is 120 volts and the current is 20 amps?
22. Identify five appliances which would require an individual appliance circuit.
23. Identify three factors that affect the size of service entrance equipment other than amperage serving the house, size of panel box, and number of branch circuits.
24. The minimum number of convenience outlets permitted in a single room is _____.
25. No point along a wall should be more than _____ ft. from a convenience outlet.

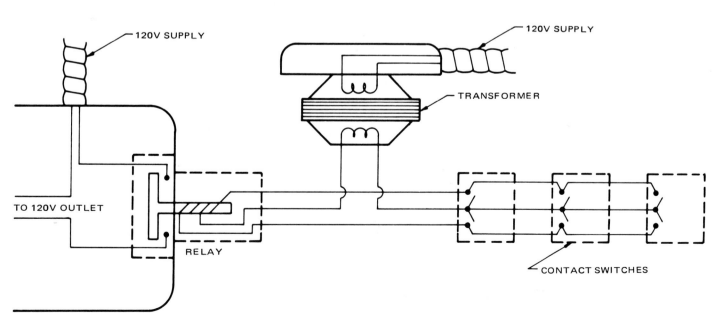

Fig. 19-21. Remote control electrical wiring diagram for a residential structure.

26. To switch a lighting fixture from two locations, you would need a _____ type of electrical switch.
27. Why would anyone use a low voltage switching system in a residence?

SUGGESTED ACTIVITIES

1. Determine the service entrance rating for your home or apartment. Count the number of 120 and 240 volt circuits. Calculate the amperage required for all the appliances, equipment, and lighting. Determine if the incoming service is sufficient to operate all requirements. Show all your work.
2. Visit a home under construction which has the rough electrical wiring in place. Count the number of convenience outlets, switches, and lighting fixtures in the house. Determine the number of circuits and size of main breaker. Organize your findings and report to the class. Is the house adequately wired? Be sure to secure permission to enter the construction site.
3. Write to manufacturers that produce residential electrical supplies. Ask for literature and specifications for electrical boxes, wire, service entrance equipment switches, and fixtures. Display the material and add it to the class collection for future use.
4. Prepare a bulletin board illustrating the circuits in a house and the equipment, appliances, and lighting they serve.

Lighting fixture placement requires planning and proper installation. (Georgia-Pacific Corporation)

The Electrical Plan

After studying this chapter, you will be able to:
- Describe an electrical plan and identify its features.
- Represent typical electrical symbols found on a residential electrical plan.
- Compile a circuit data chart.
- Draw an electrical plan for a residential structure.

The electrical plan is a plan view drawing in section similar to the floor and foundation plans. It is usually traced from the floor plan. The electrical plan shows the meter, distribution panel box, electric outlets, switches, and special electrical features. It identifies the number and types of circuits in the home. A schedule that specifies the lighting fixtures may be included.

The purpose of the electrical plan is to show the location and type of electrical equipment to be used. Convenience and trouble-free operation is dependent on a well-planned and properly installed electrical system.

REQUIRED INFORMATION

Information which should be on the electrical plan includes: service entrance capacity, meter and distribution panel location, placement and type of switches, location and type of lighting fixtures, special electrical equipment, number and types of circuits, electrical fixture schedule, symbols and legend, and notes which help to describe the system.

SERVICE ENTRANCE

The Code requires that the service entrance equipment be located as close as practical to the point where the wires attach to the house. The service conductors should not run for 15 or 20 feet inside the house before they reach the main disconnect switch. The closer the main breaker is to the meter the better.

Another factor to be considered in locating the service entrance is where the largest amounts of electricity will be used. In most houses, this is the kitchen. Try to locate the meter and distribution panel close to the area of highest usage. It is less expensive and more efficient because larger loads require larger conductors and result in larger voltage drops over a long distance.

The meter may be located inside or outside the house, however, an outside location is usually preferred because it is easier to take readings. Electric meters are weatherproof and are designed for exterior installation.

Electrical symbols commonly used on an electrical plan are shown in Fig. 20-1. Amperage rating of the service required should be designated beside the symbol representing the distribution panel.

SWITCHES

The number and placement of switches throughout the house will be related to the number of lighting fixtures, switched convenience outlets, and other equipment used. Try to select the logical location for each switch. Take into consideration the traffic patterns. The electrical plan must show whether the switches are single-pole, three-way, four-way, or another type. Use proper symbols to show types to be used.

The least expensive type of switch is a simple on-off *toggle switch.* A little more expensive, but preferred by many people, is the *quiet switch,* or the completely silent *mercury switch.*

CEILING OUTLET FIXTURE	SINGLE RECEPTACLE OUTLET	SINGLE-POLE SWITCH
RECESSED OUTLET FIXTURE	DUPLEX RECEPTACLE OUTLET	DOUBLE-POLE SWITCH
DROP CORD FIXTURE	TRIPLEX RECEPTACLE OUTLET	THREE-WAY SWITCH
FAN HANGER OUTLET	QUADRUPLEX RECEPTACLE OUTLET	FOUR-WAY SWITCH
JUNCTION BOX	SPLIT-WIRED DUPLEX RECEPTACLE OUTLET	WEATHERPROOF SWITCH
FLUORESCENT FIXTURE	SPECIAL PURPOSE SINGLE RECEPTACLE OUTLET	LOW VOLTAGE SWITCH
TELEPHONE	230 VOLT OUTLET	PUSH BUTTON
INTERCOM	WEATHERPROOF DUPLEX OUTLET	CHIMES
CEILING FIXTURE WITH PULL SWITCH	DUPLEX RECEPTACLE WITH SWITCH	TELEVISION ANTENNA OUTLET
THERMOSTAT	FLUSH MOUNTED PANEL BOX	DIMMER SWITCH
SPECIAL FIXTURE OUTLET	SPECIAL DUPLEX OUTLET	SPECIAL SWITCH

Fig. 20-1. Common electrical symbols.

Other types include **push button, dimmer,** and **delayed action** switches. A modern home may require several types of switches.

On the electrical plan switches are shown connected to the fixtures, appliances, and outlets, which they operate. A thin hidden line symbol or center line symbol is generally used. These lines **do not** represent the actual wiring, but merely indicate which switch operates a given outlet or fixture. Draw the lines using an irregular curve rather than a straightedge or freehand. Straight lines tend to become confused with other lines on the drawing and freehand lines are sloppy.

CONVENIENCE OUTLETS

Convenience outlets should be placed about 6 or 8 feet apart along the wall of all rooms. Most outlets are the 120 volt duplex type which have two receptacles. Special purpose outlets may have only one receptacle or several depending on their use. All convenience outlets should be grounded to prevent severe shock.

Convenience outlets may be switched or remain "hot" all the time. Most rooms will require at least one switched outlet for a lamp. It is wise to think about the furniture arrangement before drawing the electrical plan so that outlets and switches may be more accurately located.

Several kinds of special outlets may be desired. Each of these has a symbol to identify it. Use the proper symbol. If you are not sure the symbol is standard, identify it on the drawing.

LIGHTING

It is difficult to determine how many foot candles of light will be desirable for everyone. Some people prefer more light than others. Sufficient light should be provided for the activity to be pursued in a given area, Fig. 20-2. Basically, two

Fig. 20-2. This reading niche requires special lighting.
(Georgia-Pacific Corporation)

types of lighting fixtures are used in residences. They are the **incandescent** and the **fluorescent** types. All bulbs and tubes should be shielded in a way which will minimize glare. Exceptions are closets and storage areas. Diffusing bowls and shades are commonly used to reduce glare.

Lighting fixtures may be permanently attached to on the ceiling or wall, or they may be lamps which are plugged into convenience outlets. The trend seems to be toward more lamps and fewer ceiling mounted fixtures.

It is desirable to plan for a ceiling fixture in the dining room centered over the table. Another trend in lighting is to use fluorescent tubes above a suspended ceiling in the kitchen and bathrooms. This technique provides plenty of light and is also attractive.

Recessed lighting fixtures are suitable for certain areas of the home such as hallways, foyers, and special emphasis areas. Many varieties of recessed fixtures are available. Each should be evaluated carefully before making a selection.

Lighting fixtures that are to be located outside the house must be "exterior" fixtures. It is desirable to plan adequate lighting for walks, drives, porches, patios, and other outside areas. Exterior lighting should be used to enhance the appearance of the home as well as make it more functional.

Each lighting fixture should be represented with the proper symbol placed in the location where the fixture is to be installed. If the placement must be exact, dimension the location.

Frequently, including a lighting fixture schedule is desirable. This schedule lists fixtures to be used, Fig. 20-3.

Several other electrical devices should be shown on the electrical plan. The permanent location of the telephone and all jacks should be indicated. Differentiate between the permanent unit and jacks (other telephone outlets). Items such as an intercom system, home security devices, television antenna jack, door chimes, and stereo or hi-fi outlets should also be included.

BRANCH CIRCUITS

A well-designed electrical plan will indicate the number and type of branch circuits required for the house. These are usually specified in note or diagram form on the same sheet as the electrical plan. It is not necessary to specify the exact circuit for each outlet, but the number of

LIGHTING FIXTURE SCHEDULE						
TYPE	MANUFACTURER	CATALOG NO.	NO. REQ'D.	MOUNTING HGT.	WATTS	REMARKS
A	SEARS	34K3546	2	7 – 0	100	BRUSHED ALUM.
B	LIGHTOLIER	4107	1	CEILING	150	
C	LIGHTOLIER	4233	2	CEILING	75	
D	SEARS	34K3113C	8	CEILING	80	RAPID START 48"
E	MOLDCAST	MP 232	4	GABLE PEAK	150	TWIN FLOODS
F	PROGRESS	P–180	7	CEILING	100	RECESSED 10" SQ.
G	SEARS	34K1899C	1	CEILING	240	POLISHED CHROME CHAND.
H	LIGHTOLIER	6349	2	6" ABOVE MIRROR	60	
I	ALKCO	330–RS	1	UNDER CABINET	40	
J	EMERSON	220	2	CEILING	60	FAN AND LIGHT COMBINATION
K	PROGRESS	P–318	2	18" BELOW CEILING	100	EXTERIOR – HANGING

Fig. 20-3. A typical lighting fixture schedule which includes the necessary information about each fixture.

lighting, special appliance, and individual appliance circuits, should be listed. This information must be determined before the size of the service equipment may be specified. Follow the guidelines discussed in the previous chapter.

PROCEDURE FOR DRAWING AN ELECTRICAL PLAN

1. Trace the floor plan showing all exterior and interior walls and major appliances.

2. Locate the meter and distribution panel. Indicate the voltage and amperage rating. Check local code requirements.

3. Show all convenience outlets using the proper symbols. Be sure to indicate those which are 240 volts, split-wired (top half on different circuit from bottom or one half switched), weatherproof, or other special purpose.

4. Locate all ceiling and wall lighting outlets. Carefully check the use of symbols.

5. Show all special outlets and fixtures such as telephone, chimes, intercom, etc.

LIGHTING FIXTURE SCHEDULE

TYPE	MANUF.	CAT. NO.	NO.REQ.	MOUNTING HGT.	WATTS	REMARKS
A	PROGRESS	P4014	1	CEILING	240	CHANDELIER
B	SEARS	34 K 5165	2	CEILING	100	CERAMIC HOLDERS
C	SEARS	34 K 3113	4	CEILING	80	SUSPENDED CEILING
D	PROGRESS	P7163	2	ABOVE MIRROR	80	RAPID START
E	SEARS	34 K 2734	2	CEILING	100	
F	PROGRESS	P6406	6	CEILING	100	RECESSED 10" SQ.
G	PROGRESS	P6676	7	CEILING	100	RECESSED 8" RND.
H	PROGRESS	P4449	2	12" BELOW CEIL.	100	EXT. HANGING
I	SEARS	34 K 3546	4	7'-0"	100	BRUSHED ALUM.
J	PROGRESS	P5228	3	1'-6"	60	
K	SEARS	34 K 3622	3	GABLE PEAK	150	TWIN FLOODS
L	PROGRESS	P7002	1	UNDER CAB.	40	

CIRCUIT DATA

LIGHTING CIRCUITS:
4 CIRCUITS PROVIDING 1800 WATTS EACH = 7200 WATTS
(1785 SQ. FT. X 3 WATTS/SQ.FT. = 5355 WATTS MIN.)

SPECIAL APPLIANCE CIRCUITS:
4 CIRCUITS PROVIDING 2400 WATTS EACH = 9600 WATTS
(2 CIRCUITS IN KITCHEN, 2 CIRCUITS IN SHOP)

INDIVIDUAL APPLIANCE CIRCUITS:
1 CIRCUIT FOR REFRIGERATOR = 2400 WATTS
1 CIRCUIT FOR GARBAGE DISPOSER = 2400 "
1 CIRCUIT FOR DISHWASHER = 2400 "
1 CIRCUIT FOR WASHER = 2400 "
1 CIRCUIT FOR GAS DRYER = 2400 "
1 CIRCUIT FOR GAS RANGE = 2400 "
1 CIRCUIT FOR GAS FURNACE = 2400 "
1 CIRCUIT FOR WATER PUMP (230 VOLTS) = 4800 "
1 CIRCUIT FOR TABLE SAW (230 VOLTS) = 4800 "
2 SPARE CIRCUITS   TOTAL = 43,200 WATTS

DISTRIBUTION PANEL:
150 AMP, 20 CIRCUIT, SQUARE D NO. QOC-20 M 200

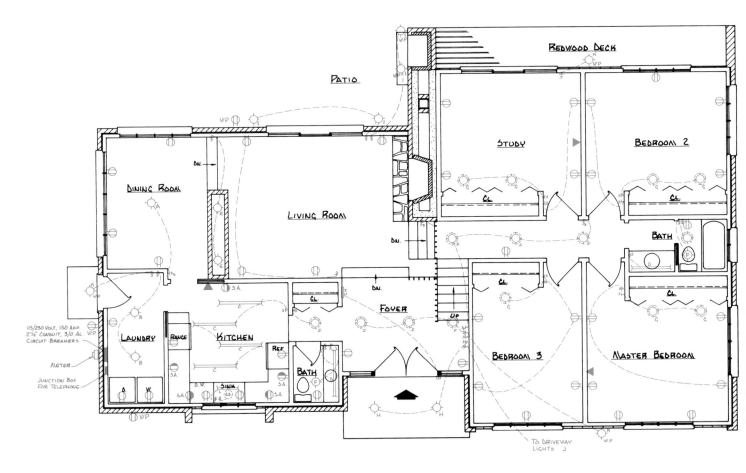

ELECTRICAL PLAN
SCALE — ¼" = 1'-0"

Fig. 20-4. A residential electrical plan showing the necessary electrical features for the first floor.

6. Locate the switches and connect them to the outlets and lighting fixtures which they operate.

7. Add the lighting fixture schedule and symbol legend if necessary.

8. Note the number and type of circuits required.

9. Letter in all other notes, title, scale, and sheet number.

10. Check the drawing carefully to be sure that all information is accurate and complete.

Fig. 20-4 shows an electrical plan for a split-level house in which the procedures just described have been followed.

REVIEW QUESTIONS – CHAPTER 20

Write your answers on a separate sheet of paper. Do not write in this book.

1. Describe the information given in an electrical plan.
2. Identify a major factor to consider when locating the service entrance equipment.
3. The best possible location for the meter is _____ the house.
4. Identify the following electrical features with the proper symbol.
   a. Flush-mounted distribution panel.
   b. Three-way switch.
   c. Push button.
   d. Telephone.
   e. Duplex convenience outlet.
5. Name three types of switches that may be used in the home.
6. Convenience outlets are grounded to prevent _____.
7. The purpose of a lighting fixture schedule is _____.
8. A lighting fixture that is switched from two locations requires two _____ switches.

SUGGESTED ACTIVITIES

1. Select a floor plan of a small house or cottage and draw an electrical plan. Show all outlets, switches, distribution panel, meter, and other required electrical fea-

tures. Identify the number of lighting, special appliance, and individual appliance circuits. Follow the procedure presented in this chapter.

2. Using the same plan as in number 1 or some other plan, develop a pictorial schematic of the circuits in the house and the appliances, fixtures, and outlets which each circuit serves. Indicate the size of conductors and overcurrent protection required.

3. Visit your local utility company, building inspector, and electrical materials distributor. Collect materials relative to house wiring, code requirements, and materials used in residential electrical systems. Bring this information to class and share it with your classmates.

4. Study the room illustrated in Fig. 20-5 to see how track lighting is used to illuminate specific areas. Collect several different applications of track lighting from magazines and manufacturers' literature. Prepare a bulletin board from the material collected.

Fig. 20-5. Track lighting allows light to be placed where it is needed. (Pella/Rolscreen Company)

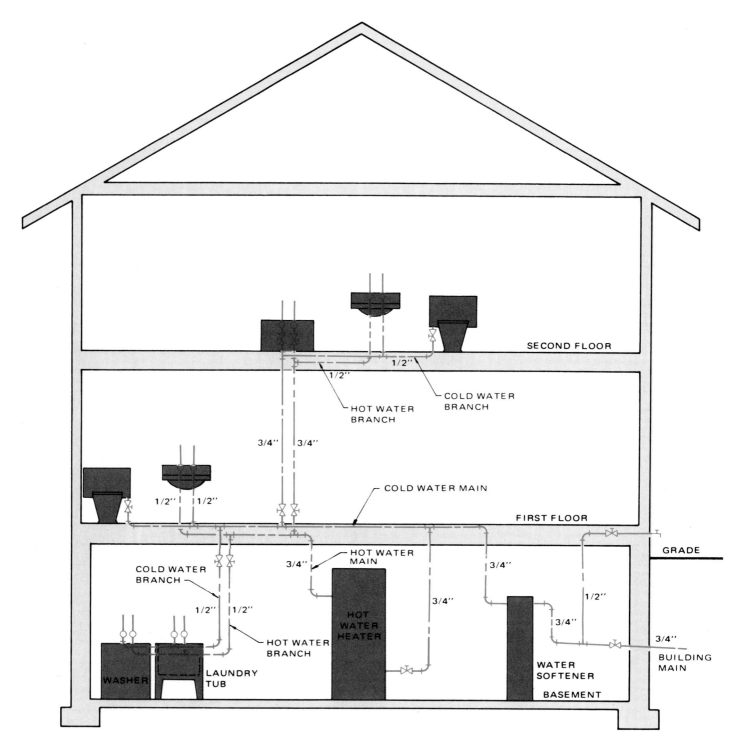

Fig. 21-1. Schematic of a residential water supply system.

21
CHAPTER

Residential Plumbing

After studying this chapter, you will be able to:
- Discuss the purpose of a residential plumbing system.
- Identify the elements contained in a residential water supply system.
- Prepare a schematic diagram of a residential water and waste removal system.
- Draft a residential water supply system.
- Explain the layout of a sewage disposal system.

The residential plumbing system is taken for granted and is seldom a concern of homeowners. Yet, it is a very important part of the house. A well-designed and efficient system is necessary if it is to be functional and remain relatively trouble-free.

A residential plumbing system provides an adequate supply of water for household use in desired locations and removes the waste through a sanitary sewer or private septic system.

There are three principal parts to a residential plumbing installation: the water supply, water and waste removal, and fixtures which facilitate the use of water.

WATER SUPPLY SYSTEM

A residential water supply system begins at the city water main or a private source such as a well, lake, or stream. The pipe that enters the house is known as the **building main,** Fig. 21-1. The building main branches into two lines--the cold water and the hot water mains. It may be necessary to include in the system a water softener, filter, or some other treatment device. It is customary to provide a branch line to hose bibbs which do not require soft or filtered water.

The cold water main extends to various parts of the house to provide water to the fixtures.

Since the water supply system is under pressure, pipes may follow any path which is convenient and practical from the viewpoint of cost. Cold water branch lines are run from the cold water main to each of the fixtures. If a branch line is to supply more than one fixture, the diameter of the pipe must be increased to provide an ample amount of water. Branch lines are smaller than mains.

The hot water main emerges from the water heater, Fig. 21-2, and usually travels parallel to

Fig. 21-2. A water heater installation using plastic pipe. (B.F. Goodrich Chemical Co.)

the cold water main where both hot and cold water are to be used. **Hot water branch lines** run from the hot water main to each fixture.

Location of piping may depend on several factors. In cold climates, care should be taken to insulate pipes along exterior walls to keep them from freezing. Frost-free hose bibbs are also available. Large, heavy pipes present a problem when they must pass through a joist. The customary solution is to place the pipe near the top of the joist and block the space above. See Fig. 21-3.

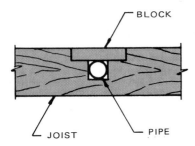

Fig. 21-3. When a large pipe such as a drain must pass through a joist, the joist should be blocked to prevent severe weakening of the member.

Pipes used in the water supply system may be threaded galvanized steel pipe, plastic, or copper tubing with soldered joints when used inside the house, Fig. 21-4. Water supply pipes underground or in concrete are usually special heavy-duty copper tubing with soldered or flare-type joints. Some codes permit the use of plastic pipe for cold water or drain lines, Fig. 21-5. Check the local code requirements before planning the system.

Today, copper tubing is used extensively for water supply systems. Rigid copper tubing (type L), copper fittings, and copper valves are used for all interior installations. Copper pipe is available in 1/2, 3/4, 1 in. and larger diameters. Main lines are usually at least 3/4 in. in diameter and branch lines are a minimum of 1/2 in. in diameter.

Shutoff valves should be supplied for each main line, branch line, and fixture. It should be possible to isolate a single fixture from the system without shutting off the entire water supply.

Many codes require that an air compression chamber be located at each faucet. The chamber cushions the water flow and reduces pipe noise during use, Fig. 21-6. Most air chambers are simply short risers constructed from pipe with the end closed.

As stated earlier, cold and hot water branch lines usually run parallel to each other. Gener-

Fig. 21-4. Galvanized steel, copper, and plastic pipe and fittings are used in residential plumbing systems.

ally, they are placed about 6 in. apart. If they must be placed closer than this, some type of insulating material should be used to prevent the transfer of heat or cold from one pipe to the other. Efficiency may be improved in any system if the hot water lines are insulated.

Fig. 21-5. This plumbing installation utilizes copper pipe and fittings for the water supply system and plastic pipe for the drain system.

Fig. 21-7. An electric heating element located under the sink provides instant hot water. A cold water line is all the plumbing needed. (In-Sink-Erator)

Fixtures such as lavatories which use small amounts of hot water may have a small, on-demand water heater located under the vanity, Fig. 21-7. These units produce instant hot water and require only a cold water line. An electric heating element provides the heat.

WATER AND WASTE REMOVAL

Used water and other waste is carried to the sanitary sewer or septic tank through the waste removal or drainage system, Fig. 21-8. These pipes are isolated from the water supply system and require sufficient capacity, proper slope and venting, and provision for cleanout.

Unlike the water supply system, the drainage system is not under pressure. It depends on gravity to carry the waste to the sewer. Waste creates gases with unpleasant odor which may be harmful. Disposing of these gases must also be provided for in the waste removal system.

All drain pipes must be pitched and large enough inside (usually 4 in.) to prevent solids from accumulating at any point within the system. Drain pipes are generally smooth inside with minimum projections and sharp turns.

In planning a residential plumbing system careful consideration should be given to the drainage network. It is practical and economical to drain as many of the fixtures as possible into a single main drain.

Fig. 21-6. A typical air chamber used at each faucet to reduce noise by cushioning the water flow.

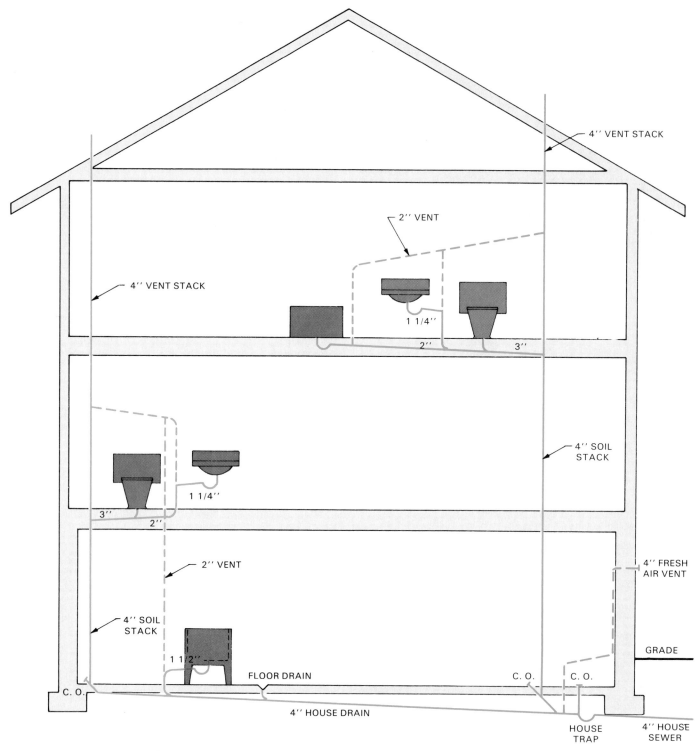

Fig. 21-8. Schematic of a residential water and waste removal system.

A vertical drain pipe that collects waste from one or more fixtures is called a **soil stack.** Stacks that have water closets draining into them are called **main stacks.** Every house must have at least one main stack. There may be several if the house has more than one bath. Main stacks are generally about 3 in. in diameter if copper is used; 4 in. if cast iron is used. Stacks which do not drain water closets are called **secondary stacks.** These stacks may be smaller in diameter than main stacks, usually 1 1/2 in. Each fixture is connected to the stack using a **branch main.** These pipes must slope toward the stack to facilitate drainage. All stacks (main stacks and secondary stacks) extend down into or below the basement or crawl space and empty into the house drain. The house drain is basically horizontal with a slight slope and must be large enough to handle the anticipated load. All houses will have at least one drain but may have several. Once the house drain passes to the outside of the house it is called a **house sewer.** The house sewer finally empties into the city sanitary sewer or a private septic system.

As indicated earlier, sewer gases are a primary consideration in all waste systems. These are dissipated into the air through the soil stack which protrudes about 12 in. above the roof. Traps are installed below each fixture (except the water closet which has a trap built internally) to prevent gases from escaping through the fixture drain into the house. The trap remains filled with water and blocks the gases, Fig. 21-9.

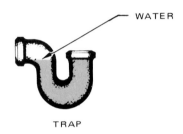

Fig. 21-9. A water trap blocks the escape of gases from the drain system.

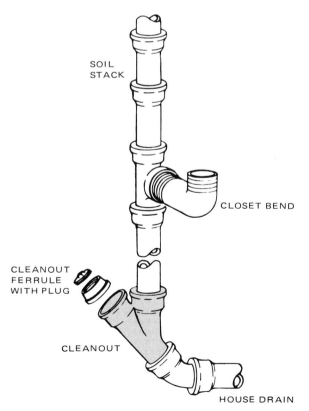

Fig. 21-10. Cleanouts are required by the National Code at the base of all stacks. This drawing illustrates a typical cleanout.

Each stack requires a **cleanout** located at the base of the stack. The cleanout permits the use of a cable to free waste from the house drain or sewer. A stack cleanout is shown in Fig. 21-10. Cleanouts should also be installed where the pipe makes a sharp bend.

In addition to providing an escape for gases, the soil stack (technically a **vent stack** from the upper floor to the roof) provides an air inlet to the drainage system. Drains must have ventilation to operate properly.

Where 4 in. cast iron pipe is used for the soil and vent stack, a 2 x 4 stud wall will not provide sufficient space to house the pipe. In this case a 2 x 6 stud should be specified. This is commonly referred to as a **stack wall.**

Several types of pipe may be used for waste removal. Cast iron pipe is used extensively. Copper and brass alloy pipes which will not rust and are easy to install are also frequently used. Other materials used include fiber and plastic. Many local codes specify the type of pipe to use, so check the code.

House sewers are frequently not as deep as basement floors. Since a drain in the basement floor is desirable, and water will not flow up hill, a pump must be used. A concrete or tile pit or "sump" is located in an inconspicuous place in the basement and the floor is usually sloped toward a drain which flows into the sump, Fig. 21-11. A sump pump which will operate automatically is installed in the sump and connected

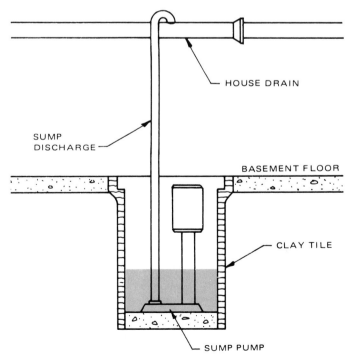

Fig. 21-11. A sump pump removes water from the basement and discharges in into the house drain or outside.

to the house drain. When water reaches a predetermined level in the sump, the pump operates and removes the water.

FIXTURES

The third part of the residential plumbing system is the fixtures. A **fixture** is any appliance such as a bathtub, shower, Fig. 21-12, water closet, sink, dishwasher, etc. that requires water. Fixtures are the most obvious part of the plumbing system, because they are visible. The choice of fixtures is important. They are expensive to install and replace. Choose them wisely.

The National Code specifies minimum clearance and location dimensions which must be adhered to when installing various fixtures. Be sure ample space is allocated for the fixture specified. Manufacturers specify roughing-in measurements for each of their fixtures. Fig. 21-13 illustrates the type of information supplied by one manufacturer.

Fig. 21-12. A prefabricated shower stall ready for installation. (Kohler Company)

PRIVATE SEWAGE DISPOSAL SYSTEM

Private sewage disposal systems (septic tank and disposal field) are used for rural and isolated home sites which cannot be connected to public sewers. Proper construction and maintenance of a private septic system are vitally important. The improper disposal of sewage may be a serious threat to the health and well being of those in the surrounding area. A large number of disease producing organisms thrive in sewage.

Usually before a building permit may be issued, the site is examined by a health department sanitarian to determine if the site is suitable for a private sewage disposal system. Suggested minimum dimensions for placement of well, septic tank, and disposal field on a one acre site are shown in Fig. 21-14. A large land area and suitable soil conditions are necessary to isolate the disposal system from all water supply wells, lakes, and streams, to prevent contamination. Septic systems should also be isolated from property lines and buildings. Check with your

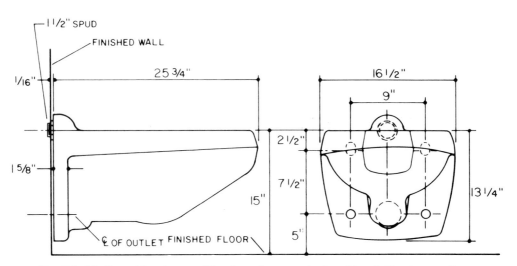

Fig. 21-13. Roughing-in specifications for a typical residential bathroom fixture. These specifications must be given consideration in the planning stages of the dwelling. (Kohler Company)

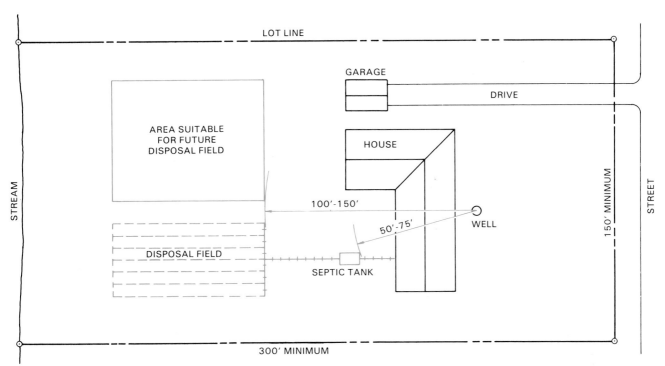

Fig. 21-14. Recommended minimum dimensions for placement of private septic system and water well with respect to the house and property lines. Minimum size site for this system is usually one acre.

local health department for minimum distances required.

SEPTIC TANK

Sewage from the house sewer first enters the septic tank. The septic tank performs two basic functions: (1) it removes about 75 percent of the solids from the sewage by bacterial action before discharging it into the disposal field; and (2) it provides storage space for the settled solids while they undergo digestive action.

A septic tank should be watertight. It is usually constructed of reinforced concrete or con-

crete blocks with mortared joints and interior surface coated with cement and sand plaster. Fig. 21-15 shows the construction of a typical septic tank.

The liquid capacity of the septic tank should be about 1 1/2 times the 24 hour sewage flow and in no case less than 750 gallons. Frequently, the number of bedrooms in a home is used as an indication of the size septic tank required. The size should be increased particularly where automatic washers and garbage disposals are used. It is customary to double the liquid capacity when a garbage disposal is used.

DISPOSAL FIELD

The function of the disposal field is to receive sewage in liquid form from the septic tank and allow it to seep into the soil. Dry and porous soil containing sand or gravel is ideal for a disposal field.

The disposal or drain field may be constructed using clay tile, or perforated fiber or plastic pipe. The drain field lines are laid nearly level (a slope of 1 in. in 50 ft. is the normal slope) about two feet below the surface of the ground. These are positioned in a bed of pebbles usually covered with straw. Fig. 21-16 shows some of the important construction features of a disposal field.

The field should be located in such a manner that surface water drainage is diverted away

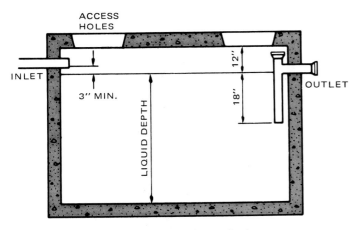

Fig. 21-15. Construction of a typical cast concrete septic tank.

from it. If it becomes flooded, it will cease to be functional. The disposal field should also be located downhill from any water supply well and never under a driveway, parking lot, paved area, or in a place where heavy vehicles may drive over it.

The suitability of the soil for a disposal field must be determined by soil tests. These tests are known as **percolation tests.** They determine how readily the soil will absorb water and provide a guide for design and size of the disposal field required. The percolation rate is determined by filling a test hole with water to completely saturate the immediate area. After complete saturation, water is added to provide 4 to 8 inches of water in the test hole. The drop in water level is measured at 30 minute intervals until the hole is dry. Drop that occurs during the final 30 minute

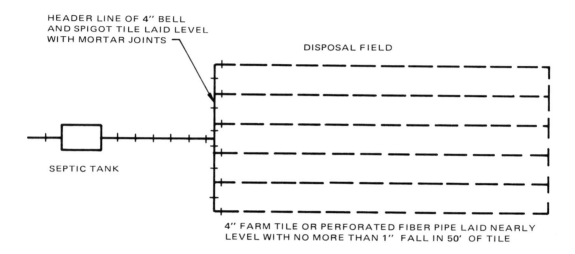

HEADER LINE OF 4" BELL AND SPIGOT TILE LAID LEVEL WITH MORTAR JOINTS

DISPOSAL FIELD

SEPTIC TANK

4" FARM TILE OR PERFORATED FIBER PIPE LAID NEARLY LEVEL WITH NO MORE THAN 1" FALL IN 50' OF TILE

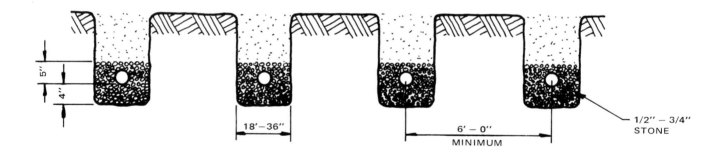

18'—36''

6' — 0''
MINIMUM

1/2'' — 3/4''
STONE

5''

4''

TILE IN INDIVIDUAL TRENCHES

STRAW OVER STONE

12'' — 24'' EARTH FILL

4' — 0''

2' — 0''

TILE IN CONTINUOUS BED

Fig. 21-16. A disposal field may be constructed using either tile in individual trenches or in a continuous bed. A continuous bed requires less space than the individual trench bed.

period is used to calculate the percolation rate for that test hole. Standard percolation rate must be no greater than 45 minutes per inch. One test hole five feet or more deep is generally required to determine groundwater level and consistency of subsoil. The following chart shows the recommended seepage area required for various percolation rates:

DISPOSAL FIELD DESIGN

Standard Percolation Rate	Soil Drainage	Required Seepage Area
Minutes Per Inch		Sq. Ft. Per Bedroom
15 or less	Good	275
16-30	Fair	375
31-45	Poor	500
Over 45	Not suitable	---

Calculation of Disposal Field Size

The following example is for a three bedroom home with a percolation rate of 25 minutes per inch.

1. If the tile is placed in individual trenches, the seepage area required would be 3 x 375 sq. ft. or 1125 sq. ft. (See chart above.) Using 2 ft. wide trenches, 562 lin. ft. of trench would be required. (1125 ÷ 2 sq. ft. per lin. ft. = 562 lin. ft.) Therefore, 8 trenches, each 70 ft. long would provide this.

2. If the tile is placed in a continuous bed, the seepage area required would be 3 x 375 sq. ft. or 1125 sq. ft. (See chart above.) A bed of 28' x 40' would provide this.

3. The minimum necessary gross area available to install the disposal field and provide space for future expansion and replacement would be:

2 1/2 x 1125 sq. ft. = 2812 sq. ft.

REVIEW QUESTIONS–CHAPTER 21

Write your answers on a separate sheet of paper. Do not write in this book.

1. Identify the three parts of any residential plumbing system.
2. The pipe that enters the house from the city water main or private well is called the _____.
3. A faucet on the outside of the house is usually called a _____.
4. The cold water line that connects to a fixture is known as a _____.
5. List two types of pipe commonly used in the water supply system.
6. Main water lines are usually at least _____ in. in diameter.
7. The purpose of an air chamber located at each faucet is _____.
8. List three places where a shutoff valve is required.
9. The force that causes water to flow in the waste removal system is _____.
10. The usual size of most main drain pipes is _____ in.
11. A vertical drain pipe that collects waste from one or more fixtures is called a _____.
12. Stacks which do not drain a water closet are known as _____ stacks.
13. All individual drains in the house empty into the _____ drain.
14. Gases are prevented from entering the house through fixture drains by _____.
15. Each stack requires a _____ at the base of the stack.
16. A wall that houses a soil and vent stack is called a _____.
17. A _____ removes water from a basement when the house drain is higher than the basement floor.
18. A _____ is any appliance which uses or helps you use water.
19. List the two main parts of a private sewage disposal system.
20. Identify two requirements that must be met before a private sewage disposal system may be installed.
21. The percentage of solids removed from sewage in the septic tank is _____ percent.
22. The minimum size septic tank is _____ gallons.
23. The addition of one appliance may double the size of the septic tank. That appliance is _____.
24. The purpose of the disposal field is _____.
25. The type of soil best suited for a disposal field is _____.
26. Recommended slope for drain lines in the septic field is _____.
27. Suitability of soil for a disposal field may be determined using a _____ test.

SUGGESTED ACTIVITIES

1. Visit a house under construction which has the rough plumbing installed. Trace the hot and cold water supply systems and the drainage system. Make notes as to the size and type of pipes used. Check to see where shutoff valves are located and determine if the house sewer is to be connected to a

public sanitary sewer or private system. Secure permission to enter the site.

2. Visit your local building or plumbing inspector. Ask for specifications and requirements for residential plumbing in your area. Invite the inspector to speak to the class.

3. Write to several manufacturers of plumbing supplies and ask for catalogs showing their products. Examine the material and add it to the class collection.

4. Using a sand box, build a scale model of a private sewage disposal system for a three bedroom house with a soil percolation rate of 25 minutes per inch. Display the model.

5. Visit a local plumbing supply store and examine materials used in residential plumbing. Report the relative cost of plastic versus copper pipe and fittings.

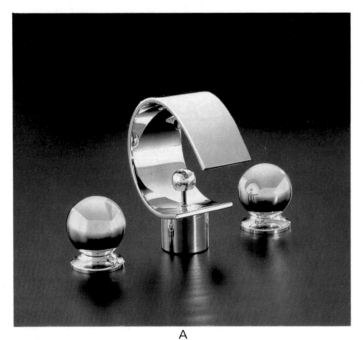

A

B

A – Contemporary styling of this polished chrome lavatory faucet creates a unique design statement. (Kohler Company)
B – The European styling of the brushed nickel and brass lavatory faucet produces a most sophisticated look for a bath or powder room. (Kohler Company)

22
CHAPTER

The Plumbing Plan

After studying this chapter, you will be able to:
- Explain the purpose and components of a residential plumbing plan.
- Draw plumbing symbols and fixtures on a plumbing plan using proper techniques.
- Develop a residential plumbing plan.
- Compile a plumbing fixture schedule.

The plumbing plan is a plan view drawing which shows the plumbing system. It is generally traced from the floor plan. The plan shows water supply lines, waste disposal lines, and fixtures. It describes the sizes and types of all piping and fittings used in the system. Gas lines, also built-in vacuum systems if required, are included on the plumbing plan.

The plumbing plan shows the location, size and type of plumbing equipment to be used. The plumbing system should be coordinated with the electrical and climate control systems. Convenience as well as health and safety depend to a considerable extent on a well-planned plumbing system which operates efficiently.

REQUIRED INFORMATION

The plumbing plan should include: waste lines and vent stacks, water supply lines, drain and fixture locations, size and type of pipe to be used, plumbing fixture schedule, symbols and legend, and notes required to describe the system.

WASTE LINES AND VENT STACKS

Proper location and sufficient size are the major considerations in planning the waste lines. This network is usually designed first, because the whole system is ordinarily planned around it.

A main stack must be designated for each water closet and a sufficient number of second-ary stacks included to properly vent other fixtures. The following chart indicates minimum sizes for residential waste and vent lines:

MINIMUM WASTE AND VENT PIPE SIZES		
KIND OF FIXTURE	MINIMUM WASTE SIZE	MINIMUM VENT SIZE
Bathtub	1 1/2 in.	1 1/4 in.
Bidet	1 1/2 in.	1 1/2 in.
Water Closet	3 in.	2 in.
Lavatory	1 1/2 in.	1 1/4 in.
Service Sink	2 in.	1 1/4 in.
Shower	2 in.	1 1/4 in.
Laundry Tub	1 1/2 in.	1 1/4 in.
Floor Drain	2 in.	1 1/4 in.

As stated in the previous chapter, waste lines are not under pressure and depend on gravity to move the waste. The lines must be sloped slightly, usually 1/4 in. per foot, to facilitate even flow. The required slope should be shown on the plumbing plan, using either a general or specific note.

Waste lines and vent stacks are larger in size than water supply lines and are usually drawn using a wider line than used for supply lines, Fig. 22-1. Try to maintain a proper size relationship between all elements of the drawing.

Care should be taken in locating the house drain and sewer so they are the desired height to properly connect with the public sewer or private septic system. The house drain should be no longer than necessary. Study all facets of the layout before deciding on the final location of the house drain and sewer.

WATER SUPPLY LINES

The water supply begins at the city water main or private water source. Show the building main on the plumbing plan with proper shutoff valves, meter, and size of pipe. Also show the water softener, filter, water storage tank, or

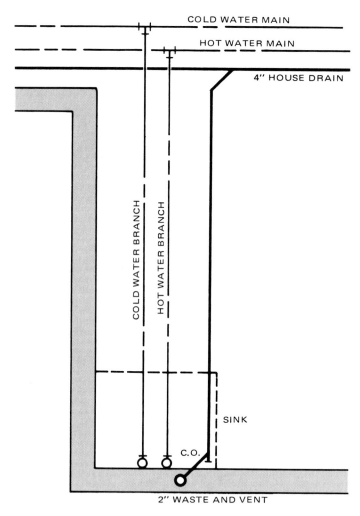

Fig. 22-1. Water supply and waste lines vary in width and are represented by different symbols.

COLD WATER MAIN

HOT WATER MAIN

4" HOUSE DRAIN

COLD WATER BRANCH

HOT WATER BRANCH

SINK

C.O.

2" WASTE AND VENT

other treatment devices positioned along the building main, Fig. 22-2.

Hose bibbs and other fixtures that do not require softened or filtered water should be connected to the building main before it reaches the

softener. Shutoff valves must be provided for each fixture in the water supply system.

Identify fixtures requiring a water supply and determine the size of pipe needed for each. Plan the size of each hot and cold water branch line so it will have the capacity to supply the amount of water needed. Show the location of the water heater and identify it.

Indicate the size of each line in the water supply system. Specify the type of pipe to be installed. Use the proper symbols.

Usually a single plumbing plan will be adequate for a ranch-type house with or without a basement. A split-level or two-story house may require two or more plans. Piping which serves a given level of the house is shown on that plan view.

DRAIN AND FIXTURE LOCATIONS

Floor drains are usually located in basements and attached garages. They are usually connected to the storm sewer or a dry well, and not to the sanitary sewer system. Indicate the drains with the proper symbol and show the location of the pipe leading to the storm sewer or dry well.

Draw the outline of all fixtures requiring plumbing. Check the local code to determine clearance dimensions and minimum space requirements for fixtures. Locate plumbing for fixtures where access may be provided for servicing. This is a requirement of the National Plumbing Code.

SIZE AND TYPE OF PIPE

The proper size pipe required for a given installation will depend on the average amount of

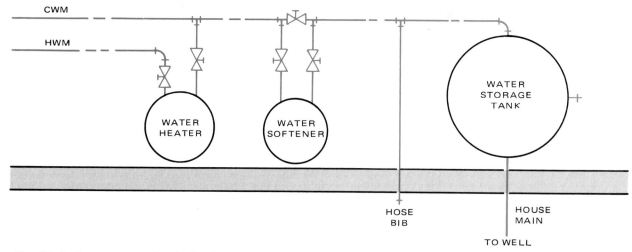

CWM

HWM

WATER HEATER

WATER SOFTENER

WATER STORAGE TANK

HOSE BIB

HOUSE MAIN

TO WELL

Fig. 22-2. Arrangement (typical) where a water storage tank, water softener, and water heater are required.

water used, peak loads, water pressure on the line, and length of the pipe run. (Friction reduces the flow of water and larger pipe should be used for long runs.) Rather than try to calculate the pipe size for each fixture and branch line in the house, it is suggested you refer to the minimum pipe sizes recommended by the Federal Housing Administration for most residences. These minimum sizes are shown in the following chart:

MINIMUM PIPE SIZES OF WATER SUPPLY LINES		
KIND OF FIXTURE	COLD WATER	HOT WATER
Bathtub	1/2 in.	1/2 in.
Bidet	1/2 in.	1/2 in.
Water Closet	3/8 in.	
Lavatory	3/8 in.	3/8 in.
Service Sink	1/2 in.	1/2 in.
Shower	1/2 in.	1/2 in.
Laundry Tub	1/2 in.	1/2 in.
Hose Bibb	1/2 in.	
Building Main	3/4 in.	
Cold Water Main	3/4 in.	
Hot Water Main		3/4 in.
Cold Water Branch	1/2 in.	
Hot Water Branch		1/2 in.

The plumbing plan should specify the type of pipe to be used throughout the system. Several types are available. It is advisable to check the local code to be sure the type you wish to use is acceptable in your locality.

Copper pipe is a frequent choice for the water supply system. The nominal diameter refers to the approximate inside diameter of the pipe. For example, a 1 in. copper pipe, Type L, is 1.025 in. inside diameter and 1.125 in. outside diameter. This is a medium weight copper pipe with Type K being heavier and Type M lighter. Type L is usually used for inside installations for hot and cold water lines. Copper tubing with a designation of DWV is also available. It is thinner than Type M and is used in the sewage disposal system. (The DWV refers to drain, waste, and vent.)

PLUMBING FIXTURE SCHEDULE

A plumbing fixture schedule is useful in planning the plumbing system, ordering the fixtures, and installing the system. Information which is customarily shown on a Plumbing Fixture Schedule includes: identifying symbol, name of the fixture, number, pipe connection sizes, and a space for remarks. A typical residential Plumbing Fixture Schedule is shown in Fig. 22-3.

SYMBOLS AND LEGEND

Whenever possible, use standard symbols. Standard symbols are those that are recognized

PLUMBING FIXTURE SCHEDULE										
IDENT. SYMB.	TYPE OF FIXTURE	NO. REQ'D.	MANUFACTURER AND CATALOG NO.	C W	H W	S & W	VENT	TRAP	GAS	REMARKS
(WC)	WATER CLOSET	1	ELJER "SILETTE" NO. E 5000 ONE-PIECE	3/8"	–	3"	2"	–	–	VITREOUS CHINA TWILIGHT BLUE
(WC)	WATER CLOSET	1	ELJER "SILETTE" NO. E 5000 ONE-PIECE	3/8"	–	3"	2"	–	–	VITREOUS CHINA TUSCAN TAN
(T)	BATHTUB	1	ELJER "RIVIERA" NO. E 1120	1/2"	1/2"	2"	1 1/2"	2"	–	ENAMELED CAST IRON TUSCAN TAN
(L)	LAVATORY	2	ELJER "BRENDA" NO. E 3328	1/2"	1/2"	2"	1 1/2"	1 1/2"	–	VITREOUS CHINA TUSCAN TAN
(L)	LAVATORY	1	ELJER "BARROW" NO. E 3471	1/2"	1/2"	2"	1 1/2"	1 1/2"	–	VITREOUS CHINA TWILIGHT BLUE
(S)	SINK	1	ELJER "KENTON" NO. E 2325	1/2"	1/2"	2"	1 1/2"	1 1/2"	–	ENAMELED CAST IRON WHITE 32 x 20"
(WS)	WATER SOFTENER	1	SEARS "SERIES 60" NO. W 42 K 3482N	3/4"	–	–	–	–	–	17 1/2" DIA. x 42" HIGH DRAIN REQUIRED
(WH)	WATER HEATER	1	SEARS "MODEL 75" NO. 42 K 33741N	3/4"	3/4"	–	4"	–	1/2"	40 GAL. CAPACITY NATURAL GAS
(CW)	CLOTHES WASHER	1	WHIRLPOOL "SUPREME 80"	1/2"	1/2"	2"	1 1/2"	1 1/2"	–	AVOCADO GREEN
(DW)	DISH WASHER	1	WHIRLPOOL SSU 80	1/2"	1/2"	2"	1 1/2"	1 1/2"	–	AVOCADO GREEN
(HB)	HOSE BIB	3	CRANE B–106	3/4"	–	–	–	–	–	

Fig. 22-3. A typical Plumbing Fixture Schedule for a residence.

and accepted by drafters, designers, contractors, and tradeworkers. If there is a chance that the symbols used may not be standard or commonly used, then a legend is used to explain each symbol. The legend should appear on the plan where the symbols are used. Fig. 22-4 shows some of the commonly accepted plumbing symbols. It is important to note that symbols usually are not drawn to the exact size of the feature which they represent. For this reason, care must be taken in choosing the appropriate symbol size.

NOTES

Frequently, information other than that represented by symbols, dimensions, and specifications is needed to describe the plumbing installation. This information is recorded in the form of general notes. The notes must appear on the drawing to which they refer. They are usually located above the title block or in some other prominent place.

Notes may refer to materials, installation procedures, or any facet of the plumbing system.

PROCEDURE FOR DRAWING PLUMBING PLAN

Several decisions and calculations must be made before the plumbing plan can be drawn. The exact fixtures to be used should be determined. Manufacturers' catalogs are good sources of this information. The exact placement of each fixture must be decided. The location of utilities such as sewer, water, storm drains, and gas must be established. (The plot plan usually provides this information.)

After initial information has been gathered, the drawing may proceed. The following steps are suggested:

1. Trace the floor plan showing only the exterior and interior walls, doors and windows, and features which relate to the plumbing plan.

2. Draw the symbols for all fixtures which are to be connected to the house plumbing system. Fixtures may be outlined using a hidden line symbol to draw attention to them. Steps 1 and 2 are shown in Fig. 22-5.

3. Locate and draw the house drain and soil and vent stacks. Be sure to include cleanouts.

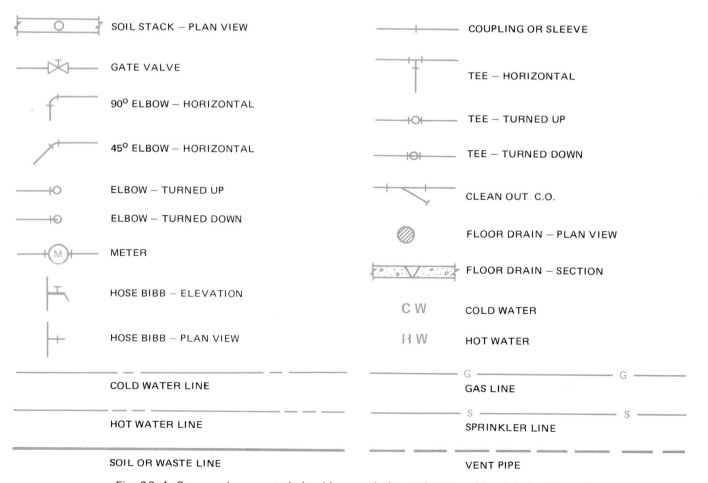

Fig. 22-4. Commonly accepted plumbing symbols used on a residential plumbing plan.

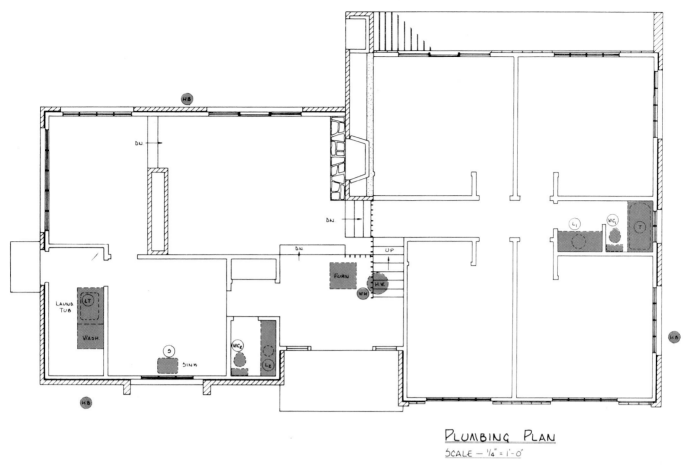

PLUMBING PLAN
SCALE — 1/4" = 1'-0"

Fig. 22-5. A floor plan showing the location of all fixtures which are to be connected to the plumbing system.

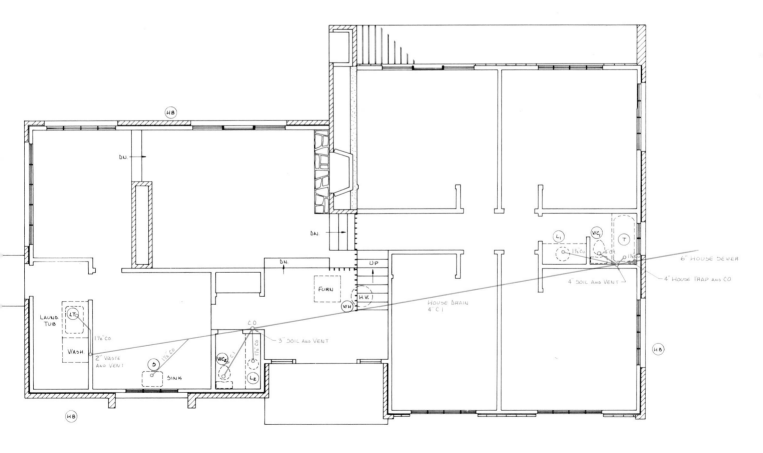

PLUMBING PLAN
SCALE — 1/4" = 1'-0"

Fig. 22-6. The plumbing system is planned around the water and waste system which includes drains, soil and vent stacks, and cleanouts.

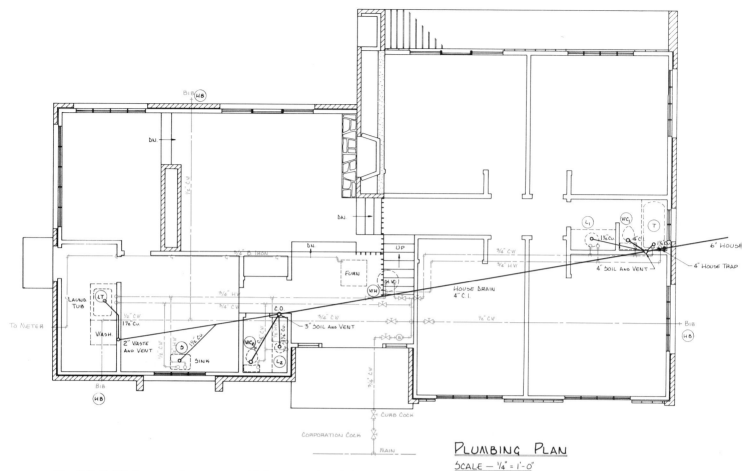

Fig. 22-7. Water supply system which traces the piping from the source to each fixture. Shutoff valves are included.

4. Connect all fixtures and floor drains to the house drain showing all fittings and secondary vents that are used. Steps 3 and 4 are shown in Fig. 22-6.

5. Locate and draw the building main for the water supply system. Connect the water supply piping to the water heater, water softener, and hose bibbs.

6. Draw the cold and hot water mains. Include shutoff valves where they are required. Draw the cold and hot water lines parallel where possible.

7. Locate and draw all cold water and hot water branch lines with shutoff valves. Use the proper symbols.

8. Identify each element of the plumbing system and show pipe sizes. Steps 5, 6, 7, and 8 are shown in Fig. 22-7.

9. Include a Plumbing Fixture Schedule, symbol legend, and general notes required.

10. Add the scale and title block. Check the entire drawing for accuracy and omissions. Fig. 22-8 shows the completed plumbing plan.

This procedure may be repeated for each floor level of the house which requires a plumbing plan.

REVIEW QUESTIONS–CHAPTER 22

Write your answers on a separate sheet of paper. Do not write in this book.
1. Explain the purpose of a plumbing plan.
2. Name two major considerations in planning the waste lines.
3. The part of the plumbing system usually designed first is _____.
4. The fixture that requires a main stack is _____.
5. A water closet requires a waste line which is a minimum of _____ in. in diameter.
6. The force which carries waste and water down the waste lines is _____.
7. Once the house drain is outside the house it becomes the house _____.
8. Most house mains for the water supply system are _____ in. in diameter.
9. Floor drains are usually connected to a dry well or _____.
10. Identify four factors which affect the size of pipe required for a given situation.
11. The nominal diameter of copper pipe refers to the _____ dimension.

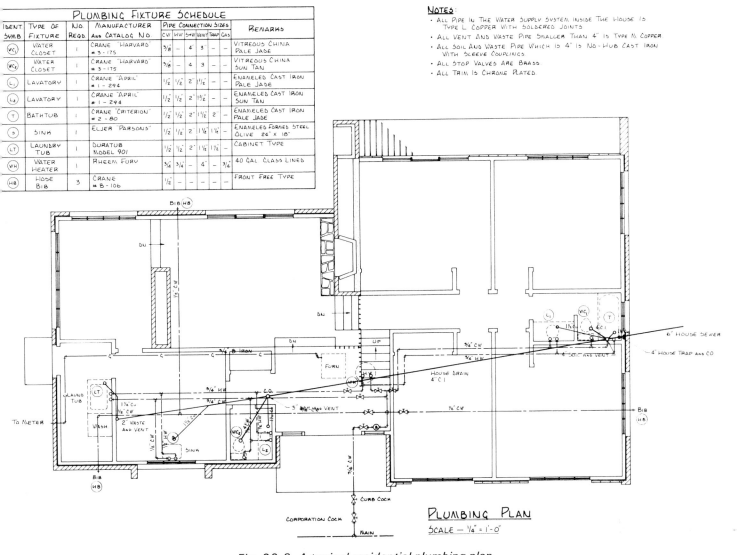

IDENT. SYMB.	TYPE OF FIXTURE	NO. REQD.	MANUFACTURER AND CATALOG NO.	CW	HW	S+W	VENT	TRAP	GAS	REMARKS
WC₁	WATER CLOSET	1	CRANE "HARVARD" # 3-175	3/8	—	4	3	—	—	VITREOUS CHINA PALE JADE
WC₂	WATER CLOSET	1	CRANE "HARVARD" # 3-175	3/8	—	4	3	—	—	VITREOUS CHINA SUN TAN
L₁	LAVATORY	1	CRANE "APRIL" # 1-294	1/2	1/2	2"	1 1/2	—	—	ENAMELED CAST IRON PALE JADE
L₂	LAVATORY	1	CRANE "APRIL" # 1-294	1/2	1/2	2"	1 1/2	—	—	ENAMELED CAST IRON SUN TAN
T	BATHTUB	1	CRANE "CRITERION" # 2-80	1/2	1/2	2"	1 1/2	2	—	ENAMELED CAST IRON PALE JADE
S	SINK	1	ELJER "PARSONS"	1/2	1/2	2"	1 1/2	1 1/2	—	ENAMELED FORMED STEEL OLIVE 24" x 18"
LT	LAUNDRY TUB	1	DURATUB MODEL 901	1/2	1/2	2"	1 1/2	1 1/2	—	CABINET TYPE
WH	WATER HEATER	1	RHEEM FURU	3/4	3/4	—	4"	—	3/4	40 GAL. GLASS LINED
HB	HOSE BIB	3	CRANE # B-106	1/2	—	—	—	—	—	FRONT FREE TYPE

PLUMBING FIXTURE SCHEDULE

NOTES:
- ALL PIPE IN THE WATER SUPPLY SYSTEM INSIDE THE HOUSE IS TYPE L COPPER WITH SOLDERED JOINTS.
- ALL VENT AND WASTE PIPE SMALLER THAN 4" IS TYPE M COPPER.
- ALL SOIL AND WASTE PIPE WHICH IS 4" IS NO-HUB CAST IRON WITH SLEEVE COUPLINGS.
- ALL STOP VALVES ARE BRASS.
- ALL TRIM IS CHROME PLATED.

PLUMBING PLAN
SCALE — 1/4" = 1'-0"

Fig. 22-8. A typical residential plumbing plan.

12. The type of copper pipe usually used for drains, vents, and waste lines is _____.

13. The legend which shows the name of fixtures, manufacturer's catalog number, pipe connection sizes, remarks, and identification symbols for fixtures is called _____.

SUGGESTED ACTIVITIES

1. Study Fig. 22-9 and list the fixtures and/or appliances that are connected to the plumbing system.
2. Select a simple floor plan and design the water and waste removal system. Determine the size pipe required for each drain and fixture. Specify the type of material to be used. Draw the plan to 1/4" = 1'-0" scale. Add necessary notes.

Fig. 22-9. Careful planning is needed to achieve a workable kitchen. Plumbing is a very important element of the kitchen plan. (Whirlpool Corporation.)

3. Using the same floor plan as above, design the water supply system. Determine the pipe size for each branch and main line. Draw the plan using the proper symbols.

4. Sometimes a pictorial schematic is drawn of the entire plumbing system to further illustrate the layout. Using the drawings constructed in 1 and 2 above, make an isometric drawing of the total plumbing system. Omit the walls and floor of the house. Identify the important features of the system.

5. Visit a local plumbing shop and obtain samples of typical plumbing materials used in residential construction. Identify each item and explain where it might be used in the system.

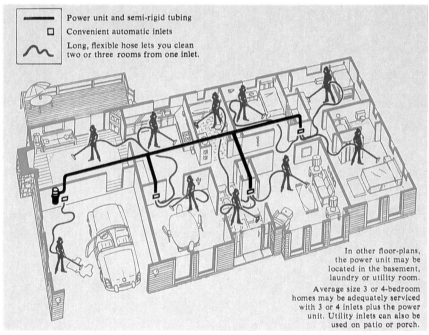

Power unit and semi-rigid tubing

☐ Convenient automatic inlets

Long, flexible hose lets you clean two or three rooms from one inlet.

In other floor-plans, the power unit may be located in the basement, laundry or utility room.

Average size 3 or 4-bedroom homes may be adequately serviced with 3 or 4 inlets plus the power unit. Utility inlets can also be used on patio or porch.

Housekeeping can be less a chore with a built-in vacuum cleaning system. The power unit (left) may be installed in any area away from normal living activities—a utility room, basement, or garage. Inlets may be placed strategically around the house. (Nutone, Inc.)

Residential Climate Control

After studying this chapter, you will be able to:
- Discuss the components of a complete climate control system.
- List the advantages and disadvantages of various types of residential heating systems.
- Perform heat loss calculations for a typical residential structure.
- Select building materials that will provide the best insulation properties.

Increasingly, modern homes are being built with complete climate control systems. A complete climate control system involves temperature control, humidity control, air circulation, and air cleaning.

TEMPERATURE CONTROL

Temperature control includes both heating and cooling. The efficiency with which the control is accomplished is dependent on several conditions. Adequate insulation properly installed is of prime importance, Fig. 23-1.

Fig. 23-1. Proper installation of adequate insulation is an important aspect of efficient temperature control. (CertainTeed Corporation)

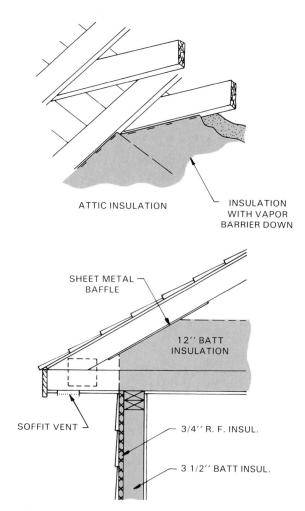

ATTIC INSULATION

INSULATION
WITH VAPOR
BARRIER DOWN

SHEET METAL
BAFFLE

12" BATT
INSULATION

SOFFIT VENT

3/4" R. F. INSUL.

3 1/2" BATT INSUL.

Fig. 23-2. Adequate insulation which is properly installed in the ceiling and soffit area will increase heating and cooling efficiency.

Insulation should be placed in the ceiling, Fig. 23-2, in the exterior walls, and under the floor when the house has a crawl space, Fig. 23-3. Houses that are built on slab foundations should have rigid foam insulation along the inside of the foundation wall and horizontally along the perimeter of the floor, Fig. 23-4.

Insulation serves to prevent the transfer of heat or cold from one location to another. It helps to keep the house warm in winter and cool in summer. Without insulation, efficiency in heating or cooling would require a much larger unit to maintain the desired temperature.

Ventilation is another important factor in an efficient temperature control system, Fig. 23-5. Ventilation reduces the temperature and moisture content in the house, crawl space, and attic. If the attic and crawl space do not have the proper amount of ventilation, moisture is likely to condense and cause damage. If the attic is hot and moist the house will be more difficult to cool. Fig. 23-6 shows how an attic fan can ventilate attic space.

A third factor that affects the efficiency of the heating or cooling system is the solar orientation of the house. The west walls of the house should be protected from the sun in the summer. In some cases this may be accomplished with trees or a garage which shades the side wall. In cold climates an attempt should be made to place all large areas of glass on the south side of the house away from the cold winter winds, and in position to take advantage of the winter sun.

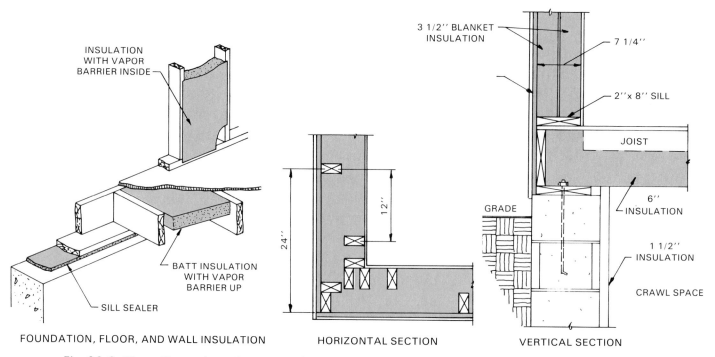

INSULATION
WITH VAPOR
BARRIER INSIDE

BATT INSULATION
WITH VAPOR
BARRIER UP

SILL SEALER

FOUNDATION, FLOOR, AND WALL INSULATION

24"

12"

HORIZONTAL SECTION

3 1/2" BLANKET
INSULATION

7 1/4"

2" x 8" SILL

JOIST

GRADE

6"
INSULATION

1 1/2"
INSULATION

CRAWL SPACE

VERTICAL SECTION

Fig. 23-3. These illustrations show several ways to provide well-insulated foundations, floors, and walls.

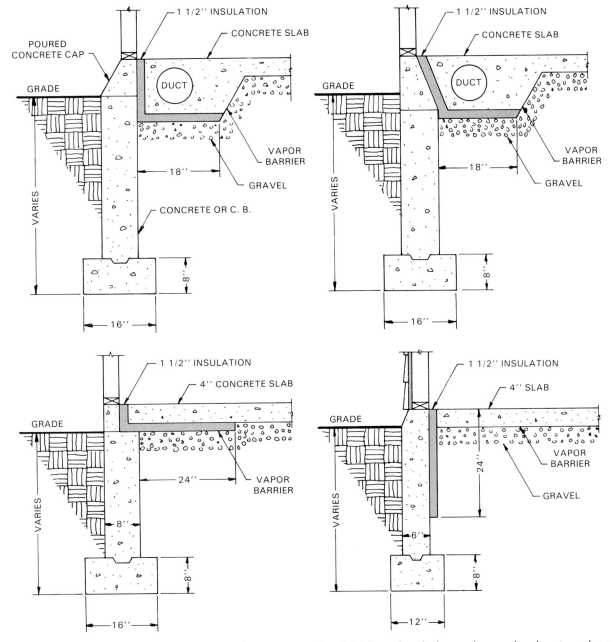

Fig. 23-4. Four types of slab foundations which utilize rigid foam insulation and vapor barriers to reduce heat loss and moisture condensation.

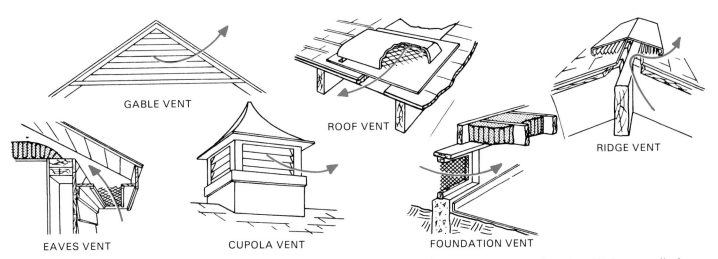

Fig. 23-5. The attic and crawl space should be ventilated for more efficient heating and cooling. Insufficient ventilation may cause damage to sheathing and other structural members due to excess moisture.

Other factors such as weather stripping, color of roofing, length of overhang, Fig. 23-7, and landscape have a bearing on the efficiency of the temperature control system. Weather stripping seals small cracks around doors and windows to reduce heat loss. Light-colored roofing materials absorb less heat from the sun than dark-colored materials. If a house located in a warm climate does not have shade trees, then a light-colored roof will most likely be preferred. Overhangs shade exterior walls and reduce the amount of heat entering the house. Landscaping not only serves to improve the appearance of a home, but may be used to block cold winds, Fig. 23-8, and provide shade. Insulated glass reduces heat loss and lowers the cost of heating and cooling, Fig. 23-9. In extremely warm climates, windows

Fig. 23-6. Proper attic ventilation is needed to reduce moisture and aid cooling in warm weather. An attic fan can improve attic ventilation. (Nutone, Inc.)

Fig. 23-8. Landscaping is an effective method to block cold winds from hitting the house. In northern climates, plants are most effective when placed on the north side of the dwelling.

Fig. 23-7. An overhang shades the sides of the house. This reduces heat gain in the summer. It may also add to the overall appearance of the structure. (California Redwood Association)

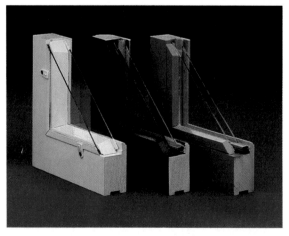

Fig. 23-9. Cut-away views of insulated glass windows. A—Single glazing with RDG. B—Insulating glass, solar gray and clear. C—Insulating glass with Low-E inside. (Marvin Windows)

with bronze glass and built-in shades reduce heat gain in the house, Fig. 23-10.

HUMIDITY CONTROL

Air in our homes contains a certain amount of water (moisture). The amount of moisture in the air related to the temperature level is called *humidity.* More specifically, humidity is the ratio (percentage) of water vapor in the atmosphere to the amount required to saturate it at the same temperature. It is properly called *relative humidity.* The air will hold more water when the temperature is high than when it is low. A comfortable humidity level is around 50 percent when the temperature is about 75 deg. During the winter months, the amount of moisture in the air indoors drops to a low level because of expanding the air during heating and the low relative humidity outside the house. If water is not added to the air to increase the humidity, throat and skin irritations are likely. Also furniture may crack and separate at the glue joints. For these reasons, humidifiers are commonly used to increase the moisture level. Humidifiers may be attached directly to the plenum or heating ducts of a forced warm air system, Fig. 23-11, or a free-standing model may be used.

In the summer the problem is too much moisture in the air. When the humidity is high, the air feels ''sticky'' and people are uncomfortable. Wood doors, windows, and drawers swell and do not operate smoothly. When the moisture content is too high water is likely to condense on windows. This condition, if allowed to persist, may cause damage in the woodwork. A *dehumidifier* may be installed to remove water from the air. This device condenses water on cold coils and thus removes it from the air and reduces the relative humidity. Humidity control is important for total comfort and should be considered when planning a climate control system.

AIR CIRCULATION AND CLEANING

If the same air in a house is used over and over without adding a fresh supply it will become stale and unhealthy. Therefore, some provision should be made to provide fresh air. Circulation helps to lessen the problems of dry air. High concentrations of moist air in the kitchen, laundry room, and bath are distributed throughout the house when the air is circulated.

The air in most homes contains a sufficient amount of dust and other foreign particles so consideration should be given to adding some type of air cleaning device. Some furnaces have

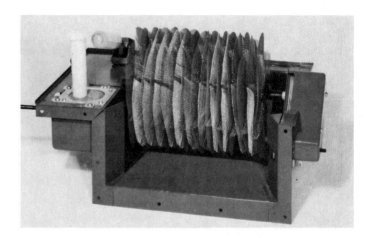

Fig. 23-10. Cut-away view of window with double glazing and built-in shade. Exterior glass is bronze. (Pella/Rolscreen Company)

Fig. 23-11. Power humidifiers may be mounted on the plenum or supply duct of a forced warm air heating system. (Whirlpool Corp.)

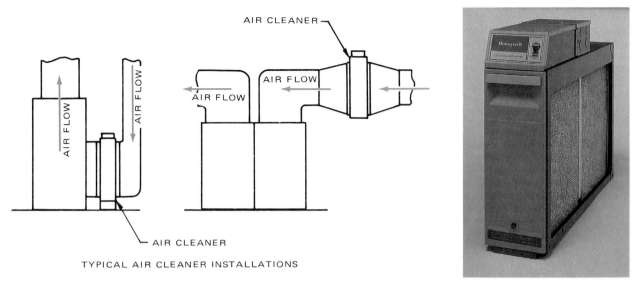

TYPICAL AIR CLEANER INSTALLATIONS

Fig. 23-12. Electronic air cleaners can be installed with most forced warm air heating, cooling, or ventilating systems. (Honeywell, Inc.)

built-in filters, some have electronic air cleaning grids, Fig. 23-12. Electronic grids are effective and will remove up to about 95 percent of the dust particles as they pass through it.

A complete climate control system heats or cools the air, cleans, circulates, and controls moisture content in the house as required for comfort, Fig. 23-13. This provides a healthful atmosphere in which to live.

TYPES OF HEATING SYSTEMS

Modern heating systems are usually one of four basic types: *forced warm air, hydronic systems, electric radiant systems,* and *heat pumps.*

FORCED WARM AIR SYSTEMS

The forced warm air system heats air in a furnace and forces it through pipes or ducts to all parts of the house, Fig. 23-14. A fan or blower is used to push the warm air. Cool air is drawn through cold air return ducts to the furnace. Before the cool air enters the heating chamber, it passes through a filter which removes dust and other particles. Some forced warm air systems have built-in humidifiers, dehumidifiers, and air cleaners.

The forced warm air system is popular because it is relatively inexpensive to purchase and install, provides heat in adequate amounts quickly, heating ducts may be used in a central air cooling system, and humidification is simple.

Air conditioners can be installed in walls, Fig. 23-15, or as part of the climate control system.

Three basic kinds of forced air furnaces are available for residential installations: *standard upflow furnace, counterflow furnace,* and *horizontal furnace.* The upflow furnace, Fig. 23-16, is designed for basement installation, because the *plenum* (chamber where warmed air is collected for distribution) is on top of the furnace.

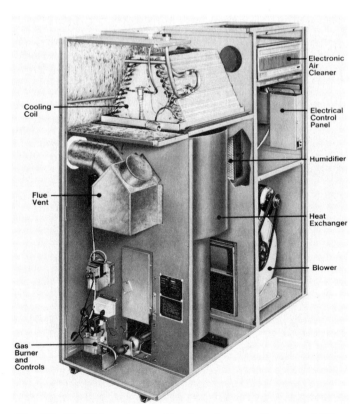

Fig. 23-13. This unit provides heating, cooling, humidification, dehumidification, and air cleaning. (The Williamson Co.)

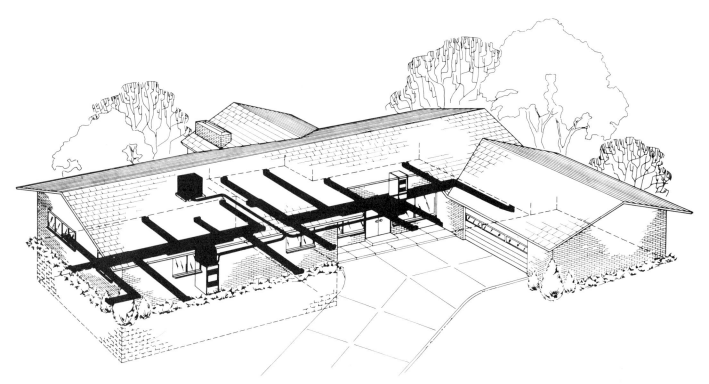

Fig. 23-14. Heating and cooling may use the same duct system or a combination of systems.

Fig. 23-15. Typical wall air conditioner.

Fig. 23-16. Upflow furnaces are designed for basement installation because the plenum is located on top of the unit. (Comfortmaker)

When the furnace is to be located on the main floor with ducts below the floor, a counterflow furnace is required, Fig. 23-17. On this type of furnace the plenum is on the bottom and the warm air is forced downward. If the furnace is to be installed in the attic or crawl space, a horizontal furnace, Fig. 23-18, is a logical choice.

Modern forced warm air systems do have some disadvantages. Rapid movement of air is objectionable to some people because drafts are created. Noise is often transmitted through the ducts and the noise level is generally higher than with other systems due to the blower.

In modern furnace installations the ducts are designed to fit between the joists and wall studs,

Fig. 23-18. Horizontal furnaces are ideally suited for crawl space or attic installation. They require only minimum clearance and can be suspended from ceilings and floor joists or installed on a concrete slab.

Fig. 23-17. Counterflow furnaces are specially designed for closet, garage, or utility room installation. The plenum is located on the bottom. (Whirlpool Corp.)

Fig. 23-19. However, the ducts are large and sometimes difficult to route to all parts of the dwelling. Furniture sometimes interferes with air movement. Furnaces may be located in the attic, crawl space, or main level, Fig. 23-20.

Furnace operation is controlled by the use of thermostats. The **thermostat** is an automatic

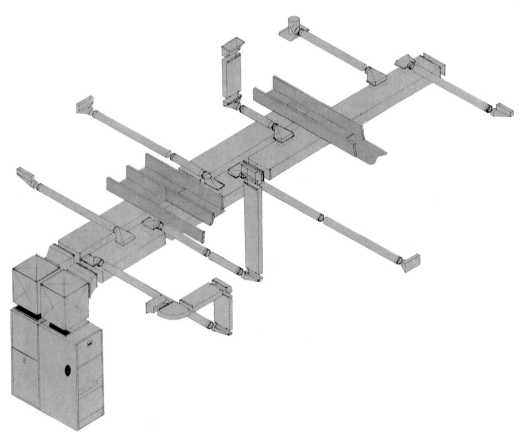

Fig. 23-19. Popular extended plenum system designed to fit within the joists and studs of a frame structure. (The Williamson Company)

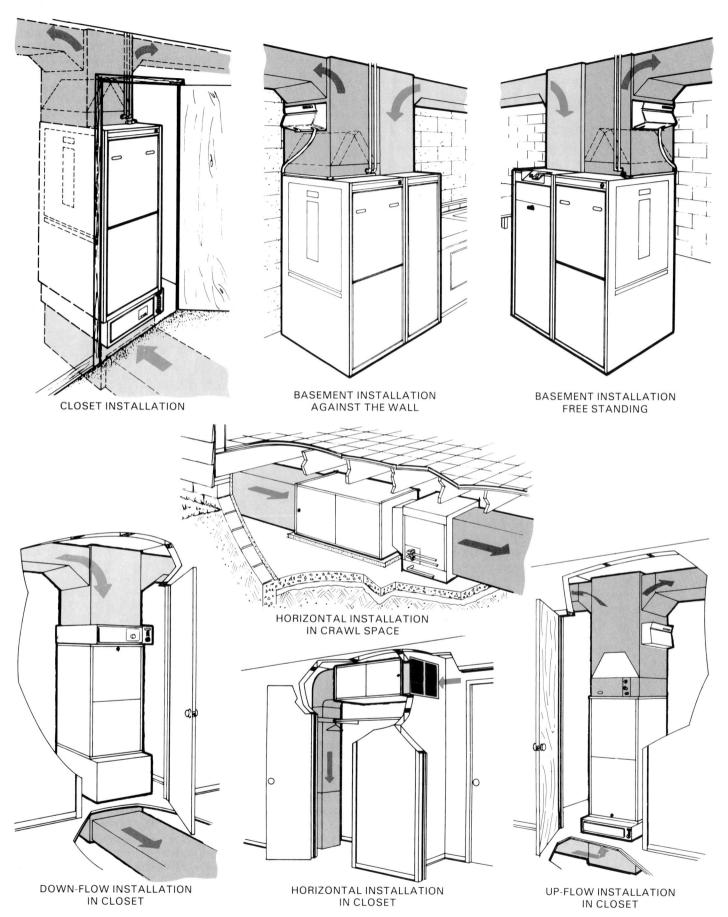

CLOSET INSTALLATION

BASEMENT INSTALLATION
AGAINST THE WALL

BASEMENT INSTALLATION
FREE STANDING

HORIZONTAL INSTALLATION
IN CRAWL SPACE

DOWN-FLOW INSTALLATION
IN CLOSET

HORIZONTAL INSTALLATION
IN CLOSET

UP-FLOW INSTALLATION
IN CLOSET

*Fig. 23-20. Typical forced warm air furnace installation in the basement, crawl space, and closet on first floor.
(Lennox Industries, Inc.)*

sensing device that may be set to activate the furnace at predetermined temperatures, Fig. 23-21. The thermostat is usually located on an inside wall of the house. It should be located where it will be free from cold air drafts and heat from lamps. A typical forced warm air system for a small home uses one thermostat which controls the heat for the entire home. Large homes frequently require zoning into heating areas and utilize separate thermostats for each of the areas. These systems usually require a separate furnace for each zone.

HYDRONIC SYSTEMS

A hydronic (hot water) system consists of a boiler to heat water, Fig. 23-22, water pipes,

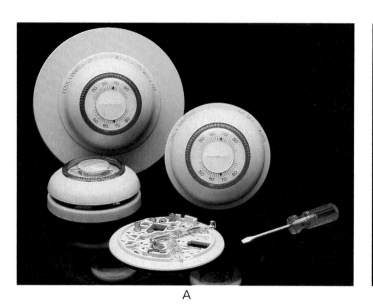
A

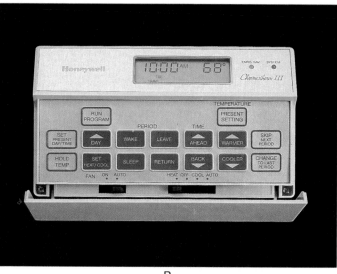
B

Fig. 23-21. Common styles of thermostats used in residential heating and cooling systems. A–Decorative round model in contemporary design. B–Programmable to maximize energy savings. (Honeywell, Inc.)

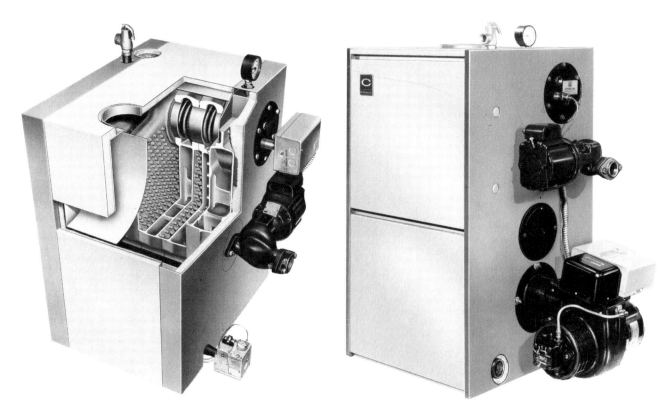

Fig. 23-22. Modern gas-fired hydronic furnaces. (Crane Co.)

and radiators or radiant panels. Hot water is pumped to the radiators which are located throughout the house. The cooled water is returned to the boiler for reheating. The type of hydronic system used in most homes is known as the **one-pipe system.** The one-pipe system uses radiators or converters, as they are sometimes called, connected in series. Heated water carried in the main pipe is diverted to the radiators and is then returned to the furnace, Fig. 23-23. Special connectors allow small amounts of hot water to enter the radiators and equalize heat in radiators throughout the home.

Old style radiators are seldom used in new homes. Baseboard convectors, Fig. 23-24, are popular. These are produced in several styles.

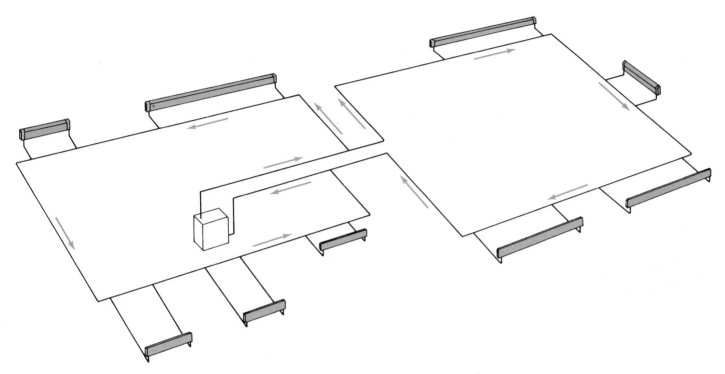

Fig. 23-23. A series loop-type hydronic system with two zones of control.

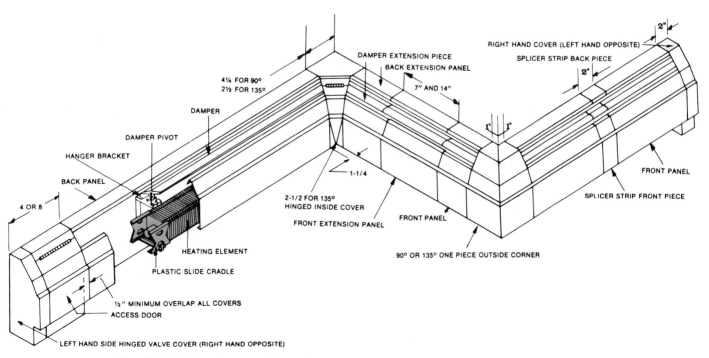

Fig. 23-24. A modern style baseboard convector for a hydronic system. (Crane Co.)

The convectors are efficient and readily transmit heat to the surrounding air.

Another type of hydronic heating system utilizes copper pipes embedded in a concrete floor or plastered ceiling. This system is often referred to as a *radiant system,* Fig. 23-25. It is popular in mild climates and locations where the temperature is not likely to drop rapidly in a short period of time. A radiant heating system is silent and is completely hidden from sight.

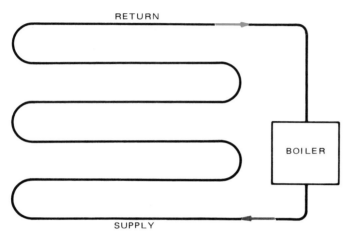

Fig. 23-25. Radiant hydronic system utilizing copper pipe embedded in concrete floor.

One of the major advantages of a hydronic heating system is that each room may be controlled individually. Frequently the home is zoned into two or three areas which require about the same temperature and each zone is controlled by a separate thermostat. This adds to the heating comfort.

Other advantages include the absence of noise transmitted from room to room, no registers to occupy wall space, and no drafts. Hydronic heat is clean, quiet, and efficient. However, it has no provision for cooling, air filtration, or humidification; and the reaction time is slow when compared to other systems. These may be considered serious deficiencies in some sections of the country.

ELECTRIC RADIANT SYSTEMS

Electric radiant systems use resistance wiring to produce heat in the wire. The wire is embedded in the ceiling, floor, or baseboards, Fig. 23-26. This system is clean, quiet, and produces a constant level of heat. The entire system is hidden if the wires are in the ceiling or floor. Heat control for each room or area is practical. No chimney is required as with most gas- or oil-fired systems. The electric radiant system is dependable and free from maintenance problems.

Disadvantages of this system include no provision for humidification, air filtration, cooling, and slow recovery if the temperature drops suddenly. In some areas of the country, electric radiant systems are expensive to operate due to the cost of electricity. Fig. 23-27 shows a typical installation.

HEAT PUMPS

Heat pumps, Fig. 23-28, serve the dual purpose of heating and cooling. They are essentially refrigeration units which pump or transfer natural heat from air or water to heat or cool the house. Heat pumps operate on the principle that there is some heat in all air and water and this heat may be removed. Heat which has been

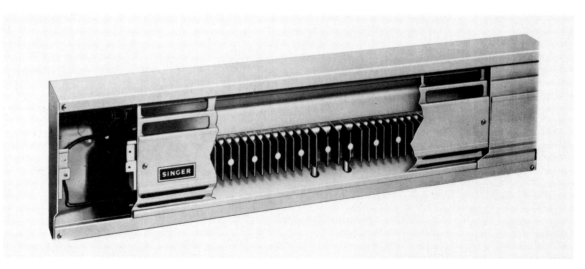

Fig. 23-26. Baseboard designed for an electric radiant heating system.

removed is pumped into the house to heat it, and pumped from the house to cool it.

The heat pump requires electricity to operate a compressor. It is clean and needs no chimney. Limited inside space is required because the main unit is located outside the house and air cleaning and humidification are easy. Heat pumps are highly efficient in mild climates. A

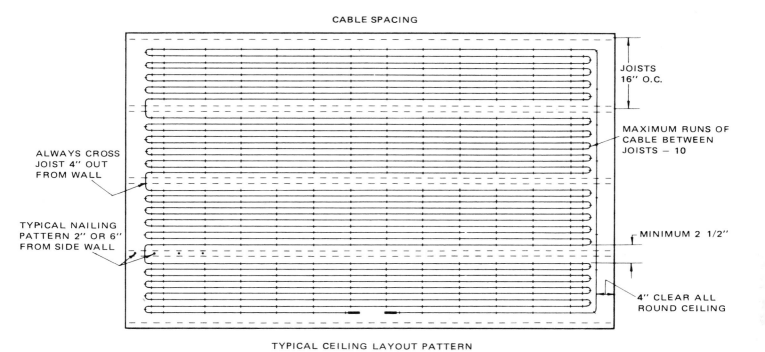

CABLE SPACING

JOISTS 16" O.C.

MAXIMUM RUNS OF CABLE BETWEEN JOISTS – 10

ALWAYS CROSS JOIST 4" OUT FROM WALL

TYPICAL NAILING PATTERN 2" OR 6" FROM SIDE WALL

MINIMUM 2 1/2"

4" CLEAR ALL ROUND CEILING

TYPICAL CEILING LAYOUT PATTERN

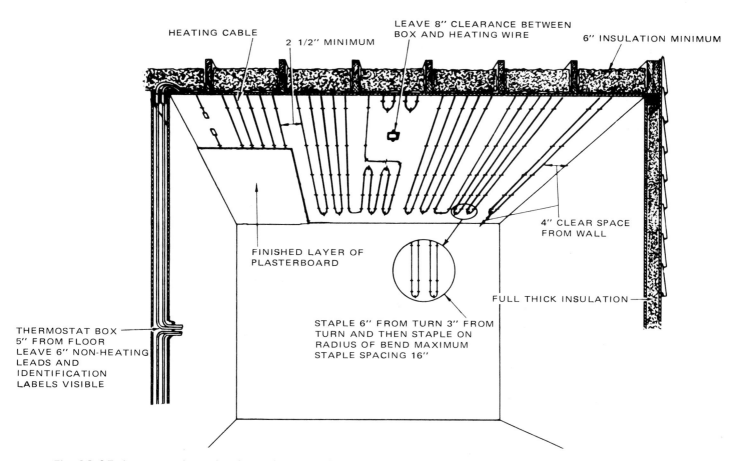

HEATING CABLE

2 1/2" MINIMUM

LEAVE 8" CLEARANCE BETWEEN BOX AND HEATING WIRE

6" INSULATION MINIMUM

FINISHED LAYER OF PLASTERBOARD

4" CLEAR SPACE FROM WALL

FULL THICK INSULATION

THERMOSTAT BOX 5" FROM FLOOR LEAVE 6" NON-HEATING LEADS AND IDENTIFICATION LABELS VISIBLE

STAPLE 6" FROM TURN 3" FROM TURN AND THEN STAPLE ON RADIUS OF BEND MAXIMUM STAPLE SPACING 16"

Fig. 23-27. Layout and spacing for resistance wiring used in radiant electrical heating systems. NOTE: 1 watt of electricity will provide 3.415 Btus of heat.

Fig. 23-28. A heat pump compressor/condenser unit designed for outside installation. (Comfortmaker)

disadvantage is that efficiency drops considerably when the temperature is below 30 degrees. For this reason, heat pumps are not practical for cold climates. This system also requires a duct system and blower to move air. Therefore, installation costs generally are higher than for other systems.

Choosing the "right" system for a particular home will depend on the availability of fuels, temperature variations, cost of installation and maintenance, type of house, and personal preference of the owner.

HEAT LOSS CALCULATIONS

Before the proper size heating or cooling unit may be determined, heat loss calculations are required for exposed surfaces of the home. Several terms with which you should become familiar are:

British thermal unit. A British thermal unit, or BTU as it is commonly called, is the quantity of heat required to increase the temperature of 1 pound of water 1 °F. Furnaces and air conditioners are rated in BTUs. Final heat loss calculation will be in BTUs.

Heat loss. The amount of heat that passes through the exposed surfaces of the house for average temperatures.

Inside design temperature. The desired room temperature level is called the inside design temperature. Seventy degrees Fahrenheit is the usual level used for calculations.

Outside design temperature. The outside design temperature is the average outdoor temperature for the winter months. An average of the coldest temperatures for the months of October

RESISTIVITY TO HEAT LOSS OF COMMON BUILDING MATERIALS

	MATERIAL	RESISTIVITY		MATERIAL	RESISTIVITY
4''	CONCRETE OR STONE	.32	1/2''	PLYWOOD	.65
6''	CONCRETE OR STONE	.48	5/8''	PLYWOOD	.80
8''	CONCRETE OR STONE	.64	3/4''	PLYWOOD	.95
12''	CONCRETE OR STONE	.96	3/4''	SOFTWOOD SHEATHING OR SIDING	.85
4''	CONCRETE BLOCK	.70		COMPOSITION FLOOR COVERING	.08
8''	CONCRETE BLOCK	1.10	1''	MINERAL BATT INSULATION	3.50
12''	CONCRETE BLOCK	1.25	2''	MINERAL BATT INSULATION	7.00
4''	COMMON BRICK	.82	4''	MINERAL BATT INSULATION	14.00
4''	FACE BRICK	.45	2''	GLASS FIBER INSULATION	7.00
4''	STRUCTURAL CLAY TILE	1.10	4''	GLASS FIBER INSULATION	14.00
8''	STRUCTURAL CLAY TILE	1.90	1''	LOOSE FILL INSULATION	3.00
12''	STRUCTURAL CLAY TILE	3.00	1/2''	GYPSUM WALLBOARD	.45
1''	STUCCO	.20	1''	EXPANDED POLYSTYRENE, EXTRUDED	4.00
15 LB.	BUILDING PAPER	.06	1''	EXPANDED POLYSTYRENE, MOLDED BEADS	3.85
3/8''	SHEET ROCK OR PLASTERBOARD	.33		SINGLE THICKNESS GLASS	.88
1/2''	SAND PLASTER	.15		GLASSWELD INSULATING GLASS	1.89
1/2''	INSULATION PLASTER	.75		SINGLE GLASS WITH STORM WINDOW	1.66
1/2''	FIBERBOARD CEILING TILE	1.20		METAL EDGE INSULATING GLASS	1.85
1/2''	FIBERBOARD SHEATHING	1.45	4''	GLASS BLOCK	2.13
3/4''	FIBERBOARD SHEATHING	2.18	1 3/8''	WOOD DOOR	1.92
	ROLL ROOFING	.15		SAME WITH STORM DOOR	3.12
	ASPHALT SHINGLES	.16	1 3/4''	WOOD DOOR	1.82
	WOOD SHINGLES	.86		SAME WITH STORM DOOR	2.94
	TILE OR SLATE	.08			

Fig. 23-29. The resistivity of various common building materials has been determined by laboratory tests to be used in heat loss calculations.

through March is used to determine the outdoor design temperature.

Design temperature difference. The difference between the outside design temperature and the inside design temperature is the design temperature difference.

U factor. The U factor, or U as it is commonly called, is the number of BTUs transmitted in 1 hour through 1 sq. ft. of a building material for each degree of temperature difference. U factors for common building materials may be determined by taking the reciprocal (dividing 1.00 by the resistance factor) of the resistivity of the material, see Fig. 23-29.

Infiltration. Heat lost through spaces around windows and doors is known as infiltration. For calculation purposes, it has been estimated that infiltration is equal to one air exchange per hour. For example, if a room is 10' x 18' and has an 8 ft. ceiling the total volume is 1440 cu. ft. This figure, 1440 cu. ft., is the amount of air infiltration.

Resistivity. Ability to resist the transfer of heat or cold. Materials which transmit heat readily are known as conductors while those that do not are called insulators.

Fig. 23-30 shows several energy-conserving exterior wall assemblies with R factors identified for each material.

CALCULATION PROCEDURE

The procedure recommended for determining heat loss for walls, ceiling, and floor of a room or the total house so the proper size heating or cooling unit may be established is:

WALLS

1. Find the total exterior wall area by multiplying the length by the height. This is the gross wall area.

2. Subtract the area filled by windows and doors in the exterior walls. The resulting area is called the net wall area.

3. Add the resistivity for each of the materials used in the construction of each wall. Take the reciprocal of the sum. This figure is the U factor for the net wall. (Each wall that is constructed differently must be calculated separately.)

4. Determine the U factor for each door and window in the exterior wall by taking the reciprocal of the resistivity.

5. Calculate the design temperature difference by subtracting the outside design temperature from the inside design temperature. Example: IDT = 70°, ODT = -10°, therefore

70° – (-10°) = 80°. The design temperature difference for this example is 80°.

6. Determine the BTU loss per hour (BTU/H) for the net wall area by multiplying the net wall area by the net wall U factor by the design temperature difference. Record this figure.

7. Determine the BTU/H for the windows by multiplying the window area by the glass U factor by the design temperature difference. Record this figure.

8. Determine the BTU/H for the doors by multiplying the door area by the door U factor by the design temperature difference. Record this figure.

CEILING

1. Find the total ceiling area by multiplying the length by the width.

2. Determine the U factor for the ceiling by adding the resistivity for each material used and taking the reciprocal.

3. Calculate the BTU/H by multiplying the ceiling area by the total ceiling U factor by the design temperature difference. Record the figure.

FLOOR

1. Find the total floor area (figure heat loss only for floors over unheated areas such as crawl space or slab-type floors) of the floor by multiplying the length by the width.

2. Determine the U factor for the floor by adding the resistivity for each material used and taking the reciprocal.

3. Calculate the BTU/H by multiplying the floor area, by the total floor U factor, by the design temperature difference. Note that the design temperature difference may not be the same here as for walls and ceiling with heating ducts and hot water pipes which are not insulated. If the area is properly vented and pipes and ducts are insulated, then some design temperature difference may be used. Record this figure.

INFILTRATION

1. Determine the volume of air in the room or home under consideration by multiplying the length by the width by the height. This volume is equal to the air infiltration.

2. Calculate the air infiltration BTU/H heat loss by multiplying the volume of air infiltration by the U factor (.018) by the design temperature difference. Note that .018 BTU/H is required to warm 1 cu. ft. of air 1 °F This is a constant and may be used in each calculation. Record this figure.

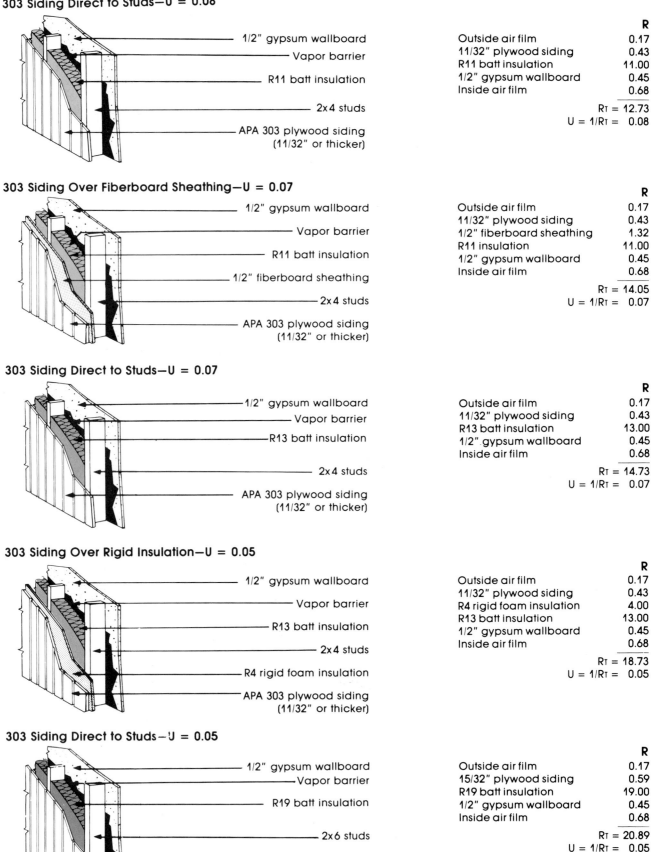

303 Siding Direct to Studs—U = 0.08

- 1/2" gypsum wallboard
- Vapor barrier
- R11 batt insulation
- 2x4 studs
- APA 303 plywood siding (11/32" or thicker)

	R
Outside air film	0.17
11/32" plywood siding	0.43
R11 batt insulation	11.00
1/2" gypsum wallboard	0.45
Inside air film	0.68
R_T =	12.73
$U = 1/R_T$ =	0.08

303 Siding Over Fiberboard Sheathing—U = 0.07

- 1/2" gypsum wallboard
- Vapor barrier
- R11 batt insulation
- 1/2" fiberboard sheathing
- 2x4 studs
- APA 303 plywood siding (11/32" or thicker)

	R
Outside air film	0.17
11/32" plywood siding	0.43
1/2" fiberboard sheathing	1.32
R11 insulation	11.00
1/2" gypsum wallboard	0.45
Inside air film	0.68
R_T =	14.05
$U = 1/R_T$ =	0.07

303 Siding Direct to Studs—U = 0.07

- 1/2" gypsum wallboard
- Vapor barrier
- R13 batt insulation
- 2x4 studs
- APA 303 plywood siding (11/32" or thicker)

	R
Outside air film	0.17
11/32" plywood siding	0.43
R13 batt insulation	13.00
1/2" gypsum wallboard	0.45
Inside air film	0.68
R_T =	14.73
$U = 1/R_T$ =	0.07

303 Siding Over Rigid Insulation—U = 0.05

- 1/2" gypsum wallboard
- Vapor barrier
- R13 batt insulation
- 2x4 studs
- R4 rigid foam insulation
- APA 303 plywood siding (11/32" or thicker)

	R
Outside air film	0.17
11/32" plywood siding	0.43
R4 rigid foam insulation	4.00
R13 batt insulation	13.00
1/2" gypsum wallboard	0.45
Inside air film	0.68
R_T =	18.73
$U = 1/R_T$ =	0.05

303 Siding Direct to Studs—U = 0.05

- 1/2" gypsum wallboard
- Vapor barrier
- R19 batt insulation
- 2x6 studs
- APA 303 plywood siding (15/32" or thicker for studs 24" oc)

	R
Outside air film	0.17
15/32" plywood siding	0.59
R19 batt insulation	19.00
1/2" gypsum wallboard	0.45
Inside air film	0.68
R_T =	20.89
$U = 1/R_T$ =	0.05

Fig. 23-30. Exterior wall assemblies showing R factors for each material. (American Plywood Association)

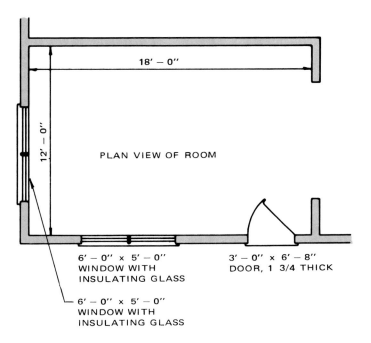

PLAN VIEW OF ROOM

18' — 0''

12' — 0''

6' — 0'' x 5' — 0''
WINDOW WITH
INSULATING GLASS

6' — 0'' x 5' — 0''
WINDOW WITH
INSULATING GLASS

3' — 0'' x 6' — 8''
DOOR, 1 3/4 THICK

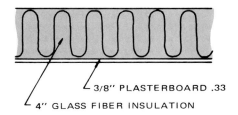

3/8'' PLASTERBOARD .33

4'' GLASS FIBER INSULATION

CEILING SECTION

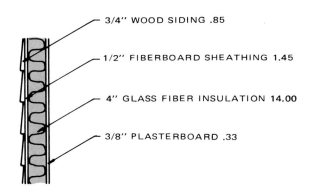

3/4'' WOOD SIDING .85

1/2'' FIBERBOARD SHEATHING 1.45

4'' GLASS FIBER INSULATION 14.00

3/8'' PLASTERBOARD .33

WALL SECTION

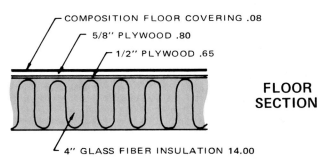

COMPOSITION FLOOR COVERING .08

5/8'' PLYWOOD .80

1/2'' PLYWOOD .65

**FLOOR
SECTION**

4'' GLASS FIBER INSULATION 14.00

Fig. 23-31. Plan view and sections of a room with resistivity of materials shown.

FINAL CALCULATIONS

1. List the BTU/H for the walls, windows, doors, ceiling, floor, and air infiltration.

2. Add the results of each together to find the total heat loss in BTUs per hour. This figure represents the size of heating units required for the room or house being calculated.

The procedure for calculating the size of cooling unit is about the same except that the design temperature difference must reflect summer temperatures rather than winter and an allowance should be made for very humid locations. A larger unit will be required.

Example of Heat Loss Calculation

The purpose of the following example is to apply the procedure just described to a room to show actual computation of heat loss. Fig. 23-31 shows the room used in the example. Details are also shown of the wall, ceiling, and floor.

CALCULATIONS FOR WALLS

1. Total exterior area –

12'-0'' x 8'-0'' =	96 sq. ft.
18'-0'' x 8'-0'' =	144 sq. ft.
Gross wall area =	240 sq. ft.

2. Window area – 6'-0'' x 5'-0'' = 30 sq. ft.
   6'-0'' x 5'-0'' = 30 sq. ft.
   Total window area = 60 sq. ft.

   Door area – 3'-0'' x 6'-8'' = 21 sq. ft.

   Net wall area = Gross wall area - doors and window area
   = 240 sq. ft. - 81 sq. ft.
   Net wall area = 159 sq. ft.

3. Resistivity of wall materials
   3/4'' wood siding .85
   1/2'' fiberboard sheathing 1.45
   4'' glass fiber insulation 14.00
   3/8'' plasterboard .33
   Total resistivity = 16.63

   1.00 ÷ 16.63 = .060
   U factor for net wall = .060

4. U factor for doors and windows
   1 3/4'' wood door .55
   insulating glass window .54 for both

5. Design temperature difference
   Inside design temperature = 70°
   Outside design temperature = -5°
   Design temperature difference = 75°

6. BTU/H for net wall
Net wall area x U factor x temperature difference
159 sq. ft. x .060 x 75° = 715.50
BTU/H for the net walls = 715.50

7. BTU/H for the windows
Window area x U factor x temperature difference
60 sq. ft. x .54 x 75° = 2430.00
BTU/H for the windows = 2430.00

8. BTU/H for the door
Door area x U factor x temperature difference
21 sq. ft. x .55 x 75° = 866.25
BTU/H for the door = 866.25

CALCULATION FOR CEILING

1. Total ceiling area—
12'-0'' x 18'-0'' = 216 sq. ft.

2. U factor for ceiling
3/8'' plasterboard = .33
4'' glass fiber insulation = 14.00
Total resistivity = 14.33

1.00 ÷ 14.33 = .070
U factor for ceiling = .070

3. BTU/H for the ceiling
Ceiling area x U factor x temperature difference
216 sq. ft. x .070 x 75° = 1134.00
BTU/H for the ceiling = 1134.00

CALCULATION FOR FLOOR

1. Total floor area—
12'-0'' x 18'-0'' = 216 sq. ft.

2. U factor for floor
Composition floor covering .08
5/8'' plywood .80
1/2'' plywood .65
4'' glass fiber insulation 14.00
Total resistivity = 15.53

1.00 ÷ 15.53 = .064
U factor for floor = .064

3. BTU/H for the floor
Floor area x U factor x temperature difference
216 sq. ft. x .064 x 75° = 1036.80
BTU/H for the floor = 1036.80

CALCULATION FOR AIR INFILTRATION

1. Volume of air
Length x width x height
18'-0'' x 12'-0'' x 8'-0'' = 1728 cu. ft.
Volume of air = air infiltration

2. BTU/H for air infiltration
Volume of air x .018 x temperature difference
1728 cu. ft. x .018 x 75° = 2332.80
BTU/H for air infiltration = 2332.80

SUMMARY CALCULATIONS

BTU/H for net walls 715.50
BTU/H for the windows 2430.00
BTU/H for the door 866.25
BTU/H for the ceiling 1134.00
BTU/H for the floor 1036.80
BTU/H for air infiltration 2332.80
Total BTU/H = 8515.35

The total room heat loss is 8,177 BTU/H. A heating unit capable of producing this amount of heat is required for the room used in this example.

REVIEW QUESTIONS—CHAPTER 23

Write your answers on a separate sheet of paper. Do not write in this book.
1. Identify the four features of a modern climate control system.
2. Name five conditions which help increase the efficiency of temperature control.
3. The amount of water in the air relative to the temperature is called _____.
4. A comfortable humidity level is about _____ percent.
5. Identify two possible outcomes from having too little moisture in the air (low humidity).
6. Name two effects of too much moisture in the house.
7. The device which removes moisture from the air in a house is called a _____.
8. List the four basic types of heating systems used in modern homes.
9. How does a forced warm air system operate?
10. Identify three types of furnaces which are used in forced warm air systems.
11. What is a thermostat?
12. List the three main parts in a hydronic system.
13. Name three advantages of the hydronic system.

14. Heat is produced in the electric radiant system by _____.
15. A heat pump is essentially a _____ unit.

SUGGESTED ACTIVITIES

1. Select a plan of a medium-size home and get an estimate from your local gas and electricity company as to the cost of heating this home. Also ask for their recommendations for insulation and ventilation. Report your findings.
2. Using a plan supplied by your instructor, calculate the total heat loss and specify the size heating unit required. Show your calculations.
3. Contact people in your community who have forced warm air, hydronic, and electric radiant heating systems and ask their opinion regarding dependability, advantages, disadvantages, economy, and serviceability. Report their reactions.
4. Visit a local heating and air conditioning equipment supplier. Ask for catalogs and other literature showing heating and cooling equipment. Add this material to the classroom collection.
5. Prepare a chart for each heating system discussed in the text showing advantages and disadvantages of each system. Display your chart.

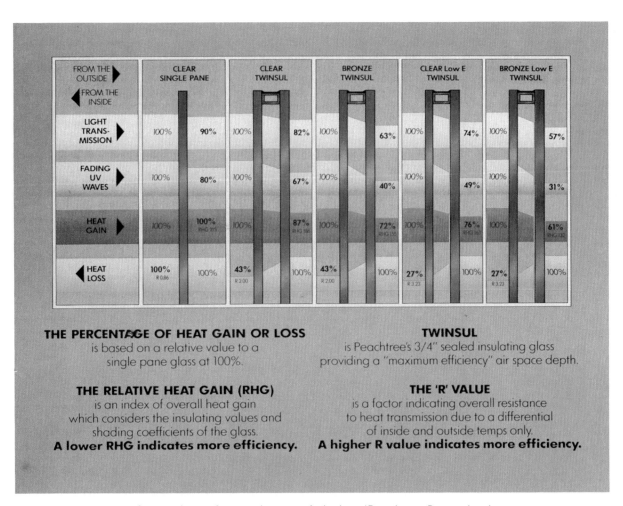

Comparison of several types of glazing. (Peachtree Doors, Inc.)

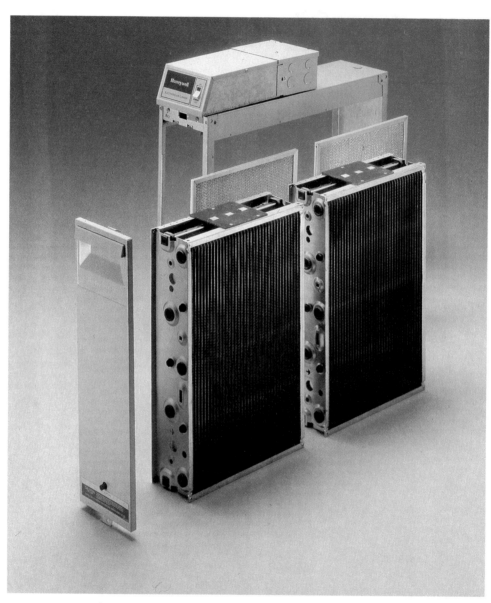

Electronic air cleaners remove dust, dirt, pollen, tobacco, and cooking odors from the home. (Honeywell, Inc.)

Climate Control Plan

After studying this chapter, you will be able to:
* List features included on a residential climate control plan.
* Plan the ductwork for a typical forced warm air system.
* Select an appropriate heating or cooling unit for a given structure.
* Draw a climate control plan using proper symbols and conventions.

A climate control plan is a plan view drawing in section of the home which shows the climate control system. It is traced from the floor plan.

The plan shows piping or heating ducts, furnace, and other climate control equipment.

A climate control plan shows the location, size, and type of heating, cooling, ventilating, humidification, and air cleaning equipment. This system should be closely coordinated with the structural, plumbing, and electrical aspects.

REQUIRED INFORMATION

The climate control plan should include information on size and location of distribution pipes

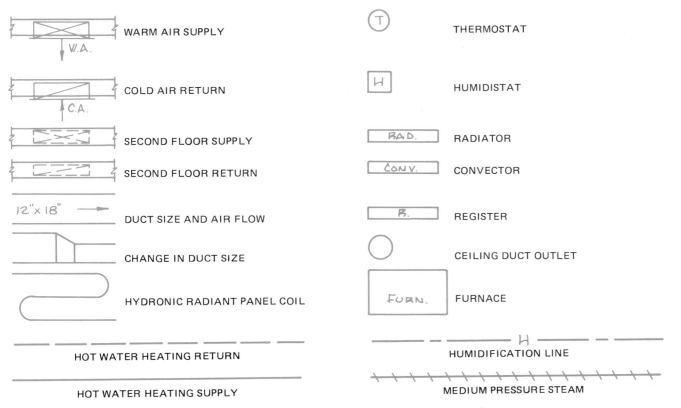

WARM AIR SUPPLY	W.A.
COLD AIR RETURN	C.A.
SECOND FLOOR SUPPLY	
SECOND FLOOR RETURN	
12" x 18"	DUCT SIZE AND AIR FLOW
	CHANGE IN DUCT SIZE
	HYDRONIC RADIANT PANEL COIL
	HOT WATER HEATING RETURN
	HOT WATER HEATING SUPPLY
(T)	THERMOSTAT
H	HUMIDISTAT
RAD.	RADIATOR
CONV.	CONVECTOR
R.	REGISTER
○	CEILING DUCT OUTLET
FURN.	FURNACE
	HUMIDIFICATION LINE
	MEDIUM PRESSURE STEAM

Fig. 24-1. Typical symbols used in a climate control system.

or ducts, location of thermostats and registers or baseboard convectors, climate control equipment location and type, equipment schedule, heat loss calculations, and general or specific notes which help to describe the system.

DISTRIBUTION SYSTEM

The distribution system usually consists of **ducts** or **pipes.** Ducts (round or rectangular) are needed to move large quantities of air for heating or cooling. Pipes are used in hydronic systems to distribute hot water or steam from the boiler to radiators, baseboard units, or radiant panels. The distribution systems to be used must be represented on the climate control plan using the proper symbols, Fig. 24-1. The ducts should be drawn as close to scale (1/4'' = 1'-0'') as possible. Sizes should be shown on the plan. Pipes are indicated by single lines and are not drawn to scale.

Planning outlet and inlet locations

A perimeter system of outlets is generally specified. This provides uniform heat (or cooling) by concentrating heat where it is needed most-- along the outside walls, Fig. 24-2. There should be at least one outlet (register or baseboard unit) in each large area to be heated or cooled. This includes rooms, halls, stairwells, etc. which are to be conditioned. An average room has up to 180 sq. ft. of floor space. Larger areas usually should be counted as two or more rooms. If a room has more than 15 ft. of exterior wall, then two or more outlets should be used.

Inlets are required for forced warm air heating systems but are not needed for hydronic or electric radiant systems. If the house is a compact one-story house, one inlet (cold air return) will usually be sufficient. However, if the house is L-shaped, U-shaped, or has several levels, then two or more inlets should be planned. Remember that closed doors and dead-end corridors block air circulation.

Registers or inlets are available in several sizes. The chart which follows shows some of the common sizes:

REGISTER SIZES		
TYPE	SIZE	SUPPLY
Floor Diffuser	4'' x 12''	6'' Pipe
Floor Diffuser	6'' x 12''	8'' Pipe
Baseboard Diffuser	2 1/4'' x 15''	6'' Pipe
Baseboard Diffuser	2 1/4'' x 24''	6'' Pipe
Floor Diffuser	2 1/4'' x 12''	6'' Pipe

INLET SIZES		
TYPE	SIZE	FURNACE SIZE
Baseboard Grille	6'' x 14''	-----
Baseboard Grille	6'' x 30''	40,000 BTU
Ceiling or Wall Grille	16'' x 20''	75,000 BTU
High Side Wall Grille	6'' x 14''	-----
Floor Grille	8'' x 30''	60,000 BTU
Floor Grille	12'' x 30''	80,000 BTU
Floor Grille	18'' x 24''	90,000 BTU

Planning ductwork

Two basic types of ductwork systems are the **radial system** and the **extended plenum system,** Fig. 24-3. The extended plenum system is usually preferred because pipes (round) do not radiate out in all directions from the furnace as they

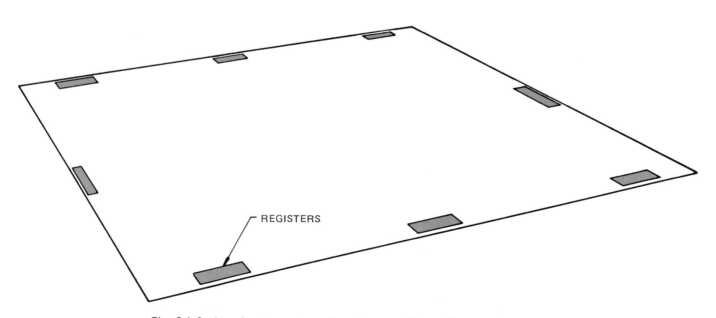

Fig. 24-2. A perimeter system of outlets provides uniform heat or cooling.

do in the radial system. The extended plenum system uses rectangular ducts for the main supply and round pipes to connect to each register, Fig. 24-4.

Round pipe used to supply a register in the extended plenum system may be 6 or 8 in. in diameter. An 8 in. pipe is generally recommended when the duct system is to be used for cooling. The larger size is necessary when the same blower is used because cool air moves slower than warm air.

The ductwork size is based on the number and size of round pipes it serves. All rectangular ducts are 8 in. deep and vary in width from 10 to 28 inches. The sectional area of the supply duct must equal the total area of all the round register pipes. The extended plenum may remain the same size throughout its entire length or may be reduced in size as fewer registers remain to be supplied.

Duct size may be determined by using the following procedure. For 6 in. pipes, multiply the number of pipes by 2 and add 2 to the product. The result is the width of the plenum duct required. Remember it is 8 in. deep. Example: A duct is to serve six 6 in. round pipes, therefore 6 x 2 = 12 + 2 = 14 in. The duct will be 8 x 14 . For 8 in. pipes, multiply the number of pipes by 3 and add 2 to the product. If the round pipes in the previous example had been 8 in. pipes, then the duct size would have been 6 x 3 = 18 + 2 = 20 in. The duct size required is 8 x 20. A vertical duct designed to fit between the studs is called a **wall stack** and is usually 12'' x 3 1/4''.

Planning piping for hydronic system.

The main hot water supply from the boiler must be large enough to provide for adequate heating. Copper pipe of these sizes is usually considered to be adequate for most installations:

1 in. main for up to 71,000 BTU

1 1/2 in. main for 72,000-160,000 BTU

2 in. main for 161,000-240,000 BTU

The size baseboard unit or convector cabinet required will depend on the heat loss for a given area. It is best to calculate the heat loss for each room and then plan the number and size outlets to match this loss. The following chart shows

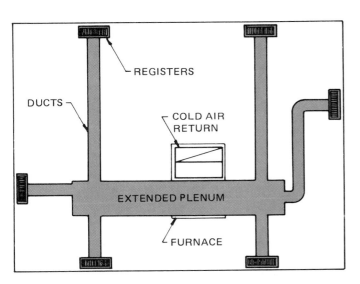

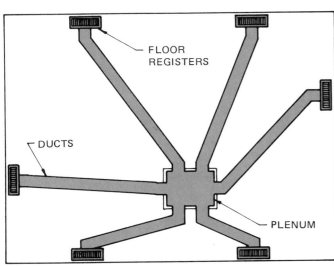

PERIMETER RADIAL SYSTEM

Fig. 24-3. Two ductwork systems are commonly used for residential climate control, radial and extended plenum systems.

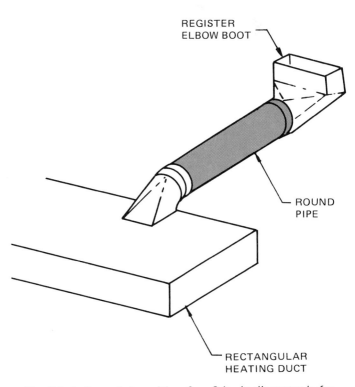

Fig. 24-4. Round pipe either 6 or 8 in. in diameter is frequently used to connect the register to the main supply duct.

the output rating for several common convector cabinets and fin-tube baseboard units.

CONVECTOR CABINETS

LENGTH	THICKNESS	BTU/H OUTPUT
24 IN.	6 3/8''	3,400
32 IN.	6 3/8''	4,800
36 IN.	8 3/8''	6,900
40 IN.	8 3/8''	7,800
48 IN.	8 3/8''	9,600
56 IN.	8 3/8''	11,400
60 IN.	10 3/8''	19,400

FIN-TUBE BASEBOARD UNITS
BTU/H OUTPUT

LENGTH	SINGLE	DOUBLE
2 FT.	-----	2,280
4 FT.	2,870	4,560
6 FT.	4,260	6,840
8 FT.	5,680	-----

Locate outlets below windows for most efficient heating. Any room that is over 15 ft. long should have at least two outlets.

THERMOSTATS AND CLIMATE CONTROL EQUIPMENT

Each automatic climate control system requires at least one thermostat. A forced warm air system will need only one thermostat if one furnace is used. Sometimes two furnaces are installed if the house is large, or if more than one zone is required. As many zones as desired may be used with electric radiant or hydronic systems. Each zone needs a thermostat to provide accurate control.

Location of the thermostat is important because it measures the temperature and activates

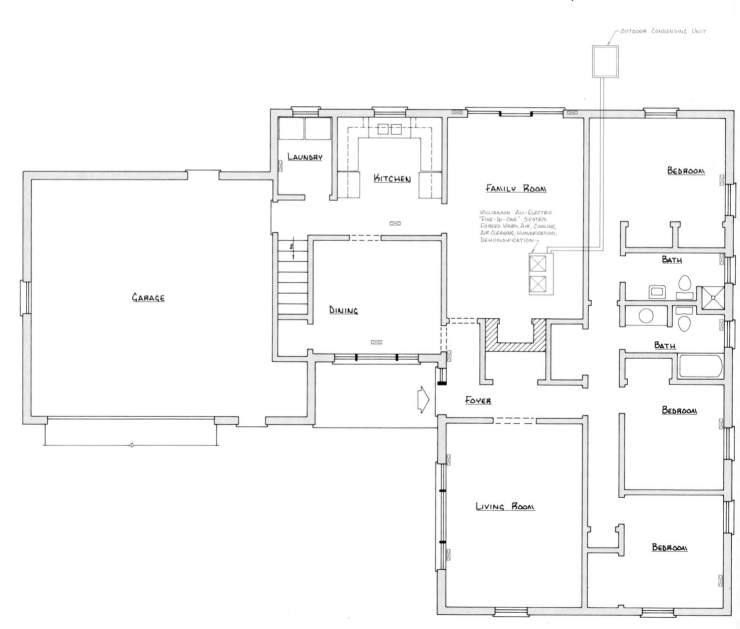

Fig. 24-5. Floor plan showing the location of the furnace, outdoor condensing unit, and registers. The furnace is in the basement below the main floor level.

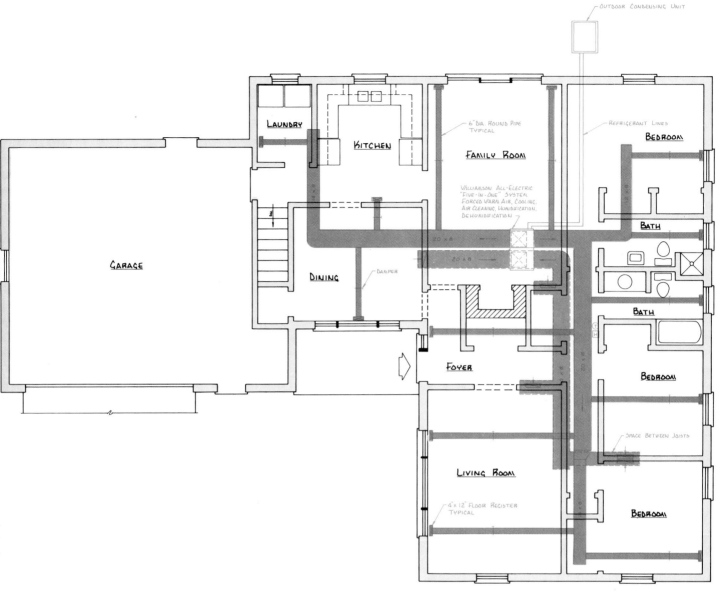

Fig. 24-6. A more complete climate control plan showing the location of supply and cold air return ducts and return registers.

the furnace. If it is placed on a wall where the sun may shine on it, in a draft, or near a lamp the performance may not be satisfactory. Locate the thermostat on an inside partition in a place where the temperature will be representative of the room as a whole. Show the location on the climate control plan.

Other equipment should be indicated on the plan using symbols or notes.

SCHEDULES, CALCULATIONS, AND NOTES

Various schedules may be useful on the climate control plan. An equipment schedule provides an orderly means of specifying equipment to be used in the system. Including a register schedule may be desirable because placing too

much information on the drawing will cause it to be crowded.

A complete climate control plan will show a summary of the heat loss calculations. These calculations form the basis for equipment selection and are important. If space permits, the summary should be located on the climate control plan.

Add any other information on the plan which you feel will be helpful or desirable to the builder or subcontractors. Notes should be short and to the point.

PROCEDURE FOR DRAWING CLIMATE CONTROL PLAN

Just as in the plumbing and electrical plans, many decisions and calculations must be made

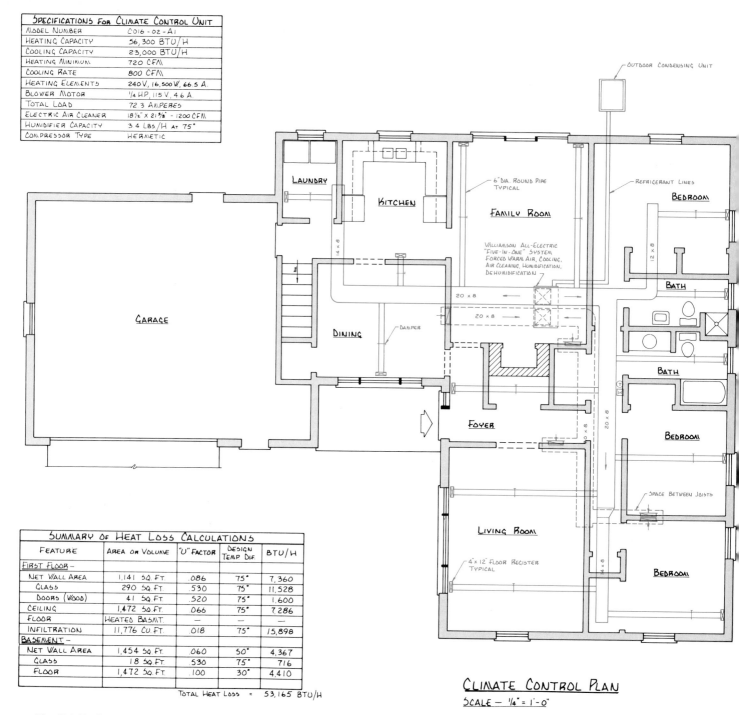

SPECIFICATIONS FOR CLIMATE CONTROL UNIT	
MODEL NUMBER	C016-02-A1
HEATING CAPACITY	56,300 BTU/H
COOLING CAPACITY	23,000 BTU/H
HEATING MINIMUM	720 CFM
COOLING RATE	800 CFM
HEATING ELEMENTS	240V, 16,500W, 66.5 A.
BLOWER MOTOR	¼ HP, 115V, 4.6 A.
TOTAL LOAD	72.3 AMPERES
ELECTRIC AIR CLEANER	18½" x 21⅝" - 1200 CFM
HUMIDIFIER CAPACITY	3.4 LBS/H AT 75°
COMPRESSOR TYPE	HERMETIC

SUMMARY OF HEAT LOSS CALCULATIONS				
FEATURE	AREA OR VOLUME	"U" FACTOR	DESIGN TEMP. DIF.	BTU/H
FIRST FLOOR -				
NET WALL AREA	1,141 SQ. FT.	.086	75°	7,360
GLASS	290 SQ. FT.	.530	75°	11,528
DOORS (WOOD)	41 SQ. FT.	.520	75°	1,600
CEILING	1,472 SQ. FT.	.066	75°	7,286
FLOOR	HEATED BASMT.	—	—	—
INFILTRATION	11,776 CU. FT.	.018	75°	15,898
BASEMENT -				
NET WALL AREA	1,454 SQ. FT.	.060	50°	4,367
GLASS	18 SQ. FT.	.530	75°	716
FLOOR	1,472 SQ. FT.	.100	30°	4,410

TOTAL HEAT LOSS = 53,165 BTU/H

CLIMATE CONTROL PLAN
SCALE — ¼" = 1'-0"

Fig. 24-7. A complete climate control plan with basement and first floor installations shown on the floor plan. The furnace and ductwork may be drawn on the foundation/basement plan and the registers shown on the floor plan if desired.

before completing the climate control plan. The type of heating and cooling system or systems must be determined, and heat loss calculated for each room. Other drawings of the structure should be studied to determine the most practical layout before starting to draw.

After the preliminary details are disposed of, then you may proceed with the drawing of the plan. This procedure is suggested:

1. Trace the floor plan showing exterior and interior walls, doors and windows, and other features which relate to the climate control system.

2. Locate on the floor plan, equipment to be used for heating, cooling, humidification, and air cleaning.

3. Locate registers, coils, baseboard units, or other means of heat exchange on the plan. Use the proper symbols. Steps 1, 2, and 3 are shown in Fig. 24-5.

4. Draw the air return ducts using a hidden line symbol. Also draw the cold air return grilles. (This step is for forced warm air systems and cooling only.)

5. Draw the supply duct or hot water main and connect it to registers, convectors, etc.

6. Locate thermostats and any other controls required.

7. Identify the size of ducts or pipe and other equipment. Steps 4, 5, 6, and 7 are shown in Fig. 24-6.

8. Draw schedules required.

9. Add necessary notes, title block, scale, and dimensions.

10. Check the drawing for accuracy and to be sure that it is complete. Steps 8, 9, and 10 are shown in Fig. 24-7.

REVIEW QUESTIONS–CHAPTER 24

Write your answers on a separate sheet of paper. Do not write in this book.

1. What is the purpose of the climate control plan?
2. Identify four features that should be included on a climate control plan.
3. The two most common devices used to distribute heat throughout a house are _____ and _____.
4. The scale of a residential climate control plan will most likely be _____.
5. Why is a perimeter heat system generally specified?
6. When should a room have more than one register?
7. Name the two basic types of ductwork systems.
8. The round pipes used to connect registers to the main heating or cooling ducts are either _____ or _____ in. in diameter.
9. A rectangular duct that will supply four 6 in. pipes should be what size?
10. A vertical duct is generally called a _____.
11. If a house has three heating zones, it will normally require _____ thermostats.
12. Name two types of schedules that may be useful on a climate control plan.

SUGGESTED ACTIVITIES

1. Locate a house under construction which has the heating equipment in place. Secure permission to enter the structure. Examine the installation carefully and report on the following points:
   a. Type and size of house.
   b. Type of heating system and comfort provisions.
   c. Number of registers or convectors (if hydronic or forced air).
   d. Number of cold air returns.
   e. Size of heating and/or cooling unit.
2. Using a simple plan provided by your instructor or designed by yourself, plan an appropriate climate control system. The system should provide for heating, cooling, humidification, and air cleaning. If one (or more) of these is not necessary in your section of the country, omit it.
3. Draw a pictorial that represents the essential elements of a heating system. You may choose a forced warm air system, hydronic, electric radiant, or heat pump system. Label the parts and prepare the pictorial for display.

Rendering of ultramodern residence shows unusual roof to take advantage of sunlight. The lake and surrounding natural landscape complement the structural features of the house.

25

CHAPTER

Solar Space Heating

After studying this chapter, you will be able to:
- Describe the two basic types of solar space heating.
- Explain how a passive solar space heating system works.
- Compare direct, indirect, and isolated passive solar gain systems.
- Identify the two most frequently used active solar systems.
- List the advantages and disadvantages of solar space heating.

Solar space heating is an important consideration to the architect because of increased heating costs and apparent dwindling fuel supplies. Using free, natural heat from the sun is prudent if it can be trapped and utilized in an efficient and practical manner. Two basic ways or systems have evolved for the utilization of solar energy for space heating. They are **passive solar systems** and **active solar systems.**

PASSIVE SOLAR SYSTEMS

Passive solar space heating involves capturing, storing, and using solar radiation (the sun's energy) to heat a dwelling without the use of fans or pumps to circulate the heat. Heat from the sun is collected by and stored in the building itself. Purely passive systems use only convection, conduction, and radiation as a means of distributing heat.

Convection refers to the transfer of heat by a moving fluid. Fluids include liquids and gases. **Conduction** is the flow of heat through an object by transferring heat from one molecule to another. **Radiation** is the flow of heat from a warm source through space in waves of infrared or visible light energy. This energy travels in straight lines from the source.

The most common types of passive solar designs may be grouped under the headings of **direct gain systems, indirect gain systems,** and **isolated gain** or **sun space systems.** The basis of these groupings is the way each system works. The word ''gain'' refers to the way heat is extracted from solar radiation.

DIRECT GAIN SYSTEMS

Direct gain systems are the most popular type of passive solar space heating systems. Direct gain systems incorporate large areas of south-facing glazing (glass or other material) that permits large amounts of sunlight to enter the interior space of the dwelling to heat the air inside, Fig. 25-1. The excess heat generated by the sunlight is usually stored in massive structures which are strategically located to receive the sunlight. During the night and periods of cloudiness, the heat stored in thick interior masonry walls, floors, and furnishings is released to

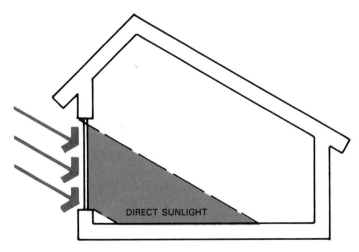

Fig. 25-1. Direct gain systems use solar radiation entering through glazing directly into the space to be heated.

the interior space. The keys to a successful direct gain passive system are large amounts of sunlight entering the living space and sufficient thermal mass to store the excess heat. If massive structures are positioned in the living space in direct sunlight they become solar collectors as well as heat storage devices, Fig. 25-2.

A large thermal mass inside the living space is necessary to help modulate temperature extremes within the structure. If insufficient mass is present, the temperature will likely rise to uncomfortable levels during the day and fall to uncomfortable levels during the night. Therefore, large amounts of stone, thick concrete walls and floors, drums filled with water or other massive structures form an integral part of a direct gain passive system, Fig. 25-3.

As with all solar systems, adequate insulation is necessary to prevent the loss of trapped interior heat. If possible, insulation should be placed on the outside of masonry walls so that their mass may be used to store heat for the interior. In most non-solar designs, insulation was generally located on the interior surface of masonry walls which released stored heat to the outside rather than the interior. Frame walls have little mass and, therefore, store small amounts of heat and the location of insulation is not as important as with masonry walls.

A large thermal mass also helps to even out indoor temperatures during the warm summer months. The large thermal mass is cooler than the interior air during the day and thus absorbs heat from the air. This, in turn, reduces the temperature of the living space. The stored heat is released during the night when temperatures drop and provides a more uniform temperature in the dwelling.

Fig. 25-3. The interior of this passive solar home integrates massive materials (stone) into the decor to store heat. (Jeff Burgin Builders)

Different materials are able to store different amounts of heat. For example, the same volume of water will store more than twice as much heat (quantity) at a given temperature as concrete, stone, or adobe. See Fig. 25-4 for a comparison of the thermal properties of typical building materials.

INDIRECT GAIN SYSTEMS

Indirect gain systems heat the interior space indirectly. In these systems, a large thermal mass is placed between the sun and the living space. Sunlight heats up the mass rather than

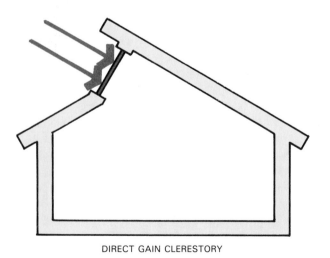

DIRECT GAIN CLERESTORY

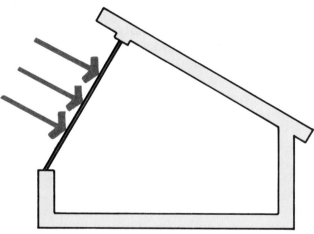

DIRECT GAIN SLOPED WALL

Fig. 25-2. These two designs illustrate some possible applications of the direct gain system with additional thermal mass to store excess heat entering the interior dwelling space. Notice they are positioned to act as solar collectors as well as provide thermal mass.

THERMAL PROPERTIES OF MATERIALS			
Material	Heat Capacity by Weight Btu/lb/ °F	Heat Capacity by Volume Btu/ft³/ °F	Density lbs/ft³
Adobe	0.24	25	106
Aluminum	0.214	36.2	169
Brick	0.20	24	120
Concrete	0.22	31	140
Rock	0.21	21	100
Steel	0.11	54	490
Water	1.00	62.4	62.4
Wood	0.60	19	32

Fig. 25-4. Thermal properties of common building materials which may be important for the thermal mass they add to the structure.

the interior space itself. Frequently, a thick masonry or concrete wall is positioned directly behind a large area of south-facing glazing to receive the solar radiation. Air is allowed to circulate around the wall to carry heat to the dwelling interior.

One popular indirect gain system utilizes a **Trombe wall,** Fig. 25-5. The massive wall is dark colored on the outside to absorb more heat and located inside the structure immediately behind a large glazed area. Vents at the top and bottom of the wall permit cool air to enter the space between the wall and glazing at the bottom, become heated, and rise by convection to the top of the wall where it reenters the dwelling interior. Heat is also transmitted by conduction through the wall to the inside surface. Radiation and convection then distribute the heat throughout the interior space.

During the heating season at night the vents in a Trombe wall must be closed to prevent reverse thermosiphoning. (Thermosiphoning is the result of a fluid expanding and rising.) Reverse thermosiphoning will cool the room by allowing the warm room air to enter the space between the Trombe wall and glazing, and be cooled as it comes in contact with the cold glass. Cold air will sink to the bottom of the wall and enter the dwelling.

The **water storage wall** is another type of indirect gain system. Water is capable of storing large amounts of heat and is inexpensive. Therefore, it is frequently used as a thermal mass. Drums, fiberglass tubes, and large pipes are typical storage containers. They are located just behind a south-facing glazed area similar to the Trombe wall. The containers are generally painted black and act as collectors and storage.

A typical drum wall will store approximately twice as much heat as a Trombe wall of the same volume, Fig. 25-6.

The drum wall, however, may not appeal to some because of its appearance and possible noise created by expansion and contraction due to heating and cooling. Further, the potential problems of evaporation, corrosion, and leaking are considerations.

A phase change material such as glauber's salt has some possible advantages as a thermal storage material. Phase change materials change from solid to liquid as they heat up. These materials are generally capable of storing more heat per unit of volume and are slow to store and release heat--a desirable trait for maintaining comfort over an extended period. The cost of these materials, however, is a negative factor as well as reduced effectiveness over a period of time.

ISOLATED GAIN SYSTEMS

Isolated gain systems collect and store solar energy in an area outside the living space. A

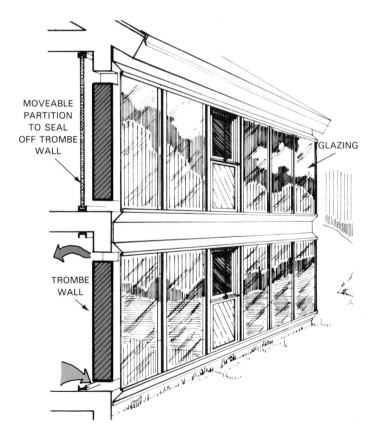

MOVEABLE PARTITION TO SEAL OFF TROMBE WALL

GLAZING

TROMBE WALL

Fig. 25-5. The Trombe wall is an example of an indirect gain solar system. The massive wall is positioned behind a large glazed area and stores heat from the sun for release during the night. (National Solar Heating and Cooling Information Center)

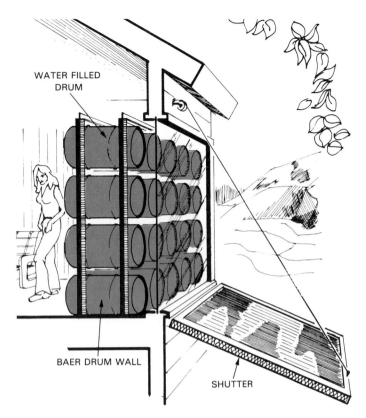

Fig. 25-6. This Baer Drum Wall, developed by Steve Baer of Zomeworks, is an example of an indirect gain system. The drums heat up during the day and act as radiators. The shutters are closed at night to prevent heat loss. (National Solar Heating and Cooling Information Center)

typical example of this type of system is shown in Fig. 25-7. Here the solar radiation is extracted using a solar collector outside the home. The storage is a rock bed located beneath the structure. Thermosiphoning moves warm air up into the dwelling while cool air returns to the rock storage and collector to be warmed again. Fig. 25-8 shows another variation with the rock storage outside the dwelling.

Advantages of the isolated gain system include less interior space dedicated to heat collection devices, large areas of interior space are not exposed to the sun, and heat collected is easier to control. Disadvantages include the generally greater expense to construct this type of isolated gain system and the difficulty of retrofitting an existing structure with it.

Another type of isolated gain system which is increasing greatly in popularity is the **attached greenhouse** or **sun space,** Fig. 25-9. A solar greenhouse must have proper orientation (south-facing) if it is to provide any solar heat to the dwelling. An attached greenhouse will reduce heat loss in the dwelling even when it is not producing usable heat by shielding the wall from winter winds. Frequently, the attached greenhouse is combined with other techniques (Trombe wall, water-filled drums, or collectors) to provide additional solar heat, Fig. 25-10.

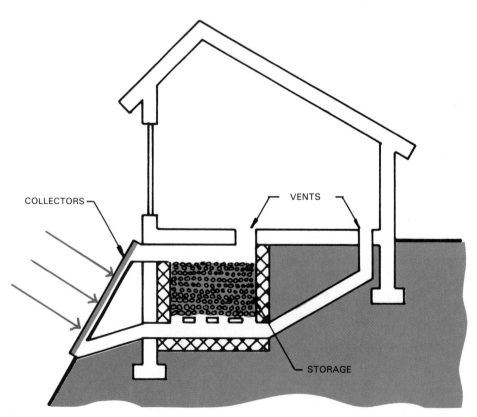

Fig. 25-7. Example of an isolated gain system utilizing a series of collectors outside the dwelling and rock storage beneath the floor.

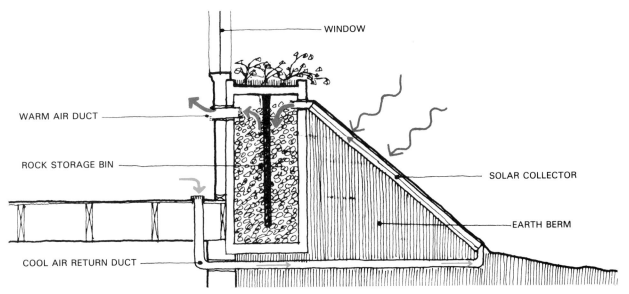

Fig. 25-8. The solar collector and rock storage are incorporated in an earth berm outside the dwelling. (National Solar Heating and Cooling Information Center)

Fig. 25-9. This large, attached greenhouse is an example of an isolated gain solar system. It extends the space of the dwelling and provides some heat. (Janco Greenhouses)

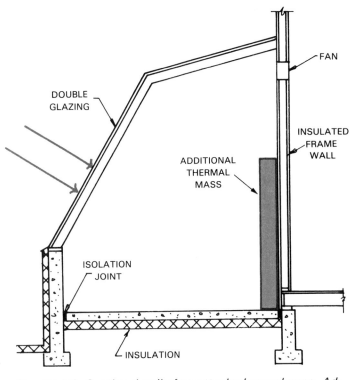

Fig. 25-10. Section detail of an attached greenhouse. Additional thermal mass has been included to provide heat for a longer period of time.

Solar greenhouses in colder climates should have a double glazing of glass, plastic, or fiberglass to reduce heat loss. Additionally, air infiltration should be reduced to the minimum to reduce further heat loss. Thick concrete floors that are insulated below and around the edges will add much heat storage, but will not be effective if not isolated from the foundation and soil below. As with other systems, a large thermal mass is required for maximum performance.

The principles utilized in the design of passive solar applications can be applied to dwellings with active solar or conventional heating systems. Such architectural considerations as proper sun orientation for large glass areas, adequate insulation, adequate thermal mass, and concern for airflow inside a structure should always be considered in the design process of any structure.

ACTIVE SOLAR SYSTEMS

Solar heating involves extracting heat from solar radiation, distributing the heat throughout the living and working space in the dwelling, and storing excess heat for future use. An **active solar heating system** utilizes pumps, fans, or other devices to distribute the heat to desired locations.

Two basic types of active solar heating systems are commonly used for residential space heating. They are **warm air systems** and **warm water systems.** Warm air systems are more popular for home heating. Warm water systems have more commercial applications.

WARM AIR SOLAR SYSTEMS

A typical warm air solar system contains a bank (array or group) of collectors, a heat storage box filled with stones or other thermal mass, and one or more blowers with controls for operating the system, Fig. 25-11.

Solar collectors for warm air systems are readily available in a wide range of sizes, quality, and price. They range in efficiency from around 15 percent to about 65 percent. Some have built-in insulation while others do not. Collectors are also made with single, double, and triple glazing. The amount of insulation and the type of glazing will greatly affect the performance in cold climates. A quality collector should form an airtight box with a highly transparent glazing and sufficient insulation to retain its heat during cold weather, Fig. 25-12.

Every solar collector has some type of absorber plate which is designed to absorb heat as the sun's rays strike it. There are many designs and styles, Fig. 25-13, but most are classified as flat plate collectors. Design characteristics which an efficient warm air absorber plate should include are:

1. It should present as much surface area to the sun as possible to receive maximum heating.

2. It should provide a large surface area to air flowing through the collector for efficient heat release.

3. Excessive turbulence should not be created in the collector by the absorber plate. This

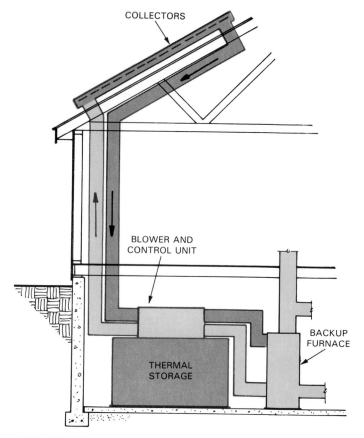

Fig. 25-11. Example of a roof-mounted, warm air active solar system. This system is connected to a backup heating system for extended cloudy periods.

Fig. 25-12. This combination warm air and domestic hot water collector has ample insulation. Note the absorber plate is isolated from the collector box frame. This reduces heat loss by conduction.

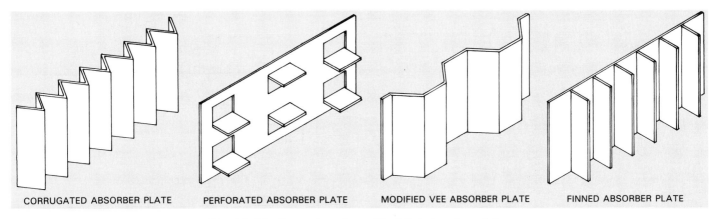

CORRUGATED ABSORBER PLATE   PERFORATED ABSORBER PLATE   MODIFIED VEE ABSORBER PLATE   FINNED ABSORBER PLATE

Fig. 25-13. Examples of modified flat absorber plates.

will reduce air flow and increase heat loss through the glazing.

4. Increased efficiency is accomplished generally by maintaining air flow behind the absorber plate and a dead air space between it and the glazing.

5. The most efficient absorber plate material is generally metal.

Copper is the most efficient (and expensive) material commonly used for warm air absorber plates. Aluminum is the most used material for absorber plates. Steel plates are used in some collectors, but they are not as efficient as aluminum. Absorber plate coatings are usually flat black, but some other colors such as dark green or purple are capable of collecting nearly as much energy.

The tilt and orientation of a solar collector is important for maximum collection of heat. Generally, a south-facing collector, Fig. 25-14, will perform best. However, a variation of up to 15 degrees will have little effect on the performance. Tilt angle of the collector is generally agreed to be between 50 and 60 degrees from the horizon for best results during the entire heating season. The objective is to position the collector so the sun's rays will strike the absorber plate at a perpendicular angle for as long as possible.

Heat storage for a warm air system is a major concern. Warm air systems generally use a large box or crawl space area filled with stone, Fig. 25-15. The thermal mass must be well insulated to reduce heat loss. The size of stone most

Fig. 25-14. Collectors have been attached to the south gable areas of this home. The vertical position will capture significant heat during winter months.

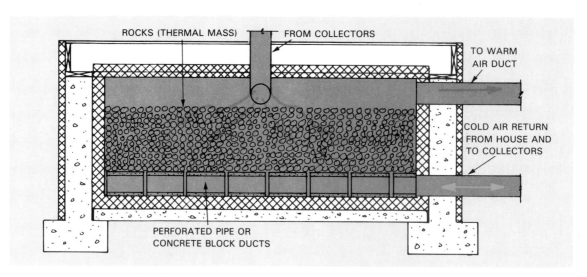

Fig. 25-15. *Typical warm air rock storage configuration.*

frequently used in the storage box is two to three inches in diameter. The size of storage needed is related to the amount of solar radiation available, area of collector surface, efficiency of storage media, heat loss in the storage area, and household needs. However, the storage should generally be large enough to store enough heat for three days of cloudy weather. A storage area that is too large can present as big a problem as one too small. If the storage is too large, a "useful" level of heat may not be attained by the system. If the storage is too small, not enough heat will be available during cloudy weather and efficiency will drop in the collectors because return air to the collectors will be too warm to efficiently remove heat. The average storage size for warm air systems usually ranges from 1/2 to 2 cubic feet of stone for each square foot of collector area.

Distribution of heat from the collectors and storage area to the living space is accomplished with a blower. The blower is similar to one used in a typical forced air heating system. Some warm air solar systems use two blowers to manage air flow more efficiently and to provide additional control. The blower system is activated by a complex set of controls that respond to temperature sensors located in the collectors, storage area, and living space. The need for a high quality control system cannot be overemphasized.

WARM WATER SOLAR SYSTEMS

A typical warm water solar system is composed of a bank of collectors, a warm water storage tank, a pump to circulate the water, some form of heat exchange device in the living space, and controls for operating the system, Fig. 25-16.

Solar collectors used with water systems are similar to flat plate warm air collectors except that tubes are attached to the absorber plate or cavities within the absorber plate. This allows

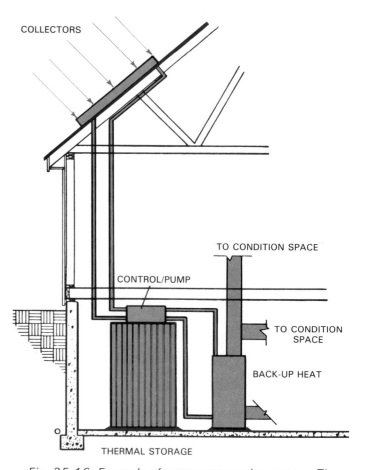

Fig. 25-16. *Example of warm water solar system. The solar system is connected to a backup furnace for extended cloudy periods.*

water to circulate over or through the heated plate, Fig. 25-17. Most care must be taken in the design and construction of water collectors because of the corrosive action of water and higher pressure than is present in an air-type system.

Another concern for a water system that is not present in an air system is the threat of freezing. If water freezes in the collectors, damage will likely result in added expense and loss of operation. Methods for preventing freezing include using a mixture of water and antifreeze, providing a draindown procedure when the temperature drops below a certain point in the collectors, and using some fluid other than water in the system. Each of these solutions to the freezing problem have drawbacks. Antifreeze tends to break down under high temperatures and forms glycolic acid which is rather corrosive. A draindown system is effective if it works every time. However, some systems will not drain down if the power is off. Nonaqueous (nonwater) fluids, such as Dow's QZ-1132 silicone-based heat-transfer fluid, can be used. However, these fluids are expensive, are more viscous requiring a larger pump, and have a lower specific heat (hold less heat) than water. A system which uses plain water and has an automatic gravity draindown system is probably the most trouble-free system.

Other considerations of water collectors such as glazing, insulation, efficiency, and quality of construction are similar to warm air collectors. The cost of water collectors is generally somewhat higher than their warm air counterparts.

Warm water solar systems generally use a large insulated tank to store the heated water. A frequent location is in the basement or crawl space, Fig. 25-18. The size of the storage tank, like the size of a rock storage, is related to the

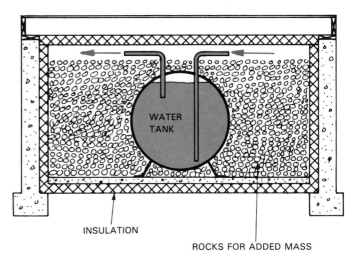

Fig. 25-18. Large warm water storage tank encased in thick insulation to prevent heat loss. The bed of stone provides additional thermal mass.

amount of solar radiation available, area of collector surface, efficiency of storage media, heat loss in the storage area, and household needs. A tank large enough to store heat for three days, assuming the proper amount of collector area has been determined, would require roughly 1 1/4 to 2 gallons of water per square foot of collector area.

Distribution of heat from the collectors and storage tank to the living space is accomplished using a pump similar to one used in a typical hydronic heating system. The pump is activated by a series of controls that respond to temperature sensors located in the collectors, storage tank, and living space.

Several liquid-to-air heat exchangers are needed to heat the air inside the dwelling. This type of heat exchanger is typically a copper tube with aluminum fins surrounding the tube. Baseboard convectors that are used for hydronic heating systems are examples of liquid-to-air heat exchangers.

ADVANTAGES OF SOLAR HEATING

Passive and active solar heating systems have some advantages over conventional systems. Some of these include:

1. Solar systems are clean, nonpolluting, and environmentally attractive.

2. Solar systems use convection, conduction, and radiation where possible to move heat to desired areas.

3. Solar systems are safe and inexpensive to operate.

4. Solar systems utilize free energy that is available for the taking.

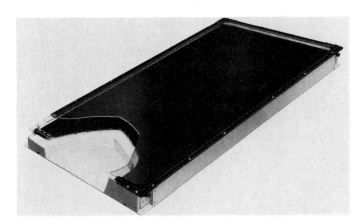

Fig. 25-17. A typical warm water solar collector with single glazing and insulation behind the absorber plate. (Lennox)

DISADVANTAGES OF SOLAR HEATING

Some disadvantages associated with passive and active solar heating systems include:

1. Solar heating systems are not as dependable as conventional heating systems. They are affected by the weather.

2. Some areas of the country have little sunshine during the coldest months and, therefore, are poor prospects for solar heating.

3. Some solar systems, especially active systems, are expensive to install and generally require a conventional backup heating system.

4. Larger temperature variations are more frequent with solar heating systems than with conventional systems.

REVIEW QUESTIONS–CHAPTER 25

Write your answers on a separate sheet of paper. Do not write in this book.

1. What are the two basic types of solar energy systems?
2. Purely passive solar energy systems use three means of distributing heat. List them.
3. Name the three basic categories that include most types of passive solar energy systems.
4. Describe how a direct gain system works.
5. What is the purpose of a large thermal mass?
6. List three building materials that are frequently used as a thermal mass.
7. A cubic foot of stone can store more heat than a cubic foot of water. True or false?
8. How do indirect and direct solar gain systems differ?
9. Drums filled with water are an example of a large thermal mass. True or false?
10. A popular example of an indirect solar gain system utilizes a _____ wall to collect heat.
11. What is thermosiphoning?
12. A water storage wall is an example of an indirect solar gain system. True or false?
13. What is unique about phase change materials such as glauber's salt?
14. Describe an isolated solar gain passive system.
15. Name two advantages of the isolated gain system.
16. An attached greenhouse or sun space is an example of an isolated gain system. True or false?
17. How is an active solar heating system different from a passive solar heating system?
18. What are the two main types of active solar systems?
19. What is the efficiency range of most solar collectors used with active systems?
20. Every solar collector has some type of _____ plate.
21. Most collectors used for residential heating systems have some type of flat plate collector. True or false?
22. What is the most popular material used for absorber plates?
23. What color are most absorber plates painted?
24. What type of thermal mass is generally used for warm air systems?
25. A solar collector facing east or west will collect as much heat as one facing south. True or false?
26. A pump is used to distribute heat in a warm air system. True or false?
27. What is the typical thermal mass used in a warm water system?
28. What is the greatest threat to a warm water solar system?
29. Generally, in cold climates, double glazing on collectors is better than single glazing. True or false?
30. What kind of device is used to heat the air inside a dwelling when a warm water system is used?

SUGGESTED ACTIVITIES

1. Contact your local meteorologist to secure weather data from the past heating season (October-April) for your local area. Specifically, request hours of sunshine per month and solar radiation available during the same months. From this data, calculate the amount of BTUs falling on each square foot of a properly positioned collector for each month of the heating season.

2. Using the data generated in #1 above, calculate the number of BTUs that might be delivered to a dwelling if the total efficiency of the system were 50 percent efficient. Assume 800 square feet of collector area.

3. Write to several companies that produce active solar systems for residential application and request technical literature related to their systems. Study this literature and report your findings to the class. (Another source of information is the Sweets Architectural File.)

4. Plan a cottage that utilizes one of the passive solar gain systems discussed in this chapter. Explain how the system works.

26
CHAPTER

Earth Sheltered Dwellings

After studying this chapter, you will be able to:
- Explain the purpose of a large thermal mass in earth sheltered dwellings.
- Review important site considerations for earth sheltered buildings.
- Explain why soil type is a major concern in the design of an earth sheltered structure.
- Summarize design variations of earth sheltered dwellings.

Architects, builders, and designers know that earth (soil) may provide a large thermal mass and may act as an insulator. Earth may be used to shield structures from cold winter winds, noise, and undesirable views. Recently, however, earth has received widespread attention and serious consideration as a major element in the basic design of housing. Increased heating costs, improved and innovative building materials, new

building technology, and the desire to find new solutions to old problems have sparked new interest in this subject. The primary considerations in planning earth sheltered dwellings will be covered in this chapter.

SITE CONSIDERATIONS

Design of an earth sheltered dwelling involves several important aspects that may not be important in the design of a conventional above-grade structure. Basic site considerations such as orientation to sun and wind, topography, Fig. 26-1, type of soil, and groundwater level are especially relevant for this type of housing structure. In addition, the load-bearing elements of the structure must be specifically designed to withstand tremendous earth pressure as well as

Fig. 26-1. The topography of this site has been utilized in the placement and orientation of this earth sheltered home. (Jeff Burgin Builders)

heavy roof loads (approximately 100-120 pounds on each square foot of the roof for each foot of earth above).

ORIENTATION ON THE SITE

Proper orientation of the structure with respect to the sun and wind will provide energy savings as well as impact the quality of life inside the dwelling. Orientation to the sun is one of the most important considerations in the design of energy efficient dwellings. Radiant energy from the sun can help heat the interior space through active and/or passive means. If sun alone were considered, the best site orientation in a northern climate for any earth sheltered dwelling would be a south-facing orientation. All windows would be on the south side and the three remaining sides of the structure covered with earth, Fig. 26-2. However, other factors sometimes prevent the optimum orientation with respect to the sun. It should be noted that maximum sunlight is desirable in the winter, but not in summer. Therefore, vegetation, shutters, and overhangs can be used to reduce solar heat gain in summer, Fig. 26-3.

Fig. 26-3. Operable "Skylids" by Zomeworks assist in controlling sunlight entering a home to improve regulating energy needs.

Fig. 26-2. All windows in this large earth sheltered home face south, with the three remaining sides of the home covered with earth. (Vermont Castings, Inc.)

Wind is also an important consideration for the orientation of an earth sheltered dwelling. Heat loss increases dramatically when a building is exposed to cold winter winds. An orientation that minimizes the effect of wind will reduce heat loss. Winter winds in the northern hemisphere are primarily from the northwest. Therefore, if energy performance is important, few

windows or doors should be placed on the north and west sides of the dwelling, Fig. 26-4. Earth sheltering provides an unique opportunity to shield the structure from winter winds and, at the same time, provide for ventilation in the summer. (Generally, summer breezes are from the southeast.)

The view may also be an orientation concern when planning for an earth sheltered dwelling. Various basic designs allow for maximization of the view or just the opposite when the view is undesirable. As in planning any dwelling, the site

Fig. 26-4. This earth sheltered dwelling shows a concern for reducing the effect of cold winter winds. The exposed side faces away from the prevailing winter winds. (Jeff Burgin Builders)

should be selected first so that the building design and site will complement each other.

TOPOGRAPHY AS A DESIGN CONSIDERATION

Topography of a site includes control of the land, trees, streams, and other natural features. The design of an earth sheltered dwelling may be affected in several ways by the site topography. For example, wind patterns and temperature around the structure may be affected by changes in the terrain, Fig. 26-5. Site contours also determine patterns of water runoff. However, the most important impact of topography on design is whether the site is sloped or flat. Flat sites present several problems for earth sheltered structures. Building codes almost always require window openings for light and ventilation and it is assumed then that the dwelling will be at least partially exposed to the outdoors.

Sloping sites provide many more opportunities in design than do flat sites for earth sheltered structures.

Vegetation on the site is desirable for beautification as well as for erosion and noise reduction. Deciduous trees provide shade in the summer and allow sun penetration in winter. Evergreens, when located properly, shield the building from winter winds.

SOIL AND GROUNDWATER

Earth sheltered structures usually require special evaluation of soils and groundwater conditions on the site. Most dwellings of this type are much heavier and generally placed deeper in the earth than conventional housing. Some sites are not suitable choices for earth sheltered dwellings because of the type of soil or groundwater conditions.

Two important soil characteristics to be evaluated are bearing capacity and tendency to expand when wet. There are many variables in determining bearing capacity such as earth loads and pressures. Calculations should not be attempted by an amateur. A professional engineer should be secured to calculate earth loading conditions and main structural elements of the building to withstand these forces, Fig. 26-6. Identify the major elements affecting the design of an earth sheltered dwelling so that a conceptual design can be developed which at least considers the proper elements.

The implications of soil type for structural components vary with the component being

Fig. 26-5. South sloping sites encourage breezes to move up the hill during the day and down the hill at night. When a body of water is nearby, breezes move from the water to land during the day and from the land toward the water at night.

Fig. 26-6. The roof of this earth sheltered home was designed by professional engineers to ensure sufficient strength to support the tremendous loads imposed on it. (Jeff Burgin Builders)

considered. The main concern of the soil on the roof is its susceptibility to frost heave and its ability to support vegetation. Fine-grained soils are most likely to prevent problems with frost heave. Fig. 26-7 shows various soil classifications which can be helpful in planning the design of an earth sheltered dwelling.

Walls present greater concerns with respect to type of soil than do roofs. Lateral pressures and ability to drain vary considerably with different soils. Generally, sand or gravel is recommended for backfill against the wall. The soil to avoid is expansive clay. It swells when wet and produces very high pressure which can cause damage to the structure.

The major concern with soil under the foundation is its bearing capacity. Remember, the foundation loads will be much higher than for a conventional structure. Soils not suitable for foundations are soft or loose deposits. Compacted sand or gravel is best. Soil under the floor slab is relatively unimportant unless expansive clay or a high water table is present, or a deep excavation is made in soft clay. These conditions can cause floor uplift loads.

Groundwater around the structure causes extra loads on the dwelling and adds to water-proofing problems. For example, if the soil is less than saturated, the weight of the water must be added to the dry weight of the soil. When the soil is saturated with water, it presents a pressure of 62.4 lbs./sq. ft. for each foot of depth. Good drainage is the most practical solution to groundwater problems. A site with a high water table or poor drainage is not a good choice for an earth sheltered dwelling.

ENERGY CONSERVATION

The primary reason for designing and building an earth sheltered dwelling is generally the potential energy savings derived from it. Energy conservation to reduce the heat loss directly affects the basic design in primarily two ways. The shape or geometry of the plan and earth mass around the structure can be used by the architect to conserve energy.

Heat loss in a building is a function of the amount of surface area through which heat can escape. Therefore, if other variables are equal, a dwelling with a larger surface area will have greater heat loss than one with a smaller surface area. Fig. 26-8 shows a comparison of four

SOIL CLASSIFICATION CHART

COARSE GRAINED SOILS (More than 50% of material is larger than a number 200 sieve size.)				FINE GRAINED SOILS (More than 50% of material is smaller than a number 200 sieve size.)	
Gravel and Gravelly Soils (more than 50% of coarse fraction retained on #4 sieve.)		Sand and Sandy Soils (More than 50% of coarse fraction passing # 4 sieve.)		Silts and Clays (Liquid limit less than 50.)	Silts and Clays (Liquid limit greater than 50.)
Clean Gravels (Little or no fines)	Gravels with Fines (Greater amount of fines)	Clean Sand (Little or no fines)	Sands with Fines (Greater amount of fines)		
GW Well-graded gravels, gravel-sand mixtures, little or no fines	GM Silty gravels, gravel-sand-silt mixtures	SW Well-graded sands, gravelly sands, little or no fines	SM Silty sands, sand-silt mixtures	ML Inorganic silts and very fine sands, rock flour, silty or clayey fine sands or clayey silts with slight plasticity	MH Inorganic silts, micaeous or diatomaceous fine sand or silty soils
GP Poorly-graded gravels, gravel-sand mixtures, little or no fines	GC Clayey gravels, gravel-sand-clay mixtures	SP Poorly-graded sands, gravelly sands, little or no fines	SC Clayey sands, sand-clay mixtures	CL Inorganic clays of low to medium plasticity, gravelly clays, sandy clays, silty clays, lean clays	CH Inorganic clays of high plasticity, fat clays
				OL Organic silts and organic silty clays of low plasticity	OH Organic clays of medium to high plasticity, organic silts

Highly organic soils (PT) include: peat, humus, swamp soils with high organic contents

Fig. 26-7. Soil classification chart showing major soil types, typical descriptions, and identifying symbols.

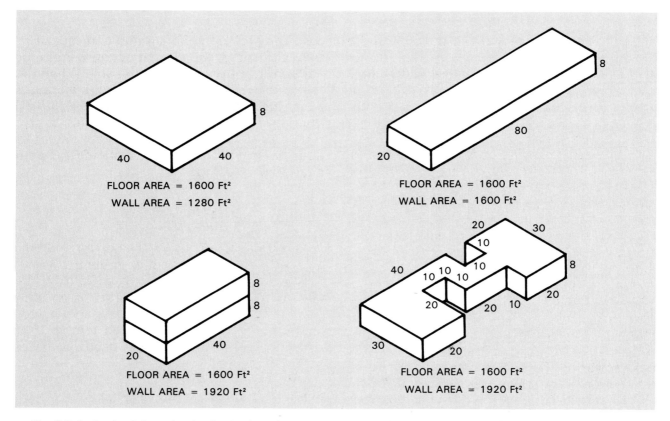

FLOOR AREA = 1600 Ft²
WALL AREA = 1280 Ft²

FLOOR AREA = 1600 Ft²
WALL AREA = 1600 Ft²

FLOOR AREA = 1600 Ft²
WALL AREA = 1920 Ft²

FLOOR AREA = 1600 Ft²
WALL AREA = 1920 Ft²

Fig. 26-8. Each of these basic shapes has the same amount of floor area–1600 square feet. Notice how the wall area varies from one design to another.

basic shapes which have exactly the same amount of floor space, but differ in the surface area exposed. If reducing heat loss is a design goal, then develop as compact a floor plan as possible to reduce surface area.

The second way that energy conservation affects the basic design is related to the earth mass encasing the earth sheltered dwelling. Earth placed against the walls and on the roof reduces heat loss in winter. The best solution to minimize heat loss would be to bury the structure deep in the earth with no area exposed. However, this would most likely be unacceptable as a living environment and would certainly not pass building code requirements. The goal then is to maximize the earth cover while meeting code requirements for ventilation, light, and escape routes, while creating a pleasant living space. (Most building codes require all habitable rooms in residential construction to have an operating window to provide light, ventilation, and a means to escape.)

STRUCTURAL SYSTEMS

The structural system is an important factor in any dwelling design. This is particularly true in an earth sheltered home because of heavy roof loads. Two basic systems are used to support the load: conventional flat roof systems and somewhat unconventional systems which use vault and dome shapes.

Conventional roof systems use cast-in-place concrete slabs, concrete planks, and wood or steel post and beam systems. The product is usually a rectangular configuration with a flat or sloping roof.

More unconventional systems are being used because they can support heavier loads and lend themselves to unique designs. These systems include concrete or steel culvert shapes and domes, Fig. 26-9. The advantage is usually greater utilization of the earth mass, but construction may be more difficult or costly.

COST OF EARTH SHELTERED DWELLINGS

The cost of construction for any type of dwelling varies considerably from one section of the country to another. For that reason, it is not practical to try to specify cost per square foot for any design. However, all indications are that the cost of earth sheltered construction is roughly comparable to good quality conventional above-grade housing. Total cost should, however, consider length of life of the dwelling (earth

Fig. 26-9. This earth sheltered dwelling, still under construction, uses the dome to provide the roof support needed. (Jeff Burgin Builders)

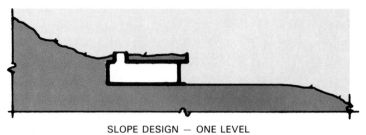

SLOPE DESIGN — ONE LEVEL

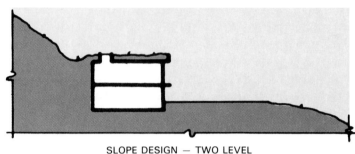

SLOPE DESIGN — TWO LEVEL

Fig. 26-10. Slope or elevational designs. All the windows are concentrated on the south side of the structure.

sheltered dwellings are usually designed to last longer than conventional construction), maintenance, and energy needs. These factors, when considered, bring the cost of an earth sheltered dwelling close to conventional construction. One other consideration related to the construction of earth sheltered dwellings is that many typical residential contractors do not have experience building this type of structure.

DESIGN VARIATIONS OF EARTH SHELTERED DWELLINGS

Most design variations of earth sheltered dwellings are one of three types: slope design, atrium design, or penetrational design. The basic difference in these types of designs is in the size and orientation of window openings and access points.

SLOPE DESIGN

The *slope design* (sometimes called elevational) maximizes earth cover around the dwelling by placing all windows and doors on one side of the structure–usually the south side, Fig. 26-10. Major living and sleeping areas are then usually arranged along the exposed elevation. Secondary areas that do not require windows such as baths, utility, and storage are located behind the living and sleeping areas. The kitchen and dining areas may be placed somewhere between if they are considered part of the front or exposed living area.

The single-level slope design does have the disadvantage that internal traffic circulation may be long, especially for a larger home. Two-level designs allow for a more compact plan which reduces the traffic circulation path. The slope of the site will largely determine which variation is most practical.

The slope design is usually a very energy efficient solution due to the continuous earth mass, windows on the south side, and reduced wind on the structure. However, suitable sites for this design are often difficult to find.

ATRIUM DESIGN

The *atrium design* places living areas around a central courtyard with all windows opening into the courtyard, Fig. 26-11. The design has more possibilities for warm climates than cool climates, because the courtyard can be used for traffic circulation. If the atrium is covered to create an interior courtyard, then the design has broader applications for cool climates. However, since the living spaces would not open directly to the outside, some codes may prohibit the

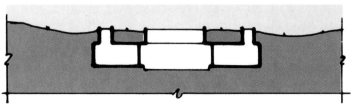

FLAT SITE — FULLY RECESSED
ATRIUM DESIGN

Fig. 26-11. Atrium design earth sheltered dwelling.

plan. At best, the atrium design for earth sheltered dwellings presents traffic circulation problems for cold climate applications.

Even though the atrium design does not face all windows to the south and does not provide for a compact plan, it does tend to hold warm air which is heated by the sun and, therefore, reduces the amount of heat loss. Further, the very private outdoor space makes it a concept worth considering.

PENETRATIONAL DESIGN

The **penetrational design** provides window openings and access at various points around the structure, Fig. 26-12. In concept, the penetrational design varies little from a conventional above-grade dwelling because windows may be located on several sides of the structure. The traffic circulation also may be located in the center of the home.

Fig. 26-12. Penetrational design earth sheltered dwelling under construction. Notice the planned openings on each side. (Jeff Burgin Builders)

Location, number, and size of windows must still be carefully evaluated if energy conservation is of primary importance. Too many openings will increase heat loss through exposure and wind turbulence. In some cases it may not be possible or desirable to face all windows to the south. In this case a penetrational design may be the best alternative.

ADVANTAGES OF EARTH SHELTERED HOUSING

As with any proposed solution to the housing problem, certain advantages become evident. Below are some of the most obvious advantages of earth sheltered housing.

1. The structure will generally be constructed of massive and relatively permanent materials. This provides a long expected life span for the building.
2. The amount of energy required to heat or cool an earth sheltered building is generally much less than a conventional above-grade dwelling because of less heat loss.
3. Maintenance costs are generally much less than for a typical dwelling because of less exposure, type of materials used, and less temperature fluctuations.
4. Earth sheltered dwellings made from concrete have a high resistance to fire damage.

DISADVANTAGES OF EARTH SHELTERED HOUSING

1. A suitable site may be difficult to locate.
2. Code restrictions frequently present problems for earth sheltered housing designs.
3. Most residential contractors are not familiar with the construction methods required for heavy loads and earth pressures.
4. A resistance may exist to "new" housing methods or solutions by banks, builders, and neighbors.

REVIEW QUESTIONS–CHAPTER 26

Write your answers on a separate sheet of paper. Do not write in this book.
1. Name several considerations that are important for earth sheltered dwellings, but may not be for conventional above-grade structures.
2. An earth sheltered dwelling should face south. True or false? Explain your answer.
3. What devices may be used to shield large glass areas in the summer?
4. Is wind an important consideration for the orientation of an earth sheltered dwelling? Why?
5. Winter winds in the northern hemisphere come from what direction?
6. What considerations are included in the topography of a site?

7. What is usually the main purpose for building an earth sheltered dwelling?
8. What type of soil should be avoided when planning an earth sheltered dwelling?
9. How much pressure does water-saturated soil exert?
10. Heat loss in a building is a function of the amount of _____ through which heat can escape.
11. Explain why earth placed against walls and on the roof reduces heat loss.
12. What two basic roof systems are used to support the roof loads in earth sheltered structures?
13. Name the three design variations used in most earth sheltered dwellings.
14. Which earth sheltered design may have openings facing several directions?
15. The _____ design has the living spaces located around a central courtyard, and all windows open to the court.

SUGGESTED ACTIVITIES

1. Plan an earth sheltered dwelling using one of the three basic types discussed as a guide. Build a model of the proposed plan and get a rough estimate of the cost to build the structure from a local builder. Report your results.
2. Visit your local building department or well drilling firm to determine the types of soil in your area. Collect samples for display and report on the acceptability of each soil type for earth sheltered dwellings.
3. Interview a local bank loan officer and a building contractor concerning earth sheltered dwellings. Obtain bank and building company policies for these homes. List major reasons for acceptance or rejection for financing, insuring, and/or constructing earth sheltered dwellings.

Earth sheltered home under construction. Building methods are much different than for conventional housing. (Jeff Burgin Builders)

Dome Structures

After studying this chapter, you will be able to:
* Explain why a dome structure generally has less heat loss than a conventional structure of comparable size.
* Diagram how a typical dome provides free interior space.
* Describe how a typical dome is constructed.
* List several advantages and disadvantages of domes.

Several variations of the geodesic dome that were developed by R. Buckminster Fuller have sprung to life on the housing scene, Fig. 27-1.

Dome structures are not new to architecture, but they are innovative with respect to residential applications.

Advocates have described them as the most efficient system of structuring yet developed for housing. This, no doubt, is supported by the fact that they provide structural superiority, unobstructed floor space, low cost, factory production, and reduced energy needs.

The basic geodesic dome that Fuller developed is an engineered system of triangular space frames that create self-reinforcing roof and wall units based on mathematically precise divisions

Fig. 27-1. A modern dome home provides an interesting architectural shape and exciting interior. Obstruction-free floor space lends itself to a wide variety of floor plans. (Monterey Domes)

of the sphere. Each triangular space frame unit may be manufactured to exact specifications in a factory and then assembled on site by simply bolting them together to form the superstructure of the building. This type of structure reduces the quantity of building materials needed per square foot of usable area by about 30 percent over conventional construction, Fig. 27-2. Heat loss is also reduced a comparable amount due to the reduced exterior exposure.

Fig. 27-2. The shape of a dome reduces energy requirements and building materials by approximately 30 percent. (Monterey Domes)

No interior or exterior support system (walls, beams, etc.) are required because the structure of a dome is self-supporting. The open interior space generated by this structure provides for a wide variety of floor plans and great flexibility, Fig. 27-3. The dome shape provides a living space that is responsive to efficient space utilization, lower energy consumption, and exciting decorative schemes. Further, a dome home can be placed on almost any site. A dome may be constructed on any typical foundation such as concrete block, cast concrete, or wood foundation.

Manufactured dome homes are available in single-story and two-story models in diameters generally ranging from 26 to 60 feet, Fig. 27-4. Two or more units can be positioned adjacent to one another or combined with a conventional structure. Typical roofing materials such as asphalt shingles and cedar shakes may be used to weatherproof the exterior.

DOME VARIATIONS

Most manufactured dome homes are not true geodesic domes, but variations which use the central idea. The true geodesic dome described by Fuller is produced by dividing the surface of a sphere into a series of small triangles. These are joined together to enclose a space resulting in a dome. Most true geodesic domes have from 60 to 120 triangles. A large number of components

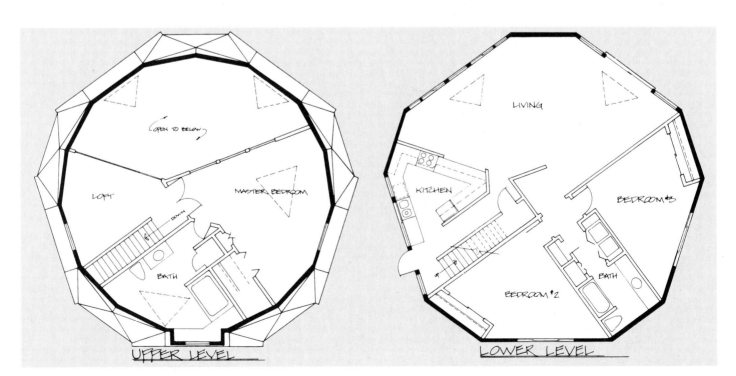

Fig. 27-3. This is a typical first and second floor layout for a 45-foot diameter dome home. (Cathedralite Domes)

Fig. 27-4. This 39-foot diameter dome provides 1500 square feet of floor space on two levels. (Domes and Homes, Inc.)

themselves to large openings for windows and doors.

Variations of the original geodesic dome which reduce the number of units and introduce new shapes have made the concept applicable to the housing market. One design called the Hexadome combines 24 triangles and 3 trapezoids to form a dome up to 32 feet in diameter. Each panel unit is constructed from standard construction lumber and plywood and is large enough to use standard windows and doors. Construction of the dome is accomplished by bolting six triangular panels together to form a raised hexagon. Four hexagons are required together with three trapezoids to complete the dome. Fig. 27-5 shows a 32 foot diameter Hexadome plan which has 1012 sq. ft. including the loft.

Another variation of the geodesic dome also uses basic triangular units, but mixes different size triangles together to form hexagons and pentagons to enclose the sphere. The appearance of this dome variation is very similar to the

may present problems for home applications. Difficulty may be encountered due to the degree of accuracy required to join a large number of triangles, and the small triangles do not lend

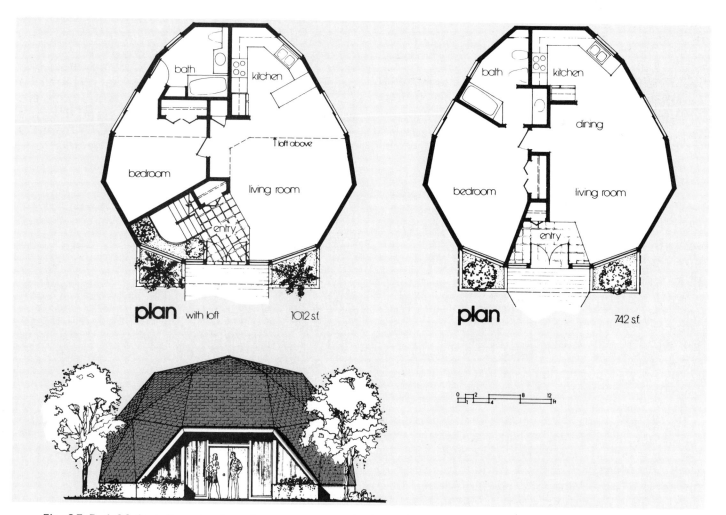

Fig. 27-5. A 32-foot diameter dome forms a cozy one-bedroom home with a loft which could be used as another bedroom. (Hexadome of American)

Fig. 27-6. Triangular panels have been combined to form raised hexagons and pentagons in this 39-foot diameter, 5/8 sphere. This model has two levels plus a loft to produce 2100 square feet of floor space. (Domes and Homes, Inc.)

Hexadome. Fig. 27-6 clearly illustrates the use of raised hexagons and pentagons in this 39 foot diameter dome.

TYPICAL DOME CONSTRUCTION

Most residential dome applications use typical construction techniques to form the basic triangular panels. The panels can be purchased complete and ready to bolt together, precut at the factory and shipped as individual pieces, or built completely on site from standard lumber and plywood. Fig. 27-7 shows typical panel designs for a 32 foot Hexadome. The frames for triangles in this example are cut from 4 x 4s and a 4 x 8 is used for the base of the trapezoid. Studs are 2 x 4s with 1/2'' construction-grade exterior plywood sheathing. The sheathing is nailed and glued to the studs.

Cutting the proper angle on each side of the triangle and trapezoid is very important if the pieces are to join together properly. For example, in the 32 foot Hexadome, the legs or sides for the 24 triangles are cut from 24 10-foot 4 x 4s lengthwise through their centers at a 7° angle. Each pair will form the sides of one triangle panel.

The base pieces for triangles are ripped in the same manner, but are cut at an angle of 15°. Twelve 4 x 4s are needed for triangle bases. The ends of the frame pieces also must be cut to fit. One end of each triangle leg should be cut at 29° as well as both ends of the base piece. The overall length of the base pieces will be 8'-11 3/8''. The remaining end of the legs are cut at

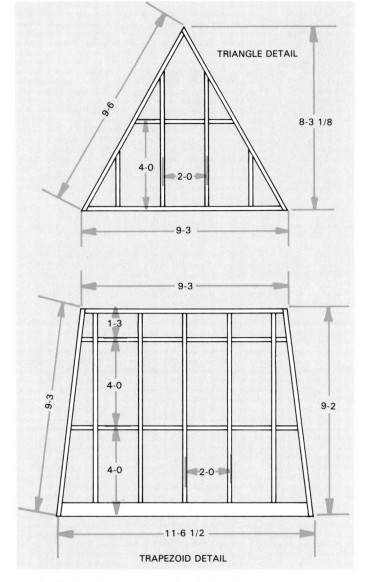

Fig. 27-7. Construction details for the two basic panel shapes used in the 32-foot diameter Hexadome.

32° to form an overall length of 9'-4'' on one and 9'-5 5/16'' on the other. The three frame pieces should then form a triangle which is 9'-6'' along the legs and 9'-3'' along the base.

Cutting the trapezoids is similar to cutting the triangle pieces except the angles are different. The top and two sides of each trapezoid are 9'-3'' long from end to end, and the base is 11'-6 1/2'' overall length. To cut the top and sides, the angle is set to 19° and five 4 x 4s are ripped lengthwise through their centers. To cut the base, the angle is set to 41° and one corner is removed from three 4 x 8s to form a header at the bottom of each trapezoid. The length of the base is 11'-6 1/2''.

Studs are spaced 24'' on center and cut to fit the triangle and trapezoid frames. Plywood sheathing is applied to the outside of each panel with glue and nails or staples. Three bolt holes are drilled along each triangle leg and sides of the trapezoid, except the base.

Once the dome panels are constructed and bolted together, the entire shell of the dome is ready to be placed on the foundation. A crane will be required for this operation. Another procedure is to erect the panels of the dome directly on the foundation, however, a crane will still be required to place the top hexagon in place.

The foundation for a dome structure may be any one of the standard types used for conventional construction. A basement, crawl space, or slab foundation is also compatible with dome construction. Once the type of foundation is decided upon and the basic size and style of dome is chosen, the foundation shape may be located on the site.

Again, the 32-foot diameter Hexadome is used to illustrate the typical procedure for laying out the foundation for a dome dwelling. Fig. 27-8 shows the basic foundation shape with openings and walls indicated. Fig. 27-9 gives the dimensions for locating the three primary dome support walls. Fig. 27-10 provides the location and lengths of all edges of the foundation for cross checking the accuracy.

Riser walls support the entire structure while providing additional headroom on the second floor. The Hexadome, Fig. 27-5, requires three riser walls to support the dome. Each is 9'-3'' long made from 2 x 6 construction lumber with plywood sheathing, concrete blocks, or cast

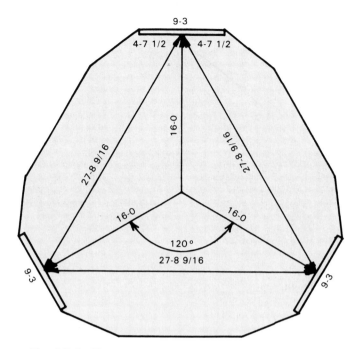

Fig. 27-9. These dimensions are typical for a 32-foot diameter Hexadome foundation layout.

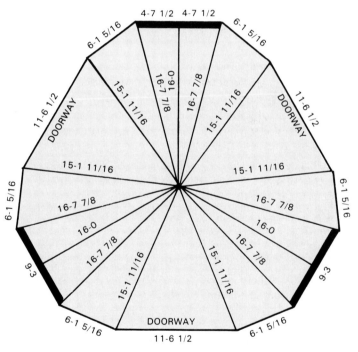

Fig. 27-10. Illustration of the dimensions for cross checking the foundation layout of a 32-foot Hexadome.

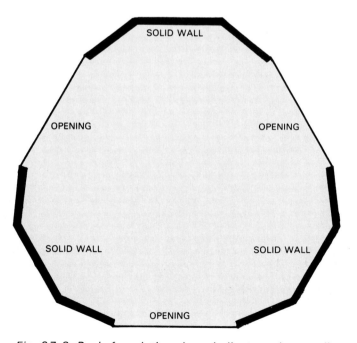

Fig. 27-8. Basic foundation shape indicates where walls and openings are located.

concrete. They must be strong and solidly attached to the foundation, Fig. 27-11. Wooden riser walls must be solidly braced during placement of the dome to prevent movement and a possible accident. **Wing walls** on either side of the riser walls will completely enclose the structure. Wing walls are shown in Fig. 27-5 on both sides of the entry door.

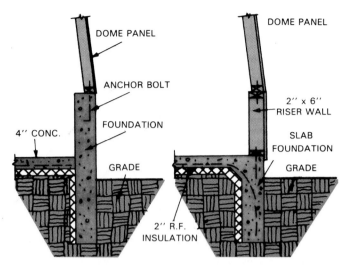

Fig. 27-11. Typical foundation details. Left–Raised concrete foundation wall with slab floor. Right–Thickened-edge slab with a wood riser wall.

The construction and erection of most dome structures is similar to the example discussed here. Completion of the home is the same as for any frame structure.

ADVANTAGES OF DOMES

Dome structures have some advantages when compared with typical residential construction. Following are some of the most obvious advantages of domes.

1. Domes form a very efficient system which is strong and versatile.

2. Domes provide an open, obstruction-free floor space that lends itself to a wide variety of floor plans, Fig. 27-12.

3. Factory production makes it possible to erect a dome from standard panels in just a few hours.

4. The basic dome shape requires less energy for heating and air conditioning than conventional rectangular shapes which cover the same floor space.

5. Domes are economical to build since less materials are required.

6. The interior of a dome home is exciting and fun to decorate due to the varied shapes and surfaces, Fig. 27-13.

DISADVANTAGES OF DOMES

Some disadvantages of dome homes include the following.

1. Walls that are not vertical or form square corners may present some problems with typical furniture and appliances.

2. More custom built-ins may be required due to the unique design of the structure. Custom work adds cost.

3. The dome design may not be compatible with surrounding homes and, therefore, not a good choice in some communities.

4. Banks, insurance companies, and building departments are generally not familiar with this type of construction. They may be reluctant to lend money, insure it, or approve the design for construction.

5. Resale may be more difficult than a conventional home because it is different.

REVIEW QUESTIONS–CHAPTER 27

Write your answers on a separate sheet of paper. Do not write in this book.

1. What person is generally associated with geodesic domes?
2. Most dome homes are not true geodesic domes. True or false?
3. Name several attributes of the dome structure as a building superstructure.

Fig. 27-12. The interior space of a dome may be used in any manner since no interior structural support is needed for the shell. (Monterey Domes)

*Fig. 27-13. The interior of this dome is interesting and exciting. It provides many opportunities for decorating.
(Monterey Domes)*

4. Domes have less heat loss per square foot of floor space because the walls are thicker. True or false? Explain your answer.
5. Manufactured dome homes usually range in size from about 26 to 60 ft. True or false?

6. The basic modular shape used in most domes is the _____.
7. One variation of the geodesic dome mixes different size triangles to form _____ and _____ to enclose the sphere.
8. What materials are used in the construction of most commercially produced residential domes?
9. One piece of heavy equipment may be required on site to assemble a dome home. Name it and explain why it is needed.
10. A dome structure can be built on most any conventional type foundation. Give two examples.
11. What is the purpose of a riser wall, other than to support the dome?

SUGGESTED ACTIVITIES

1. Go to your local library, bookstore, or magazine stand and secure several books or magazines which list manufacturers of dome homes. Write to three manufacturers and request information about their products. Study the literature and share it with your classmates.
2. Plan a simple dome structure and build a scale model of the plan. Explain the advantages and disadvantages of this type of structure.
3. Using a plan supplied by your instructor, obtain information from your local gas and electric company on the cost of heating and cooling a dome home. If needed, modify the plan to increase its energy efficiency. Report your findings to the class.

These are examples of custom precut homes which show a diversity of shapes and sizes.
(Photos courtesy of Lindal Cedar Homes, Inc., Seattle, Washington)

Modular Applications

After studying this chapter, you will be able to:
- List the advantages of modular applications in the construction industry.
- Apply modular concepts to the design of a simple residence.
- Explain the term "industrialized housing."
- Describe the primary differences between panelized construction, precuts, and modular components.

Traditionally, residential structures have been built by fastening thousands of small pieces (boards, bricks, etc.) together on the job site. This type of construction is generally known as **stick-built.** This requires a great deal of time and labor and is costly. In recent years much experimentation has been underway in an effort to speed up the process of building a house and reduce the cost. Experiments have involved pre-cut lumber, factory wall assemblies, modular components, and industrialized housing. Each of these has helped to further the technology of modern home construction, but the big pay off is still to be realized. Industries are just beginning to be truly successful in applying mass production techniques to house construction and home designers are using modular sizes in their plans.

In the past, people associated factory-built houses with cheap, poorly constructed and designed boxes, but today this is no longer true. The modular concept can be applied to any style or house design, Figs. 28-1 and 28-2.

Fig. 28-1. This beautiful factory-built home is a prime example of good quality and design which applies the principles of modular construction. (Photo courtesy of Lindal Cedar Homes, Inc., Seattle, Washington)

Fig. 28-2. This striking chalet-style home was constructed using factory precut components. (Photo courtesy of Lindal Cedar Homes, Inc., Seattle, Washington)

STANDARD MODULE
4" x 4" x 4"

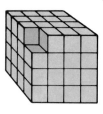

MINOR MODULE
16" x 16" x 16"

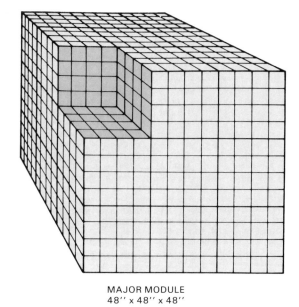

MAJOR MODULE
48" x 48" x 48"

Fig. 28-3. All modules are multiples of 4 in. and each is a cube.

STANDARDIZATION

Application of the modular concept to on-site construction or factory-built homes necessarily involves standardization. Manufacturers are moving toward standard size building materials which lend themselves to modular construction. Some of the common size materials which are modular include:

4" x 8"	16" x 32"	48" x 48"
4" x 12"	16" x 48"	48" x 96"
8" x 16"	16" x 96"	48" x 120"
16" x 16"	48" x 32"	48" x 144"

Plywood sheets, interior paneling, floor tiles, etc. are all designed to be integrated into modular systems. Other materials will most likely join the ranks in the future.

The modular plan includes length, width, and height using the *standard module,* a 4 in. cube. The 4 in. cubes are combined to produce larger units. For example, the *major module* is 4'-0" or 12 standard modules. Cubes which are 16 and 24 in. are *minor modules,* Fig. 28-3. It is evident then, that a modular length must be a multiple of 4 inches. Minor modules of 16 and 24 in. are important because studs and joists are spaced those distances.

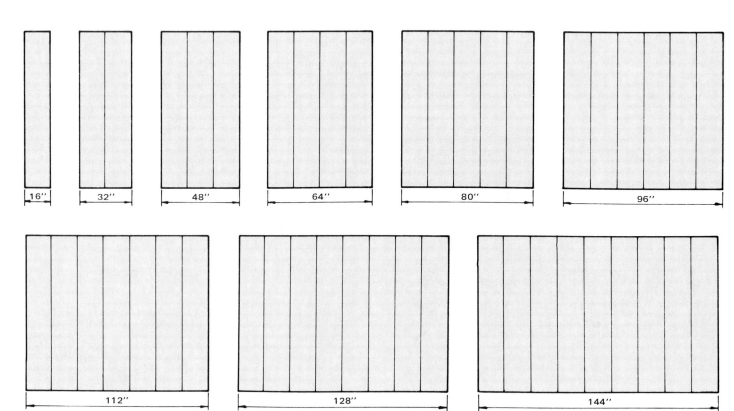

16" 32" 48" 64" 80" 96"

112" 128" 144"

Fig. 28-4. Standard factory-built panels are produced in 16 in. increments. Windows are located in the panels with the top at a constant height.

Modular panel components are usually produced in widths ranging from 16 to 196 in. in multiples of 16 inches, Fig. 28-4. These panels are then fastened together to form a wall. Exterior walls are generally multiples of 4'-0'' if feasible, in the modular system. This saves materials and reduces cutting time.

A structure that incorporates modular principles must be designed with definite modules in mind. Lengths, widths, and heights must be planned to coincide with modular size materials and specifications given for materials to be used. The drafter should use a modular grid as a guide in designing and dimensioning the structure. A typical modular grid is shown in Fig. 28-5.

A few simple rules have been devised for modular planning and dimensioning:

1. Lengths must be multiples of 4 inches.

2. Details of the structure should begin and terminate on a grid line, Fig. 28-6.

3. Grid dimensions are shown on the plan.

4. Floor levels are located on grid lines. The top of the subfloor and top of a finished concrete slab are located on the grid line, Fig. 28-7.

5. Dimensions terminating on a grid line are shown with an arrow. Dimensions terminating off the grid line are shown with a dot, Fig. 28-8.

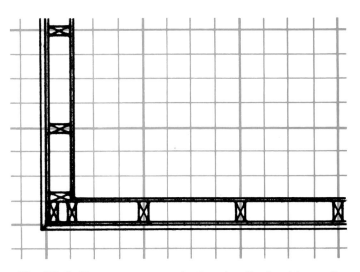

Fig. 28-6. House corners and other details should coordinate with the grid lines. Grid lines are shown on the plan.

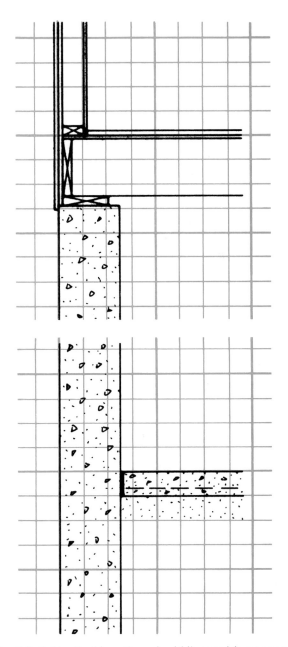

Fig. 28-7. Vertical location of grid lines with respect to frame floor above and slab floor below.

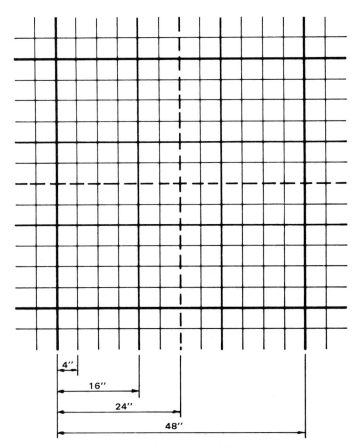

Fig. 28-5. A typical modular grid with three different weight lines to represent 4, 16, and 48 inches.

6. Partitions are usually centered on grid lines, Fig. 28-9, but modular length interior walls are not nearly as important as outside walls.

MODULAR COMPONENTS

Modular components are building parts which have been preassembled either in a plant or on-site. They are parts such as floor panels, roof panels, wall sections, or roof trusses, Figs. 28-10 and 28-11. They may be constructed from wood, concrete, plywood, plastics, fiberglass, steel, aluminum, paper, or most any other building material. Panels may also be made from layers of different materials, Fig. 28-12.

Some of the advantages of prefabricated panels (panelized construction) are: design freedom and aesthetic appeal, high strength-to-weight ratios, uniform quality, more efficient use of materials, lower cost, and reduced time required for installation. Several companies are producing modular components in this growing field.

Fig. 28-10. The frame of this home will be covered with factory-built insulated modular panels. (Northern Energy Homes)

Fig. 28-11. A prefabricated wall panel being installed. It has a thick rigid foam core which produces a high R-value. (Associated Foam Manufacturers, Inc.)

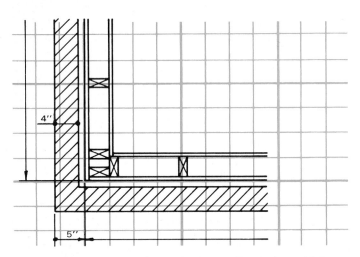

Fig. 28-8. In modular dimensioning, a dimension which terminates on a grid line is shown with an arrow. Dimensions which terminate off a grid line are shown with a dot.

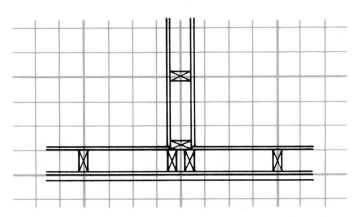

Fig. 28-9. Partitions are usually centered on a grid line.

Fig. 28-12. A thick core of rigid expanded polystyrene insulation is adhesively welded between two building panels, or facings. This forms a single structure that resists twisting, warping, and racking. Available core thicknesses include 3 1/2, 5 1/2, 7 1/4, 9 1/4, and 11 1/4 in. (Associated Foam Manufacturers, Inc.)

Fig. 28-13. A factory-built ranch-style house which was erected on a regular foundation.

INDUSTRIALIZED HOUSING

The term industrialized housing refers to houses built in a factory. Many types of houses are being built in plants today, all composed of modules, Fig. 28-13. Modules range in size from 12' x 20' to 14' x 40' and larger. A width of 14 ft. seems to be ideal because it is large enough for a fair size room and 14 ft. is the maximum width that most states will allow on the highway. The larger modules are generally built on a production line much the same as an automobile, Fig. 28-14. Some facilities are so advanced that computer-directed systems are being used. The computer calculates placement of studs for each wall panel and automatic nailers fasten the materials together. The trend toward more

Fig. 28-14. Wall panels under construction on a production line.

automatic equipment will continue as factory-built houses receive public acceptance and production increases. Fig. 28-15 shows some of the operations involved in producing a factory-built home.

The quality of many factory-built homes is better than traditional construction. Jigs and fixtures are used to cut and fit parts together and accuracy is improved. Better quality lumber is usually used because a warped board will not fit the jig properly.

These large modules are usually more than just a shell, Fig. 28-16. Most have the plumbing, wiring, finished floors, and doors installed. They may be shipped to the site and lifted into place by a large crane one day, and be ready to move into in the next few days. Most are set on a regular foundation and ready to be connected to the water, sewer, gas, and electricity as soon as they are located.

The versatility of these modules is evidenced by the fact that they may be set side-by-side, end-to-end, directly on top of each other, or cantilevered to form interesting and functional shapes.

Modules within modules are also popular, Fig. 28-17. For example, a kitchen module which is complete with cabinets, range, refrigerator, and floor covering may be plugged into a larger half-house size module. Bathroom modules are also being produced in the same manner, Fig. 28-18. As selection becomes greater, one will be able to

A

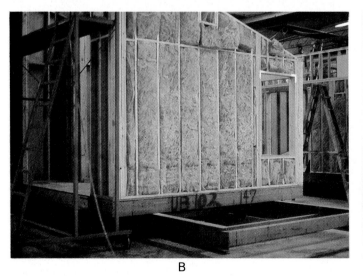

B

C

Fig. 28-15. A—Factory-built modular homes are completely constructed in a factory using high quality and material standards. B—Each module is built on a heavy steel frame for easy handling and transportation. This module is ready for exterior siding. C—A factory-built module being placed on the foundation using a large crane.
(Select Housing Associates)

Fig. 28-16. A modular house constructed from modular components. Most of the interior trim and mechanical equipment is already installed. (Wausau Homes)

Fig. 28-17. These kitchen modules are reaching completion on the production line. They will be complete with plumbing, wiring, cabinets, and appliances.

Fig. 28-18. A bathroom module on the production line about to receive its drain and vent system. (Wausau Homes)

select the kitchen, bath, and living room modules that he/she wishes to make up the total house, Fig. 28-19. A house may then be ordered just as a new car is now.

Factory-built houses of the future will not necessarily look like they do today. As new materials (new to the housing industry) are used for various house components and new processes are developed, complex shapes and rounded corners will be commonplace. The house of tomorrow should be more functional and afford a wider variety of configurations to choose from. If predictions are realized, the relative cost of housing will decline as factories move into full swing of home production.

Fig. 28-19. This kitchen module is being lifted into place. Other walls of the house will be located around it. Note the dishwasher, sink, and lighting fixtures have been installed.

REVIEW QUESTIONS—CHAPTER 28

Write your answers on a separate sheet of paper. Do not write in this book.

1. Name techniques that have been tried in an effort to reduce the cost and time required to build a residential structure.
2. In designing a structure that incorporates modular principles, the lengths, widths, and heights must be planned to coincide with _____ materials.
3. Building parts that have been preassembled in a plant are called _____.
4. Identify four advantages of using prefabricated panels.
5. Identify the standard sizes of modules.
6. All modules should be a multiple of _____ inches.
7. Modular panels are usually produced in multiples of _____ inches.
8. When drawing a modular plan, dimensions terminating on a grid line are represented with a(n) _____ while dimensions terminating off a grid line terminate with a(n) _____.
9. With respect to a frame floor, the grid line is located _____.
10. The term industrialized housing refers to _____.
11. List two reasons why a 12'-0" width appears ideal for industrialized housing modules.
12. List two reasons why the quality of a factory-built home is likely to be better than a stick-built home?

SUGGESTED ACTIVITIES

1. Choose a non-modular floor plan and redesign it following the principles of modular construction. Dimension the plan and present both drawings for a comparison.
2. Invite a local builder to class to discuss methods which may be used in the design process that will conserve materials when building a house.
3. Design a residence that follows the principles of modular construction and makes use of standard roof and wall panels. Information about these panels may be secured from the American Plywood Association, the National Lumber Manufacturing Association, the Weyerhaeuser Company, and others.
4. Design a modern two-car garage that makes use of formed roof modules. The modules may be plywood curved or flat stressed skin panels or precast concrete modules. Use your imagination and try for a unique but functional design.
5. Design a modular unit boat dock that may be expanded by simply adding more modules. Choose your own materials.

Perspective Drawings

After studying this chapter, you will be able to:
- Explain the purpose of using a perspective drawing.
- Explain the difference between one-, two-, and three-point perspectives.
- Prepare a one- or two-point perspective drawing using the office method.
- Explain how changing the viewing position, angle, and height changes the perspective.
- Make a simple perspective using a grid.

A type of pictorial drawing commonly used for communication purposes is the **perspective.** This type of drawing provides a realistic picture of the object, Fig. 29-1. The result gives a three-dimensional representation showing more than one side of the object. We know that things appear smaller when they are farther away. Perspective drawing applies this and other principles to achieve an accurate representation of the object.

Two other types of pictorial drawings are also used as presentation (communication) drawings, *isometric* and *oblique* drawings. Fig. 29-2 shows an isometric, oblique, and perspective of the same object to illustrate the difference between the three methods. Isometric and oblique drawings do not show a building as realistically

Fig. 29-1. This perspective rendering is a true representation of the actual home. (The Garlinghouse Company)

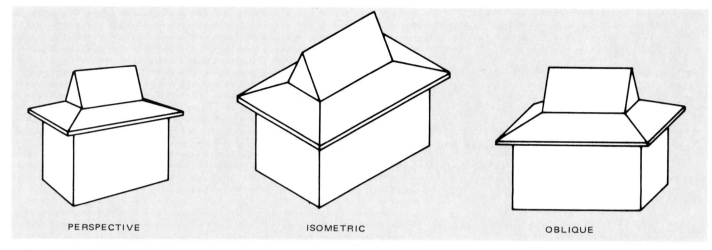

| PERSPECTIVE | ISOMETRIC | OBLIQUE |

Fig. 29-2. Any of these pictorial methods may be used for presentation drawings, however, the perspective produces a more realistic representation.

as a perspective. However, both are useful for some types of presentations and are generally much easier to draw.

PERSPECTIVES

There are three basic types of perspectives: **one-point** or parallel perspective, **two-point** or angular perspective, and **three-point** or oblique perspective, Fig. 29-3. One- and two-point perspectives are commonly used for residential structures. Three-point perspectives are generally used for tall, commercial type buildings and are, therefore, of little interest here.

A perspective drawing differs from an orthographic drawing in the position of the station point. The **station point** is the location of the observer's eye. See Fig. 29-4. In orthographic projection, the station point is infinitely far away. Therefore, all visual rays or projection lines are parallel to one another. In perspective, the station point is a finite distance (measurable distance) away from the object or picture plane, Fig. 29-5. In all types of drawing the object is drawn as it would appear on an imaginary transparent picture plane. The picture plane could be in front of, behind, or pass through the object.

Several terms related to perspectives should be clarified before the procedure for drawing perspectives is discussed.

Ground line (G.L.). The ground line represents a horizontal plane which is called the ground plane. In the least complex situation, the object to be drawn is positioned so that the foremost corner touches this plane. The ground line is drawn in the elevation part of the perspective layout. There are three parts to a perspective layout—**elevation, plan,** and **perspective draw-**

ing. When the object touches the picture plane in the plan view, it must also touch the ground line in the perspective drawing. If the object is placed behind the picture plane, then the object will be above the ground line. Objects that pass through the picture plane will also extend below the ground line.

Horizon line (H.L.). The horizon line represents the place where the ground and sky meet. It is therefore drawn in the elevation part of the layout. The distance between the ground line and horizon line represents the height of the observer's eye above the ground. This may be measured at the same scale as the plan view and elevation.

Picture plane (P.P.). The picture plane is a transparent plane on which the perspective is drawn. It is a vertical plane and therefore perpendicular to the ground plane. It is represented as a line (picture plane line) on the plan part of the layout and normally is located between the object and the station point or the observer's eye.

Any portion of the object that touches the picture plane will be true size in the perspective drawing. Any portion of the object that is behind the picture plane will appear smaller than scale on the perspective drawing. Parts of the object that are in front of the picture plane (between the plane and the station point) will appear larger than scale in the perspective drawing.

Station point (S.P.). The station point is the location of the observer's eye and therefore the beginning point of the visual rays or sight lines. The rays radiate out from the station point to the object which is represented in the plan view. They pass through the picture plane and locate the various points of the object on the picture plane.

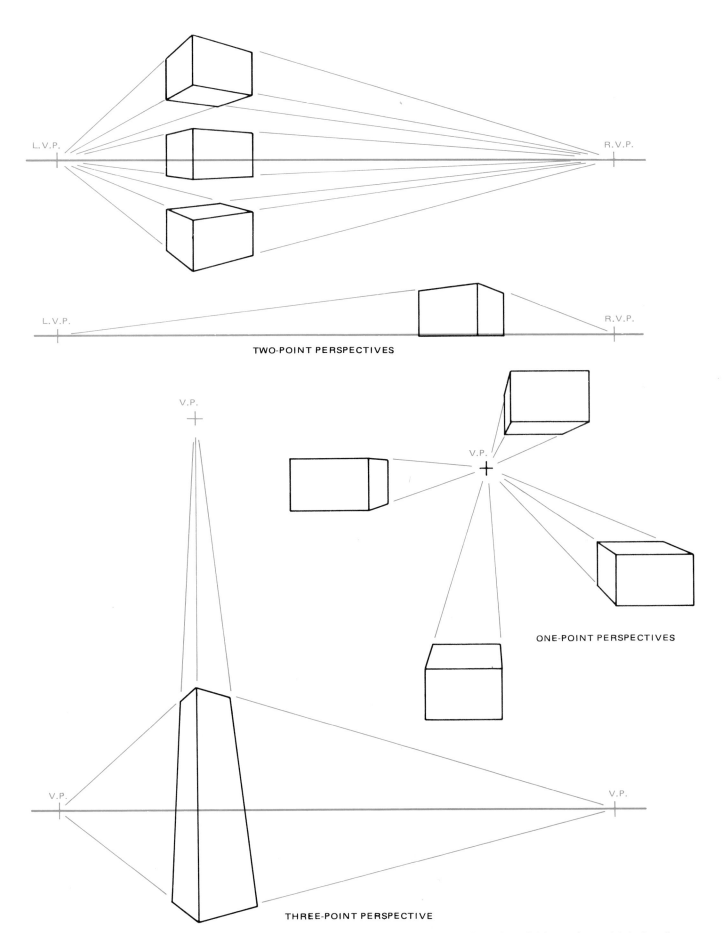

TWO-POINT PERSPECTIVES

ONE-POINT PERSPECTIVES

THREE-POINT PERSPECTIVE

Fig. 29-3. These three basic types of perspectives are so named for the number of vanishing points which they have. Notice how the object lines converge at the vanishing points.

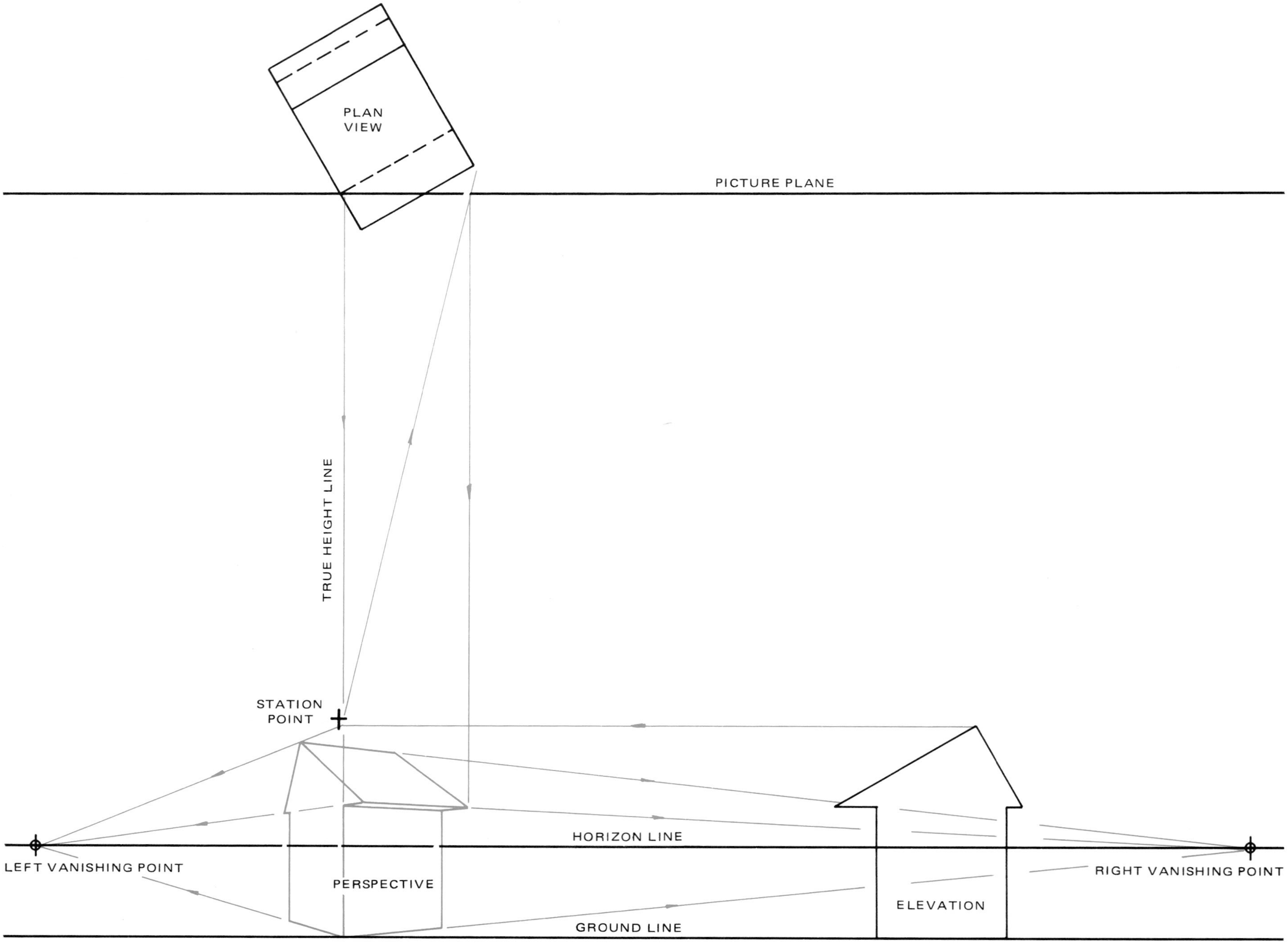

Fig. 29-4. A typical two-point perspective with the parts identified.

PICTURE PLANE

PLAN VIEW

TRUE HEIGHT LINE

STATION POINT

LEFT VANISHING POINT

PERSPECTIVE

HORIZON LINE

GROUND LINE

ELEVATION

RIGHT VANISHING POINT

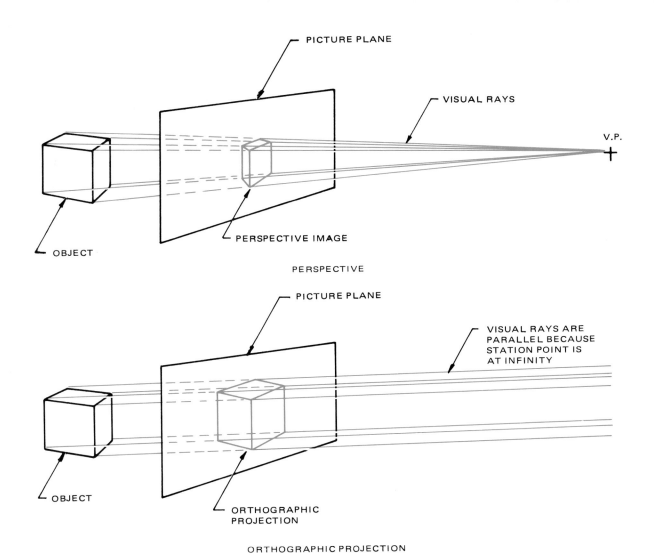

PERSPECTIVE

ORTHOGRAPHIC PROJECTION

Fig. 29-5. In an orthographic projection drawing the station point is infinitely far away. However, it is a finite (measurable) distance in perspective. In both types of drawings the object is drawn as it would appear on an imaginary picture plane.

In two-point perspective, the station point is located only in the plan view. In a one-point perspective it is located in the elevation view as well. In both instances, the distance that the station point is positioned from the picture plane may be measured using the same scale as the plan and elevation drawings.

True length line (T.L.). A true length line or true height line as it is frequently called, is established where the object touches the picture plane. This true length line is used to project heights to the perspective drawing. It is always necessary to find at least one true length line in the perspective drawing so that height measurements may be made. If the object does not touch the picture plane then a side may be extended until it touches the picture plane thus establishing a true length corner.

Vanishing points. One-, two-, or three-point perspectives are named for the number of vanishing points they include. Vanishing points are always located on the horizon line. The sides of

the object recede toward the vanishing points. The sides also become smaller as they approach the point.

A two-point perspective has a right and left vanishing point (R.V.P. and L.V.P.). The procedure for locating these will be discussed later in this chapter. The one-point perspective has one vanishing point and it need not be formally identified, using popular construction techniques, unless desired.

TWO-POINT PERSPECTIVES

Two-point perspectives are especially appropriate for exterior views. They produce a photolike result which is quite accurate in detail. An architectural drafter should be able to draw objects similar to the way they would appear in real life, as this provides an effective way to communicate with prospective clients and other interested parties.

Before beginning to draw a perspective you should be aware that several relationships affect the final perspective drawing and these must be understood and controlled if the resulting drawing is to be satisfactory. These relationships include:

1. *The distance the station point is from the picture plane.* Fig. 29-6 shows how the perspective grows larger as the station point is moved farther away from the picture plane. Proper location of the station point is critical to the final perspective. If it is too close, the drawing will be distorted and unrealistic. In most instances, a station point positioned so that it forms a cone of vision between 30 and 45 degrees is desirable. The procedure for determining this cone of vision is to draw a vertical line down from the corner of the object which touches the picture plane and place a 30 or 45 degree triangle over the line so that 15° or 22 1/2°, depending on the triangle used, fall on either side of the line. When the entire object is within the cone of vision represented by the triangle, the minimum distance has been established for the station point. Fig. 29-7 illustrates the procedure.

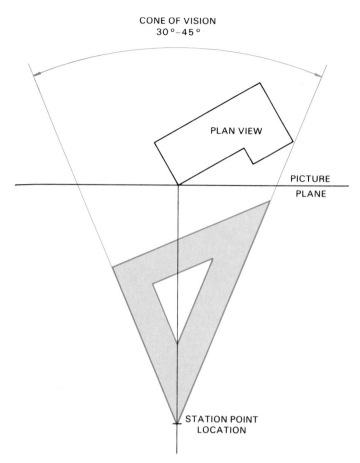

Fig. 29-7. The station point should be far enough away from the picture to include the entire object in the cone of vision.

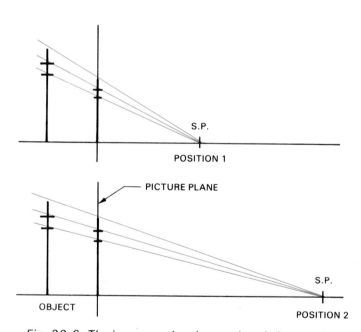

Fig. 29-6. The image on the picture plane is larger when the station point is moved from position 1 farther away to position 2.

The station point may also be moved from side to side. This may improve the viewing position but should not be moved too far either way because distortion will result. The same effect may be accomplished by changing the angle of the plan view with respect to the picture plane, rather than move the station point.

2. *The position of the object with respect to the picture plane.* Two factors are at work. First, the angle that the object forms with the picture plane will affect the portions of the finished drawing, Fig. 29-8. An angle of 30° on one side and 60° on the other is the most common position. This may be varied to suit the particular object.

The second factor relating to the position of the object with respect to the picture plane is whether the object is behind, in front of, or passing through the picture plane, Fig. 29-9. When the object is behind the picture plane, it will appear smaller than one in front of the picture plane. Therefore, size will be dependent on this placement. Also, if the station point is not sufficiently far away when the object is in front of the picture plane, distortion is greatly increased and will likely spoil the drawing.

3. *The vertical height of the station point or horizon line.* The finished result will vary greatly depending on the height of the station point. (Remember that this height is the distance from the ground line to the horizon line in a two-point perspective.) The horizon line may be located

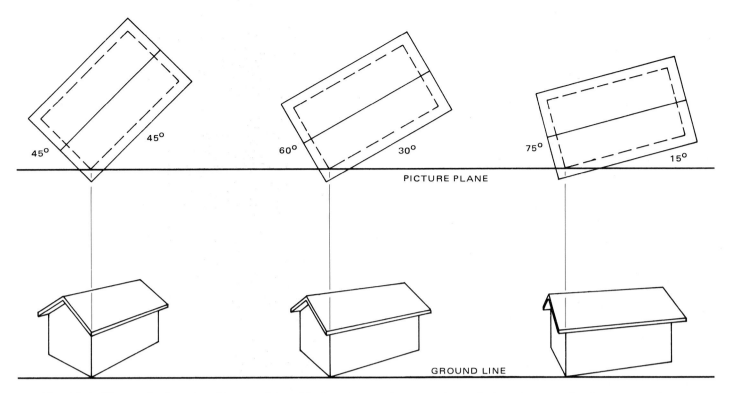

Fig. 29-8. The angle that the object makes with the picture plane may be varied to place emphasis on a certain part of the object.

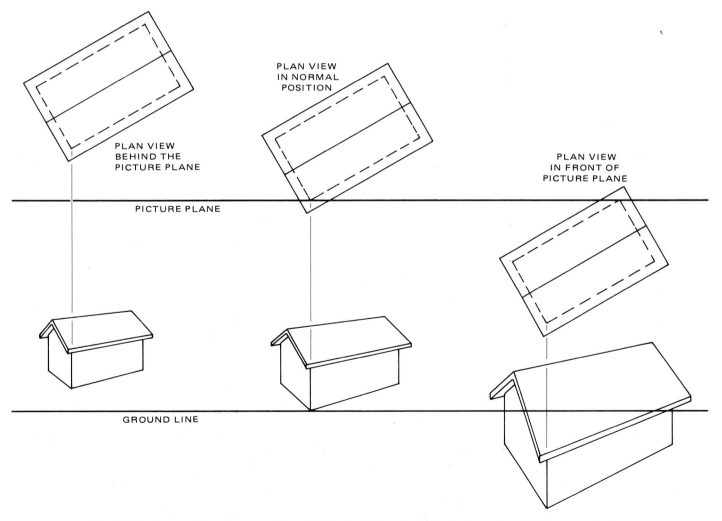

Fig. 29-9. As an object is moved from behind to in front of the picture plane, it increases in size.

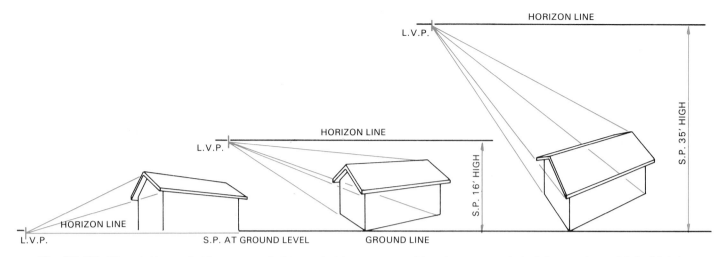

Fig. 29-10. *The station point is commonly located either at ground level, a person's height, or about 30 ft. high in residential perspectives.*

well above the ground line (20-30 ft.), a conventional height of 5 or 6 ft., on the ground line, or below the ground line, Fig. 29-10. Names have been attached to some of these relative positions such as "bird's eye view" and "worm's eye view." The proper height will depend on the particular object and what features are to be emphasized.

These relationships must be kept in mind when laying out a perspective. In starting out only one factor should be varied at a time, to see the effect each has on the final outcome. If several things are changed at once, the effect of a single factor may never be known.

Several methods for drawing two-point perspectives are in use, but the method most frequently used is the **common** or **office method**. The following procedure is used for drawing this type of two-point perspective.

Two-point perspective drawing sequence

1. Draw the plan view or roof. plan of the object on a sheet of drawing paper. Draw an elevation view on a separate sheet of paper. See Fig. 29-11.

2. Secure a large sheet of paper to the drawing table and draw the picture plane line near the top of the sheet, the ground line near the bottom of the sheet, and the horizon line the desired distance above the ground line. These lines must be parallel, Fig. 29-12.

3. Place the plan view or roof plan at a 30° angle with the picture plane so the front corner touches the picture plane. Locate the elevation on the ground line to the extreme right or left side of the paper, Fig. 29-13.

4. Draw a vertical line down from the point where the object touches the picture plane and

PLAN VIEW

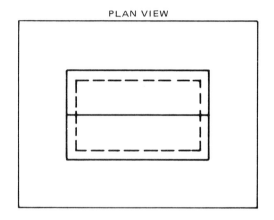

ELEVATION

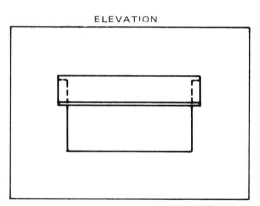

Fig. 29-11. *Procedure for drawing two-point perspective–Step 1.*

locate the station point using the 30 or 45 degree cone of vision procedure, Fig. 29-14.

5. Determine the location of the right and left vanishing points by drawing two construction lines from the station point, parallel to the sides of the object (in the plan view), to the picture plane line. Drop a vertical line from the point where each of these lines intersects the picture plane down to the horizon line. This is the

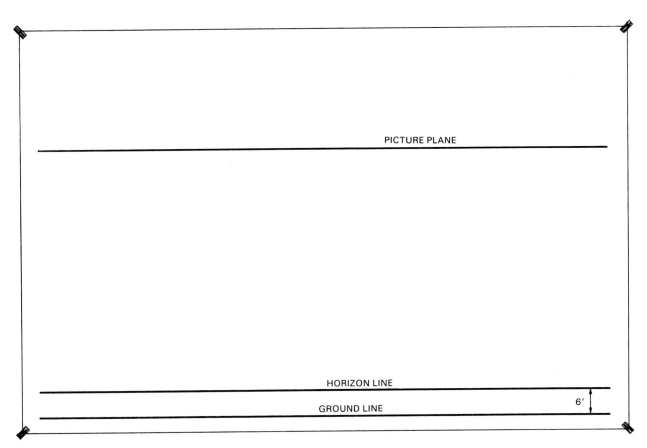

PICTURE PLANE

HORIZON LINE

GROUND LINE

6'

Fig. 29-12. Procedure for drawing two-point perspective–Step 2.

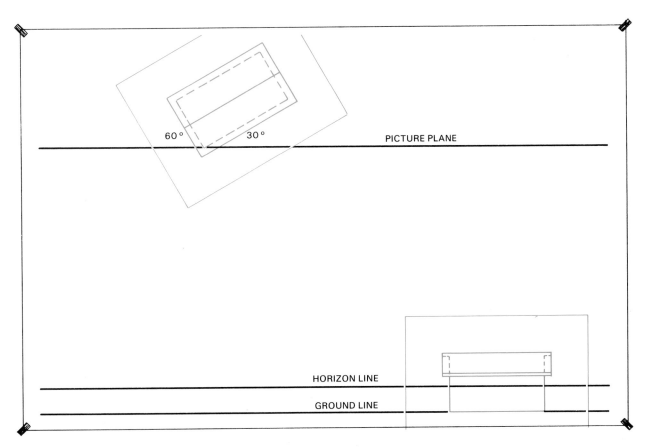

60° 30°

PICTURE PLANE

HORIZON LINE

GROUND LINE

Fig. 29-13. Procedure for drawing two-point perspective–Step 3.

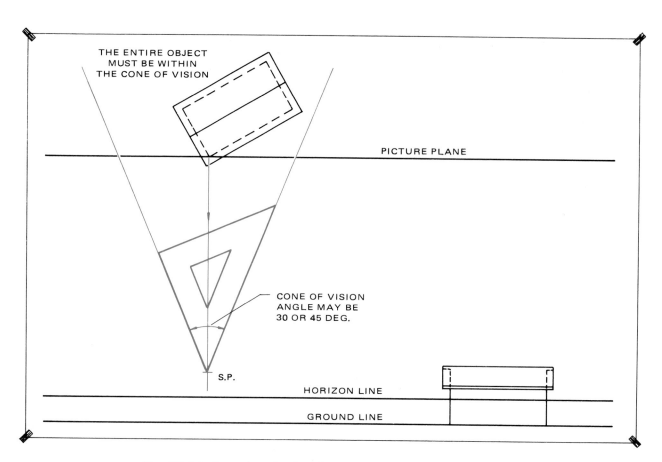

Fig. 29-14. Procedure for drawing two-point perspective—Step 4.

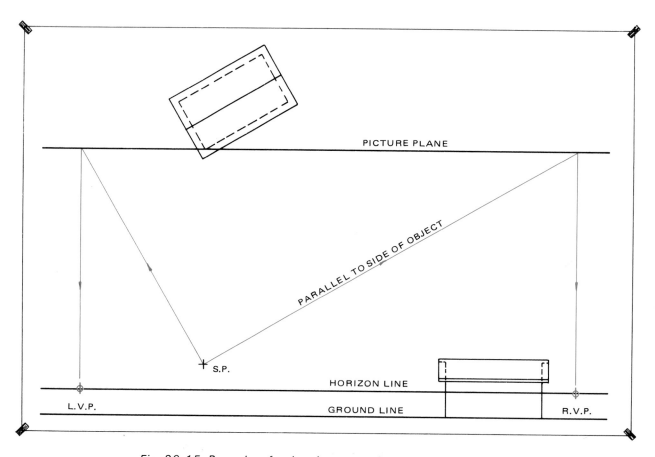

Fig. 29-15. Procedure for drawing two-point perspective—Step 5.

location of the right and left vanishing points, Fig. 29-15.

6. Draw a true height line from the corner of the object which touches the picture plane down to the ground line. Project the object height of that corner to the T.L. line. The distance from the ground line to this point is the true height and location of the object corner in the perspective drawing, Fig. 29-16.

7. Determine the location of the other corners of the object by drawing sight lines from the station point to each corner in the plan view. The place where the sight line crosses the picture plane is projected down to the perspective. Each corner of the object will be on one of these lines, Fig. 29-17.

8. The length and vertical location of these corners may be found by projecting the vertical true length from the true height corner to the vanishing points. Sides of the object that extend away to the right are projected to the right vanishing point and sides which extend to the left are projected to the left vanishing point. Inclined or oblique lines may not be projected to either vanishing point. Their end points must be located and simply connected, Fig. 29-18.

9. The back two sides of the object may be completed by projecting the corners to the van-ishing points. The location where the projection lines cross is the fourth corner. Check the accuracy of your work by drawing a vertical line down from the point where the sight line for the remaining corner crosses the picture plane. It should pass through the point where the two projection lines cross, Fig. 29-19. This corner will not be visible in the finished drawing.

10. The ridge of this object may be found by extending it until it touches the picture plane. This procedure establishes a new T.L. line. Project the height of the ridge over to the T.L. line and project this point to the right vanishing point. The right vanishing point is used because the ridge extends away to the right, Fig. 29-20.

11. Find the length of the ridge in the perspective by extending sight lines from the station point to the ends of the ridge on the plan view. The point where each sight line crosses the picture plane determines the length of the ridge, Fig. 29-21.

12. The roof overhang height may be determined by drawing a new T.L. line down from the point where the overhang crosses the picture plane in the plan view. Project the fascia board width on the elevation over to this T.L. line. The top and bottom edge of the fascia passes through these two points. Project these points to

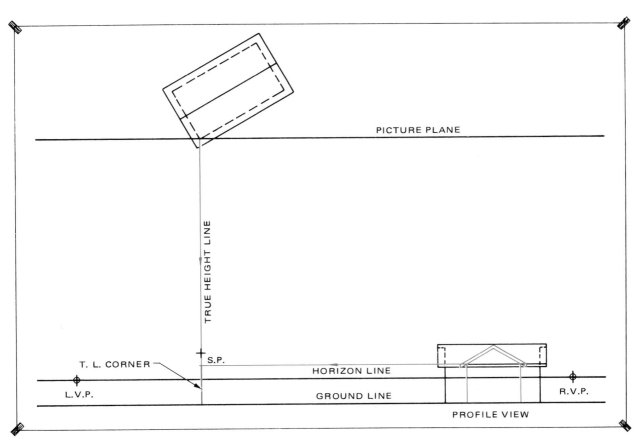

Fig. 29-16. Procedure for drawing two-point perspective—Step 6.

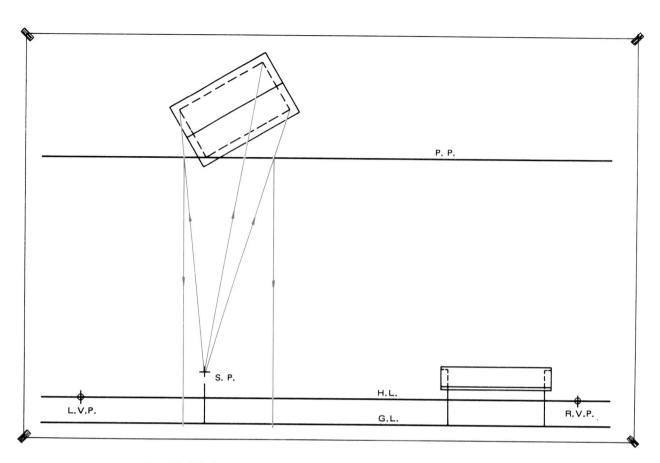

Fig. 29-17. Procedure for drawing two-point perspective—Step 7.

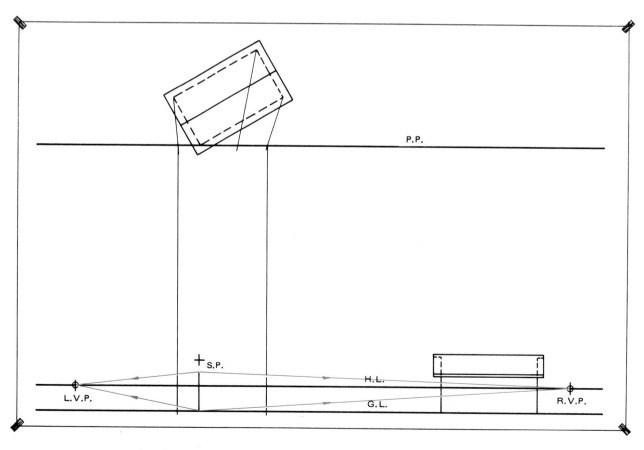

Fig. 29-18. Procedure for drawing two-point perspective—Step 8.

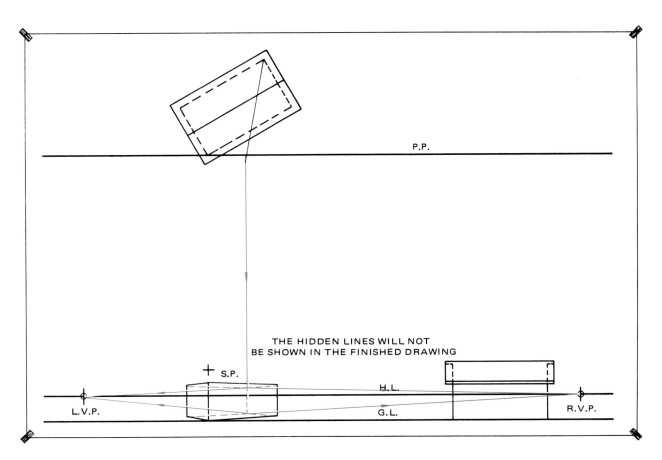

THE HIDDEN LINES WILL NOT
BE SHOWN IN THE FINISHED DRAWING

Fig. 29-19. Procedure for drawing two-point perspective–Step 9.

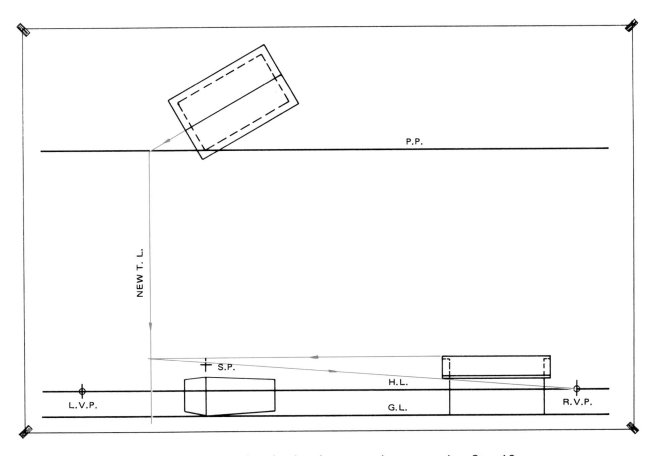

Fig. 29-20. Procedure for drawing two-point perspective–Step 10.

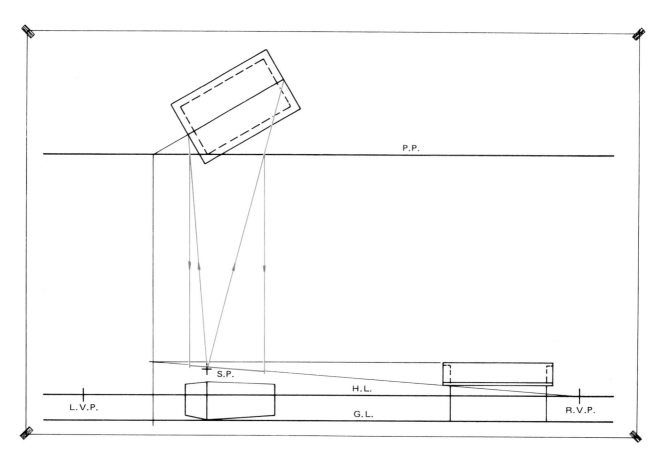

Fig. 29-21. Procedure for drawing two-point perspective—Step 11.

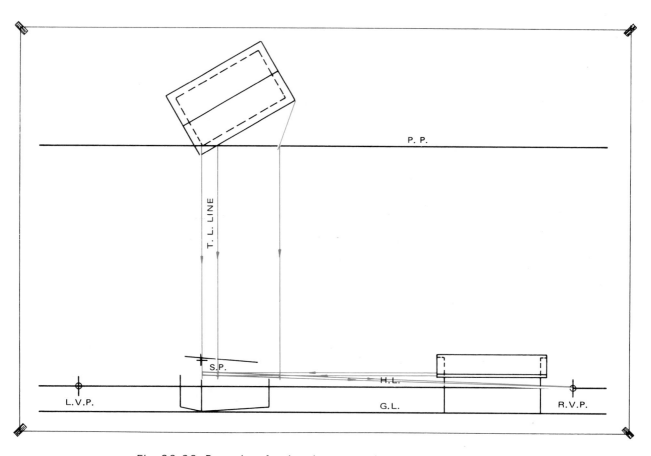

Fig. 29-22. Procedure for drawing two-point perspective—Step 12.

the right vanishing point. The length of the fascia may be determined by extending sight lines from the station point to the corners on the plan view. The points where the sight lines cross the picture plane give the horizontal location for each corner, Fig. 29-22.

13. The perspective may be completed by locating the remaining roof corner and connecting

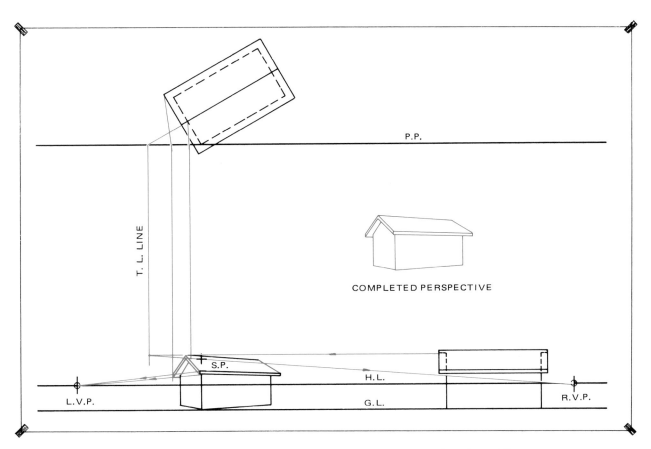

Fig. 29-23. Procedure for drawing two-point perspective–Step 13.

Fig. 29-24. A typical two-point perspective of a residence. This drawing was made by following the steps previously described.

the ridge to the three visible corners. The extreme left corner height is drawn by projecting the top and bottom of the fascia board at the front corner to the left vanishing point and dropping the sight line location from the plan view. Where they cross is the roof corner. Connect the roof corner to the roof ridge. Draw the gable trim boards as shown in Step 6 of the procedure. The peak point of the gable under the roof may be located by finding the point on the plan view and dropping a line down to the perspective. Connect the top of the left corner to this peak point, Fig. 29-23.

Establishing a new T.L. line is useful in rapidly determining the height of features which are not located on the principal sides of the object. Examples of these features are roof ridges, overhangs, and chimneys.

A perspective of a more complex house is shown in Fig. 29-24. Note that the same procedures have been followed in drawing this perspective as the previous example.

ONE-POINT PERSPECTIVES

One-point perspectives are not used as frequently as two-point perspectives, but they are well suited for interior drawings. Room and furniture layouts, kitchen cabinet pictorial details, and interior space studies are all candidates for one-point perspective techniques, Fig. 29-25.

One-point perspectives may also be used for some exterior situations, Fig. 29-26. Entries, courts, porches, and exterior architectural details may sometimes be shown best in one-point perspective, Fig. 29-27.

The procedure for drawing a one-point perspective using the common or office method is similar in some respects to the two-point perspective, but there are several differences. One of the most important differences is the selection of an elevation to provide height measurements. Any elevation was acceptable for the two-point perspective, but a specific elevation is necessary for the one-point perspective. Another difference is that the vanishing point does not have to be located unless desired, in drawing the one-point perspective. The main difference is the most frequent position of the plan view which is placed parallel to the picture plane so that the horizontal and profile planes project to the vanishing point.

One-point perspective drawing sequence

These steps are presented to help clarify the procedure for drawing a common one-point perspective:

1. Select a sheet of drawing paper (about the size of a large drawing board) and draw the plan view near the top left side. With the paper in the same position, draw the right side elevation in the lower right corner. The picture plane should be drawn so that it touches the front of the plan

Fig. 29-25. A room layout drawn in angular one-point perspective.

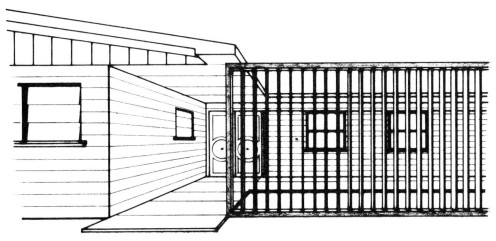

Fig. 29-26. This entrance detail in one-point perspective captures the major design elements as well or better than a two-point perspective could.

Fig. 29-27. An example of the type of exterior layout which lends itself to one-point perspective.

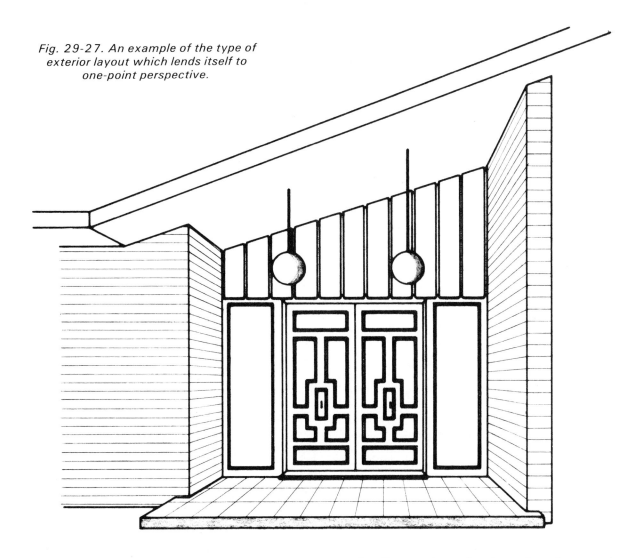

view and the left side of the elevation. Draw the picture plane line in both the plan and elevation views. Study Fig. 29-28 carefully to be sure that you understand which elevation is to be drawn. The space between these drawings (lower left corner) is where the perspective will be drawn.

2. Determine the location from where you wish to view the object. If one side should be emphasized more than the other then move the S.P. to the opposite side slightly. Locate the plan view of the S.P. first. Label it S.P. . This view of the station point indicates how far away and

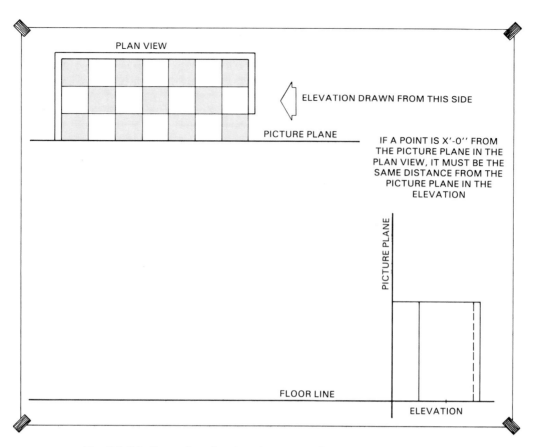

Fig. 29-28. Procedure for drawing one-point perspective–Step 1.

how much to the right or left you are viewing the object. Next, locate the elevation view of the S.P. This view shows the heights of the viewing position. The height is measured from the ground line or floor line vertically. Label this station point S.P., Fig. 29-29. **Both views of the station point must be the same distance from the picture plane.**

3. Any wall or other feature which touches the picture plane will be true size. You may project these points down from the plan view and across from the elevation. Where the lines cross is the location of each feature, Fig. 29-30.

4. Parts which are behind the picture plane will appear smaller than scale in the perspective. They may be drawn by projecting a sight line from the S.P. to each point of the detail in the plan view. Where the sight line crosses the picture plane is the horizontal location of the feature. The vertical location is determined by projecting sight lines from the S.P. to the elevation drawing. Where these lines cross the profile view of the picture plane is the height of each feature. Connect the points together in the perspective to outline each detail, Fig. 29-31.

5. The floor grid may be located by projecting the points which touch the picture plane in the plan view down to the floor line. The grid line ends that touch the back wall must be located by drawing a sight line from the station point to each end. The place where the sight line crosses the picture plane is the horizontal location of the point. The same procedure is followed in the elevation to determine the vertical location of each point. Connect the points, Fig. 29-32.

6. Trace all object lines using the appropriate weight line for each feature. Fig. 29-33 shows the completed perspective.

Fig. 29-34 shows a typical one-point perspective of a kitchen. The procedures involved in this drawing were exactly the same as those shown in the step-by-step drawing sequence.

PERSPECTIVE GRIDS

One of the problems in constructing a two-point perspective is the large size layout. It is not uncommon for the vanishing points to be five feet or more apart for a residence. The use of a perspective grid, Fig. 29-35, will reduce the size of work space needed and time required to draw a large perspective. The chief disadvantage is the limited freedom in choosing the position of the station point and placement of the picture plane. Many grid variations are available, but

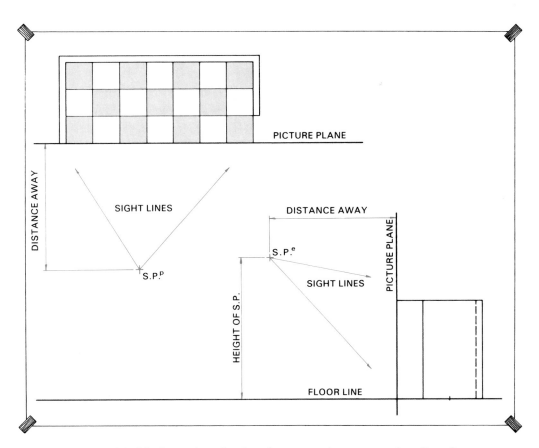

PICTURE PLANE

DISTANCE AWAY

SIGHT LINES

S.P.^{p}

DISTANCE AWAY

S.P.^{e}

SIGHT LINES

PICTURE PLANE

HEIGHT OF S.P.

FLOOR LINE

Fig. 29-29. Procedure for drawing one-point perspective–Step 2.

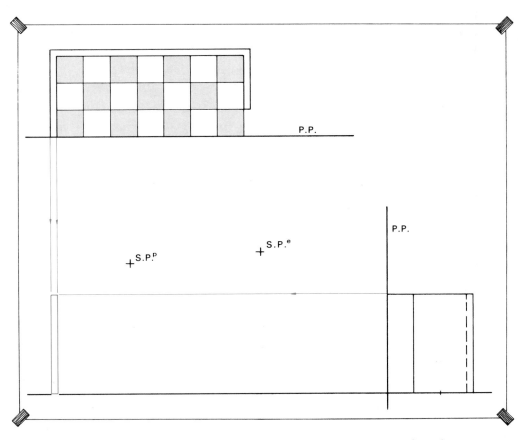

P.P.

+S.P.^{p}

+S.P.^{e}

P.P.

Fig. 29-30. Procedure for drawing one-point perspective–Step 3.

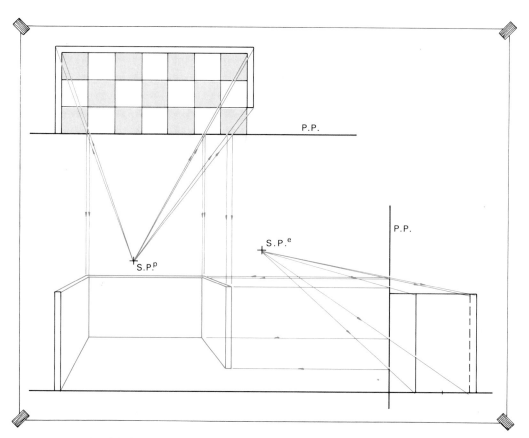

Fig. 29-31. Procedure for drawing one-point perspective—Step 4.

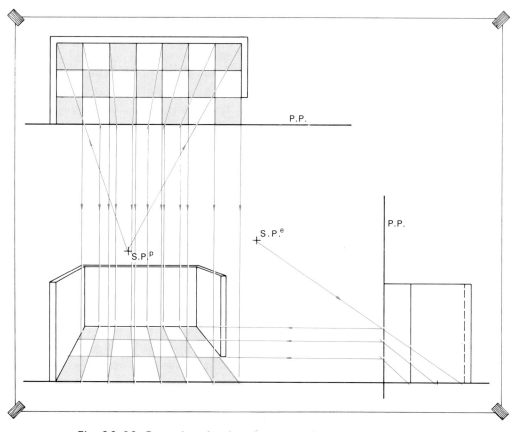

Fig. 29-32. Procedure for drawing one-point perspective—Step 5.

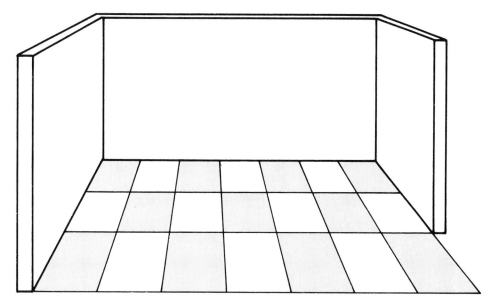

Fig. 29-33. Procedure for drawing one-point perspective – Step 6.

each is for a specific layout and several would be required if the best position were to be achieved in each drawing.

A thorough understanding of perspectives is necessary before grids may be used effectively. A grid will not ensure a successful drawing if the person using it is not skillful in drawing perspectives beforehand.

PERSPECTIVES OF COMPLEX FEATURES

Frequently, objects to be drawn in perspective contain elements that are not parallel to any of the principle reference planes, or are circular or curved. Such features may appear to be difficult to draw. Described in the following paragraphs

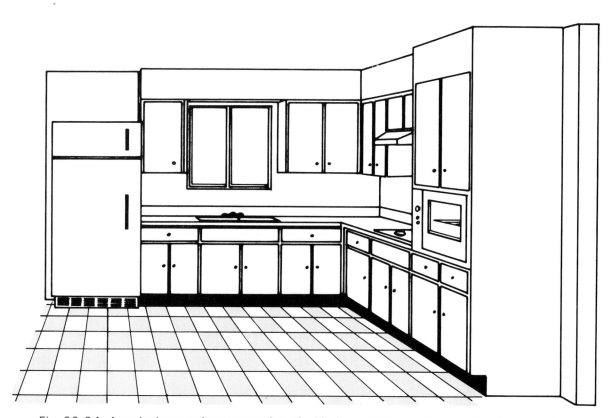

Fig. 29-34. A typical one-point perspective of a kitchen which was drawn using the procedure presented in steps 1 through 6. (David Brownlee)

Fig. 29-35. A perspective grid used for drawing two-point perspectives.

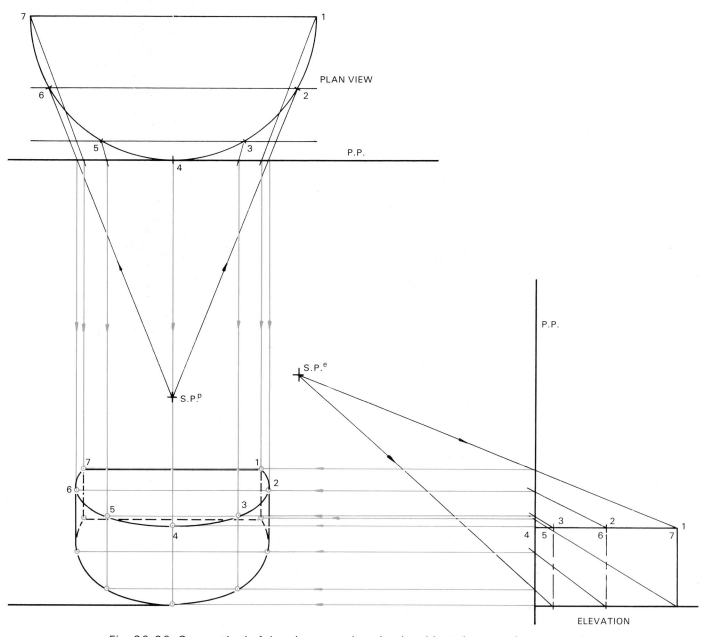

Fig. 29-36. One method of drawing curved or circular objects in one-point perspective.

are simple techniques which should be helpful:

Objects that are circular such as a round top table or oval area rug may be easily drawn if a series of points or a grid is superimposed over the surface to be drawn, Fig. 29-36. Several points on the curve may be located which define the details of the surface. Locate the points and draw the curve with a French or irregular curve. Other objects that have a series of soft curves such as a sofa or chair may be drawn as though they had hard and sharp lines and then softened freehand, Fig. 29-37. Still other objects which involve a great deal of free form must be boxed in and then drawn freehand within the space designated, Fig. 29-38.

Remember that the drawing of any object is only a series of connected points. If a sufficient number of points are located and connected accurately, the result will be true to form. Reduce

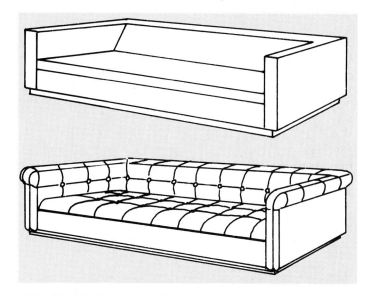

Fig. 29-37. An object with soft curves such as this sofa, may be ''blocked in'' first and then softened freehand.

Fig. 29-38. The details of this sofa and chair were drawn freehand after the basic shapes were boxed in perspective. (Darlana Fowler)

complex objects to simple parts and construct them one at a time rather than try to locate all points and then connect them. Once you understand the procedure used in drawing perspectives you will be able to draw complex objects by applying the procedure over and over again.

REVIEW QUESTIONS—CHAPTER 29

Write your answers on a separate sheet of paper. Do not write in this book.
1. Name three types of pictorial drawings that are used as presentation drawings.
2. Identify the three basic types of perspectives.
3. The type of perspective commonly used for exterior views is _____.
4. The ground line is drawn in the _____ part of the perspective layout.
5. The distance between the ground line and the horizon line represents the _____.
6. An edge in the perspective view is true height when _____.
7. Parts of the object which are in front of the picture plane appear _____ than scale.
8. The position of the observer's eye is called the _____.
9. In a perspective layout, how do you show the distance that an observer is standing away from the picture plane?
10. All heights on a perspective must be measured on the _____.
11. Vanishing points are always located on the _____ line.
12. A two-point perspective has _____ vanishing points.
13. If a station point were moved from 20 ft. to 30 ft. away from the picture plane, the perspective would _____ in size.
14. The standard angle at which objects are usually placed with respect to the picture plane is _____.
15. One may determine the closest place to stand to draw a perspective by _____.
16. If the station point is too close to the picture plane, the perspective may be spoiled because of _____.
17. Identify three common heights used in drawing two-point perspectives.
18. If the station point is moved closer to the picture plane, how will this affect the distance between the vanishing points in a two-point perspective?
19. One-point perspectives are well suited for _____ type views.
20. Heights are determined in a one-point perspective by _____.
21. The main disadvantage of using a perspective grid is _____.
22. The construction technique that may be used to draw a circular object in perspective is _____.

SUGGESTED ACTIVITIES

1. Using a simple straight-line object supplied by your instructor, draw several two-point perspectives from different distances and positions. Identify how far away and how high the station point was in each drawing.
2. Draw a two-point perspective of a small residence. Trace the finished drawing on vellum in ink. Display your work in class.
3. Look through old issues of Better Homes and Gardens, House and Home, House Beautiful, Home Modernizing Guide, or similar magazines and cut out perspective drawings of homes. Mount these pictures for display.
4. Select a large photograph (not a drawing) of a home or building from a magazine and mount it on a piece of illustration board or stiff paper. Locate the horizon line and vanishing points and label each.

Presentation Drawings

After studying this chapter, you will be able to:
- List methods commonly used to increase the degree of realism in a presentation plan.
- Render common materials using a variety of techniques.
- Demonstrate ability to ink a rendering.
- Devise a typical presentation floor plan.
- Demonstrate the ability to represent typical entourage' symbols.

The purpose of a presentation drawing is to show the finished structure. It can also present various parts of the building in a form that is more meaningful than construction drawings. Presentation drawings are shown to those people who are interested in the structure, such as the owner. They are generally rendered to enhance their appearance.

RENDERING

Presentation plans require a degree of realism which may be accomplished through rendering,

Fig. 30-1. Shades, shadows, and textures provide much more realism that just clear sharp lines. For this reason, presentation drawings are usually rendered using one or more of the common techniques.

Several methods of rendering presentation drawings are popular. They include:

Pencil	Water Color
Ink	Scratch Board
Tempera	Applique'
Colored Pencils	Air Brush
Magic Markers	Combination of Techniques

Each of these methods has advantages which should be considered before beginning the project.

PENCIL RENDERING

Pencil rendering is popular and probably the easiest. No special materials are needed and the product is highly acceptable if well done. Pencils softer than those generally used for construction type drawings are used. One of the problems

Fig. 30-1. This two-point perspective rendering shows a realistic picture of a Spanish design home.
(Ken Hawk)

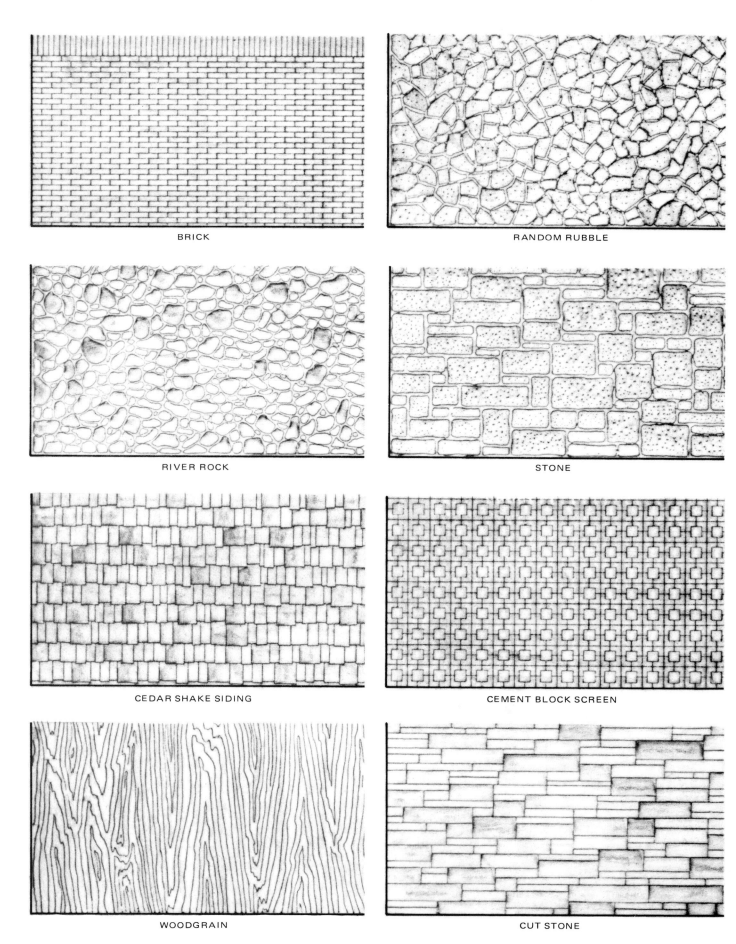

BRICK

RANDOM RUBBLE

RIVER ROCK

STONE

CEDAR SHAKE SIDING

CEMENT BLOCK SCREEN

WOODGRAIN

CUT STONE

Fig. 30-2. Common exterior materials rendered in pencil.

encountered in pencil rendering is the difficulty in keeping the drawing clean. A good procedure is to cover the surrounding area to prevent smudges and smears.

Several common exterior materials are shown in Fig. 30-2 to illustrate the effect that may be achieved by using a pencil rendering technique. An ink drawing rendered in pencil by a student is shown in Fig. 30-3.

INK RENDERING

Renderings to be used for reproduction are best done in ink. Lines are sharper and fine detail is possible with ink, Fig. 30-4. Ink can be used to shade areas also. This is accomplished with a series of parallel lines, dot pattern, or solid shading. Drawing inks are produced in a broad spectrum of colors which are also quite useful in rendering, Fig. 30-5. Various materials and techniques are often combined in a single rendering.

WATER COLOR RENDERING

Water color rendering is one of the most effective forms, Fig. 30-6. Vivid colors or broad expanses of light wash (very little paint with lots of water) are possible with water color. This type

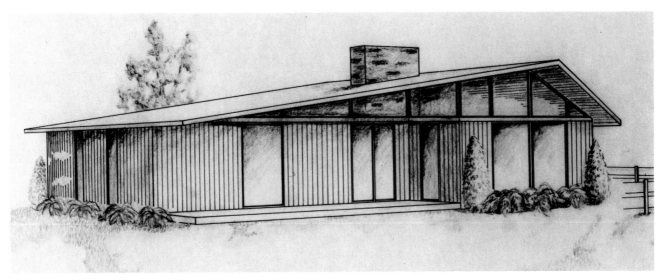

Fig. 30-3. An inked drawing rendered in pencil by a beginning student.

Fig. 30-4. A pen and ink drawing with tremendous detail and depth. (The Garlinghouse Company)

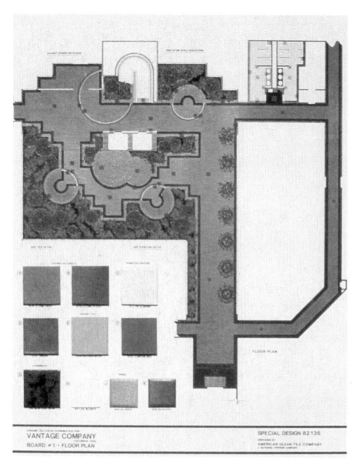

Fig. 30-5. Bright colors and striking contrasts were achieved using colored drawing inks in this illustration. (American Olean Tile Company)

Fig. 30-7. Water color rendering produces a very realistic effect. (The Garlinghouse Company)

TEMPERA RENDERING

Tempera paint is also a type of water soluble paint. It differs from water color (transparent) in that it is opaque. Tempera is frequently used for monotone renderings as shown in Fig. 30-8. Advantages of this technique include a broad selection of colors which maybe obtained by mixing and the ease of mending mistakes if the brush slips or the color is not satisfactory.

COLORED PENCIL RENDERING

Colored pencils may be used to obtain satisfactory rendering. Light shades or strong strokes

of rendering is one of the most difficult to execute. Practice and patience are necessary to develop this technique. A water color rendering is shown in Fig. 30-7.

Fig. 30-6. A faithful reproduction of a house in water colors. (Ken Hawk)

are easily accomplished. Even the beginning student can achieve success with this technique, Fig. 30-9. Either regular colored pencils or water color pencils may be used. Drawings rendered in water color pencil may be presented simply as a colored pencil rendering or transformed into a water color by adding water with a brush.

MAGIC MARKER RENDERING

Certain types of presentation drawings may be effectively rendered using magic markers or felt tip pens. Presentation plot plans are frequently rendered using these types of pens. The result is distinct and differs greatly from other

Fig. 30-8. A monotone type rendering in tempera. (The Aladdin Co.)

Fig. 30-9. The basic technique used in this rendering is colored pencil. It has been combined with ink and water colors.
(Ed Fegan)

techniques. Fine detail may be accomplished by mixing other techniques with the marker. Fig. 30-10 shows a perspective loosely rendered in felt tip pen.

SCRATCH BOARD RENDERING

Scratch board rendering produces a drawing with a great deal of character. Lines are scratched through a special black-coated illustration board-type material. The result is a drawing of white lines on a black background. Such a rendering commands attention from the viewer. Figs. 30-11 shows one type of scratch board rendering.

APPLIQUE' RENDERING

Applique' rendering is accomplished by attaching a pressure-sensitive transparent film over a drawing. The film may be a series of dots, lines, symbols, or color. Several manufacturers

are producing these films and it is possible to achieve striking results with them. Fig. 30-12 shows a computer drawing rendered using applique'-like technique.

AIR BRUSH RENDERING

Air brush renderings are frequently produced by professional illustrators. Again, a great deal of practice is required to be able to produce a fine quality rendering using this technique. An air brush is simply an air nozzle which sprays paint or colored ink. If examined closely you will find the surface of the rendering is covered with many small dots of color which form subtle shades and shadows, Fig. 30-13. Areas not be sprayed should be blocked out with paper or rubber cement since it is difficult to accurately control the spray.

Techniques described here represent the majority used for rendering presentation plans. Each requires a certain amount of artistic ability and skill to produce a satisfactory rendering. The

Fig. 30-10. Felt tip pen has been used in this loose but effective rendering.

Fig. 30-11. Scratch board rendering.

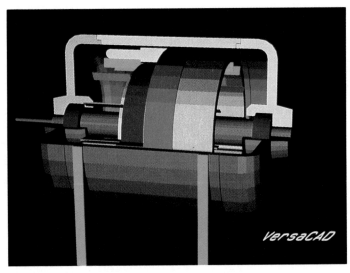

Fig. 30-12. An example of a computer-generated applique' illustration created using VersaCAD DESIGN software. (Versacad Corporation, Huntington Beach, CA)

ability to prepare renderings is well worth developing.

ENTOURAGE'

Entourage' (pronounced ''n-tur-ahge'') refers to surroundings such as trees, shrubs, cars, people, and terrain. These features add to the realism of a drawing and show an architectural structure in its proper setting. Entourage' is usually drawn to represent objects in simplified form rather than trying to make them look exactly as they would appear. Architects usually develop a personal style of drawing entourage'. For those who feel inadequate in drawing these features; appliques', rub-on symbols, and rubber stamps

Fig. 30-13. These air brush renderings illustrate the realism possible using this technique. (Progress Lighting)

are available which may be used to add a professional appearance to their drawings. Fig. 30-14 shows some entourage' symbols that are representative of those commonly used by architects. Always draw surroundings to the proper scale.

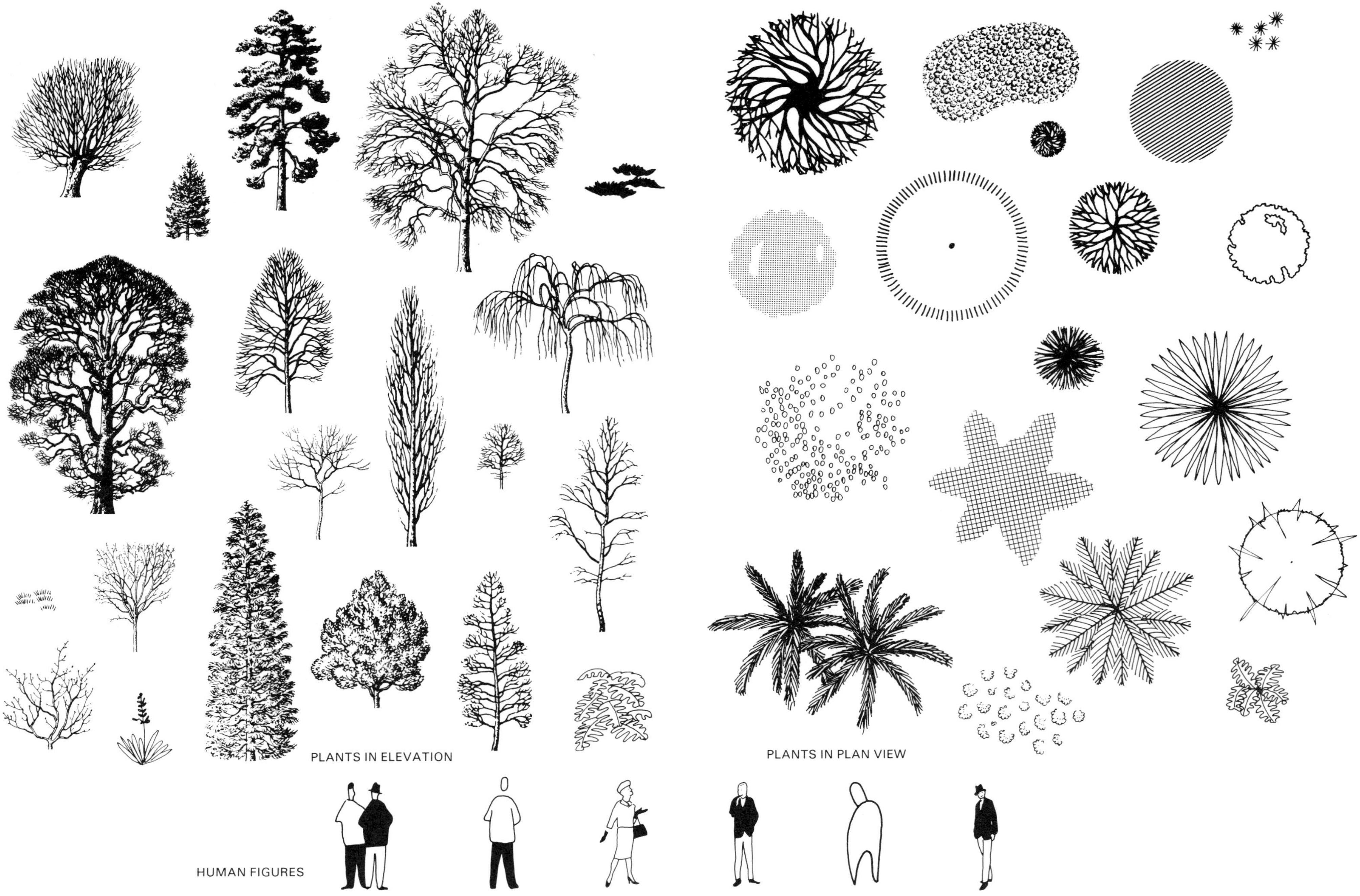

PLANTS IN PLAN VIEW

PLANTS IN ELEVATION

HUMAN FIGURES

Fig. 30-14. Typical entourage' symbols.

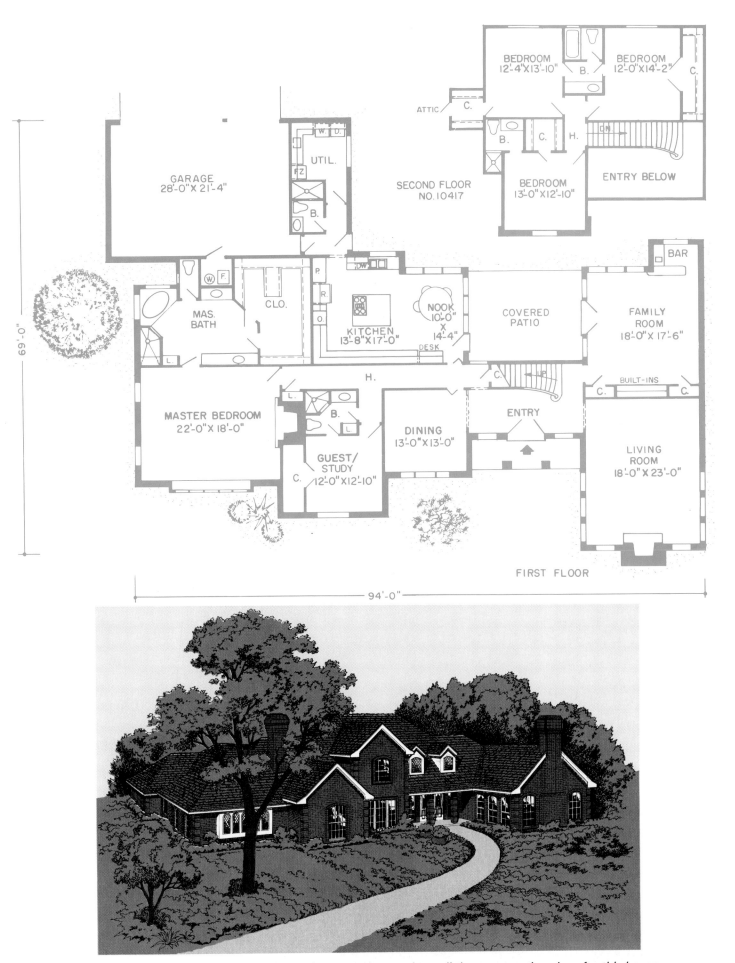

SECOND FLOOR
NO. 10417

BEDROOM
12'-4"X13'-10"

BEDROOM
12'-0"X14'-2"

B.

C.

ATTIC

C.

B.

C.

H.

DN

BEDROOM
13'-0"X12'-10"

ENTRY BELOW

GARAGE
28'-0" X 21'-4"

UTIL.

W. D.

FZ

B.

MAS.
BATH

W.

F.

CLO.

P.

R.

O.

DW

KITCHEN
13'-8"X17'-0"

NOOK
10'-0"
X
14'-4"

DESK

COVERED
PATIO

BAR

FAMILY
ROOM
18'-0" X 17'-6"

BUILT-INS

C.

C.

C.

UP

H.

MASTER BEDROOM
22'-0"X 18'-0"

L.

B.

L.

GUEST/
STUDY
12'-0"X12'-10"

C.

DINING
13'-0"X13'-0"

ENTRY

LIVING
ROOM
18'-0" X 23'-0"

69'-0"

94'-0"

FIRST FLOOR

Fig. 30-15. A presentation floor plan and perspective used to sell the construction plans for this house. (The Garlinghouse Company)

Information regarding appropriate sizes of surroundings may be obtained from the Architectural Graphic Standards.

TYPES OF PRESENTATION PLANS

Several types of presentation drawings are used to represent a structure. Exterior and interior perspectives, rendered elevations, presentation plot plans, floor plans, and sections are commonly prepared to help ''sell'' the plan to a prospective client. These drawings are designed to present the structure to the layperson who may not understand a set of construction drawings in an accurate and honest manner. They may also be used for advertising and other purposes, Fig. 30-15.

EXTERIOR PERSPECTIVES

The exterior perspective should present the structure as accurately as possible. Distortion, if permitted, could misrepresent the appearance and create a false impression. Fig. 30-16 shows a home which is faithfully represented. Fig. 30-17 shows an elaborate home rendered in such a

Fig. 30-16. A two-point exterior perspective of an earth sheltered home. (The Garlinghouse Company)

Fig. 30-17. This rendering emphasizes the luxury of this modern home. (Larry Campbell)

NORTH

WEST

SOUTH

EAST

Fig. 30-18. Presentation elevations are sometimes used to represent a residential structure rather than a perspective, as this example of the home in Fig. 30-17 shows.

manner that the exquisite design is emphasized. Both examples are accurate representations of the actual homes.

RENDERED ELEVATIONS

An elevation is an orthographic-type drawing which shows no depth. The addition of material symbols, trees, and other surrounding features can transform an elevation into an effective presentation drawing, Fig. 30-18. Even though no depth is shown in the structure, the feeling of depth is accomplished through shades, shadows, textures, and surroundings. Presentation elevations are frequently used instead of exterior perspectives because they are faster to draw and if presented well, are usually quite satisfactory, Fig. 30-19.

PRESENTATION PLOT PLANS

Presentation plot pans are used to show the site and structure relationship. This is essentially a plan view of the site showing important topo-

Fig. 30-19. A presentation elevation rendered in colored pencil by a student. (A. Sewell)

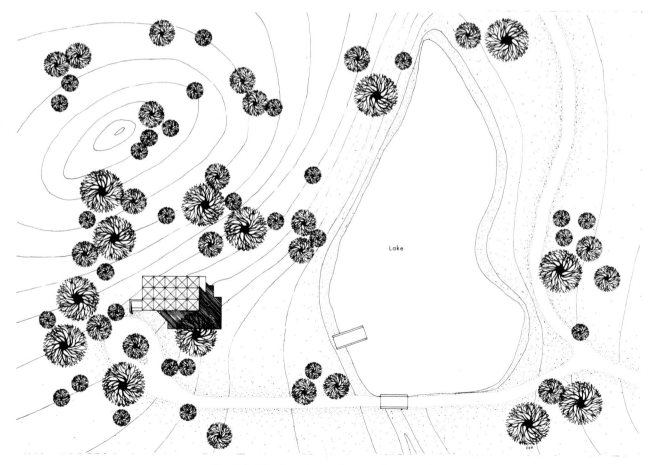

Fig. 30-20. An ink rendering of a site plan.

Fig. 30-21. Presentation plot plan of residence in Fig. 30-17 drawn over elevation of the plot.

graphical features, house location, and property boundaries. The presentation plot plan gives a "bird's eye" view of the layout and provides an opportunity to show off the type of living afforded by the surroundings.

Several styles of presentation plot plans are possible. Figs. 30-20 and 30-21 show two different treatments.

PRESENTATION FLOOR PLANS

Presentation floor plans may be used to emphasize features such as furniture arrangement, area utilization, and conveniences, Fig. 30-22. Color may be utilized to call attention to similar features or to separate areas. The color should be functional if possible rather than used just to "color" the drawings. The specific use intended for the drawing should be evident by the presentation technique utilized. Figs. 30-23 and 30-24 show contrasting styles of presentation floor plans.

RENDERED SECTIONS

Frequently, a complex structure requires a longitudinal section to emphasize the various levels. Such a plan is effective in communicating the internal layout of the house. Fig. 30-25 is an example of such a drawing. The realistic way in which information is presented helps to clarify the plan.

Presentation plans are being used more and more to communicate ideas. People understand

Lower floor plan

Upper floor plan

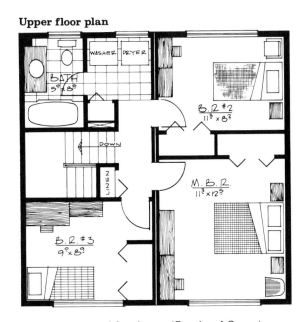

Fig. 30-22. A presentation floor plan with emphasis on space and furniture. (Fruehauf Corp.)

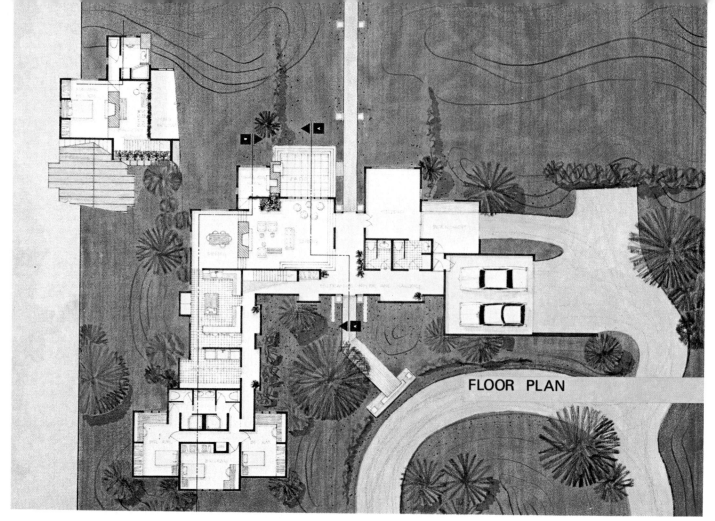

FLOOR PLAN

Fig. 30-23. This presentation floor plan of the home in Fig. 30-17 is rendered in ink and colored chalk. (Larry Campbell)

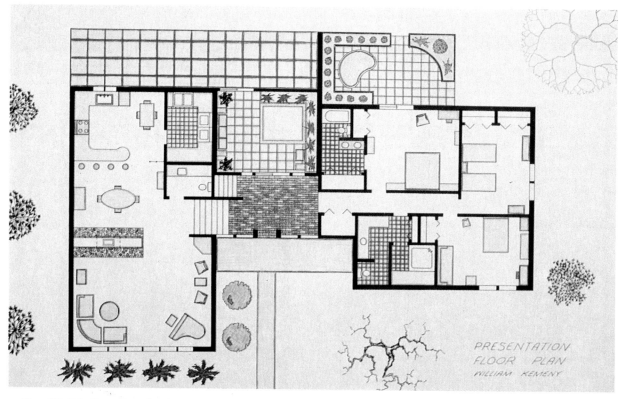

PRESENTATION
FLOOR PLAN
WILLIAM KEMENT

Fig. 30-24. Functional color was used in this presentation floor plan to achieve greater communication.
(William Kement)

SECTION ◼AA◼

SECTION ◼BB◼

Fig. 30-25. Rendered sections of residence shown in Fig. 30-17 provide an effective means of illustrating complex structures. (Larry Campbell)

Fig. 30-26. Computer-generated perspective created using VersaCAD DESIGN software. (Versacad Corporation, Huntington Beach, CA)

architectural ideas better if they are presented in a manner in which they are accustomed. Presentation plans do just that and are therefore very useful, Figs. 30-26 and 30-27. They do require talents and skills which technical drawings do not, but they are definitely an integral part of architectural drawing and should be mastered by the architect.

REVIEW QUESTIONS–CHAPTER 30

Write your answers on a separate sheet of paper. Do not write in this book.
1. The purpose of rendering is _____.
2. Identify six common methods of rendering.
3. The most popular rendering technique is _____.
4. Renderings to be used for reproduction are best done in _____.
5. A rendering which uses a pressure-sensi-

tive transparent film over the drawing is called _____ rendering.
6. Professional illustrators frequently use _____ rendering for their work.
7. What is entourage'?
8. What is the function of entourage' on a presentation drawing.
9. Identify the five types of presentation plans which may be used to ''sell'' a residential structure.
10. A rendered elevation is a(n) _____-type drawing which shows no depth.
11. Name three features commonly represented by presentation floor plans.

SUGGESTED ACTIVITIES

1. Place a piece of tracing paper over the photograph used in Activity No. 4 in Chapter 29 and make a rendering in pencil. Do the

Patio Deck
16' x 12'

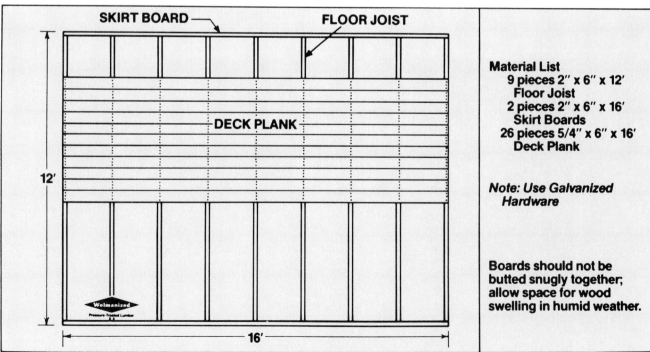

SKIRT BOARD — **FLOOR JOIST**

DECK PLANK

12'

16'

Wolmanized
Pressure Treated Lumber

Material List
9 pieces 2" x 6" x 12' **Floor Joist**
2 pieces 2" x 6" x 16' **Skirt Boards**
26 pieces 5/4" x 6" x 16' **Deck Plank**

Note: Use Galvanized Hardware

Boards should not be butted snugly together; allow space for wood swelling in humid weather.

Fig. 30-27. These drawings are effective communication devices because they are easily understood. (The Wolman Group)

drawing freehand. Compare your drawing with the photograph.

2. Collect renderings of architectural structures from magazines or brochures. Display these for style and inspiration in the drawing room.

3. Select a simple construction-type floor plan and develop a presentation floor plan which emphasizes the furniture layout.

4. Render the two-point perspective that you drew for Activity No. 2 in Chapter 29. Use a technique specified by your instructor or one of your choice.

5. Draw a one-point perspective of one of the rooms in the house used for the presentation floor plan in No. 3 above or one of your own design. Illustrate the furniture in your perspective.

6. Render the interior perspective above in color. Mount it on illustration board if drawn on paper. Display your drawing on the bulletin board.

7. Develop a presentation plot plan showing property boundaries, house location, drive, walks, and topographical features. Present the plan in color and display.

This collage of photos shows the detail possible in an architectural model. These photos are of the interior of the dome home shown in Fig. 31-5. The scale of this model is 1'' = 1'-0''.

Architectural Models

After studying this chapter, you will be able to:
* Explain the various types of architectural models used to represent residential structures.
* List the features commonly included in a presentation model.
* Summarize the steps for constructing a balsa wood model.

An architectural model provides the ultimate means of showing how the finished home will look in all three dimensions. The model may be viewed from any position and greatly increases the amount of information communicated. Models are useful in checking the finished appearance of an architectural design and ''selling'' a design to a client.

TYPES OF MODELS

Several types of models are used to represent architectural structures. One type is the **small scale solid model,** Fig. 31-1. This is frequently used to show how a building will relate to surrounding buildings. Scales used range from 1/32'' = 1'-0'' to 1/8'' = 1'-0''. Very little detail is shown on solid models.

Structural models are frequently used to show features of a residence. All structural materials used should be cut to scale and proper building methods represented, Fig. 31-2. Structural models are usually 1/2'' = 1'-0'' or 1'' = 1'-0'' scale. If the scale is too small, the materials will be difficult to work with. Since the purpose of a structural model is to show the basic construction, most siding and roofing materials are left off to expose the structural aspects, Fig. 31-3. This type of model is useful when unique construction procedures are to be used, Fig. 31-4.

Most residential models are **presentation models.** The purpose of a presentation model is to

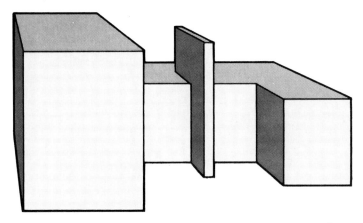

Fig. 31-1. A small scale solid model is frequently used to study the mass of a building or show its relation to surrounding buildings.

Fig. 31-2. A structural model under construction using materials cut to the proper scale. (Harry Smith)

Fig. 31-3. Structural models show the framing of a building.

Fig. 31-4. This A-frame cottage has unique construction. Students are working as a group on this model.
(Harry Smith)

show appearance of the finished building as realistically as possible, Fig. 31-5. A primary concern is to select materials that will closely resemble materials used in actual construction. Presentation models are usually 1/4'' = 1'-0'' scale. They may be larger or smaller depending on the amount of detail desired, size of the structure, and funds available for model construction.

MATERIALS USED IN MODEL CONSTRUCTION

There are several basic materials which are commonly used for architectural model construction. Some model builders prefer Styrofoam® sheets. This material is easy to cut and may be made to resemble various exterior building materials. Styrofoam® is easy to glue and may be painted with various kinds of paint. However, it is soft and may be scratched or easily broken. Fig. 31-6 shows a residential model made from foam board and illustration board.

Another popular material for architectural models is cardboard or illustration board. This material is easy to obtain, glues well, and may be painted with almost any type of paint. Two disadvantages are: cardboard warps easily and it must be cut with a knife or razor-type blade rather than by sawing. Pin holes are also more visible than with other materials.

A popular material for building models of homes is balsa wood. Balsa is available in a wide variety of sizes and is easy to cut with a sharp knife. It receives a finish well, and may be sawed or sanded and scored to represent exterior mate-

rials. A balsa model does not warp as much as cardboard and is stronger.

Procedure for constructing balsa model

The following procedure (typical) is presented as an aid to building a presentation-type balsa model with a removable roof:

1. Obtain a set of plans for the home which is to be built. If the plans are not 1/4'' = 1'-0'' then they should be drawn to that scale. (In some instances it may be desirable to build a model to some other scale, but the majority of residential models are 1/4'' = 1'-0'' scale.) In most instances only the floor plan, Fig. 31-7, and elevations, Fig. 31-8, will be needed to build the model. However, if the building site is not flat, a plot plan should be drawn using the same scale as the other plans. It is usually not necessary to draw the entire site at 1/4'' = 1'-0'' scale, but only the portion represented by the model. If the roof is complex, it may be desirable to develop a roof plan, Fig. 31-9, to aid in building the roof.

2. A decision must be made concerning the site of the base for the model. A prime consideration to be remembered is storage and handling.

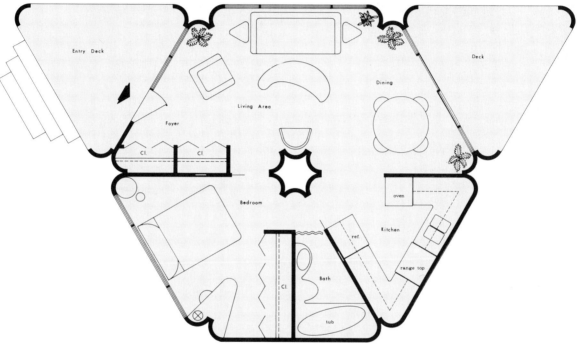

Fig. 31-5. New and unique types of construction frequently are modeled before actual construction.

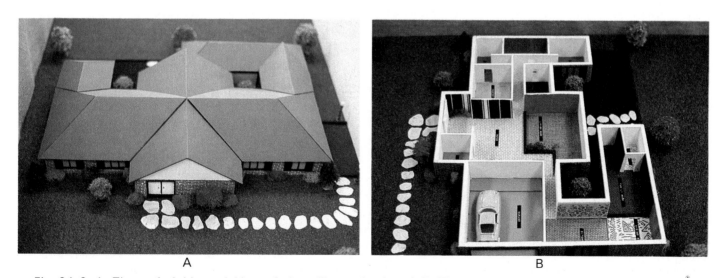

A   B

Fig. 31-6. A–The roof of this model is made from illustration board. B–The exterior walls are made from Styrofoam® sheets. Interior walls are illustration board.

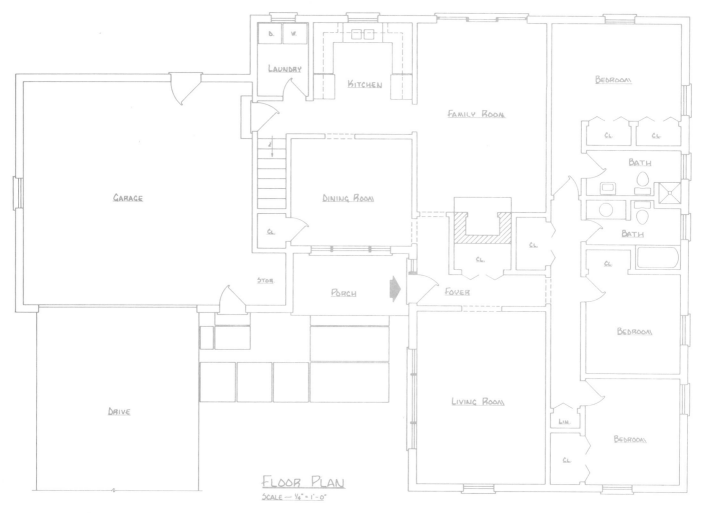

FLOOR PLAN
SCALE — 1/4" = 1'-0"

Fig. 31-7. A floor plan drawn at 1/4'' = 1'-0'' scale to be used in building a presentation model.

LEFT SIDE ELEVATION
SCALE — 1/4" = 1'-0"

FRONT ELEVATION   SCALE — 1/4" = 1'-0"

Fig. 31-8. A front and left side elevation of the house shown in the floor plan.

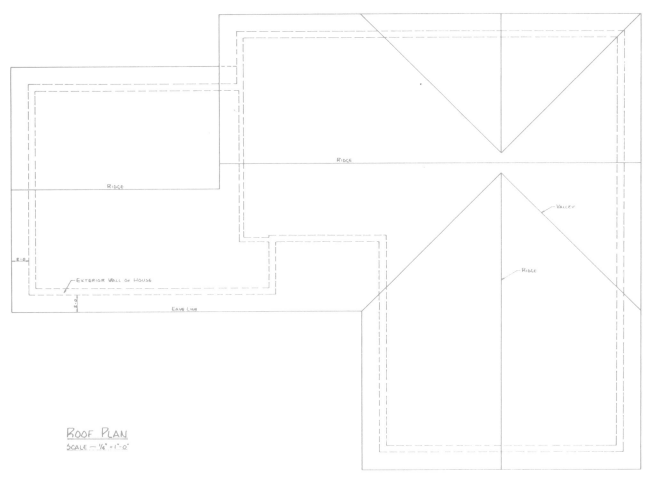

ROOF PLAN
SCALE — ¼" = 1'-0"

Fig. 31-9. Roof plan of the same house to be used in constructing the model roof.

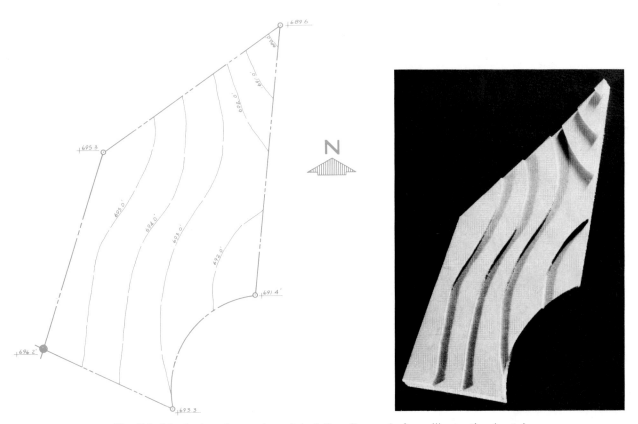

Fig. 31-10. A site plan and model of the site made from illustration board.

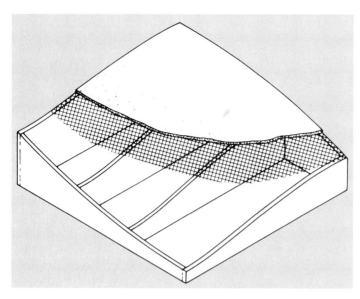

Fig. 31-11. A rolling site may be modeled by building a frame support, cut to the proper contour, and covered with screen and plaster of paris.

If the base is large it may be hard to store and transport. A good size base for an average residence is 30″ X 30″ or 30″ X 36″. The base should be 3/4″ plywood if the site is relatively smooth. If the site is rolling, then a lighter base should be used to reduce weight. A rolling site must be accurately represented by building up the high spots with plaster of paris, Styrofoam®, or cardboard, Fig. 31-10. It should be noted that if the site is flat, the model may be completed on a workbench and placed on the base. If the site is rolling, Fig. 31-11, it may be easier to build the model on the base. (The procedure presented here relates to a house on a flat site.)

3. After studying the floor plan and elevations, select a piece of balsa which is about the thickness for the exterior walls of the model. Usually 3/16 or 1/4 in. thick material is used. Lay out the length of one exterior wall and openings in the wall such as windows and doors. Cut this piece accurately paying close attention to details. The corners may be mitered or butt jointed. A mitered corner is usually neater.

Proceed with the next exterior wall by cutting it to length and locating the windows and doors. Construct all the exterior walls in the same manner. The walls may then be glued together. Place them on the floor plan to insure accuracy. See Fig. 31-12.

4. Lay out each section of interior wall on a piece of 1/8″ thick balsa. This thickness closely approximates the thickness of an interior wall

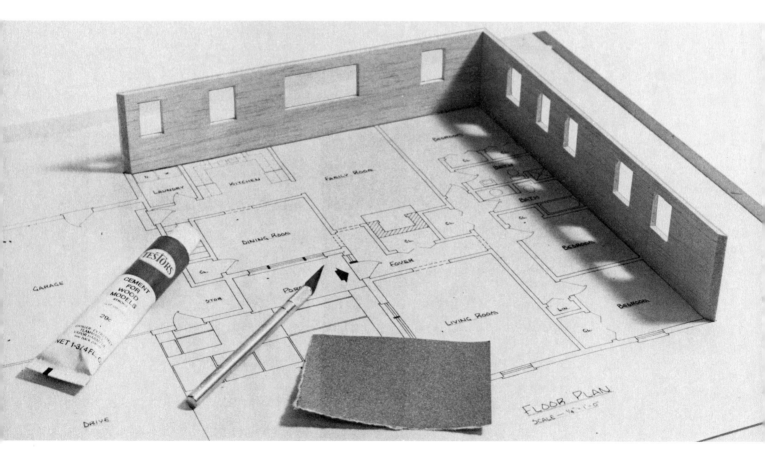

Fig. 31-12. Two exterior walls have been completed. Tools used included X-Acto knife, scale, square, and metal straightedge.

drawn to scale. Cut out each interior wall segment and glue the pieces together in their proper locations on the plan.

5. Apply the trim around windows and doors and insert exterior doors (usually 1/8'' thick). The window glass may also be installed now or after the interior is painted. For best results, 1/16'' thick Plexiglass may be used for windows. Exterior siding, brick, or other material may be applied to the walls.

You may wish to make your own siding or represent other materials by scoring the board or gluing on thin strips. If you cut your own strips of siding be sure to make them to scale. Commercial materials are available at hobby and model train shops. Again, choose materials which are to scale. If materials in sheet form are to be used, rubber cement will work fine for applying them to the walls. If individual strips are to be used, model cement or other fast drying cement is recommended. Fig. 31-13 shows the model after step 5 has been completed.

6. Paint the interior walls with tempera paint. The walls may be painted in soft pastels or white. Dark colors usually do not look realistic and should be avoided. Any wood siding or three-dimensional brick, stone, or shingles used, should also be painted or stained. Exterior materials are available on plastic sheets which are embossed to provide a three-dimensional effect. These should be finished with enamel. The mortar joints should be painted with a water base paint and wiped. This technique produces a realistic appearance. Fig. 31-14 shows the walls after painting.

7. Roof construction comes next. The roof may be assembled on the roof plan or on the model. Experience has shown that the most satisfactory results are usually obtained by assembling the roof on the roof plan. Since the roof framing will not be seen in a presentation model it is not necessary to cut each rafter and ceiling joist. Lay out the gables on 1/4'' balsa and cut them out. Cut ridge boards from similar stock and glue in place at the peaks of the gables. Use straight pins to hold the pieces in place. The roof sheathing may be 1/4'' balsa glued to the gables and ridge board. This thickness will approximate the thickness of the raters and sheathing on the house. Use a strip of 1/16'' thick balsa to represent a fascia board. If the home has a chimney, build a chimney to scale and accurately locate it on the roof, Fig. 31-15. Finish the roof by gluing strips of sandpaper or fine gravel to the sheathing. Be sure to represent the flashing. This may be aluminum foil or dark colored sandpaper.

8. After the floor area has been painted, or covered with an appropriate material, locate the model on the base and glue it in place. Next, paint the area surrounding the house bright green. For best results apply two coats and sprinkle grass flock before the second coat dries.

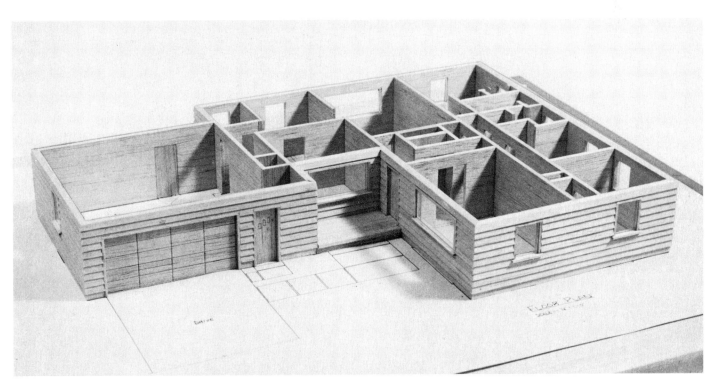

Fig. 31-13. Model with interior and exterior walls and siding in place. The siding was made from individual strips of balsa 1/4 in. wide by 1/32 in. thick and overlapped.

Add trees, shrubs, drive, and walk. The plants may be bought commercially or fabricated from a sponge and/or twigs. Use your imagination to develop a landscape that looks realistic. Do not add so many plants that the landscape appears to be cluttered. The walk and drive may be painted balsa or sandpaper glued in place.

9. Check the model to be sure all details are complete. Fig. 31-16 shows the completed model.

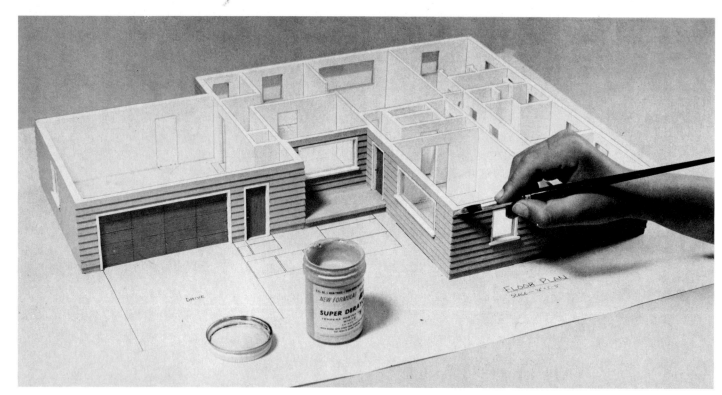

Fig. 31-14. The model has been painted both inside and out using tempera colors. Painting must be carefully done.

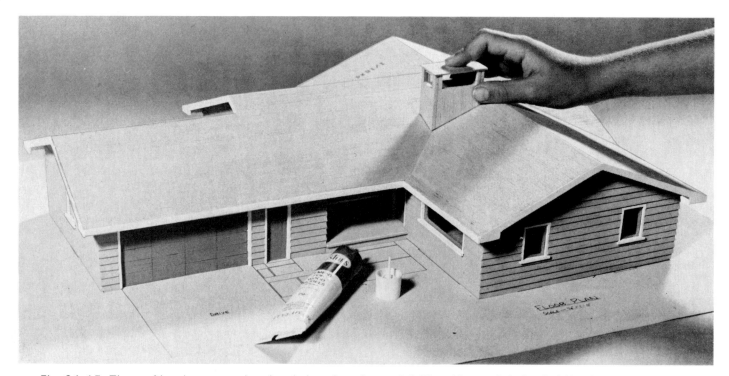

Fig. 31-15. The roof has been completed and placed on the model. The chimney is being held in place for glue to dry. Small blocks have been attached to the underside of the roof to insure proper placement of the roof on the house.

Fig. 31-16. The completed model with landscape, drive, and walk. The model was mounted on a piece of 3/4'' x 24'' x 30'' plywood. The tree and plants were made from lichen purchased from the local hobby store. The grass is bright green flock made especially for models.

Furniture and major fixtures can be carved out of soap or wood and glued into place for added attraction. Again, the main consideration is scale. There is no limit to the amount of realism that may be incorporated in a model. Use your imagination. Be creative and develop a truly realistic presentation model. Fig. 31-17 shows a residential model made from plaster of paris. The shrubbery is lichen.

REVIEW QUESTIONS—CHAPTER 31

Write your answers on a separate sheet of paper. Do not write in this book.
1. Name three types of architectural models that may be used for homes.
2. The scale of most residential models is _____.

Fig. 31-17. This residential model with floor plan was constructed from 12 identical plaster castings. Two castings form each room module, which are the same shape. Two slightly modified modules form the decks. Each module is supported by a foundation pedestal.

3. Identify the three types of materials that are commonly used in the construction of a model house.
4. The first step in getting ready to build a model is _____.
5. A plot plan would be a necessity for building a model when _____.
6. The size of base for an average-size residence usually is about _____.
7. Because the base must be strong, _____ in. thick plywood is commonly used.
8. Exterior walls are usually thicker than interior walls. What is the thickness of most exterior walls on house models that are constructed at 1/4″ = 1′-0″ scale? _____.
9. Interior walls are usually _____ in. thick on a 1/4″ = 1′-0″ scale model.
10. The type of paint frequently used for house models is _____.
11. Soap may be used for _____ in a house model.

SUGGESTED ACTIVITIES

1. Visit a hobby shop and examine materials available for model home construction. Make a list of the materials and record prices. Also write down the address of the shop. Compare your findings with other members of the class.
2. Secure the plan of a modern free-standing garage and construct a balsa model to scale. A scale of 1/4″ = 1′-0″ is suggested. Mount the model on a base 12 in. square. Record the time required to build the model and total cost.
3. Obtain the plans for an attractive one-story type home. Build a presentation model of the home. Mount it on a suitable base and landscape the site. Display the model along with the plans.
4. Carve a permanent fixture such a bathtub or water closet from soap. Check dimensions of the carving for accuracy.
5. Build a structural model of a modern storage or garden house of your design. Present your design and model for analysis.

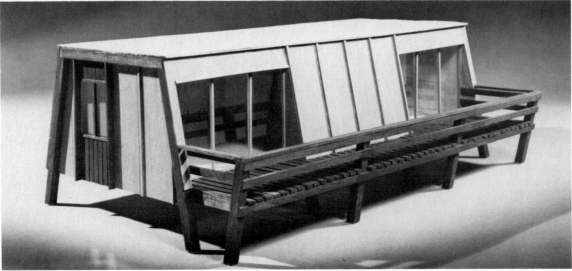

Architectural models can be unique in design. The model builder has created the effect of stone and wood siding.

32
<u></u>

CHAPTER

Material and Tradework Specifications

After studying this chapter, you will be able to:
- Explain the purpose of material and tradework specifications.
- List the sources of specification guides.
- Recognize the format followed by typical contract specification sheets.
- Use a "description of materials" form.

The architect is generally responsible for the preparation of material and tradework specifications for residential structures. The specifications provide written information on details and products which supplement the drawings and become part of the complete set of building plans. When the house is to be constructed for sale, the architect supplies the specifications needed. When the home is being designed and constructed for a particular client, the architect and customer usually develop a "specifications outline" together, Fig. 32-1.

PURPOSE OF SPECIFICATIONS

Both working drawings and specification sheets (specs) become part of the total contract between the builder and owner and are legal and binding on both parties. This illustrates the necessity of carefully preparing specifications for materials, fixtures, and tradework that leaves little or no chance for misunderstandings between the contractor and owner.

The owner should carefully discuss the details of construction with the architect and, in most cases, rely upon the architect's judgment and suggestions for structural materials. On the other hand, the architect should accept the client's desires in such details as floor coverings, paint colors, type and style of hardware, plumbing fixtures, wallpaper, and other items involving

individual taste. Various forms for developing specifications are available. Some of these are short while others are long and highly detailed. In some instances the architect simply prepares specifications to the agreement of both parties.

While material specifications are quite factual, the question of tradework and quality of construction is more difficult to define. What may appear to be a quality job of cabinet construction to one person may appear sloppy to another. It is the purpose of the specifications to include what both the contractor and owner agree on as an acceptable degree of tradework quality. The contractor should employ or subcontract only to qualified skilled tradeworkers.

Fig. 32-1. The architect, left, goes over details of the working drawings for a new residence with a client.

CONTRACT SPECIFICATIONS

Mr. & Mrs. Frank E. Smith Residence
1103 Douglas Street
Glendale, GA

Date _____

EXCAVATION: House to be excavated to depths shown on drawings, backfilled and graded with existing soil. Excavation overcut in garage and lower level to be filled with sand. Twelve inches of sand to be furnished under garage floor. Tree removal is included only within building or drive area.

CONCRETE: All concrete to be 5 bag mix. Included is all foundation work, front sidewalk, garage floor, lower level floor, basement floor, and front stoop. Garage floor to have 6/6 wire mesh. All tie rods in lower level and basement are to be broken off on the inside and outside of foundation and inside of walls to have brushed cement finished coat. Furnish and install Andersen basement windows complete with area wells and grates.

WATERPROOFING: Exterior of lower level and basement to receive two coats of Portland Cement plaster and one spray coat of bituminous waterproofing.

STEEL: All steel beams, angles, plates, columns, and lintels are a part of this contract.

LUMBER: All floor joists are to be 2 x 10 kiln-dried Southern Yellow Pine. All studs to be 2 x 4 white fir precuts. Ceiling joists and roof rafters to be 2 x 6 white fir. Roof sheathing and subfloor to be 4 x 8 x 1/2 C-D plywood. Exterior siding to be channel type prestained rough sawn cedar. Fascia and soffit to be 1 x 8 prestained rough sawn cedar. Basement and lower level stairs to have 2 x 10 oak treads, pine risers, and stringers. Two rows of 1 x 3 cross bridging to be installed.

MASONRY: Residence to have face brick four sides with an allowance of $500/3000. Fireplace to be face brick at $500/3000 allowance with slate hearth, colonial damper, cast iron ash drop and cleanout, 13/13 tile flue. Color mortar or raked joints will be extra.

CARPENTRY: All carpentry labor is included for all rough and trim work, including installation of all cabinets, tops, appliances, and hardware. Front door, garage service door, and door from garage to lower level to be weatherstripped, and to have aluminum thresholds.

STAIRWAY: Stairway from first to second floor to be mill made with oak treads and pine or white wood risers and stringers. Furnish railings for foyer and dining room.

MILLWORK: All trim to be Colonial white pine; all interior doors to be Colonial pine panel (first and second floor) 1 3/8 in. flush white birch on lower level; front and garage service doors to be 1 3/4 in. pine panel; door from garage to lower level to be 1 3/4 in. solid core birch. All windows to be Andersen casements in insulating glass with screens on operating windows and muntin bars where indicated on drawings. All windows to have birch stools.

CABINETS: All kitchen and vanity cabinets to be birch or oak, prefinished, with ranch or provincial grooves and lap type doors with flush surface. Purchaser to select from standard finishes.

COUNTERTOPS: Kitchen and vanity countertops to be post formed one piece Formica and scribed to the wall. Maple cutting block to be included over dishwasher.

FLOORING: Floors for living room, dining room, upper hall, and bedrooms to be 5/8 in. plywood. Floors under ceramic tile in second floor baths and foyer to be 1/2 in. plywood. Floors in kitchen to be 5/8 in. underlayment plywood screwed in place. All floors to be laid directly on top of subfloors.

CERAMIC TILE: Foyer, lower hall, and closet to have ceramic floor with an allowance of $10 per sq. ft. in place. Baths No. 1 and No. 2 to have ceramic floors and base with an allowance of $10 per sq. ft. in place. Ceramic tile walls and ceiling of 2 showers and walls only at 1 tub with an in place allowance of $10 per sq. ft. All ceramic to be laid in mastic.

RESILIENT FLOORS: Kitchen floor to be vinyl inlaid with an installed allowance of $20 per sq. yd. Stairway from kitchen to lower hall, lower hall, laundry room, and future powder room to have vinyl asbestos tile floor with an allowance of $1.50 per sq. ft. installed. Rubber base to be installed in workshop, lower hall, laundry room, future powder room, and den. Five chrome fixtures to be supplied and installed in second floor hall bath, 4 chrome fixtures in master bath, and 2 chrome fixtures in lower powder room.

DRYWALL: All drywall to be 1/2 in. adhesive applied before nailing (3 coat finish) garage ceiling and firewall to be 5/8 in. fire code with three exterior walls to be 1/2 in. regular drywall.

INSULATION: Ceiling of house to have 12 in. fiberglass insulation except cathedral ceiling in living and dining room to have 4 in. fiberglass batt insulation. Walls of house to have 3 1/2 in. fiberglass batts and 3/4'' rigid foam weatherboard. Garage ceiling and garage exterior walls are insulated similar to house.

GLAZING: Obscure D.S. glass to be installed in basement sash. A 54'' x 48'' plate glass mirror to be installed in upper hall bath. Decorative glass panels to be installed in garage.

SHINGLES: All shingles to be 235 lb. asphalt with adhesive tabs laid over 15 lb. roofing felt.

HEATING AND SHEET METAL: A Carrier or Bryant gas forced air furnace and electric air conditioner to be installed with deluxe high wall returns on the second floor. A power humidifier, copper gutters and downspouts and flashing, exhaust ducts for fans are a part of this contract.

WROUGHT IRON: A wrought iron railing is to be supplied and installed at stairway in garage.

PLUMBING: All plumbing fixtures to be Kohler in almond except blue in bath No. 2. Two water closets to be ''Willworth'' model. Two lavatories to be ''Castelle,'' one tub to be ''Caribbean,'' two prefab shower bases, one 32'' x 21'' stainless steel kitchen sink, one single compartment standard laundry tub. Water heater to be Rheem Fury 40 gal. glass lined. All faucets to be Moen mixing valve type. Shutoff valves are included at all sinks, lavatories, and water closets. Three hose bibbs to be installed (front free type). Floor drain to be installed in basement, laundry room, and garage. Drain tile to be installed around lower level and deep basement leading into a submersible sump pump for grade discharge. Gas lines to be run to furnace and water heater. Install dishwasher and disposal. All water lines to be copper and all sewer lines to be P.V.C. Install bypass for future softener by owner. Rough in only for powder room lavatory and water closet.

ELECTRICAL: 150 amp. underground electrical service with circuit breakers, one recessed chime with front and rear button. Install 220 volt outlet for range and oven. Provide electrical installation of furnace, power humidifier, dishwasher, and disposal. Light fixture allowance is $1250.00.

HARDWARE: Interior and exterior door locks to be Schlage A Series. Kitchen cabinet and vanity hardware to be Amerock. Allowance for all finish hardware is $800.00 which includes closet rods,, hinges, locks, latches, pulls, door bumpers, etc.

PAINTING: First floor and lower level trim to be stained; sealed, and varnished. Walls and ceilings of house to receive a prime and finish coat. Exterior trim on windows and doors to receive two coats. Walltex is included at $16.00 per roll for baths No. 1 and No.2. Second floor trim and doors to be painted (bedroom level).

APPLIANCES: Kitchenaid dishwasher No. KUDS215, Kitchenaid Disposal No. KBDS200, Kitchenaid Range top No. KECG260 with Grille, Kitchenaid Double Oven No. KEMS376. All are part of contract.

DRIVEWAY: A blacktop drive is to be installed over blacktop base.

MEDICINE CABINETS: None in contract.

GARAGE DOOR: A 16'-0'' x 7'-0'' x 1 3/8 in. flush Masonite overhead garage door to be installed as manufactured by the Overhead Door Co.

SHOWER DOORS: Two shower doors are to be provided.

PATIO DOOR: An Arcadia aluminum framed patio door 8'-0'' wide with insulating glass and screen to be installed in kitchen.

GAS LIGHT: A standard gas post light is to be installed at front of driveway.

PERMIT: All permits and inspection fees are included in this contract.

SURVEY: Topography, survey, and building site are a part of this contract.

INSURANCE: Contractor to carry builders risk, covering fire, theft, liability, and property damage. Purchaser to insure building upon final closing.

QUALITY: Contractor to provide all material necessary to build on real estate in a good, substantial, and quality tradeworker manner.

Fig. 32-2. A set of contract specifications for a home designed specifically for the owner. Details of the specifications are planned by hours of discussions between the architect and client.

SPECIFICATION FORMATS

There are many types and styles of standard long and short form specification formats. Specification guides or outlines may be purchased locally or supplied by the architect. Standard forms are also available from such organizations as the American Institute of Architects and the Veterans Administration. The V.A. form has become one of the leading guides for writing specifications.

Information provided by specification forms should include:

1. A description of the materials to be used. This includes sizes, quality, brand names, style, and specification numbers.

2. List of required building operations. These are usually described under major headings such as excavation, masonry, carpentry, millwork, plumbing, electrical, insulation, etc.

3. Notes relative to cash allowances for such items as lighting fixtures and hardware which are to be selected by the owner. Expenditures over the cash allowance must be paid by the owner.

4. An indication that all of the specifications refer to the detailed plans of the working drawings.

5. A statement or agreement on quality of tradeworker's skill. This statement or agreement is often drawn up as a separate part of the contract.

6. Liability covered by the contractor during construction.

EXAMPLES OF SPECIFICATIONS

Fig. 32-2 shows a typical contract specification sheet prepared by an architect. The architect and owner went over the working drawings together and came to an agreement on details of construction, design, and appliances.

A standard form as shown in Fig. 32-3 provides the necessary major headings for specifications. Each section may be filled in or left blank as agreed to by the architect and client. Each topic on this standard specification form should be carefully discussed with the architect, and in some cases the builder, so that all understand and agree to its content.

FHA Form 2005
VA Form 26-1852
Rev. 3/68

☐ Proposed Construction

☐ Under Construction

For accurate register of carbon copies, form may be separated along above fold. Staple completed sheets together in original order.

DESCRIPTION OF MATERIALS   No. _____
(To be inserted by FHA or VA)

Form approved.
Budget Bureau No. 63-R055.11.

Property address _____ City _____ State _____

Mortgagor or Sponsor _____ (Name) _____ (Address)

Contractor or Builder _____ (Name) _____ (Address)

INSTRUCTIONS

1. For additional information on how this form is to be submitted, number of copies, etc., see the instructions applicable to the FHA Application for Mortgage Insurance or VA Request for Determination of Reasonable Value, as the case may be.
2. Describe all materials and equipment to be used, whether or not shown on the drawings, by marking an X in each appropriate check-box and entering the information called for in each space. If space is inadequate, enter "See misc." and describe under item 27 or on an attached sheet.
3. Work not specifically described or shown will not be considered unless required, then the minimum acceptable will be assumed. Work exceeding minimum requirements cannot be considered unless specifically described.
4. Include no alternates, "or equal" phrases, or contradictory items. (Consideration of a request for acceptance of substitute materials or equipment is not thereby precluded.)
5. Include signatures required at the end of this form.
6. The construction shall be completed in compliance with the related drawings and specifications, as amended during processing. The specifications include this Description of Materials and the applicable Minimum Construction Requirements.

1. EXCAVATION:

Bearing soil, type _____

2. FOUNDATIONS:

Footings: concrete mix _____ ; strength psi _____   Reinforcing _____

Foundation wall: material _____   Reinforcing _____

Interior foundation wall: material _____   Party foundation wall _____

Columns: material and sizes _____   Piers: material and reinforcing _____

Girders: material and sizes _____   Sills: material _____

Fig. 32-3. This standard Veterans Administration and Federal Housing Administration form lends itself well to all types of specifications for residential construction. (Continued)

Basement entrance areaway _____   Window areaways _____
Waterproofing _____   Footing drains _____
Termite protection _____
Basementless space: ground cover _____ ; insulation _____ ; foundation vents _____
Special foundations _____
Additional information: _____

3. CHIMNEYS:

Material _____   Prefabricated *(make and size)* _____
Flue lining: material _____   Heater flue size _____   Fireplace flue size _____
Vents *(material and size)*: gas or oil heater _____ ; water heater _____
Additional information: _____

4. FIREPLACES:

Type: ☐ solid fuel; ☐ gas-burning; ☐ circulator *(make and size)* _____   Ash dump and clean-out _____
Fireplace: facing _____ ; lining _____ ; hearth _____ ; mantel _____
Additional information: _____

5. EXTERIOR WALLS:

Wood frame: wood grade, and species _____   ☐ Corner bracing. Building paper or felt _____
    Sheathing _____ ; thickness _____ ; width _____ ; ☐ solid; ☐ spaced _____" o. c.; ☐ diagonal; _____
    Siding _____ ; grade _____ ; type _____ ; size _____ ; exposure _____"; fastening _____
    Shingles _____ ; grade _____ ; type _____ ; size _____ ; exposure _____"; fastening _____
    Stucco _____ ; thickness _____"; Lath _____ ; weight _____ lb.
    Masonry veneer _____   Sills _____   Lintels _____   Base flashing _____
Masonry: ☐ solid ☐ faced ☐ stuccoed; total wall thickness _____"; facing thickness _____"; facing material _____
    Backup material _____ ; thickness _____"; bonding _____
    Door sills _____   Window sills _____   Lintels _____   Base flashing _____
    Interior surfaces: dampproofing, _____ coats of _____ ; furring _____
Additional information: _____
Exterior painting: material _____ ; number of coats _____
Gable wall construction: ☐ same as main walls; ☐ other construction _____

6. FLOOR FRAMING:

Joists: wood, grade, and species _____ ; other _____ ; bridging _____ ; anchors _____
Concrete slab: ☐ basement floor; ☐ first floor; ☐ ground supported; ☐ self-supporting; mix _____ ; thickness _____";
    reinforcing _____ ; insulation _____ ; membrane _____
Fill under slab: material _____ ; thickness _____". Additional information: _____

7. SUBFLOORING: *(Describe underflooring for special floors under item 21.)*

Material: grade and species _____ ; size _____ ; type _____
Laid: ☐ first floor; ☐ second floor; ☐ attic _____ sq. ft.; ☐ diagonal; ☐ right angles. Additional information: _____

8. FINISH FLOORING: *(Wood only. Describe other finish flooring under item 21.)*

Location	Rooms	Grade	Species	Thickness	Width	Bldg. Paper	Finish
First floor							
Second floor							
Attic floor _____ sq. ft.							

Additional information: _____

FHA Form 2005
VA Form 26–1852
1
DESCRIPTION OF MATERIALS

DESCRIPTION OF MATERIALS

9. PARTITION FRAMING:

Studs: wood, grade, and species _____   size and spacing _____   Other _____
Additional information: _____

10. CEILING FRAMING:

Joists: wood, grade, and species _____   Other _____   Bridging _____
Additional information: _____

11. ROOF FRAMING:

Rafters: wood, grade, and species _____   Roof trusses (see detail): grade and species _____
Additional information: _____

Fig. 32-3. (Continued) Standard VA and FHA specification form.

12. ROOFING:
Sheathing: wood, grade, and species _____; ☐ solid; ☐ spaced _____" o.c.
Roofing _____; grade _____; size _____; type _____
Underlay _____; weight or thickness _____; size _____; fastening _____
Built-up roofing _____; number of plies _____; surfacing material _____
Flashing: material _____; gage or weight _____; ☐ gravel stops; ☐ snow guards
Additional information: _____

13. GUTTERS AND DOWNSPOUTS:
Gutters: material _____; gage or weight _____; size _____; shape _____
Downspouts: material _____; gage or weight _____; size _____; shape _____; number _____
Downspouts connected to: ☐ Storm sewer; ☐ sanitary sewer; ☐ dry-well. ☐ Splash blocks: material and size _____
Additional information: _____

14. LATH AND PLASTER
Lath ☐ walls, ☐ ceilings: material _____; weight or thickness _____ Plaster: coats _____; finish _____
Dry-wall ☐ walls, ☐ ceilings: material _____; thickness _____; finish _____;
Joint treatment _____

15. DECORATING: *(Paint, wallpaper, etc.)*

ROOMS	WALL FINISH MATERIAL AND APPLICATION	CEILING FINISH MATERIAL AND APPLICATION
Kitchen _____		
Bath _____		
Other _____		

Additional information: _____

16. INTERIOR DOORS AND TRIM:
Doors: type _____; material _____; thickness _____
Door trim: type _____; material _____ Base: type _____; material _____; size _____
Finish: doors _____; trim _____
Other trim *(item, type and location)* _____
Additional information: _____

17. WINDOWS:
Windows: type _____; make _____; material _____; sash thickness _____
Glass: grade _____; ☐ sash weights; ☐ balances, type _____; head flashing _____
Trim: type _____; material _____ Paint _____; number coats _____
Weatherstripping: type _____; material _____ Storm sash, number _____
Screens: ☐ full; ☐ half; type _____; number _____; screen cloth material _____
Basement windows: type _____; material _____; screens, number _____; Storm sash, number _____
Special windows _____
Additional information: _____

18. ENTRANCES AND EXTERIOR DETAIL:
Main entrance door: material _____; width _____; thickness _____". Frame: material _____; thickness _____"
Other entrance doors: material _____; width _____; thickness _____". Frame: material _____; thickness _____"
Head flashing _____ Weatherstripping: type _____; saddles _____
Screen doors: thickness _____"; number _____; screen cloth material _____ Storm doors: thickness _____"; number _____
Combination storm and screen doors: thickness _____"; number _____; screen cloth material _____
Shutters: ☐ hinged; ☐ fixed. Railings _____, Attic louvers _____
Exterior millwork: grade and species _____ Paint _____; number coats _____
Additional information: _____

19. CABINETS AND INTERIOR DETAIL:
Kitchen cabinets, wall units: material _____; lineal feet of shelves _____; shelf width _____
Base units: material _____; counter top _____; edging _____
Back and end splash _____ Finish of cabinets _____; number coats _____
Medicine cabinets: make _____; model _____
Other cabinets and built-in furniture _____
Additional information: _____

20. STAIRS:

STAIR	TREADS		RISERS		STRINGS		HANDRAIL		BALUSTERS	
	Material	Thickness	Material	Thickness	Material	Size	Material	Size	Material	Size
Basement _____										
Main _____										
Attic _____										

Disappearing: make and model number _____
Additional information: _____

2

Fig. 32-3. (Continued) Standard VA and FHA specification form.

21. SPECIAL FLOORS AND WAINSCOT:

	Location	Material, Color, Border, Sizes, Gage, Etc.	Threshold Material	Wall Base Material	Underfloor Material
Floors	Kitchen ___				
	Bath ___				

	Location	Material, Color, Border, Cap. Sizes, Gage, Etc.	Height	Height Over Tub	Height in Showers (From Floor)
Wainscot	Bath ___				

Bathroom accessories: ☐ Recessed; material _____ ; number _____ ; ☐ Attached; material _____ ; number _____

Additional information: _____

22. PLUMBING:

Fixture	Number	Location	Make	Mfr's Fixture Identification No.	Size	Color
Sink ___						
Lavatory ___						
Water closet ___						
Bathtub ___						
Shower over tub △ ___						
Stall shower △ ___						
Laundry trays ___						

△☐ Curtain rod   △☐ Door   ☐ Shower pan: material _____

Water supply: ☐ public; ☐ community system; ☐ individual (private) system.★

Sewage disposal: ☐ public; ☐ community system; ☐ individual (private) system.★

★Show and describe individual system in complete detail in separate drawings and specifications according to requirements.

House drain (inside): ☐ cast iron; ☐ tile; ☐ other _____   House sewer (outside): ☐ cast iron; ☐ tile; ☐ other _____

Water piping: ☐ galvanized steel; ☐ copper tubing; ☐ other _____   Sill cocks, number _____

Domestic water heater: type _____ ; make and model _____ ; heating capacity _____

_____ gph. 100° rise.   Storage tank: material _____ ; capacity _____ gallons.

Gas service: ☐ utility company; ☐ liq. pet. gas; ☐ other _____   Gas piping: ☐ cooking; ☐ house heating.

Footing drains connected to: ☐ storm sewer; ☐ sanitary sewer; ☐ dry well.   Sump pump; make and model _____

_____ ; capacity _____ ; discharges into _____

23. HEATING:

☐ Hot water.   ☐ Steam.   ☐ Vapor.   ☐ One-pipe system.   ☐ Two-pipe system.

☐ Radiators.   ☐ Convectors.   ☐ Baseboard radiation.   Make and model _____

Radiant panel: ☐ floor; ☐ wall; ☐ ceiling.   Panel coil: material _____

☐ Circulator.   ☐ Return pump.   Make and model _____ ; capacity _____ gpm.

Boiler: make and model _____   Output _____ Btuh.; net rating _____ Btuh.

Additional information: _____

Warm air: ☐ Gravity.   ☐ Forced.   Type of system _____

Duct material: supply _____ ; return _____   Insulation _____ , thickness _____   ☐ Outside air intake.

Furnace: make and model _____   Input _____ Btuh.; output _____ Btuh.

Additional information: _____

☐ Space heater; ☐ floor furnace; ☐ wall heater.   Input _____ Btuh.; output _____ Btuh.; number units _____

Make, model _____   Additional information: _____

Controls: make and types _____

Additional information: _____

Fuel: ☐ Coal; ☐ oil; ☐ gas; ☐ liq. pet. gas; ☐ electric; ☐ other _____ ; storage capacity _____

Additional information: _____

Firing equipment furnished separately: ☐ Gas burner, conversion type.   ☐ Stoker: hopper feed ☐; bin feed ☐

Oil burner: ☐ pressure atomizing; ☐ vaporizing _____

Make and model _____   Control _____

Additional information: _____

Electric heating system: type _____   Input _____ watts; @ _____ volts; output _____ Btuh.

Additional information: _____

Ventilating equipment: attic fan, make and model _____ ; capacity _____ cfm.

kitchen exhaust fan, make and model _____

Fig. 32-3. (Continued) Standard VA and FHA specification form.

Other heating, ventilating. or cooling equipment _____

24. ELECTRIC WIRING:

Service: ☐ overhead; ☐ underground.   Panel: ☐ fuse box; ☐ circuit-breaker; make_____AMP's_____No. circuits_____

Wiring: ☐ conduit; ☐ armored cable; ☐ nonmetallic cable; ☐ knob and tube; ☐ other _____

Special outlets: ☐ range; ☐ water heater; ☐ other _____

☐ Doorbell.   ☐ Chimes.   Push-button locations _____   Additional information: _____

25. LIGHTING FIXTURES:

Total number of fixtures_____   Total allowance for fixtures, typical installation, $_____

Nontypical installation _____

Additional information: _____

DESCRIPTION OF MATERIALS

DESCRIPTION OF MATERIALS

26. INSULATION:

LOCATION	THICKNESS	MATERIAL, TYPE, AND METHOD OF INSTALLATION	VAPOR BARRIER
Roof			
Ceiling			
Wall			
Floor			

HARDWARE: (make, material, and finish.) _____

_____

SPECIAL EQUIPMENT: (State material or make, model and quantity.   Include only equipment and appliances which are acceptable by local law, custom and applicable FHA standards.   Do not include items which, by established custom, are supplied by occupant and removed when he vacates premises or chattles prohibited by law from becoming realty.)_____

_____

_____

_____

_____

_____

_____

_____

27. MISCELLANEOUS: (Describe any main dwelling materials, equipment, or construction items not shown elsewhere; or use to provide additional information where the space provided was inadequate.   Always reference by item number to correspond to numbering used on this form.) _____

_____

_____

_____

_____

_____

_____

_____

_____

PORCHES:

_____

_____

TERRACES:

_____

_____

GARAGES:

_____

_____

_____

Fig. 32-3. (Continued) Standard VA and FHA specification form.

WALKS AND DRIVEWAYS:

Driveway: width _____ ; base material _____ ; thickness _____" ; surfacing material _____ ; thickness _____"

Front walk: width _____ ; material _____ ; thickness _____". Service walk: width _____ ; material _____ ; thickness _____"

Steps: material _____ ; treads _____"; risers _____". Cheek walls _____

OTHER ONSITE IMPROVEMENTS:

(Specify all exterior onsite improvements not described elsewhere, including items such as unusual grading, drainage structures, retaining walls, fence, railings, and accessory structures.)

_____

_____

_____

LANDSCAPING, PLANTING, AND FINISH GRADING:

Topsoil _____" thick: ☐ front yard; ☐ side yards; ☐ rear yard to _____ feet behind main building.

Lawns (seeded, sodded, or sprigged): ☐ front yard _____ ; ☐ side yards _____ ; ☐ rear yard _____

Planting: ☐ as specified and shown on drawings; ☐ as follows:

_____ Shade trees, deciduous, _____" caliper. _____ Evergreen trees. _____' to _____', B & B.

_____ Low flowering trees, deciduous, _____' to _____' _____ Evergreen shrubs. _____' to _____', B & B.

_____ High-growing shrubs, deciduous, _____' to _____' _____ Vines, 2-year _____

_____ Medium-growing shrubs, deciduous, _____' to _____' _____

_____ Low-growing shrubs, deciduous, _____' to _____' _____

IDENTIFICATION.—This exhibit shall be identified by the signature of the builder, or sponsor, and/or the proposed mortgagor if the latter is known at the time of application.

Date_____   Signature _____

Signature _____

FHA Form 2005
VA Form 26-1852   4   GPO 1968 c48—16—80081-1 296-152

Fig. 32-3. (Continued) Standard VA and FHA specification form.

REVIEW QUESTIONS—CHAPTER 32

Write your answers on a separate sheet of paper. Do not write in this book.

1. Briefly list the six major types of information that should be included in any set of specifications for a residential structure.
2. Why is it important that the architect listen carefully to the desires of the client when writing specifications?
3. The architect often writes the complete specifications for a house when _____.
4. Specification sheets and working drawings become part of the _____ between the builder and the owner.
5. A cash allowance is often provided for what items?
6. Why is an agreement on tradeworker quality an important item on a specification sheet?
7. Explain why many of the details of the actual building construction do not show up on the specification sheets.

SUGGESTED ACTIVITIES

1. Prepare a specification sheet, as illustrated in Fig. 32-2, for one of the homes you have designed during the course or from a set of working drawings supplied by your instructor. Have another person be the client and use this person's suggestions for appliances, floor coverings, and other items.
2. Write to manufacturers of appliances and plan a bulletin board display of the latest fixtures a client has to select from when planning a new home.
3. Visit a brick supplier to gain information as to types of face brick available for residential construction and present prices. Write a short report on how you would present the selection of face brick and cost allowance to a client when planning specifications.
4. Using the Veterans Administration "Description of Materials" form as a format, secure a set of working drawings for a residence from your instructor, or other source, and fill in all necessary information. Plan the specifications as if you were to be the owner and make selections as listed in current catalogs and manufacturers' literature.

Estimating Building Cost

After studying this chapter, you will be able to:
- Explain what is involved in developing an estimate of building costs.
- Generate a typical materials list for a simple structure.
- Estimate the cost of a residential structure using the square foot or cubic foot method.

After the house has been designed, construction drawings completed, and material and quality tradework specifications prepared, an estimate of cost should be made.

Estimating refers to an organized effort to determine the cost of materials and labor and other services required to build a house.

PRELIMINARY ESTIMATES

Two methods of estimating the cost of building a home are the **square foot method** and the **cubic foot method.** A rough estimate of the cost may be determined by using either method. In using the square foot method the first step is to compute the number of square feet in the house, then multiply this product by a constant which is determined by local conditions. The number of square feet is determined by multiplying the length of the house by the width. (All wall thicknesses are included in the total.) Garages, porches, and basements are figured separately since they are not as expensive to construct as the living part of the house. (These are usually figured one half the cost per square foot of the living area.) For example, if a house is 24' x 60' and has a 20' x 20' garage, the area of living space would be 1,440 sq. ft. plus the garage area of 400 sq. ft. If the cost per square foot is $50 in a given area, then the living area would be 1,440 x $50 or $72,000. The cost of the

garage would be 400 x $25 or $10,000. The estimated cost of the complete home then is $82,000. This price does not include the land. The constant of $50/sq. ft. (used for comparative purposes) is reasonable for some areas, but may vary several dollars in different localities and for different styles of homes and materials specified. For example, a ranch-style home is more expensive to build than a two-story home which provides the same area of living space. Most builders use a different constant for each style house and add various amounts for special features such as an extra bath or fireplace. Before trying to calculate the cost of a home check with local builders to determine the constant for your area.

In estimating by the cubic foot method, volume is used rather than area. The volume of a house is determined by finding the area and then multiplying this by the height. The height is figured from the basement floor to the ceiling. The attic volume is also included. It is calculated by finding the area (length by the width) and multiplying this figure by 1/2 the rise. The rise of the roof is the distance from the ceiling to the ridge. This procedure takes into account the volume lost due to the sloping roof.

If the 24' x 60' house is again used for the cubic foot method, the area is 1,440 sq. ft. and the height is 8 ft. Therefore, 1,440 x 8 = 11,520 cu. ft. for the living space, not including the attic. The area of the attic is 1,440 sq. ft. and the rise is 4 ft. Therefore, 1,440 x 2 = 2,800 cu. ft. for the attic. The total cu. ft. for the house then is 11,520 + 2,880 or 14,440 cu. ft. If the cost for a cubic foot is $5, then the estimated cost for the house would be 14,440 x 5 or $72,200.

The volume of the garage must also be computed and added to this figure. The volume is

400 x 8 or 3,200 cu. ft. The attic is 400 x 1 1/2 (the rise was 3 ft.) or 600 cu. ft. The total volume of the garage is 3,200 plus 600 or 3,800 cu. ft. The estimated cost of the garage is 3,800 x 2 1/2 or $9,500. The cost per cu. ft. of garage space is figured at one half the cost per cu. ft. of living space.

Total estimated cost of the house using the cubic foot method is $72,200 + $9,500 or $81,700. The difference in estimated cost between the two methods in this case is $300. Remember that you must use an accurate constant.

ESTIMATES THAT ARE MORE ACCURATE

There are so many variables involved in the cost of a home that cost estimates obtained by the square foot or cubic foot method may vary considerably. A cost estimate that is more accurate may be obtained by determining the quantity, quality and cost of materials to be used, and cost of labor required by installation. You must also include an allowance for material waste, and for supervision and overhead.

The first step in compiling an accurate estimate is to study the construction drawings very carefully to become fully acquainted with the various elements of the structure. The specifications must also be examined carefully to determine the quality of materials and tradework specified. Both of these factors will affect the final cost.

After one is intimately familiar with the plans, a list of materials may be compiled which will be required to construct the house. Most estimates follow the headings as listed on a good set of specifications. The order of the headings usually coincides with the construction sequence. When all the materials have been listed and priced, a total cost for materials may be identified. Prices should be secured from sources where the materials will be purchased to get an accurate price. A typical materials list is shown in Fig. 33-1.

Now that the cost of materials has been determined, the labor cost must be calculated. As recent as a few years ago, the labor cost was less than half the total cost of building a house, but today in most sections of the country it ranges from 60 to 80 percent of the total cost. The labor cost involved in building a house has steadily increased year after year and it would be wise to research this area carefully before trying to estimate that cost. Publications such as the Building Construction Cost Data Book are available which give detailed information on labor costs for various areas of the country. General contractors and sub-contractors also can provide help in arriving at the projected cost. Their experience will enable them to make an accurate estimate of labor costs for a given job.

Another cost that must be included is the fee for permits. Most areas require a building permit, a plumbing permit, an electrical permit, and a

Non-standard sizes and unique styles will increase expenses considerably.
(IBG International)

Article And Description	Price	Amount

General Information

Area of Basement, 1240 Sq. Ft. _____
Area of First Floor, 2250 Sq. Ft. _____
Height of Basement Floor to First Floor, 9'1-5/8" and 10'1-5/8" _____
First Floor Ceiling Height 8'0", 7'0" and Slopes _____
Ceiling to Roof, 4'6" and 3'1" _____
Size of Garage and/or Carport, 24'1"x22'10" _____

Excavating and Grading (will vary with local site conditions)

Rough Excavating, depends on site _____
Trench Excavating (wall footings), 19 Cu. Yds. _____
Backfill, depends on site and soil _____
Finished Grading, depends on site _____
Hand Excavating (column footings), 1/2 Cu. Yd. _____

Material Sub Total _____
Labor Sub Total _____

Masonry

Concrete Footings, 19.5 Cu. Yds. _____
Concrete Walls
  4" Block, 40 Sq. Ft. _____
  8" Block, 1600 Sq. Ft. _____
  10" Block, 40 Sq. Ft. _____
  12" Block, 420 Sq. Ft. _____
Exposed Concrete above Grade (block), 60 Sq. Ft. _____
Reinforcing Rods
  2 - #4x4'0" _____
  18 - #3x30'0" _____
Wire Mesh Reinforcing, 2100 Sq. Ft. _____
Concrete Basement Floor 4" Thickx1200 Sq. Ft. _____
Patio Floor 4"Thick x 225 Sq. Ft. _____
Concrete Platforms on Ground (@ garbage cans), 4" Thick x 15 Sq. Ft. _____
Concrete Sidewalks (under flagstone walk), 4" Thick x 70 Sq. Ft. _____
Garage Floor, 4" Thick x 600 Sq. Ft. _____
Concrete Steps (under flagstone), 7 Sq. Ft. _____
Concrete Hearth setting bed for flagstone for fireplace, 3" Thick x 6 Sq.Ft
Flue Lining
  12"x16" T.C., 21 Ft. _____
  8"x8" T.C., 19 Ft. _____
220 Firebrick _____
2400 Common Brick and Chimney _____
Mortar, 8.2 Cu. Yds. _____
Drain Tile (depends on site), as required _____
Chimney Cap, 15 Sq. Ft. _____
Supported Concrete Slabs, 1" setting bed x 185 Sq. Ft. _____
Supported Concrete Slabs, 4" Thick x 175 Sq. Ft. _____
Stone Veneer, 8" Thick x 34'0"x10'0" _____
Pea Gravel Patio and Walk, 3 Cu. Yds. _____
19,000 Exterior Face Brick _____
Flagstones, 250 Sq. Ft. _____
6 Vents in Foundation Walls _____
Cement Block Quoins
  160, 8" Blocks _____
  15, 10" Blocks _____
  45, 12" Blocks _____
Water Proofing Foundation Walls, 850 Sq. Ft. _____

Material Sub Total _____
Labor Sub Total _____

Carpenter's Lumber List

Joists
  42 Pcs., 2x12x20'0" _____
  38 Pcs., 2x12x18'0" _____
  23 Pcs., 2x12x16'0" _____
  3 Pcs., 2x12x8'0" _____
Bridging 1x4, 340 Sq. Ft. _____
Sub Flooring, 2010 Sq. Ft. _____
Ceiling Joists
  13 Pcs., 2x8x20'0" _____
  27 Pcs., 2x6x18'0" _____
  8 Pcs., 2x6x16'0" _____
  50 Pcs., 2x6x12'0" _____
  23 Pcs., 2x6x8'0" _____
  8 Pcs., 2x6x14'0" _____
Deck Beams
  2 Pcs., 2x10x14'0" _____
  2 Pcs., 2x10x12'0" _____
  4 Pcs., 2x10x8'0" _____
  2 Pcs., 2x8x18'0" _____
  12 Pcs., 2x8x14'0" _____
  10 Pcs., 2x8x10'0" _____
  4 Pcs., 2x8x6'0" _____
Deck Flooring
  21 Pcs., 2x6 (redwood) x14'0" _____
  18 Pcs., 2x6 (redwood) x12'0" _____
  18 Pcs., 2x6 (redwood) x10'0" _____
  18 Pcs., 2x6 (redwood)x 8'0" _____

Article And Description	Price	Amount

Carpenter's Lumber List (Cont'd.)

Lintels
  2 Pcs., 2x12x15'0" (Flitch beams) _____
  8 Pcs., 2x12x18'0" (Flitch beams) _____
  6 Pcs., 2x12x3'4" _____
  2 Pcs., 2x12x3'8" _____
  2 Pcs., 2x12x5'0" _____
  2 Pcs., 2x12x7'0" _____
  8 Pcs., 2x12x9'0" _____
  2 Pcs., 2x12x10'0" _____
Stair Stringers
  3 Pcs., 2x12x16'0" _____
Exterior Wall Plates, 2x4, 1260 Ft. _____
Exterior Wall Plates, 2x6x150 Ft. _____
Exterior Studs
  180 Pcs., 2x4x8'0" _____
  93 Pcs., 2x4x9'0" _____
  7 Pcs., 2x4x10'0" _____
  9 Pcs., 2x4x11'0" _____
  6 Pcs., 2x4x12'0" _____
Interior Plates
  2x4, 800 Ft. _____
  2x6, 30 Ft. _____
  2x8, 105 Ft. _____
Interior Studs
  55 Pcs., 2x4x9'0" _____
  7 Pcs., 2x6x9'0" _____
  10 Pcs., 2x8x9'0" _____
  210 Pcs., 2x4x8'0" _____
  11 Pcs., 2x6x8'0" _____
  25 Pcs., 2x8x8'0" _____
Headers
  2 Pcs., 2x12x4'0" _____
  18 Pcs., 2x4x3'0" _____
  16 Pcs., 2x4x2'8" _____
  6 Pcs., 2x6x4'4" _____
  2 Pcs., 2x8x6'4" _____
Roof Sheathing 1/2" Plywood, 3850 Bd. Ft. _____
Ridge Boards, 2x10, 110 Ft. _____
Rafters
  60 Pcs., 2x8x22'0" _____
  97 Pcs., 2x8x16'0" _____
  14 Pcs., 2x8x12'0" _____
  4 Pcs., 2x8x10'0" _____
Fascia Cornice 1x10, 340 Ft. _____
Porch Steps
  2 Pcs., 2x12x10'0" _____
Waterproof Roofing Paper, 38-1/2 Sqs. _____
Building Paper under Wood Floor, 21-1/2 Sqs. _____
Posts
  1 Pc., 4x4x8'0" _____
Girders Laminated Beams
  1 Pc., 5-1/4x14-1/2x24'0" _____
  1 Pc., 5-1/4"x14-1/2"x24'0" _____
Porch Posts
  8 Pcs., 4x4x8'0" _____
Porch Railing 2x4, 128 Lin. Ft. _____
Porch Cap 2x6, 64 Lin. Ft. _____
Exterior Sheathing 1/2" Insulating Board, 2400 Sq. Ft. _____
Siding, 1250 Sq. Ft. _____
Basement Stair Posts
  1 Pc., 4x4x8'0" _____
Basement Stair Railings
  1 Pc., 2x4x6'0" _____
Soffits or Roof Overhang
  1/2" Plywood, 3'4"x205' _____
  1/2" Plywood, 2'0"x145' _____
Scaffolding and Extra Joists (approx.), as required _____
Plastic Ceiling at Kitchen and Master Bath
  3 Pcs., 1x12x14'0" _____
Valance
  1x6, 126 Ft. _____
  1x10, 132 Ft. _____
Furring Strips, as required _____
Wind Stops at Eaves, 300 Ft. _____
Battens 1x2, 1100 Ft. _____
Shelving
  10 Pcs., 1x10x10'0" _____
  8 Pcs., 1x10x8'0" _____
Rafter Ties
  2x4, 70 Ft. _____
  24 Pcs., 2x4x10'0" _____

Material Sub Total _____
Labor Sub Total _____

MILLWORK

Windows And Screens (as selected)

Window Frames
  4 4'0"x6'0" Vertical Sliding Steel Windows _____
        (Continued on next page)

Fig. 33-1. Typical list for materials, fixtures, and finishes. (Continued)

Article And Description	Price	Amount	Article And Description	Price	Amount

Windows and Screens (Cont'd.)

 3   Double 4'0"x6'0" Vertical Sliding Steel Windows _____
 4   4'0"x5'0" Vertical Sliding Steel Windows _____
 1   3'0"x3'0" Horizontal Sliding Steel Windows _____

Fixed Plastic Screens (weather resistant)

Note: Provide frames for above plastic screens.

Storm Sash and Window screens or Rolling Metal Screens, as required _____

Doors And Trim

Exterior Door Frames
 4   Frames for 2'8"x6'8"x1-3/4" Solid Core Wood Doors _____
 1   Frame for 2-2'8"x6'8"x1-3/4" Solid Core Wood Doors _____
 1   Frame for 2'8"x6'8"x1-3/8" Hollow Core Wood Doors _____
 1   Frame for 16'0"x8'0" Sliding Glass Door _____
 3   Frames for 8'0"x6'8" Sliding Glass Door _____

Interior Door Frames
 8   Frames for 2'8"x6'8"x1-3/8" Hollow Core Wood Doors _____
 7   Frames for 2'4"x6'8"x1-3/8" Hollow Core Wood Doors _____
 3   Frames for 4'0"x6'8"x1-3/8" Hollow Core Wood Doors (folding)
 2   Frames for 6'0"x6'8"x1-3/8" Hollow Core Wood Doors (folding)

Special Door Frames
 1   Frame for 2'0"x6'8" Shower Door (master bath) _____

Exterior Doors
 6   2'8"x6'8"x1-3/4" Solid Core Doors _____
 1   2'8"x6'8"x1-3/8" Hollow Core Door _____
 1   16'0"x8'0" Sliding Glass Door _____
 3   8'0"x6'8" Sliding Glass Doors _____

Interior Doors
 8   2'8"x6'8"x1-3/8" Hollow Core Doors _____
 7   2'4"x6'8"x1-3/8" Hollow Core Doors
 6   2'0"x6'8"x1-3/8" Hollow Core Folding Doors (louvered) ____
 4   3'0"x6'8"x1-3/8" Hollow Core Folding Doors (louvered) _____
Interior Door Trim, 330 Lin. Ft. _____
Screen Doors, as required

Cabinets and Miscellaneous Millwork

Room Base, 375 Ft. _____
Clothes Closet Hook Strips, 75 Ft._____
(Including Storage Closet but not Kitchen)
At other shelving, 125 Ft. _____
Closet Shelving, 1'6"x115 Ft. _____
Closet Shelving, 1'8"x12'6" _____
Closet Poles, 50 Ft. _____
Outside Door Thresholds, Entry – Bronze Thresholds ,x5'4" _____
Ceiling Mold around Chimney, 30'0" _____
Kitchen Broom Closet and Pantry
    5 Shelves 1'8"x3/4"x2'6" _____
    2 Sides 1'8"x3/4"x8'0" _____
    10 Cleats, 1'2"x1'8"_____
Kitchen Cupboards
    Doors and Exposed Faces, 180 Sq. Ft. _____
    Sides and Partitions, 100 Sq. Ft. _____
    Shelves, 115 Sq. Ft. _____
    Backs, Sides and Bottom, 90 Sq. Ft. _____
    Tops (Plastic Laminated), 65 Sq. Ft. _____
    1x2 Framing, 220 Ft. _____
    Wood Legs at Island, 7 _____
    Drawer Track, 20 Ft. _____
Basement Stairs
    16 Pine Risers 7-1/2"x3/4"x3'4" _____
    15 Oak Treads 10-1/2"x1-1/4"x3'4" _____
Decorative Screen–In Foyer, 7'0"x11'0" _____
Clothes Chute Door 3/4" Plywood, 1'0"x2'6" _____
Bathroom Cabinets (1st floor)
    1x2 Frame, 53' _____
    1x4 Kickboard, 12'4" _____
    Doors, etc., 31 Sq. Ft. _____
    Shelves, etc., 67 Sq. Ft. _____
Special Beams (false)
    2 Pcs., 2x4x18'0" _____
    5 Pcs., 4x4x18'0" _____
Window Valances
    1x10, 130 Ft. _____
    1x6, 130 Ft. _____
China Closets
    3   16"x28"x1/4" Plate Glass Shelves _____
    2   54" Adjustable Shelf Standards _____
    6   16" Adjustable Shelf Brackets _____
    3"x1-1/8"x2'4" Plate Glass Shelves _____
    2-1/4"x1-1/8"x4'8" Plate Glass Shelves _____
    3/4"x3/4"x9'0" Plate Glass Shelves _____
    15"x24"x1/4" Frosted Plastic Top _____
    3/4" Plywood, 40 Sq. Ft. _____
    2x6 - 4'8" _____
    1x3 - 5'0" _____
    2x3 - 2'4" _____
Breakfast Room Cabinets
    Kickboard 1x4, 8 Ft. _____
    Doors and Sides, 56 Sq. Ft. _____

Cabinets and Miscellaneous Millwork (Cont'd.)

Shelves, 53 Sq. Ft. _____
Frame 1x2, 53 Ft. _____
Full Length Mirror
Baths
    1   80x50 _____
    1   68x50 _____
Basement
    1   68x50 _____

        Material Sub Total _____
        Labor Sub Total _____

Insulation

Batt Type Ceilings, 2230 Sq. Ft. _____
Batt Type Walls, 1650 Sq. Ft. _____

        Material Sub Total _____
        Labor Sub Total _____

Weatherstripping and Calking

Windows, 275 Ft. _____
Exterior Doors, 205 Ft. _____

        Material Sub Total _____
        Labor Sub Total _____

Plastering or Dry Wall

Living Room Walls, 340 Sq. Ft. _____
Living Room Ceiling, 530 Sq. Ft. _____
Dining Room Walls, 290 Sq. Ft. _____
Dining Room Ceiling, 215 Sq. Ft. _____
Foyer Walls, 31 Sq. Ft. _____
Foyer Ceiling, 102 Sq. Ft. _____
Hall Walls, 250 Sq. Ft. _____
Hall Ceiling, 80 Sq. Ft. _____
Basement Stairway Walls, 300 Sq. Ft. _____
Basement Stairway Ceiling, 35 Sq. Ft._____
Kitchen Walls, 490 Sq. Ft. _____
Kitchen Ceiling, 290 Sq. Ft. _____
Bathroom Walls
    Basement, 65 Sq. Ft. _____
    1st Floor, 230 Sq. Ft. _____
Bathroom Ceiling
    Basement, 50 Sq. Ft. _____
    1st Floor, 85 Sq. Ft. _____
Bedroom Walls
    Basement, 410 Sq. Ft. _____
    1st Floor, 780 Sq. Ft. _____
Bedroom Ceilings
    Basement, 245 Sq. Ft. _____
    1st Floor, 480 Sq. Ft. _____
Closet Walls
    Basement, 120 Sq. Ft. _____
    1st Floor, 610 Sq. Ft. _____
Closet Ceilings
    Basement, 16 Sq. Ft. _____
    1st Floor, 105 Sq. Ft. _____
Garage Walls, 600 Sq. Ft. _____
Garage Ceiling, 515 Sq. Ft. _____
Laundry Walls Basement, 195 Sq. Ft. _____
Laundry Ceiling Basement, 65 Sq. Ft._____
Storage Room Walls, 120 Sq. Ft. _____
Storage Room Ceiling, 21 Sq. Ft. _____
Study Walls, 350 Sq. Ft._____
Study Ceiling, 170 Sq. Ft. _____

        Material Sub Total _____
        Labor Sub Total _____

Finish Flooring

Living Room, 408 Sq. Ft. _____
Dining Room, 201 Sq. Ft. _____
Foyer, 102 Sq. Ft. _____
Halls, 80 Sq. Ft. _____
Basement Stairway, 50 Sq. Ft. _____
Kitchen, 290 Sq. Ft. _____
Bathrooms, 115 Sq. Ft._____
Bedrooms, 450 Sq. Ft. _____
Closets, 100 Sq. Ft. _____
Storage Room, 22 Sq. Ft. _____
Study, 155 Sq. Ft. _____

        Material Sub Total _____
        Labor Sub Total _____

(Continued on next page)

Fig. 33-1. (Continued) Typical list for materials, fixtures, and finishes.

Article And Description	Price	Amount	Article And Description	Price	Amount

Painting And Finishing

Exterior Siding, 1250 Sq. Ft. _____
Exterior Cornice, 360 Ft. _____
Exterior Doors (both sides), 230 Sq. Ft. _____
Basement Doors (both sides), 270 Sq. Ft. _____
Basement Stairs (top sides), 94 Sq. Ft. _____
Interior Doors (both sides), 720 Sq. Ft. _____
Interior Door Trims, 330 Ft. _____
Sheet Metal Items
  Chimney Flashing, 16 Ft. _____
  Wall Flashing @ Decks, 41 Ft. _____
  Ridge Vent, 116 Ft. _____
Kitchen Cupboards (including Shelves and Interior), 650 Sq. Ft. _____
Linen Closets (including Shelves), 145 Sq. Ft. _____
Broom Closet and Pantry (including Shelves), 200 Sq. Ft. _____
Closet Shelving (both sides), 150 Sq. Ft. _____
Closet Poles, 50 Ft. _____
Closet Hook Strip (clothes closets), 75 Ft. _____
Wood Base, 375 Ft. _____
Porch Posts (pipe columns), 35 Ft. _____
Garage Doors (both sides), 225 Sq. Ft. _____
Exposed Bricks
  Interior, 200 Sq. Ft. _____
  Exterior, 1250 Sq. Ft. _____
Interior Beams
  4x4 False Beams, 112 Ft. _____
  5-1/4x14-1/2 Laminated Beams, 48 Ft. _____
Exterior Cinder Block Walls, 60 Sq. Ft. _____
Living Room Walls, 340 Sq. Ft. _____
Living Room Ceiling (including top side of Valance), 615 Sq. Ft. _____
Living Room Floor
  Flagstone, 38 Sq. Ft. _____
  Carpeted, 408 Sq. Ft. _____
Dining Room Walls, 290 Sq. Ft. _____
Dining Room Ceiling, 215 Sq. Ft. _____
Dining Room Floor
  Flagstone Passage, 14 Sq. Ft. _____
  Carpeted, 201 Sq. Ft. _____
Foyer Walls, 31 Sq. Ft. _____
Foyer Ceiling, 102 Sq. Ft. _____
Foyer Floor Flagstone, 102 Sq. Ft. _____
Hall Walls, 250 Sq. Ft. _____
Hall Ceiling, 80 Sq. Ft. _____
Hall Floor, 80 Sq. Ft. _____
Basement Stairway Walls, 300 Sq. Ft. _____
Basement Stairway Ceiling, 35 Sq. Ft. _____
Kitchen Walls, 325 Sq. Ft. _____
Kitchen Plastic Ceiling, 48 Sq. Ft. _____
Kitchen Ceiling, 240 Sq. Ft. _____
Kitchen Floor, 290 Sq. Ft. _____
Bathroom Walls
  Basement, 60 Sq. Ft. _____
  1st Floor, 230 Sq. Ft. _____
Bathroom Ceilings
  Plastic Ceiling, 51 Sq. Ft. _____
  Basement, 50 Sq. Ft. _____
  1st Floor, 105 Sq. Ft. _____
Bathroom Floors
  Basement, 20 Sq. Ft. _____
  1st Floor, 115 Sq. Ft. _____
Bedroom Walls
  Basement, 410 Sq. Ft. _____
  1st Floor, 780 Sq. Ft. _____
Bedroom Ceilings (including valances)
  Basement, 245 Sq. Ft. _____
  1st Floor, 480 Sq. Ft. _____
Bedroom Floors
  Basement, 245 Sq. Ft. _____
  1st Floor, 450 Sq. Ft. _____
Closet Walls
  Basement, 120 Sq. Ft. _____
  1st Floor, 520 Sq. Ft. _____
Closet Ceilings
  Basement, 16 Sq. Ft. _____
  1st Floor, 90 Sq. Ft. _____
Closet Floors
  Basement, 18 Sq. Ft. _____
  1st Floor, 90 Sq. Ft. _____
Garage Walls, 600 Sq. Ft. _____
Garage Ceiling, 515 Sq. Ft. _____
Laundry Walls
  Concrete Block, 80 Sq. Ft. _____
  Other, 195 Sq. Ft. _____
Laundry Ceiling, 65 Sq. Ft. _____
Laundry Floor, 65 Sq. Ft. _____
Breakfast Room Walls, see Kitchen _____
Breakfast Room Ceiling, see Kitchen _____
Breakfast Room Floor, see Kitchen _____
Storage Room Walls, 120 Sq. Ft. _____
Storage Room Ceiling, 21 Sq. Ft. _____
Storage Room Floor, 21 Sq. Ft. _____

Painting And Finishing (Cont'd.)

Study Walls, 350 Sq. Ft. _____
Study Ceiling (including Valance), 170 Sq. Ft. _____
Study Floor, 155 Sq. Ft. _____
Special Mold Quarter Round, 500 Ft. _____
Bathroom Cabinets (including shelves and interior)
  Basement, 105 Sq. Ft. _____
  1st Floor, 210 Sq. Ft. _____
China Cabinet (including shelves and interior), 35 Sq. Ft. _____
Deck Steps (one side), 20 Sq. Ft. _____
Full Length Mirrors
Baths
  1   80x50 _____
  1   68x50 _____
Basement
  1   68x50 _____
Square Edge Trim 3/4x3/4, 10 Ft. _____
Battens 1x2, 1100 Ft. _____
Wood Decks
  2x6 Flat 3/16" Spacers, 365 Sq. Ft. _____
  2 2x10 Beams, 42 Sq. Ft. _____
  2 2x8 Beams, 132 Ft. _____
  1 2x8 Beams, 14 Ft. _____
Guard Rail, 190 Ft. _____

            Material Sub Total _____
            Labor Sub Total _____

Miscellaneous Hardware

40 Foundation Anchor Bolts 1/2" Diam.   A.B.'s to Sill _____
1 Clean out Door Frame Unit _____
1 Ash Dump Unit _____
1 Fireplace Damper Unit _____
2 Angle Iron Fireplace Lintels 3-1/2"x3-1/2"x1/2"x5'4" _____
1 Angle Iron Fireplace Lintel 3-1/2"x3-1/2"x1/2"x6'0" _____
Nails approximately 400 Lbs. _____
1 Dowel for Wood Post Anchors and Footings _____
Lally Columns 3" Diam. Pipe Columns
  1   2'0" _____
  1   7'0" _____
  3   8'6" _____
Miscellaneous Builders Hardware, as required _____
250 Wall Ties
Roof Beams Flitch Plates
  4   11"x3/8"x18'0" _____
  1   11"x3/8"x15'0" _____
  1   Angle 3-1/2"x3-1/2"x3/8"x3'0" _____
  1   Angle 3-1/2"x3-1/2"x1/2"x4'4" _____
5 Column Caps for 3" Diam. Pipe Column Units _____
5 Column Bases for 3" Diam. Pipe Column Units _____
Wire Mesh Reinforcement, (see Masonry Section) _____
Steps down to Living Room Floor
  4 Angles 1-1/2"x1-1/2"x3'0" _____
  2 Junior Channels 12"x1-1/2"x5'0" _____
Miscellaneous Bolts at Deck Rail 32 Machine Bolts 3/4" Diam. x 6" _____
Extra Heavy Corrugated Sheets Metal Forming, 180 Sq. Ft. _____
Reinforcement Bars, see Masonry Section _____

            Material Sub Total _____
            Labor Sub Total _____

Finish Hardware

2 Basement Doors
  2 Pr. 3-1/2x3-1/2 Butts _____
  2 Latch Sets _____
1 Pr. Front Entrance Doors
  3 Pr. 4x4 Butts _____
  1 Lockset _____
1 Rear Entrance Doors
  1-1/2 Pr. 4x4 Butts _____
  1 Lockset _____
4 Side Doors (including Doors from Garage)
  6 Pr. 4x4 Butts _____
  4 Locksets _____
Screen Doors (as required) _____
4 Bathroom Doors
  4 Pr. 3-1/2x3-1/2 Butts _____
  4 Locksets (Bath) _____
  3 - 8'0"x6'8" Glass Sliding Door Unit _____
  1 - 16'0"x8'0" Glass Sliding Door Unit _____
Double Acting Doors
  1   2'8"x6'8" _____
  1   Pr. 3-1/2x3-1/2 Double Acting _____
  1   Push Plate each Side _____
9 Interior Doors
  9 Pr. 3-1/2x3-1/2 Butts _____
  9 Latch Sets _____
Storm Sashes, as required _____

(Continued on next page)

Fig. 33-1. (Continued) Typical list for materials, fixtures, and finishes.

Article And Description	Price	Amount

Finish Hardware (Cont'd.)

Kitchen Cabinets (Storage and Bathroom included)
41 Pr. Cabinet Hinges
95 Knobs or Pulls
42 Friction Catches
Closets Folding Wood (4 panel)
  3   4'0"x6'8"
  2   6'0"x6'8"
 20 Pr. 3-1/2x3-1/2 Butts
 10 Pulls
 10 Catches
Miscellaneous Cabinets - Dining Room
  2   Pr. Cabinet Hinges
  2   Pulls
  2   Catches
1 Mail Box Unit
5 Floor Door Stops
16 Regular Door Stops
1 Doz. Coat and Hat Hooks
Miscellaneous Small Hardware, as required
1 Overhead Garage Door Unit 16'0"x7'0"
Shower Door (Master Bath)
  1   Pr. Metal Hinges
  1   Knob Set Unit
  1   Friction Catch

      Material Sub Total
      Labor Sub Total

Sheet Metal Work

Flashing around Chimney, 16 Lin. Ft.
Flashing at Vertical Walls at Exterior Decks, 41 Ft.
Exhaust Fan Grills
  3   Bathroom required
  1   Kitchen required
4 - 8" Diam. Ducts to Roof Vents
Valleys, 40 Ft.
Ridge Vent, 116 Ft.
1 Metal Clothes Chute Unit 12"x16"
Metal Lined Bread Drawer, 12 Sq. Ft.

      Material Sub Total
      Labor Sub Total

Floor Finishing Material

Resilient
Tile
Wood
Carpet
Tile Fireplace Hearth
Cove Base
Miscellaneous

      Material Sub Total
      Labor Sub Total

Wall Finishing Material

Work Table Tops and Backs Plastic Laminated, 90 Sq. Ft.
Tile Base in Bathroom, 80 Ft.
Tile or Chrome inserts in Bathroom
  3   Toilet Paper Holders
  3   Soap Dishes and Grab Bars
 10 Towel Bars
  3   Robe Hooks
Bathroom Tile Wainscot, 270 Sq. Ft.

      Material Sub Total
      Labor Sub Total

Roofing

38-1/2 Sqs. Owner' Choice

      Material Sub Total
      Labor Sub Total

Plumbing

Note: This survey does not list the quantities of each item required for the mechanical equipment, as there is a variation in any system chosen. However, the form given will be of assistance to your dealer in arriving at an accurate estimate.

1 Double Kitchen Sink
3 Water Closet Units
2 Bath Tubs
3 Shower Head Units
3 Floor Drain Units
4 Top Mounted Lavatories
Automatic Washer Outlet
4 Hose Bib Units
Hot Water Heater 40 Gallons Gas Fired Unit (50 Gallons Electric)
1 Garbage Disposer Unit
Miscellaneous
Gas Range, Grill with Cover and Rotisserie, Hood with 2 Dual Blowers (1200 CFM), Built-In Refr.-Freezer

      Material Sub Total
      Labor Sub Total

Electric Wiring

21 Ceiling Outlets (6 Spots)
4 Bracket Outlets, Outside Fixtures
57 Duplex Receptacles
10 Water-proof Receptacles
32 Wall Switches
1 Dimmer Switch Dining Room Spots
10 Three-way Switches
1 Set Entrance Chime
1 Ceiling Outlet (vapor-proof) over Master Bath Shower
2 Push Buttons
7 Porch Lights Twin Floods @ each Unit
7 Hall and Entrance Lights 150 W Ceiling Flush Mounted Units
1 Kitchen Fan - Hood-Fan Combination Unit
1 Bathroom Exhaust Fan
1 Bathroom Combination Heater and Ventilator
1 Bathroom Combination Heater, Ventilator and Light
2 - 220V Receptacles (Dryer and Range)
Special Tubular Light Installations
  2   2'0" Single Tube Units (20W)
 11 4'0" Single Tube Units (40W)
  2   23'0" Single Tube Units (Living Room)
  1   14'0" Single Tube Unit (Bedroom)
  1   13'0" Single Tube Unit (Bedroom)
  1   12'6" Single Tube Unit (Bedroom)

      Material Sub Total
      Labor Sub Total

Telephone Wiring

Note: Call the nearest telephone company business office for assistance in planning adequate built-in telephone facilities. These will include the following items:

1. Entrance pipe or underground entrance conduit
2. Galvanized iron protector cabinet
3. Interior thin-wall conduit to all outlets
4. Standard outlet boxes with telephone cover
5. Telephone or jack locations
6. Miscellaneous or special items

      Material Sub Total
      Labor Sub Total

Heating

A heating unit will be required of sufficient size for a house with 3490 Sq. Ft. and/or 30250 Cu. Ft.

      Material Sub Total
      Labor Sub Total

Fig. 33-1. (Continued) Typical list for materials, fixtures, and finishes.

health permit. The cost of these permits may be as small as a few dollars or as much as several hundred dollars. Also, there may be a fee for electrical, gas, sewer, telephone, and water hookup. Again, this may be a small amount or total several hundred dollars. Investigate these areas to determine their exact costs.

Many builders add the cost of insurance to protect materials and workers in the event of an accident or damage. This cost should also be added to the cost of construction. Once all these elements have been evaluated, the total cost of building the house may be calculated.

This estimate will most likely be more accurate than the approximate methods presented earlier, but it may still be a few hundred dollars off. It is impossible to calculate exactly the cost of building a house. Even builders who have been in the business for years sometimes fail to accurately estimate the cost of a job. Therefore, it is extremely important that you learn to prepare drawings and specifications accurately. Be sure all specifications are complete and easy to understand.

REVIEW QUESTIONS—CHAPTER 33

Write your answers on a separate sheet of paper. Do not write in this book.
1. List two methods commonly used for preliminary cost estimates.
2. If the estimated cost of a house with 1,500 sq. ft. is $75,000, what would be the cost per square foot?
3. Explain how a more accurate estimate than the square or cubic foot method may be computed.
4. Name the permits usually required for building a new home.
5. The cost of labor to construct a house may be determined accurately by _____.
6. The cost of materials required to build a house may be secured from _____.

SUGGESTED ACTIVITIES

1. Using a plan that you have designed or one supplied by your instructor, calculate the cost using the square foot method. Your instructor will help you determine the price per square foot in your area.
2. Using the same plan in No. 1 above, calculate a more accurate estimate for materials only by listing the materials to be used and pricing them in detail. Use prices from a local lumber company and other material suppliers.
3. Establish current rate for carpenters, plumbers, electricians, masons, and all other skilled tradeworkers who work together to build a house. Record rates and sources used and prepare a report to be presented to your class.

The computer is an important tool of the designer and architect. (McDonnell-Douglas, St. Louis)

Computer Applications

After studying this chapter, you will be able to:
- Discuss a variety of broad areas where computers are being used in architecture and construction.
- Recognize the advantages of computer analysis for the constructor or designer.
- Define terms related to computer applications in architecture.
- Discuss the type of information generally shown on a PERT chart.

The availability of computers and specialized software programs has a significant impact on the architect's planning, designing, and building of structures. The computer provides the potential for powerful analyses and graphic representations of many aspects of architecture and construction, Fig. 34-1. With the availability of minicomputers and microcomputers, most every architect and builder can have access to powerful, time-saving assistance. The computer is another tool of the architect and like all other tools of the trade, improved results are achieved with practice.

The computer is only as useful as the programs the architect runs on the hardware. Many commercial computer programs are available in the field of residential and commercial architecture and construction. Software can be purchased or developed to assist in the areas of estimating, site planning and mapping, structural analysis, computer-aided drafting and design (CADD), computer graphic presentations, energy analysis, project management, and computer simulations. The software allows the architect to ''test'' designs, to call-up previously

Fig. 34-1. A typical color workstation used to create advanced color graphics, perform sophisticated analyses, and generate conventional drawings. (Auto-trol Technology Corporation)

designed components, and to call up data from memory that would take considerable research time to locate in traditional resources.

This chapter gives a brief introduction to computer applications in the architectural field. By further study, you may become proficient in using and applying the computer to design and drafting applications.

SITE PLANNING AND MAPPING

Site planning and mapping are required for most large scale projects such as subdivisions, multifamily complexes, and nonconventional construction. One example of applying the computer to automated contour mapping is shown in Fig. 34-2. The computer was used to display all accumulated data and provide a visual display for the site planner. Another application of the computer is illustrated in Fig. 34-3. This generation of site grading plans will be useful to the contractors of the development. Fig. 34-4 shows some other computer applications used in site planning and mapping.

Fig. 34-2. Computer generated pictorial representation of contours derived from X, Y, Z coordinate data. (Bruning)

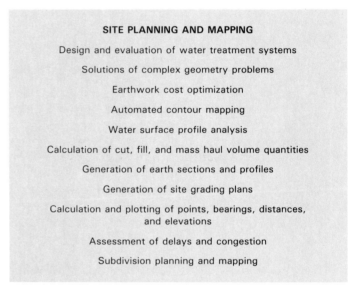

SITE PLANNING AND MAPPING

Design and evaluation of water treatment systems

Solutions of complex geometry problems

Earthwork cost optimization

Automated contour mapping

Water surface profile analysis

Calculation of cut, fill, and mass haul volume quantities

Generation of earth sections and profiles

Generation of site grading plans

Calculation and plotting of points, bearings, distances, and elevations

Assessment of delays and congestion

Subdivision planning and mapping

Fig. 34-4. Site planning and mapping applications, using the computer.

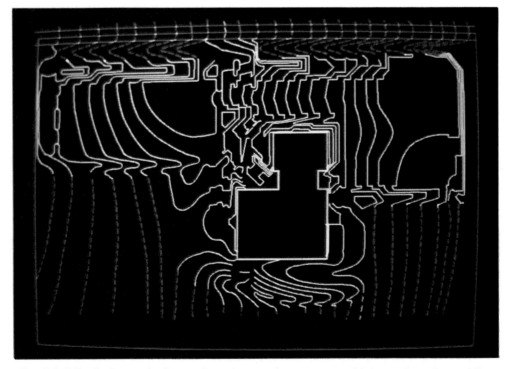

Fig. 34-3 Preliminary site layout is an interactive process which requires the melding of land form and structure with a CADD system. (Auto-trol Technology Corporation)

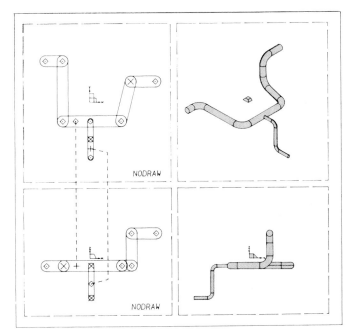

Fig. 34-5. A pipe model developed using standard software functions. (MEDUSA 3-D)

Structural analysis is an important aspect of the design process used by the architect in creating a wide range of buildings, from single-family residences to commercial complexes. Structural analysis allows the architect to design building components able to withstand stress and weight from the building and from any use the structure experiences. As an example, structural analysis is used to design the massive concrete shells used in earth sheltered homes. Most post-and-beam construction, along with most non-traditional building designs, also require some structural analysis to insure design integrity.

The designer may use structural analysis to assist in designing components by using step-by-step model generation as shown in Fig. 34-5. An architect uses descriptive analysis to

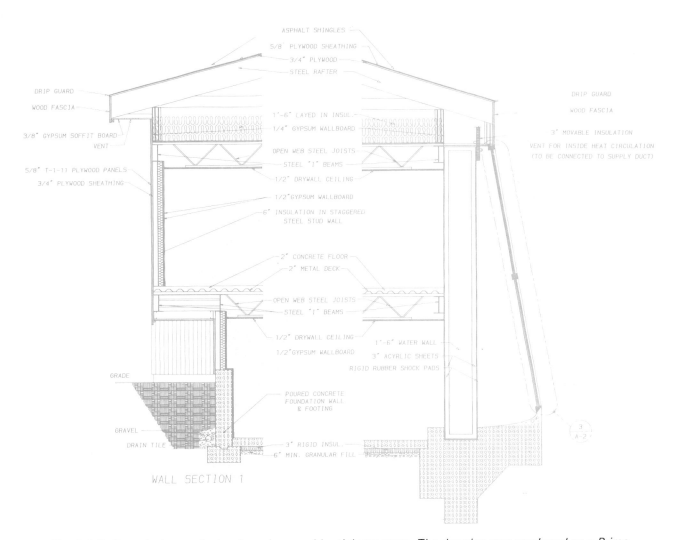

Fig. 34-6. Descriptive analysis of a unique residential structure. The drawing was produced on a Prime computer using MEDUSA software. (Prime Computer, Inc.)

calculate geometrics and stress forces in unique residential structures, Fig. 34-6. The list in Fig. 34-7 includes some of the more common computer applications of structural analysis.

STRUCTURAL ANALYSIS

Finite element analysis

Analysis of fixed arches, frames, or rings

Calculation and graphics of loading conditions, geometrics, stress forces, and deflected shapes

Steel structure design and analysis

Strength analysis including static and fatigue calculations, local buckling, and deformations

Elastic stability analysis

Step-by-step model generation

Heat transfer and analysis

Truss evaluation with 2-D and 3-D elements

Pipe rupture and fluid flow analysis

Analysis of arbitrary shell structures

Analysis of structural members and frames including cables, beams-columns, grillages, rings, plane and space frames

Fig. 34-7. Structural analysis applications using the computer.

COMPUTER-AIDED DRAFTING AND DESIGN (CADD)

Computer-aided drafting and design is the largest and most familiar area of computer application in architecture, design, and construction. By being able to call-up standard components or drawings, the architect is able to save time while improving accuracy. Previously, traditional drawings were drawn exclusively by hand. This process was very labor intensive and costly for large scale projects.

By using the computer to speed up drawing and to provide uniform components, the drafting and design process has harnessed the power of the computer. One example of a computer-generated architectural drawing is shown in Fig. 34-8. This foundation detail is typical of the type of drawing that can be developed rapidly by a skilled operator of CADD equipment.

Fig. 34-9 shows a typical menu of standard symbols and shading that the architect or designer can choose from when creating a drawing. Rapid access to such menu items permits the operator to complete complex drawings quickly. A listing of some other possible applications of CADD are shown in Fig. 34-10.

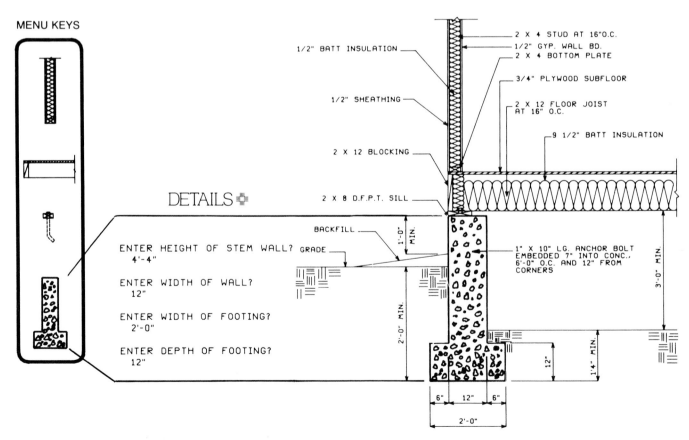

Fig. 34-8. Typical computer-generated foundation detail. Standard symbols and conventions are stored in a library accessible to the CAD software program. (Sigma Design, Inc.)

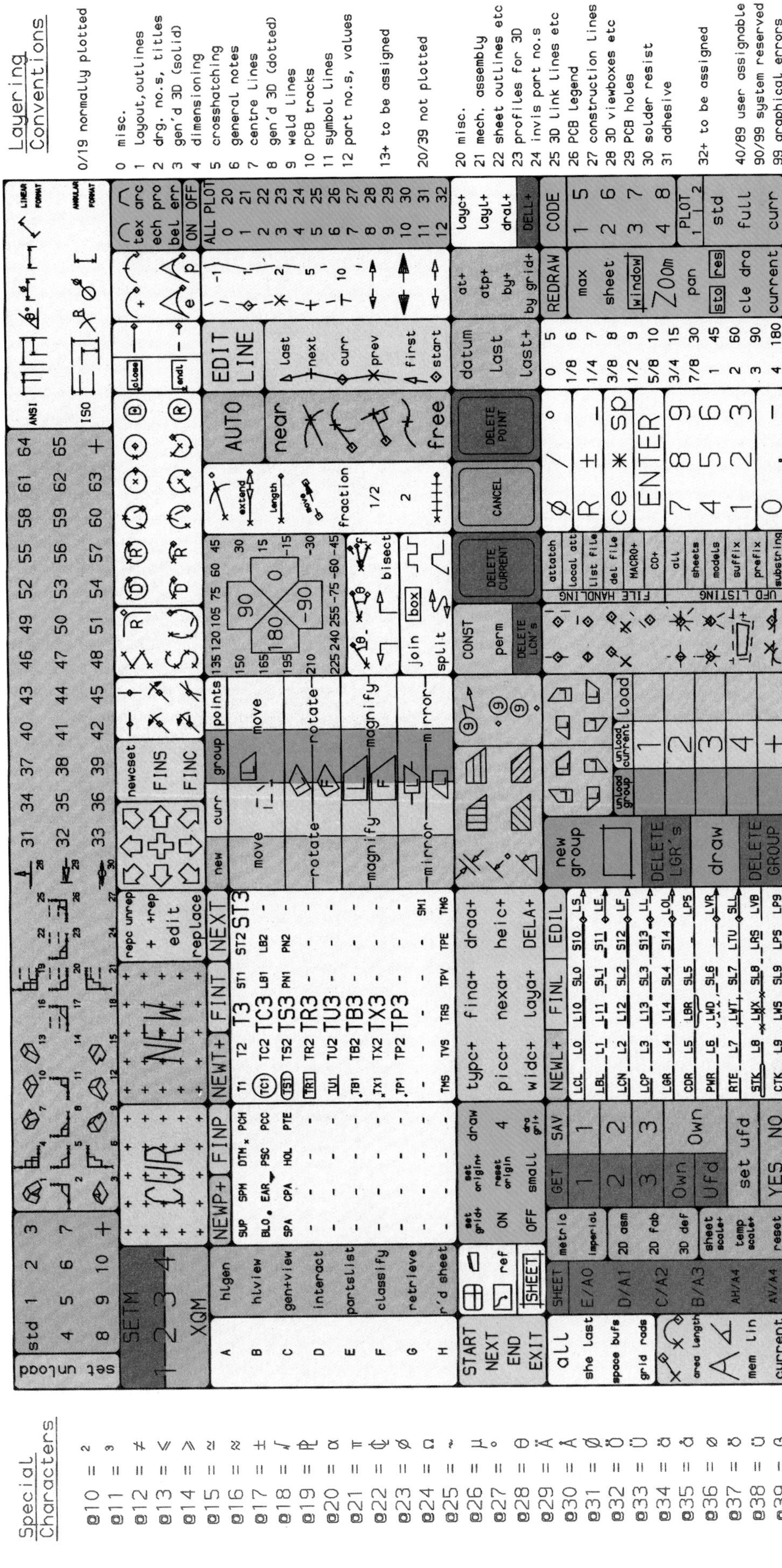

Fig. 34-9. Color graphics menu for MEDUSA software driven by a Prime computer. A digitizing device is used to enter commands or draw symbols shown on the menu. This technique speeds the process of drafting and design. (Prime Computer, Inc.)

COMPUTER-AIDED DRAFTING AND DESIGN

Creation of a two-dimensional data base accessible for all phases of design, drafting, and management interrogation

Creation and storage of drawings with easy modifications

Applications in black and white or color graphics

Graphic system dealing with all stages of design, from project inception, concept, and final design, to a working drawing, through the use of a three-dimensional data base

Drafting capabilities including hatching, area calculation, automatic dimensioning, and layering

Geometric modeling such as sweep and slide operation, ruled surfaces, volumes of revolution, and completely automatic hidden line removal

Definition of planes, cylinders, cones, spheres, ruled surfaces, and double curved surfaces

Production of drawings related to specific trades or professions, schedules, quantity take-offs, costs, and system audit changes

Generation of standard symbols and shading

Fig. 34-10. Computer-aided drafting and design (CADD) applications.

COMPUTER GRAPHICS REPRESENTATION

Graphic presentations are important tools of communication for architects and designers. A strong picture can often ''sell'' an idea or project. Conventional techniques generally require significant skill and time to draw or assemble attractive and accurate graphic representations.

By using the power of a minicomputer or microcomputer to drive plotters and dot matrix printers, the operator is capable of producing exact representations of complex objects in a relatively short time. For example, Fig. 34-11 shows a pictorial of a small office building that was computer generated. Using special software, an architect is able to create a graphic representation of a building. Once the data for the structure is stored in the computer, the architect can view the building from any position. The data may be represented as an isometric, oblique, or perspective drawing, Fig. 34-12.

Interior designs can be represented as shown in Fig. 34-13. Computer graphics allows the designer to see the results of designs quickly. If the results are not exactly what the customer desires, the designer can immediately alter the data to produce a design acceptable to the client. The listing in Fig. 34-14 contains examples of typical computer graphic applications.

ENERGY ANALYSIS

Since energy costs today are so significant, a complete energy analysis should be performed for most structures planned for construction. An energy analysis is also important for all remodeling construction projects. Computer software programs are designed to analyze all aspects of energy efficiency. Using these programs, the architect is able to plan and draw energy-efficient

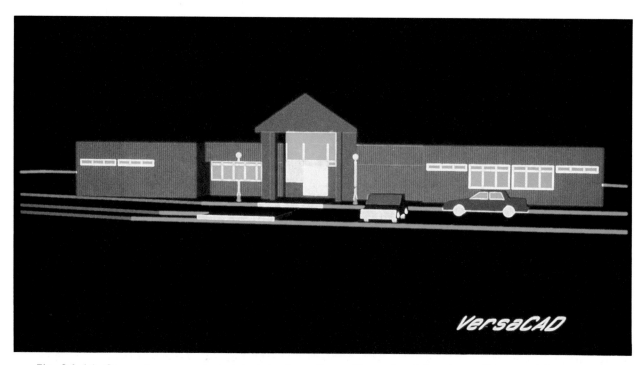

Fig. 34-11. Computer-generated pictorial using a three-dimensional data base. (Versacad Corporation)

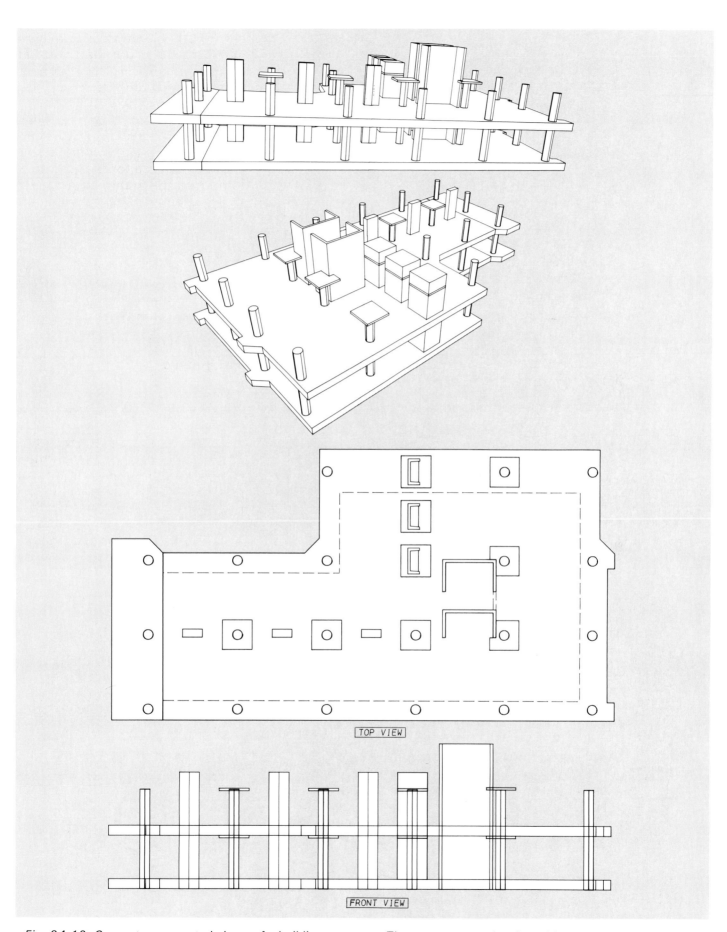

TOP VIEW

FRONT VIEW

Fig. 34-12. Computer-generated views of a building structure. The structure may be viewed from any position once the data base is complete. (Prime Computer, Inc.)

Fig. 34-13. Computer-enhanced line drawing. An ARTRON Computer generated this lifelike room setting using the ''image grabber'' like a stat camera to capture the original drawing. A light pen was used to select the colors, textures, and shapes from a menu to complete the illustration. (Marbaugh Engineering, Tim Trovillion)

COMPUTER GRAPHICS

Drawing two-dimensional, orthogonal views, with shifting, scaling, and rotational routines

Produce color contouring and shading.

Generate orthographic, isometric, oblique, and perspective drawings

Produce ruled line drawings

Draw line graphs, bar charts, pie charts, scatter diagrams, and finite element analysis

Generate color graphic visuals

Fig. 34-14. Computer graphics representation.

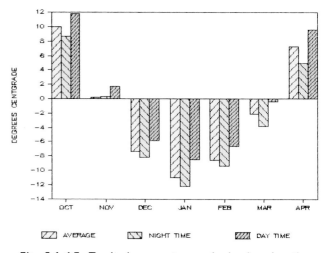

Fig. 34-15. Typical computer analysis showing the average monthly outdoor temperature for a specific area of the country. An IBM PC with compatible software was used to perform the analysis and generate the graphics.

structures. One example of the type of information that can be accessed by a computer is the outdoor temperatures for a certain location in the country, Fig. 34-15. Using this information, the architect can design a building with the most efficient combination of insulation and heating system.

Some typical programs for analyzing energy efficiency are listed in Fig. 34-16. By using these resources, the plans for a building may be drawn to provide energy conservation and cost savings to the owner.

Fig. 34-16. Energy analysis computer applications.

PROJECT MANAGEMENT WITH THE COMPUTER

After building plans are completed and the contractor starts on the actual construction, the computer may assist in planning the management, cost estimates, financial models, and

Fig. 34-17. Project management computer applications.

scheduling for the building. Frequently the difference between profit and loss on a project lies in the area of project management. The use of software programs, such as those listed in Fig. 34-17 allow contractors to improve productivity and efficiency. As an example, a ***Project Evaluation and Review Technique (PERT) chart,*** shown in Fig. 34-18, provides step-by-step guidance in the construction of a new sidewalk. This simplified example allows us to understand how a PERT chart works by providing both a plan to complete the project and checkpoints to monitor progress of the project. Complex projects such as an entire housing development will require extremely large charts that can be very useful to the contractor. The number and variety of software programs available to contractors and

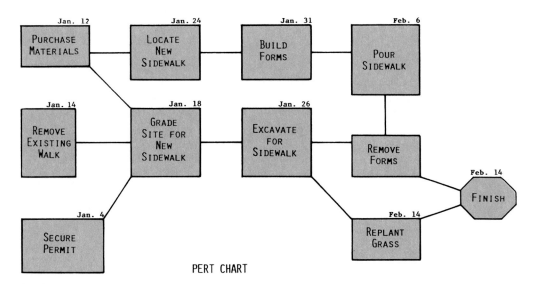

PERT CHART

Fig. 34-18. A simple PERT chart representing the operations necessary for a construction project. PERT stands for Project Evaluation and Review Technique. PERT chart programs are available to generate charts and monitor progress of the job as well as calculate costs.

planners in the area of project management is rapidly increasing.

COMPUTER SIMULATION

One of the more useful applications of the computer for the architect is the ability to simulate results. The planner or designer is able to visualize the outcome of various design solutions. By altering the input, the operator is capable of viewing the design solutions to various problems. One example of simulation is shown in Fig. 34-19, where a patio has been projected off one room of a home. By changing the dimensions, the patio can be designed to fit the client's needs while blending into the site. Typical areas that are receiving considerable attention from the simulation technique are listed in Fig. 34-20.

REVIEW QUESTIONS – CHAPTER 34

Write your answers on a separate sheet of paper. Do not write in this book.
1. List seven areas where computers are being used to assist the architect or planner.

COMPUTER SIMULATIONS

Generation of a mathematical description or model of a relationship or situation

Modeling behavior of continuous systems

Parameter estimation

Data summarization or transformation

Statistical as well as visual goodness-of-fit testing

Perform parametric studies

Analyze time-series observations

Presentation of system scenarios

Fig. 34-20. Typical computer simulation applications.

2. Give an example of where site planning and mapping may be required.
3. Explain the importance of structural analysis in planning an earth sheltered home. How can the computer assist the architect?
4. List advantages of using CADD over the conventional methods of drafting.
5. Designers use computer software to generate graphic representations to aid in _____.
6. List three applications of computer pro-

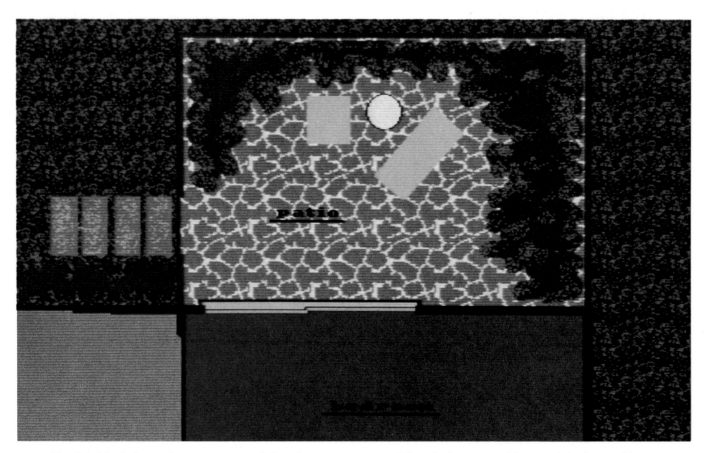

Fig. 34-19. Color and texture are useful tools to present possible solutions to architectural design problems. (Marbaugh Engineering, Tim Trovillion)

grams used to analyze energy efficiency.

7. There are computer programs that help in the planning and analysis of scheduling, cost estimating, and financial modeling. These may be grouped under the heading of _____.

SUGGESTED ACTIVITIES

1. Arrange for a demonstration of a computer-driven graphics system which is capable of generating architectural drawings. Check with your local college or university, engineering or architectural firms, or a computer store.

2. Research the names and addresses of sources of computer programs related to architecture and construction. Request descriptions of their programs. Share the information with your class.

3. Organize your class into a fund raising event with the proceeds targeted to purchasing software for the school's microcomputer or minicomputer. Ask for a demonstration of the software package before the fund raising event to prepare the class for the project.

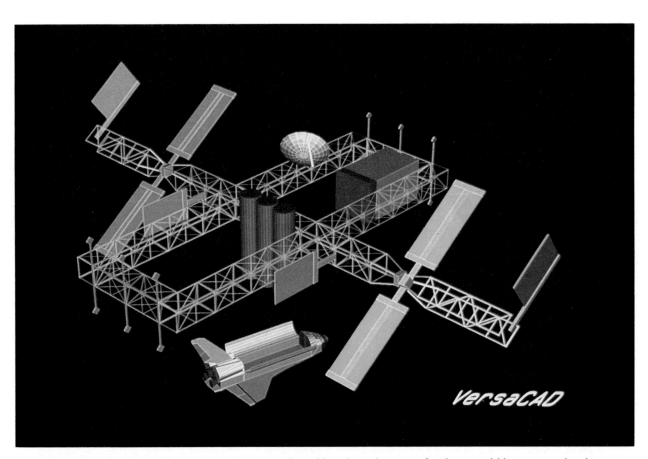

Computer-generated images may be reproduced in a broad range of colors to aid in communication. (Versacad Corporation)

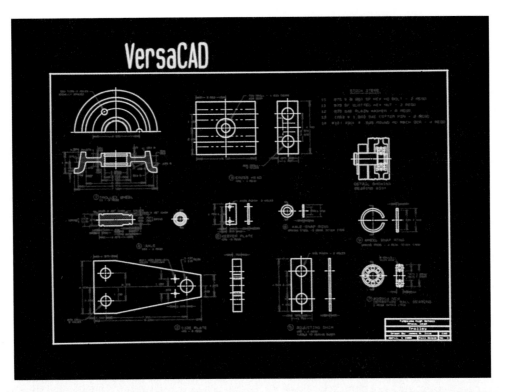

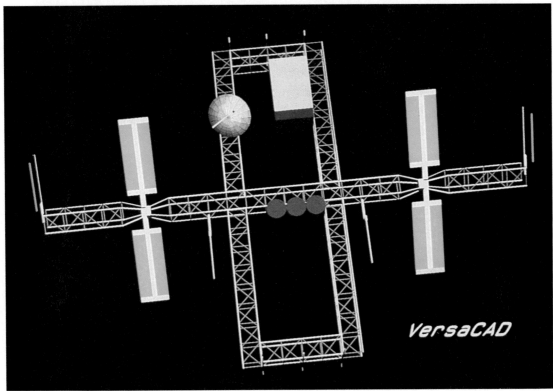

Computer-generated drawings using a CADD system. (Versacad Corporation)

Introduction to Computer-Aided Drafting and Design

After studying this chapter you will be able to:
- Explain why CADD is important to the fields of architecture and construction.
- List the components of modern microcomputers and explain their basic functions.
- Specify the characteristics of monitors that are important for a CADD system.
- Recognize common input and pointing devices used with a CADD system.
- Discuss several graphics output devices that are installed for CADD applications.

CADD is an acronym for computer-aided drafting and design. Initially, the letters CAD referred to computer-aided (or assisted) drafting, but now they can mean computer-aided drafting, computer-aided design, or both. CADD (with two Ds) better describes current technology since many popular software packages include both two-dimensional drafting and three-dimensional design functions. In addition, many CADD systems provide analysis capabilities, schedule production, and reporting. All are part of the design process, Fig. 35-1.

CADD has dramatically changed the way that designers develop and record their ideas. Even though the principles of graphic communication have not changed, the method of creating, manipulating, and recording design concepts has changed with computers, Fig. 35-2. The techniques of drafting, organization of views, projection, representation of elements in a design, dimensioning, etc. are the same. Yet, drawing boards, triangles, scales, and other traditional drafting equipment are no longer required to communicate a design idea. A designer/drafter

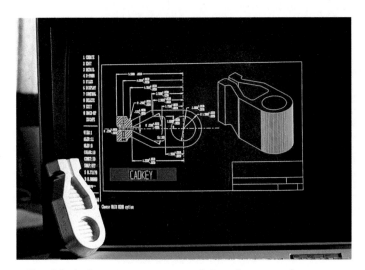

Fig. 35-1. Computer-generated drawings may be two- or three-dimensional.
(CADKEY, Division of Micro Control System, Inc.)

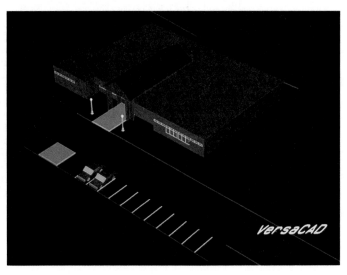

Fig. 35-2. Computer-generated pictorial model of a planned design. (Versacad Corporation)

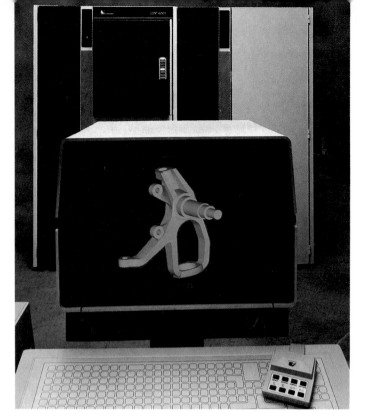

Fig. 35-3. Complex, three-dimensional modeling frequently requires the capacity of a large computer. (Computervision Corporation)

using a computer system and the appropriate software can:
- Plan a part, structure, or whatever product is needed.
- Modify the design without having to redraw the entire plan.
- Call up symbols or base drawings from computer storage.

- Automatically duplicate forms and shapes commonly used.
- Produce schedules or analyses.
- Produce hardcopies of complete drawings or drawing elements in a matter of minutes.

Just a few short years ago CADD programs were crude and clumsy, not user friendly, and difficult to use. Most of the early packages required a mainframe computer or powerful minicomputer to handle the calculations. Even then, they were extremely slow. The cost of such a system was so high that only large companies or school systems could afford to purchase one.

Today, this has all changed. Some very large and complex applications still require mainframe, super-minicomputers, or minicomputers, Fig. 35-3. Plus, these systems have become easier to use, faster, and even more powerful. However, microcomputer-based CADD (micro-CADD) systems have steadily improved. Now, they meet the needs of most users. These newer systems are packed with features. Their cost is only a small fraction of a mainframe system, making them affordable for almost every classroom and small business. The trend is toward smaller computers running specialized software programs.

Popular microCADD systems offer high performance at an affordable price. Increased performance improves productivity and helps to produce more accurate drawings. All types of architectural, engineering, and construction (AEC) drawings may be produced with a CADD system, Fig. 35-4.

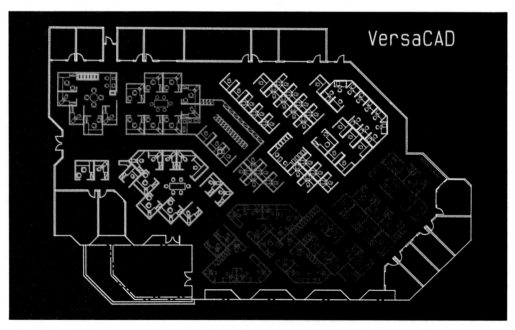

Fig. 35-4. Using functional color, this office complex layout clearly explains the design to the client. (Versacad Corporation)

Once a design has been completed and stored in the computer, it can be called up whenever needed for copies or revisions. Revising CADD drawings is where the true time savings is realized. Frequently, a revision that requires several hours to complete using traditional drafting methods can be done in a few minutes on a CADD system. In addition, some CADD packages automatically produce updated schedules after you revise the original plan.

Another benefit of CADD is symbol libraries. Inserting standard symbols and shapes is quick, easy, and accurate. Once a standard symbol has been drawn and stored in the library, it can be called up and placed as many times, in as many drawings, as required. For example, symbols for trees, Fig. 35-5, furniture, doors and windows, and common appliances are usually included in an architectural symbol library. During insertion, the symbol may be scaled, rotated, or mirrored to meet a specific need. In addition, unique symbols may be designed and added to the library for local applications, Fig. 35-6.

Chapters 35 through 38 will examine computer-aided design and drafting hardware, software, commands, functions, and applications.

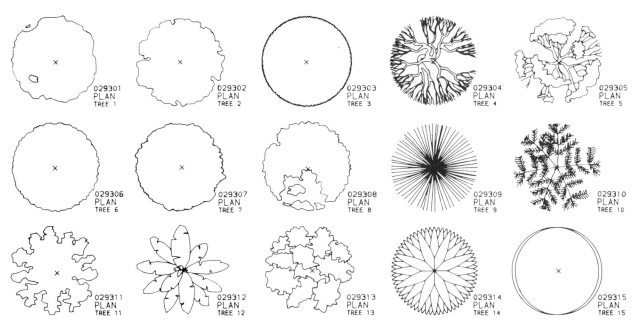

Fig. 35-5. Each of these tree symbols is stored in the computer library for easy access. All can be inserted on the drawing as many times as desired. (Prime Computer, Inc.)

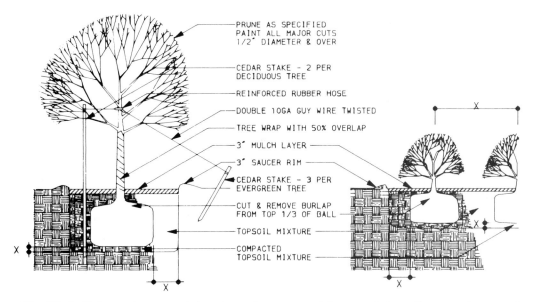

Fig. 35-6. Unique shapes and drawings that are used frequently by a firm may be stored as symbols and incorporated in other drawings. (Prime Computer, Inc.)

Much of the discussion will relate to microcomputer systems since most businesses, schools, and individuals have access to these computers.

A CADD system generally consists of the following hardware: computer or processor, monitor, graphics adapter, input and pointing device, and hardcopy device, Fig. 35-7. Each of these components serves a unique purpose in the system.

Fig. 35-7. The CADD system includes all the necessary hardware to produce complex designs. (Computervision Corporation)

COMPUTER

The heart of a CADD system is the computer. It serves as the center of activity since all information flows through it. Peripheral devices (plotters, digitizing tablets, monitors, etc.) are connected to the computer. Most CADD systems require computers that can process a large amount of information very rapidly. Processing speed is an important consideration when choosing a CADD system computer. The same computer may be used for non-CADD applications, such as word processing and accounting, or the computer may be specially ''dedicated'' to drafting and design functions.

Computers are manufactured in many sizes and configurations. Generally, they are grouped as **mainframe computers, super-minicomputers, minicomputers,** and **microcomputers.**

Mainframe computers are very large and usually able to handle many users at the same time (time sharing) without sacrificing speed. The cost of these systems is extremely high–hundreds of thousands to millions of dollars.

Super-minicomputers, like the Prime 750, are large computers that can handle several users at once, Fig. 35-8. They typically have 8 to 30 megabytes (million bytes) of main memory. They operate very similar to a mainframe computer.

Minicomputers, on the other hand, are generally **turnkey systems** (self-contained). They may or may not serve more than one user. Minicomputer systems are popular for mid-size to large companies, design firms, and schools. The cost for a complete minicomputer CADD system may be over $50,000, depending on the peripheral equipment and software selected.

Fig. 35-8. This CADD workstation is connected to a Prime 750 super-minicomputer. Several other workstations are also connected to the computer. All can be used at the same time.

Microcomputers, sometimes known as **personal computers (PC),** are the smallest computers that support CADD programs. They are self-contained units that are designed primarily for a single user, Fig. 35-9. They may contain several megabytes of **RAM** (Random Access Memory), but most microCADD software packages require no more than 640K RAM. (K means kilobytes, a unit of measurement equal to 1024 characters of information.)

Examples of popular microcomputers for CADD applications include: IBM PC and PS/2 series, Apple Macintosh series, Zenith series, and Compaq series. Those dedicated to CADD generally include a high performance CPU chip,

Fig. 35-9. This microcomputer system is dedicated to CADD and can generate complex drawings in color. (CADKEY)

components synchronized and operating in harmony. Three basic computer CPUs are found in microcomputers today. They are rated according to the size of instruction they can process at one time—8, 16, and 32 bits. Processing power beyond 16 bits has, until recently, been found only in the larger mini-, super-mini-, and mainframe systems. In general, the more powerful the CPU, the faster the computer. Fig. 35-10 shows the type, size, and clock speed of various processor chips used in typical microcomputers.

RAM

The CPU stores data and programs in another hardware component, called **Random Access Memory (RAM)**. Memory is for short term storage and should not be confused with disk storage. The amount of memory is important when choosing CADD programs. Some require larger amounts of storage than your computer can handle. Microcomputers should have a minimum of 640K RAM for most CADD software. Once a computer is turned off, all the information contained in RAM is lost. This is why you store data on permanent storage devices such as floppy disks and hard disks.

MATH COPROCESSORS

Math coprocessors are ''number crunchers'' that take some of the work load off the CPU. With CADD, the coprocessor speeds up the generation of on-screen graphics and is required to operate many CADD software programs. The execution of display commands such as Redraw, Pan, and Zoom are very slow if the computer does not have a math coprocessor. The advent of the math coprocessor is one main factor that led to the sudden popularity of CADD on microcomputers.

additional ports to support pointing devices and plotters, a math coprocessor, and preferably a large capacity hard disk drive and one floppy drive.

CPU

The engine or ''brain'' of the computer system is the CPU (central processing unit). The CPU, also known as a microprocessor in microcomputers, is a computer chip that executes the software program and keeps the various system

Computer	Chip	Clock Speed	Size
IBM PC	8088 (Intel)	4.77 MHz	16 bit
IBM XT	8088 (Intel)	4.77 MHz	16 bit
IBM AT	80286 (Intel)	6 MHz	16 bit
Most PC Clones	8088 (Intel)	5-6 MHz	16 bit
Turbo PC Clones	8088 (Intel)	6-8 MHz	16 bit
AT Clones	80286 (Intel)	8 Mhz	16 bit
IBM PS/2 80	80386 (Intel)	16 MHz	32 bit
Apple MACII	68020 (Motorola)	16 MHz	32 bit

Fig. 35-10. A comparison of CPU chips, their clock speeds, and sizes for several popular microcomputers.

The math coprocessor speeds up processing because graphics information is stored as coordinate data. These data (numbers) require rapid calculation to be useful. The speed using a math coprocessor is about five times that of the same machine without this chip.

PERMANENT STORAGE DEVICES

Permanent storage devices store data and programs. Two basic types of devices are commonly used with microCADD systems: *floppy disks* and the *hard disk,* Fig. 35-11. Floppy disks are available in three diameters: 3 1/2, 5 1/4, and 8 in. The 8 in. disk is least popular, while the 3 1/2 in. disk is gaining popularity over 5 1/4 in. disks due to its large storage capacity and rigid case. The 5 1/4 in. disk is available in 360KB as well as 1.2MB capacities. Most CADD applications use the 1.2MB size disk.

Fig. 35-12. Typical 5 1/4 in. and 3 1/2 in. floppy disks used with a microcomputer.

Fig. 35-11. This microcomputer has a 20MB hard disk (below) and a 1.2MB floppy disk.

Hard disks, or fixed disk units, are much faster than floppies. They are also capable of storing much larger amounts of data. Graphics applications require huge amounts of storage space for the software as well as drawings. For example, about 55 floppy disks would be required to store the same amount of data that can be stored on a 20MB hard disk. Most popular CADD software packages require (or strongly suggest) including a hard disk as well as one floppy disk unit in the system.

Backup files should be made to prevent loss due to damage of the hard disk. Backups should also be made of all floppy disks. The contents of a hard disk can be backed up on floppies, Fig.

35-12. However, a streaming tape system is preferred by most users. Some systems have a built-in tape backup for regular use.

STANDARD PORTS

Connected to the computer are input and output devices such as a plotter, digitizing tablet, and monitor. These connect to ports on the back of the computer. Two types of ports are generally used with microcomputers: *parallel* and *serial.* Parallel ports have a 25 pin connector. Serial ports have 9 or 25 pin connectors. Most input and output devices, such as the plotter and digitizing tablet, connect to a standard RS-232 serial port. However, most dot matrix and daisy wheel printers require a parallel port. The ports, located at the rear of the computer, use standard multipin connectors for easy attachment. See Fig. 35-13.

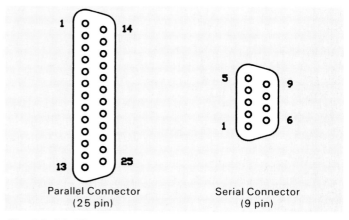

Parallel Connector
(25 pin)

Serial Connector
(9 pin)

Fig. 35-13. The two types of ports used to attach peripherals. Left. Parallel port. Right. Serial port.

Each device requires its own port. It is important to identify all of the intended peripherals when purchasing the computer so that it can be configured properly. However, most computers have space (expansion slots) for future use. Printed circuit boards (cards) may be inserted in these slots to expand memory, increase speed, add ports, etc.

MONITORS

The monitor, or display, allows the computer to communicate with the operator. Monitors are available in a broad spectrum of sizes, prices, quality, and applications. Important considerations include: compatibility with the computer you are using, color or monochrome, physical size of the monitor, and character resolution.

Monitors for microCADD applications can be divided into two main categories, *color* or *monochrome.* Monochrome monitors are generally used for word processing and similar applications where color is not important. Color monitors are popular for CADD since color is functional and supported by many CADD software programs, Fig. 35-14. The trend in CADD systems is to have a large color monitor for graphics and a smaller monochrome monitor for text material. This arrangement lets you see more of the drawing on the color monitor. The monochrome monitor shows previously executed commands and prompts.

Monitors range in size from 5 in. to over 25 in. The most popular size is 13 in. This size offers an adequate viewing area for most CADD applications. However, a 15 in. monitor helps reduce eyestrain and speeds work when drawing many small details. Large monitors do require extra space and are significantly more expensive.

Resolution is often more important than size. Resolution refers to the sharpness of detail displayed on the screen. A CADD monitor should have at least a resolution of 640 x 480 pixels, if possible. A *pixel,* or picture element, is one dot of light emitted from the screen. Low-resolution displays produce coarse images with stair-step diagonal lines and curves. High-resolution monitors produce smooth lines at any angle. Monitors are available with a resolution over 1000 pixels in both vertical and horizontal directions. These monitors are considerably more expensive, but produce very sharp images.

Most monitors have a slightly curved screen surface. This makes lines on the displayed image look curved rather than straight. Newer monitors are flat and eliminate this problem. Glare has also been reduced in newer models. With less glare, an operator can work for longer periods without eyestrain, Fig. 35-15.

GRAPHICS ADAPTERS

The graphics monitor requires a special circuit board in the computer called a *graphics adapter* or *controller.* The adapter should be compatible with the resolution and color characteristics required by the monitor. This lets the monitor display its best color and resolution capabilities. Typical graphics adapters include: EGA (enhanced graphics adapter), CGA (color graphics

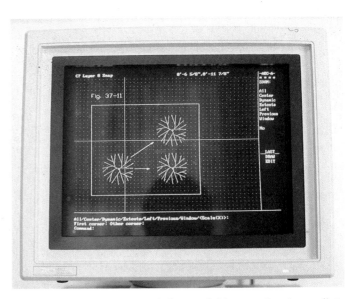

Fig. 35-14. A typical CADD monitor with good resolution and sharp color.

Fig. 35-15. This state-of-the-art 14 in. monitor has a flat screen that eliminates distortion, reduces glare, and provides high (640 X 480) resolution. It is an excellent monitor for CADD applications.

Introduction to Computer-Aided Drafting and Design   515

adapter), MDA (monochrome display adapter), and VGA (video graphics array).

INPUT AND POINTING DEVICES

All CADD systems require one or more input devices. Typical input devices include: keyboard, mouse, digitizing tablet and puck or stylus, light pen, joystick, thumb wheels, and track ball.

Keyboard

The keyboard is the most common and universal input device, Fig. 35-16. It provides an excellent way to input numbers and letters (alphanumeric information). Typing skills are almost a necessity to use the keyboard efficiently.

There are three common kinds of keyboards available: membrane, calculator-style, and typewriter-style. The membrane type is touch sensitive with no moving parts. It is found in certain industrial environments where the membrane cover protects the keyboard from dirt and debris. The calculator-style keyboard is most popular for microCADD applications. It provides for easy input of text as well as numeric data. This keyboard also has special function keys that allow you to perform several commands or a unique function with a single keystroke. The typewriter-style keyboard is designed for word processing applications and is not as fully functional for CADD as the calculator-style. Since the keyboard is such an important element of a CADD system, it should be comfortable and suited for the specific application.

Mouse

The mouse is a popular input device for CADD programs. Often called a pointing device, it is used to pick objects and identify points on the screen, Fig. 35-17. Although inexpensive, it is an effective way to issue commands and draw. Some CADD programs are designed specifically for this type of input device.

Fig. 35-17. A mouse is one type of input and pointing device.

Two types of mice are common. One type has a small ball on the underside that rolls as the mouse moves across a smooth surface, Fig. 35-18. The cursor on screen moves with the mouse's movement. Another type of mouse has a small light source that shines on a metal pad that contains a metal grid. The mouse detects movement when the light passes over a grid line.

Fig. 35-16. This keyboard is especially suited for CADD work. It has 101 keys arranged in five groups—alphanumeric keys, numeric keys, control keypad, cursor control keypad, and function keys.

Fig. 35-18. This underside view of a mouse shows the ball that senses motion.

Digitizing Tablet

Digitizing tablets and larger digitizing tables are a vital part of most large CADD systems. A digitizing tablet consists of a large, smooth surface and a cursor control. When used with a menu overlay, digitizing tablets can speed the design and drafting process greatly, Fig. 35-19. Many popular CADD packages are developed around menu overlays and require a digitizing tablet for efficient use.

Basically, a puck or stylus on the digitizing tablet converts graphic data or X-Y coordinates for point entry. Digitizers can be used in several ways. Without a menu overlay, they function much like a mouse. With a menu overlay, they can be used to select commands as well as

draw. In addition, you can sketch (digitize) existing drawings placed on the tablet.

Digitizing tablets are available in several sizes. The most popular are: 9 x 9, 12 x 12, and 12 x 18 in. However, digitizing tables can be several feet wide and long, Fig. 35-20. The resolution of the tablet is a consideration. For example, a tablet with good resolution would be able to discern over 1,000 lines per inch (.001 in. resolution). High resolution is necessary for digitizing existing hardcopy drawings.

A stylus or puck cursor control is used with a digitizing tablet to select items and locate points, Fig. 35-21. The puck is more popular

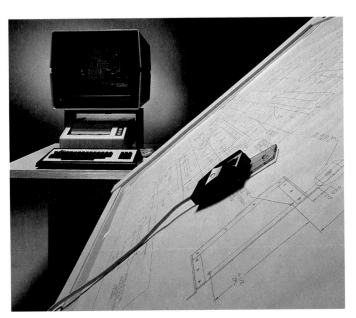

Fig. 35-20. A digitizing table used to input large drawings. (Computervision Corporation)

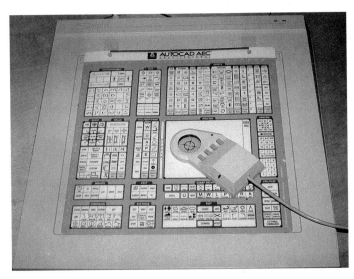

Fig. 35-19. This 12 x 12 in. digitizing tablet, with a menu overlay, provides a convenient and efficient way to enter commands, move the cursor, and digitize drawings.

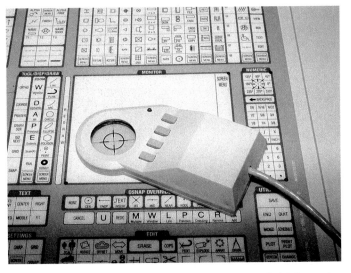

Fig. 35-21. A four-button puck used with a digitizing tablet. The buttons can be assigned certain commands or functions by the software.

Introduction to Computer-Aided Drafting and Design 517

because it also has buttons that perform functions. For example, the buttons might activate commands such as Erase, Pan, or Line.

Miscellaneous Input Devices

Several other input devices may be used with various CADD software. They include: light pen, joystick, thumb wheels, and track ball. These devices are not as popular, but are preferred by some CADD operators.

GRAPHICS OUTPUT DEVICES

The information created on a CADD system may be classified as *softcopy* or *hardcopy.* Softcopy includes user prompts, instructions, and a visual record of the operations as they are performed. This information is output to the monitor. Hardcopy output includes drawings, parts lists, bills of materials, and specifications. These are produced on paper, vellum, or film using a plotter or printer, Fig. 35-22.

The hardcopy device you have depends on the intended use of the output. The most common devices used to produce hardcopy output in-clude: pen plotters, laser printers, thermal plotters, electrostatic plotters, color impact printers, daisy wheel printers, and film recorders. When evaluating these devices, consider their accuracy, quality of lines and text, speed, plot size, and color possibilities.

Pen Plotters

The pen plotter is the most popular device for producing high-quality CADD line drawings, Fig. 35-23. It is the easiest for experienced drafters

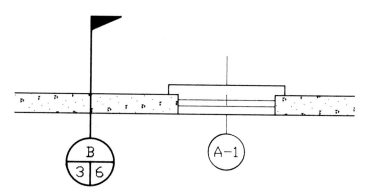

Fig. 35-23. This drawing was made by a multipen plotter at a speed of 16 in./sec.

DOOR SCHEDULE

DOOR NO.	W	H	T	MAT.	TYPE	FRAME MAT.	REMARKS
05 01	3'-0"	7'-0"	1 3/4"	WD.	A	H.M.	SOLID CORE
05 02	3'-0"	7'-0"	1 3/4"	WD.	A	H.M.	SOLID CORE
05 03	PR3'-6"	7'-0"	1 3/4"	WD.	B	H.M.	
05 04	3'-6"	7'-0"	*	H.M.	–	H.M.	
05 05	3'-6"	7'-0"	*	H.M.	–	H.M.	
05 06	3'-6"	7'-0"	*	H.M.	–	H.M.	
05 07	3'-0"	7'-0"	1 3/4"	WD.	A	H.M.	SOLID CORE
05 08	3'-0"	7'-0"	1 3/4"	WD.	A	H.M.	SOLID CORE
05 09	3'-6"	7'-0"	1 3/4"	WD.	C	H.M.	

ABBREVIATIONS:

H.M. – HOLLOW METAL
PR – PAIR
ST. – STAIR

Fig. 35-22. This door schedule is an example of hardcopy output. (Sigma Designs, Inc.)

to understand because it produces drawings in much the same way they do. The pen plotter will create a finished document drawing, parts list, bill of materials, or specifications on most any traditional drafting medium such as tracing paper, vellum, or film.

Pen plotters are made in two basic styles--flatbed and drum. Flatbed plotters resemble drafting tables that are electronically operated. They are available in several sizes to handle ''A'', ''B'', ''C'', ''D'', and ''E'' size drawings. Some flatbed plotters are several feet long for special applications. A flatbed plotter holds the drawing medium stationary and moves the pen across the sheet. This makes it easy to monitor the drawing while it is being created, Fig. 35-24.

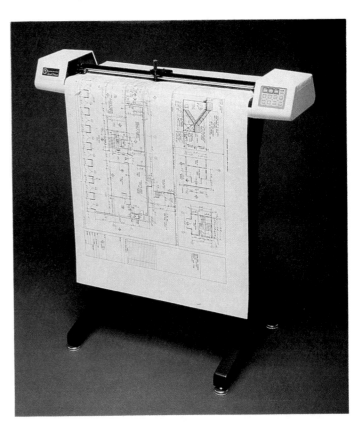

Fig. 35-25. A drum-type pen plotter capable of drawing on 24 x 36 in. paper, vellum, or film. This machine is available with 14 pen stalls.
(Houston Instrument, Division of AMETEK, Inc.)

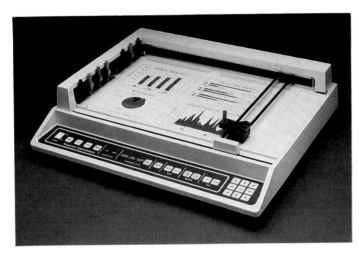

Fig. 35-24. A small flatbed pen plotter used for ''A'' size drawings. (Houston Instrument, Division of AMETEK, Inc.)

Drum-type pen plotters operate on a different principle than flatbed plotters. Drum plotters move both the pen and the medium, Fig. 35-25. A drum rolls the paper or other medium forward and backward. A pen carriage slides across a rail to move the pen from one side to the other. Angles and curves are produced by moving the pen and medium simultaneously. Drum plotters do not let you inspect the drawing in process as easily as flatbed plotters because the paper is constantly moving. Some drum plotters can handle standard size sheets up to ''E'' size. Their performance is comparable to flatbed plotters. While the flatbed plotter is usually placed on a table, the drum plotter stands on the floor.

Most modern pen plotters are available as single- or multi-pen models. Some have as many as 14 stalls for a variety of pen sizes and colors. Pen plotters run at different speeds depending on the application, drafting medium, pens, and ink used. Speeds run as high as 15 to 25 in./sec.

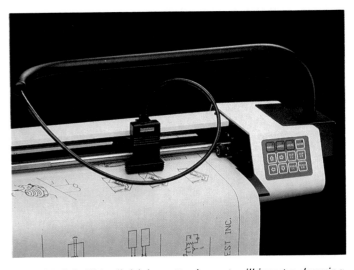

Fig. 35-26. This digitizing attachment will input a drawing into the computer in a fraction of the time required to enter it manually.
(Houston Instrument, Division of AMETEK, Inc.)

while the plotter maintains an accuracy of 0.001 in. repeatability. A digitizing attachment, available for some pen plotters, lets the plotter input drawings into the computer. Fig. 35-26 shows a digitizing attachment for a drum pen plotter.

Laser Printers

Laser printers are very popular where line drawings and text material is integrated together, such as in desktop publishing. These printers provide a quiet and fast means of producing quality black and white documents. The

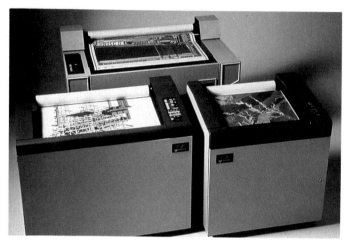

Fig. 35-27. This electrostatic plotter will produce drawings up to "D" size. (Versatec)

quality of line drawings is not as sharp as those made with a pen plotter, but good enough for many applications. One disadvantage, however, is that laser printers cannot handle large sheets. They may be used for small format "check" plots.

Electrostatic Plotters

The electrostatic plotter is often considered the most versatile type of plotter, Fig. 35-27. It can function as a plotter or a printer. Although it is over 75 times as fast as a pen plotter, a drawback is that the accuracy is much less than a pen plotter. When operated in the printer mode, it can produce over 2,500 individual characters per second.

The electrostatic plotter converts vector data into a pattern of dots, or rasters. The small dots, arranged in a matrix or array, creates the text or drawing. Electrostatic plotters can handle large sheets, but traditional drafting paper is generally unacceptable. They use a special electrographic paper which produces a copy similar to a typical duplicating machine.

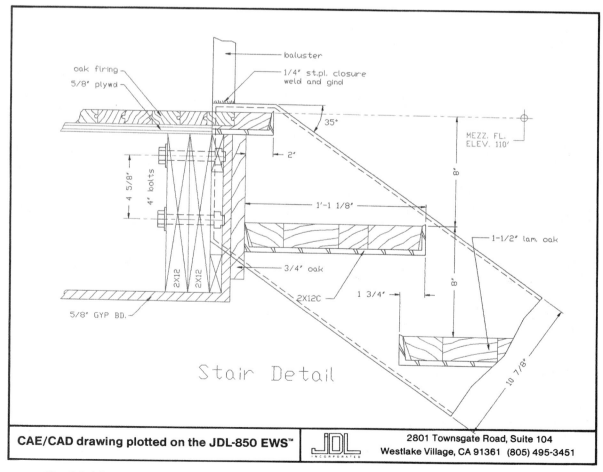

Fig. 35-28. A detail drawing produced with a 24 pin color impact printer/plotter. (JDL, Inc.)

Color Impact Printers

The color impact printer provides a less expensive alternative to color plotting. Although the quality is less than that of a pen plotter, it is acceptable for some applications, Fig. 35-28. A major disadvantage of the color impact printer is that it cannot handle sheets larger than ''C'' size. These printers are fast and provide good preliminary drafts.

Daisy Wheel Printers

Daisy wheel printers produce letters and numbers in the same way as typewriters by striking character keys against an inked ribbon or film. These units produce high quality drafts of text material, but cannot produce line drawings.

Film Recorders

Film recorders produce 35 mm slides, color prints, and transparencies for overhead projectors. The slide, print, or transparency is made by a camera unit photographing an image displayed inside the device. The entire unit is attached to the computer, Fig. 35-29. The computer can control the exposure and automatically advances the film as each photo is made. The quality of these visuals is good and may be used for presentations, Fig. 35-30.

Fig. 35-29. Film recorder unit and computer used to produce slides of computer-generated drawings. (Bruning)

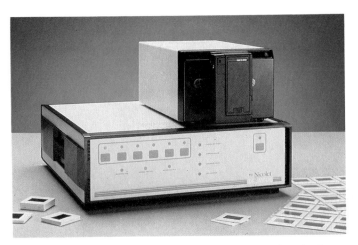

Fig. 35-30. Closeup of the film recorder. (Bruning)

REVIEW QUESTIONS—CHAPTER 35

Write your ansers on a separate sheet of paper. Do not write in this book.

1. _____ is the modern acronym for computer-aided drafting and design.
2. Identify the four basic categories of computers discussed in this chapter.
3. How may a computer symbol library be used?
4. Name the four basic parts of a CADD hardware system.
5. What type of computer is self-contained and designed primarily for a single user?
6. A unit of measurement equal to 1024 characters of information is represented with the following symbol _____.
7. What do the letters CPU stand for?
8. The largest CPUs have _____ bits of processing power.
9. Two types of permanent storage devices used in a computer are _____ and _____.
10. What is the purpose of a math coprocessor?
11. A CADD computer usually has a parallel port and a _____ port to connect input and output devices.
12. The _____ allows the computer to communicate with the operator.
13. Name the two basic types of monitors that are available for CADD work.
14. Which of the following monitors would produce the sharpest image on the screen, assuming they were all the same size?
    a. 320 X 200 pixels.
    b. 640 X 350 pixels.
    c. 640 X 480 pixels.
15. The _____ is the most common and universal input device for use with a computer.

Introduction to Computer-Aided Drafting and Design 521

16. Which of the following is not a computer input device?
    a. light pen.
    b. stylus.
    c. pen ball.
    d. joystick.
    e. mouse
    f. keyboard
17. How can a digitizing tablet be used?
18. The output generated on a CADD system may be classified as _____ copy and _____ copy.
19. The _____ is the most popular device for producing high-quality CADD line drawings.
20. The _____ plotter is considered by some to be the most versatile type of plotter because it can function as a plotter or printer.

SUGGESTED ACTIVITIES

1. Collect as many examples of computer-generated graphics (hardcopy output) as possible. Compare the line quality produced by each machine.
2. Visit your local computer store and examine the CADD hardware available. Collect specification sheets, descriptive literature, and price lists about the hardware components and share this with your class.
3. Arrange a field trip to see a demonstration of a large (mini-, super-mini-, or mainframe) CADD system. Take notes during the demonstration and prepare a summary of the basic capabilities of the system. Compare your list with lists prepared by other members of the class.

A visual (slide) created with a film recorder. (Versacad Corporation)

CADD Software

After studying this chapter you will be able to:
* Explain the benefits of using CADD in generating architectural designs.
* Identify several factors that should be considered when purchasing a CADD system.
* Describe the characteristics of a general-purpose CADD program.
* Describe the features of an AEC architectural CADD program.
* Select a CADD package to perform certain tasks based on characteristics of software presented in the chapter.

Software is the program or series of instructions that makes the hardware perform the intended tasks. Selecting a specific software package is probably the single most important decision in putting together a CADD system. Not only is the decision important, it is tough. There are many CADD packages available. They range widely in price, speed, capability, ease of use, and required hardware. Yet, if the proper decision is made, you will find yourself in a wonderful new world–the world of computer-aided drafting and design.

BENEFITS OF CADD IN ARCHITECTURE

Granted, the computer has proven its worth in scientific applications such as space flight, biotechnology, and atomic research. It has conquered the tasks of word processing, spreadsheets, and file management. But, has the computer overcome the obstacles inherent in the creative process of design? The answer to this question is definitely, yes.

The computer itself has changed in the last 10 or 15 years. It is faster, more user friendly, and more colorful. However, the big advances have been in software. Good CADD software is abun-

dant and economical today, Fig. 36-1. There is a package to perform most any task that you can imagine. The problem is to choose the right one.

Modern CADD programs let the drafter/designer develop and communicate ideas in precise and attractive computer-generated graphics, Fig. 36-2. Once an operator learns how to use a given system, increased productivity and higher quality work will be recognized. All types of mechanical, architectural, construction, and engineering drawings can be made on a CADD system. Plus, the drafter does not make an endless number of revised drawings for each small change required. In fact, editing drawings is where CADD earns its cost. Changes are easy to make and some software makes the corrections in every drawing or schedule affected. Even the simplest CADD packages speed the change process.

Once a design is complete, plots of all or selected parts of the design can be made in

Fig. 36-1. Many CADD software packages are available, and the number constantly increases.

ENTER MAXIMUM RISE (INCHES)
7.75

ENTER MINIMUM RUN (INCHES)
9

ENTER WIDTH OF STAIRS
3'1

ENTER TYPE OF STAIRS - METAL PAN (M), CONCRETE (C) OR WOOD (W)
W

ENTER CONFIGURATION OF STAIRS - STRAIGHT (S), L OR U SHAPE
L

STARTING POINT OF STAIRS
(CROSS HAIRS)

ENTER SIZE OF LANDING
3'1

SECOND POINT AT LANDING
(CROSS HAIRS)

ENDING POINT OF STAIRS
(CROSS HAIRS)

Fig. 36-2. Precise drawings, such as this stair detail, represent the quality of modern computer-generated drawings. (Sigma Design Inc.)

minutes. Depending on the equipment being used, a drawing may be:
- Plotted at any scale which will fit on the drafting medium.
- Plotted in several colors.
- Developed in sequential steps.
- Presented on different media depending on the intended use.

Flexibility is definitely one advantage of using a CADD system to generate drawings, Fig. 36-3.

Architectural and construction applications can benefit from a CADD system in several other ways. Various CADD packages will automatically generate window and door schedules, kitchen cabinet schedules, plumbing fixture schedules, lighting fixture schedules, and various reports, Fig. 36-4. This function does require preplanning so that the appropriate attributes can be identified during the design process. Yet, the time savings of having window and door information collected automatically is overshadowed by another feature. Most CADD systems have automatic correction in the event a window or door is changed. The time required to redraw a schedule or floor plan because of a simple change would be significant using traditional drafting methods. Using CADD, such a change would require only a few minutes to complete.

Drawings produced on a CADD system will possess a high degree of uniformity regardless of who makes the drawings. (Of course, this

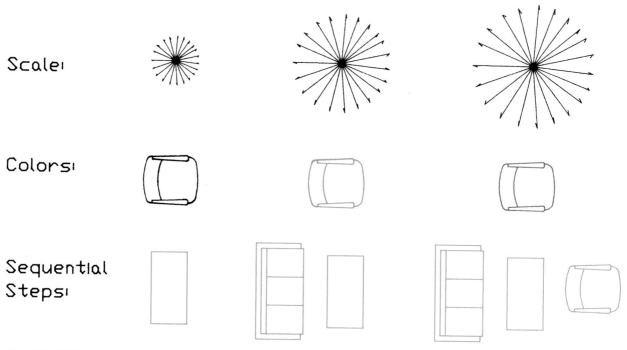

Scale:

Colors:

Sequential Steps:

Fig. 36-3 This drawing represents some of the flexibility provided by CADD. It represents varied scale, multiple colors, and drawing in sequential steps.

CIRCUIT DATA

LIGHTING CIRCUITS:
    4 CIRCUITS PROVIDING 1800 WATTS EACH

SPECIAL APPLIANCE CIRCUITS:
    4 CIRCUITS PROVIDING 2400 WATTS EACH

INDIVIUAL APPLIANCE CIRCUITS:
    1 CIRCUIT FOR REFRIGERATOR
    1 CIRCUIT FOR GARBAGE DISPOSAL
    1 CIRCUIT FOR DISHWASHER
    1 CIRCUIT FOR WASHER
    1 CIRCUIT FOR FURNACE
    1 CIRCUIT FOR WATER PUMP (230 V)
    1 CIRCUIT FOR RANGE (230 V)
    1 CIRCUIT FOR TABLE SAW
    1 CIRCUIT FOR AIR COMPRESSOR (230 V)

2 SPARE CIRCUITS

DISTRIBUTION PANEL:
    150 AMP, 20 CIRCUITS

Fig. 36-4. A computer-generated circuit data chart.

assumes each drafter has the technical knowledge to select the proper symbol, size, etc.) For example, every time tree symbol ''X'' is placed on the drawing, it is reproduced exactly the same as before. Every single-pole light switch drawn will be identical, Fig. 36-5. The length of

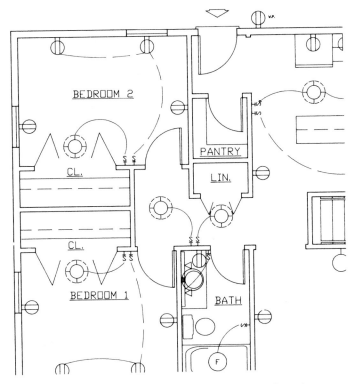

Fig. 36-5. The symbols used in CADD drawings have a high degree of uniformity.

every dash in a hidden line will be the same. Such uniformity greatly improves communication among those who use the final drawings. Yet, uniformity need not reduce creativity or personal style because users can develop and store personalized symbols. But, just as before, each symbol ''X'' placed on the drawing will look exactly like the previous one.

Poor line quality that will not reproduce does not exist with CADD. All lines drawn by the plotter will be reproducible. Proper line widths, Fig. 36-6, require no more time than making sure the lines are the same on screen. Smudged lines or sloppy lettering, which often leads to errors on the construction site, is not a problem with CADD-generated drawings. In short, the benefits gained from sharp, crisp, clean, and accurate drawings is reason enough to use a CADD system.

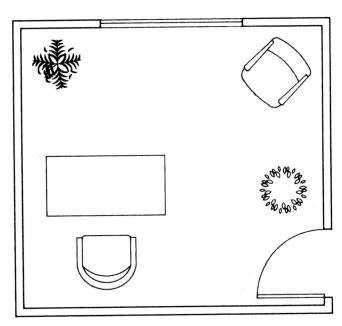

Fig. 36-6. How many different line widths can you count in this drawing? There are many used.

The time saved by CADD in making drawings with many repetitive features is impressive. For example, the time required to draw the brick symbol around a foundation wall by hand would be significant. Using a CADD software package, the symbol could be called up from the library and applied to the proper area in minutes. A site plan requiring several complex tree symbols might require an hour or more to draw by hand. The trees could be added almost instantly using symbols from the CADD library.

Greater savings in time can be realized by drawing complex details only once and then storing them on disk. Using CADD functions to

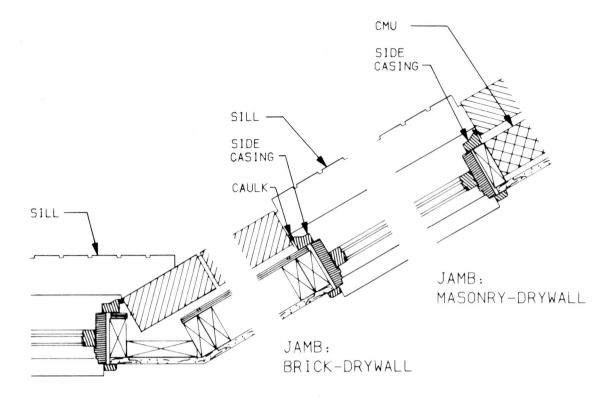

Fig. 36-7. This complex window framing detail is stored in the computer for use whenever it is needed.

add stored shapes, you simply insert the details on drawings where needed. Examples include window details, typical wall sections, stair designs, cabinet details, paving and gutter sections, culverts, roof and floor truss details, and so on, Fig. 36-7. One can readily see that using standard details, with only minor changes, could save many hours in a single set of drawings.

CADD has reached a high level of sophistication, dependability, and ease of use. Almost anyone wishing to use it can justify the cost. Companies of all sizes as well as individuals are using CADD to produce top-rate drawings.

SELECTING A CADD PACKAGE

All CADD packages are not alike. Some are designed for very specific applications. For example, Andersen's CADD-I program is used to draw Andersen windows and prepare schedules and specifications for their windows, Fig. 36-8. Other packages are specific for a field. An example is AutoCAD's AEC architecture package. This program is specifically designed for persons who design residential or light commercial buildings, Fig. 36-9. Still other packages, such as

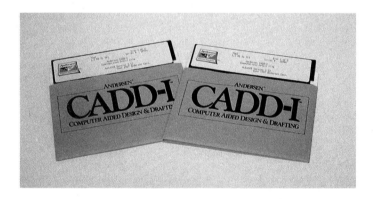

Fig. 36-8. This CADD program draws the plan view, elevation, and detail of Andersen's windows. It also generates a window schedule. (Andersen Corporation)

CADKEY, are broader in scope, Fig. 36-10. This package is aimed at general engineering design and provides full 3D object generation. The best advice is that you know what you need in a CADD package before buying one.

The answers to these basic questions may help you select the best package for you:
- How easy is the program to use? Does it provide help/screens and clear instructions?
- Does the program require special hardware not common to other packages? If so, you

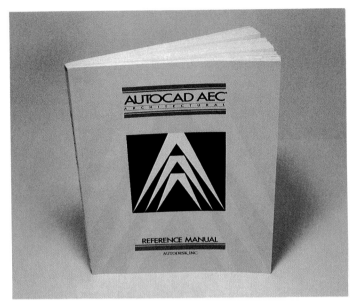

Fig. 36-9. AutoCAD's AEC Architecture CADD program is specifically designed for persons that design residential and light commercial buildings. (Autodesk, Inc.)

Fig. 36-10. CADKEY is designed for general engineering applications. It has full 3D capabilities. (CADKEY, Division of Micro Control System, Inc.)

might want to think twice before purchasing the package.

- How well does the package meet your needs? Is it useful to you? Just because it is a ''neat'' package is not a good reason to purchase it.
- What kind of support does the company provide after you purchase it? Do they provide updates—either free or for a reasonable cost? Will they answer your questions over the phone? Remember these programs are complex and you may need some help in using them.

- What are the hardware requirements of the package? Determine whether expanded memory, special cards, or a math coprocessor is needed or recommended.
- Check the warranty. What does it provide? What is the length of time covered?
- What are specific features of the software? Is it broad or narrow in application? Is it 2D or 3D? Is it a design or support package? Is it compatible with other popular packages?
- How much does it cost? How does the cost compare with other similar packages? Consider a price-to-performance ratio.

You may be able to think of other questions to add to this list. These should be helpful in weeding out packages that do not fit your needs. If possible, use the program before you purchase it. At least talk to someone who has used it.

GENERAL-PURPOSE CADD PACKAGES

General-purpose CADD packages are usually designed for making typical mechanical drawings and other general drafting applications. Although architectural/construction drawings can be made using these packages, an AEC (architectural, engineering, and construction) software program is more suited to architectural work.

General-purpose CADD packages are available to meet a wide range of needs. Some are very comprehensive and used by major industries. Others are used purely for CADD education, home use, and less demanding drawings. See Fig. 36-11.

Fig. 36-11. AutoSketch is an inexpensive, general-purpose CADD program. (Autodesk, Inc.)

It would be impossible to describe the capabilities, strengths, and weaknesses of all general-purpose CADD packages. A brief description of the main features of popular CADD packages is provided here to show the range of capabilities. The features chosen offer a rather comprehensive view of general-purpose CADD.

General-purpose CADD package characteristics

A study of any CADD package should review certain features, regardless of the intended use. Other characteristics may be important or not depending on specific needs of the user. The following list provides a rather broad basis for comparing most general-purpose CADD packes.

- **Basic system requirements.** This ranges from mainframe to microcomputer. The cost of a complete CADD system is most affected by the hardware required to run the software.
- **Supported hardware.** Examples of supported hardware include a math coprocessor, digitizing tablet or mouse, plotter, and EMS memory. Speed and flexibility of the system are greatly affected by these hardware items.
- **Number of Dimensions.** The basic categories include 2D, 2.5D, and 3D, Fig. 36-12. Some software programs are limited to two-dimensional drafting while others create a true three-dimensional design. 3D programs store a three-dimensional database for each point on an object. The number of dimensions greatly affects the ability to view and display pictorial views of the object.
- **Entities.** Entities are the basic elements used to create objects. They include such things as lines, points, circles, arcs, boxes, etc. However, other entities such as polylines, fillets, chamfers, and freehand sketching add function to the program. The number and type of entities included in the program are very important for speed and ease of drawing. See Fig. 36-13.
- **Compound entities.** Compound entities refer to the ability to manipulate several entities as a group, block, attribute, or symbol. Compound entities add considerable flexibility in manipulating entities.
- **Entity editing.** Entity editing includes tools to copy, erase, move, scale, rotate, trim, break, explode, array, divide, mirror, extend, and stretch shapes, Fig. 36-14. Having several entity editing tools to choose from is an advantage.
- **Layers.** Layers are similar to transparent drawing sheets on which you can draw. They allow various parts of a drawing to be placed on different ''sheets'' or layers. This feature is especially useful in creating several drawings that must relate in some way to each other. Layers also help when plotting a variety of outputs from a single complex drawing. The number of layers available in typical general-purpose CADD packages range from zero to unlimited.
- **Colors.** Adding color can be very useful when designing objects on a CADD system. For example, certain features can be assigned a certain color for easy viewing. In addition, color

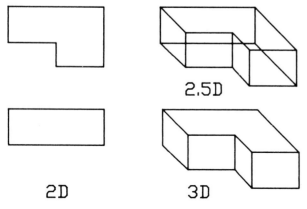

Fig. 36-12. Comparison of 2D, 2.5D, and 3D drawings.

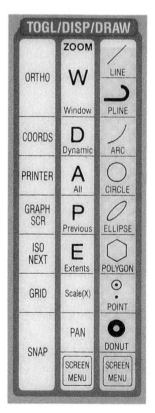

Fig. 36-13. Available entities that you can add to the drawing are clearly indicated on this digitizing template. (Autodesk, Inc.)

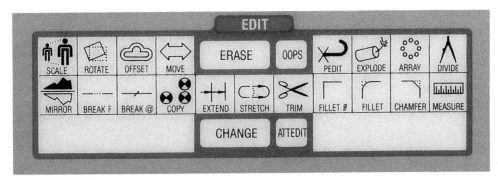

Fig. 36-14. The edit section of this template is used for entity editing.
(Autodesk, Inc.)

aids communication. Most CADD packages provide a number of colors, Fig. 36-15.
- **Standard linetypes.** Mechanical drawings as well as specialized drawings generally require several standard linetypes. Those most frequently found in general-purpose CADD packages include: continuous (solid), dashed, hidden, center, phantom, border, dot, and dashdot. A broad assortment of standard linetypes saves time when creating drawings that should conform to standard format.
- **Indicating position.** To make drawings, the user must be able to indicate where to begin, end, or place an entity. You can do this with the digitizing tablet, some type of pointing device, or keyboard. A good CADD package will provide for more than one method to enter location and distance.
- **Linear units.** The unit of linear measurement is used to place points and locate straight line distance. Several systems of assigning linear units are common—architectural, engineering, scientific, decimal, and fractional. A powerful

CADD package will include several linear units for broad base application.
- **Angular units.** Angular units are also possible in several formats. Some of the common ones include: decimal degrees, degrees/minutes/seconds, grads, radians, and surveyor's units. Several formats are useful for multiple applications.
- **Command entry.** Because most CADD programs are command driven, the method(s) of invoking commands is very important. Common methods of entering commands include: keyboard, screen menu, tablet menu, and button menu. The ability to enter commands several ways speeds work and makes operation easier.
- **Display Controls.** The computer communicates with the operator through the monitor, or display. Display controls help the operator better see what is being drawn. Functions such as zoom, pan, view, redraw, and fill help the operator see the desired area on the screen, Fig. 36-16.
- **Drawing aids.** Drawing aids help you locate position on screen and on existing entities. They make the task of drawing easier, faster, and more accurate. The more common drawing aids included in CADD packages are: grid, snap, orthogonal mode, object snap, axis, isometric mode, dynamic location, and attach, Fig. 36-17. The absence of these drawing aids would make the drawing process considerably more difficult.
- **Dimensioning.** Dimensioning has always been a problem for manual drafters. Most CADD packages make it a simple two-step operation. You simply pick the distance to measure and locate where the dimension should appear. The dimension numeral can be shown using several standard formats. Dimensioning approaches and options available with most CADD packages include: linear (aligned, horizontal, vertical), angular, diameter/radius,

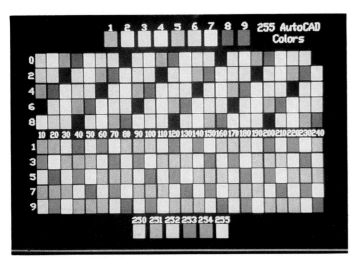

Fig. 36-15. These colors, photographed from the screen display, are supported by this CADD package and hardware setup.

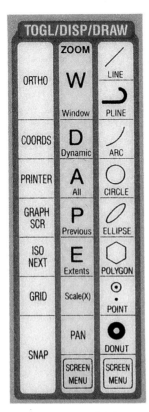

Fig. 36-16. The display section of the template determines how much and what parts of the drawing are displayed. (Autodesk, Inc.)

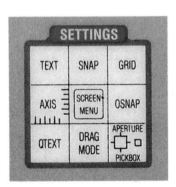

Fig. 36-17. This digitizing template incorporates a section called "settings." Note the commands included in this block. (Autodesk, Inc.)

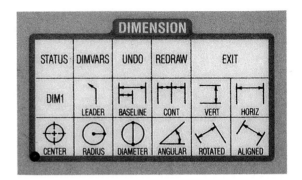

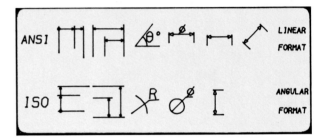

Fig. 36-18. Most digitizing templates include a section for dimensioning commands. These illustrate two common approaches. (Autodesk, Inc., Prime Computer, Inc.)

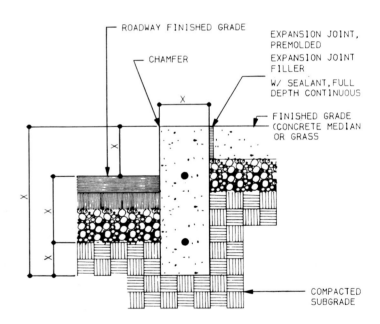

Fig. 36-19. Note the different hatch patterns in this section view. These are provided by many CADD packages. (Prime Computer, Inc.)

leader, alternate units (English/metric), arrow styles, dimension settings, and tolerancing. A full range of options is desirable for various applications, Fig. 36-18.

- **Standard hatch patterns.** Drawings are usually composed of lines, standard symbols, and notes. Hatching using the proper symbol is an important feature of any drawing requiring a sectioned view. Common CADD packages may include several standard hatch symbols, Fig. 36-19. Most also allow you to design your own pattern. Creating custom symbols is very time consuming. The broader the selec-

tion of patterns the software includes, the greater the savings in time.

- **Text fonts.** A text font provides a certain overall "style" to a drawing. A variety of fonts is not essential, but does allow the user to personalize his/her work. Some CADD packages not only provide several standard fonts, but allow you to design new fonts.
- **Geometric analysis.** Geometric analysis is important for certain types of drawings and

applications. Typical geometric-supported analyses by CADD programs include area, distance, and angles, Fig. 36-20. More sophisticated programs also include centroid, moment, and section modulus. The importance of this feature will depend on the application.

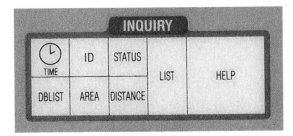

Fig. 36-20. The ''inquiry'' section of this template provides for distance and area analyses. (Autodesk, Inc.)

- **On-line printing or plotting.** On-line printing or plotting is a convenience that can save time when generating drawings to see the hardcopy output during the creation process.
- **Digitizing.** Digitizing a hardcopy drawing is one way to enter an existing drawing into the computer without having to redraw it. This is an important timesaver for some types of applications.
- **3D shading.** Three-dimensional shading adds a true-to-life appearance to a 3D drawing. Shaded drawings are useful for communicating overall designs, generating publicity materials, and presentation models, Fig. 36-21.
- **Drawing interchanges.** A CADD program's ability to communicate with other packages or databases is important for many users. Some of the common drawing interchanges supported by CADD packages are: IGES (Initial Graphics Exchange Specification), DXF (Drawing Interchange Format), and DXB (Drawing Interchange Binary format).
- **Program customization.** The degree to which the user can customize the software is especially important to the experienced CADD user. Customization allows the user to modify the program to suit his/her purposes. Some areas of customization that may be important are: menus, fonts, hatch patterns, linetypes, system variables, prototype drawing directories, tablet menus, shapes, help files, macros, and system messages.
- **Schedule generation.** Most full-function CADD packages provide for ''automatic'' schedule generation. The data is taken from entity or symbol attributes that were identified at the time the symbol was inserted into the drawing. The ability to generate schedules may be an important capability for some applications.
- **Programming.** Programming allows you write a program that performs a series of functions with one key press or command. Some CADD systems have internal programming, otherwise known as macro programs. Examples of common microcomputer programming languages include AutoLISP for AutoCAD and CPL for VersaCAD.
- **3D primitives.** Primitives are three-dimensional shapes used to create 3D models just as lines, rectangles, and circles are used in 2D drawing. Common 3D primitives are: boxes, cylinders, cones, spheres, and custom primitives.

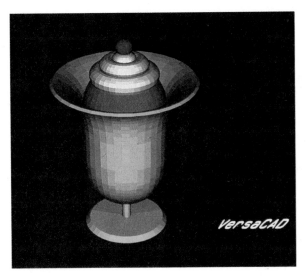
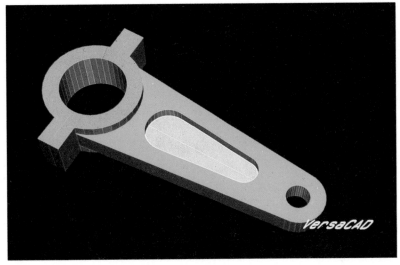

Fig. 36-21 Examples of computer 3D color shading. The computer images were photographed using a special film recorder attached to the computer. (Versacad Corporation)

- **Model building.** Modeling is one of the strengths of a computer when the software provides it. Typical CADD packages use extrusion, sweeping a plane, digitizing a multiview drawing, and 3D object creation to build models.
- **3D viewing modes.** Viewing three-dimensional models varies considerably among CADD packages. Some provide simple wireframe, while the most sophisticated packages also include hidden line removal, color shading, isometric, and perspective viewing modes.
- **Special features.** Each CADD package has special features that may or may not be important to a particular user. Check other users to see what they believe is the CADD program's special features.

AEC CADD PACKAGES

Architectural, engineering, and construction (AEC) CADD packages are programs designed for a specific field. The scope of these programs is narrower than that of general-purpose programs, but broader than the single-purpose CADD programs that draw windows, produce charts, or produce reports. Some AEC programs are complete packages. Examples are CAD-VANCE by Calcomp, DataCAD by Microtecture, and CADSolutions by Sigma Design. Others are extensions of general-purpose CADD packages.

AutoCAD AEC Architecture by Autodesk, VersaCAD/Architect by Versacad, and Medusa AEC Architectural Design by Prime Computer are examples of add-on program modules. AEC CADD packages designed for architectural applications generally contain certain features or functions in addition to those offered in general-purpose CADD packages. The extra functions improve their use for design work in architecture. The following list of features provides a basis for comparing general capabilities of AEC programs.

- **Hardware requirements.** Hardware is a prime cost consideration. AEC packages generally require about the same hardware as general-purpose CADD packages.
- **General CADD program dependence.** An AEC package that depends on a general CADD program provides an advantage and disadvantage. The advantage is that you have all the functions of the general package. The disadvantage is that you must purchase both programs. This could increase the cost considerably.

- **Database dimensions.** The database dimensions determine whether or not the program can produce only two-dimensional drawings, two-dimensional drawings with elevation thickness, or full three-dimensional models. The database dimensions will be important for certain modeling and pictorial applications.
- **Space diagram generation.** Space diagrams are useful planning tools. Some AEC programs will automatically convert a space diagram to a floor plan, complete with wall thicknesses, Fig. 36-22.
- **Methods of wall generation.** Architectural packages generally provide more than one method of generating a wall thickness. Common methods include: from space diagrams, continuous walls, and from dimensions.
- **Drawing walls.** Walls are an important element of most architectural structures. Most AEC systems offer a variety of methods for manipulating, constructing, and hatching walls. Features such as intersection cleanup, wall thickness specification, and alignment are important time savers. A large selection of standard hatch symbols is also necessary to produce top-rate drawings, Fig. 36-23.

Fig. 36-22. Example of a space diagram converted automatically to a plan view with assigned wall thicknesses.

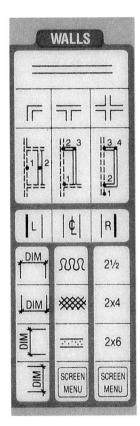

Fig. 36-23. This digitizing template provides several commands to assist in drawing, manipulating, and hatching walls. (Autodesk, Inc.)

- **Wall modification.** Modifying existing walls is frequently necessary. The ability to stretch walls and add interior spaces is important.
- **3D viewing.** Three-dimensional viewing is a useful design tool for many applications. A variety of 3D viewing modes are provided by some packages. Typical modes include standard top, front, rear, right, and left sides. Also, views may be offered from each principal corner, global viewpoint, solid modeling, isometric, and perspective. See Fig. 36-24.

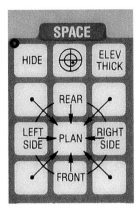

Fig. 36-24. An object may be viewed from several positions using these template picks. (Autodesk, Inc.)

Additional features available in some programs are hidden line removal, dynamic positioning, and color shading.

- **Standard door types.** Doors require a considerable amount of time to draw unless appropriate symbols are in the symbols library. A good AEC architecture package should include all of the standard door symbols to speed drawing and insure uniformity, Fig. 36-25.

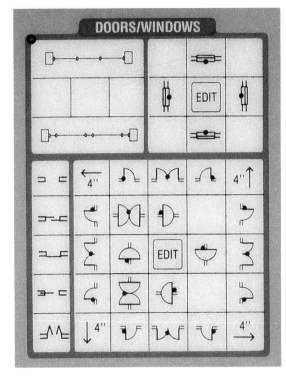

Fig. 36-25. Standard door and windows symbols are included in this CADD program library. (Autodesk, Inc.)

- **Standard window types.** Look for programs that include standard plan view symbols, elevation views, and large-scale details of most standard window types. These can save many hours in drawing time.
- **Structural symbols.** Structural symbols are generally limited in typical microcomputer-based AEC CADD programs, Fig. 36-26. However, minicomputer and mainframe systems frequently provide a large number of these symbols. You may be able to purchase add-on structural symbol libraries for a microCADD system. Structural symbols are needed more for commercial work than for residential design.
- **Plumbing symbols.** Standard plumbing symbols may be a needed feature for certain companies or individuals. Typical symbols include: tub, lavatory, shower stall, toilet, bidet, plumbing lines, and valves. See Fig. 36-26.

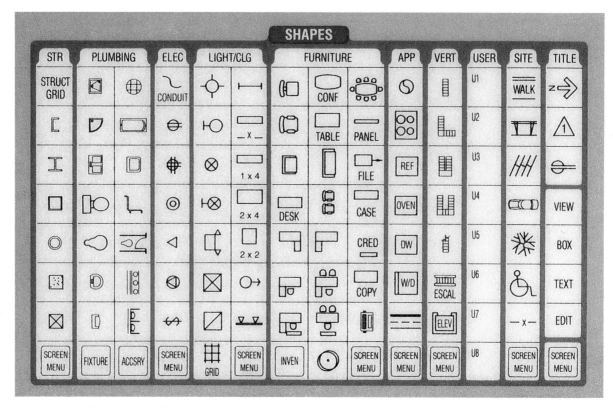

Fig. 36-26. The "shapes" section of this digitizing template includes a representative selection of symbols included in the library. Note the various types included. (Autodesk, Inc.)

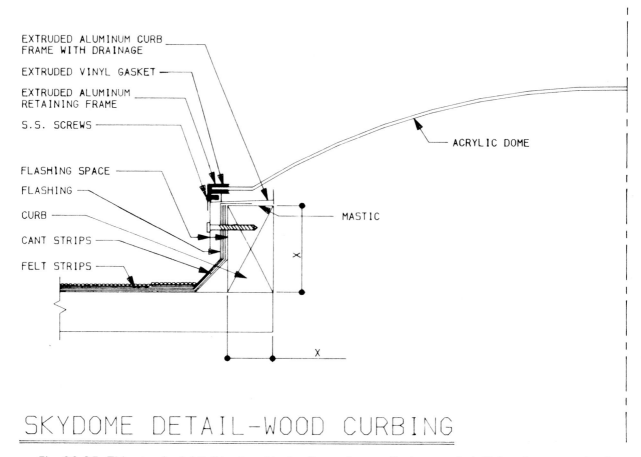

SKYDOME DETAIL-WOOD CURBING

Fig. 36-27. This standard detail is stored in the library for recall when needed. (Prime Computer, Inc.)

- **Electrical and lighting symbols.** Most residential construction plans include an electrical plan. These symbols are time consuming to draw if the program does not include the standard symbols. Most AEC architectural packages include several electrical and lighting symbols. See Fig. 36-26.
- **HVAC symbols.** Heating, ventilating, and air conditioning symbols are valuable to the designer of commercial structures. These symbols are frequently omitted from smaller packages.
- **Construction details.** Construction details are generally much larger and more complex than other symbols. Smaller packages do not typically include these. Yet, they can save many hours of work for a designer who uses them frequently, Fig. 36-27.
- **Furniture symbols.** The plan view symbols of typical furniture pieces are part of most AEC

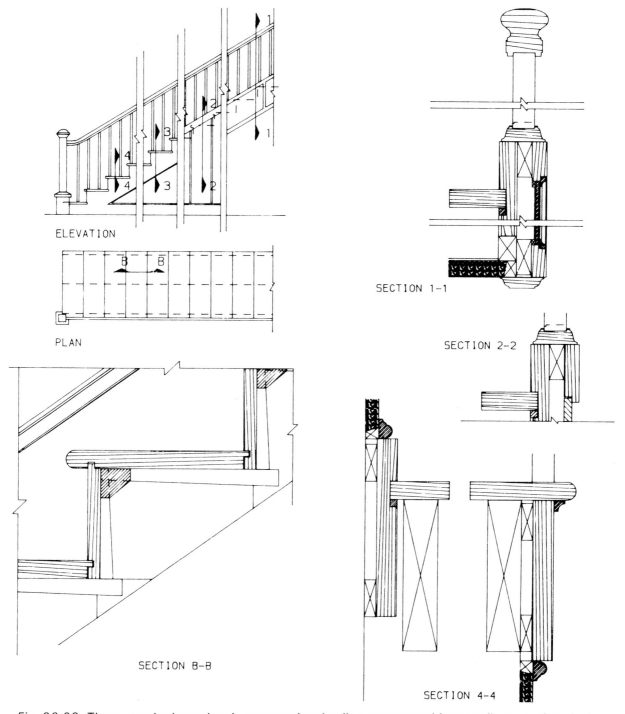

Fig. 36-28. These standard wood stair construction details are generated from attributes assigned when planning the stairs. (Prime Computer, Inc.)

packages. Office furniture and elevation views are generally restricted to larger packages. See Fig. 36-26.

- **Tree and plant symbols.** Several plan view plant symbols are generally included in typical AEC programs. Elevation views, planters, and landscaping details generally are not.
- **Appliance symbols.** These symbols are likely to be included in programs designed more for residential design than for commercial buildings. See Fig. 36-26.
- **Site symbols.** Most packages include several general site symbols. See Fig. 36-26. Special libraries for mapping, site development, and highway design are also available.
- **Vehicle symbols.** This is a popular symbol category even though its use is limited.
- **Title symbols.** The most basic symbols—north arrow, revision triangle, drawing title, scale, and tags—are likely to be included in an AEC architectural package.
- **Stair generation.** Stair design requires a considerable effort and a package which includes a stair design module is desirable. Some larger packages also include metal stairs, concrete/steel stairs, elevators, and escalators, Fig. 36-28.
- **Hatch patterns.** Authentic hatch patterns are a necessary element of an architectural package. These symbols are very difficult to develop if not included in the program. They should be clearly recognized standard patterns—many are not.
- **Ability to add user-defined shapes to library.** A good architectural package will allow you to add custom symbols to the library.
- **Creating background drawings.** Background drawings are used as underlays to construct other plans or compare certain features. An example is a structural grid that would affect the placement of members on each floor of a multifloor building.
- **Schedule generation.** A CADD systems ability to generate schedules—for doors, windows, lighting, appliances, furniture, etc.—is a necessity. Most packages provide some schedule generation.
- **Customization.** Customization allows the operator to make changes in menus, predefined shapes, scale factors, attributes, etc. Most users want the program to suit his/her particular needs.
- **Database interface.** More and more packages are now able to exchange data using standard interfaces. A typical database interface in a microcomputer-based AEC CADD package might be dBase IV or Lotus. These are popular database and spreadsheet programs. Larger systems will provide for others.

REVIEW QUESTIONS-CHAPTER 36

Write your answers on a separate sheet of paper. Do not write in this book.

1. What is probably the single most important decision in putting together a CADD system?
2. What kinds of drawings can be made on a CADD system?
3. Name eight ways that a CADD system can benefit the user.
4. Identify eight questions that you should answer before purchasing a CADD system.
5. What type of CADD package is designed for making typical mechanical drawings and general drafting applications?
6. For what areas are AEC CADD packages designed?
7. Name two items that are considered to be supported hardware in a CADD system.
8. The number of dimensions that a CADD program can represent are 2D, 3D, and _____.
9. Give four examples of entities found in most CADD programs.
10. Which of the following is an example of entity editing?
    a. Trim.
    b. Scale.
    c. Rotate.
    d. All of the above.
11. How many layers might a CADD program have?
    a. 0 to unlimited.
    b. 1 to 56.
    c. 2 to 256.
    d. 1 to 1024.
12. Name six standard linetypes supported by a typical CADD program.
13. Several systems of linear units are supported by most CADD programs. Which of the following is an example of architectural units?
    a. 10.6'.
    b. 12'-6''.
    c. N 45 E 110.6'.
14. The computer communicates with the operator through the _____.
15. Which of the following is not an example of a CADD drawing aid?
    a. Snap.
    b. Axis.
    c. Redraw.
    d. Grid.

16. What type of drawings require hatching?
17. _____ adds a true-to-life appearance to a 3D drawing.
18. Which of the following is an example of a 3D primitive?
    a. Rectangle.
    b. Line.
    c. Cone.
19. Identify three methods of wall generation used in common AEC CADD packages.
20. Name five basic symbol categories that are generally included in an AEC package. These probably would be absent from a general-purpose CADD package.
21. A structural grid is an example of a _____ drawing when it is used to create other drawings or to check particular relationships.

SUGGESTED ACTIVITIES

1. Examine the program documentation for a microCADD package. Determine the hardware requirements. Obtain an estimated cost for these components at your local computer store.
2. Visit or call several architectural firms in your city or general area. Determine:
   a. How many are using a CADD system to generate drawings?
   b. What CADD packages they are using?
   c. What are their feelings toward using CADD in architecture? Report your findings to the class.
3. Use the characteristics described within this chapter to evaluate either a general-purpose CADD or an AEC architectural package that runs on a microcomputer. See how it compares with the characteristics described in this chapter.

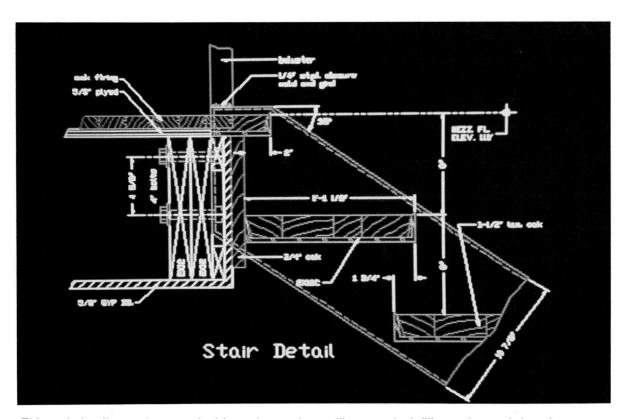

This stair detail was photographed from the monitor to illustrate the brilliant colors and sharp image possible with a 640 x 480 pixel resolution.

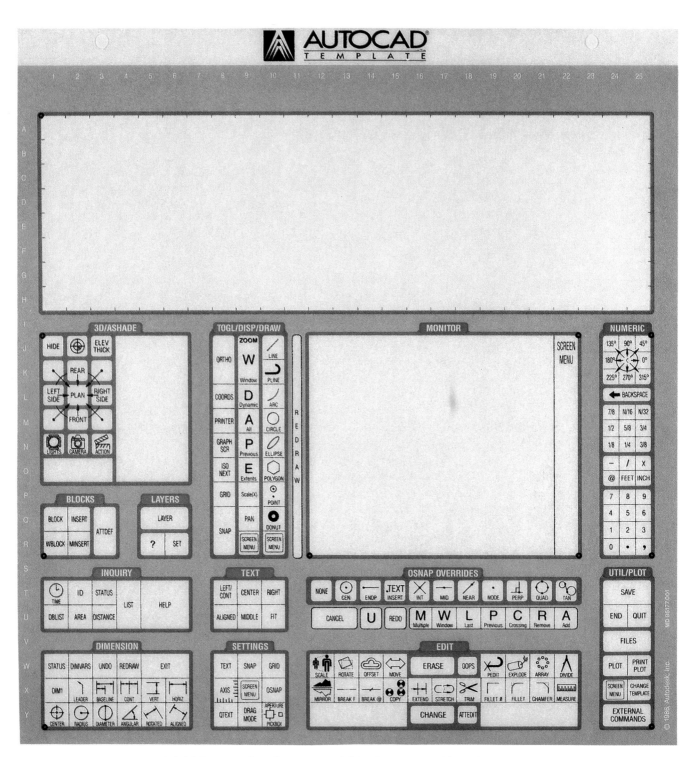

Digitizing template for a general CADD package. (Autodesk, Inc.)

CADD Commands and Functions

After studying this chapter you will be able to:
* Explain the difference between CADD commands and functions.
* List several typical drawing commands used in popular CADD programs.
* Describe how ZOOM and PAN commands are used when making a drawing on a CADD system.
* Sketch an example of each of the following basic forms of dimensioning–linear, angular, and leader.
* Discuss the purpose of layers in typical CADD programs.
* List several drawing aids that are provided by most CADD programs.

Most CADD programs provide several entities (lines, circles, text, etc.) for use in constructing a drawing. Commands tell the computer which entity to draw. Commands can be entered (typed) from the keyboard, selected from a screen menu, picked from a digitizing tablet overlay, or entered using a multibutton pointing device. After the entity is selected, certain parameters can be chosen for it. For example, the parameters always include the location where the entity is to be placed. Other parameters may include sizes or rotation angle. Once the parameters are chosen, the entity is drawn as specified and appears on the monitor. Successive commands can then be entered to add other entities or perform other functions.

Most CADD programs include functions that provide for the modification of a drawing in a variety of ways. For instance, erase, move, and copy are examples of functions that modify drawings. Other functions allow the operator to change the view displayed on the monitor or display certain information about the drawing. Drawing aids help position entities accurately.

When a hardcopy is desired, the "plot" function can be used to produce the drawing. Commands allow all of these functions (and others) to be performed.

Several common commands and functions found in most CADD programs will be discussed in this chapter to describe how drawings are made and modified using the computer. The commands included are not meant to be an exhaustive list, but are representative of popular CADD packages. Command names also vary from package to package which may be confusing to the beginner, but there are many similarities between various products.

DRAWING COMMANDS

Drawing commands include several commands and their associated functions which together compose the heart of a CADD system's drawing capability. The commands to be discussed include the following: LINE, ARC, CIRCLE, POLYGON, RECTANGLE, DOUBLE LINE, SKETCH, TEXT, DRAG, and HATCH.

LINE

The LINE command is the most frequently used command in a CADD program because it is the basic element of most drawings. Each line requires information as to the placement of the first point (one end) and then the second point (other end). Most programs use a "rubber band" approach to show where the line will be drawn. This command generally remains active to allow several line segments to be constructed in a sequential fashion. This saves time and increases accuracy. Each line may also have one or more attributes specified. These may include linetype, width, or color, Fig. 37-1. Using the LINE command produces lines that remain as separate entities for easy modification.

ARC

The ARC command draws partial circles. Several methods of drawing arcs are usually provided. Examples include:
• Three points on the arc, Fig. 37-2.
• Starting point, center, and end point.
• Starting point, center, and included angle.

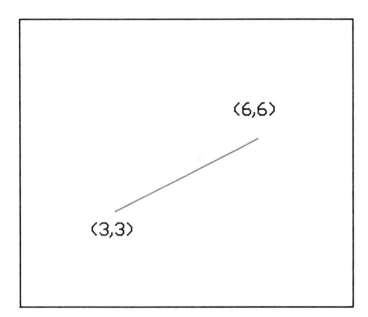

Fig. 37-1. The following attributes may be identified for this LINE (entity): coordinates (3,3) (6,6), width (0.07''), linetype (continuous), and color (red).

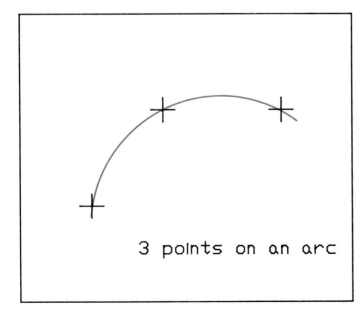

Fig. 37-2. Three points were identified to draw this arc.

• Starting point, center, and length of chord.
• Starting point, end point, and radius.
• Starting point, end point, and included angle.
• Starting point, end point, and a starting direction.
• Continuation of a previous line or arc.

CIRCLE

The CIRCLE command allows circles to be drawn using several common methods. These methods include:
• Center and radius, Fig. 37-3.
• Center and diameter.
• Three points on the circle.
• Two points on the circle.
• Two lines or two circles to which the circle should be tangent, and radius.
• Dynamic circle specification by dragging.

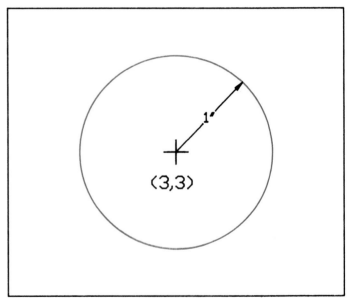

Fig. 37-3. The center and radius were specified to draw this circle.

POLYGON

The POLYGON command enables the construction of a *regular polygon* (an object with equal length, sides, and angles) which has from three to almost any number of sides required. A common approach used by many programs is to either ''inscribe'' or ''circumscribe'' the polygon in (or about) a circle, Fig. 37-4. The information required in these instances is radius of the circle, method desired, and number of sides. Another method used is to define the end points of one side or edge and then the computer generates the remaining sides in some predefined fashion.

RECTANGLE

The RECTANGLE command usually provides at least two methods of construction–specifying the width and height of the rectangle or specifying a corner and dragging the opposite corner to the desired location, Fig. 37-5. Both methods are useful in the design process.

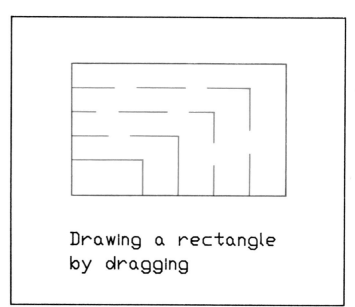

Fig. 37-5. One method of constructing a rectangle is to specify one corner and then dragging the opposite corner to the desired location.

DOUBLE LINE

Some CADD packages provide a DOUBLE LINE command. This command is useful in creating walls on floor plans and similar applications, Fig. 37-6. The prompt asks for the thickness of walls. Some programs provide a facility for proper joining of wall corners and intersections.

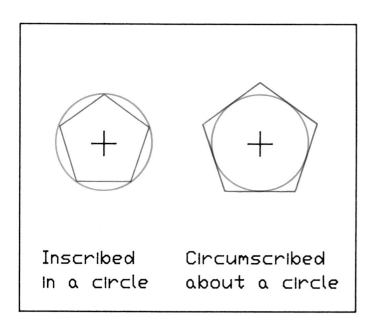

Fig. 37-4. Polygons are frequently constructed inscribed in a circle or circumscribed about a circle.

Fig. 37-6. The DOUBLE LINE command can be used to construct walls with various widths.

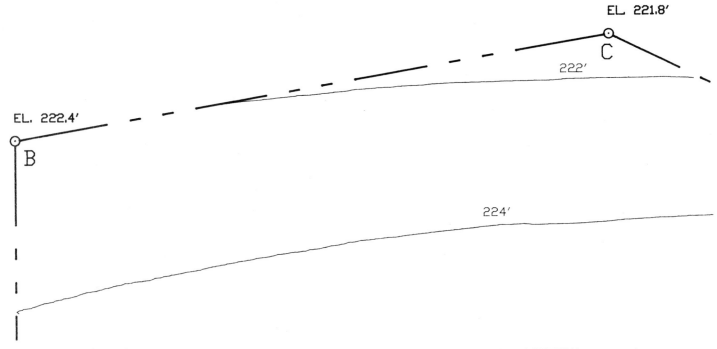

EL. 221.8'

C

222'

EL. 222.4'

B

224'

Fig. 37-7. The contour lines on this drawing were created using the freehand SKETCH command.

SKETCH

The SKETCH command allows a freehand line to be drawn with the pointing device. This capability is especially useful in creating contour lines, Fig. 37-7, short break lines, and the like. The creation of freehand lines does, however, generally create a large amount of data for each line and, therefore, require significant storage capacity.

TEXT

You can add text to a drawing using the TEXT command. Most CADD packages provide several standard text fonts which can be stretched, compressed, obliqued, or mirrored. Placement can be justified left, right, or centered, Fig. 37-8. Rotation is also supported.

PROPERTY LINE DATA

AB DUE NORTH 95.0'

BC N 80° E 63.0'

CD S 65° E 60.0'

DE S 7° W 75.0'

EA S 86° W 107.0'

Fig. 37-8. The text in this data chart was left justified so that the left margin would be straight.

DRAG

The DRAG function permits moving an image on the screen to a desired location. This function is frequently embedded in commands such as CIRCLE, ARC, AND RECTANGLE. For example, once the location of the center of a circle is indicated, then the cursor is used to "drag" the radius out to the desired size.

HATCH

The HATCH command is used to hatch an area of a drawing, Fig. 37-9. Most CADD programs include several standard hatch (or stipple) patterns for use with the command. Areas to be hatched are selected with the pointing device and elements within the boundary can be excluded, if desired.

EDITING AND INQUIRY COMMANDS

Editing commands allow the user to modify drawings in several ways. Inquiry commands are designed to list the selected database records for selected objects; calculate distances, areas, and perimeters; and convert points on the screen to absolute coordinates (or the reverse). Common editing and inquiry commands that will be described in this section include the following: ERASE, UNERASE, MOVE, COPY, MIRROR, ROTATE, FILLET, CHAMFER, EXTEND, STRETCH, ARRAY, SCALE, WINDOW, LIST, DISTANCE, AREA, and PERIMETER.

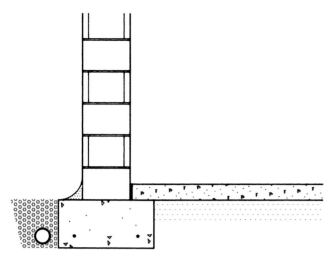

Fig. 37-9. The HATCH command was used to section this area. The desired symbol was called up from the symbols library.

ERASE

The ERASE command asks for identification of specific entities that are to be removed permanently from the drawing. Many programs provide a SELECT command to make this choice. Also, many programs provide for erasing the last entity drawn as an alternative to the previous approach.

UNERASE

This command restores an entity inadvertently erased. Certain limits are usually associated with this command.

MOVE

The MOVE command allows one or more entities to be moved from the present location to a new one without changing their orientation or size. Relative displacement is the method usually indicated for this operation, Fig. 37-10.

COPY

The COPY command is similar to MOVE except that it places "copies" of the selected entities at the specified location, leaving the original drawing(s) in place, Fig. 37-11.

MIRROR

This command draws a mirror image of an existing object, Fig. 37-12. The original may be retained or deleted during the operation. The mirror line can generally be designated.

ROTATE

The ROTATE command can be used to alter the orientation of entities on the drawing. Rotation about a specified point is the usual method, Fig. 37-13.

SCALE

The size of existing entities may be changed using the SCALE command. The size may be

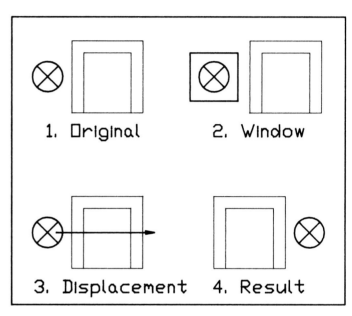

Fig. 37-10. This four-step sequence shows how an object is moved on the drawing using the displacement method.

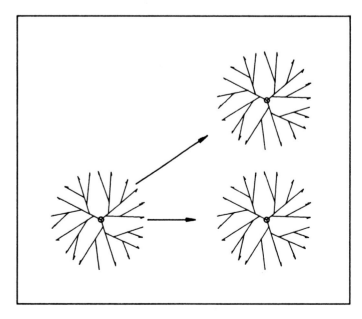

Fig. 37-11. The original tree was copied and moved to two additional locations. All three symbols are identical.

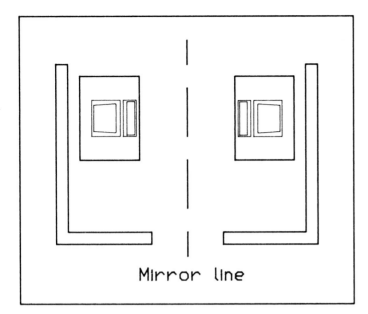

Fig. 37-12. The mirror image was created of the arrangement on the left. Note the mirror line which is equidistant from both drawings.

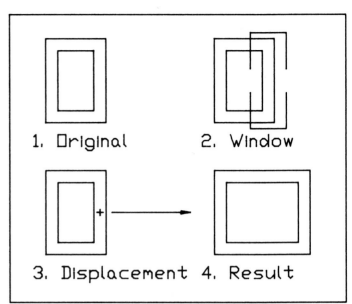

Fig. 37-14. The STRETCH command was used to change the size of this object. Notice how all the connections were maintained.

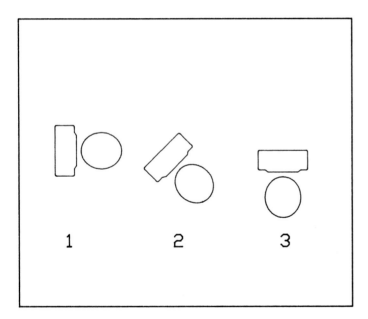

Fig. 37-13. This drawing illustrates how an object may be rotated into a new position.

increased or decreased and repositioned, if desired.

STRETCH

The STRETCH command is designed to move a selected portion of a drawing while maintaining connections to parts of the drawing left in place. The general procedure is to place a box (window) around the portion to be stretched and select a base point and destination, Fig. 37-14.

FILLET

The FILLET command generates a smoothly fitted arc of a specified radius between two lines, arcs, or circles, Fig. 37-15.

CHAMFER

The CHAMFER command is very similar to FILLET. It trims two intersecting lines a specific

Fig. 37-15. The FILLET command was used to generate a smoothly fitted arc of a specified radius in both of these examples.

distance from the intersection and then connects the trimmed ends with a new line.

EXTEND

Using EXTEND, an existing object can be lengthened to end precisely at a boundary edge. This edge (or edges) is generally defined by one or more objects in the drawing.

ARRAY

The ARRAY command is essentially a copy function. It makes multiple copies of selected objects in a rectangular or circular pattern. See Fig. 37-16.

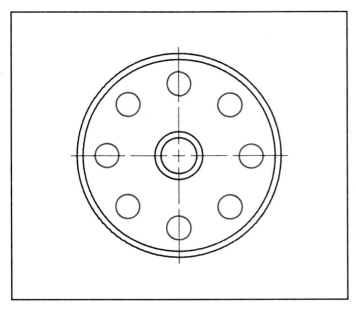

Fig. 37-16. The eight holes in this bolt hole circle were created using the ARRAY command.

WINDOW

The WINDOW function allows the operator to place a box (window) around an object or group of objects. Frequently, this function is embedded in other commands such as SCALE, MOVE, ERASE, and ROTATE. It saves time when several objects are to be selected for an operation.

LIST

The LIST command permits the examination of data stored for an entity. For example, the report for a LINE entity may include the coordinates of the end points, length, angle from start

point, and change in X and Y coordinates from the start point.

DISTANCE

The DISTANCE command measures the distance and angle between two points. The result is displayed in drawing units.

AREA

This command allows any number of points to be selected to enclose a space on the drawing. The program then calculates the area of the enclosed space, Fig. 37-17.

PERIMETER

The PERIMETER command is frequently a part of the AREA command, but may be treated separately in some programs. It computes the distance around any space specified on the drawing.

DISPLAY CONTROL COMMANDS

Display control commands govern how a drawing is displayed on the monitor. These

Fig. 37-17. This space diagram shows the use of the AREA command.

commands control the position and magnification of the screen window, specify the degree to which time-consuming entities are drawn, and explicitly request the screen to be redrawn. Commands in this section which are common to CADD packages include: ZOOM, PAN, VIEW, REDRAW, and REGENERATE.

ZOOM

The ZOOM command increases or decreases the apparent size of objects on the screen even though their actual size remains constant. The total area viewed is related to the apparent size of the objects, Fig. 37-18. Generally, several options are available as part of the ZOOM command and may include: entire drawing to drawing limits, center point and height, dynamic zoom, entire drawing to current extents, lower left corner and height, restore previous view, change size of window, and a magnification factor.

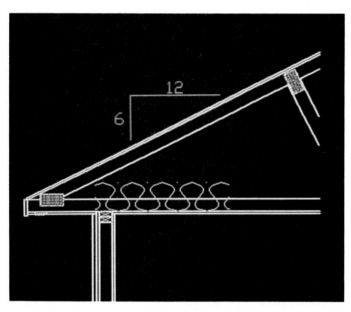

Fig. 37-18. This photo of the screen shows a detail more clearly using ZOOM.

PAN

The PAN command moves the display window from one location to another. It lets you see a different portion of the drawing without changing the magnification. In other words, PAN lets you see details that were off the screen. This command may be used instead of zooming on different parts of the drawing which would require more time.

VIEW

When constant switching back and forth between views on a large drawing is required, the VIEW command can be used to speed the process. However, the views must be identified, Fig. 37-19. This is an alternative to using ZOOM and PAN.

Top	Isometric
Front	Right Side

Fig. 37-19. Note how the drawing area has been divided up to accommodate four named views. The VIEW command requires that views be identified.

REDRAW

The REDRAW command ''cleans up'' the display by removing marker blips, etc. Some commands automatically redraw the screen as when a grid is removed or visible layers are changed, but sometimes it is useful to request a redraw when other operations are being performed.

REGENERATE

This command forces the program to regenerate the entire drawing and redraw the screen. This operation takes longer than REDRAW.

DIMENSIONING COMMANDS

One of the advantages of using a CADD program to generate drawings is the dimensioning routines which speed this process and reduce errors. In most applications, notations must be added to drawings which show lengths and distances or angles between objects. Dimensioning is the process of adding this information. Most CADD packages provide for semi-automatic dimensioning. The five basic types of dimensioning that will be discussed here are the following: LINEAR, ANGULAR, DIAMETER, RADIUS, and LEADER.

LINEAR

This command represents a group of commands which relate to linear dimensioning, Fig. 37-20. They may include:

HORIZONTAL—a linear dimension with a horizontal dimension line.

VERTICAL—a linear dimension with a vertical dimension line.

ALIGNED—a linear dimension with the dimension line parallel to the specified extension line origin points.

ROTATED—a linear dimension with the dimension line drawn at a specific angle.

BASELINE—continues a linear dimension from the baseline of the previous dimension.

CONTINUE—continues a linear dimension from the second extension line of the previous dimension.

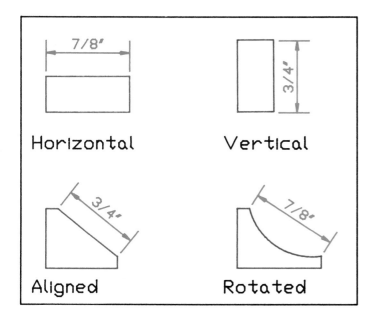

Fig. 37-20. Examples of four types of linear dimensions.

ANGULAR

This command generates an arc to indicate the angle between two non-parallel lines. The ANGULAR command is used to dimension angles, Fig. 37-21.

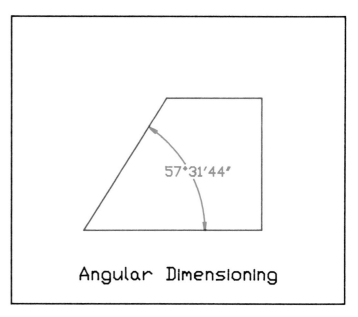

Fig. 37-21. An angular dimension is used between two non-parallel lines.

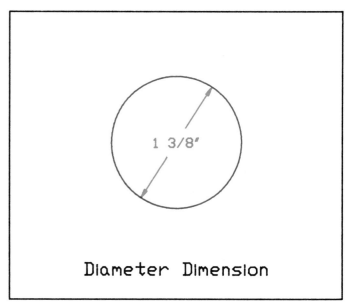

Fig. 37-22. Example of a diameter dimension using the DIAMETER command.

DIAMETER

Diameter dimensioning for circles and arcs can be accomplished using the DIAMETER command, Fig. 37-22. The usual steps include first, pointing to a circle or arc, then specifying the diameter length or accepting the computed length. The computer will then draw the dimension.

RADIUS

The RADIUS command performs radius dimensioning. It is almost identical to the

DIAMETER command except that a radius is drawn instead of a diameter, Fig. 37-23.

LEADER

A leader is used to provide a specific or local note. Most CADD programs provide an automatic leader capability. Complex leaders may be constructed using the LEADER command, Fig. 37-24. With this command, all aspects of leader construction may be specified.

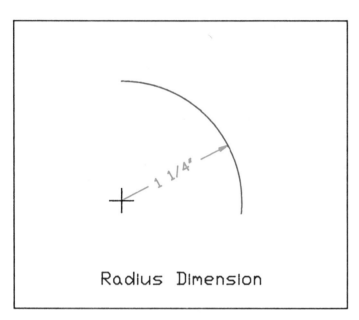

Fig. 37-23. The RADIUS command was used to dimension this arc.

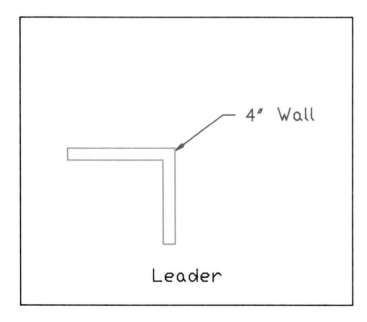

Fig. 37-24. A specific or local note requires a leader. The LEADER command was used to construct this example.

LAYERS, COLORS, AND LINETYPES

Commands related to layers, colors, and linetypes permit the user to group associated objects in a drawing, control the visibility of those groups, and provide additional visual information through color and a variety of linetypes.

Entities in a drawing can be placed on one or more drawing layers. Layers are like transparent overlays. All layers are always perfectly registered with one another. The same drawing limits, coordinate system, and zoom factor apply to all layers in a drawing. The number of layers that may be used in a drawing is only limited by the software itself. The number of layers commonly available range from one to unlimited. Generally, you can assign a name to each layer and any number of layers can be displayed at once. Layers and their properties are saved as part of the drawing database.

As a general rule, each entity and each layer in a drawing has an associated color number. Several layers or entities may have the same color number and are controlled by the operator. In order to facilitate exchange of drawings between different computer systems, seven color numbers have been assigned standard meanings. They are:

1 - Red	5 - Blue
2 - Yellow	6 - Magenta
3 - Green	7 - White
4 - Cyan	

Each entity in a drawing has an associated linetype. A linetype is a combination of dashes, dots, and blank spaces. A name has been assigned to several standard linetypes and each is produced the same each time it is used. Most CADD programs permit custom linetypes as well. By-in-large, these linetypes are compatible with the typical alphabet of lines used in architectural drawing, Fig. 37-25.

DRAWING AIDS

Drawing aids are designed to speed up the drawing process and at the same time, maintain accuracy. Most CADD packages provide for most of the drawing aids discussed below. They include: GRID, SNAP, OBJECT SNAP, ORTHO, and ISOMETRIC drawing.

GRID

The GRID function causes a reference grid of dots to be displayed on the screen, Fig. 37-26.

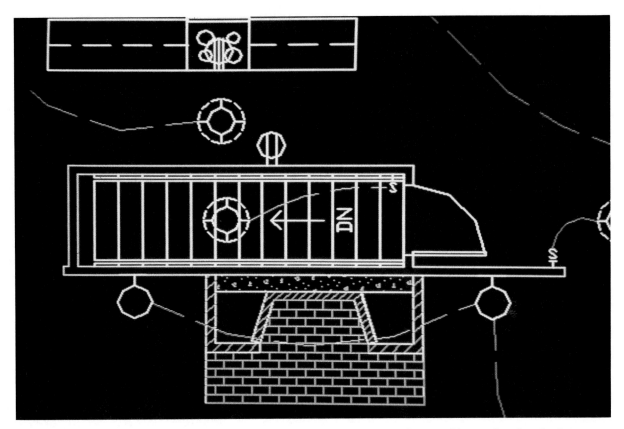

Fig. 37-25. This photo of a drawing on the monitor shows the use of several layers (each color is a separate layer), colors, and linetypes. Note how the use of these features helps to visualize the different elements in the design.

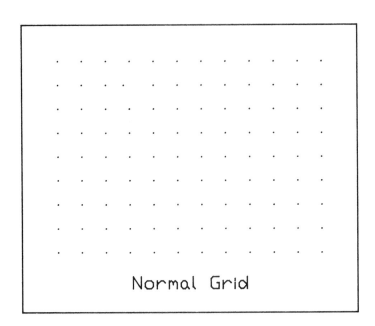

Normal Grid

Fig. 37-26. This is a normal (not rotated) grid which was created with the GRID command.

The user can specify any desired spacing that is useful for a particular drawing. The grid is a useful device for creating various drawings and provides a "feel" for sizes of drawing entities used. The grid may be turned on or off or the spacing

changed as desired. Some programs also have an AXIS command that display ruler lines along the vertical and horizontal axes of the screen to aid in drawing.

SNAP

The SNAP function is similar to GRID except that the grid is not visible and is generally used with some type of pointing device. The "snap resolution" defines the spacing of this grid and the crosshairs of all input coordinates are "snapped" or locked to the nearest point on the grid. This function is very useful for highly precise drawing creation.

OBJECT SNAP

The OBJECT SNAP function allows the drafter to connect to points already in the drawing. For example, a line could be "snapped" to the end of a previous line to continue it. A line could also be connected to an existing corner of one object and then snapped to a corresponding point on another. This function provides a quick and accurate way of connecting two existing points.

ORTHO

The ORTHO mode insures that all lines and traces drawn using a pointing device will be orthogonal (vertical or horizontal) with respect to the current snap grid, assuming it has not been rotated, Fig. 37-27. ORTHO mode does not affect explicit keyboard entries of coordinate data.

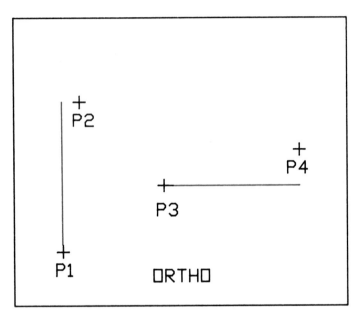

Fig. 37-27. Even though the cursor (P2) is too far right for the line on the left to be vertical, ORTHO draws it properly. The line on the right is drawn horizontally using ORTHO even though the cursor (P4) is too high.

ISOMETRIC DRAWING

Some CADD packages have a grid or facility for making isometric drawings. The procedure for making isometric drawings using a CADD system is very similar to manual drafting unless the program provides for automatic 3D representation from the database. The isometric snap grid has three axes—vertical, 30 degrees, and 150 degrees.

3D FUNCTIONS

As discussed in the CADD software chapter, some CADD software is 2D, 2.5D, and 3D. The 2D packages store data for the X and Y coordinates of all points. Packages which are 2.5D also store data points for the X and Y coordinates, but they also provide simplified 3D visualization for objects where the thickness has been stored earlier, Fig. 37-28. The 3D programs store data for the X, Y, and Z coordinates of

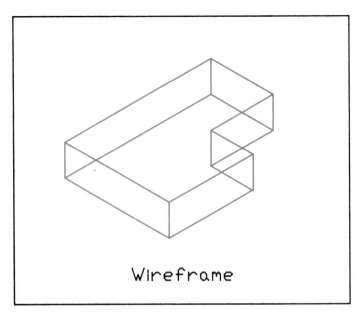

Fig. 37-28. This is a 2.5D wireframe drawing with no lines removed.

each data point. They provide full 3D capabilities from the 3D database.

Packages having 2.5D and 3D capabilities generally offer a feature referred to as hidden line removal. **Hidden lines** (lines which would not be visible in the pictorial view) are removed in wireframe models using the hidden line removal facility. This produces a more realistic picture of the object, Fig. 37-29. Some of the more sophisticated CADD packages also take the "cleaned up" wireframe model one step further. The next step is called **surface modeling.** Essentially, a skin is placed over the wireframe model to

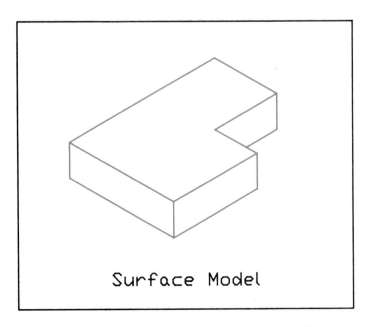

Fig. 37-29. The hidden line facility was used to "clean-up" this drawing to produce a more realistic illustration.

Fig. 37-30. Colors and textures were applied to this pictorial drawing to illustrate the effect of surface modeling. (Marbaugh Engineering, Tim Trovillion)

greatly enhance the appearance. This "skin" may provide a variety of textures and colors. These drawings are very useful in presenting conceptual models to clients and in producing advertising literature, Fig. 37-30.

A still more advanced technique of producing 3D representations of objects is **solids modeling.** The end product appears similar to one produced using surface modeling, but in solids modeling, the object is treated as though it were solid instead of a wireframe. Programs for solids modeling require much more power and memory and are, therefore, usually run on larger computers.

The most sophisticated 3D representations are **shaded solids modeling.** The product of these programs is very realistic. They are shaded and shadowed as though a specific light source were illuminating the object, Fig. 37-31. As would be expected, these programs are designed today mainly for larger computers.

UTILITY COMMANDS AND FUNCTIONS

Utility commands are those functions that load and save drawings, provide help, and give you the status of the drawing.

HELP

The HELP command provides user assistance. Usually, a list of commands will be presented as well as format or options if you need them. Most

Fig. 37-31. A 3D shaded model representing a high level of sophistication in pictorial illustration. (Created using VersaCAD DESIGN software–Versacad Corporation)

CADD programs also allow use of the HELP command even when in the middle of a command to get assistance for the current command.

END

The END command returns to the Main Menu and updates the drawing file. The updated drawing is then the drawing file so it can be edited.

QUIT

This command returns to the Main Menu but does not update the drawing. All changes to the drawing are discarded.

SAVE

The SAVE command is useful to save a new or modified drawing while you are working to avoid loss due to power failure, editing errors, etc. This command writes the current state of the drawing to the disk, but remains in the Drawing Editor for further work.

STATUS

The STATUS command generally displays the defaults, modes, and extents used by the program and denotes the current settings.

LIMITS

The LIMITS command allows the designation of drawing limits or boundaries for the current drawing. It also controls the checking of those limits in certain CADD programs.

UNITS

Most microcomputer CADD programs use ordinary decimal notation for coordinates, distances, and angles. Some applications, however, require other forms of notation. This command accommodates these requirements.

MENU

The MENU command directs the program to load a new menu from the disk. Typical menus include: the screen menu, the pointer device but-ton menu, an auxiliary function box menu, and various digitizer menus.

FILES

The FILES command on some CADD packages allows you to list, delete, rename, and copy files while still in the Drawing Editor.

TIME

The TIME command typically provides access to the following data: current date and time, drawing creation time, time of last update, amount of time spent editing the current drawing, and total elapsed time in the Drawing Editor.

SYSTEM VARIABLES

This command may be identified by several names, but essentially is used to set various modes, sizes, and limits that remain in effect until changed. This command can usually be invoked anytime desired.

RENAME

The RENAME command permits changing the name of a block, layer, linetype, text style, or named view.

REVIEW QUESTIONS–CHAPTER 37

Write your answers on a separate sheet of paper. Do not write in this book.
1. Commands tell the computer which _____ to draw.
2. Most CADD programs include _____ that provide for the modification of a drawing.
3. Commands such as LINE, ARC, CIRCLE, and POLYGON are examples of what type of commands?
   a. Editing.
   b. Display.
   c. Inquiry.
   d. Drawing.
4. Name three attributes that may be identified for each line.
5. Which of the following is not a recognized method of drawing a circle using CADD?
   a. Center and radius.
   b. Starting point, end point, and radius.

c. Center and diameter.
d. Dynamic specification by dragging.

6. Name a common architectural application for the DOUBLE LINE command.

7. Which of the following commands should be used to apply a brick pattern to a sectioned wall?
   a. HATCH.
   b. BRICK.
   c. FILL.

8. The _____ command can be used to alter the orientation of entities on a drawing.

9. A(n) _____ is a smoothly fitted arc of a specified radius which is drawn between two lines, arcs, or circles.

10. Which command should you select if you want to know the distance and angle between two points?

11. Display control commands govern how a drawing is displayed on the _____.

12. The _____ command lets you see a different portion of the drawing without changing the magnification.

13. The five basic types of dimensions discussed in this chapter included LINEAR, DIAMETER, RADIUS, LEADER, and _____.

14. What is the maximum number of layers a drawing can have?

15. Each layer in a CADD package has an assigned color. The first seven are standard. Fill in the missing colors.
    1 - Red
    2 - _____
    3 - Green
    4 - _____
    5 - Blue
    6 - _____
    7 - White

16. _____ is a combination of dashes, dots, and blank spaces.

17. Which of the following is not considered to be a CADD drawing aid?
    a. Grid.
    b. Object Snap.
    c. Ortho.
    d. Symbol template.

18. An isometric drawing has _____ (number) axes.

19. A CADD program that stores only X and Y coordinate data is a _____-dimensional package.

20. The most sophisticated type of 3D representation is a _____.
    a. Wireframe model.
    b. Solids model.
    c. Shaded solids model.

SUGGESTED ACTIVITIES

1. Go to your school, county, or city library and find at least one article which discusses the capabilities of a specific CADD program. Record any references made in the article to the commands and functions discussed in this chapter. Report your findings to the class.

2. Using the library and/or community sources, record as many different types of dimensions as possible. For example, illustrate decimal dimensions, dimensions with fractions, architectural style dimensions, surveyors' units, scientific units, etc. Explain the use of each. Display your work.

3. Collect as many different examples of 3D computer-generated illustrations as you can. Search through books and magazines and bring them to class to share with your classmates. Try to classify each one as to wireframe, surface modeling, solids modeling, or shaded solids modeling.

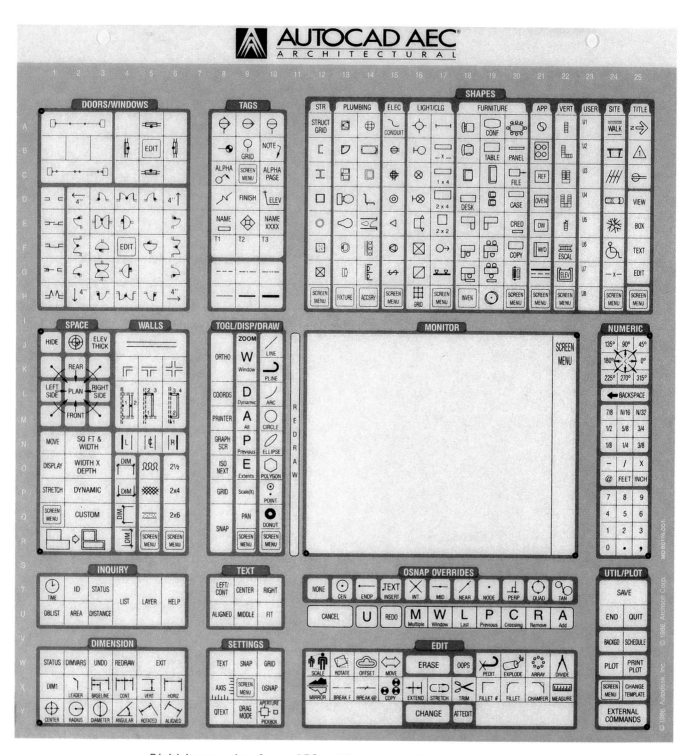

Digitizing template for an AEC architectural package. (Autodesk, Inc.)

Architectural CADD Applications

After studying this chapter you will be able to:
* Understand the major preliminary steps in getting ready to use a CADD package to make drawings.
* Explain the advantages of using several layers while making a CADD drawing.
* Outline the basic steps in producing floor plans, elevations, foundation plans, plot plans, electrical plans, and details.
* Apply the steps for making standard drawings to your own specifications.

The focus of the preceding four chapters has progressively led to the subject of this one—architectural CADD applications. If you have studied those chapters carefully, then you should now understand the basics of CADD and possess enough knowledge to appreciate the opportunities afforded by this exciting ''new'' technology.

As with any field of study, mastery of some skills and knowledge is required for success. The field of architectural design is no different. In fact, it is more demanding than most imagine. For example, not only must you know the symbols and conventions used in architecture so that you can communicate precisely and accurately; but you must know how structures are constructed so that your designs will be sound and efficient, and be prepared to provide the information needed by the various tradespeople, loan agencies, inspection departments, clients, etc. In addition, you must understand the graphic language so that you can present your ideas in a form that communicates well and is familiar to those who will depend on your work to answer their questions regarding a proposed structure. In effect, several fields must be mastered to perform effectively in architectural design.

Architectural computer-aided design and drafting is a field in its own right. It requires knowledge and understanding of all of the above plus a working knowledge of the computer—how to install a program, copy diskettes, use a hard disk, set or change variables in a program, print or plot files, and so on. In fact, a basic course in computer operation is invaluable before trying to use a CADD package. Lastly, even the simplest CADD program is complicated to use and, therefore, adds another degree of complexity to the task of producing designs and drawings. (Some of the larger packages require formal instruction before use.) Even so, the result is worth the effort for most who master the task.

GETTING READY TO USE A CADD PACKAGE

The proper system configuration and setup is prerequisite to successful CADD work. If you are not very familiar with the use of computers, you should seek help in configuring a microcomputer to run a CADD program. Larger systems will require a technician to configure the equipment.

Once all of the equipment is properly connected, tested, and in good working order, then the CADD software program can be installed. Every program has unique features and, therefore, a complete examination of the manuals accompanying the program is a necessity. Proper installation of the program on your computer will take a while, but it is important to follow every step and double check your work. This is the time to study every detail and understand how the program operates in your computer.

When the program is successfully installed and operates as described in the specifications, then the tutorial (if one is provided) is a good place to begin. A *tutorial program* is a brief lesson on how the program works and a demonstration of some of its primary capabilities. Most tutorials are very easy to use and well worth the time spent going through them. By this time, most new CADD operators are beginning to build some confidence and are anxious to make a drawing. If a booklet of sample drawing lessons is provided, then this would be the next logical step. Follow the step-by-step procedures to see how various operations work. You are now drawing, but someone else is making the decisions as to what to do next. You may want to go through the sample lesson several times if this is all new to you. Experienced computer users will no doubt skip the sample lessons. After a few hours following the steps provided in the sample lessons and building confidence, you will be ready to make ''your'' first drawing.

DRAWING SETUP

Even though every CADD package is different, most all provide opportunities to change certain variables relating to drawing setup. You should take full advantage of this opportunity to select the size drawing sheet desired, scale of the drawing, layers to be used, colors, linetypes, etc. Thorough planning at this point will pay off later.

SCALE

Most every construction drawing has a specified scale. For example, residential plans are basically 1/4'' = 1'-0'' scale.

Exceptions include the plot plan and details. If a residential floor plan is to be drawn, then quarter scale is appropriate. Frequently, at this point you will have to decide what drawing units will be used. In architecture, two basic types are common—standard architectural form (feet and inches) and feet in decimal form for lengths on plot plans. (Surveyors measure in feet and tenths of feet.) Choosing the proper scale will not only produce a final drawing (hardcopy) that complies with standard practice, but will let you see how it fits on the drawing sheet as you proceed through the design process.

SHEET SIZE

Early in the drawing setup process a decision should be made as to the sheet size, orientation, borders, title block, etc. Selection of the sheet size will depend on several factors: accepted practice, size of the drawing, and capacity of the plotter. Most residential plans are drawn on ''C'' or ''D'' size paper. Large homes may require the larger size, but most average-size homes will fit on ''C'' size paper.

Paper size can be confusing. There are two basic systems of paper size that are in common use—engineering sizes based on 8 1/2'' x 11'' multiples and architectural sizes based on 9'' x 12'' multiples. Some plotters will handle either size, but none will plot to the very edge of the sheet. Study the manual for your plotter to determine the effective plotting area. This may affect your choice of sheet size.

LAYERS, COLORS, AND PEN SIZES

Using a number of layers while making a drawing can be a great advantage, but it requires some planning. If your CADD program has layers, then you should learn how to make them work for you. It is not necessary to put all components of a drawing on separate layers, but you might want to think along the following lines:

1. Layers will assist you in plotting several versions of the final drawing, because any of the layers may be turned off when plotting.

2. Layers, colors, and pen size go hand-in-hand. You should form the habit of thinking of all three when considering any one of them.

3. Most CADD packages have preassigned layers and colors for certain drawing characteristics. For example, the ''dimensions layer'' may have red assigned to it and be designated as #1 pen. Take advantage of options which save you work.

4. Try to work out a pattern of assigning layers, colors, and pens that suits your needs. If you change every time you make a new drawing, you may have problems later if you try to merge two or more of these drawings together and no consistent pattern is followed.

5. Have an overall scheme in mind before you begin to draw. In other words, plan the layers, colors, and pen sizes before hand.

Following is an example of how you might plan the use of layers, colors, and pen sizes before you start to draw a floor plan:

Features requiring extra fine lines (1st pen, 0.25mm) [former #000]
Dimensions, layer 1, red
Hatching, layer 2, blue
Features requiring fine lines (2nd pen, 0.35mm) [former #0]
Glazing, layer 3, yellow

Door symbols, layer 4, yellow
Wall cabinets (hidden), layer 5, green
Stairs, layer 6, green
Appliances and fixtures, layer 7, green
Features requiring medium lines (3rd pen, 0.50mm) [former #1]
Wall thickness, layer 8, white
Porch boards, layer 9, white
Closet rods and shelves, layer 10, white
Room names, layer 11, cyan
Entry arrow, layer 12, cyan
Notes, layer 13, cyan
Scale, layer 14, cyan
Features requiring broad lines (4th pen, 0.70mm) [former #2 1/2]
Border, layer 15, magenta
Title, layer 16, magenta

Using a plan such as this will permit the plotting of a drawing that has the proper width lines, provide for easy modification of the drawing, and allow several different versions of the drawing to be plotted.

Different line widths can be generated two ways. First, and most logical, is to use a different pen size for each width of line, Fig. 38-1. In the chart above, four pens would be required to produce the lines as specified. The second approach is to specify the line width at the time it is drawn and let the plotter trace over it until the desired width is achieved. Either method will produce the desired results, but if you have a multipen plotter the first method is faster and more consistent.

Once the preliminary planning is done, the drawing setup completed and scale designated,

STANDARD RAPIDOGRAPH		METRIC
6x0		.13
4x0		.18
3x0		.25
00		.30
0		.35
1		.50
2		.60
2½		.70
3		.80
3½		1.00
4		1.20
6		1.40
7		2.00

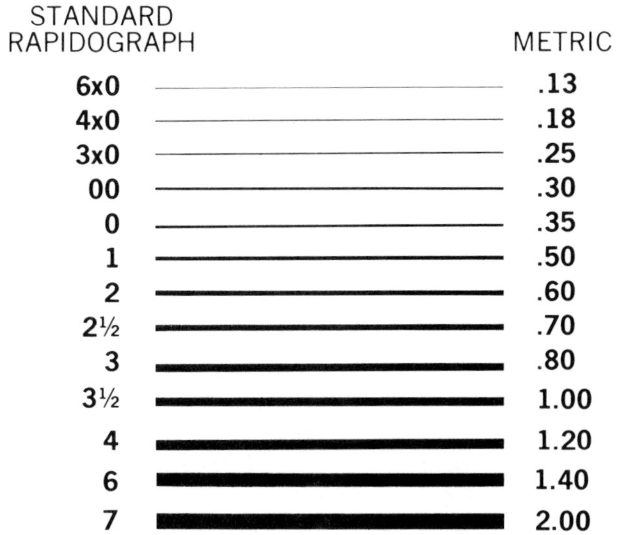

Approximate only, (Line widths will vary depending on surface, ink, speed at which line is drawn, etc.).

Fig. 38-1. Standard drawing pen widths. All may not be available for CADD plotters. (Koh-I-Noor Rapidograph, Inc.)

you are ready to begin. The procedure for making CADD drawings is very similar to making drawings manually. The same rules for good planning and communication also apply. The remainder of this chapter will be devoted to the step-by-step procedure for drawing a residential floor plan, foundation plan, front elevation, plot plan, electrical plan, and detail. The procedure will relate to the logical steps in making each drawing rather than how to use a particular CADD software program. For the record, these drawings were produced using AutoCAD's AEC Architectural package and were plotted on a Houston Instrument DMP-52 MP plotter using four different pen widths.

DRAWING FLOOR PLANS

Refer to Chapter 16 for a complete discussion of the definition and purpose; required information; location of walls, windows and doors, cabinets, appliances, fixtures, stairs, fireplaces, etc.; and dimensioning and symbols used on floor plans.

The first step in designing a residential structure is generally to determine the basic requirements and record them as sketches and/or notes. The house about to be designed must provide the following: 3 bedrooms, 2 baths, living room, kitchen/dining area, den, pantry, and ample closet space. Basic room sizes have been determined and recorded as well as the general arrangement of space.

SEQUENTIAL STEPS

1. *Prepare a space diagram.* A space diagram is an effective technique to determine how the various areas desired might fit together. The diagram should be drawn to scale with each room or area identified and the number of square feet noted for each. Select a layer for this drawing even though you may not want to plot it. Fig. 38-2 shows a completed space diagram which meets the criteria identified. The total area occupied by the plan is 1778.91 sq. ft.

2. *Drawing the exterior and interior walls.* Two approaches are commonly used to draw the walls on a floor plan. The first is to convert a space diagram into a floor plan using a facility provided by the CADD program. Fig. 38-3 illustrates the steps involved when using this method. The second approach is to use the DOUBLE LINE command to draw the walls. Fig. 38-4 shows the steps for this approach. Two of

the key advantages to using the automatic procedure are speed and wall corner and intersection cleanup. Some programs also clean up walls developed using the double line procedure. Fig. 38-5 illustrates four typical wall areas that require cleanup. Two important things to remember when locating and drawing exterior and interior walls on a floor plan is their proper thickness and measurement location. The thickness of all walls should be drawn as accurately as possible. Interior walls are generally 4 1/2'' thick which allows for drywall on both sides of a 3 1/2'' stud. Exterior walls vary considerably depending on type and construction technique. A typical exterior frame wall might be 5 3/32'' in actual thickness (1/2'' drywall, 3 1/2'' stud, 3/4'' R.F. insulation, and 11/32'' P.W. siding). The computer can draw this thickness as easily as 6 inches. The second important consideration, measurement location, is where the wall is dimensioned. Interior walls are generally dimensioned to the center of the wall. Therefore, the center of an interior wall should produce a reasonable dimension like 6'-2'' or 12'-3'', but not

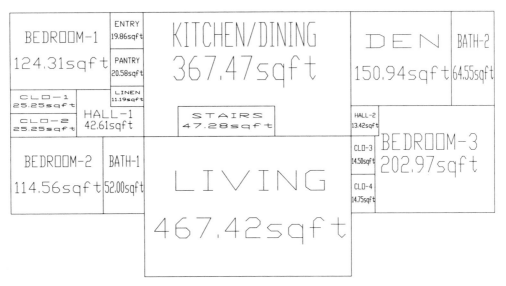

Fig. 38-2. Example of a computer-generated space diagram which shows the designated room name and area. (Step 1.)

Fig. 38-3. These drawings represent the steps involved in converting a space diagram into a floor plan. (Step 2.)

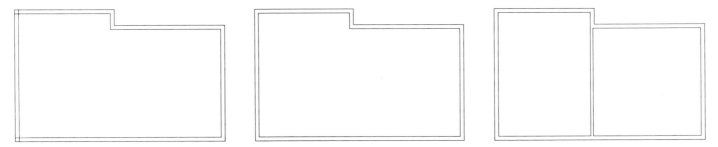

Fig. 38-4. Steps in developing a floor plan using the DOUBLE LINE method. (Step 2.)

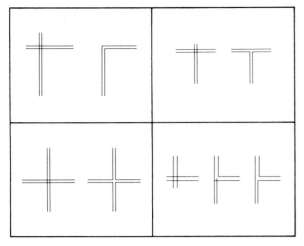

Fig. 38-5. Four typical wall areas that require "cleanup" after the DOUBLE LINE command is used.

10'-1 7/16". Exterior frame walls are usually dimensioned to the outside of the rough frame wall which includes the weatherboard or rigid foam insulation on the outside of the studs, but not the siding or veneer. These lengths should also be reasonable. Try to plan a structure so that the overall length and width are multiples of 2 feet if possible.

Fig. 38-6 shows the results of converting a space diagram into a floor plan. Note the difference in thickness of the exterior and interior walls. Also see how the intersections are handled where an interior wall becomes an exterior wall in the large center area. Be sure to remember to select an appropriate layer, color, and pen size for the drawing.

3. **Locate the windows and doors.** When windows and doors are located in a frame wall structure, they are dimensioned to the center of the unit. (A unit may have one or more doors or windows.) Plan the location of these elements so that they complement the overall design, but also use location dimensions that are at least multiples of 1 inch. Window sills may or may not be included depending on the desires of the designer. Fig. 38-7 shows the plan with windows and doors added. Can you see that these elements use thinner lines than the walls? Doors and windows should be on a different layer than the walls.

4. **Draw the stairs.** This one-story house has a basement, therefore, the total finished floor (basement)-to-finished floor (first floor) distance must be determined before the stairs can be designed. The total rise for this house is 10'-2". This is greater than usual because rather large wood floor trusses will be used. Put the stairs on a layer by itself for easy modification of the floor plan. Consider pen width and color.

Some CADD programs calculate the tread width and riser height for each step and draw the stairs. Whether or not you have this facility, the stairs should conform to good design principles. See Chapter 14 for complete details on stair design. The stair treads, handrails, and direction of travel should be shown on the floor plan.

5. **Locate and draw the fireplace.** Study Chapter 15 before drawing the fireplace. Proper design is essential to satisfactory operation. Identify the type (single-face, double-face, etc.)

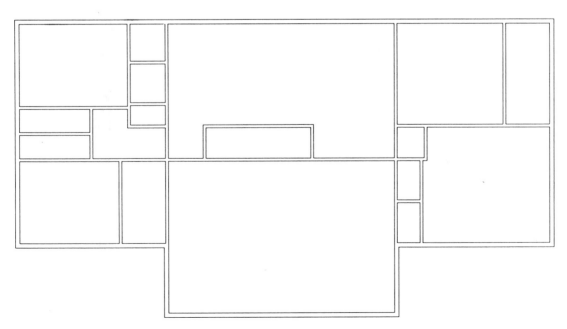

Fig. 38-6. A floor plan generated from a space diagram. All wall intersection cleanup was automatic.

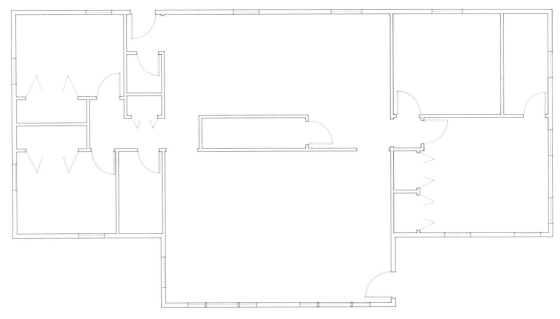

Fig. 38-7. Windows and doors have been added using picks from a digitizing overlay. (Step 3.)

and size of fireplace to be designed. Find the necessary dimensions in the Reference Section or Chapter 15 and record them for use in this drawing. Draw the fireplace in its proper location using appropriate hatch symbols and line thickness. The fireplace should have its own layer.

6. *Locate and draw walks, patios, and porches.* Elements in the plan such as walks, patios, and porches should be thought of as extensions of the floor plan. Careful thought should go into their design and placement. Draw these elements on the floor plan. You may want to use a separate layer for these elements.

7. *Draw the kitchen cabinets, appliances, and bathroom fixtures.* Review the sections in the text dealing with the layout and design of kitchens and baths before adding these elements. Good planning in these areas is essential. Add the kitchen cabinets, appliances, and bathroom fixtures to the floor plan using standard symbols from the symbols library and the appropriate linetypes. Fig. 38-8 includes steps 4-7.

8. *Add dimensions to the plan.* All construction features on the floor plan should be dimensioned unless the location or size is very obvious. For example, a door placed at a stan-

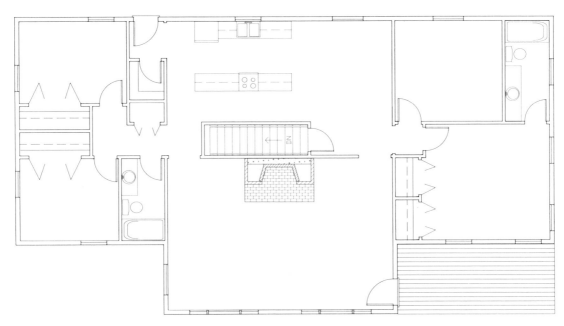

Fig. 38-8. This drawing shows steps 4 through 7 of the sequence.

dard 4'' offset need not be dimensioned or a set of bi-fold doors that fills the space in front of the closet need not be dimensioned. However, if there is any doubt, dimension the feature. Remember, the extension lines begin at the outside of the rough stud wall and do not include the thickness of the siding or veneer. Every window, door, intersecting wall, or offset in the exterior wall must be dimensioned. Each exterior segment should have partial dimensions as well as an overall length dimension. Study the arrangement of dimensions in Fig. 38-9 to see how dimensions should be arranged on a drawing. Be sure your dimensions are accurate and add up properly. Use the dimensioning capabilities of your CADD program to accomplish this task. Be sure to assign the correct layer and color for these items.

9. *Add room names, notes, material symbols, scale, and title.* Use the TEXT command to enter room names and sizes, scale, notes, and title. Think about which pen you want to use for each of these items so they will be on the proper layer and use the appropriate color. Use any material symbols that are appropriate for this drawing, but do not overdo it. Construct a title block, if you desire.

10. *Check over the entire drawing.* Examine all aspects of the drawing for accuracy, good design, and missing items. When you are sure it is complete, save it for plotting. Steps 9 and 10 are shown in Fig. 38-10.

DRAWING ELEVATIONS

Chapter 18 in the text describes the purpose of and information required on exterior elevations. Please study that material before attempting to draw an elevation using the computer.

An exterior elevation is usually drawn for each side of the house. These views are generally identified as front, rear, left side, and right side. Occasionally, they are identified by the direction they face—north side, south side, etc. Whichever method is used is not important, but each elevation should be labeled to avoid confusion.

The design of any structure should take into account the site characteristics. The ''lay of the land,'' physical features such as the presence of groundwater, a variety of soils, and frost penetration depth have definite implications for the building substructure. The elevation will be affected to some extent by these features because

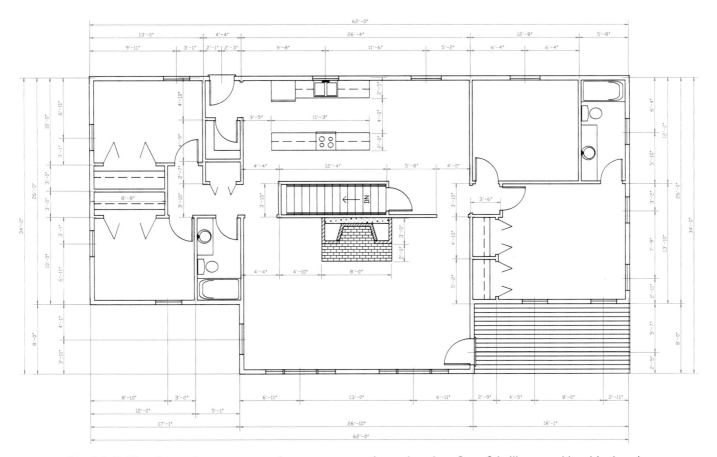

Fig. 38-9. The dimensions are a very important part of any drawing. Step 8 is illustrated by this drawing.

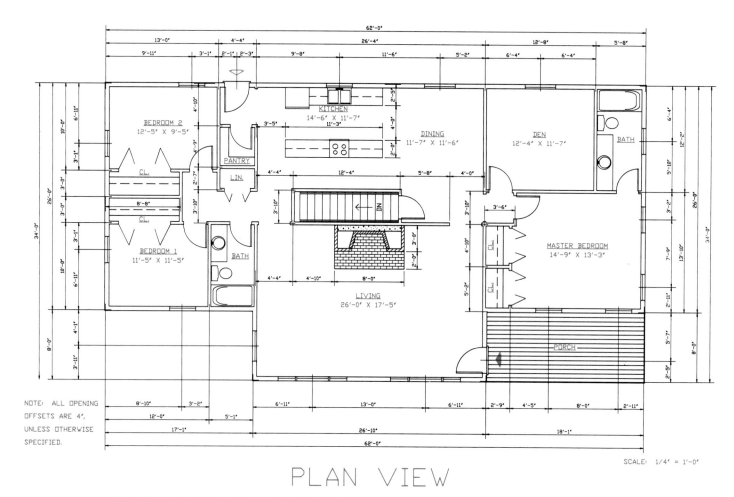

PLAN VIEW

Fig. 38-10. Steps 9 and 10 of the drawing sequence are added to complete the floor plan.

the reference point for most elevations is the grade line.

SEQUENTIAL STEPS

1. ***Draw a typical wall section to provide height measurements.*** Many questions will need answers before an accurate typical wall section can be drawn. Here are some of them:
- Will the house have a basement, crawl space, or slab foundation?
- How will the house relate to the present grade?
- Must the grade be modified to accommodate the structure?
- What are the finished floor-to-finished ceiling heights?
- How thick is the floor(s)?
- What type of roof construction is planned?
- Will standard rough opening heights be used for windows and doors?
- What kind of exterior materials will be used?
- What type of soffit will be used?

Once these questions are answered, an accurate typical wall section can be drawn to provide the height measurements needed to draw an elevation. Figure 38-11 shows a typical wall sec-

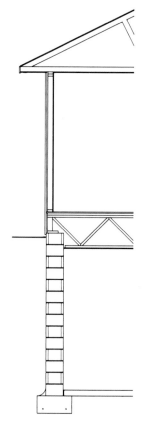

Fig. 38-11. This typical wall section will be used to construct the front elevation. (Step 1.)

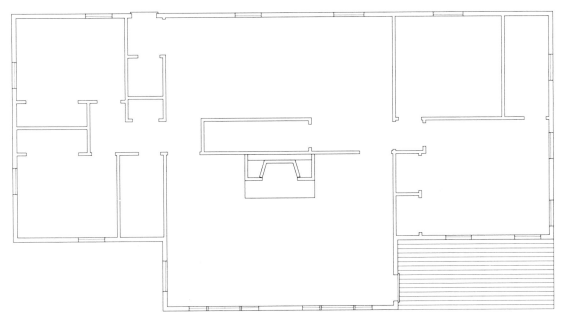

Fig. 38-12. The floor plan properly positioned to draw the front elevation. (Step 2.)

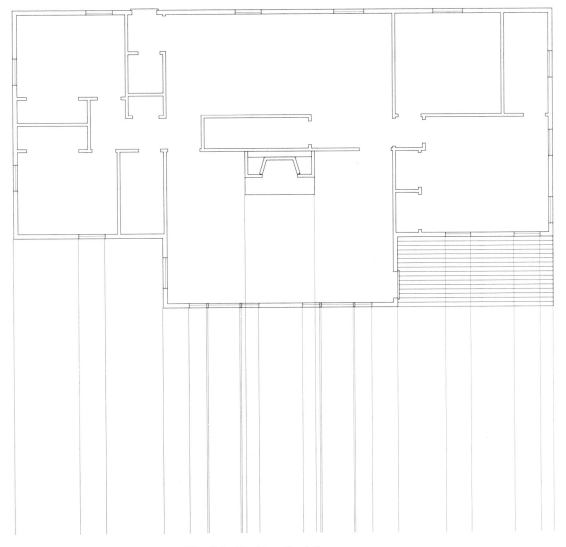

Fig. 38-13. Step 3 of the sequence.

tion with sufficient information to construct a front elevation. The scale of this drawing should be 1/4″ = 1′-0″ if the drawing is to be used to project the various heights.

If only the dimensions are to be used then the scale is normally larger. The 1/4″ scale section drawing will be discarded after the elevations are completed, but the larger scale detail may be used in the detail section.

2. *Place a copy of the floor plan above the space where the elevation is to be drawn.* The arrangement of the floor plan should be such that the side to be drawn faces down toward the elevation. Fig. 38-12 shows the floor plan properly positioned to draw the front elevation. Note: Only the information needed to draw the elevation is included on the floor plan copy. This is easily done using CADD by turning off those layers that contain unwanted material.

3. *Project features to be drawn on the elevation from the floor plan.* This operation can be performed as each projection line is needed or all elements can be projected at this time. The illustration in Fig. 38-13 shows all of the vertical projection lines completed. Projection lines should be placed on a separate layer to facilitate removal when you are finished with them. Note the typical wall section is off the screen at this point to show details of the floor plan more clearly. It can be called up as needed.

4. *Locate the foundation wall, footings, and grade line heights on the elevation.* The first lines to be drawn on the front elevation will be the footings, foundation walls, floor slab, and grade line. All of these lines will be dashed (hidden) lines except the grade line. Make separate layers for these two linetypes since both will be different widths than the projection lines. Fig. 38-14 shows the foundation (substructure) completed up to the grade line.

5. *Locate the wall height and roof lines on the elevation.* The exterior walls above the grade

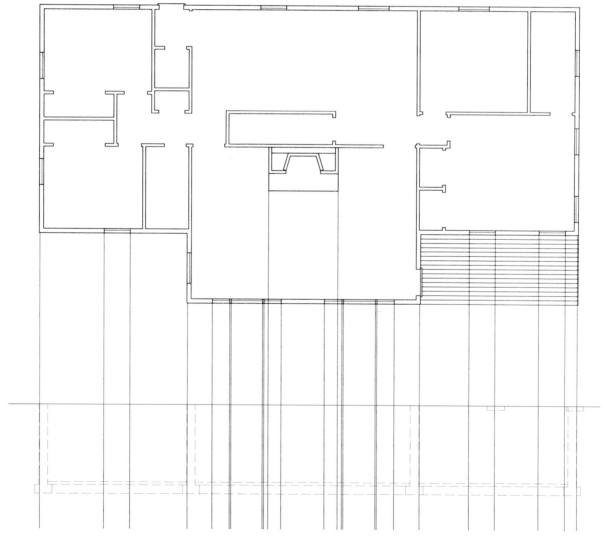

Fig. 38-14. Foundation substructure completed to the grade. (Step 4.)

can now be drawn as well as the roof. Notice in Fig. 38-15 that the finished floor and finished ceiling on the first floor are represented using a center line symbol. These lines will be used for dimensioning, so they may be located on the dimension layer. The exterior wall lines should have a layer of their own since they will be a different width than any of the previous lines. The chimney has been added so that it is 3'-0'' above the highest point of the roof.

This a good place to sit back and look at the overall proportions of the house. Changes can be made easily at this point. You will notice the elevation overlaps the floor plan at this point. This presents no problem as the floor plan will be turned off when the elevation is plotted.

6. *Locate the height of windows, doors, and any other features.* The remaining elements of the house can now be located and drawn in place. Windows are time consuming to draw one at a time so they should be developed and stored

in the symbols library for use when needed. Placing them on a separate layer would make it easy to call up different window styles for compatibility with the house style. Fig. 38-16 shows the windows completed. Now all of the exterior features have been added.

7. *Add dimensions, material symbols, notes, scale, and title.* The remaining information may be added to the elevation at this point. Notes and dimensions are best added first so they will not interfere with material symbols. The scale and title can be added last. Fig. 38-17 shows the completed front elevation with sufficient detail to accurately communicate the intended design. Again, separate layers were used for the siding, dimensions, notes, scale, and title.

Elevations for the remaining sides of the house should be drawn using the same procedure for each one. Generally, not as much material symbol is used on these elevations especially if the same material is used on all sides.

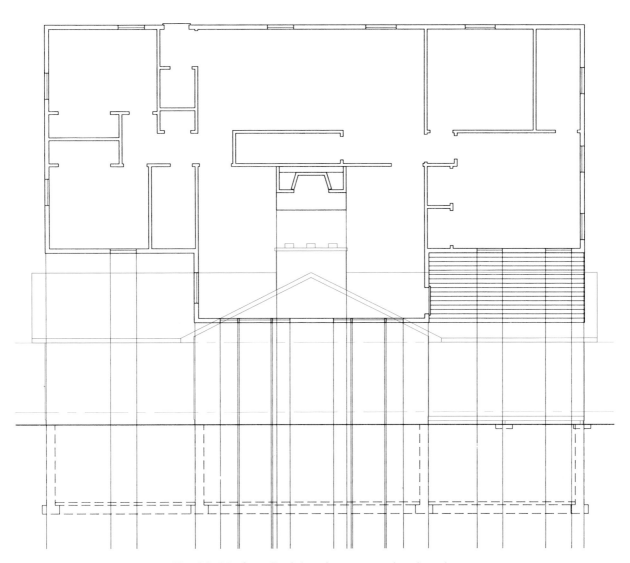

Fig. 38-15. Step 5 of drawing an exterior elevation.

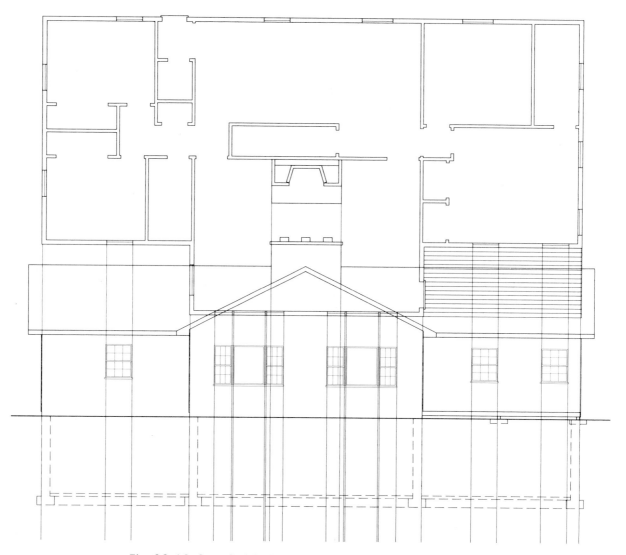

Fig. 38-16. Step 6. All of the exterior features have been added.

3'-4"

12
6

235# ASPHALT SHINGLES WITH
ADHESIVE TABS ON 15# FELT

1" X 6" REDWOOD FASCIA

F.C.

REDWOOD
SIDING

1'-6"

6'-10"

8'-0"

F.F.

1'-4"

BASEMENT FLOOR 4" CONC. ON 4" SAND

10'-2 3/4"

1'-0"

F.F.

SCALE: 1/4" = 1'-0"

FRONT ELEVATION

Fig. 38-17. Completed front elevation. (Step 7.)

DRAWING FOUNDATION/BASEMENT PLANS

Chapter 10 describes in detail the purpose of a foundation plan and the features shown on it. Study Chapter 10 before beginning the foundation plan.

Many of the questions that need to be answered will have already been dealt with during the construction of the typical wall section, but some will still remain. For example, are any special footings required inside the foundation perimeter to support columns, chimneys, etc.? If so, where are they located and what are their sizes? Will any beam supports (pilasters) be required? Are any stepped footings or retaining walls required? Are there any problems with the grade? These and other questions should be answered before starting this drawing.

SEQUENTIAL STEPS

1. *Call up a copy of the floor plan to use as an underlay.* Once again, the floor plan should be used as a guide for the construction of the foundation plan. The same copy that was used for the elevations can be used for this drawing. The foundation plan is also drawn at 1/4'' = 1'-0'' scale.

2. *Locate the outline of the foundation walls and footings.* Generally, the outside of the foundation walls are identical to the outside of the rough stud walls on the floor plan in a frame structure with siding. Brick or other veneer is added to the outside of this point. (See the typical wall section in Fig. 38-11). The foundation wall is wider than a frame wall, therefore, the inside line will fall inside the floor plan. Generally, the foundation wall will be 8'', 10'', or 12'' thick, but there are exceptions. A 12'' thick wall will be used in this example. Fig. 38-18 shows the foundation wall, footings, and chimney located and drawn. The footings and foundation walls should be drawn on separate layers since the line widths and symbols are different. Piers and their footings may be added to these layers since they use similar symbols and are part of the foundation.

3. *Draw the stairs, interior walls, windows, and doors.* The stairs should be drawn at this point since they will directly affect the basement layout. They can be recalled and positioned in the proper location, but some modification will be required since the opposite end of the floor plan is visible in the basement. Also, the direction arrow points in the wrong direction. Keep the stairs on another layer for easy future modification. This is the appropriate time to turn off the floor plan underlay, since it will not be needed for the remaining elements.

Draw all interior walls showing their openings. Insert doors and windows in the plan. Each of these elements should be on separate layers. Use symbols from the library or construct your own. Add other features such as joist direction arrow and window wells. Fig. 38-19 shows the plan to this point.

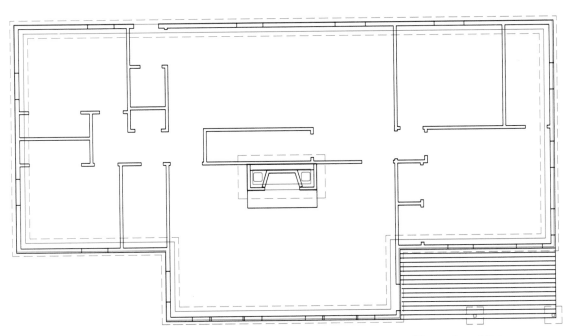

Fig. 38-18. Foundation/basement plan drawing sequence. (Steps 1 and 2.)

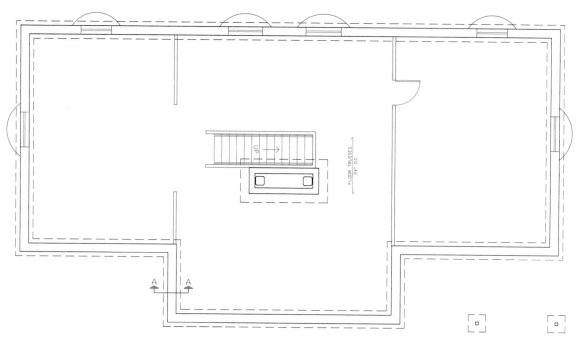

Fig. 38-19. Foundation/basement plan drawing sequence. (Step 3.)

4. *Dimension the foundation plan.* Use the DIMENSION command to add the appropriate dimensions to the plan. The approach is similar to dimensioning the floor plan except that openings in the wall are located to the edge of the openings rather than the center. Also dimensions inside the perimeter of the wall are dimensioned to the inside surface of the wall. Frame

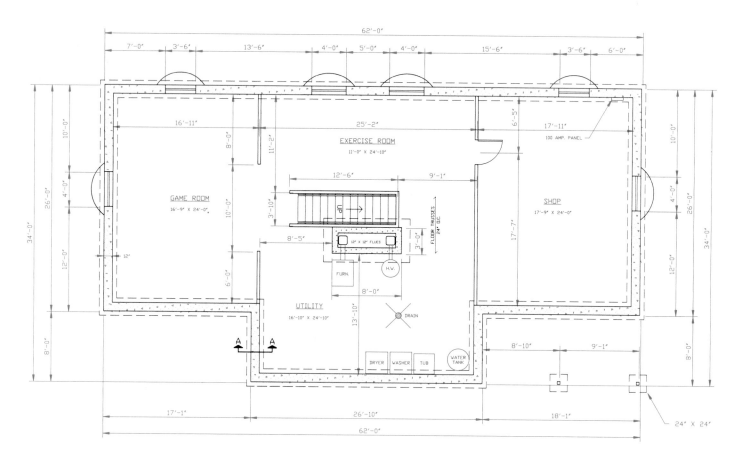

FOUNDATION PLAN

Fig. 38-20. Completed foundation/basement plan. (Step 4.)

walls are dimensioned in the normal manner. Exterior dimensions are to the very outside of the masonry wall.

Interior features such as appliances, fixtures, and furnace may now be added to the plan and identified. Be sure to use appropriate layers so line widths and linetypes will be correct. Add cutting plane symbol and room names and sizes. Look over the plan to be sure it is complete before adding the scale and title. Fig. 38-20 shows the completed basement plan.

DRAWING ELECTRICAL PLANS

A residential electrical plan shows the location and type of all electrical features in the home. Chapter 20 describes the purpose of the electrical plan and describes all of the information required on it. Study this chapter before starting the drawing.

SEQUENTIAL STEPS

1. ***Copy the floor plan showing all exterior and interior walls and major appliances.*** Call up the floor plan that was used for the foundation underlay and copy it for the electrical plan. It should not include dimensions, notes, and room sizes. The scale of the electrical plan is 1/4″ =

1'-0''. Fig. 38-21 shows the floor plan to be used for the electrical plan. Note, the room names are retained since they should be included on the electrical plan.

2. ***Locate the meter and distribution panel.*** Some thought should be given to the proper location of the meter and distribution panel. The distribution panel is frequently located in the basement and the meter is shown on that electrical plan, particularly if underground service is provided. (Neither are shown on this plan, but would be included on the basement electrical plan.)

3. ***Show all convenience outlets, switches, and fixtures.*** Assign a layer for these electrical elements. Take one room at a time and add the outlets, switches, and ceiling outlet fixtures. Include telephone or other special devices using symbols from the library or custom symbols. Proceed one room at a time until the inside of the house is completed. Note the 230-volt outlet for the range. Then add outside lighting and weatherproof outlets as needed. Fig. 38-22 shows the electrical plan to this point.

4. ***Connect switches to lighting fixtures and switched outlets.*** Use another layer for the connecting conductors (wires). The linetype used for this purpose is the long dashed line. It merely shows which fixtures or outlets are connected to a given switch—not where the conductors are

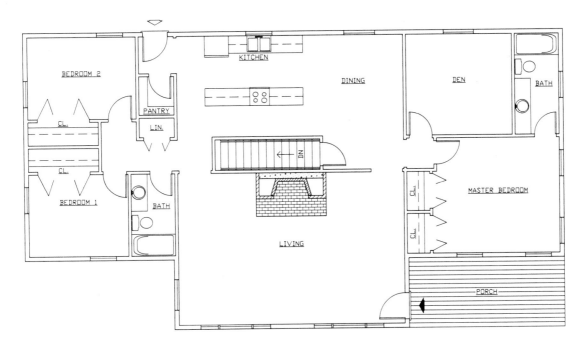

PLAN VIEW

Fig. 38-21. Electrical plan drawing sequence. (Step 1.)

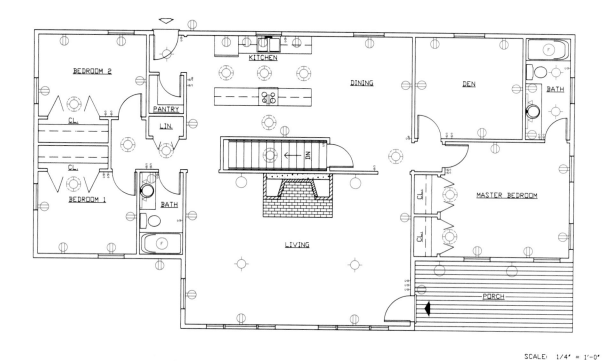

Fig. 38-22. Electrical plan drawing sequence. (Steps 2 and 3.)

actually located. These lines (symbols) are usually curved so they are easier to see. They can be drawn by locating three points (both ends and a point between).

5. ***Add a circuit data chart, lighting fixture schedule, and symbol legend, if desired.*** The circuit data chart is especially useful in planning and communicating the electrical needs of the structure. Add the scale and title to complete the drawing. Fig. 38-23 shows the completed electrical plan which includes most of the typical features.

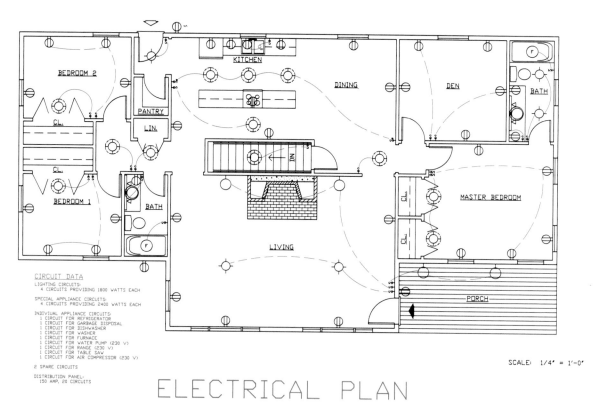

Fig. 38-23. Completed electrical plan. (Steps 4 and 5.)

DRAWING PLOT PLANS

The plot plan is a plan view drawing which shows the site and location of the buildings on the property. Chapter 8 describes in detail the features shown on a plot plan. Study this chapter before attempting to draw a plot plan using the computer.

The plot plan lends itself to freehand sketching of contour lines using a pointing device and the use of surveyor's units (if your CADD package provides this option) for location of the property lines. Also, this plan is usually drawn at a scale of 1'' = 10'-0'', 1'' = 20'-0'', or 1'' = 30'-0'' depending on the size of paper used, complexity of the site, and size of the property.

SEQUENTIAL STEPS

1. **Select a scale for the plot plan.** Select a scale that will provide the largest drawing on the size of paper that you have chosen for the set of construction drawings. All sheets should be the same size for easy handling.

2. **Lay out the property lines.** Plan to draw the property lines on their own layer since the linetype is unique and very wide. The property line description is generally supplied by surveyors in the form of a site plan, word description, or legal description. A typical property line description is N 45° 15' 45'' W for a distance of 162.43'.

Start at the reference corner if there is one, and lay out each line in a clockwise manner until you reach the starting point. Extreme accuracy is required to produce a satisfactory property line layout. The end of each property line should terminate with a small circle with a point in the center which represents the end of the line. Use the CIRCLE command.

3. **Locate the building(s) on the site.** Be careful to position it according to code. Some communities require setbacks from the street and property lines. The driveway, patios, walks, and other flatwork may also be located at this time. Add property corner elevation. Use a separate layer for the building perimeter, drive, and walks. Fig. 38-24 shows the first three steps completed.

4. **Draw the contour lines and add elevations.** The contour lines should be placed on a layer by themselves because they will use a different linetype and be freehand lines. (The contour lines may also be drawn by locating several points from an elevation grid data chart for each line and have the computer generate the best line of fit.) Choose an appropriate contour interval for your site. Label the elevation of each contour line.

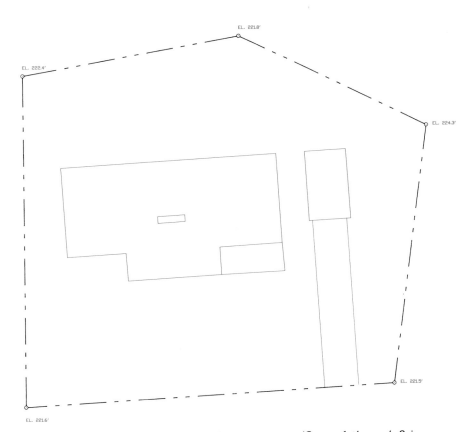

Fig. 38-24. Plot plan drawing sequence. (Steps 1 through 3.)

5. ***Add house reference corner location dimensions.*** The reference corner of the house should be selected so the structure can be properly located on the site and placed correctly with respect to the grade. Locate the corner relative to a property corner or in relation to two property lines, if they form a right angle. Label the reference corner and identify the elevation. Dimensions should be located on the "Dimension" layer.

6. ***Add other house features as desired.*** Additional features of the house such as rooflines may be added at this time. The rooflines are particularly useful if a roof plan is not intended or the roof is complicated. Long dashed lines are appropriate for the roofline. It will also need a separate layer. The overall dimensions of the house should be shown on the plot plan to aid in staking out the house location on the site. Fig. 38-25 shows steps 4-6.

7. ***Add other topographical features.*** Other topographical features such as trees, streams, and right-of-ways can be added to the drawing now. Choose appropriate layers for these features. Use symbols from the library or design your own.

8. ***Include property line data and north arrow.*** Property line data may be added to the drawing in the form of a chart or placed along each prop-erty line. The north symbol or meridian arrow is a very important information device on a plot plan. This is the one place where it must appear.

9. ***Add the scale, title, and features unique to the situation.*** All plot plans should include the scale and title, but some may not require the utilities, septic tank and field, lot number, and well. Add these items as the situation dictates. Fig. 38-26 shows a reasonably complete plot plan.

DRAWING DETAILS

Every set of construction drawings requires several individual details. They are usually drawn where more information is needed to fully describe the construction intended. Some of the areas of the house that typically require details are the stairs, kitchen, fireplace, windows, doors, foundation walls, roof, and special construction.

Each detail will involve unique drawing procedures and problems. Some will be very time consuming while others will be simple. Frequently, you will want to save these details for future use since only minor changes may be required for use with another set of plans. Some CADD packages include a significant number of standard

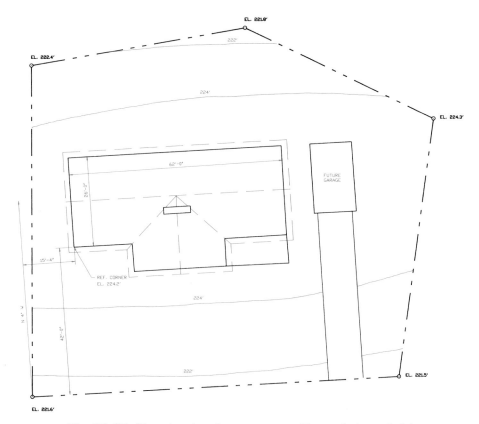

Fig. 38-25. Plot plan drawing sequence. (Steps 4 through 6.)

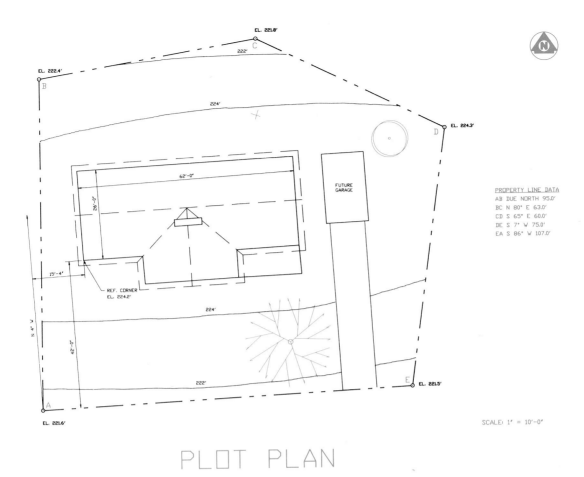

FUTURE
GARAGE

PROPERTY LINE DATA
AB DUE NORTH 95.0'
BC N 80° E 63.0'
CD S 65° E 60.0'
DE S 7° W 75.0'
EA S 86° W 107.0'

62'-0"

26'-0"

15'-4"

REF. CORNER
EL. 224.2'

224'

N 4° W

4'-0"

222'

E
EL. 221.5'

A
EL. 221.6'

SCALE: 1" = 10'-0"

PLOT PLAN

Fig. 38-26. Completed plot plan. (Steps 7 through 9.)

details which are often used in a typical set of drawings. If you have such a package, your work will be greatly reduced. If not, the procedure shown for constructing a typical wall section may be helpful to you in making similar drawings for other areas of the house.

SEQUENTIAL STEPS OF DRAWING A TYPICAL WALL SECTION

1. ***Gather the necessary information and choose a scale.*** The first step in drawing any detail is to determine the necessary information. A guess is not good enough. You must know the specific dimensions, construction procedure, etc. to draw a detail. Once you have the information, you can begin to communicate it to others. Plan to use a scale which will show the elements of the detail. Common scales used include: 1/2'' = 1'-0'', 3/4'' = 1'-0'', and 1'' = 1'-0''.

2. ***Layout the footing, foundation wall, and floor slab.*** If you have not studied Chapter 9 Footings, Foundations, and Concrete, this would be an ideal place to begin. Select an appropriate layer for the footing and foundation wall and draw these elements. Locate the basement slab

and show a portion of it. Fig. 38-27 shows a foundation wall, footing, and floor slab for the house used throughout this chapter.

3. ***Draw the first floor, wall, and roof structure.*** Once the foundation wall is properly constructed, the floor joists or trusses may be located and drawn. Be sure to consider the layers, linetypes, and colors you wish to use. Fig. 38-28 shows a photo of the screen taken during this construction. The use of different colors helps to define the different parts of the

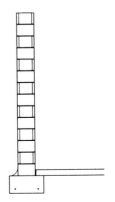

Fig. 38-27. Typical wall section detail drawing sequence. (Steps 1 and 2.)

Architectural CADD Applications 573

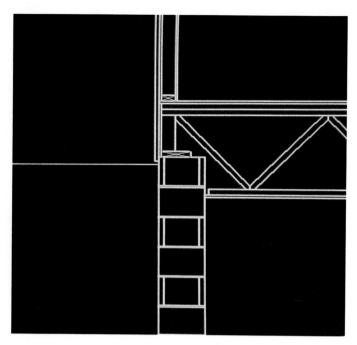

Fig. 38-28. Photo of the screen showing the construction of Step 3 in progress.

drawing. Also, each color represents a different layer and pen size.

Continue drawing the first floor exterior wall and roof trusses. Use actual sizes rather than nominal sizes. Zoom in on small parts so that they may be more easily seen and manipulated. Once the wall is completed (roughed in), it is wise to sit back and look it over carefully to be sure it represents good building practice. Fig. 38-29 shows the wall section to this point.

4. *Add details and hatch symbols.* Position the grade line (remember the layer) and draw it in place. Add details such as gusset plates, drain tile, and a roof slope triangle. Include insulation, concrete symbol, sand, and gravel. Earth can also be included, if you desire. Fig. 38-30 shows these symbols and details.

5. *Add dimensions and notes.* A typical wall section should include all of the required dimensions—finished floor-to-ceiling height, thickness of the floor system, thickness and width of footing, height of foundation wall, overhang length, and so on. Try to be thorough. Use local notes to identify materials. Identify the grade elevation. Add other information that is pertinent for your drawing.

6. *Add scale and title.* When all the information desired has been added to the drawing, then add the scale and title on the appropriate layers. Look over your work to be sure that you are finished. Fig. 38-31 shows the completed wall section.

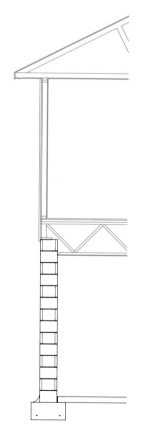

Fig. 38-29. Typical wall section detail drawing sequence. (Step 3.)

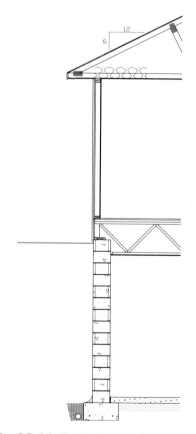

Fig. 38-30. Typical wall section detail drawing sequence. (Step 4.)

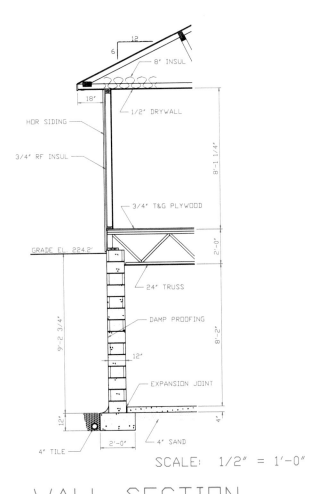

SCALE: 1/2" = 1'-0"

WALL SECTION

Fig. 38-31. Completed typical wall section.
(Steps 5 and 6.)

REVIEW QUESTIONS—CHAPTER 38

Write your answers on a separate sheet of paper. Do not write in this book.

1. What four things must you know in order to be successful in architectural CADD?
2. Once a CADD program is successfully installed and operates properly, where should you begin?
3. Which of the following is an example of architectural drawing units?
   a. 12'-6''.
   b. 12.6'.
   c. Both of the above.
4. Most residential construction drawings are made on _____ or _____ size paper.
5. Most CADD packages have preassigned _____ and colors for certain drawing characteristics.
6. Which of the following best describes the proper use of pen sizes to produce architectural drawings?
   a. #000 for dimensions and object lines.
   b. #0 for door symbols, glazing, and wall cabinets.
   c. #1 for wall thicknesses and border line.
   d. #2 1/2 for wall thicknesses and text.
7. The recommended first step in designing a floor plan is to:
   a. Draw the exterior walls first.
   b. Use the sketch command to rough in the basic shape.
   c. Prepare a space diagram.
   d. None of the above.
8. Which of the following standard symbols are frequently included in the symbols library of common CADD packages:
   a. Doors, windows, plants, furniture, stairs.
   b. Appliances, fixtures, electrical symbols.
   c. North symbol, user-defined symbols, vehicles.
   d. All of the above.
9. The _____ command is used to enter room names and titles on a drawing.
10. The reference point of most exterior elevations is the _____ line.
11. What device is used to provide heights for drawing exterior elevations?
12. How can you temporarily remove unwanted material from a drawing displayed on the monitor?
13. Why should a footing be placed on a different layer than the foundation wall?
14. The foundation plan is usually drawn using the floor plan as a _____ to provide location of walls and other features.
15. Why can't the stairs that were developed for the floor plan be used exactly as they are in the basement plan?
16. Name two basic differences in dimensioning a foundation plan as opposed to a floor plan using frame walls.
17. Which of the following commands would you most likely use first to begin the electrical plan?
   a. COPY.
   b. MOVE.
   c. ZOOM.
   d. PAN.
18. Which linetype should you use to connect a switch to a ceiling outlet fixture?
   a. Continuous.
   b. Dotted.
   c. Dashed.
   d. Phantom.
19. The SKETCH command would most likely be used to draw the _____ lines on a plot plan.
20. Which layer are dimensions usually located on?

21. List five standard details described in this chapter that might be developed and saved for future use.
22. What type of symbol is used to show concrete, brick, or other building material?

SUGGESTED ACTIVITIES

1. If you do not have access to a CADD system in your school, contact your local community college, state university technology department, or local firm that uses this equipment and arrange for a ''hands-on'' experience with a CADD tutorial program.

Have a simple design sketched out beforehand to try with the CADD system if time permits.
2. If you have access to a CADD system, use the steps presented in this chapter to design a simple floor plan from a prepared sketch. Present a printed or plotted copy of your computer drawing to the class and explain how you proceeded.
3. If you have used a CADD system before, develop a detail that might be used in future plans. Ask your instructor to evaluate the use of symbols, dimensions, notes, and method of construction.

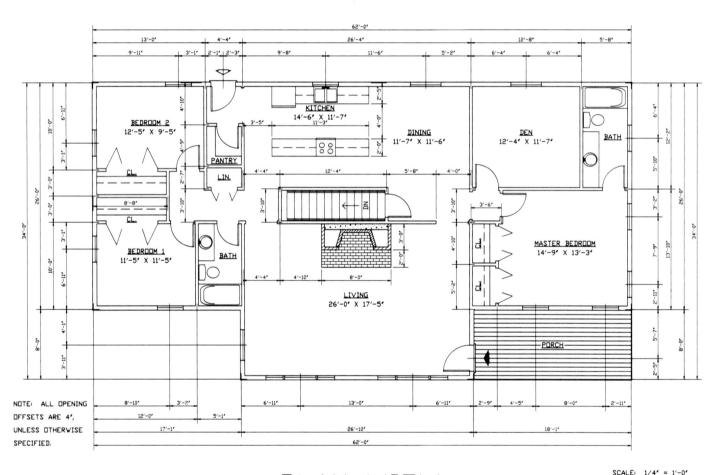

PLAN VIEW

SCALE: 1/4" = 1'-0"

Fig. 38-32. Set of working drawings created by the activities in this chapter. Add your standard title block and border. (Continued)

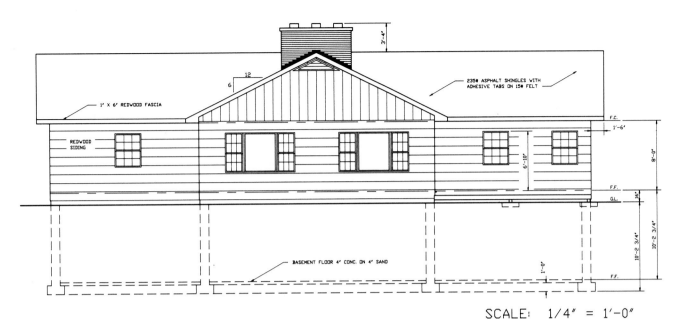

SCALE: 1/4" = 1'-0"

FRONT ELEVATION

Fig. 38-32. (Continued)

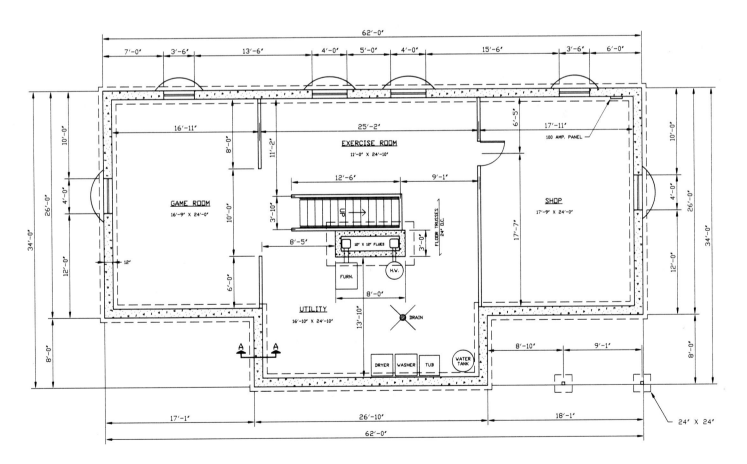

FOUNDATION PLAN

Fig. 38-32. (Continued)

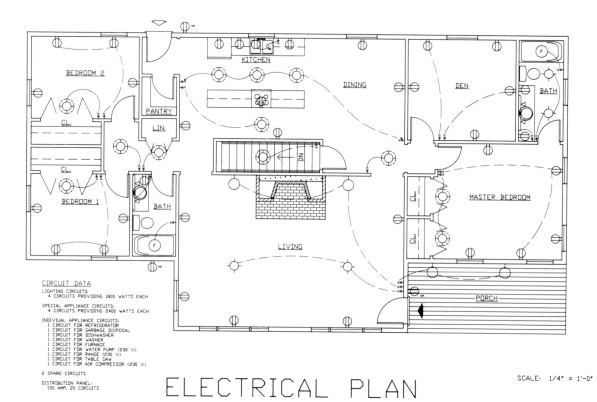

CIRCUIT DATA

LIGHTING CIRCUITS:
 4 CIRCUITS PROVIDING 1800 WATTS EACH

SPECIAL APPLIANCE CIRCUITS:
 4 CIRCUITS PROVIDING 2400 WATTS EACH

INDIVIUAL APPLIANCE CIRCUITS:
 1 CIRCUIT FOR REFRIGERATOR
 1 CIRCUIT FOR GARBAGE DISPOSAL
 1 CIRCUIT FOR DISHWASHER
 1 CIRCUIT FOR WASHER
 1 CIRCUIT FOR FURNACE
 1 CIRCUIT FOR WATER PUMP (230 V)
 1 CIRCUIT FOR RANGE (230 V)
 1 CIRCUIT FOR TABLE SAW
 1 CIRCUIT FOR AIR COMPRESSOR (230 V)

2 SPARE CIRCUITS

DISTRIBUTION PANEL:
 150 AMP, 20 CIRCUITS

SCALE: 1/4" = 1'-0"

ELECTRICAL PLAN

Fig. 38-32. (Continued)

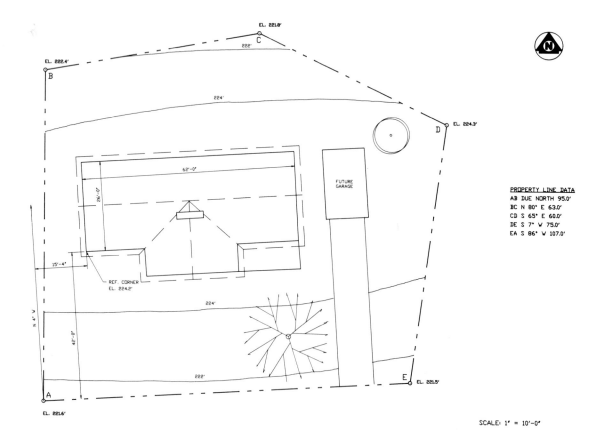

PROPERTY LINE DATA

AB DUE NORTH 95.0'
BC N 80° E 63.0'
CD S 65° E 60.0'
DE S 7° W 75.0'
EA S 86° W 107.0'

SCALE: 1" = 10'-0"

PLOT PLAN

Fig. 38-32. (Continued)

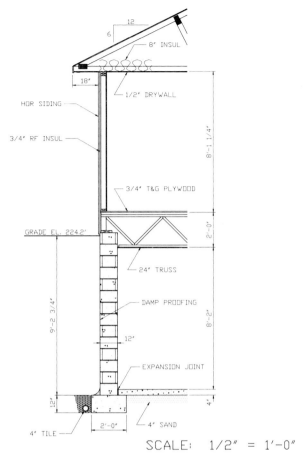

12
6

8" INSUL

18"

HOR SIDING

1/2" DRYWALL

3/4" RF INSUL

8'-1 1/4"

3/4" T&G PLYWOOD

GRADE EL. 224.2'

2'-0"

24" TRUSS

DAMP PROOFING

9'-2 3/4"

8'-2"

12"

EXPANSION JOINT

12"

4"

4' TILE

2'-0"

4" SAND

SCALE: 1/2" = 1'-0"

WALL SECTION

Fig. 38-32. (Continued)

Computers are being integrated into a variety of occupational settings, including architects, illustrators, and estimators. (Courtesy of International Business Machines Corporation)

Career Opportunities

After studying this chapter, you will be able to:
- List various career options in architecture and residential construction.
- Compare the duties and educational requirements of various occupations in architecture and construction.

The fascinating world of architecture and residential construction has been illustrated throughout this text by many related career and job opportunities. Home construction requires the knowledge and skills of a variety of tradeworkers and professionals. To some people, certain occupations will be more interesting and exciting than others. It is this concept that persons should carefully analyze as they contemplate a career in any phase of architecture and the variety of related occupational fields.

Take a close look at the duties, functions, responsibilities, and educational requirements of a number of possible employment opportunities in residential architecture. If your interests and abilities are in any of the architecture and residential construction areas, a close examination of the qualifications for particular job opportunities should be made. The following brief descriptions of a number of career opportunities should prove of value in gaining an overall picture of the role people play in residential architecture, designing, and construction.

ARCHITECT

The architect's jobs include a great deal of creativity and sensitivity to form and materials, Fig. 39-1. An architect generally work closely with the client in making preliminary drawings, sketches, and suggestions for materials to be used. When the architect and client mutually

Fig. 39-1. Architect checks on the work in progress.

agree upon a final design for the structure, working drawings are prepared as described throughout the previous chapters.

An architect may also have the responsibility of assisting the client in selecting a building contractor and represent the owner in dealing with the contractor during construction. It is usually the architect's duty to periodically check construction as it proceeds to see that the plan is being followed and the materials specified are being used.

Education requirements for an architect may vary according to the background of the individual. However, the general practice requires a bachelor's degree from an accredited college or university. In many cases a master's degree for advanced study is obtained. In some instances, a two-year program along with a number of years of practical experience will meet the necessary requirements. All states require an examination to obtain a license. The license indicates that the person is a registered architect. This means that the person is qualified to design structures that meet the standards for safety, health, and property. Job opportunities for an architect appear to be very favorable. However, relatively few architects are employed full time in residential home design. Most architects work for large firms which design commercial buildings.

ARCHITECTURAL DRAFTERS

Architectural drafters generally draw the details of working drawings and make tracings from original drawings that the architect or designer has prepared, Fig. 39-2. They often begin as junior drafters and, as they gain experience, are given more difficult assignments in the architectural firm.

Fig. 39-2. CADD workstations are becoming commonplace tools for the architectural drafter.

Many architectural drafters who are satisfied with their position retain this job as a career. Others may take the licensing examinations with the goal of becoming architects or beginning new firms on their own.

Educational requirements for the architectural drafter usually require graduation from high school with some courses in architectural drawing and the use of CADD systems. Extensive study at a technical institute, vocational school, or community college is desirable for further experience and better job placement. Those who have experience in using the computer to make drawings will have an advantage since this technology is gaining broad acceptance in the field of architecture.

ARCHITECTURAL ILLUSTRATOR

Architectural illustration requires a high degree of skill and study to become readily employable. Architectural illustrators usually begin their study in architectural drawing or art and branch off into this specialized field, Fig. 39-3. The chapter on presentation drawings provides a good opportunity to recognize the various techniques used by architects and illustrators in preparing presentations and renderings. Drawings, sketches, renderings, and illustrations are generally prepared to present ideas to potential clients and as advertisements for commercial catalogs and publications.

In more recent years, the use of photographs and models has replaced some of the work the architectural illustrator has done. However, there is still great need for people who are highly skilled in this area. As persons study architectural design and find they have a flair for preparing illustrations, it may well be occupationally profitable to pursue this goal. Educational requirements are similar to those of the architectural drafter or commercial artist and resulting

Fig. 39-3. Architectural illustrators use many techniques to communicate the plan to others.

job opportunities are normally found in larger architectural firms.

SPECIFICATION WRITER

The job of the specification writer is to prepare all the necessary written information needed to describe materials, methods, and fixtures to be used in the structure, Fig. 39-4. A review of the chapter on residential specifications provides a broad coverage of the specification writer's responsibilities.

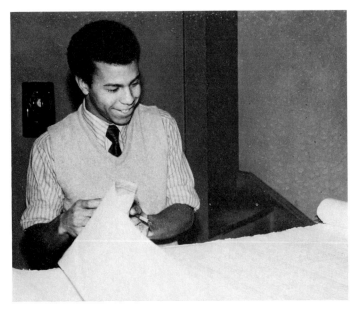

Fig. 39-4. A specification writer checking the exacting details of all requirements to go into the contract of an architectural project.

Just as for architects, the specification writer must be knowledgeable in all phases of construction, building materials, hardware, tradework, and fixtures. A college degree is normally required with emphasis on drawings, industrial materials, and building construction. In some cases, a specification writer may advance to this position from experience in the construction industry and related study. There are many job opportunities for people with skill in specification writing.

ESTIMATOR

Persons who calculate the costs of materials and labor for a building structure are called estimators, Fig. 39-5. Their responsibilities are extremely important, since any error in judgment

Fig. 39-5. An estimator reviewing a set of plans to prepare the cost of materials.
(Smith, Hinchman, and Grylls, Assoc.)

or material estimates could prove very costly to the company. They must prepare all the paperwork necessary to inform the architect or builder of what the total cost of the structure will be. Selling prices and profits are then determined from this information.

An architectural estimator for a large company or corporation will normally have a college degree with emphasis on mathematics and the use of computers. Experience with a computer-based estimating package would be advisable. A good background in economics and structural materials is also of extreme value. In smaller concerns, an estimator is often selected from drafting work or the building trades and given additional training to master the necessary skills required on the job.

SURVEYOR

In architectural work, land surveyors are primarily concerned with establishing areas and boundaries of real estate property. They are involved with the planning and subdivision of land, Fig. 39-6, and the preparation of descriptions of property. It is also their responsibility to prepare maps and plats which show defined areas as well as natural or artificially created features above and below the ground level. These include

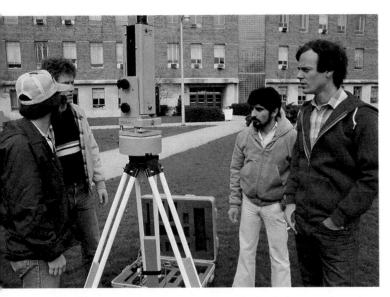

Fig. 39-6. A surveying team usually includes a rod worker, chain worker, instrument worker, and party chief.

the principles of real estate property law. Many features of a residential structure will be dependent upon the skills of the surveyor as to grade level, property lines, and building code requirements.

Educational requirements to become a surveyor normally require a bachelor's degree in surveying or civil engineering. Many technical institutes and community colleges offer two year programs which, along with practical experience, one may become a surveying technician.

TEACHING ARCHITECTURAL DRAWING

A teaching career in architectural drawing is a very interesting and rewarding experience for many people. There are considerable opportunities to teach architecture in high schools, trade or vocational schools, and community colleges or universities, Fig. 39-8.

both drawings and written specifications, Fig. 39-7. The American Society of Civil Engineers identify four major categories in the field of surveying: land surveying, engineering surveying, geodetic surveying, and cartographic surveying.

The surveyor should be skilled in the use of surveying equipment, be exacting in collecting data, knowledgeable about mapping, and know

The educational requirements will vary according to the type of school and program. However, one should possess a bachelor's degree in architecture or industrial technology. Teaching in architectural technology or graduate programs in architectural drawing will normally require an advanced degree, either a master's or doctorate and practical experience.

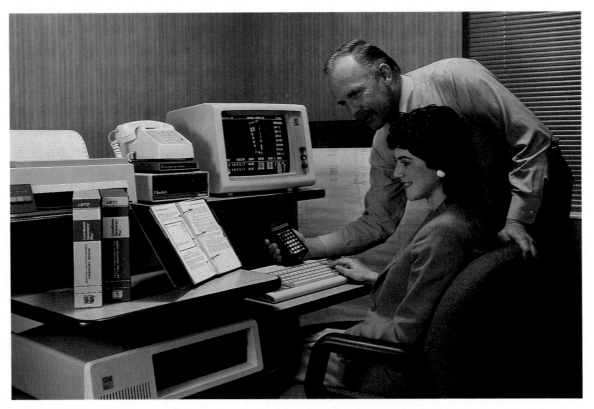

Fig. 39-7. A modern surveying software computer workstation used to calculate traverse, least squares, and coordinate geometry. (Lietz Corporation)

CONSTRUCTION TECHNOLOGIST

Construction technologists are qualified for both supervisory and technical roles in the construction industry. Areas of specialization of the construction technologist include managing construction, purchasing, expediting, specification writing, estimating and bidding, quality control, and site supervision, Fig. 39-9.

Fig. 39-8. Teaching architectural drawing is a very interesting and rewarding career.

A construction technologist typically has a bachelor's degree in construction technology. This major requires a strong background in science and knowledge of construction methodology. Experience in construction, although not essential, is extremely helpful.

REVIEW QUESTIONS–CHAPTER 39

Write your answers on a separate sheet of paper. Do not write in this book.
1. An architect usually checks the progress of the construction of a residence to see that _____ and _____.
2. Give reasons why state laws require an architect to be registered (licensed).
3. List some of the career opportunities for teaching architecture.
4. A person who calculates the costs of materials and labor for a residential structure is known as a(n) _____.
5. Name four areas of work in which the surveyor must be highly skilled.
6. The architectural drafter usually has what two duties to perform?
7. Many architects have the responsibility of assisting the client in selecting a _____.

Fig. 39-9. Close supervision on the job is necessary to insure quality construction.

8. A person who prepares all the written information needed to describe the materials, methods, and fixtures to be used for a house is known as _____.

SUGGESTED ACTIVITIES

1. Using library references, such as the Occupational Outlook Handbook, select a career related to architecture and write a report including such topics as job opportunities, educational requirements, job responsibilities, and predicted factors for success.
2. Prepare a bulletin board display that depicts the many jobs involved in architecture. Make use of pictures, magazine clippings, industrial literature, and actual drawings to illustrate the ways in which the architect influences the construction of a residential structure.
3. Make a visit to a local architect's office or an architectural firm to ask questions and observe their operation. Prepare a list of the various responsibilities and skills required by those involved with residential architecture and construction. Make note of the use of any new techniques or equipment in architectural designing.
4. To become better acquainted with educational offerings in architecture, obtain catalogs from community colleges, technical schools, and universities and write down the names of courses available. Discuss with your class the many directions a person may take in making architecture a career.

Reference Section

BUILDING MATERIAL SYMBOLS

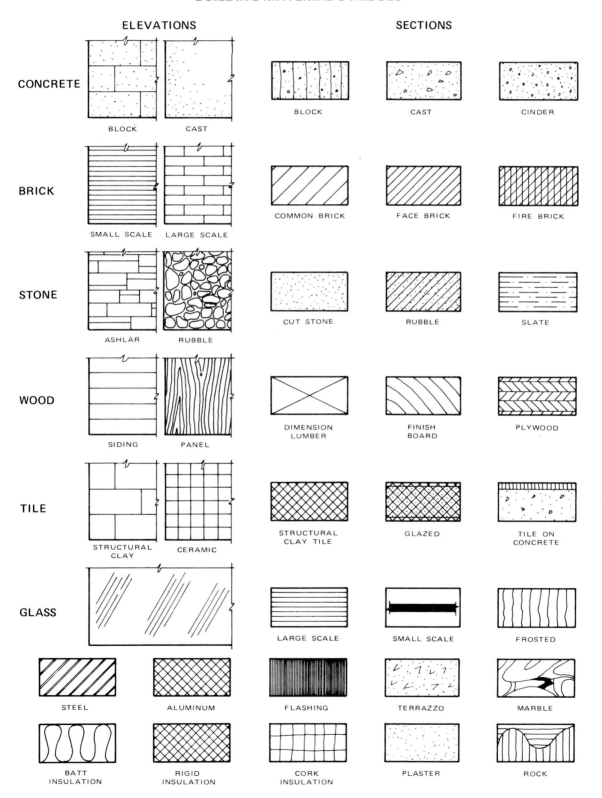

ELEVATIONS

SECTIONS

CONCRETE — BLOCK, CAST | BLOCK, CAST, CINDER

BRICK — SMALL SCALE, LARGE SCALE | COMMON BRICK, FACE BRICK, FIRE BRICK

STONE — ASHLAR, RUBBLE | CUT STONE, RUBBLE, SLATE

WOOD — SIDING, PANEL | DIMENSION LUMBER, FINISH BOARD, PLYWOOD

TILE — STRUCTURAL CLAY, CERAMIC | STRUCTURAL CLAY TILE, GLAZED, TILE ON CONCRETE

GLASS | LARGE SCALE, SMALL SCALE, FROSTED

STEEL, ALUMINUM, FLASHING, TERRAZZO, MARBLE

BATT INSULATION, RIGID INSULATION, CORK INSULATION, PLASTER, ROCK

TOPOGRAPHICAL SYMBOLS

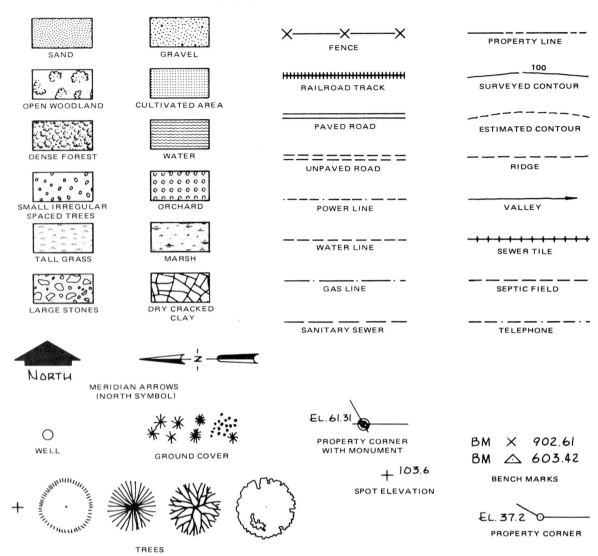

SAND

GRAVEL

OPEN WOODLAND

CULTIVATED AREA

DENSE FOREST

WATER

SMALL IRREGULAR SPACED TREES

ORCHARD

TALL GRASS

MARSH

LARGE STONES

DRY CRACKED CLAY

FENCE

PROPERTY LINE

RAILROAD TRACK

100

SURVEYED CONTOUR

PAVED ROAD

ESTIMATED CONTOUR

UNPAVED ROAD

RIDGE

POWER LINE

VALLEY

WATER LINE

SEWER TILE

GAS LINE

SEPTIC FIELD

SANITARY SEWER

TELEPHONE

NORTH

MERIDIAN ARROWS
(NORTH SYMBOL)

WELL

GROUND COVER

EL. 61.31

PROPERTY CORNER
WITH MONUMENT

+ 103.6

SPOT ELEVATION

BM ✗ 902.61
BM △ 603.42

BENCH MARKS

EL. 37.2

PROPERTY CORNER

TREES

PLUMBING SYMBOLS

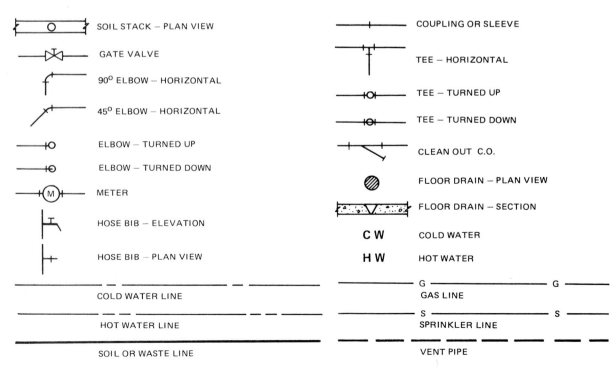

SOIL STACK – PLAN VIEW

GATE VALVE

90° ELBOW – HORIZONTAL

45° ELBOW – HORIZONTAL

ELBOW – TURNED UP

ELBOW – TURNED DOWN

METER

HOSE BIB – ELEVATION

HOSE BIB – PLAN VIEW

COLD WATER LINE

HOT WATER LINE

SOIL OR WASTE LINE

COUPLING OR SLEEVE

TEE – HORIZONTAL

TEE – TURNED UP

TEE – TURNED DOWN

CLEAN OUT C.O.

FLOOR DRAIN – PLAN VIEW

FLOOR DRAIN – SECTION

C W   COLD WATER

H W   HOT WATER

G   G
GAS LINE

S   S
SPRINKLER LINE

VENT PIPE

CLIMATE CONTROL SYMBOLS

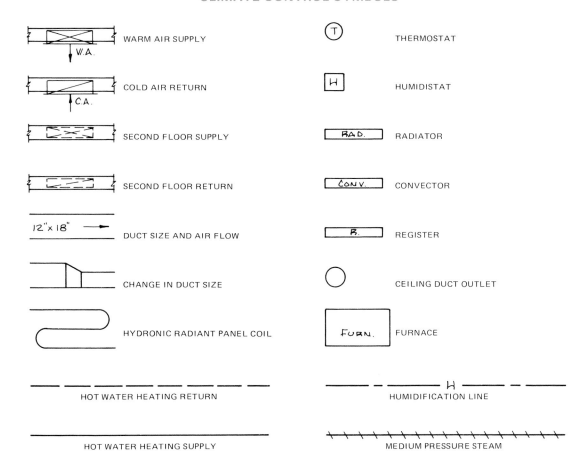

WARM AIR SUPPLY

COLD AIR RETURN

SECOND FLOOR SUPPLY

SECOND FLOOR RETURN

DUCT SIZE AND AIR FLOW

CHANGE IN DUCT SIZE

HYDRONIC RADIANT PANEL COIL

HOT WATER HEATING RETURN

HOT WATER HEATING SUPPLY

THERMOSTAT

HUMIDISTAT

RADIATOR

CONVECTOR

REGISTER

CEILING DUCT OUTLET

FURNACE

HUMIDIFICATION LINE

MEDIUM PRESSURE STEAM

ELECTRICAL SYMBOLS

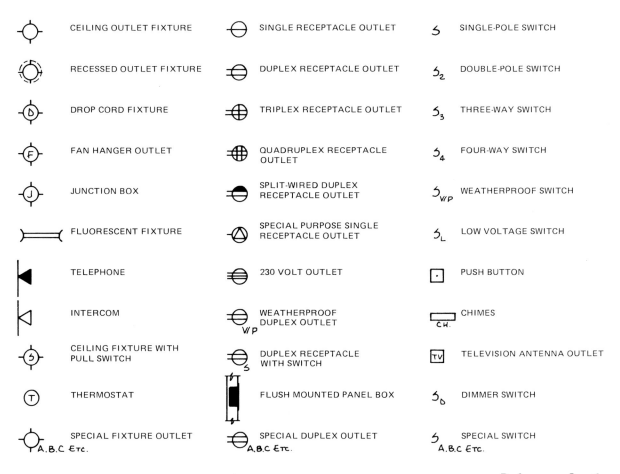

CEILING OUTLET FIXTURE

RECESSED OUTLET FIXTURE

DROP CORD FIXTURE

FAN HANGER OUTLET

JUNCTION BOX

FLUORESCENT FIXTURE

TELEPHONE

INTERCOM

CEILING FIXTURE WITH PULL SWITCH

THERMOSTAT

SPECIAL FIXTURE OUTLET

SINGLE RECEPTACLE OUTLET

DUPLEX RECEPTACLE OUTLET

TRIPLEX RECEPTACLE OUTLET

QUADRUPLEX RECEPTACLE OUTLET

SPLIT-WIRED DUPLEX RECEPTACLE OUTLET

SPECIAL PURPOSE SINGLE RECEPTACLE OUTLET

230 VOLT OUTLET

WEATHERPROOF DUPLEX OUTLET

DUPLEX RECEPTACLE WITH SWITCH

FLUSH MOUNTED PANEL BOX

SPECIAL DUPLEX OUTLET

SINGLE-POLE SWITCH

DOUBLE-POLE SWITCH

THREE-WAY SWITCH

FOUR-WAY SWITCH

WEATHERPROOF SWITCH

LOW VOLTAGE SWITCH

PUSH BUTTON

CHIMES

TELEVISION ANTENNA OUTLET

DIMMER SWITCH

SPECIAL SWITCH

STANDARD VANITY SIZES AND DESIGNS

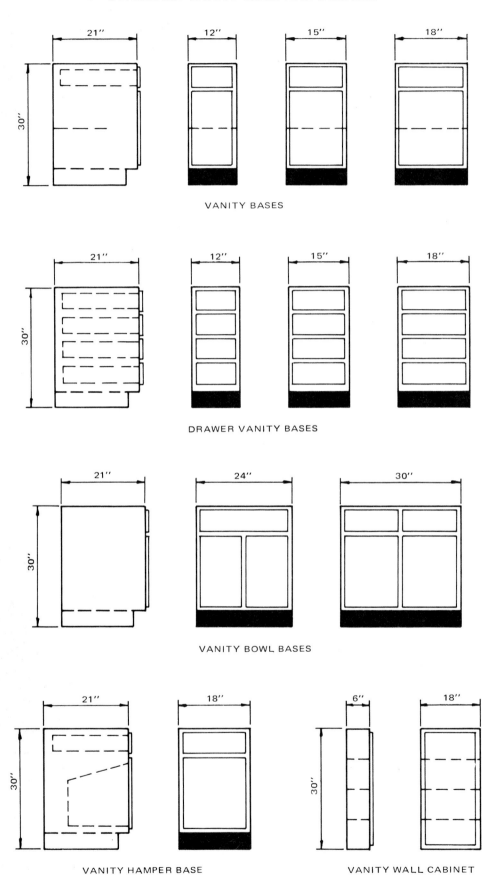

VANITY BASES

DRAWER VANITY BASES

VANITY BOWL BASES

VANITY HAMPER BASE

VANITY WALL CABINET

STANDARD WALL CABINET SIZES AND DESIGNS

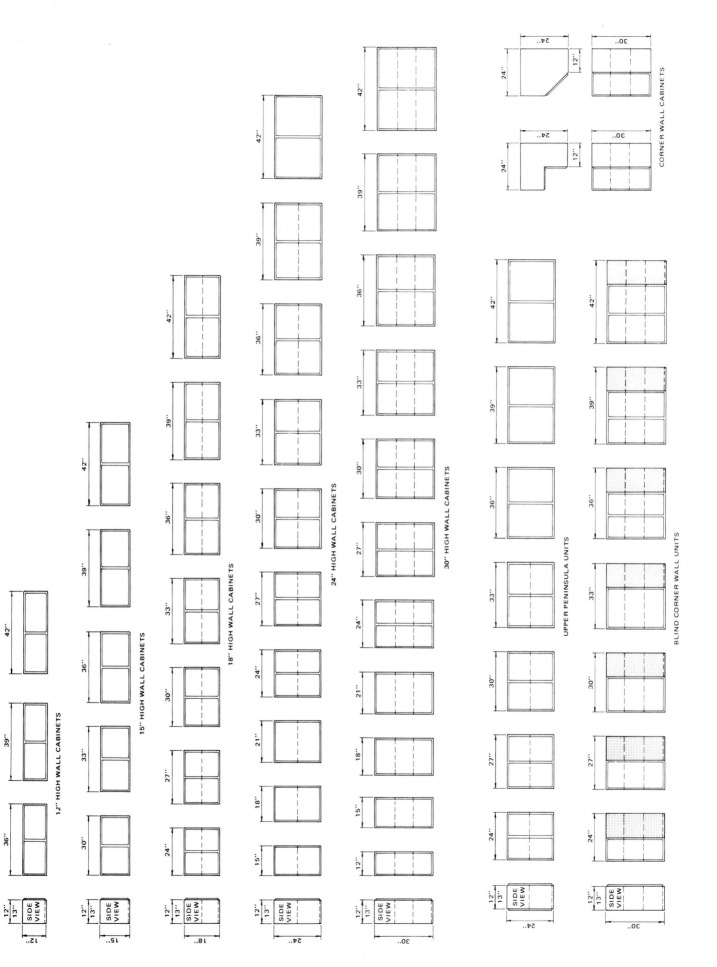

12" HIGH WALL CABINETS

15" HIGH WALL CABINETS

18" HIGH WALL CABINETS

24" HIGH WALL CABINETS

30" HIGH WALL CABINETS

UPPER PENINSULA UNITS

BLIND CORNER WALL UNITS

CORNER WALL CABINETS

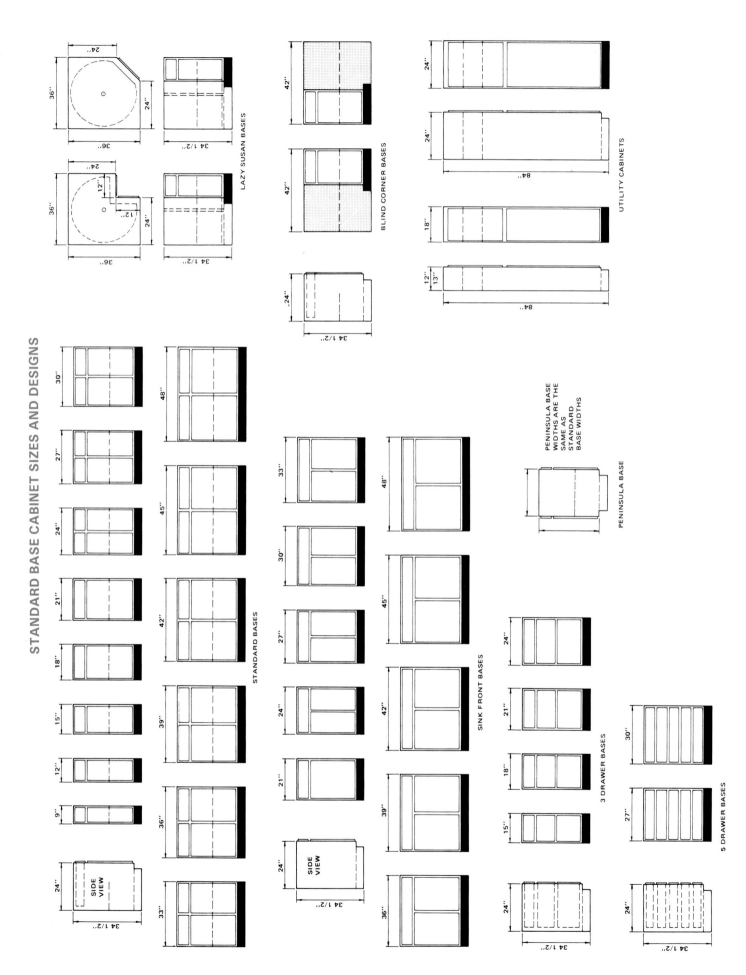

STANDARD BASE CABINET SIZES AND DESIGNS

LAZY SUSAN BASES

24″

36″

36″

24″

12″

12″

24″

36″

34 1/2″

34 1/2″

BLIND CORNER BASES

42″

42″

24″

34 1/2″

UTILITY CABINETS

24″

24″

18″

84″

12″

13″

84″

STANDARD BASES

30″

27″

24″

21″

18″

15″

12″

9″

24″

SIDE VIEW

34 1/2″

48″

45″

42″

39″

36″

33″

33″

30″

27″

24″

21″

24″

SIDE VIEW

34 1/2″

48″

45″

42″

39″

36″

SINK FRONT BASES

PENINSULA BASE WIDTHS ARE THE SAME AS STANDARD BASE WIDTHS

PENINSULA BASE

3 DRAWER BASES

24″

21″

18″

15″

24″

34 1/2″

5 DRAWER BASES

30″

27″

24″

34 1/2″

DOUBLE-HUNG WINDOWS—STANDARD SIZES

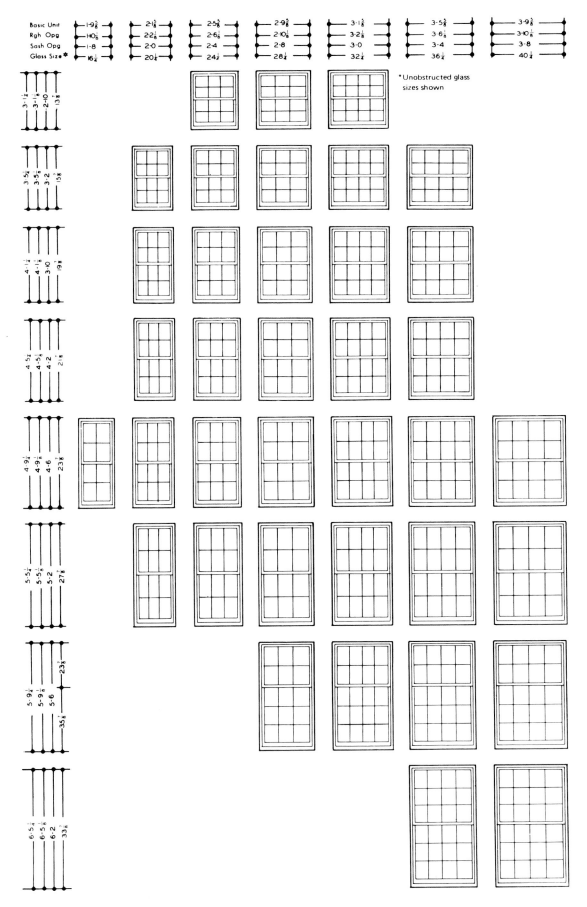

*Unobstructed glass sizes shown

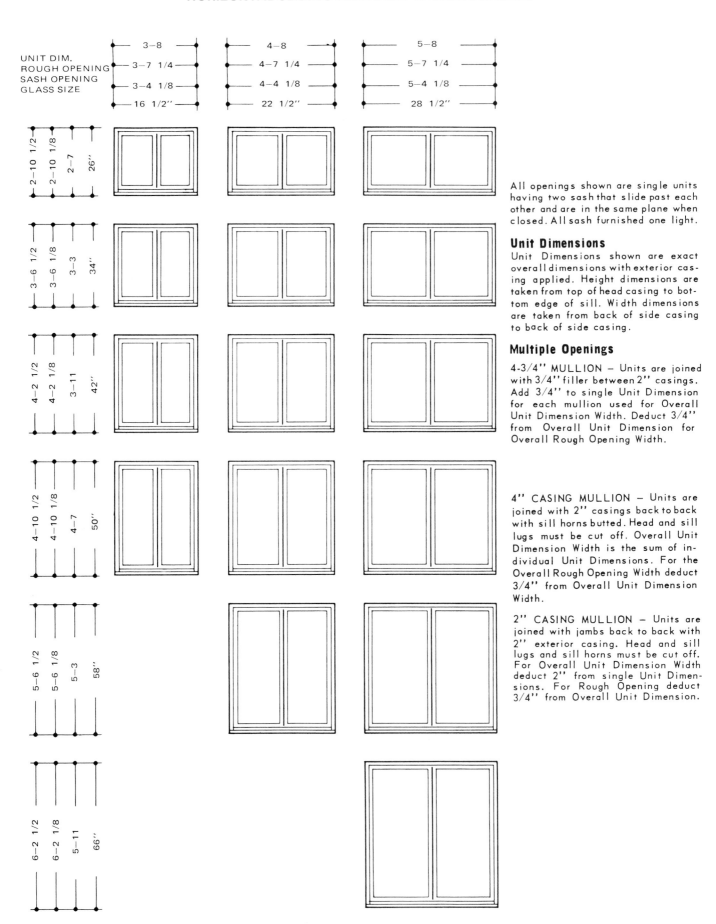

UNIT DIM.
ROUGH OPENING
SASH OPENING
GLASS SIZE

3—8 / 3—7 1/4 / 3—4 1/8 / 16 1/2"
4—8 / 4—7 1/4 / 4—4 1/8 / 22 1/2"
5—8 / 5—7 1/4 / 5—4 1/8 / 28 1/2"

2—10 1/2 / 2—10 1/8 / 2—7 / 26"

3—6 1/2 / 3—6 1/8 / 3—3 / 34"

4—2 1/2 / 4—2 1/8 / 3—11 / 42"

4—10 1/2 / 4—10 1/8 / 4—7 / 50"

5—6 1/2 / 5—6 1/8 / 5—3 / 58"

6—2 1/2 / 6—2 1/8 / 5—11 / 66"

All openings shown are single units having two sash that slide past each other and are in the same plane when closed. All sash furnished one light.

Unit Dimensions

Unit Dimensions shown are exact overall dimensions with exterior casing applied. Height dimensions are taken from top of head casing to bottom edge of sill. Width dimensions are taken from back of side casing to back of side casing.

Multiple Openings

4-3/4" MULLION — Units are joined with 3/4" filler between 2" casings. Add 3/4" to single Unit Dimension for each mullion used for Overall Unit Dimension Width. Deduct 3/4" from Overall Unit Dimension for Overall Rough Opening Width.

4" CASING MULLION — Units are joined with 2" casings back to back with sill horns butted. Head and sill lugs must be cut off. Overall Unit Dimension Width is the sum of individual Unit Dimensions. For the Overall Rough Opening Width deduct 3/4" from Overall Unit Dimension Width.

2" CASING MULLION — Units are joined with jambs back to back with 2" exterior casing. Head and sill lugs and sill horns must be cut off. For Overall Unit Dimension Width deduct 2" from single Unit Dimensions. For Rough Opening deduct 3/4" from Overall Unit Dimension.

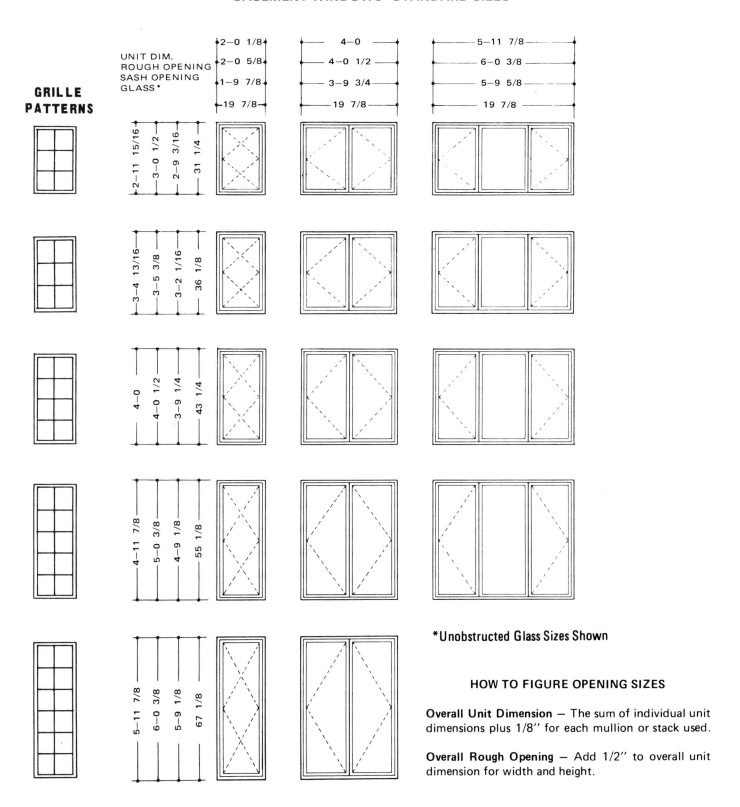

GRILLE PATTERNS

UNIT DIM.
ROUGH OPENING
SASH OPENING
GLASS*

*Unobstructed Glass Sizes Shown

HOW TO FIGURE OPENING SIZES

Overall Unit Dimension — The sum of individual unit dimensions plus 1/8″ for each mullion or stack used.

Overall Rough Opening — Add 1/2″ to overall unit dimension for width and height.

AWNING WINDOWS—STANDARD SIZES

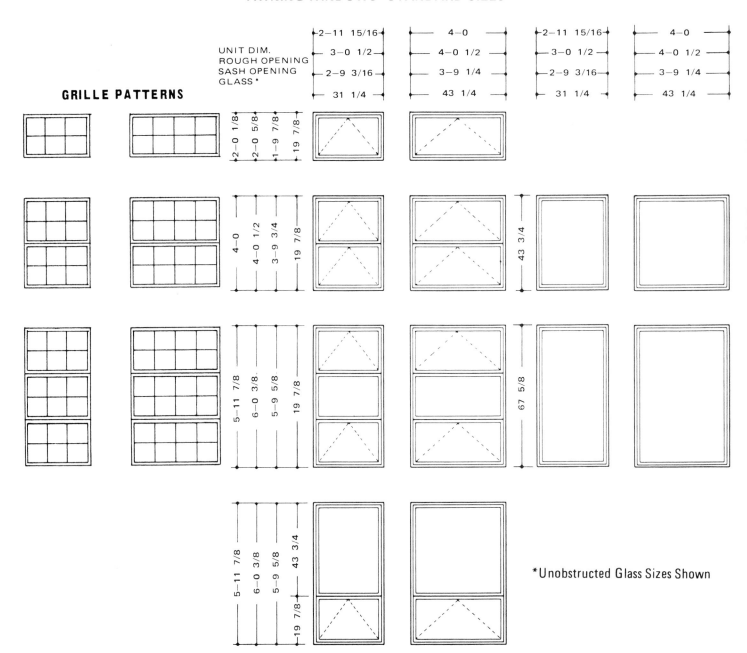

GRILLE PATTERNS

UNIT DIM.
ROUGH OPENING
SASH OPENING
GLASS *

2—11 15/16
3—0 1/2
2—9 3/16
31 1/4

4—0
4—0 1/2
3—9 1/4
43 1/4

2—11 15/16
3—0 1/2
2—9 3/16
31 1/4

4—0
4—0 1/2
3—9 1/4
43 1/4

2—0 1/8   2—0 5/8   1—9 7/8   19 7/8

4—0   4—0 1/2   3—9 3/4   19 7/8

43 3/4

5—11 7/8   6—0 3/8   5—9 5/8   19 7/8

67 5/8

5—11 7/8   6—0 3/8   5—9 5/8   43 3/4   19 7/8

*Unobstructed Glass Sizes Shown

HOPPER WINDOW SIZES

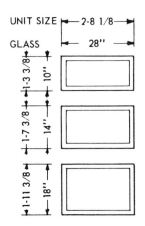

UNIT SIZE   2-8 1/8

GLASS   28"

1-3 3/8   10"

1-7 3/8   14"

1-11 3/8   18"

PICTURE WINDOWS—STANDARD SIZES

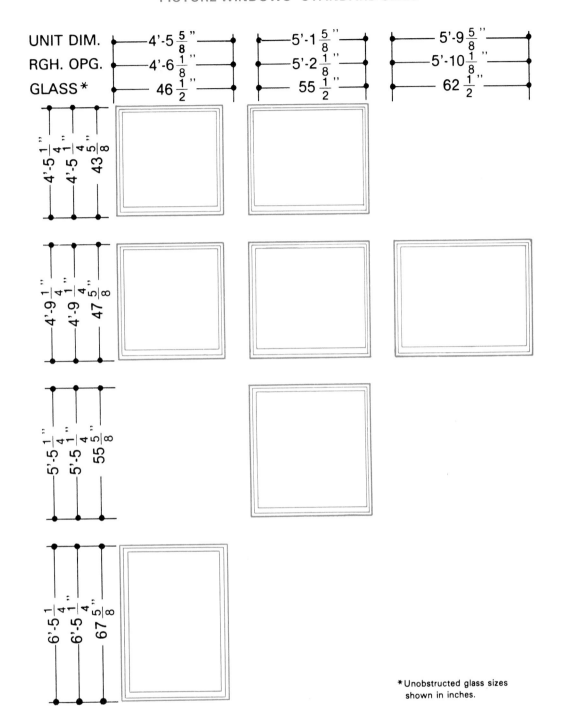

UNIT DIM. 4'-5 5/8 "   5'-1 5/8 "   5'-9 5/8 "
RGH. OPG. 4'-6 1/8 "   5'-2 1/8 "   5'-10 1/8 "
GLASS*   46 1/2 "   55 1/2 "   62 1/2 "

4'-5 1/4 " | 4'-5 1/4 " | 43 5/8 "

4'-9 1/4 " | 4'-9 1/4 " | 47 5/8 "

5'-5 1/4 " | 5'-5 1/4 " | 55 5/8 "

6'-5 1/4 " | 6'-5 1/4 " | 67 5/8 "

*Unobstructed glass sizes
shown in inches.

GLASS SLIDING DOORS—STANDARD SIZES

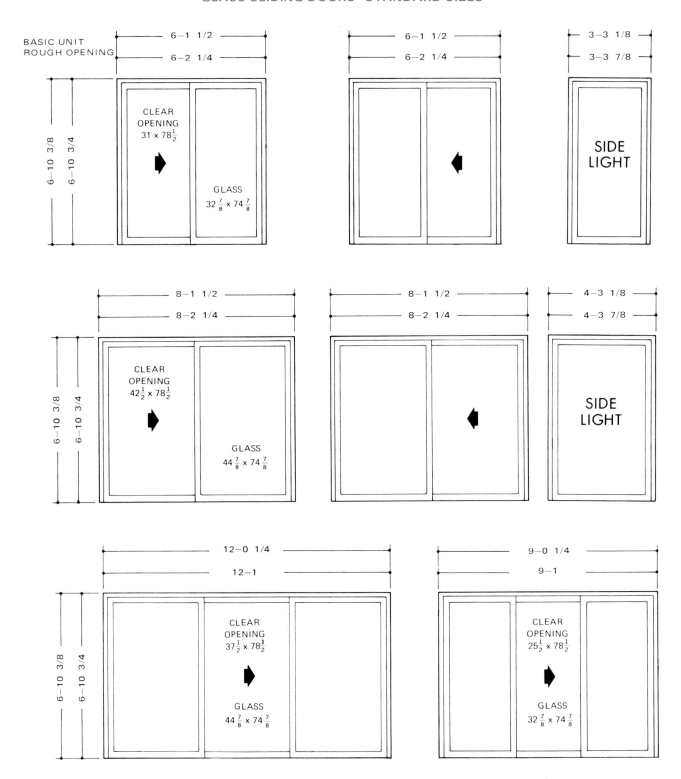

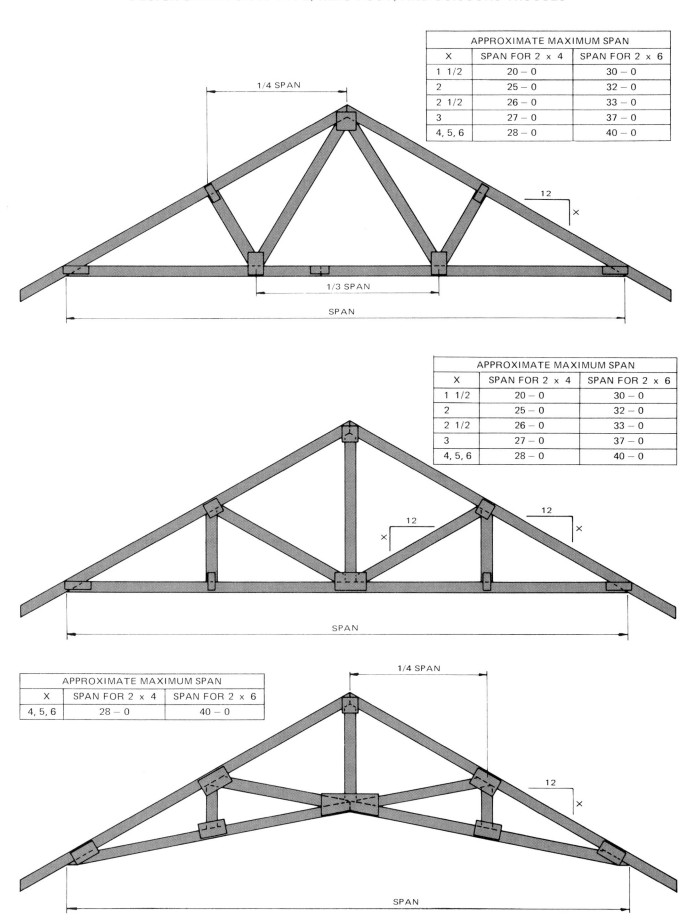

APPROXIMATE MAXIMUM SPAN		
X	SPAN FOR 2 x 4	SPAN FOR 2 x 6
1 1/2	20 — 0	30 — 0
2	25 — 0	32 — 0
2 1/2	26 — 0	33 — 0
3	27 — 0	37 — 0
4, 5, 6	28 — 0	40 — 0

1/4 SPAN

12

1/3 SPAN

SPAN

APPROXIMATE MAXIMUM SPAN		
X	SPAN FOR 2 x 4	SPAN FOR 2 x 6
1 1/2	20 — 0	30 — 0
2	25 — 0	32 — 0
2 1/2	26 — 0	33 — 0
3	27 — 0	37 — 0
4, 5, 6	28 — 0	40 — 0

12

12

SPAN

APPROXIMATE MAXIMUM SPAN		
X	SPAN FOR 2 x 4	SPAN FOR 2 x 6
4, 5, 6	28 — 0	40 — 0

1/4 SPAN

12

SPAN

Douglas Fir — Larch — 30 lbs./Ft² — Live Load

	"F_b"	"E"*	2 x 6			2 x 8			2 x 10			2 x 12		
			12"	16"	24"	12"	16"	24"	12"	16"	24"	12"	16"	24"
Select Structural	2050	1.8	12-3	11-2	9-9	16-2	14-8	12-10	20-8	18-9	16-5	25-1	22-10	19-11
Dense #1	2050	1.9	12-6	11-4	9-11	16-6	15-0	13-1	21-0	19-1	16-8	25-7	23-3	20-3
Dense #2	1700	1.7	12-0	10-11	9-7	15-10	14-5	12-7	20-3	18-5	16-1	24-8	22-5	19-7
#2	1450	1.7	12-0	10-11	9-7	15-10	14-5	12-7	20-3	18-5	16-1	24-8	22-5	19-7
#3	850	1.5	10-4	9-0	7-2	13-8	11-10	9-8	17-5	15-1	12-3	21-3	18-3	15-0

Douglas Fir — Larch — 40 lbs./Ft² — Live Load

	"F_b"	"E"*	2 x 6			2 x 8			2 x 10			2 x 12		
			12"	16"	24"	12"	16"	24"	12"	16"	24"	12"	16"	24"
Select Structural	2050	1.8	11-2	10-2	8-10	14-8	13-4	11-8	18-9	17-0	14-11	22-10	20-9	18-1
Dense #1	2050	1.9	11-4	10-4	9-0	15-0	13-7	11-11	19-1	17-4	15-2	23-3	21-1	18-5
Dense #2	1700	1.7	10-11	9-11	8-8	14-5	13-1	11-5	18-5	16-9	14-7	22-5	20-4	17-9
#2	1450	1.7	10-11	9-11	8-6	14-5	13-1	11-4	18-5	16-9	14-5	22-5	20-4	17-6
#3	850	1.5	9-2	7-11	6-7	12-3	10-7	8-8	15-7	13-6	11-0	18-11	16-4	13-5

Southern Yellow Pine — 30 lbs./Ft² — Live Load

	"F_b"	"E"*	2 x 6			2 x 8			2 x 10			2 x 12		
			12"	16"	24"	12"	16"	24"	12"	16"	24"	12"	16"	24"
Select Structural	2150	1.8	12-3	11-2	9-9	16-2	14-8	12-10	20-8	18-9	16-5	25-1	22-10	19-11
#1 Dense	2150	1.9	12-6	11-4	9-11	16-6	15-0	13-1	21-0	19-1	16-8	25-7	23-3	20-3
#2 Dense	1750	1.7	12-0	10-11	9-7	15-10	14-5	12-7	20-3	18-5	16-1	24-8	22-5	19-7
#2	1500	1.6	11-10	10-9	9-4	15-7	14-2	12-4	19-10	18-0	15-9	24-2	21-11	19-2
#3	875	1.5	10-6	9-0	7-4	14-0	11-11	9-9	17-7	15-3	12-5	21-9	18-7	15-1

Southern Yellow Pine — 40 lbs./Ft² — Live Load

	"F_b"	"E"*	2 x 6			2 x 8			2 x 10			2 x 12		
			12"	16"	24"	12"	16"	24"	12"	16"	24"	12"	16"	24"
Select Structural	2150	1.8	11-2	10-2	8-10	14-8	13-4	11-8	18-9	17-0	14-11	22-10	20-9	18-1
#1 Dense	2150	1.9	11-4	10-4	9-0	15-0	13-7	11-11	19-1	17-4	15-2	23-3	21-1	18-5
#2 Dense	1750	1.7	10-11	9-11	8-8	14-5	13-1	11-5	18-5	16-9	14-7	22-5	20-4	17-9
#2	1500	1.6	10-9	9-9	8-6	14-2	12-10	11-3	18-0	16-5	14-4	21-11	19-11	17-5
#3	875	1.5	9-4	7-11	6-8	12-4	10-10	8-9	15-9	13-9	11-0	19-3	16-7	13-8

California Redwood — 30 lbs./Ft² — Live Load

	"F_b"	"E"*	2 x 6			2 x 8			2 x 10			2 x 12		
			12"	16"	24"	12"	16"	24"	12"	16"	24"	12"	16"	24"
Cl. Heart Struct.	2650	1.4	11-3	10-3	8-11	14-11	13-6	11-10	19-0	17-3	15-1	23-1	21-0	18-4
Select Structural	2000	1.4	11-3	10-3	8-11	14-11	13-6	11-10	19-0	17-3	15-1	23-1	21-0	18-4
#1	1700	1.4	11-3	10-3	8-11	14-11	13-6	11-10	19-0	17-3	15-1	23-1	21-0	18-4
#2	1400	1.25	10-10	9-10	8-7	14-4	13-0	11-4	18-3	16-7	14-6	22-2	19-2	17-8
#3	800	1.1	10-0	8-8	7-1	13-3	11-6	9-4	16-11	14-9	11-11	20-7	17-8	14-7

California Redwood — 40 lbs./Ft² — Live Load

	"F_b"	"E"*	2 x 6			2 x 8			2 x 10			2 x 12		
			12"	16"	24"	12"	16"	24"	12"	16"	24"	12"	16"	24"
Cl. Heart Struct.	2650	1.4	10-3	9-4	8-2	13-6	12-3	10-9	17-3	15-8	13-8	21-0	19-1	16-8
Select Structural	2000	1.4	10-3	9-4	8-2	13-6	12-3	10-9	17-3	15-8	13-8	21-0	19-1	16-8
#1	1700	1.4	10-3	9-4	8-2	13-6	12-3	10-9	17-3	15-8	13-8	21-0	19-1	16-8
#2	1400	1.25	9-10	8-11	7-10	13-0	11-10	10-4	16-7	15-1	13-2	20-2	18-4	16-0
#3	800	1.1	9-0	7-10	6-5	11-9	10-3	8-5	15-0	13-1	10-8	18-2	15-10	13-2

*Modulus of Elasticity "E" in 1,000,000 psi. or 1.0 is equal to 1,000,000 psi.

Span data in feet and inches for floor joists of Douglas Fir — Larch, Southern Yellow Pine and California Redwood. Spans are calculated on the basis of dry sizes with a moisture content equal to or less than 19 percent. Floor joist spans are for a single span with calculations performed based on the modulus of elasticity (E) and maximum fiber bending stress (F_b) allowed. Deflection is limited to 1/360 of the span. Span data assumes a dead load of 10 lbs./Ft². For other species and applications see "Span Table for Joists and Rafters, American Softwood Lumber Standard Sizes PS 20-70." (National Forest Products Association)

CEILING JOIST SPAN DATA

Limited Attic Storage Where Development of Future Rooms is Not Possible
Douglas Fir — Larch — 20 lbs./Ft² — Live Load

	"Fb"	"E"	2 x 4			2 x 6			2 x 8			2 x 10		
			12"	16"	24"	12"	16"	24"	12"	16"	24"	12"	16"	24"
Select Structural	2050	1.8	10-3	9-4	8-1	16-1	14-7	12-9	21-2	19-3	16-10	27-1	24-7	21-6
Dense #1	2050	1.9	10-5	9-6	8-3	16-4	14-11	13-0	21-7	19-7	17-2	27-6	25-0	21-10
Dense #2	1700	1.7	10-0	9-1	7-7	15-9	14-4	11-11	20-10	18-11	15-9	26-6	24-1	19-10
#2	1450	1.7	9-11	8-8	7-0	15-7	13-6	11-0	20-7	17-10	14-5	26-3	22-8	18-6
#3	850	1.5	7-8	6-7	5-5	11-11	10-7	8-5	15-8	13-8	11-4	20-2	17-5	14-2

Limited Attic Storage Where Development of Future Rooms is Not Possible
Southern Yellow Pine — 20 lbs./Ft² — Live Load

	"Fb"	"E"	2 x 4			2 x 6			2 x 8			2 x 10		
			12"	16"	24"	12"	16"	24"	12"	16"	24"	12"	16"	24"
Select Structural	2150	1.8	10-3	9-4	8-1	16-1	14-7	12-9	21-2	19-3	16-10	27-1	24-7	21-6
#1 Dense	2150	1.9	10-5	9-6	8-3	16-4	14-11	13-0	21-7	19-7	17-2	27-6	25-0	21-10
#2 Dense	1750	1.7	10-0	8-1	7-9	15-9	14-4	12-1	20-10	18-11	16-4	26-6	24-1	20-4
#2	1500	1.6	9-10	8-9	7-2	15-6	13-9	11-3	20-5	18-2	14-9	26-0	23-2	18-10
#3	875	1.5	7-9	6-8	5-6	12-0	10-8	8-6	15-9	13-9	11-5	20-3	17-6	14-3

Maximum Deflection is 1/240 of span.

ALLOWABLE RAFTER SPANS

Flat or Sloped Rafters (Flat Roof or Cathedral Ceiling with no Attic Space) Supporting Drywall Ceiling
Douglas Fir — Larch — Live Load = 20 lbs./Ft²

	"Fb"	"E"	2 x 6			2 x 8			2 x 10			2 x 12		
			12"	16"	24"	12"	16"	24"	12"	16"	24"	12"	16"	24"
Select Structural	2050	1.8	16-1	14-6	12-2	21-2	19-1	16-0	27-0	24-7	20-6	32-10	29-9	24-10
Dense #1	2050	1.9	16-5	14-10	12-2	21-7	19-7	16-0	27-6	25-0	20-6	33-4	30-5	24-10
Dense #2	1700	1.7	15-8	13-7	11-1	20-8	17-10	14-7	26-4	22-10	18-7	32-0	27-9	22-8
#2	1450	1.7	14-5	12-6	10-2	19-1	16-6	13-5	24-4	21-0	17-2	29-7	25-7	20-10
#3	850	1.5	11-1	9-7	7-10	14-7	12-7	10-3	18-7	16-2	13-1	22-6	19-7	16-0

Flat or Sloped Rafters (Flat Roof or Cathedral Ceiling with no Attic Space) Supporting Drywall Ceiling
Southern Yellow Pine — Live Load = 20 lbs./Ft²

	"Fb"*	"E"	2 x 6			2 x 8			2 x 10			2 x 12		
			12"	16"	24"	12"	16"	24"	12"	16"	24"	12"	16"	24"
Select Structural	2150	1.8	16-1	14-6	12-5	21-3	19-2	16-5	27-0	24-5	20-11	32-10	29-9	25-5
#1 Dense	2150	1.9	16-4	14-10	12-5	21-6	19-7	16-5	27-5	25-0	20-11	33-4	30-5	25-5
#2 Dense	1750	1.7	15-10	13-9	11-3	20-11	18-1	14-9	26-8	23-1	18-10	31-7	28-1	22-11
#2	1500	1.6	14-8	12-9	10-5	19-5	16-9	13-8	24-9	21-5	17-6	30-1	26-0	21-3
#3	875	1.5	11-3	9-8	7-11	14-9	12-10	10-5	18-10	16-4	13-3	23-0	19-11	16-3

Flat or Low Sloped Rafters (No Attic Storage) Slope 3 in 12 or less
Douglas Fir — Larch — Live Load = 20 lbs./Ft²

	"Fb"*	"E"	2 x 6			2 x 8			2 x 10			2 x 12		
			12"	16"	24"	12"	16"	24"	12"	16"	24"	12"	16"	24"
Select Structural	2050	1.8	16-2	14-7	12-10	21-3	19-3	16-10	27-1	24-7	21-6	33-0	29-11	26-1
Dense #1	2050	1.9	16-5	14-10	13-1	21-7	19-7	17-3	27-7	24-10	22-1	33-6	30-4	26-10
Dense #2	1700	1.7	15-10	14-6	11-11	20-10	19-0	15-9	26-7	24-2	20-1	32-5	29-6	24-5
#2	1450	1.7	15-7	13-6	11-0	20-7	17-10	14-7	26-3	22-9	18-7	31-11	27-8	22-7
#3	850	1.5	11-11	10-4	8-6	15-9	13-6	11-2	20-1	17-5	14-2	24-5	21-1	17-3

Flat or Low Sloped Rafters (No Attic Storage) Slope 3 in 12 or less
Southern Yellow Pine — Live Load = 20 lbs./Ft²

	"Fb"*	"E"	2 x 6			2 x 8			2 x 10			2 x 12		
			12"	16"	24"	12"	16"	24"	12"	16"	24"	12"	16"	24"
Select Structural	2150	1.8	16-2	14-7	12-10	21-3	19-3	16-10	27-1	24-7	21-6	33-0	29-11	26-1
#1 Dense	2150	1.9	16-5	14-10	13-1	21-7	19-7	17-3	27-7	24-10	22-1	33-6	30-4	26-10
#2 Dense	1750	1.7	15-10	14-6	12-1	20-10	19-0	16-0	26-7	24-2	20-4	32-5	29-6	24-9
#2	1500	1.6	15-7	13-9	11-3	20-9	18-2	14-10	26-6	23-2	18-11	31-5	28-2	23-0
#3	875	1.5	12-0	10-5	8-7	15-10	13-7	11-3	20-2	17-5	14-3	24-6	21-2	17-4

Medium or High Sloped Rafters (No Attic Storage) Slope over 3 in 12
Douglas Fir — Larch — Live Load = 20 lbs./Ft²

	"Fb"*	"E"	2 x 4			2 x 6			2 x 8			2 x 10		
			12"	16"	24"	12"	16"	24"	12"	16"	24"	12"	16"	24"
Select Structural	2050	1.8	11-2	10-3	8-10	17-9	16-0	13-10	23-5	21-2	18-2	29-11	27-0	23-4
Dense #1	2050	1.9	11-6	10-7	8-10	18-0	16-6	13-10	23-10	21-9	18-2	30-5	29-9	23-4
Dense #2	1700	1.7	11-2	9-10	8-0	17-4	15-5	12-7	22-10	20-4	16-7	29-2	25-3	21-2
#2	1450	1.7	10-5	9-1	7-4	16-5	14-3	11-7	21-8	18-9	15-4	27-8	24-0	19-7
#3	850	1.5	8-0	7-0	5-8	12-7	10-11	8-11	16-7	14-4	11-9	21-2	18-4	15-0

Medium or High Sloped Rafters (No Attic Storage) Slope over 3 in 12
Southern Yellow Pine — Live Load = 20 lbs./Ft²

	"Fb"*	"E"	2 x 4			2 x 6			2 x 8			2 x 10		
			12"	16"	24"	12"	16"	24"	12"	16"	24"	12"	16"	24"
Select Structural	2150	1.8	11-2	10-3	9-0	17-9	16-0	14-2	23-5	21-2	18-6	29-11	27-0	23-8
#1 Dense	2150	1.9	11-6	10-7	9-0	18-0	16-6	14-2	23-10	21-9	18-8	30-5	29-9	23-10
#2 Dense	1750	1.7	11-2	9-11	8-1	17-4	15-8	12-9	22-10	20-7	16-10	29-2	25-3	21-6
#2	1500	1.6	10-8	9-3	7-6	16-8	14-6	11-10	22-1	19-1	15-7	28-2	24-5	19-11
#3	875	1.5	8-1	7-1	5-9	12-8	11-0	9-0	16-8	14-5	11-10	21-3	18-5	15-1

*The required extreme fiber stress in bending, "Fb", in pounds/In². Modulus of elasticity is in 1,000,000 psi where 1.8 is equal to 1,800,000 psi.

Ceiling joist and rafter span data in feet and inches for Douglas Fir — Larch and Southern Yellow Pine. Spans are based on dry lumber size with a moisture content equal to or less than 19 percent. Calculations were based on the modulus of elasticity (E) and maximum fiber bending stress (Fb) allowed for ceiling joists. Rafter spans were based on the fiber bending stress (Fb) and allowable modulus of elasticity (E). Rafter spans are horizontal distances. See page 468 for a rafter conversion table.

SPAN DATA FOR GLUED LAMINATED ROOF BEAMS*
MAXIMUM DEFLECTION 1/240TH OF THE SPAN

BEAM SIZE (ACTUAL)	WGT. OF BEAM PER LIN. FT. IN POUNDS	SPAN IN FEET											
		10	12	14	16	18	20	22	24	26	28	30	32
		POUNDS PER LIN. FT. LOAD BEARING CAPACITY											
3 x 5 1/4	3.7	151	85										
3 x 7 1/4	4.9	362	206	128	84								
3 x 9 1/4	6.7	566	448	300	199	137	99						
3 x 11 1/4	8.0	680	566	483	363	252	182	135	102				
4 1/2 x 9 1/4	9.8	850	673	451	299	207	148	109					
4 1/2 x 11 1/4	12.0	1,036	860	731	544	378	273	202	153				
3 1/4 x 13 1/2	10.4	1,100	916	784	685	479	347	258	197	152	120		
3 1/4 x 15	11.5	1,145	1,015	870	759	650	473	352	267	206	163	128	104
5 1/4 x 13 1/2	16.7	1,778	1,478	1,266	1,105	773	559	415	316	245	193	154	124
5 1/4 x 15	18.6	1,976	1,647	1,406	1,229	1,064	771	574	438	342	269	215	174
5 1/4 x 16 1/2	20.5	2,180	1,810	1,550	1,352	1,155	933	768	586	457	362	290	236
5 1/4 x 18	22.3	2,378	1,978	1,688	1,478	1,308	1,113	918	766	598	478	382	311

```
EXAMPLE:  CLEAR SPAN     = 20'-0''
          BEAM SPACING   = 10'-0''
          DEAD LOAD      = 8 LBS./SQ. FT. (ROOFING AND DECKING)
          LIVE LOAD      = 20 LBS./SQ. FT. (SNOW)
          TOTAL LOAD     = LIVE LOAD + DEAD LOAD x BEAM SPACING
                         = (20 + 8) x 10 = 280 LBS./LIN. FT.
THE BEAM SIZE REQUIRED IS 3 1/4'' x 13 1/2'' WHICH SUPPORT 347 LBS./LIN. FT. OVER A SPAN OF 20'-0''
```

*BEAMS MAY BE DOUGLAS FIR, LARCH OR SOUTHERN YELLOW PINE.

SPAN DATA FOR GLUED LAMINATED FLOOR BEAMS*
MAXIMUM DEFLECTION 1/360TH OF THE SPAN

BEAM SIZE (ACTUAL)	WGT. OF BEAM PER LIN. FT. IN POUNDS	SPAN IN FEET											
		10	12	14	16	18	20	22	24	26	28	30	32
		POUNDS PER LIN. FT. LOAD BEARING CAPACITY											
3 x 5 1/4	3.7	114	64										
3 x 7 1/4	4.9	275	156	84	55								
3 x 9 1/4	6.7	492	319	198	130	89							
3 x 11 1/4	8.0	590	491	361	239	165	119						
4 1/2 x 9 1/4	9.8	738	479	298	196	134	96						
4 1/2 x 11 1/4	12.0	900	748	541	359	248	178	131	92				
3 1/4 x 13 1/2	10.4	956	795	683	454	316	228	169	128	98			
3 1/4 x 15	11.5	997	884	756	626	436	315	234	178	137	108		
5 1/4 x 13 1/2	16.7	1,541	1,283	1,095	732	509	367	271	205	158	123	96	
5 1/4 x 15	18.6	1,713	1,423	1,219	1,009	703	508	376	286	221	173	137	109
5 1/4 x 16 1/2	20.5	1,885	1,568	1,340	1,170	939	678	505	384	298	235	187	151
5 1/4 x 18	22.3	2,058	1,710	1,464	1,278	1,133	886	660	503	391	309	247	200

```
EXAMPLE:  CLEAR SPAN     = 20'-0''
          BEAM SPACING   = 10'-0''
          DEAD LOAD      = 7 LBS./SQ. FT. (DECKING AND CARPET)
          LIVE LOAD      = 40 LBS./SQ. FT. (FURNITURE AND OCCUPANTS)
          TOTAL LOAD     = LIVE LOAD + DEAD LOAD x BEAM SPACING
                         = (40 + 7) x 10 = 470 LBS./LIN. FT.
THE BEAM SIZE REQUIRED IS 5 1/4'' x 15'' WHICH WILL SUPPORT 508 LBS./LIN. FT. OVER A SPAN OF 20'-0''
```

*BEAMS MAY BE DOUGLAS FIR, LARCH OR SOUTHERN YELLOW PINE.

MANUFACTURED 2''x 4'' WOOD FLOOR TRUSSES

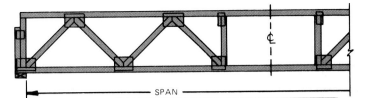

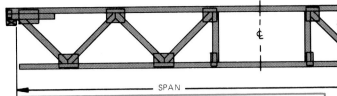

Bottom Chord Bearing Type			
DEPTH	CLEAR SPANS	# DIAGONAL WEBS	CAMBER
12''	7'-2''	4	0.063''
	9'-8''	6	0.063''
	12'-2''	8	0.063''
	14'-8''	10	0.134''
	17'-2''	12	0.237''
	19'-8''	14	0.365''
	21'-4''	16	0.507''
14''	9'-8''	6	0.063''
	12'-2''	8	0.063''
	14'-8''	10	0.095''
	17'-2''	12	0.178''
	19'-8''	14	0.288''
	22'-7''	16	0.449''
	24'-0''	18	0.569''
16''	12'-2''	8	0.065''
	14'-8''	10	0.070''
	17'-2''	12	0.132''
	19'-8''	14	0.228''
	22'-2''	16	0.346''
	25'-1''	18	0.505''
	26'-1''	20	0.596''
18''	14'-8''	10	0.065''
	17'-2''	12	0.120''
	19'-8''	14	0.176''
	22'-2''	16	0.268''
	24'-8''	18	0.367''
	27'-6''	20	0.600''
	27'-10''	22	0.630''
20''	14'-8''	10	0.063''
	17'-2''	12	0.081''
	19'-8''	14	0.140''
	22'-2''	16	0.226''
	24'-8''	18	0.327''
	27'-6''	20	0.451''
	29'-6''	22	0.630''
22''	17'-2''	10	0.066''
	19'-8''	12	0.114''
	22'-2''	14	0.184''
	24'-8''	16	0.266''
	27'-6''	18	0.367''
	30'-0''	20	0.520''
	31'-1''	22	0.630''
24''	17'-2''	12	0.063''
	19'-8''	14	0.095''
	22'-2''	16	0.153''
	24'-8''	18	0.235''
	27'-2''	20	0.325''
	30'-0''	22	0.431''
	32'-6''	24	0.630''

Top Chord Bearing Type			
DEPTH	CLEAR SPANS	# DIAGONAL WEBS	CAMBER
12''	6'-10''	4	0.063''
	9'-4''	6	0.063''
	11'-10''	8	0.063''
	14'-4''	10	0.122''
	16'-10''	12	0.233''
	19'-10''	14	0.376''
	21'-4''	16	0.507''
14''	9'-5''	6	0.063''
	11'-11''	8	0.063''
	14'-5''	10	0.088''
	16'-11''	12	0.167''
	19'-5''	14	0.273''
	21'-4''	16	0.429''
	24'-0''	18	0.569''
16''	12'-0''	8	0.063''
	14'-6''	10	0.067''
	17'-0''	12	0.126''
	19'-6''	14	0.219''
	22'-4''	16	0.337''
	24'-10''	18	0.489''
	26'-1''	20	0.596''
18''	14'-6''	10	0.063''
	17'-0''	12	0.098''
	19'-6''	14	0.170''
	22'-0''	16	0.260''
	24'-10''	18	0.378''
	27'-8''	20	0.617''
	27'-10''	22	0.630''
20''	14'-6''	10	0.063''
	17'-0''	12	0.079''
	19'-6''	14	0.136''
	22'-0''	16	0.221''
	24'-10''	18	0.337''
	27'-4''	20	0.442''
	29'-6''	22	0.630''
22''	17'-1''	12	0.065''
	19'-7''	14	0.112''
	22'-1''	16	0.181''
	24'-10''	18	0.275''
	27'-4''	20	0.381''
	30'-2''	22	0.534''
	31'-1''	24	0.630''
24''	17'-1''	12	0.063''
	19'-7''	14	0.093''
	22'-1''	16	0.150''
	24'-7''	18	0.231''
	27'-5''	20	0.335''
	30'-2''	22	0.443''
	32'-6''	24	0.630''

Wood floor trusses are typically manufactured from #3 Southern Yellow Pine. Pieces are joined together with 18 and 20 gauge galvanized steel plates applied to both faces of the truss at each joint. Where no sheathing is applied directly to top chords, they should be braced at intervals not to exceed 3'-0''. Where no rigid ceiling is applied directly to bottom chords, they should be braced at intervals not to exceed 10'-0''.

Manufactured wood floor trusses are generally spaced 24'' o.c. and are designed to support various loads. Typical trusses shown here were designed to support 55 psf (live load - 40 psf, dead load - 10 psf, ceiling dead load - 5 psf). A slight bow (camber) is built into each joist so that it will produce a level floor when loaded. Allowable deflection is 1/360 of the span.

Some of the longer trusses require one or more double diagonal webs at both ends. Wood floor trusses are a manufactured product which must be engineered and produced with a high degree of accuracy to attain the desired performance. See your local manufacturer or lumber company for trusses available in your area.

BEAM DATA

MAXIMUM ALLOWABLE UNIFORM LOADS FOR AMERICAN STANDARD I-BEAMS WITH LATERAL SUPPORT

SPAN IN FEET

SIZE OF BEAM	WEIGHT OF BEAM PER FT.	4	6	8	10	12	14	16	18	20	22	24	26	28	30	32	34	36	38	40
4 x 2 3/4	7.7	10	7	5																
	9.5	11	7	6																
5 x 3	10.0	16	11	8	6															
	11.3	20	13	10	8															
6 x 3 1/8	12.5	24	16	12	10	8														
	17.3	29	19	15	12	10														
7 x 3 3/4	15.3	35	23	17	14	12	10													
	20.0	40	27	20	16	15	13													
8 x 4	18.4	47	32	24	19	16	14	12												
	23.0	53	36	27	21	18	15	13												
10 x 4 3/4	25.4	80	54	41	33	27	23	20	18	16										
	35.0	97	65	49	39	32	28	24	22	20										
12 x 5	31.8	110	80	60	48	40	34	30	27	24	22	20								
	35.0	126	84	63	50	42	36	32	28	25	23	21								
12 x 5 1/4	40.8	144	100	75	60	50	43	37	33	30	27	25								
	50.0	168	112	84	67	56	48	42	37	34	31	28								
15 x 5 1/2	42.9	160	131	98	79	65	56	49	44	39	36	33	30	28	26	25				
	50.0	214	143	107	86	71	61	54	48	43	39	36	33	31	29	27				
18 x 6	54.7		196	147	118	98	84	74	66	59	54	49	45	42	39	37	35	33	31	
	70.0		226	170	136	113	97	85	76	68	62	57	52	49	45	43	40	38	36	
20 x 6 1/4	65.4		260	195	156	130	111	97	87	78	71	65	60	56	52	49	46	43	41	39
	75.0		281	211	169	140	120	105	94	84	77	70	65	60	56	53	50	47	44	42

LOADS ARE IN KIPS. 1 KIP = 1,000 POUNDS   (American Institute of Steel Construction)

MAXIMUM ALLOWABLE UNIFORM LOADS FOR WIDE FLANGE I-BEAMS WITH LATERAL SUPPORT

SPAN IN FEET

SIZE OF BEAM	WEIGHT OF BEAM PER FT.	4	6	8	9	10	12	14	18	20	22	24	26	28	30	32	34	36	38	40
8 x 5 1/4	17	47	31	24	19	16	13	12												
8 x 6 1/2	24		46	35	28	23	20	17												
8 x 8	31		60	46	37	30	26	23	20	18	16									
10 x 5 1/4	21	62	48	36	29	24	21	18	16	14										
10 x 8	33			74	58	47	39	33	29	26	23									
10 x 10	49				88	73	61	52	46	40	36	33	30	28	26					
12 x 6 1/2	27			74	57	45	38	32	28	25	23	21	19							
12 x 8	40			87	69	58	49	43	38	35	32	29								
12 x 10	53				108	94	79	67	59	52	47	43	39							
12 x 12	65					117	98	84	73	65	59	53	49	45	42	39				
14 x 6 3/4	30			93	70	56	46	40	35	31	28	25	23	21	20	19				
14 x 8	43				105	84	70	60	52	46	42	38	35	32	30	28				
14 x 10	61					123	102	88	77	68	62	56	51	47	44	41				
14 x 12	78					156	135	115	101	90	81	73	67	62	58	54				
14 x 14 1/2	87						152	132	115	102	92	84	77	71	66	61	57	54	51	
16 x 7	36		124	94	75	63	54	47	42	38	34	31	29	27	25	24	22			
16 x 8 1/2	58					157	126	105	90	78	70	63	57	52	48	45	42	39	37	
16 x 11 1/2	88						202	168	144	126	112	101	92	84	78	72	67	63	59	
18 x 7 1/2	50			148	119	99	85	74	66	59	54	49	46	42	40	37	35	33	31	
18 x 8 3/4	64				188	156	130	111	98	87	78	71	65	60	56	52	49	46	43	41
18 x 11 3/4	96				224	189	176	154	137	123	112	103	95	88	82	77	72	68	65	
21 x 8 1/4	62			211	169	141	120	105	94	84	77	70	65	60	56	53	50	47	44	42

LOADS ARE IN KIPS. 1 KIP = 1,000 POUNDS   (American Institute of Steel Construction)

PLANKING SPAN DATA

SPAN DATA FOR ROOF DECKING
WITH A MAXIMUM DEFLECTION OF 1/240TH OF THE SPAN
LIVE LOAD = 20 LBS./SQ. FT.

THICKNESS IN INCHES (NOMINAL)	LUMBER GRADE	SIMPLE SPANS	
		DOUGLAS FIR, LARCH, SOUTHERN YELLOW PINE	WESTERN RED CEDAR
		SPAN	SPAN
2	CONSTRUCTION	9'- 5''	8'- 1''
2	STANDARD	9'- 5''	6'- 9''
3	SELECT DEX.	15'- 3''	13'- 0''
3	COMPL. DEX.	15'- 3''	13'- 0''
4	SELECT DEX.	20'- 3''	17'- 3''
4	COMPL. DEX.	20'- 3''	17'- 3''

THICKNESS IN INCHES (NOMINAL)	LUMBER GRADE	RANDOM LENGTHS	
		DOUGLAS FIR, LARCH, SOUTHERN YELLOW PINE	WESTERN RED CEDAR
		SPAN	SPAN
2	CONSTRUCTION	10'- 3''	8'- 10''
2	STANDARD	10'- 3''	6'- 9''
3	SELECT DEX.	16'- 9''	14'- 3''
3	COMPL. DEX.	16'- 9''	13'- 6''
4	SELECT DEX.	22'- 0''	19'- 0''
4	COMPL. DEX.	22'- 0''	18'- 0''

THICKNESS IN INCHES (NOMINAL)	LUMBER GRADE	COMB. SIMPLE AND TWO-SPAN CONTINUOUS	
		DOUGLAS FIR, LARCH, SOUTHERN YELLOW PINE	WESTERN RED CEDAR
		SPAN	SPAN
2	CONSTRUCTION	10'- 7''	8'- 9''
2	STANDARD	10'- 7''	6'- 9''
3	SELECT DEX.	17'- 3''	14'- 9''
3	COMPL. DEX.	17'- 3''	13'- 6''
4	SELECT DEX.	22'- 9''	19'- 6''
4	COMPL. DEX.	22'- 9''	18'- 0''

RESISTIVITY TO HEAT LOSS OF COMMON BUILDING MATERIALS

	MATERIAL	RESISTIVITY		MATERIAL	RESISTIVITY
4''	CONCRETE OR STONE	.32	1/2''	PLYWOOD	.65
6''	CONCRETE OR STONE	.48	5/8''	PLYWOOD	.80
8''	CONCRETE OR STONE	.64	3/4''	PLYWOOD	.95
12''	CONCRETE OR STONE	.96	3/4''	SOFTWOOD SHEATHING OR SIDING	.85
4''	CONCRETE BLOCK	.70		COMPOSITION FLOOR COVERING	.08
8''	CONCRETE BLOCK	1.10	1''	MINERAL BATT INSULATION	3.50
12''	CONCRETE BLOCK	1.25	2''	MINERAL BATT INSULATION	7.00
4''	COMMON BRICK	.82	4''	MINERAL BATT INSULATION	14.00
4''	FACE BRICK	.45	2''	GLASS FIBER INSULATION	7.00
4''	STRUCTURAL CLAY TILE	1.10	4''	GLASS FIBER INSULATION	14.00
8''	STRUCTURAL CLAY TILE	1.90	1''	LOOSE FILL INSULATION	3.00
12''	STRUCTURAL CLAY TILE	3.00	1/2''	GYPSUM WALLBOARD	.45
1''	STUCCO	.20	1''	EXPANDED POLYSTYRENE, EXTRUDED	4.00
15 LB.	BUILDING PAPER	.06	1''	EXPANDED POLYSTYRENE, MOLDED BEADS	3.85
3/8''	SHEET ROCK OR PLASTERBOARD	.33		SINGLE THICKNESS GLASS	.88
1/2''	SAND PLASTER	.15		GLASSWELD INSULATING GLASS	1.89
1/2''	INSULATION PLASTER	.75		SINGLE GLASS WITH STORM WINDOW	1.66
1/2''	FIBERBOARD CEILING TILE	1.20		METAL EDGE INSULATING GLASS	1.85
1/2''	FIBERBOARD SHEATHING	1.45	4''	GLASS BLOCK	2.13
3/4''	FIBERBOARD SHEATHING	2.18	1 3/8''	WOOD DOOR	1.92
	ROLL ROOFING	.15		SAME WITH STORM DOOR	3.12
	ASPHALT SHINGLES	.16	1 3/4''	WOOD DOOR	1.82
	WOOD SHINGLES	.86		SAME WITH STORM DOOR	2.94
	TILE OR SLATE	.08			

THE METRIC SYSTEM

LINEAR MEASURE

10 millimeters	=	1 centimeter
10 centimeters	=	1 decimeter
10 decimeters	=	1 meter
10 meters	=	1 decameter
10 decameters	=	1 hectometer
10 hectometers	=	1 kilometer

LIQUID MEASURE

10 milliliters	=	1 centiliter
10 centiliters	=	1 deciliter
10 deciliters	=	1 liter
10 liters	=	1 decaliter
10 decaliters	=	1 hectoliter
10 hectoliters	=	1 kiloliter

SQUARE MEASURE

100 sq. millimeters	=	1 sq. centimeter
100 sq. centimeters	=	1 sq. decimeter
100 sq. decimeters	=	1 sq. meter
100 sq. meters	=	1 sq. decameter
100 sq. decameters	=	1 sq. hectometer
100 sq. hectometers	=	1 sq. kilometer

WEIGHTS

10 milligrams	=	1 centigram
10 centigrams	=	1 decigram
10 decigrams	=	1 gram
10 grams	=	1 decagram
10 decagrams	=	1 hectogram
10 hectograms	=	1 kilogram
100 kilograms	=	1 quintal
10 quintals	=	1 ton

CUBIC MEASURE

1000 cu. millimeters	=	1 cu. centimeter
1000 cu. centimeters	=	1 cu. decimeter
1000 cu. decimeters	=	1 cu. meter

WEIGHTS AND MEASURES CONVERSION TABLE

LINEAR MEASURE

1 inch	=		= 2.54 centimeters
1 foot	= 12 inches		= 0.3048 meter
1 yard	= 3 feet		= 0.9144 meter
1 rod	= 5 1/2 yds. or 16 1/2 ft.		= 5.029 meters
1 furlong	= 40 rods		= 201.17 meters
1 mile (statute)	= 5280 ft. or 1760 yds.		= 1609.3 meters
1 league (land)	= 3 miles		= 4.83 kilometers

CHAIN LINEAR MEASURE
(FOR SURVEYOR'S CHAIN)

1 link	= 7.92 inches		= 20.12 centimeters
1 chain	= 66 feet or 100 links		= 20.12 meters
1 furlong	= 10 chains		= 201.17 meters
1 mile	= 80 chains		= 1609.3 meters

SQUARE MEASURE

1 sq. inch	=		= 6.452 sq. centimeters
1 sq. foot	= 144 sq. inches		= 929 sq. centimeters
1 sq. yard	= 9 sq. feet		= 0.8361 sq. meter
1 sq. rod	= 30 1/4 sq. yards		= 25.29 sq. meters
1 acre	= 43,560 sq. feet or 160 sq. yds.		= 0.4047 hectare
1 sq. mile	= 640 acres		= 259 hectares or 2.59 sq. kilometers

CHAIN SQUARE MEASURE

1 sq. pole	= 625 sq. links		= 25.29 sq. meters
1 sq. chain	= 16 sq. poles		= 404.7 sq. meters
1 acre	= 10 sq. chains		= 0.4047 hectare
1 sq. mile or section	= 640 acres		= 259 hectares
1 township	= 36 sq. miles		= 9324.0 hectares

ANGULAR AND CIRCULAR MEASURE

1 minute	=	60 seconds
1 degree	=	60 minutes
1 right angle	=	90 degrees
1 straight angle	=	180 degrees
1 circle	=	360 degrees

CUBIC MEASURE

1 cu. inch	=		= 16.387 cu. centimeters
1 cu. foot	= 1728 cu. inches		= 0.0283 cu. meter
1 cu. yard	= 27 cu. feet		= 0.7646 cu. meter

WEIGHTS OF BUILDING MATERIALS

MATERIAL	WEIGHT		MATERIAL	WEIGHT	
CONCRETE			**WOOD CONSTRUCTION (CONTINUED)**		
With stone reinforced	150	pcf	Ceiling, joist and plaster	10	psf
With stone plain	144	pcf	Ceiling, joist and 1/2'' gypsum board	7	psf
With cinders, reinforced	110	pcf	Ceiling, joist and acoustic tile	5	psf
Light concrete (Aerocrete)	65	pcf	Wood shingles	3	psf
(Perlite)	45	pcf	Spanish tile	15	psf
(Vermiculite)	40	pcf	Copper sheet	2	psf
			Tar and gravel	6	psf
METAL AND PLASTER					
Masonry mortar	116	pcf	**STONE**		
Gypsum and sand plaster	112	pcf	Sandstone	147	pcf
			Slate	175	pcf
BRICK AND BLOCK MASONRY (INCLUDING MORTAR)			Limestone	165	pcf
4'' brick wall	35	psf	Granite	175	pcf
8'' brick wall	74	psf	Marble	165	pcf
8'' concrete block wall	100	psf			
12'' concrete block wall	150	psf	**GLASS**		
4'' brick veneer over 4'' concrete block	65	psf	1/4'' plate glass	3.28	psf
			1/8'' double strength	1.63	psf
WOOD CONSTRUCTION			1/8'' insulating glass with air space	3.25	psf
Frame wall, lath and plaster	20	psf	4'' block glass	20.00	psf
Frame wall, 1/2'' gypsum board	12	psf			
Floor, 1/2'' subfloor + 3/4'' finished	6	psf	**INSULATION**		
Floor, 1/2'' subfloor and ceramic tile	16	psf	Cork board 1'' thick	.58	psf
Roof, joist and 1/2'' sheathing	3	psf	Rigid foam insulation 2'' thick	.3	psf
Roof, 2'' plank and beam	5	psf	Blanket or bat 1'' thick	.1	psf
Roof, built-up	7	psf			

BRICK AND BLOCK COURSES

BLOCK NO. OF COURSES	BRICK NO. OF COURSES*	HEIGHT OF COURSE	BLOCK NO. OF COURSES	BRICK NO. OF COURSES*	HEIGHT OF COURSE
	1	0' – 2 5/8''		37	8' – 2 5/8''
	2	0' – 5 3/8''		38	8' – 5 3/8''
1	3	0' – 8''	13	39	8' – 8''
	4	0' – 10 5/8''		40	8' – 10 5/8''
	5	1' – 1 3/8''		41	9' – 1 3/8''
2	6	1' – 4''	14	42	9' – 4''
	7	1' – 6 5/8''		43	9' – 6 5/8''
	8	1' – 9 3/8''		44	9' – 9 3/8''
3	9	2' – 0''	15	45	10' – 0''
	10	2' – 2 5/8''		46	10' – 2 5/8''
	11	2' – 5 3/8''		47	10' – 5 3/8''
4	12	2' – 8''	16	48	10' – 8''
	13	2' – 10 5/8''		49	10' – 10 3/8''
	14	3' – 1 3/8''		50	11' – 1 3/8''
5	15	3' – 4''	17	51	11' – 4''
	16	3' – 6 5/8''		52	11' – 6 5/8''
	17	3' – 9 3/8''		53	11' – 9 3/8''
6	18	4' – 0''	18	54	12' – 0''
	19	4' – 2 5/8''		55	12' – 2 5/8''
	20	4' – 5 3/8''		56	12' – 5 3/8''
7	21	4' – 8''	19	57	12' – 8''
	22	4' – 10 5/8''		58	12' – 10 5/8''
	23	5' – 1 3/8''		59	13' – 1 3/8''
8	24	5' – 4''	20	60	13' – 4''
	25	5' – 6 5/8''		61	13' – 6 5/8''
	26	5' – 9 3/8''		62	13' – 9 3/8''
9	27	6' – 0''	21	63	14' – 0''
	28	6' – 2 5/8''		64	14' – 2 5/8''
	29	6' – 5 3/8''		65	14' – 5 3/8''
10	30	6' – 8''	22	66	14' – 8''
	31	6' – 10 5/8''		67	14' – 10 5/8''
	32	7' – 1 3/8''		68	15' – 1 3/8''
11	33	7' – 4''	23	69	15' – 4''
	34	7' – 6 5/8''		70	15' – 6 5/8''
	35	7' – 9 3/8''		71	15' – 9 3/8''
12	36	8' – 0''	24	72	16' – 0''

*Individual course heights are only approximations. They will not add up mathematically since mortar joints may vary in thickness. It is only important that courses average 2 2/3 in. over heights such as 4 ft., 6 ft., and 8 ft. Mortar joint is about 3/8 in.

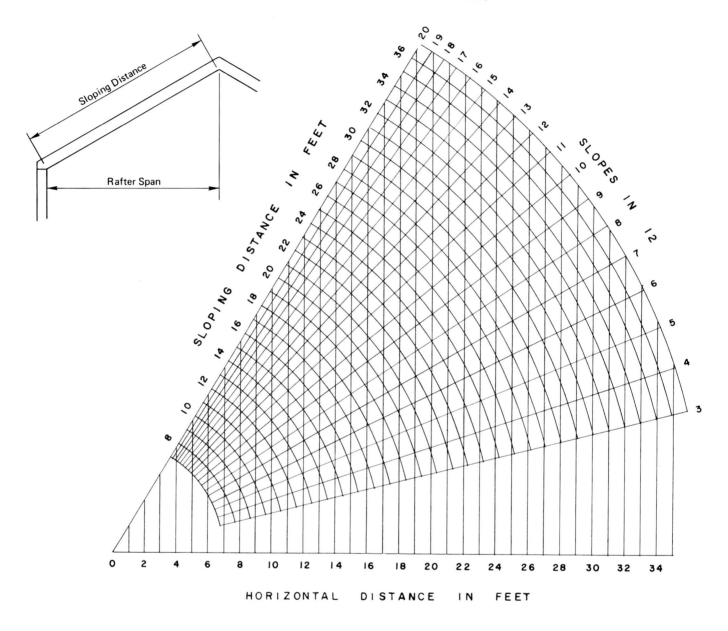

To use the diagram select the known horizontal distance and follow the vertical line to its intersection with the radial line of the specified slope, then proceed along the arc to read the sloping distance. In some cases it may be desirable to interpolate between the one foot separations. The diagram also may be used to find the horizontal distance corresponding to a given sloping distance or to find the slope when the horizontal and sloping distances are known.

Example: With a roof slope of 8 in 12 and a horizontal distance of 20 feet the sloping distance may be read as 24 feet.

Classification of Species

Group 1	Group 2	Group 3	Group 4	Group 5
Apitong	Cedar, Port	Alder, Red	Aspen	Basswood
Beech,	Orford	Birch, Paper	Bigtooth	Poplar,
American	Cypress	Cedar, Alaska	Quaking	Balsam
Birch	Douglas	Fir,	Cativo	
Sweet	Fir 2[a]	Subalpine	Cedar	
Yellow	Fir	Hemlock,	Incense	
Douglas	Balsam	Eastern	Western	
Fir 1[a]	California	Maple	Red	
Kapur	Red	Bigleaf	Cottonwood	
Keruing	Grand	Pine	Eastern	
Larch,	Noble	Jack	Black	
Western	Pacific	Lodgepole	(Western	
Maple, Sugar	Silver	Ponderosa	Poplar)	
Pine	White	Spruce	Pine	
Caribbean	Hemlock,	Redwood	Eastern	
Ocote	Western	Spruce	White	
Pine, South.	Lauan	Engelmann	Sugar	
Loblolly	Almon	White		
Longleaf	Bagtikan			
Shortleaf	Mayapis			
Slash	Red			
Tanoak	Tangile			
	White			
	Maple, Black			
	Mengkulang			
	Meranti,			
	Red[b]			
	Mersawa			
	Pine			
	Pond			
	Red			
	Virginia			
	Western			
	White			
	Spruce			
	Black			
	Red			
	Sitka			
	Sweetgum			
	Tamarack			
	Yellow-			
	Poplar			

(a) Douglas Fir from trees grown in the states of Washington, Oregon, California, Idaho, Montana, Wyoming, and the Canadian Provinces of Alberta and British Columbia shall be classed as Douglas Fir No. 1. Douglas Fir from trees grown in the states of Nevada, Utah, Colorado, Arizona and New Mexico shall be classed as Douglas Fir No. 2.

(b) Red Meranti shall be limited to species having a specific gravity of 0.41 or more based on green volume and oven dry weight.

American Plywood Association's Product
Guide, Grades and Specifications

Typical APA Registered Trademarks

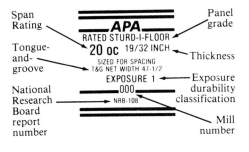

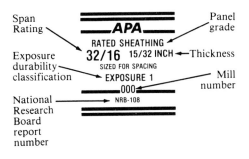

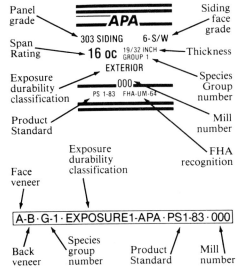

American Plywood Association's Product
Guide, Grades and Specifications

VENEER GRADES

A	Smooth, paintable. Not more than 18 neatly made repairs, boat, sled, or router type, and parallel to grain, permitted. May be used for natural finish in less demanding applications.
B	Solid surface. Shims, circular repair plugs and tight knots to 1 inch across grain permitted. Some minor splits permitted.
C Plugged	Improved C veneer with splits limited to 1/8 inch width and knotholes and borer holes limited to 1/4 x 1/2 inch. Admits some broken grain. Synthetic repairs permitted.
C	Tight knots to 1-1/2 inch. Knotholes to 1 inch across grain and some to 1-1/2 inch if total width of knots and knotholes is within specified limits. Synthetic or wood repairs. Discoloration and sanding defects that do not impair strength permitted. Limited splits allowed. Stitching permitted.
D	Knots and knotholes to 2-1/2 inch width across grain and 1/2 inch larger within specified limits. Limited splits allowed. Stitching permitted. Limited to Interior, Exposure 1 and Exposure 2 panels.

GRADE

The term "grade" may refer to *panel* grade or to *veneer* grade. Panel grades are generally identified in terms of the veneer grade used on the face and back of the panel (e.g., A-B, B-C, etc.), or by a name suggesting the panel's intended end use (e.g., APA Rated Sheathing, Underlayment, etc.).

Veneer grades define veneer appearance in terms of natural unrepaired growth characteristics and allowable number and size of repairs that may be made during manufacture. The highest quality veneer is "A," the lowest "D." The minimum grade of veneer permitted in Exterior plywood is "C." "D" veneer is used only in panels intended for interior use or for applications protected from permanent exposure to the weather or moisture.[1]

EXPOSURE DURABILITY

APA trademarked panels may be produced in four exposure durability classifications — Exterior, Exposure 1, Exposure 2, and Interior.

Exterior panels have a fully waterproof bond and are designed for applications subject to continuous exposure to the weather or to moisture.

(1) Some manufacturers also produce a premium "N" grade (natural finish) veneer, available only on special order.

(2) An exception may be made in the case of plywood used for the All-Weather Wood Foundation, which may be Exposure 1, provided it is pressure-preservative-treated in accordance with the treating and drying provisions of the AWPB-FDN Standard. Exposure 1 panels may also be used when exposure to the outdoors is on the underside only, such as at roof overhangs.

```
___APA___
RATED SHEATHING
48/24  23/32 INCH
SIZED FOR SPACING
EXTERIOR
___000___
PS 1-83 C-C  NRB-108
```

```
___APA___
A-C    GROUP 1
EXTERIOR
___000___
PS 1-83
```

Exposure 1 panels are highly moisture resistant and are designed for applications where ability to resist moisture during long construction delays or where exposure to conditions of similar severity is required. Exposure 1 panels are made with the same exterior phenolic resin adhesive used in Exterior panels. However, because other compositional factors (such as the lower grade of veneer ["D"] permitted in plywood panels) may affect bond performance, only Exterior panels should be used for permanent exposure to the weather or moisture.[2]

```
___APA___
RATED SHEATHING
32/16  15/32 INCH
SIZED FOR SPACING
EXPOSURE 1
___000___
NRB-108
```

```
___APA___
A-D    GROUP 1
EXPOSURE 1
___000___
PS 1-83
```

NOTE: All-veneer APA Rated Sheathing Exposure 1, commonly called "CDX" in the trade, is frequently mistaken as an Exterior panel and erroneously used in applications for which it does not possess the required moisture resistance. "CDX" is, in fact, an Interior panel with exterior glue and should only be used for applications as outlined under Exposure 1 above. For sheathing grade panels that will be exposed permanently to the weather or moisture, specify APA Rated Sheathing Exterior (C-C Exterior under PS 1.)

American Plywood Association's Product Guide, Grades and Specifications

Exposure 2 panels (identified as Interior type with intermediate glue under PS 1) are intended for protected construction applications where only moderate delays in providing protection from moisture may be expected.

Interior panels which lack further glueline information in their trademarks are manufactured with interior glue and are intended for interior applications only.

A-B · G-1 · INT-APA · 000 · PS1-83

SPECIES GROUP NUMBER

Plywood manufactured under U.S. Product Standard PS 1-83 may be made from over 70 species of wood. These species are divided according to strength and stiffness properties into five groups. Group 1 species are the strongest and stiffest, Group 2 the next strongest and stiffest, and so on. The Group number appearing in an APA trademark is based on the species used for face and back veneers.[1] Some species are used widely in plywood manufacture; others rarely. Check local availability if a particular species is desired.

SPAN RATINGS

Some APA trademarked panels — APA Rated Sheathing, APA Rated Sturd-I-Floor and APA 303 Siding — carry numbers in their trademarks called Span Ratings. These denote the maximum recommended center-to-center spacing in inches of supports over which the panel should be placed in construction applications.

APA Rated Sheathing Span Ratings appear as two numbers separated by a slash, such as 32/16, 48/24, etc.[2] The left-hand number denotes the maximum

recommended spacing of supports when the panel is used for roof sheathing with the long dimension of the panel across three or more supports. The right-hand number indicates the maximum recommended spacing of supports when the panel is used for subflooring with the long dimension of the panel across three or more supports. A panel marked 32/16, for example, may be used for roof sheathing over supports 32 inches on center or for subflooring over supports 16 inches on center.

APA Rated Sturd-I-Floor panels are designed specifically for single-floor (combined subfloor-underlayment) applications under carpet and pad and are manufactured with Span Ratings of 16, 20, 24 and 48 inches. These, like those for APA Rated Sheathing, are based on application of the panel with the long dimension across three or more supports.

APA 303 Sidings are produced with Span Ratings of 16 and 24 inches and may be used direct to studs or over nonstructural wall sheathing (Sturd-I-Wall construction), or over nailable panel or lumber sheathing (double-wall construction). Panels with a Span Rating of 16 inches may be applied vertically direct to studs spaced 16 inches on center. Panels bearing a Span Rating of 24 inches may be used vertically direct to studs 24 inches on center. All 303 Siding panels may be applied horizontally direct to studs 16 or 24 inches on center provided horizontal joints are blocked. When used over nailable structural panel or lumber sheathing, the 303 Siding Span Rating refers to the maximum recommended spacing of vertical rows of nails rather than to stud spacing.

(1) Where face and back veneers are not from the same species group, the higher Group number is used, except for sanded panels 3/8 inch thick or less and Decorative (including APA 303 Siding) panels of any thickness. These are identified by face species because they are chosen primarily for appearance and used in applications where structural integrity is not critical. Sanded panels greater than 3/8 inch are identified by face species if C or D grade backs are at least 1/8 inch thick and are not more than one species group number larger.

(2) An exception is APA Rated Sheathing intended for use as wall sheathing only. The trademarks for these panels contain a single number similar to the Span Rating for APA 303 Sidings.

American Plywood Association's Product Guide, Grades and Specifications

GUIDE TO APA PERFORMANCE-RATED PANELS

Trademarks Shown Are Typical Facsimiles

APA
RATED SHEATHING
32/16 15/32 INCH
SIZED FOR SPACING
EXPOSURE 1
000
NRB-108

APA RATED SHEATHING

Specially designed for subflooring, wall sheathing and roof sheathing, but also used for broad range of other construction, industrial and do-it-yourself applications. Can be manufactured as conventional plywood, as a composite, or as a reconstituted wood panel (waferboard, oriented strand board, structural particleboard). For special engineered applications, veneered panels conforming to PS 1 may be required. SPAN RATINGS: 16/0, 20/0, 24/0, 24/16, 32/16, 40/20, 48/24. EXPOSURE DURABILITY CLASSIFICATIONS: Exterior, Exposure 1, Exposure 2. COMMON THICKNESSES: 5/16, 3/8, 7/16, 15/32, 1/2, 19/32, 5/8, 23/32, 3/4.

APA
RATED STURD-I-FLOOR
20 oc 19/32 INCH
SIZED FOR SPACING
EXPOSURE 1
000
NRB-108

APA RATED STURD-I-FLOOR

Specially designed as combination subfloor-underlayment. Provides smooth surface for application of carpet and possesses high concentrated and impact load resistance. Can be manufactured as conventional plywood, as a composite, or as a reconstituted wood panel (waferboard, oriented strand board, structural particleboard). Available square edge or tongue-and-groove. SPAN RATINGS: 16, 20, 24. EXPOSURE DURABILITY CLASSIFICATIONS: Exterior, Exposure 1, Exposure 2. COMMON THICKNESSES: 19/32, 5/8, 23/32, 3/4.

APA
RATED SHEATHING
STRUCTURAL I
48/24 23/32 INCH
SIZED FOR SPACING
EXTERIOR
000
PS 1-83 C-C NRB-108

APA STRUCTURAL I AND II RATED SHEATHING

Unsanded all-veneer PS 1 plywood grades for use where cross-panel strength and stiffness or shear properties are of maximum importance, such as box beams, gusset plates, stressed-skin panels, containers, pallet bins. All plies in Structural I panels are special improved grades and limited to Group 1 species. All plies in Structural II panels are special improved grades and limited to Group 1, 2, or 3 species. Structural I more commonly available. SPAN RATINGS: 20/0, 24/0, 32/16, 40/20, 48/24. EXPOSURE DURABILITY CLASSIFICATIONS: Exterior, Exposure 1. COMMON THICKNESSES: 5/16, 3/8, 15/32, 1/2, 19/32, 5/8, 23/32, 3/4.

APA
RATED STURD-I-FLOOR
48 oc 1-1/8 INCH
2-4-1
SIZED FOR SPACING
EXPOSURE 1
T&G
000
PS 1-83 UNDERLAYMENT
NRB-108 FHA-UM-64

APA RATED STURD-I-FLOOR 48 oc (2-4-1)

For combination subfloor-underlayment on 32- and 48-inch spans and for heavy timber roof construction. Manufactured only as conventional plywood. Available square edge or tongue-and-groove. SPAN RATING: 48. EXPOSURE DURABILITY CLASSIFICATIONS: Exposure 1. THICKNESS: 1-1/8.

NOTE: Specify Performance-Rated Panels by thickness and Span Rating. Span Ratings are based on panel strength and stiffness. Since these properties are a function of panel composition and configuration as well as thickness, the same Span Rating may appear on panels of different thicknesses. Similarly, panels of the same thickness may be marked with different Span Ratings.

American Plywood Association's Product Guide, Grades and Specifications

TYPICAL ASPHALT PREPARED ROOFING PRODUCTS

PRODUCT	Approx. Shipping Weight Per Square	Packages Per Square	Length	Width	Shingles Per Square	Side or End Lap	Top Lap	Head Lap	Exposure
3 Tab Self Sealing Strip Shingle	235 lb. / 300 lb.	3 or 4	36" / 36"	12" / 12"	80 / 80		7" / 7"	2" / 2"	5" / 5"
2 and 3 Tab Hex Strip	195 lb.	3	36"	11-1/3"	86		2"	2"	5"
Individual Lock Down	145 lb.	2	16"	16"	80	$2\frac{1}{2}$"			
Individual Staple Down	145 lb.	2	16"	16"	80	$2\frac{1}{2}$"			
Giant Individual American	330 lb.	4	16"	12"	226		11"	6"	5"
Giant Individual Dutch Lap	165 lb.	2	16"	12"	113	3"	2"	2"	10"

PRODUCT	Approx. Shipping Weight Per Square	Packages Per Square	Length	Width	Units Per Square	Side or End Lap	Top Lap	Head Lap	Exposure
Saturated Felt	15 lb. / 30 lb.	1/4 / 1/2	144' / 72'	36" / 36"		4" to 6" / 4" to 6"	2" / 2"		34" / 34"
Smooth Roll	65 lb. / 50 lb.	1 / 1	36' / 36'	36" / 36"		6" / 6"	2" / 2"		34" / 34"
Mineral Surfaced Roll	90 lb. / 90 lb. / 90 lb.	1.0	36'	36"	1.0 / 1.075 / 1.15	6" / 6" / 6"	2" / 3" / 4"		34" / 33" / 32"
Pattern Edge Roll	105 lb. / 105 lb.	1 / 1	42' / 48'	36" / 32"			2" / 2"		16" / 14"
19" Selvage Double Coverage	110 lb. to 120 lb.	2	36'	36"			19"	2"	17"

RECOMMENDED STYLES OF WELDED WIRE FABRIC
REINFORCEMENT FOR CONCRETE

TYPE OF CONSTRUCTION	RECOMMENDED STYLE	REMARKS
Barbecue Foundation Slab	6x6-8/8 to 4x4-6/6	Use heavier style fabric for heavy, massive fireplaces or barbecue pits.
Basement Floors	6x6-10/10, 6x6-8/8 or 6x6-6/6	For small areas (15-foot maximum side dimension) use 6x6-10/10. As a rule of thumb, the larger the area or the poorer the sub-soil, the heavier the gauge.
Driveways	6x6-6/6	Continuous reinforcement between 25- to 30-foot contraction joints.
Foundation Slabs (Residential only)	6x6-10/10	Use heavier gauge over poorly drained sub-soil, or when maximum dimension is greater than 15 feet.
Garage Floors	6x6-6/6	Position at midpoint of 5- or 6-inch thick slab.
Patios and Terraces	6x6-10/10	Use 6x6-8/8 if sub-soil is poorly drained.
Porch Floor a. 6-inch thick slab up to 6-foot span b. 6-inch thick slab up to 8-foot span	6x6-6/6 4x4-4/4	Position 1 inch from bottom form to resist tensile stresses.
Sidewalks	6x6-10/10 6x6-8/8	Use heavier gauge over poorly drained sub-soil. Construct 25- to 30-foot slabs as for driveways.
Steps (Free span)	6x6-6/6	Use heavier style if more than five risers. Position fabric 1 inch from bottom form.
Steps (On ground)	6x6-8/8	Use 6x6-6/6 for unstable sub-soil.

GYPSUM WALLBOARD APPLICATION DATA

THICKNESS	APPROX. WEIGHT LBS./SQ. FT.	SIZE	LOCATION	APPLICATION METHOD	MAX. SPACING OF FRAMING MEMBERS
¼″	1.1	4′ x 8′ to 12′	Over Existing Walls & Ceilings	Horizontal or Vertical	
⅜″	1.5	4′ x 8′ to 14′	Ceilings	Horizontal	16″
⅜″	1.5	4′ x 8′ to 14′	Sidewalls	Horizontal or Vertical	16″
½″	2.0	4′ x 8′ to 14′	Ceilings	Vertical Horizontal	16″ 24″
½″	2.0	4′ x 8′ to 14′	Sidewalls	Horizontal or Vertical	24″
⅝″	2.5	4′ x 8′ to 14′	Ceilings	Vertical Horizontal	16″ 24″
⅝″	2.5	4′ x 8′ to 14′	Sidewalls	Horizontal or Vertical	24″
1″	4.0	2′ x 8′ to 12′		For Laminated Partitions	

SIZES AND DIMENSIONS FOR REINFORCING BARS

WEIGHT LB PER FT	NOMINAL DIAMETER INCHES	SIZE	NUMBER	NOMINAL CROSS SECT AREA SQ IN.	NOMINAL PERIMETER
.376	.375	⅜	3	.11	1.178
.668	.500	½	4	.20	1.571
1.043	.625	⅝	5	.31	1.963
1.502	.750	¾	6	.44	2.356
2.044	.875	⅞	7	.60	2.749
2.670	1.000	1	8	.79	3.142
3.400	1.128	1*	9	1.00	3.544
4.303	1.270	1⅛*	10	1.27	3.990
5.313	1.410	1¼*	11	1.56	4.430
7.650	1.693	1½*	14	2.25	5.320
13.600	2.257	2*	18	4.00	7.090

These sizes rolled in rounds equivalent to square cross section area.

RECOMMENDED FOOT CANDLE LEVELS

AREA	LEVEL
TV Viewing	5 FC
Storage	10 FC
Stairway	20 FC
Dining	20 FC
Bedroom	20 FC
Bath	30 FC
Living	30 FC
Den	30 FC
Reading	50 FC
Sewing	50 FC
Kitchen	50 FC
Shop	70 FC
Drawing	100 FC

DESIGN TEMPERATURES AND DEGREE DAYS
(Heating Season)

State	City	Outside Design Temperature (°F)	Degree Days (°F-Days)
Alabama	Birmingham	19	2,600
Alaska	Anchorage	-25	10,800
Arizona	Phoenix	31	1,800
Arkansas	Little Rock	19	3,200
California	San Francisco	35	3,000
California	Los Angeles	41	2,000
Colorado	Denver	-2	6,200
Connecticut	Hartford	1	6,200
Florida	Tampa	36	600
Georgia	Atlanta	18	3,000
Idaho	Boise	4	5,800
Illinois	Chicago	-3	6,600
Indiana	Indianapolis	0	5,600
Iowa	Des Moines	-7	6,600
Kansas	Wichita	5	4,600
Kentucky	Louisville	8	4,600
Louisiana	New Orleans	32	1,400
Maryland	Baltimore	12	4,600
Massachusetts	Boston	6	5,600
Michigan	Detroit	4	6,200
Minnesota	Minneapolis	-14	8,400
Mississippi	Jackson	21	2,200
Missouri	St. Louis	4	5,000
Montana	Helena	-17	8,200
Nebraska	Lincoln	-4	5,800
Nevada	Reno	2	6,400
New Hampshire	Concord	-11	7,400
New Mexico	Albuquerque	14	4,400
New York	Buffalo	3	7,000
New York	New York	12	5,000
North Carolina	Raleigh	16	3,400
North Dakota	Bismark	-24	8,800
Ohio	Columbus	2	5,600
Oklahoma	Tulsa	12	3,800
Oregon	Portland	21	4,600
Pennsylvania	Philadelphia	11	4,400
Pennsylvania	Pittsburg	5	6,000
Rhode Island	Providence	6	6,000
South Carolina	Charleston	23	2,000
South Dakota	Sioux Falls	-14	7,800
Tennessee	Chattanooga	15	3,200
Texas	Dallas	19	2,400
Texas	San Antonio	25	1,600
Utah	Salt Lake City	5	6,000
Vermont	Burlington	-12	8,200
Virginia	Richmond	14	3,800
Washington	Seattle	28	5,200
West Virginia	Charleston	9	4,400
Wisconsin	Madison	-9	7,800
Wyoming	Cheyenne	-6	7,400

A more complete listing of monthly and yearly degree days and outside design temperatures can be found in the ASHRAE Guide and Data Book.

This list of U.S. cities, with their outside design temperatures and degree days, is a useful resource for computer aided energy analysis.

Typical Wood Foundation

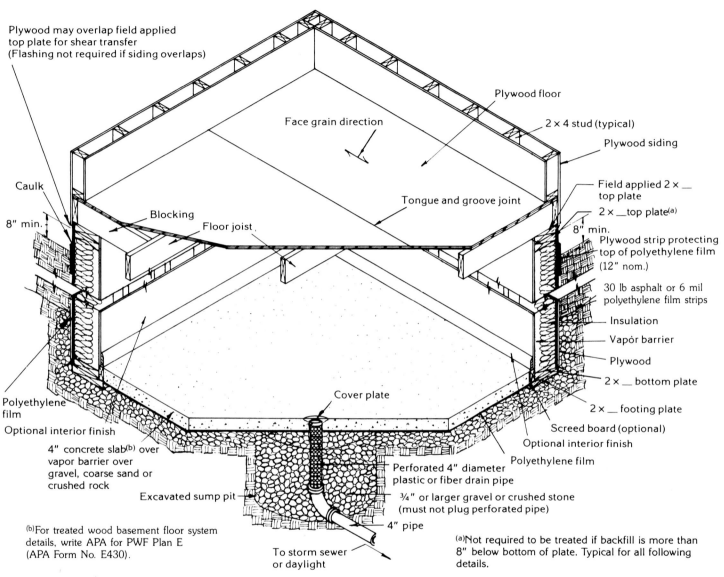

Plywood may overlap field applied top plate for shear transfer (Flashing not required if siding overlaps)

Caulk

8″ min.

Blocking

Floor joist

Polyethylene film

Optional interior finish

4″ concrete slab(b) over vapor barrier over gravel, coarse sand or crushed rock

Excavated sump pit

(b)For treated wood basement floor system details, write APA for PWF Plan E (APA Form No. E430).

Face grain direction

Plywood floor

Tongue and groove joint

Cover plate

To storm sewer or daylight

Perforated 4″ diameter plastic or fiber drain pipe

¾″ or larger gravel or crushed stone (must not plug perforated pipe)

4″ pipe

2 × 4 stud (typical)

Plywood siding

Field applied 2 × __ top plate

2 × __ top plate(a)

8″ min.

Plywood strip protecting top of polyethylene film (12″ nom.)

30 lb asphalt or 6 mil polyethylene film strips

Insulation

Vapor barrier

Plywood

2 × __ bottom plate

2 × __ footing plate

Screed board (optional)

Optional interior finish

Polyethylene film

(a)Not required to be treated if backfill is more than 8″ below bottom of plate. Typical for all following details.

American Plywood Association

Crawl Space

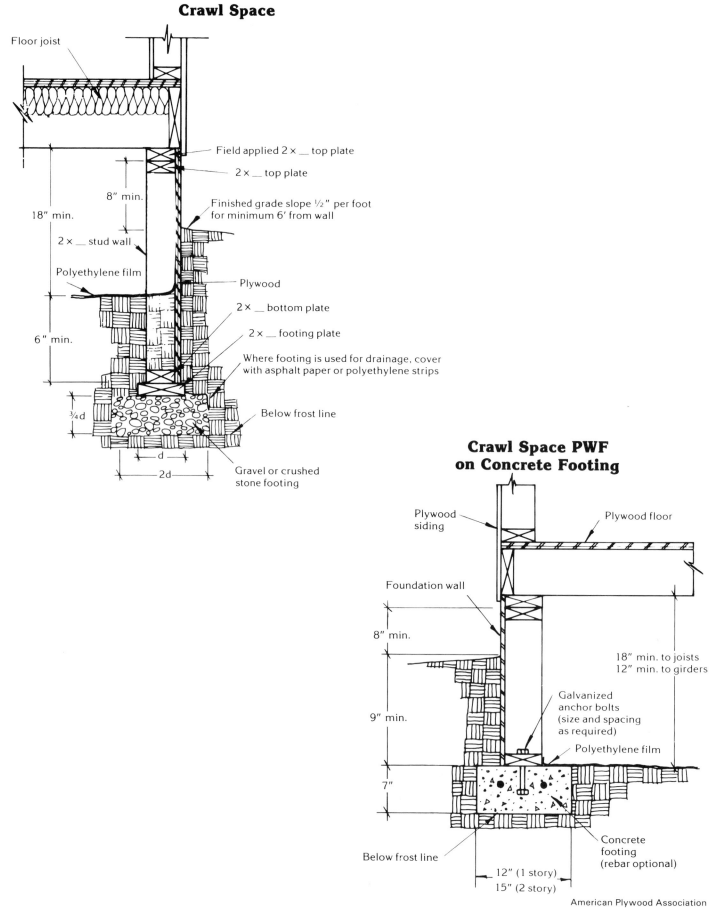

Floor joist

Field applied 2 × __ top plate

2 × __ top plate

8" min.

18" min.

Finished grade slope ½" per foot for minimum 6' from wall

2 × __ stud wall

Polyethylene film

Plywood

2 × __ bottom plate

2 × __ footing plate

Where footing is used for drainage, cover with asphalt paper or polyethylene strips

6" min.

¾ d

Below frost line

d

2d

Gravel or crushed stone footing

Crawl Space PWF on Concrete Footing

Plywood siding

Plywood floor

Foundation wall

8" min.

18" min. to joists
12" min. to girders

9" min.

Galvanized anchor bolts (size and spacing as required)

Polyethylene film

7"

Below frost line

12" (1 story)
15" (2 story)

Concrete footing (rebar optional)

American Plywood Association

WOOD FOUNDATIONS

Basement Wall

Finish grade slope ½" per foot min. 6' from wall

1 × _____ or plywood strip protecting top of polyethylene film (12" nom.)

Plywood may overlap field applied top plate for shear transfer (Flashing not required if siding overlaps)

Floor joist

Plywood siding

Field applied 2 × __ top plate

2 × __ top plate*

Insulation as appropriate

2 × __ stud wall

Vapor barrier

Asphalt or polyethylene film strips

Optional interior finish

3" or 4" concrete slab

Polyethylene film

8" min.

Caulk

Plywood

Polyethylene film

2 × __ bottom plate

2 × __ footing plate

¾ d

d

2d

Below frost line

1 × __ screed board (optional)

Gravel, coarse sand, or crushed stone fill (4" for Group I and II soils, 6" for Group III)

Backfill w/crushed stone or gravel 12" for Group I soils, and half the backfill height for Groups II and III soils.

*Not required to be treated if backfill is more than 8 in. below bottom of plate. Typical for all following details.

Knee Wall with Brick Veneer

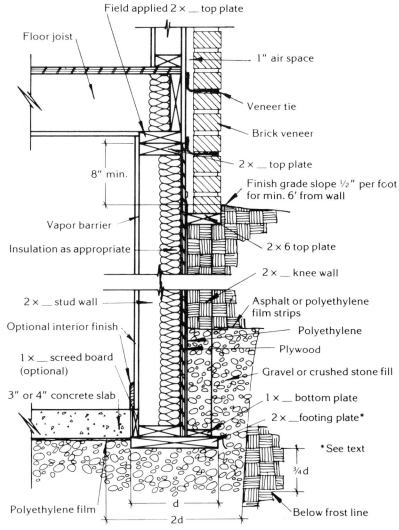

Field applied 2 × __ top plate

Floor joist

1" air space

Veneer tie

Brick veneer

2 × __ top plate

Finish grade slope ½" per foot for min. 6' from wall

2 × 6 top plate

2 × __ knee wall

8" min.

Vapor barrier

Insulation as appropriate

2 × __ stud wall

Optional interior finish

1 × __ screed board (optional)

3" or 4" concrete slab

Polyethylene film

Asphalt or polyethylene film strips

Polyethylene

Plywood

Gravel or crushed stone fill

1 × __ bottom plate

2 × __ footing plate*

*See text

¾ d

d

2d

Below frost line

American Plywood Association

Garage PWF Details

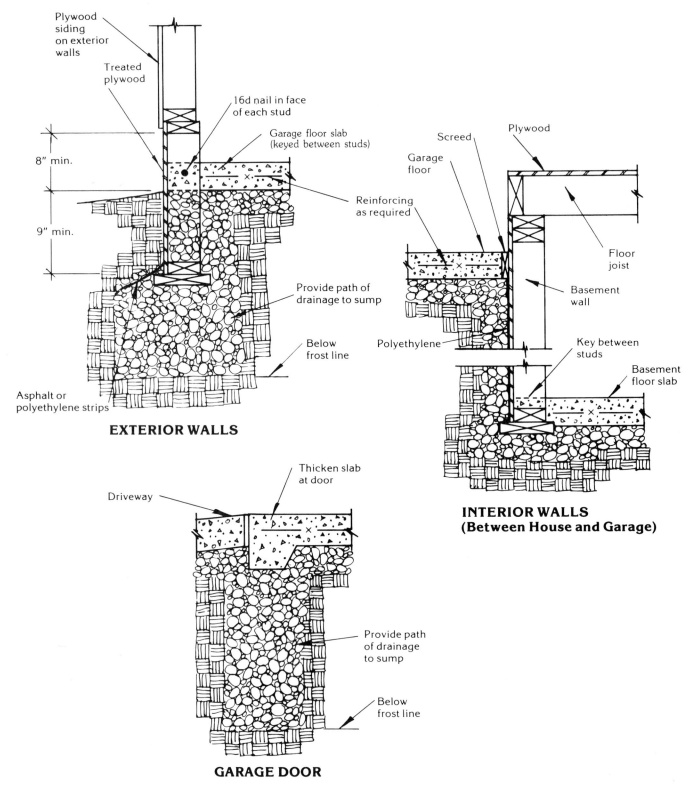

EXTERIOR WALLS

- Plywood siding on exterior walls
- Treated plywood
- 16d nail in face of each stud
- Garage floor slab (keyed between studs)
- 8" min.
- 9" min.
- Reinforcing as required
- Provide path of drainage to sump
- Below frost line
- Asphalt or polyethylene strips

INTERIOR WALLS (Between House and Garage)

- Screed
- Garage floor
- Plywood
- Floor joist
- Basement wall
- Polyethylene
- Key between studs
- Basement floor slab

GARAGE DOOR

- Driveway
- Thicken slab at door
- Provide path of drainage to sump
- Below frost line

American Plywood Association

2 X 4 Wood Stud Partition

2 X 4 wood studs 16″ o.c.
CertainTeed 3½″ (R-11) Sound
Control Batts or
Insul-Safe III fiber glass insulation
½″ regular gypsum wallboard

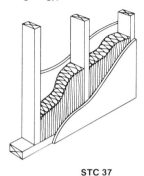

STC 37

2 X 4 Wood Stud Resilient Channel Partition

2 X 4 wood studs 16″ o.c.
CertainTeed 3½″ (R-11) Sound
Control Batts
Resilient channels 24″ o.c.
one side
⅝″ type "X" gypsum wallboard

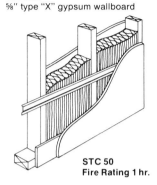

STC 50
Fire Rating 1 hr.

2 X 4 Wood Stud Partition

2 X 4 wood studs 24″ o.c.
CertainTeed 3½″ (R-11) Sound
Control Batts
2 layers ⅝″ type "X" gypsum
wallboard each side

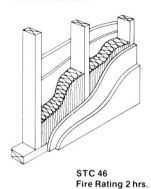

STC 46
Fire Rating 2 hrs.

Staggered Wood Stud Partition

2 X 4 wood studs staggered
16″ o.c.
2 X 6 wood plates
CertainTeed 2½″ (R-8) Sound
Control Batts all stud spaces
½″ regular gypsum wallboard

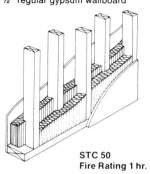

STC 50
Fire Rating 1 hr.

Double Wood Stud Partition

2 X 4 wood studs 16″ o.c. (double
row)
Separate 2 X 4 wood plates
CertainTeed 3½″ (R-11) Sound
Control Batts all stud spaces
½″ regular gypsum wallboard

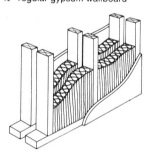

STC 55
Fire Rating 1 hr.

Exterior Wood Stud Wall

2 X 4 studs 16″ o.c.
CertainTeed 3½″ (R-11) Sound
Control Batts
Interior: ½″ regular gypsum
wallboard
Exterior: ½″ gypsum sheating
⅜″ exterior plywood

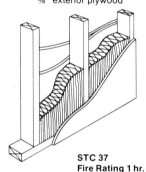

STC 37
Fire Rating 1 hr.

Exterior Wood Stud Wall

2 X 4 wood studs 16″ o.c.
CertainTeed 3½″ (R-11) Sound
Control Batts
Interior: resilient channel
⅝″ type "X" gypsum
wallboard
Exterior: ½″ gypsum sheathing
⅜″ exterior plywood

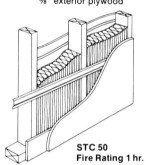

STC 50
Fire Rating 1 hr.

2½″ & 3⅝″ Steel Stud Partitions

2½″ or 3⅝″ steel studs 24″ o.c.
CertainTeed 2½″ (R-8) or 3½″
(R-11) Sound Control Batts
½″ regular gypsum wallboard

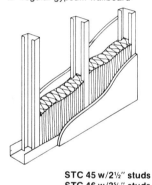

STC 45 w/2½″ studs
STC 46 w/3⅝″ studs

Steel Stud Partition

2½″ steel studs 24″ o.c.
CertainTeed 2½″ (R-8) Sound
Control Batts
⅝″ type "X" gypsum wallboard

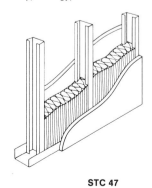

STC 47
Fire Rating 1 hr.

Steel Stud Partition

2½″ steel studs 24″ o.c.
CertainTeed 2½″ (R-8) Sound
Control Batts
2 layers ½″ type "X" gypsum
wallboard each side

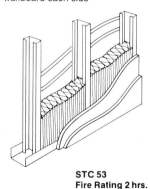

STC 53
Fire Rating 2 hrs.

Floor/Ceiling Construction

Wood joists 16″ o.c.
CertainTeed 3½″ (R-11) Sound
Control Batts
Resilient channel
½″ type "X" gypsum wallboard
⅝″ plywood subfloor
⅜″ particle board underlayment
carpet & pad

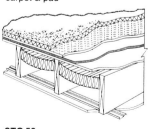

STC 53
IIC 73
Fire Rating 1 hr.

Floor/Ceiling Construction

Wood joists 16″ o.c.
CertainTeed 3½″ (R-11) Sound
Control Batts
Resilient channel
½″ type "X" gypsum wallboard
⅝″ plywood subfloor
1½″ cellular or light weight
concrete
carpet & pad

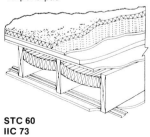

STC 60
IIC 73
Fire Rating 1 hr.

Certain-Teed Corp.

WALL SYSTEM SELECTION CHART FOR WOOD STUD WALLS

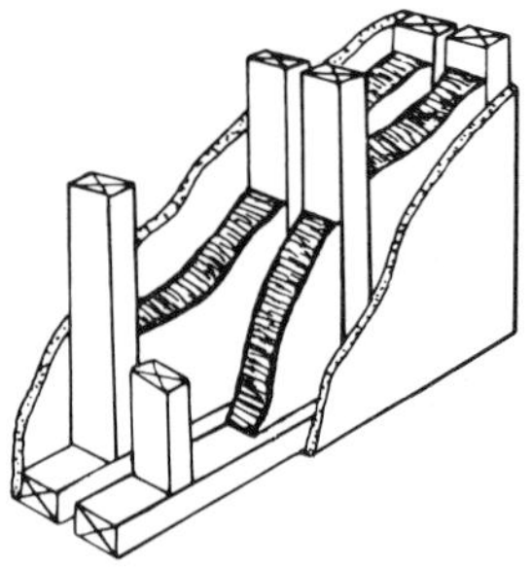

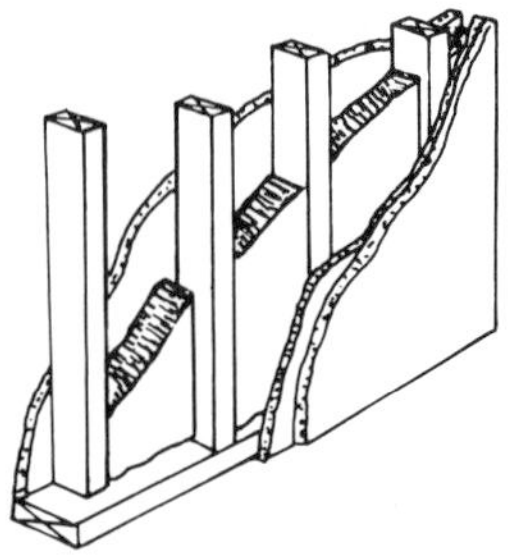

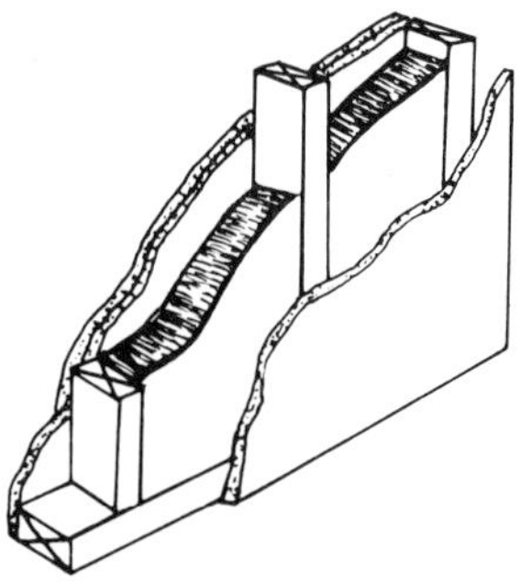

Fire Rating	Test No.	STC	Construction Description		
1 Hr.*	W01480	64	Double wood studs 16" o.c.; double layer ½" type "x" gypsum board each side, one thickness R-11 Fiberglas insulation		**Double Wood Studs**
1 Hr.*	W01080	60	Double wood studs 16" o.c.; double layer ½" type "x" gypsum board one side, single layer other side; two thicknesses R-11 Fiberglas insulation		
1 Hr.	W2869	59	Double wood studs 16" o.c.; single layer ½" type "x" gypsum board each side; two thicknesses R-11 Fiberglas insulation		
2 Hr.	W4269	58	Double wood studs 16" o.c.; double layer ⅝" type "x" gypsum board one side; no insulation		
1 Hr.*	W01180	57	Double wood studs 16" o.c.; double layer ½" type "x" gypsum board one side, single layer other side; one thickness R-11 Fiberglas insulation		
N.A.	W2969	56	Double wood studs 16" o.c.; single layer ½" type "x" gypsum board each side; one thicknesses R-11 Fiberglas insulation		
1 Hr.*	OCF448	56	Double wood studs 16" o.c.; single layer ⅝" type "x" gypsum board each side; one thickness R-11 Fiberglas insulation		
1 Hr.	W01580	54	Double wood studs 16" o.c.; double layer ½" type "x" gypsum board each side; no insulation		
N.A.	W00980	48	Double wood studs 16" o.c.; double layer ½" type "x" gypsum board one side; single layer other side; no insulation		
1 Hr.*	W4169	52	Double wood studs 16" o.c.; double layer ⅝" type "x" gypsum board one side; single layer other side; no insulation		
N.A.	W3469	47	Double wood studs 16" o.c.; single layer ½" type "x" gypsum board each side; no insulation		
1 Hr.*	W06282	46	Double wood studs 16" o.c.; single layer ⅝" type "x" gypsum board each side; no insulation		
1 Hr.*	W4869	55	Staggered wood studs 24" o.c.; double layer ½" type "x" gypsum board each side; one thickness R-11 Fiberglas insulation		**Staggered Wood Studs**
N.A.	W4769	53	Staggered wood studs 24" o.c.; double layer ½" type "x" gypsum board one side; single layer other side; one thickness R-11 Fiberglas insulation		
1 Hr.*	W4669	52	Staggered wood studs 24" o.c.; double layer ½" type "x" gypsum board each side; no insulation		
1 Hr.	OC5FC	51	Staggered wood studs 16" o.c.; single layer ½" gypsum board each side; two thicknesses R-11 Fiberglas insulation		
N.A.	OC4FC	49	Staggered wood studs 16" o.c.; single layer ½" type "x" gypsum board each side; one thickness R-11 Fiberglas insulation		
N.A.	W4569	47	Staggered wood studs 24" o.c.; double layer ½" type "x" gypsum board one side; single layer other side; no insulation		
1 Hr.*	W5769	46	Staggered wood studs 16" o.c.; single layer ⅝" type "x" gypsum board one side; one thickess R-11 Fiberglas insulation		
1 Hr.*	W5869	43	Staggered wood studs 16" o.c.; single layer ⅝" type "x" gypsum board each side; no insulation		
N.A.	OC3FC	39	Staggered wood studs 16" o.c.; single layer ½" type "x" gypsum board each side; no insulation		
1 Hr.*	W2569	45	Single wood studs, 16" o.c.; double layer ½" type "x" gypsum board each side; one thickness R-11 Fiberglas insulation		**Single Wood Studs**
N.A.	W2469	40	Single wood studs 16" o.c., double layer ½" gypsum board one side; single layer ½" gypsum board other side; one thickness R-11 Fiberglas insulation		
N.A.	W2069	39	Single wood studs, 16" o.c., single layer ½" type "x" gypsum board each side; one thickness R-11 Fiberglas insulation		
N.A.	W2269	38	Single wood studs, 16" o.c.; double layer ½" type "x" gypsum board one side; single layer other side; no insulation		
N.A.	W2169	35	Single wood studs, 16" o.c.; single layer ½" type "x" gypsum board each side; no insulation		
1 Hr.	OCF424	34	Single wood studs 16" o.c., single layer ⅝" type "x" gypsum board each side; no insulation		

Owens-Corning Fiberglas Corp.

*Some of the above test results are estimated. Where specific test references are available, they will be provided upon request.

CLEARANCE REQUIREMENTS

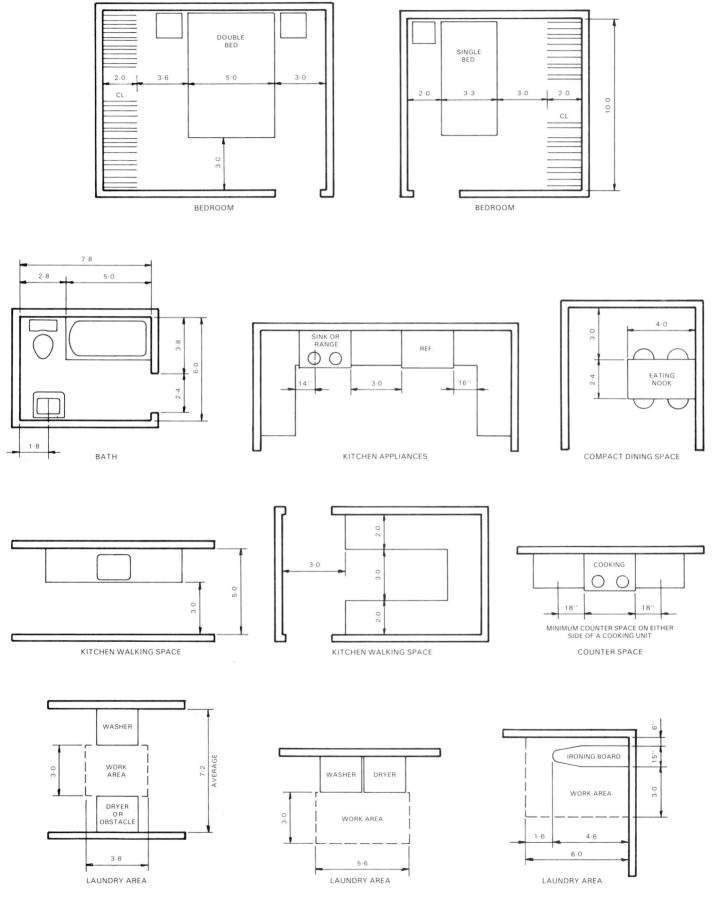

BEDROOM

BEDROOM

BATH

KITCHEN APPLIANCES

COMPACT DINING SPACE

KITCHEN WALKING SPACE

KITCHEN WALKING SPACE

MINIMUM COUNTER SPACE ON EITHER
SIDE OF A COOKING UNIT

COUNTER SPACE

LAUNDRY AREA

LAUNDRY AREA

LAUNDRY AREA

303 Siding Direct to Studs—U = 0.08

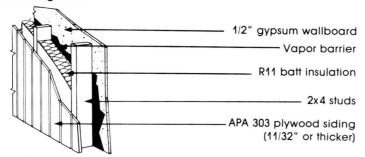

- 1/2" gypsum wallboard
- Vapor barrier
- R11 batt insulation
- 2x4 studs
- APA 303 plywood siding (11/32" or thicker)

	R
Outside air film	0.17
11/32" plywood siding	0.43
R11 batt insulation	11.00
1/2" gypsum wallboard	0.45
Inside air film	0.68
R_T =	12.73
$U = 1/R_T$ =	0.08

303 Siding Over Fiberboard Sheathing—U = 0.07

- 1/2" gypsum wallboard
- Vapor barrier
- R11 batt insulation
- 1/2" fiberboard sheathing
- 2x4 studs
- APA 303 plywood siding (11/32" or thicker)

	R
Outside air film	0.17
11/32" plywood siding	0.43
1/2" fiberboard sheathing	1.32
R11 insulation	11.00
1/2" gypsum wallboard	0.45
Inside air film	0.68
R_T =	14.05
$U = 1/R_T$ =	0.07

303 Siding Direct to Studs—U = 0.07

- 1/2" gypsum wallboard
- Vapor barrier
- R13 batt insulation
- 2x4 studs
- APA 303 plywood siding (11/32" or thicker)

	R
Outside air film	0.17
11/32" plywood siding	0.43
R13 batt insulation	13.00
1/2" gypsum wallboard	0.45
Inside air film	0.68
R_T =	14.73
$U = 1/R_T$ =	0.07

303 Siding Over Rigid Insulation—U = 0.05

- 1/2" gypsum wallboard
- Vapor barrier
- R13 batt insulation
- 2x4 studs
- R4 rigid foam insulation
- APA 303 plywood siding (11/32" or thicker)

	R
Outside air film	0.17
11/32" plywood siding	0.43
R4 rigid foam insulation	4.00
R13 batt insulation	13.00
1/2" gypsum wallboard	0.45
Inside air film	0.68
R_T =	18.73
$U = 1/R_T$ =	0.05

303 Siding Direct to Studs—U = 0.05

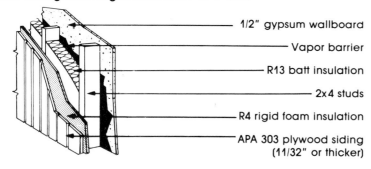

- 1/2" gypsum wallboard
- Vapor barrier
- R19 batt insulation
- 2x6 studs
- APA 303 plywood siding (15/32" or thicker for studs 24" oc)

	R
Outside air film	0.17
15/32" plywood siding	0.59
R19 batt insulation	19.00
1/2" gypsum wallboard	0.45
Inside air film	0.68
R_T =	20.89
$U = 1/R_T$ =	0.05

ABBREVIATIONS

Acoustic	ACST	Drywall	D W	Plaster	PLAS
Acrylonitrile butadiene styrene	ABS	Elbow	ELL	Plate glass	PL GL
Actual	ACT	Electric	ELEC	Plates	PLTS
Addition	ADD	Elevation	EL or ELEV	Platform	PLATF
Adhesive	ADH	Enhanced graphics adapter	EGA	Plumbing	PLMB
Aggregate	AGGR	Entrance	ENT	Plywood	PLY
Air conditioning	AIR COND	Estimate	EST	Polyvinyl chloride	PVC
Alternate	ALT	Excavate	EXC	Prefabricated	PREFAB
Aluminum	AL	Exterior	EXT	Property	PROP
American Association of Registered Architects	ARA	Fabricate	FAB	Push button	PB
		Family room	FAM R	Radiator	RAD
American Institute of Architects	AIA	Federal Housing Authority	FHA	Random access memory	RAM
American Society for Testing and Materials	ASTM	Finish	FIN	Random length and width	RL & W
		Firebrick	FBRK	Range	R
American wire gage	AWG	Fireproof	FP	Read-only memory	ROM
Amount	AMT	Fitting	FTG	Receptacle	RECP
Ampere	AMP	Fixture	FIX	Recessed	REC
Anchor bolt	AB	Flange	FLG	Red-Green-Blue	RGB
Approximate	APPROX	Flashing	FLSHG	Reference	REF
Architectural	ARCH	Floor	FL	Refrigerator	REF
Area	A	Floor drain	F D	Register	REG
Asbestos	ASB	Flooring	FLG	Reinforce	REINF
Asphalt	ASPH	Footing	FTG	Return	RET
Assembly	ASSY	Foundation	FDN	Riser	R
Automatic	AUTO	Frame	FR	Roof	RF
Average	AVG	Full size	FS	Roofing	RFG
Balcony	BALC	Gallon	GAL	Rough	RGH
Basement	BSMT	Galvanized	GALV	Round	RD
Bathroom	B	Glass	GL	Schedule	SCH
Beam	BM or BMS	Grade	GR	Section	SECT
Bedroom	BR	Gypsum	GYP	Self-closing	SC
Bench mark	BM	Hall	H	Service	SERV
Between	BET	Hardware	HDW	Sewer	SEW
Bits per inch	bpi	Header	HDR	Sheet metal	SHT'G
Blocking	BLKG	Heater	HTR	Shelves	SM
Board feet	BD FT	Horizontal	HORIZ	Shower	SHVL'S
Bottom	BOT	Hose bibb	HB	Siding	SH
Bracket	BRKT	Inside diameter	ID	Sill cock	SDG
British thermal unit	BTU	Insulation	INS	Sink	SC
Broom closet	BC	Integrated circuit	IC	Socket	SOC
Building	BLDG	Interior	INT	Soil pipe	SP
Buzzer	BUZ	International Standards Organization	ISO	Specification	SPEC
Cabinet	CAB			Square	SQ
Casing	CSG	Joint	JT	Stairs	ST
Cast iron	CI	Joist	JST	Standpipe	ST P
Cathode ray tube	CRT	Kiln dried	KD	Station point	SP
Caulking	CLKG	Kitchen	K	Steel	STL
Ceiling	CL	Kitchen cabinets	KC	Structural	STR
Cement	CEM	Kitchen sink	KS	Surface	SUR
Center line	CL or ℄	Laminated	LAM	Surface four sides	S4S
Center to center	C to C	Landing	LDG	Surface two sides	S2S
Central processing unit	CPU	Laundry	LAU	Suspended ceiling	SUSP CLG
Ceramic	CER	Lavatory	LAV	Switch	S or SW
Circuit	CKT	Leader	LDR	Symbol	SYM
Circuit breaker	CIR BKR	Level	LEV	Tee	T
Cleanout	CL or CO	Light	LT	Telephone	TEL
Closet	CLOS or CL	Linen closet	L CL	Television	TV
Clothes dryer	CL D	Linoleum	LINO	Temperature	TEMP
Column	COL	Living room	LR	Terra-cotta	TC
Composition	COMP	Lumber	LBR	Thermostat	THERMO
Concrete	CONC	Manufacture	MFR	Thickness	THK
Concrete block	CONC B	Material	MATL	Tongue and groove	T & G
Construction	CONST	Maximum	MAX	Tread	TR
Copper	COP or CU	Medicine cabinet	MC	Unfinished	UNFIN
Counter	CTR	Metal	MET	Vanishing point	VP
Courses	C	Minimum	MIN	Vanity	VAN
Cross section	X-SECT	Modular	MOD	Ventilation	VENT
Cubic feet	CU FT	Molding	MLDG	Ventilator	V
Cubic yard	CU YD	National Electric Code	NEC	Vertical	VERT
Damper	DMPR	National Lumber Manufacturer's Association	NLMA	Wall cabinet	W CAB
Decorative	DEC			Wall vent	W V
Detail	DET	Nominal	NOM	Water	W
Diagram	DIA	North	N	Water closet	W C
Dimension	DIM	Number	NO	Water heater	W H
Dining room	DR	Office	OFF	Waterproof	WP
Dishwasher	D W	On center	OC	Weep hole	W H
Disk operating system	DOS	Opening	OPG	Wide flange	WF
Door	DR	Outside diameter	OD	Window	WDW
Double hung	D H	Painted	PTD	With	W/
Down	D N	Panel	PNL	Wood	WD
Downspout	DS	Parallel	PAR	Wrought iron	WI
Drain	D or DR	Partition	PTN	Zinc	Z or ZN
Drawing	DWG	Perpendicular	PERP		

TJI® joists are the essential ingredient to constructing today's highest quality floors and roofs with the greatest of ease. Lightweight, long lengths, and the unique I-configuration make for fast, efficient construction. Precision-engineered design is the key to stiff, silent floors.

Joists in lengths to 60′ speed installation by eliminating laps over beams or walls, and, since a TJI® joist is only about half the weight of an ordinary joist, a typical floor or roof can be put in place in a fraction of the time. The I-shape makes nailing to the plate much easier, too.

TJI® joists are available from Trus Joist stocking lumber dealers throughout the United States and Canada in four depths, 9½″, 11⅞″, 14″, and 16″.

9½″ TJI®/25 Joist   11⅞″ TJI®/25 Joist   14″ TJI®/35 Joist   16″ TJI®/35 Joist

CODE EVALUATIONS: FHA 689, NER 119.

NOTE: NER Evaluation includes BOCA, ICBO and SBCCI.

MICRO = LAM® L.V.L. HEADERS & BEAMS

High strength, consistent dimensions, and exceptional workability make MICRO=LAM® laminated veneer lumber (L.V.L.) the perfect material for almost every header and beam application in residential construction.

MICRO=LAM® L.V.L. is available in 1¾″ thicknesses and seven depths from 5½″ to 18″ and in lengths to 60′ from Trus Joist stocking dealers throughout the United States and Canada. Two or more pieces can be nailed or bolted together right on the job site to form a header or beam for almost any load condition found in residential construction. Two 1¾″ thick pieces match conventional 2x4 wall framing to eliminate shimming.

MICRO=LAM® L.V.L.'s unique manufacturing process eliminates many of the problems caused by twisting, shrinking, splitting, and checking, and thus reduces material waste.

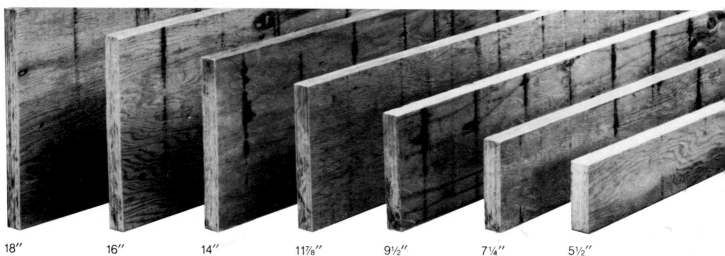

18″   16″   14″   11⅞″   9½″   7¼″   5½″

CODE EVALUATIONS: NER 119, NER 126, FHA 925.

NOTE: NER evaluation includes BOCA, ICBO, and SBCCI.

TYPICAL FLOOR FRAMING

FOR INSTALLATION STABILITY:
Temporary strut lines (1x4 min.) 8' on center max. Fasten at each joist with 2-8d nails min. ——

MICRO=LAM® L.V.L. header or TJI® joist header. ——

NOTE: Bridging is not required.

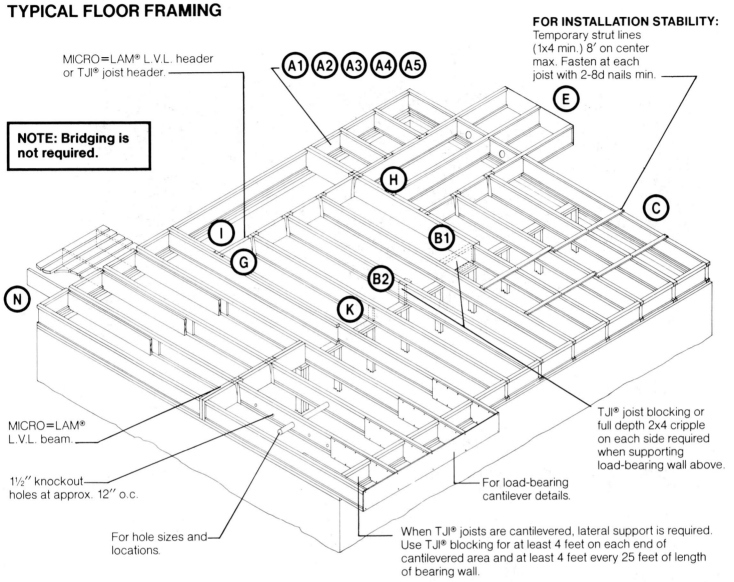

MICRO=LAM® L.V.L. beam. ——

1½'' knockout holes at approx. 12'' o.c.

For hole sizes and locations.

TJI® joist blocking or full depth 2x4 cripple on each side required when supporting load-bearing wall above.

For load-bearing cantilever details.

When TJI® joists are cantilevered, lateral support is required. Use TJI® blocking for at least 4 feet on each end of cantilevered area and at least 4 feet every 25 feet of length of bearing wall.

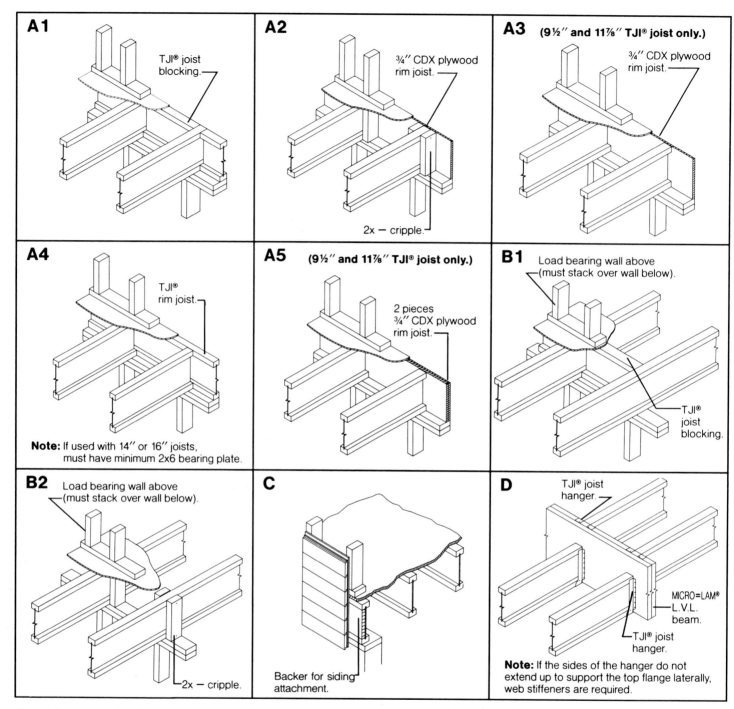

A1
TJI® joist blocking.

A2
¾″ CDX plywood rim joist.
2x — cripple.

A3 (9½″ and 11⅞″ TJI® joist only.)
¾″ CDX plywood rim joist.

A4
TJI® rim joist.
Note: If used with 14″ or 16″ joists, must have minimum 2x6 bearing plate.

A5 (9½″ and 11⅞″ TJI® joist only.)
2 pieces ¾″ CDX plywood rim joist.

B1
Load bearing wall above (must stack over wall below).
TJI® joist blocking.

B2
Load bearing wall above (must stack over wall below).
2x — cripple.

C
Backer for siding attachment.

D
TJI® joist hanger.
MICRO=LAM® L.V.L. beam.
TJI® joist hanger.
Note: If the sides of the hanger do not extend up to support the top flange laterally, web stiffeners are required.

GENERAL NOTES

MINIMUM BEARING LENGTH
1¾″ minimum bearing required at joist ends; 3½″ minimum bearing at intermediate supports.

RIM JOISTS OR BLOCKING
1. For single story applications and second floors of two story applications, use detail A1, A2, A3, A4, or A5.
2. For main floor rim of two story applications, use detail A1, A2, A4 or A5.
3. Assumes 1000 PLF vertical load transfer for each layer of ¾″ CDX plywood rim joist.
4. Assumes 2000 PLF vertical load transfer for each TJI® joist blocking panel or rim joist.
5. When plywood rim is used, bracing complying with code shall be carried to the foundation or TJI® joist solid blocking used for a minimum of 4′ at each end and at least 4′ every 25′ of length of bearing wall.
6. 2x — cripples for details A2 and B2 must be 1/16″ longer than depth of joist. Web stiffeners may also be required.
7. Other ¾″ APA 48/24 rated sheathing may be used for rim joist in lieu of ¾″ CDX plywood.

NAILING REQUIREMENTS
1. Nail joists at bearings with 2-8d nails (1 each side), 1½″ minimum from end to avoid splitting.
2. Nail TJI® joist blocking or rim to bearing plate with 8d nails at 6″ on center. When used for shear transfer, nail to bearing plate with same nailing as the plywood shear schedule.
3. Nail TJI® rim joist, ¾″ CDX plywood rim, or plywood closure to TJI® joist with 2-8d nails, one each at top and bottom flange. With 14″ and 16″ TJI® rim joists, use 16d nails.

FILLER AND BACKER BLOCKS
9½″ and 11⅞″ TJI® joist:
Filler block — 2x6
Backer block — ¾″ plywood
14″ and 16″ TJI® joist:
Filler block — 2x8 + ½″ plywood
Backer block — 2 pieces ½″ plywood

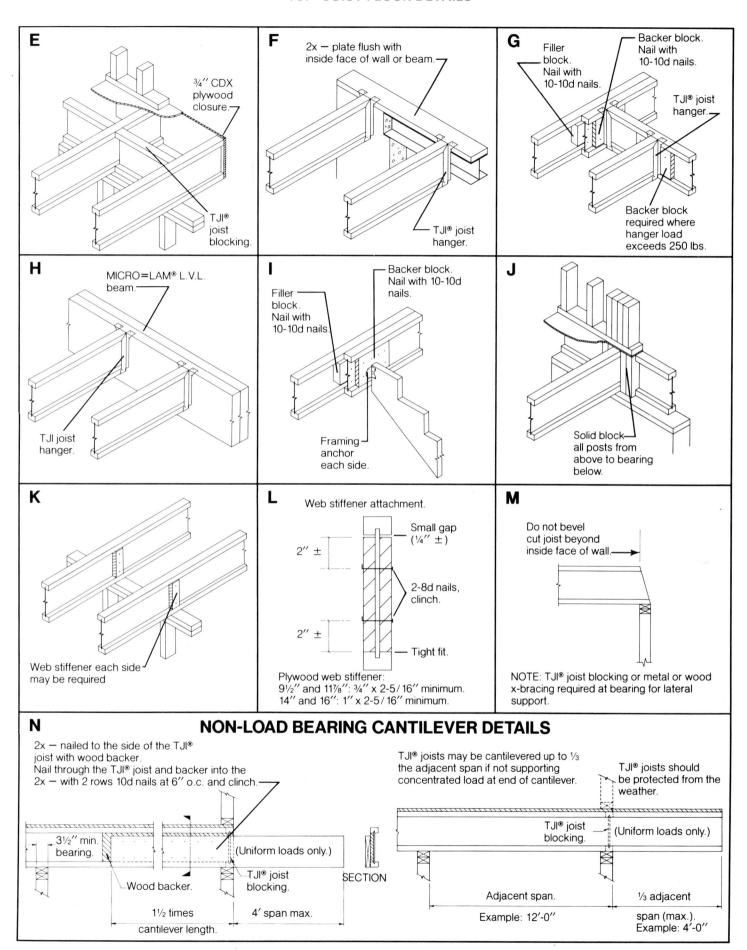

E

¾" CDX plywood closure.

TJI® joist blocking.

F

2x — plate flush with inside face of wall or beam.

TJI® joist hanger.

G

Filler block. Nail with 10-10d nails.

Backer block. Nail with 10-10d nails.

TJI® joist hanger.

Backer block required where hanger load exceeds 250 lbs.

H

MICRO=LAM® L.V.L. beam.

TJI joist hanger.

I

Filler block. Nail with 10-10d nails.

Backer block. Nail with 10-10d nails.

Framing anchor each side.

J

Solid block all posts from above to bearing below.

K

Web stiffener each side may be required

L

Web stiffener attachment.

Small gap (¼" ±)

2" ±

2-8d nails, clinch.

2" ±

Tight fit.

Plywood web stiffener:
9½" and 11⅞": ¾" x 2-5/16" minimum.
14" and 16": 1" x 2-5/16" minimum.

M

Do not bevel cut joist beyond inside face of wall.

NOTE: TJI® joist blocking or metal or wood x-bracing required at bearing for lateral support.

N NON-LOAD BEARING CANTILEVER DETAILS

2x — nailed to the side of the TJI® joist with wood backer. Nail through the TJI® joist and backer into the 2x — with 2 rows 10d nails at 6" o.c. and clinch.

3½" min. bearing.

(Uniform loads only.)

Wood backer.

TJI® joist blocking.

1½ times cantilever length.

4' span max.

SECTION

TJI® joists may be cantilevered up to ⅓ the adjacent span if not supporting concentrated load at end of cantilever.

TJI® joists should be protected from the weather.

TJI® joist blocking.

(Uniform loads only.)

Adjacent span.

Example: 12'-0"

⅓ adjacent span (max.). Example: 4'-0"

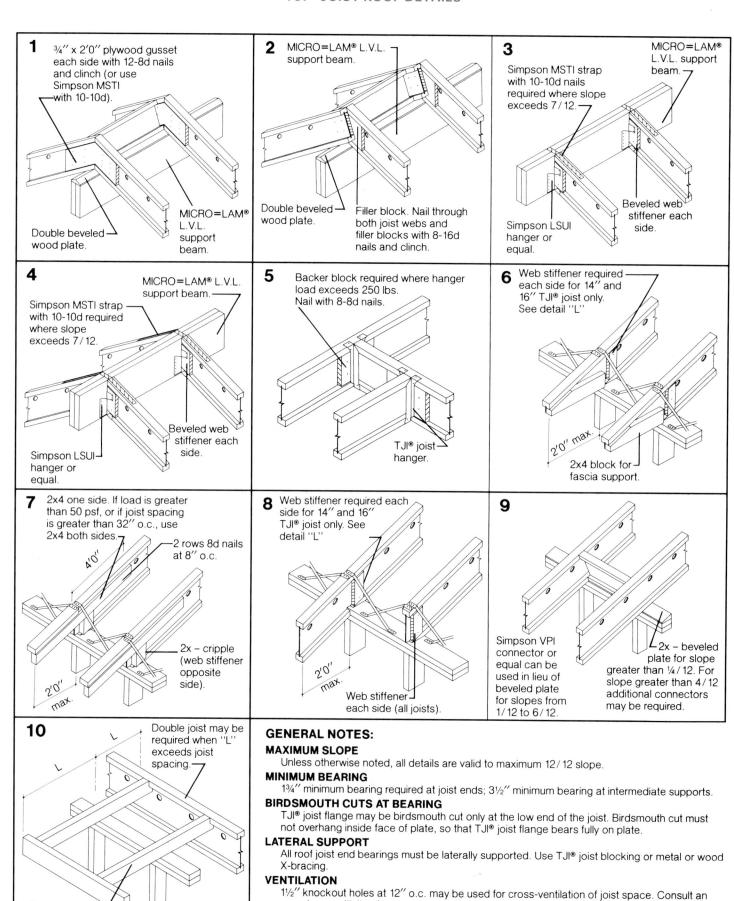

1 ¾'' x 2'0'' plywood gusset each side with 12-8d nails and clinch (or use Simpson MSTI with 10-10d).

MICRO=LAM® L.V.L. support beam.

Double beveled wood plate.

2 MICRO=LAM® L.V.L. support beam.

Double beveled wood plate.

Filler block. Nail through both joist webs and filler blocks with 8-16d nails and clinch.

3 MICRO=LAM® L.V.L. support beam.

Simpson MSTI strap with 10-10d nails required where slope exceeds 7/12.

Simpson LSUI hanger or equal.

Beveled web stiffener each side.

4 MICRO=LAM® L.V.L. support beam.

Simpson MSTI strap with 10-10d required where slope exceeds 7/12.

Simpson LSUI hanger or equal.

Beveled web stiffener each side.

5 Backer block required where hanger load exceeds 250 lbs. Nail with 8-8d nails.

TJI® joist hanger.

6 Web stiffener required each side for 14'' and 16'' TJI® joist only. See detail ''L''

2'0'' max.

2x4 block for fascia support.

7 2x4 one side. If load is greater than 50 psf, or if joist spacing is greater than 32'' o.c., use 2x4 both sides.

4'0''

2 rows 8d nails at 8'' o.c.

2x – cripple (web stiffener opposite side).

2'0'' max.

8 Web stiffener required each side for 14'' and 16'' TJI® joist only. See detail ''L''

2'0'' max.

Web stiffener each side (all joists).

9 Simpson VPI connector or equal can be used in lieu of beveled plate for slopes from 1/12 to 6/12.

2x – beveled plate for slope greater than ¼/12. For slope greater than 4/12 additional connectors may be required.

10 Double joist may be required when ''L'' exceeds joist spacing.

L L L

2x – outrigger. Notch around flange.

End wall.

GENERAL NOTES:

MAXIMUM SLOPE
Unless otherwise noted, all details are valid to maximum 12/12 slope.

MINIMUM BEARING
1¾'' minimum bearing required at joist ends; 3½'' minimum bearing at intermediate supports.

BIRDSMOUTH CUTS AT BEARING
TJI® joist flange may be birdsmouth cut only at the low end of the joist. Birdsmouth cut must not overhang inside face of plate, so that TJI® joist flange bears fully on plate.

LATERAL SUPPORT
All roof joist end bearings must be laterally supported. Use TJI® joist blocking or metal or wood X-bracing.

VENTILATION
1½'' knockout holes at 12'' o.c. may be used for cross-ventilation of joist space. Consult an expert on ventilation for specific requirements.

TJI® JOIST ROOF SPAN CHART

Low slope (6/12 or less) and high slope (over 6/12 through 12/12)
Max. clear span in feet and inches (based on horizontal spans)

JOIST SPACING		LIVE LOAD / DEAD LOAD P.S.F.	9½" TJI®/25 LOW SLOPE	9½" TJI®/25 HIGH SLOPE	11⅞" TJI®/25 LOW SLOPE	11⅞" TJI®/25 HIGH SLOPE	14" TJI®/35 LOW SLOPE	14" TJI®/35 HIGH SLOPE	16" TJI®/35 LOW SLOPE	16" TJI®/35 HIGH SLOPE
12" o.c.	Non-Snow (125%)	20/10	23'-10"	21'-5"	28'-4"	25'-6"	35'-3"	31'-9"	39'-1"	35'-2"
		20/15	22'-6"	20'-1"	26'-9"	23'-11"	33'-4"	29'-9"	36'-11"	33'-0"
		20/20	21'-5"	19'-0"	25'-6"	22'-7"	31'-9"	28'-2"	35'-2"	31'-3"
	Snow (115%)	25/10	22'-7"	20'-5"	26'-11"	24'-4"	33'-6"	30'-4"	37'-1"	33'-7"
		25/15	21'-6"	19'-3"	25'-7"	23'-0"	31'-11"	28'-7"	35'-4"	31'-8"
		30/10	21'-7"	19'-7"	25'-9"	23'-4"	32'-0"	29'-1"	35'-6"	32'-2"
		30/15	20'-8"	18'-7"	24'-7"	22'-2"	30'-8"	27'-7"	33'-11"	30'-7"
		40/10	19'-9"	18'-3"	23'-6"	21'-9"	29'-3"	27'-1"	32'-5"	30'-0"
		40/15	19'-4"	17'-6"	23'-0"	20'-10"	28'-8"	25'-11"	31'-9"	28'-9"
		50/10	18'-3"	17'-0"	21'-9"	20'-3"	27'-1"	25'-2"	30'-0"	27'-11"
		50/15	18'-3"	16'-7"	21'-9"	19'-9"	27'-1"	24'-7"	30'-0"	27'-3"
16" o.c.	Non-Snow (125%)	20/10	21'-6"	19'-5"	25'-8"	23'-1"	31'-11"	28'-9"	35'-4"	31'-10"
		20/15	20'-4"	18'-2"	24'-3"	21'-8"	30'-2"	26'-11"	33'-5"	29'-10"
		20/20	19'-4"	17'-2"	23'-0"	20'-6"	28'-8"	25'-6"	31'-9"	28'-3"
	Snow (115%)	25/10	20'-5"	18'-6"	24'-4"	22'-0"	30'-4"	27'-5"	33'-7"	30'-5"
		25/15	19'-5"	17'-5"	23'-2"	20'-9"	28'-10"	25'-11"	31'-11"	28'-8"
		30/10	19'-6"	17'-9"	23'-3"	21'-1"	29'-0"	26'-4"	32'-1"	29'-2"
		30/15	18'-8"	16'-10"	22'-3"	20'-1"	27'-8"	25'-0"	30'-8"	27'-8"
		40/10	17'-10"	16'-6"	21'-3"	19'-8"	26'-5"	24'-6"	29'-4"	27'-2"
		40/15	17'-5"	15'-10"	20'-9"	18'-10"	25'-10"	23'-6"	28'-8"	26'-0"
		50/10	16'-6"	15'-4"	19'-7"	18'-3"	24'-5"	22'-9"	26'-9"	25'-3"
		50/15	16'-5"	15'-0"	19'-6"	17'-10"	24'-5"	22'-3"	24'-8"	23'-3"
19.2" o.c.	Non-Snow (125%)	20/10	20'-2"	18'-2"	24'-1"	21'-8"	30'-0"	27'-0"	33'-2"	29'-11"
		20/15	19'-1"	17'-1"	22'-9"	20'-4"	28'-3"	25'-3"	31'-4"	28'-0"
		20/20	18'-2"	16'-2"	21'-7"	19'-3"	26'-11"	23'-11"	29'-10"	26'-6"
	Snow (115%)	25/10	19'-2"	17'-4"	22'-10"	20'-8"	28'-5"	25'-9"	31'-6"	28'-6"
		25/15	18'-3"	16'-5"	21'-9"	19'-6"	27'-0"	24'-4"	29'-11"	26'-11"
		30/10	18'-4"	16'-8"	21'-10"	19'-10"	27'-2"	24'-8"	30'-1"	27'-4"
		30/15	17'-6"	15'-10"	20'-10"	18'-10"	26'-0"	23'-5"	28'-9"	26'-0"
		40/10	16'-8"	15'-6"	19'-11"	18'-5"	24'-9"	23'-0"	26'-8"	25'-4"
		40/15	16'-4"	14'-10"	19'-2"	17'-8"	24'-0"	22'-0"	24'-3"	22'-8"
		50/10	15'-5"	14'-5"	17'-10"	17'-1"	22'-5"	21'-4"	22'-8"	21'-8"
		50/15	15'-0"	14'-1"	16'-6"	15'-7"	20'-8"	19'-6"	20'-11"	19'-9"
24" o.c.	Non-Snow (125%)	20/10	18'-8"	16'-10"	22'-3"	20'-1"	27'-8"	25'-0"	30'-8"	27'-8"
		20/15	17'-7"	15'-9"	21'-0"	18'-9"	26'-2"	23'-5"	29'-0"	25'-11"
		20/20	16'-9"	14'-11"	20'-0"	17'-9"	24'-10"	22'-1"	27'-6"	24'-6"
	Snow (115%)	25/10	17'-9"	16'-1"	21'-1"	19'-1"	26'-3"	23'-10"	29'-2"	26'-5"
		25/15	16'-10"	15'-2"	20'-1"	18'-0"	25'-0"	22'-6"	26'-2"	23'-10"
		30/10	16'-11"	15'-5"	20'-2"	18'-4"	25'-1"	22'-10"	26'-6"	24'-11"
		30/15	16'-2"	14'-7"	18'-8"	17'-2"	23'-4"	21'-6"	23'-7"	21'-9"
		40/10	15'-5"	14'-4"	17'-2"	16'-3"	21'-6"	20'-5"	21'-9"	20'-8"
		40/15	14'-2"	13'-2"	15'-7"	14'-7"	19'-6"	18'-3"	19'-10"	18'-6"
		50/10	13'-2"	12'-8"	14'-7"	14'-0"	18'-3"	17'-6"	18'-6"	17'-9"
		50/15	12'-2"	11'-6"	13'-6"	12'-9"	16'-10"	15'-11"	17'-1"	16'-2"

1. Roof joists to be sloped ¼" in 12" minimum. No camber provided.
2. Maximum deflection is limited to L/180 at total load, L/240 at live load.

3. Tables are based on a support beam or wall at the high end. Applications utilizing ridge boards are not covered by these tables.

DEPTH (INCHES)	WEIGHT (PLF)[1]	EI* 10⁶IN²LBS.	MAXIMUM VERTICAL SHEAR (LBS.)			MAXIMUM RESISTIVE MOMENT (FT.-LBS.)		
			100%	115%	125%	100%	115%	125%
9½″ TJI/25 Joist	1.9	170	805	925	1006	2940	3380	3675
11⅞″ TJI/25 Joist	2.2	285	875	1006	1094	3935	4525	4920
14″ TJI/35 Joist	2.8	550	1100	1265	1375	6450	7420	8060
16″ TJI/35 Joist	3	745	1100	1265	1375	7570	8705	9460

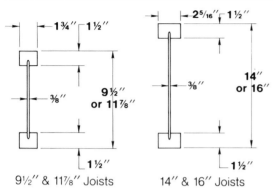

9½″ & 11⅞″ Joists   14″ & 16″ Joists

*The following formula approximates the uniform load deflection of Δ (inches)

$$\Delta = \frac{5w\ell^4}{384\,EI} + \frac{w\ell^2}{2.7d \times 10^5}$$

w = uniform load in pounds per lineal inch
ℓ = clear span in inches
d = out to out depth of the joist
EI = value from table

NOTE: The shear values above are based on an assumed minimum bearing length of 1¾″.

[1] Weights shown are for Douglas Fir MICRO = LAM® L.V.L. flanges. For Southern Yellow Pine MICRO = LAM® L.V.L. flanges, increase weight approximately 20%.

RESIDENTIAL FLOOR SPAN CHARTS

MINIMUM CRITERIA PER CODE

o.c. spacing	JOIST DEPTH			
	9½″	11⅞″	14″	16″
12″	18′-7″		27′-3″	30′-1″
16″	16′-10″	20′-2″	24′-8″	27′-4″
19.2″	15′-11″	18′-11″	23′-2″	25′-8″
24″	14′-9″	17′-6″	20′-3″	21′-10″

(watermark overlaid: CODE ALLOWED MINIMUM)

NOTE: Based on minimum code deflection criteria of L/360 at live load. For stiffer floors, please see "Trus Joist Recommended Span" table. See "A Word About Floor Performance" below.

GENERAL NOTES:
1. Based on residential floor load of 40 PSF live load and 10 PSF dead load.
2. Assumes composite action with single layer of glue-nailed plywood decking for deflection only. **Spans shall be reduced 5″ where sheathing panels are nailed only.**
3. Spans are based on clear distance between supports.

TRUS JOIST RECOMMENDED SPANS

o.c. spacing	JOIST DEPTH			
	9½″	11⅞″	14″	16″
12″	16′-10″	20′-0″	24′-6″	27′-1″
16″	15′-4″	18′-2″	22′-3″	24′-8″
19.2″	14′-5″	17′-1″	20′-11″	23′-2″
24″	13′-4″	15′-10″	19′-4″	21′-5″

NOTE: Based on L/480 live load deflection.

4. Web stiffeners (see detail "K") are required at intermediate supports where joists are continuous span, bearing width is less than 5¼″ and either span is greater than:
   - 13′-8″: for 9½″ and 11⅞″ TJI® joists @ 24″ o.c.
   - 17′-2″: for 11⅞″ TJI® joists @ 19.2″ o.c.
   - 19′-2″: for 14″ and 16″ TJI® joists @ 24″ o.c.
   - 24′-0″: for 16″ TJI® joists @ 19.2″ o.c.

A WORD ABOUT FLOOR PERFORMANCE

The spans indicated in the "Minimum Criteria Per Code" chart above meet or exceed all code requirements and may provide acceptable performance to the user. But, in addition to safely supporting the loads to be imposed on it, a floor system must perform to the satisfaction of the end user. Since expectancy levels may vary from one user to another, designing a floor system becomes a subjective issue requiring judgement as to the sensitivity of the occupant.

The second span chart above entitled "Trus Joist Recommended Spans" has been developed as a guide to help builders construct higher quality floors. Spans in the "Trus Joist Recommended Spans" chart were developed using stricter deflection limits (see note under chart) to limit deflection over longer spans.

In addition to joist deflection, several other factors may affect the performance of the floor system. A glue-nailed

floor system will perform better than a nailed floor. Deflection of the sheathing material between the joists can be reduced by increasing the thickness of sheathing or decreasing the spacing of the joist. Proper installation, including adequate and level support for the joists, and care in fastening of the joists and sheathing are essential to the system performance.

In some cases where the system is stiff and very little dead load (i.e. partition walls, ceilings, furniture, etc.) exists, vibrations may occur. Vibrations are generally sufficiently dampened when a ceiling is directly attached to the bottom flange of the joists. When the joists occur in a crawl space or over an unfinished basement, the vibration can be minimized by nailing a continuous 2x4 (flat) perpendicular to the joists' bottom flanges at midspan and tying off to the end walls.

BEARING @ EXTERIOR WALL

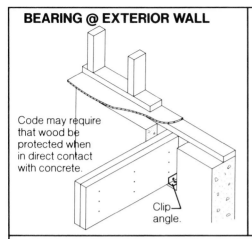

Code may require that wood be protected when in direct contact with concrete.

Clip angle.

BEARING FOR DOOR OR WINDOW HEADER

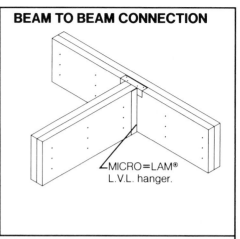

Trimmers. See table below for minimum bearing length.

BEAM TO BEAM CONNECTION

MICRO=LAM® L.V.L. hanger.

NOTE: BEARING LENGTH IS EXTREMELY CRITICAL AND MUST BE CONSIDERED FOR EACH APPLICATION.

BEARING @ WOOD COLUMN

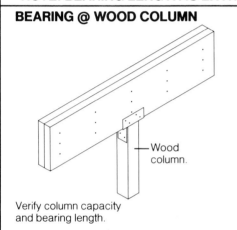

Wood column.

Verify column capacity and bearing length.

BEARING @ STEEL COLUMN

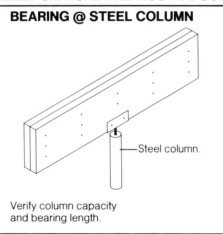

Steel column.

Verify column capacity and bearing length.

NAILING PATTERN FOR MULTIPLE PIECES

For Top Loaded Beams
Minimum of 2 rows 16d nails @ 12″ o.c.

3 rows of 16d nails @ 12″ o.c. for 14″, 16″, and 18″ beams.

NOTE: For side loaded multiple member beams, additional nailing or bolting may be required.

BEARING LENGTH REQUIREMENTS

MINIMUM BEARING LENGTH IN INCHES									
	ONE PIECE BEAM			TWO PIECE BEAM			THREE PIECE BEAM		
REACTION (POUNDS × 1,000)	100%	115%	125%	100%	115%	125%	100%	115%	125%
1	1.5″	1.5″	1.5″	1.5″	1.5″	1.5″	1.5″	1.5″	1.5″
2	3″	2.5″	2.5″	1.5″	1.5″	1.5″	1.5″	1.5″	1.5″
3	4″	3.5″	3″	2″	1.5″	1.5″	1.5″	1.5″	1.5″
4	5″	4.5″	4″	3″	2.5″	2.5″	2″	1.5″	1.5″
5	6″	5.5″	5″	3.5″	3″	3″	2.5″	2″	2″
6	7.5″	6.5″	6″	4″	3.5″	3″	3″	2.5″	2.5″
7	8.5″	7.5″	7″	4.5″	4″	3.5″	3″	3″	2.5″
8	9.5″	8.5″	8″	5″	4.5″	4″	3.5″	3″	3″
9				5.5″	5″	4.5″	4″	3.5″	3″
10				6″	5.5″	5″	4.5″	4″	3.5″
11				6.5″	6″	5.5″	4.5″	4″	4″
12				7.5″	6.5″	6″	5″	4.5″	4″
13				8″	7″	6.5″	5.5″	5″	4.5″
14				8.5″	7.5″	7″	6″	5″	5″
15				9″	8″	7.5″	6″	5.5″	5″
16				9.5″	8.5″	8″	6.5″	6″	5.5″
17							7″	6″	5.5″
18							7.5″	6.5″	6″
19							7.5″	7″	6.5″
20							8″	7″	6.5″
21							8.5″	7.5″	7″
22							9″	8″	7″

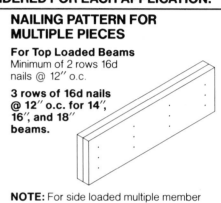

DO NOT CUT OR NOTCH

NO DRILLING UNLESS APPROVED BY TRUS JOIST CORPORATION.

NOTES

1. A minimum of 1.5″ of bearing length is required.
2. Bearing across full width of beam is assumed.
3. Assumes structural adequacy of supporting member.
4. Assumes 500 psi bearing stress on beam. May be further limited by bearing stress on supported member.
5. **16″ and 18″ deep beams are to be used in multiple member units only.**
6. Lateral support required at bearing points.
7. Nails installed on the narrow face (top edge) shall not be spaced any closer than 4″ for 10d common and 3″ for 8d common.

Reference manufacturer's current literature for additional sizing and installation information.
Copyright TJ International, Inc. Reprinted by permission of Trus Joist Corporation, a division of TJ International.

ALLOWABLE LOAD LBS./LIN. FT. (PLF)

Total load column limits deflection to L/180. For stiffer criteria, check L/240 column.
CHECK LOCAL CODE FOR DEFLECTION CRITERIA.

SPAN (ft.)	One-1¾"x5½" Snow (115%)	One-1¾"x5½" Non-Snow (125%)	One-1¾"x5½" DEFL. L/240	One-1¾"x7¼" Snow (115%)	One-1¾"x7¼" Non-Snow (125%)	One-1¾"x7¼" DEFL. L/240	One-1¾"x9½" Snow (115%)	One-1¾"x9½" Non-Snow (125%)	One-1¾"x9½" DEFL. L/240	One-1¾"x11⅞" Snow (115%)	One-1¾"x11⅞" Non-Snow (125%)	One-1¾"x11⅞" DEFL. L/240
4	1348	1465	1402	1986	2159		3006	3268		4494	4885	
5	863	938	764	1432	1556		2126	2311		3006	3268	
6	599	611	458	994	1081	989	1632	1774		2259	2455	
7	393	393	295	730	794	646	1199	1303		1805	1962	
8	267	267	201	559	591	444	918	998	943	1382	1502	
9	190	190	142	423	423	317	725	788	681	1092	1187	
10	139	139	104	312	312	234	587	639	507	884	961	943
11	105	105	79	236	236	177	486	516	387	731	795	725
12	81	81	61	183	183	138	402	402	301	614	668	569
13	64	64	48	145	145	109	319	319	239	523	569	454
14	52	52	39	117	117	88	257	257	193	451	490	367
15	42	42	31	95	95	71	211	211	158	393	402	301
16				79	79	59	174	174	131	334	334	250
17				66	66	49	146	146	109	280	280	210
18				56	56	42	123	123	93	237	237	178
19				47	47	35	105	105	79	203	203	152
20				41	41	30	90	90	68	174	174	131
21							78	78	59	151	151	113
22							68	68	51	132	132	99
23							60	60	45	116	116	87
24							53	53	40	102	102	77
25							47	47	35	90	90	68
26							42	42	31	81	81	60
27										72	72	54
28										65	65	49
29										58	58	44
30										53	53	40

MICRO=LAM® L.V.L. DESIGN PROPERTIES

SIZE	Maximum Vertical Shear (lbs.) 100%	115%	125%	Maximum Resistive Moment (ft.-lbs.) 100%	115%	125%	Moment of Inertia (in.⁴)	Weight (lbs./ft.) [1]
1¾"x5½"	1830	2105	2285	2345	2695	2930	25	2.50
1¾"x7¼"	2410	2770	3010	3890	4475	4860	55	3.25
1¾"x9½"	3160	3630	3950	6385	7345	7980	125	4.25
1¾"x11⅞"	3950	4540	4940	9615	11055	12015	245	5.30
1¾"x14"	4655	5355	5820	13000	14950	16250	400	6.25
1¾"x16"	5320	6120	6650	16605	19100	20760	595	7.15
1¾"x18"	5985	6880	7480	20610	23700	25760	850	8.00

ALLOWABLE DESIGN STRESSES

Modulus of elasticity	E	$= 2.0 \times 10^6$ psi
Flexural stress	F_b^*	$= 2800$ psi
Tension parallel to grain	F_t	$= 1850$ psi
Compression perpendicular to grain parallel to glue line	F_c	$= 500$ psi
Compression parallel to grain	$F_{c\parallel}$	$= 2700$ psi
Horizontal shear perpendicular to glue line	F_v	$= 285$ psi

*For 12-inch depth. For other depths, multiply by $\left[\frac{12}{d}\right]^{\frac{1}{6}}$

*See NER 126 for additional design information.

*Assumes continuous lateral support of top of beam (simple span applications).

[1] Weights shown are for Douglas Fir MICRO = LAM® L.V.L. For Southern Yellow Pine MICRO = LAM® L.V.L., increase weight approximately 10%.

Reference manufacturer's current literature for additional sizing and installation information.
Copyright TJ International, Inc. Reprinted by permission of Trus Joist Corporation, a division of TJ International.

MICRO = LAM® L.V.L. ALLOWABLE LOAD (ROOF)

One-1¾"x14"			One-1¾"x16"*			One-1¾"x18"*			
TOTAL LOAD		DEFL.	TOTAL LOAD		DEFL.	TOTAL LOAD		DEFL.	
Snow (115%)	Non-Snow (125%)	L/240	Snow (115%)	Non-Snow (125%)	L/240	Snow (115%)	Non-Snow (125%)	L/240	SPAN (ft.)
6424	6983		9177	9975					4
4015	4364		5244	5700		6883	7481		5
2920	3174		3671	3990		4588	4988		6
2294	2494		2824	3069		3441	3741		7
1869	2031		2294	2494		2753	2993		8
1477	1605		1886	2050		2294	2494		9
1196	1300		1528	1661		1896	2061		10
988	1074		1263	1372		1567	1703		11
831	903	899	1061	1153		1317	1431		12
708	769	720	904	983		1122	1219		13
610	663	586	779	847		967	1051		14
532	578	482	679	738	701	843	916		15
467	508	401	597	649	586	741	805		16
414	450	338	529	575	494	656	713	687	17
369	382	286	472	513	420	585	636	586	18
327	327	245	423	460	360	525	571	503	19
282	282	211	382	414	311	474	515	435	20
244	244	183	346	360	270	430	467	379	21
213	213	160	315	315	236	392	426	331	22
187	187	141	277	277	207	358	389	292	23
166	166	124	244	244	183	329	344	258	24
147	147	110	217	217	163	303	306	229	25
131	131	98	194	194	145	273	273	205	26
117	117	88	173	173	130	244	244	183	27
105	105	79	156	156	117	220	220	165	28
95	95	71	141	141	105	198	198	149	29
86	86	64	127	127	95	180	180	135	30

NOTES
- This table is based on uniform loads and simple spans.
- Table is for one beam. When properly fastened together, double the values for two beams, triple for three. When top loaded, fasten together with a minimum of two rows of 16d nails at 12" o.c. **Use three rows of 16d nails at 12" o.c. for 14", 16" and 18" beams.**

- MICRO-LAM® lumber beams are made without camber; therefore, in addition to complying with the deflection limits of the applicable Building Code, other deflection considerations

should be evaluated such as ponding (positive drainage is essential) and aesthetics.
- Roof members should either be sloped for drainage or designed to account for load and deflection as specified in the applicable Building Code.
- Assumes continuous lateral support of the top edge of beam.
- Lateral support required at bearing points.
- Bearing area to be calculated for specific application.

*16" and 18" deep beams are to be used in multiple member units only.

Reference manufacturer's current literature for additional sizing and installation information.
Copyright TJ International, Inc. Reprinted by permission of Trus Joist Corporation, a division of TJ International.

ALLOWABLE LOAD LBS./LIN. FOOT (PLF)

SPAN (ft.)	One-1¾"x5½" LIVE LOAD	One-1¾"x5½" TOTAL LOAD	One-1¾"x7¼" LIVE LOAD	One-1¾"x7¼" TOTAL LOAD	One-1¾"x9½" LIVE LOAD	One-1¾"x9½" TOTAL LOAD	One-1¾"x11⅞" LIVE LOAD	One-1¾"x11⅞" TOTAL LOAD	One-1¾"x14" LIVE LOAD	One-1¾"x14" TOTAL LOAD	One-1¾"x16"* LIVE LOAD	One-1¾"x16"* TOTAL LOAD	One-1¾"x18"* LIVE LOAD	One-1¾"x18"* TOTAL LOAD
6	305	458	660	865	1353	1419		1964		2539		3192		3990
7	197	295	431	635	903	1043		1570		1995		2455		2993
8	134	201	296	444	629	798	1144	1202		1625		1995		2394
9	95	142	211	317	454	631	837	949		1284		1640		1995
10	70	104	156	234	338	507	629	769	981	1040		1329		1649
11	53	79	118	177	258	387	484	636	760	860	1085	1098		1363
12	41	61	92	138	201	301	379	534	599	722	861	923		1145
13			73	109	160	239	302	454	480	615	694	786	952	976
14			58	88	129	193	245	367	390	531	566	678	781	841
15			48	71	105	158	201	301	321	462	468	590	647	733
16			39	59	87	131	167	250	268	401	390	519	542	644
17					73	109	140	210	225	338	329	460	458	570
18					62	93	119	178	191	286	280	410	390	509
19					53	79	101	152	163	245	240	360	335	457
20					45	68	87	131	141	211	207	311	290	412
21					39	59	76	113	122	183	180	270	252	374
22									107	160	157	236	221	331
23									94	141	138	207	194	292
24									83	124	122	183	172	258
25											109	163	153	229
26											97	145	136	205

1. To size a beam for use in a floor it is necessary to check both live load and total load. Make sure the selected beam will work in both columns.

2. Live load column is based on deflection of L/360. Check local code for other deflection criteria.

3. Total load column limits deflection to L/240.

4. For deflection limits of L/240 and L/480 multiply loads shown in L/360 column by 1.5 and 0.75 respectively.

NOTES
- This table is based on uniform loads and simple spans.
- Table is for one beam. When properly fastened together, double the values for two beams, triple for three, etc. When top loaded, fasten together with a minimum of two rows of 16d nails at 12" o.c. **Use three rows of 16d nails at 12" o.c. for 14", 16" and 18" beams.**
- MICRO=LAM® L.V.L. beams are made without camber and will deflect under load.
- Assumes continuous lateral support of the top edge of beam.
- Lateral support required at bearing points.
- Bearing area to be calculated for specific application.

*16" and 18" deep beams are to be used in multiple member units only.

SIDE LOADED MICRO=LAM® L.V.L. CONNECTION FOR MULTIPLE MEMBER UNITS

No. of pieces	MAXIMUM UNIFORM LOAD APPLIED TO OUTSIDE MEMBER (lbs. per lin. foot)				
	NAILED CONNECTION(1)		THROUGH BOLTED CONNECTION(2)		
	2 rows 16d common wire at 12" o.c.	3 rows 16d common wire at 12" o.c.	2 rows ½" bolts at 24" o.c. staggered	2 rows ½" bolts at 12" o.c.	2 rows ½" bolts at 6" o.c.
2	420	630	580	1160	2320
3	320	480	440	880	1760
4	NOT RECOMMENDED		Should only be used when loads are applied to both sides of the members.		
			390	780	1560

NOTES
- Verify adequacy of beam in Table 6 or Table 8.
- Values listed are for 100% stress level. Increase 15% for snow loaded roof conditions; increase 25% for non-snow roof conditions.
- Other connections are possible with specific design by the design professional.

(1) For a three-piece member, the nailing specified is from each side for a total of 6 nails/foot (3 from each side).

(2) Bolt holes are to be the same diameter as the bolt and located 2" from the top and bottom of the member.

Glossary

A

ACRE: A plot of land comprising a total area of 43,560 sq. ft.

ADHESIVE: A natural or synthetic material, generally in paste or liquid form, used to fasten or glue boards together, lay floor tile, fabricate plastic laminates, etc.

AIR-DRIED LUMBER: Lumber that has been piled in yards or sheds for a length of time. The minimum moisture content of thoroughly air-dried lumber is usually 12 to 15 percent.

ALCOVE: A recessed opening off a wall of a larger room. Often used as a sitting area, coat room, or storage area.

ALPHANUMERIC: Letters, numbers, punctuation marks, and symbols used to represent information or data.

ANCHOR: Any fastener (usually metal) used to attach parts, such as joists, trusses, posts, etc., to masonry or masonry materials.

ANCHOR BOLT: A threaded rod inserted in masonry construction to anchor the sill plate to the foundation.

ANSI: American National Standards Institute.

APRON: Trim used under the stool on interior windows.

ARCADE: A series of arches supported by columns or piers to provide an open passageway.

ARCH: A curved structure that will support itself and the weight above its curved opening by mutual pressure.

AREAWAY: Below-grade recessed area around the foundation to allow light and ventilation into basement window.

AROMATIC RED CEDAR: Similar characteristics to (Western) red cedar. Primarily used in construction for chests and closet linings for its moth-proof value.

ARRIS: A sharp edge formed when two planes or surfaces meet. Found on edges of moldings, doors, shelves, and in cabinet construction.

ASCII: American Standard Code for Information Interchange. An industry standard used in transmitting information between computers, printers, and peripheral devices.

ASH PIT: The area below the hearth of a fireplace, which collects the ashes.

ASPHALT SHINGLES: Composition roof shingles made from asphalt-impregnated felt covered with mineral granules.

ASSESSMENT: The levy of a tax or charge on property, usually according to established rates.

ASSESSOR: A public official responsible for the evaluation of property for the purposes of taxation.

ASSIGNEE: A person to whom a transfer of interest is made in connection with a mortgage or contract for a home or piece of property.

ASSIGNOR: A person who makes an assignment for a mortgage or contract for a home or piece of property.

ASTM: American Society of Testing and Materials.

ATRIUM: A central hall or open court within a structure.

ATTACHMENT: The legal seizure of property to require payment of a debt.

ATTIC: The space between the roof and the ceiling.

ATTIC VENTILATORS: In houses, screened openings provided to ventilate an attic space. They are located in the soffit area as inlet ventilators and in the gable end or along the ridge as outlet ventilators. They can also consist of power-driven fans used as an exhaust system. See LOUVER.

ATTRIBUTE: The line or color characteristics assigned to an entity or group of entities.

AWNING WINDOW: An outswinging window hinged at the top.

B

BACKFILL: The replacement of excavated earth into a trench around and against a basement foundation.

BACKUP: A copy of data or programs that is saved in case the original is damaged or destroyed. Floppy disks are generally used to save backup copies.

BALCONY: A deck projecting from the wall of a building above ground level.

BALUSTERS: Usually small vertical members in a railing used between a top rail and the stair treads or a bottom rail.

BALUSTRADE: A series of balusters connected by a rail; generally used for porches and balconies.

BANISTER: A handrail with supporting posts used alongside a stairway.

BASEBOARD: The finish board covering the interior wall where the wall and floor meet.

BASE SHOE: A molding used next to the floor in interior baseboards.

BATT: A roll or sheet of insulation designed to be installed between members of frame construction.

BATTEN: Narrow strips of wood used to cover joints or as decorative vertical members over plywood or wide boards.

BATTER BOARD: One of a pair of horizontal boards nailed to posts set at the corners of an excavation, used to indicate the desired level, also used for fastening stretched strings to indicate outlines of foundation walls.

BAY WINDOW: Any window space projecting outward from the walls of a building, either square or polygonal in plan.

BEAM: A structural member transversely supporting a load.

BEAM CEILING: A ceiling in which the ceiling beams are exposed to view.

BEARING PARTITION: A partition that supports any vertical load in addition to its own weight.

BEARING WALL: A wall that supports any vertical load in addition to its own weight.

BEECH: A whitish- to reddish-brown hardwood used especially in construction for interior and exterior cabinet parts. Blends well with birch for stained kitchen cabinets and vanities.

BENCH MARK: A mark on some permanent object fixed to the ground from which land measurement and elevations are taken.

BIRCH: Hard and heavy light reddish-brown hardwood. The most widely used hardwood veneer for flush doors, cabinetwork, and paneling. Mill products include interior trim, flooring, sash, and trim.

BIT: A binary digit. The smallest unit of information used by a computer, expressed by a 0 or a 1.

BLIND NAILING: A method of nailing so that the nail is not visible.

BOARD, ELECTRICAL: A printed circuit assembly that is mounted onto the chassis of the computer or other electronic device.

BOARD FOOT: A method of lumber measurement using nominal dimensions of 1'' thick, 12'' wide, and 12'' long, or the equivalent.

BOOT: The process of loading or transferring the operating system from disk into the computer's memory. Also referred to as booting up.

BRICK: A solid masonry unit composed of clay or shale. Formed into a rectangular prism while soft and burned or fired in a kiln.

BRICK VENEER: A facing of brick laid against and fastened to sheathing of a frame wall or tile wall construction.

BRIDGING: Small wood or metal members that are inserted in a diagonal position between the floor joists at midspan to act both as tension and compression members for the purpose of bracing the joists and spreading the action of loads.

BTU (British Thermal Unit): The amount of heat required to raise one pound of water one degree Fahrenheit (F).

BUFFER: An auxiliary storage area for data. Many peripherals have buffers used to temporarily store data.

BUG: The cause of a computer malfunction. The term ''bug'' refers to hardware faults as well as to errors in software and programs which prevent them from executing properly.

BUILT-UP ROOF: A roofing composed of three to five layers of asphalt felt laminated with coal tar, pitch, or asphalt. The top is finished with crushed slag or gravel. Generally used on flat or low-pitched roofs.

BUREAU OF LAND MANAGEMENT: The branch of government in charge of surveying public lands.

BYTE: A group of eight consecutive bits. A computer uses bytes for addresses, instructions, and data words.

C

CALL UP: The process of entering a command or series of commands that cause the CPU to start a particular program and make it ready for your use.

CARD: A printed circuit assembly that plugs into a printed circuit board.

CARPORT: A garage not fully enclosed.

CARTESIAN COORDINATES: X,Y,Z absolute coordinates used to locate position in space.

CASEMENT WINDOW: A hinged window, usually metal, that opens out.

CASING: Molding of various widths and thicknesses used to trim door and window openings at the jambs.

CAULKING: A waterproof material used to seal cracks.

CENTRAL HEATING: A system by which the heat from a single source is distributed with ducts.

CGA: Color Graphics Adapter. A type of video display that has been accepted as a standard through common usage by a number of manufacturers. It refers to the resolution of the display, number of colors, and graphics and text modes available.

CHAIN: A unit of land measurement 66 ft. in length.

CHAMFER: A beveled edge on a board formed by removing the sharp corner. Generally used on moldings, edges of drawer fronts, and cabinet doors.

CHARACTER: One of a set of symbols (letters, numbers, punctuation marks) used to express information.

CHASE: A slot or continuous groove built in a masonry wall to accommodate ducts, pipes, or conduits.

CHIMNEY: A vertical flue for passing smoke from a heating unit fireplace, or incinerator.

CHIP: An integrated circuit or the package that contains an integrated circuit. A chip is sometimes called an IC.

CHIPPED GRAIN: Wood surface that has been roughened by the action of cutting tools. Considered a defect when surfaces are to be smoothly finished.

CHORD: The horizontal member of a truss connecting the lower corners.

CLEAR TITLE: A title to property that is free of any defects.

CLEAT: A piece of wood, normally used in frame construction, fastened to another member to serve as a brace or support.

COLLAR BEAM: Nominal 1 or 2 in. thick members connecting opposite roof rafters. They serve to stiffen the roof structure.

COMMAND: A code that directs the computer to perform a particular operation or sequence of operations.

COMPUTER-AIDED DESIGN: Using the computer to perform drafting and design functions.

CONCRETE: A mixture of cement, sand, and gravel with water.

CONDITIONS AND RESTRICTIONS: The term used to designate any conditions to which the use of land may not be put and the penalties for failure to comply.

CONDUCTION: The flow of heat through an object by transferring heat from one molecule to another.

CONDUIT, ELECTRICAL: A pipe, usually metal, in which wire is installed.

CONFIGURATION: The specific number and type of major components that make up a computer system. Examples are disk drives, memory banks, circuit cards, and peripheral devices. Hardware programming jumper blocks and switches and operating system configuration are all used to notify the microprocessor of your computer's configuration.

CONTRACT: An agreement between a seller and purchaser. The title is withheld from the purchaser until all required payments to the seller have been completed.

CONVECTION: Refers to the transfer of heat by a moving fluid (liquids and gases).

COPING: A cap or top course of a masonry wall used to protect areas beneath it from water penetration.

COPROCESSOR: An auxiliary microprocessor dedicated to a particular function, such as a numeric coprocessor, that works in conjunction with the microprocessor to speed up the processing of information.

CORBEL: A ledge or shelf constructed by laying successive courses of masonry out from the face of the wall.

CORE: The inner layer or layers of plywood. The core may consist of veneer, solid lumber, or composition board.

CORNER BRACES: Diagonal braces at the corners of frame structure to stiffen and strengthen the wall.

CORNICE: The part of a roof that projects out from the wall.

CORNICE RETURN: That portion of the cornice that returns on the gable end of a house.

COUNTERFLASHING: A flashing used under the regular flashing.

COVE: Molded trim of a concave shape used around cabinet construction and other built-ins.

CPU (Central Processing Unit): The circuitry that processes information, performs arithmetic functions, and controls the rest of the computer system.

CRAWL SPACE: The shallow space below the floor of a house built above the ground. Generally it is surrounded with the foundation wall.

CRICKET: A device used at roof intersections to divert water.

CRIPPLE: A structural member that is cut less

than full length, such as a stud above a window or door.

CROSS BRACING: Boards nailed diagonally across studs or other boards to make framework rigid.

CROWN MOLDING: A decorative molding used at the top of cabinets, at ceiling corners, and under a roof overhang.

CUL-DE-SAC: A street or court with no outlet, which provides a circular turn around for vehicles.

CULL: Building material (especially boards) that is rejected because of defects or below usable grade.

CUPOLA: A small, decorative structure built on the roof of a house. It is often placed over an attached garage and may also be used for ventilating purposes.

CURSOR: A character, usually an underline or block, used to indicate a position on the CRT.

CURSOR BUTTON: A button assigned on the digitizer stylus or mouse which denotes a selection or position when pressed.

CURTAIN WALL: An exterior wall that provides no structural support.

D

DADO JOINT: A groove cut across the face of a pieceof stock to receive the end of another board. Often used in quality shelf and cabinet construction.

DAMPER: A movable plate that regulates the draft of a stove, fireplace, or furnace.

DEAD LOAD: All the unmovable weight in a structure and the weight of the structure itself.

DEED: A document indicating that the ownership of land has been transferred from one person to another.

DEFAULT: A standard value or condition under which the computer operates, unless specifically directed to do otherwise.

DENSITY: The number of bits per inch (bpi) that can be stored on a disk.

DIGITIZER: A tablet or pad that converts graphic information into digital values.

DIMENSION LUMBER: Framing lumber that is 2 in. thick and from 4 to 12 in. wide.

DISK: A mass storage device.

DISK DRIVE: A device used to read and write information on disks.

DISPLAY: The video screen used by the computer to present information to the operator.

DOME: A roof used over an entryway or a complete structure in the form of a hemisphere.

DOME STRUCTURES: Structures incorporating design elements of the geodesic dome or triangular space frames.

DOORJAMB: Two vertical pieces held together by a head jamb forming the inside lining of a door opening.

DOORSTOP: The strips on the doorjamb against which the door closes.

DORMER: An opening in a sloping roof, the framing of which projects out to form a vertical wall suitable for windows or other openings.

DOS: Disk Operating System.

DOUBLE GLAZING: Making a pane of two pieces of glass with air space between and sealed to provide insulation.

DOUBLE HEADER: Two or more timbers joined for strength.

DOUBLE-HUNG WINDOW: Refers to a window having top and bottom sashes, each capable of movement up and down.

DOUGLAS FIR: A yellow to pale reddish softwood. The leading veneer wood primarily converted into plywood and widely used in building and construction. Lumber used in general construction. Mill products used for sash, flooring, and doors.

DOWNSPOUT: A pipe, usually of metal, for carrying rainwater from roof gutters.

DRESSED SIZE: The actual size of lumber after jointing and surfacing.

DRIP CAP: A molding placed on the exterior top side of a door or window frame to cause water to drip beyond the outside of the frame.

DRYWALL: Interior covering material, such as gypsum board or plywood, which is applied in large sheets or panels.

DRY WELL: A pit located on porous ground, walled up with rock, which allows water to seep through; used for the disposal of rainwater or the effluent from a septic tank.

DUCTS: In a house, usually round or rectangular metal pipes for distributing warm air from the heating plant to rooms, or air from a conditioning device or as cold air returns. Ducts are also made of composition materials.

DUPLEX OUTLET: Electrical wall outlet having two plug receptacles.

DWARF WALL: A low wall built to retain an excavation or embankment.

E

EARNEST MONEY: A partial payment made as part of the purchase price to bind a contract for property.

EARTH SHELTERED DWELLING: A structure which uses soil to reduce heat loss (or gain).

EASEMENT: An area of a piece of property given rights to another for the purpose of placing power lines, drains, and other specified uses.

EASTERN FIR: A softwood similar to spruce in its general characteristics. Used for siding, moldings, and general construction.

EAVES: The lower portion of the roof that overhangs the wall.

EGA: Enhanced Graphics Adapter. A type of video display that has been accepted as a standard through common usage by a number of manufacturers. It refers to the resolution of the display, number of colors, and graphics and text modes available.

ELL: An extension or wing of a building at right angles to the main section.

ENTITY: Basic, individual drawing component such as a line or circle.

ESCUTCHEON: Door hardware that accommodates the knob and keyhole.

EXCAVATION: A cavity or pit produced by digging the earth in preparation for construction.

EXPANSION JOINT: A bituminous fiber strip used to separate blocks or units of concrete to prevent cracking due to expansion as a result of temperature changes.

EXPANSION MEMORY: Read/write memory installed in addition to base memory.

EXPANSIVE CLAY: A type of soil that swells when wet and produces very high pressure against underground walls.

F

FACADE: The front elevation or face of a structure.

FACE BRICK: Brick of better quality used on the face of a wall.

FACE SIZE: The exposed width of a molded piece of lumber after installation.

FACE VENEER: Veneer selected for exposed surfaces in plywood. Especially selected for fancy paneling.

FACING: Any material attached to the outer portion of a wall used as a finished surface.

FASCIA: A vertical board nailed onto the ends of the rafters.

FIBERBOARD: A building board made with fibrous material and used as an insulating board.

FILL: Sand, gravel, or loose earth used to bring a subgrade up to a desired level around a house.

FILLED INSULATION: A loose insulating material poured from bags or blown by machine into walls.

FIREBRICK: A brick that is especially hard and heat resistant; used in fireplaces.

FIRECLAY: A refractory mortar used to lay firebrick in the bed and walls of a fireplace.

FIRECUT: The angular cut at the end of a joist designed to rest on a brick wall.

FIRESTOP: A solid, tight closure of a concealed space, placed to prevent the spread of fire and smoke through such a space. In a frame wall, this will usually consist of 2 x 4 cross blocking between studs.

FIREWALL: Any wall designed to resist the spread of fire between sections of a house or other structure. Firewalls are commonly used between the main structure and an attached garage. Fire-resistant materials are designed specifically for this purpose.

FLAGSTONE: Flat stone used for floors, steps, walks, or walls.

FLASHING: Sheet metal or other material used in roof and wall construction to protect a building from water seepage.

FLOPPY DISK: A thin, flexible, plastic disk, coated with magnetic material and enclosed in a plastic jacket. It is used to store application programs and data and to transport information from one computer to another. Floppy disks are also called floppy diskettes, flexible disks, or flexible diskettes and come in various sizes and capacities.

FLUE: The space or passage in a chimney through which smoke, gas, or fumes ascend. Each passage is called a flue, which together with any others and the surrounding masonry make up the chimney.

FLUE LINING: Fireclay or terra-cotta pipe, round or square, usually made in all ordinary flue sizes and in 2 ft. lengths. Used for the inner lining of chimneys with the brick or masonry work around the outside. Flue lining in chimneys runs from about a foot below the flue connection to the top of the chimney.

FLY RAFTERS: End rafters of the gable overhang supported by roof sheathing and lookouts.

FONT: Represents the style of text.

FOOTING: A masonry section, usually concrete, in a rectangular form. Wider than the bottom of the foundation wall or pier it supports.

FORM, CONCRETE: A temporary structure built to contain concrete during placement and initial hardening.

FOUNDATION: The supporting portion of a structure below the first-floor construction, or below grade, including the footings.

FRAMING, BALLOON: A system of framing a building in which all vertical structural elements of the bearing walls and partitions consist of single pieces extending from the top of the foundation sill plate to the roof plate and to which all floor joists are fastened.

FRAMING, PLATFORM: A system of framing a building in which floor joists of each story rest on the top plates of the story below or on the foundation sill for the first story, and the bearing walls and partitions rest on the subfloor of each story.

FRIEZE: In house construction, a horizontal member connecting the top of the siding with the soffit of the cornice.

FROST LINE: The depth of frost penetration in soil. This depth varies in different parts of the country. Footings should be placed below this depth to prevent movement.

FURRING: The use of wood strips (or other materials) as a method of finishing the interior face of a masonry wall. Furring provides a space for insulation, helps prevent moisture transmission, and provides a level surface for paneling or other surface finishing treatment.

G

GABLE: The portion of the roof above the eaves line of a double-sloped roof.

GAIN: (a) A recess or notch into which a door hinge fits flush with the surface. (b) Refers to the way heat is extracted from solar radiation.

GARRETT: An attic or unfinished part of a house just under the roof.

GIRDER: A large or principle beam of wood or steel used to support concentrated loads at isolated points along its length.

GLAZING: Placing of glass in windows or doors.

GRADE: The surface of the ground around a building.

GRADE, WOOD: A designation given to the quality of manufactured lumber.

GRAVEL STOP: A strip of metal with a vertical lip used to retain the gravel around the edge of a built-up roof.

GROUT: A plaster-like material used to seal between ceramic and other tile in kitchens, showers, and baths.

GUSSET: A plywood or metal plate used to strengthen the joints of a truss.

GUTTER: A trough for carrying off water.

H

HANGER: A metal strap used to support piping or the ends of joists.

HARDCOPY: A paper copy of a computer's output.

HARD DISK: A carefully machined and polished nonmagnetic metal platter, coated with magnetic material, used for the storage of computer programs and data. Hard disks may be permanently mounted inside the disk drive or are available as removable cartridges.

HARDWARE: The electronic and mechanical parts of your computer system. Includes the disk drives, circuit boards and cards, cables, cabinet, power supply, and peripheral devices.

HARDWOOD: Wood produced from broad-leaved trees or trees that lose their leaves annually. Examples include oak, maple, walnut, and birch.

HEADER: (a) A beam placed perpendicular to joists and to which joists are nailed in framing for chimney, stairway, or other opening. (b) A wood lintel.

HEARTH: The inner or outer floor of a fireplace, usually made of brick, tile, or stone.

HEAT EXCHANGER: A device for removing heat from water or air and transferring the heat to another medium. Baseboard convectors are water-to-air heat exchangers.

HEXADOME: One variation of the geodesic dome.

HICKORY: A hard and heavy brown to reddish-brown hardwood. Used as face veneer for decorative interior plywood paneling and as solid lumber in special flooring applications. Pecan, a variety of the hickory family, has similar properties and construction applications.

HIP RAFTER: The diagonal rafter that extends from the plate to the ridge to form the hip.

HIP ROOF: A roof that rises by inclined planes from all four sides of a building.

HOSE BIBB: A water faucet made for the threaded attachment of a hose.

HOUSE DRAIN: A horizontal sewer piping within a building, which receives waste from the soil stacks.

HOUSE SEWER: The watertight soil pipe extending from the exterior of the foundation wall to the public sewer.

HUMIDIFIER: A device, generally attached to a furnace, to supply or maintain humidity in a home.

HUMIDISTAT: A controlling device to regulate or maintain the desired degree of humidity in a house.

I

I-BEAM: A steel beam with a cross section resembling the letter I. It is used for long spans as basement beams or over wide wall openings, such as a double garage door when wall and roof loads are imposed on the opening.

IMPROVEMENTS: Any additions to property which tends to increase its value, such as buildings, streets, sewers, etc.

INCANDESCENT LAMP: A lamp in which a filament gives off light when sufficiently heated by an electric current.

INPUT: Information transferred into the computer via keyboard or other input device.

INSULATING BOARD: Any board suitable for insulating purposes; usually manufactured broad made from vegetable fibers, such as fiberboard.

INSULATION: Materials for obstructing the passage of sound, heat, or cold from one surface to another.

INTERFACE: A term used to describe the connection of one component, assembly, or circuit board to another. Interface is also used to describe the connection of a peripheral device to a computer. It applies to both the physical connector and the electronic signals at the connector.

INTERIOR TRIM: General term for all the finish molding, casing, baseboard, and cornice applied within the building by finish carpenters.

ISO: International Standards Organization.

J

JACK RAFTER: A rafter that spans the distance from the wall plate to a hip, or from a valley to a ridge.

JALOUSIE: A type of window consisting of a number of long, thin, hinged panels.

JAMB: The side and head lining of a doorway, window, or other opening.,

JOIST: A horizontal structural member that supports the floor or ceiling system.

K

KEYBOARD: A device used to enter information into a computer. The keys are often arranged like those on a typewriter or calculator.

KILN-DRIED LUMBER: Lumber that has been kiln-dried, generally to a moisture content of 6 to 12 percent.

KILOBYTE (K): A unit of measurement of computer memory that equals 1024 bytes.

KING POST: The center upright piece in a roof truss.

KNEE WALL: A low wall resulting from one-and-one-half-story construction.

L

LALLY COLUMN: A steel column used as a support for girders and beams.

LAMINATED BEAM: A beam made of superimposed layers of similar materials by joining them with glue and pressure.

LANDING: A platform between flights of stairs or at the termination of a flight of stairs.

LATH: A building material of wood, metal, gypsum, or insulating board that is fastened to the frame of a building to act as a plaster base.

LATTICE: A framework of crossed wood or metal strips.

LEADER: A vertical pipe or downspout that carries rainwater from the gutter to the ground or storm sewer.

LEASE: A contract for the use of land for a period of years with a designated payment of a monthly or annual rental.

LEDGER STRIP: A strip of lumber nailed along the bottom of the side of a girder on which joists rest.

LEGAL DESCRIPTION: A written indication of the location and boundaries of a parcel of land. Reference is generally made to a recorded plat of survey.

LIGHT PEN: A hand-held data-entry device used only with refresh displays. It consists of an optical lens and photocell, with associated circuitry mounted in a wand. Most light pens have a switch allowing the pen to be sensitive to light from the screen.

LINTEL: A horizontal structural member that supports the load over an opening such as a door or window.

LOOKOUT: A short wooden framing member used to support an overhanging portion of a roof. It extends from the wall to the underside surfacing of the overhang.

LOT: A measured amount of property (land) having fixed boundaries.

LOT LINE: The line forming the legal boundary of a piece of property.

LOUVER: An opening with a series of horizontal slats so arranged as to permit ventilation but to exclude rain, sunlight, or vision. See ATTIC VENTILATORS.

M

MANTEL: The shelf above a fireplace. Also used in referring to the decorative trim around a fireplace opening.

MAPLE: Both hard and soft maple are generally light tan and used in construction where hardness is a major factor. Used for expensive cabinetwork, flooring, doors, and trim. Often used for interior railings, posts, and furniture.

MASONRY: Stone, brick, concrete, hollow tile, concrete block, gypsum block, or other similar building units or materials or a combination of the same, bonded together with mortar to form a wall, pier, buttress or similar mass.

MASTIC: A flexible adhesive for adhering building materials.

MEGABYTE (MB): A unit of measurement of computer memory that equals 1,048,576 bytes.

MEMORY: Integrated circuits used to store data and programs.

METAL WALL TIES: Strips of corrugated metal used to tie a brick veneer wall to a framework.

MICROPROCESSOR: An integrated circuit package that operates as a CPU.

MILLWORK: Lumber that is shaped to a given pattern or molded form. It includes dressing, matching, and machining. Examples include casing, base, panel door parts, and stair rails.

MITER JOINT: A joint made with the ends or edges of two pieces of lumber cut at a 45° angle and fitted together.

MODEM: A device that converts digital signals from a computer to signals that are compatible with telephone lines or other communications facilities.

MODULAR CONSTRUCTION: Construction in which the size of all the building materials is based on a common unit of measure.

MOISTURE BARRIER: A material such as specially treated paper that retards the passage of vapor or moisture into walls, and prevents condensation within the walls.

MONITOR: A control program resident in your computer's ROM. Also, a peripheral device used to display information, such as a CRT.

MONOCHROME DISPLAY: A single-color video display, usually black and white, black and green, or black and amber.

MORTAR: A mixture of cement, sand, and water, used by a mason as a bonding agent for brick and stone.

MORTGAGE: A document used to hold property as security for a debt.

MORTISE: A slot cut into a board, plank, or timber, usually edgewise, to receive the tenon of another board, plank, or timber to form a joint.

MULLION: A vertical bar or divider in the frame between windows, doors, or other openings.

MUNTIN: A small member which divides the glass or openings of sash or doors.

N

NEWEL: A post supporting the handrail at the top or bottom of a stairway.

NOMINAL SIZE: The size of lumber before dressing, rather than its actual size.

NON-BEARING WALL: A wall supporting no load other than its own weight.

NOSING: The rounded edge of a stair tread.

NUMERIC KEYPAD: A set of keys, printed with arrows, found to the right of the keyboard, which are used to direct the cursor on the screen.

O

OAK, RED: Hard and tough hardwood used for flooring, interior trim, stair treads, and railings. Popular as a face veneer plywood for paneling and cabinetwork. A rich light to medium brown in color. White oak has similar characteristics and applications.

OAK, WHITE: See OAK, RED.

ON CENTER, OC: The measurement of spacing for studs, rafters, joists, and other framing members from the center of one member to the center of the next.

OPERATING SYSTEM: A collection of programs stored on disk that provides instructions for the basic operation and management of a computer system.

OUTLET: Any type of electrical box allowing current to be drawn from the electrical system for lighting or appliances.

OUTPUT: Information transferred from the computer to a disk drive, video display, other peripheral device, or another computer.

OVERHANG: The projecting area of a roof or upper story beyond the wall of the lower part.

P

PALLET: An inexpensive wood skid used to stack and ship construction materials such as brick or concrete block.

PANEL: In residential construction, a thin flat piece of wood, plywood, or similar material, framed by stiles and rails as in a door or fitted into grooves of thicker material with molded edges for decorative wall treatment.

PAPER, BUILDING: A general term for paper, felt, or similar sheet materials used in buildings without reference to their properties or uses.

PARAPET: A low wall or railing around the edge of a roof.

PARGE COAT: A thin coat of cement plaster applied to a masonry wall for refinement of the surface or for dampproofing.

PARTICLEBOARD: A composition board made of wood chips or particles bonded together with an adhesive under high pressure.

PARTITION: A wall that subdivides spaces within any story of a building.

PASSIVE SOLAR HEATING: Involves capturing, storing, and using solar radiation (the sun's energy) to heat a dwelling without the use of fans or pumps to circulate the heat.

PECAN: See HICKORY.

PERIPHERAL: Any equipment that is connected to the computer, including video monitors, printers, and modems.

PERIPHERY: The boundary or the complete

outside edge of a parcel of land or an object on a drawing.

PHASE CHANGE MATERIAL: A material capable of storing large amounts of heat as they change from solid to liquid. They are slow to release the stored heat and are, therefore, interesting as possible thermal mass materials.

PIER: A masonry pillar usually below a building to support the floor framing.

PILASTER: A portion of a square column, usually set within or against a wall for the purpose of strengthening the wall; also, a decorative column attached to a wall.

PINE, PONDEROSA: Light reddish-colored softwood used especially for sash, doors, and screens in the softer grades. Harder grades are used for joists, rafters, studs, sills, sheathing, porch columns, posts, balusters, and stair rails.

PINE, WHITE: Softwood of light tan color used for door, sash, interior and exterior trim, siding, and panels. Lower grades are used for sheathing subflooring and roofing.

PINE, YELLOW: Softwood of medium texture, moderately hard, and a yellow to reddish-brown color. Used for joists, rafters, studs, and general construction where extra strength and stiffness are required.

PITCH: The slope of a roof usually expressed as a ratio.

PLASTER: A mortar-like composition used for covering walls and ceilings, usually made of portland cement mixed with sand and water.

PLAT: A drawing of surveyed land indicating the location, boundaries, and dimensions of the parcel. The recorded plat, usually sent to an appropriate governmental office or the county record office, also contains information as to easements, restrictions, and lot number.

PLATE: Sill plate is a horizontal member anchored to a masonry wall. Sole plate is bottom horizontal member of a frame wall. Top plate is top horizontal member of a frame wall supporting ceiling joists, rafters or other members.

PLENUM SYSTEM: A system of heating or air conditioning in which the air is forced through a chamber connected to distributing ducts.

PLUMB: Exactly perpendicular; vertical.

PLYWOOD: A piece of wood made of three or more layers of veneer joined with glue, and usually laid with the grain of adjoining plies at right angles. Almost always an odd number of plies are used to provide balanced construction.

PORT: The connector and associated circuitry through which information is transferred into and out of the computer.

PORTICO: A covered entryway attached to house, usually open on three sides and sup-

ported by posts or columns.

POST AND BEAM CONSTRUCTION: Wall construction consisting of posts rather than studs.

PRECAST: Concrete shapes that are made before being placed into a structure.

PREFABRICATED HOUSES: Houses that are built in sections or component parts in a plant, and then assembled at the site.

PREFRAMED PANELS: Fabricated panels consisting of precut lumber and plywood manufactured to standard dimensions ready for structural use.

PRESERVATIVE: Any substance that, for a reasonable length of time, will prevent the action of wood-destroying fungi, various kinds of borers, and similar destructive agents when the wood has been properly coated or impregnated with it.

PROGRAM: A set of computer instructions that, when executed, results in the computer performing an operation.

PROMPT: A symbol or message indicating that the computer is ready for operator input.

PURLINS: Horizontal roof members laid over trusses to support rafters.

Q

QUARTER ROUND: A small molding that has the cross section of a quarter circle.

QUARTER-SAWED LUMBER: Lumber that has been sawed so that the medullary rays showing on the end grain are nearly perpendicular to the face of the lumber.

QUOINS: Stone or other building materials set in the corners of masonry sections of a house for appearance.

R

RABBET: A groove cut along the edge of a board producing an L-shaped strip. Used as trim and for jointery in cabinet construction.

RADIANT HEATING: A method of heating, usually consisting of a forced hot water system with pipes placed in the floor, wall, or ceiling; or with electrically heated panels.

RADIATION: The flow of heat from a warm source through space in waves of infrared or visible light energy. Sometimes called ''isolation.''

RAFTER: One of a series of structural members of a roof designed to support roof loads. The rafters of a flat roof are sometimes called roof joists.

RAM (Random Access Memory): You can change the information stored in this type of computer memory. It is also known as read/write memory. The contents of RAM are lost when you turn your computer off.

RANDOM RUBBLE: Stonework having irregular shaped units and no indication of systematic course work.

RED CEDAR: A reddish to dull brown softwood. The premier wood for shingles used in the United States because of its durability, ease of working, and light weight. Also used for interior and exterior trim, sash, doors, and siding.

REDWOOD: Light to deep reddish-brown softwood. Mill products include sash, doors, blinds, siding, and trim. Extensively used for garden furniture and exterior decking.

REGISTER: The open end of a duct for warm or cool air; usually covered with screening.

REINFORCED CONCRETE: Concrete with steel bars or webbing embedded for strength.

RESOLUTION: Refers to the sharpness of the display on a video monitor.

RETAINING WALL: A wall that holds back an earth embankment.

REVEAL: The side of an opening for a window or door, between the frame and the outer surface of the wall.

RGB: Red-Green-Blue Intensity. A set of separate video signals used by color video monitors to produce a color display, and by monochrome monitors to produce different shades of one color.

RHEOSTAT: An instrument used for regulating electric current.

RIDGE: The top edge of the roof where two slopes meet.

RIDGE BOARD: The board placed on edge at the ridge of the roof into which the upper ends of the rafters are fastened.

RIPRAP: A sustaining wall or foundation of random stone that is used to prevent erosion on an embankment.

RISE: In stairs, the vertical height of a step or flight of stairs.

RISER: Each of the vertical boards closing the spaces between the treads of stairways.

RISER WALL: A short wall.

ROM (Read-Only Memory): Memory that can be read but not altered. The contents of ROM are not lost when you turn your computer off.

ROOF SHEATHING: The boards or sheet material fastened to the roof rafters on which the shingles or other roof covering is laid.

ROUGH OPENING: A framed opening in a structure into which doors, windows, and other finished trim are set.

RUN: In stairs, the net width of a step or the horizontal distance covered by a flight of stairs.

S

SADDLE: Two sloping surfaces meeting in a horizontal ridge, used between the back side of a chimney or other vertical surface and a sloping roof. Also called a cricket.

SASH: A single-light frame containing one or more lights of glass.

SCUTTLE: A small opening in a ceiling which provides access to an attic or roof.

SECTION: A rectangular area of land used in the survey system which is approximately one mile square bounded by section lines. The section system may then be divided into halves, quarters, or smaller units. One square mile comprises 640 acres.

SEPTIC TANK: A concrete or steel tank where sewage is partially reduced by the action of bacteria.

SETBACK LINES: Lines that indicate the required distances of the location of a structure in relation to the boundaries of the property.

SHEATHING: The structural covering, usually wood boards or plywood, used over studs or rafters of a structure. Structural building board is normally used only as wall sheathing.

SHED ROOF: A flat roof, slanting in only one direction.

SHIPLAP: Wood sheathing that is rabbeted so that the edges of the boards make a flush joint.

SHOE MOLD: The small mold against the baseboard at the floor.

SIDING: The finish covering of the outside wall of a frame building, whether made of horizontal weatherboards, vertical boards with battens, shingles, or other material.

SILL: The lowest member of the frame of a structure, resting on the foundation and supporting the floor joists or the uprights of the wall. The member forming the lower side of an opening, as a door sill.

SKYLIGHT: An opening in a roof covered by glass or plastic material to admit natural light.

SLEEPER: Usually a wood member embedded in concrete, as in a floor, that serves to support and to fasten subfloor or flooring.

SMOKE CHAMBER: The portion of a chimney flue located directly over the fireplace.

SOFFIT: Usually the underside of an overhanging cornice.

SOFTWARE: Any applications program that can be loaded into a computer.

SOFTWOOD: Wood produced from coniferous trees or trees that bear cones. Most commonly used as the pines, but also includes such trees as fir, spruce, redwood, and cedar. The term has no reference to the actual hardness or softness of the wood.

SOIL STACK: The main vertical pipe which receives waste water from fixtures in a building.

SOLAR COLLECTOR: Device for trapping the sun's energy.

SOLAR RADIATION: The sun's energy.

SOLID BRIDGING: A solid member placed between adjacent floor joists near the center of the span to prevent joists from twisting.

SPRUCE: Pale yellowish softwood used for general building purposes as planks, dimension stock, and joists. Millwork products include doors, sash, casing, and trim.

SQUARE: A unit of measurement—100 sq. ft. Usually applied to roofing material. Sidewall coverings are sometimes packed to cover 100 sq. ft. and are sold on that basis.

STOOL: The horizontal ledge or strip as part of the frame below an interior window.

STRETCHER COURSE: A row of masonry in a wall with the long side of the units exposed to the exterior.

STUCCO: Most commonly refers to an outside plaster made with portland cement as its base.

STUD: The vertical framing member of a wall.

STYLUS: A pointing device used with a digitizer to specify position and location.

SUBFLOORING: Any material, usually 1/2 in. plywood, nailed directly to floor joists. The finish floor is attached over the subflooring.

SUBGRADE: A fill or earth surface upon which concrete is placed.

SUMP: A pit in a basement floor which collects water and into which a sump pump is placed to remove the water.

SURVEY: A description of the measure and marking of land, including maps and field notes, which describe the property.

SUSPENDED CEILING: A ceiling system supported by hanging from the overhead structural framing.

T

TAIL BEAM: A relatively short beam or joist supported in a wall on one end and by a header at the other.

TERMITE SHIELD: A shield, usually of noncorrosive metal, placed in or on a foundation wall or other mass of masonry or around pipes to prevent passage of termites.

TERRAZZO FLOORING: Wear-resistant flooring made of marble chips or small stones embedded in concrete and polished smooth.

THERMAL MASS: Materials which can store large amounts of heat such as stone, masonry, or concrete.

THERMAL SIPHONING: Is the result of a fluid expanding and rising.

THERMOSTAT: Automatic device for controlling temperature.

THRESHOLD: A strip of wood or metal with beveled edges used over the finish floor and the sill of exterior doors.

TITLE: Evidence indicating the rights a person has to the ownership and possession of land.

TOPOGRAPHY: Usually refers to site characteristics such as contour of the land, trees, or other natural features.

TRACT: A specified area of land.

TRANSOM: A window placed above a door or permanent window which is hinged for ventilation purposes.

TRAP: A U-shaped pipe below plumbing fixtures designed to create a water seal and prevent sewer odors and gases from being released into habitable areas.

TREAD: The horizontal board in a stairway on which the foot is placed.

TRIM: The finish materials in a building, such as moldings, applied around openings (window trim, door trim) or at the floor and ceiling of rooms (baseboard, cornice).

TRIMMER: The longer floor framing member around a rectangular opening into which a header is joined.

TROMBE WALL: A popular passive solar design technique for trapping and storing the sun's energy.

TROWELING: The finishing operation which produces a smooth, hard surface on concrete slab.

TRUSS: Structural members arranged and fastened in triangular units to form a rigid framework for support of loads over a long span.

U

UNDERLAYMENT: A material placed under finish coverings, such as floor or shingles, to provide a smooth, even surface for applying the finish.

UTILITY: A program that accomplishes a specific computer management purpose. Most utilities are included as a part of an operating system. However, some, like SORT routines, are sold as separate packages.

V

VALLEY: The internal angle formed by the junction of two sloping sides of a roof.

VALLEY RAFTER: The diagonal rafter at the intersection of two intersecting sloping roofs.

VENEER: Extremely thin sheets of wood produced by slicing or rotary cutting a log.

VENEER CONSTRUCTION: Type of wall construction in which frame or masonry walls are faced with other exterior surfacing materials.

VENT STACK: A vertical soil pipe connected to the drainage system to allow ventilation and pressure equalization.

W

WAINSCOT: Surfacing on the lower part of an interior wall when finished differently from the remainder of the wall.

WALL TIE: A small metal strip or steel wire used to bind tiers of masonry in cavity wall and veneer construction.

WATER CONDITIONER: A device used to remove dissolved minerals from water to make it soft. Generally used in houses supplied by well water, which contains calcium, magnesium, and other minerals, to remove hardness that causes scale buildup in plumbing.

WEATHERSTRIP: Strip of metal or fabric fastened along the edges of windows and doors to reduce drafts and heat loss.

WEEP HOLE: An opening at the bottom of a wall which allows the drainage of water.

WYTHE: Pertaining to a single-width masonry wall.

Z

ZONING: Building restrictions which regulate size, location, and type of structures to be built in specific areas.

Index